D1707504

Fundamentals of Transportation Systems Analysis

MIT Press Series in Transportation Studies
Marvin L. Manheim, editor
Center for Transportation Studies, MIT

1. *The Automobile and the Environment: An International Perspective,*
edited by Ralph Gakenheimer, 1978

2. *The Urban Transportation System: Politics and Policy Innovation,*
Alan Altshuler with James P. Womack and John R. Pucher, 1979

3. *Planning and Politics: The Metro Toronto Transportation Review,*
Juri Pill, 1979

4. *Fundamentals of Transportation Systems Analysis. Volume 1:
Basic Concepts,* Marvin L. Manheim, 1979

Fundamentals of Transportation Systems Analysis
Volume 1: Basic Concepts

Marvin L. Manheim

The MIT Press
Cambridge, Massachusetts, and London, England

Library of Congress Cataloging in Publication Data

Manheim, Marvin L
  Fundamentals of transportation systems analysis.

  Bibliography: p.
  Includes index.
  CONTENTS: v. 1.   Basic concepts.
    1.   Transportation planning.   2.   Transportation—
Mathematical models.   3.   System analysis.   I.   Title.
HE199.9.M34   380.5   78–11535
ISBN 0–262–13129–3

To Margaret and Susannah, who share with me the sheer delight that this volume is finally done

Contents

Preface

This textbook provides a basic introduction to the field of transportation systems analysis. We shall treat this subject as a coherent field of study and shall employ an approach that will be applicable to many different types of transportation systems problems. This approach incorporates concepts from economics, engineering, operations research, and public policy analysis. Our hope is that the resulting synthesis will be intellectually coherent and stimulating, comprehensive, and pragmatic.

Enough details and numerical examples will be provided to build understanding of the concepts and to indicate how they can be applied in practice to various modes and problems. We have not, however, attempted to survey all of the models and analytical techniques that have been developed in recent years. Rather, our objective is to provide the reader with a basic framework onto which many different areas of specialization can be added by later coursework and practical experience.

Our approach integrates a number of methods from diverse areas of analysis that are now widely accepted in the profession. For example, the techniques that have been employed in most urban transportation planning studies are here described in the context of more fundamental methods of travel forecasting. Similarly, transportation systems technologies are viewed from the perspective of a unified theory, without undue concentration on the specific details of vehicle kinematics or traffic flow theory.

The theory presented in this book builds upon many current research results. For example, the approach to travel demand modeling is based upon techniques now moving from the frontiers of research into the arena of professional practice. Thus the material is sufficiently new in its perspective that professionals already working in transportation—whether their backgrounds are in engineering, economics, or other fields—should find it useful.

We expect the book to be used primarily for introductory courses in transportation systems analysis for undergraduate or graduate students.

No prerequisites are assumed except a facility with mathematical notation.

Since 1967 more than seven hundred such students have used versions of this material as it has evolved. Typical classes have included students majoring in transportation systems analysis with engineering or systems analysis preparations and also students with backgrounds in political science, urban studies, economics, management, and other fields. As we shall emphasize throughout the text, this mixture of backgrounds is an essential and exciting part of the field.

The material has also been used in intensive training programs for midcareer professionals. Two-week courses taught annually at MIT since 1970 have been taken by over five hundred professionals from more than thirty countries. Attendees have come from national, state, and local governments and from private industry. In addition, special versions of this material have been presented in intensive courses in Israel, Spain, and Switzerland.

We have not endeavored to give uniform coverage to all aspects of transportation systems analysis in this text. Our primary consideration was, rather, to identify and present concepts that are truly fundamental, in that understanding them is a prerequisite for any serious work in the field.

Our secondary consideration was to emphasize, through more detailed treatment, certain topics which are basic yet are treated insufficiently or even erroneously in much of the technical literature. These topics include transportation demand and performance and the processes of evaluation and choice. Particular attention is given to demand for several reasons. First, it is very important. Second, there is a substantial behavioral component to the determination of demand, and this has often been slighted in transportation courses in favor of more technical matters that build on the engineering or systems analysis backgrounds of most present students and practitioners in the field.

In contrast, topics that are covered briefly here—or not at all— because they are treated effectively in other texts or in the technical literature include optimization models, especially for network analysis, such as minimum-path and related algorithms; statistics; economic evaluation methods; and the details of present urban transportation forecasting models. Instead, key references are supplied at appropriate points.

The development of models is an important part of any analysis, but we have here chosen just a few basic models to illustrate the concepts we present. In the case of demand and technology models, this approach is justified by the sheer abundance and diversity of available models, so that a comprehensive inventory would require an effort quite outside the range of the book. In the case of activity-shift models, on the other hand, there is an abundant and diverse technical literature but no outstanding synthesis, so we have chosen to leave this important and complex topic for a later volume.

In order to emphasize the range of the field, we have deliberately chosen examples from a wide variety of modes and problem contexts. Even in courses on particular fields such as urban transportation, we believe that it is important for the student to understand that the methods he or she is learning are general and applicable to many other contexts. Instructors are encouraged to modify examples to fit local circumstances and the particular problems in which the class is most interested. The bibliography and guides to further reading found at the end of each chapter should provide useful starting points for such adaptations.

This volume is self-contained. Volume 2 will present in-depth coverage of selected topics and is intended as an advanced and supplementary text.

The text has been designed to be used flexibly for a variety of teaching and self-study approaches, as indicated on the accompanying figure. For example, one sequence of chapters (prologue, 1–5, 8–10, epilogue) covers fundamentals plus two case studies; this would be suitable for a one-semester introductory course. The remaining chapters form two additional sequences, one modeling-oriented (6, 7, 11–13) and one policy-oriented (14–16). The material can also be used for specialized courses: for example, a course on transportation engineering or transportation technology might include the prologue, chapters 1–3, 5–8, 10, and the epilogue plus portions of volume 2, which will present in-depth coverage of selected topics.

The three case study chapters form the bases for practical exercises. Although they focus on urban transportation, applications to other modes and contexts are stressed in the exercises. The first case study, on disaggregate prediction (chapter 3), provides an elementary introduction to predicting consumer response to system changes. Especially useful is the introduction of the idea of employing worksheets to organize calculations.

The second case study, on carrier operations planning (chapter 10), complements the concepts presented in the fundamentals sequence and

Fundamentals　　　　　　　　**Other Basic Topics**

Modeling-oriented:　　　Policy-oriented:

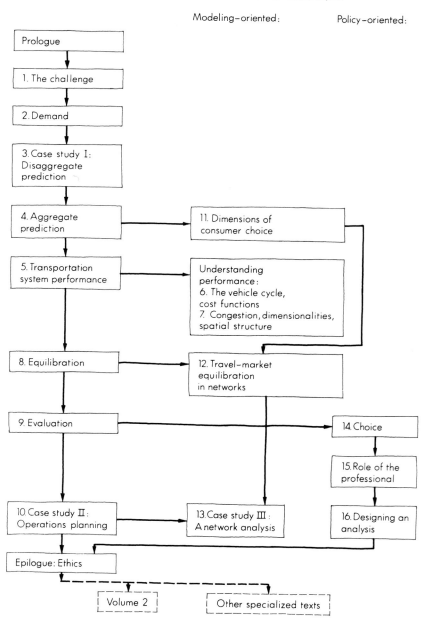

Teaching paths.

demonstrates the application of these concepts without elaborate computer models. It also demonstrates an operator's perspective. This study is designed so that the early portions can be done after chapters 1 and 2 and prior to, or in the course of, chapters 5 and 9.

The third case study, on network analysis (chapter 13), complements the modeling-oriented chapters (especially chapters 11 and 12). In order to focus the student's attention on the substance of the concepts rather than on calculational details, a simple Fortran program is used (see the Teacher's Manual). The case study includes a sequence of questions. The reader studying the volume alone should pause at each question, study it, and write out an answer before proceeding. In a class, the questions can be used as a basis for discussions.

A variety of study materials are included to further the goal of establishing a style of thinking about transportation systems problems. Aside from the case studies and self-checking questions included in the text, there are a number of exercises at the end of most chapters. Some of these exercises are relatively straightforward, requiring either algebraic manipulations or numerical calculations and judgments; these are meant to reinforce or test basic analytical concepts. To assist students to begin thinking about broader issues, many of the exercises are relatively open-ended and more qualitative than quantitative. To differentiate the exercises, we use the following symbols:

E: Simple exercises, usually involving numerical calculations.
C: Conceptual exercises, usually requiring substantial thought.
P: Projects, usually requiring a substantial amount of independent work.

We believe that transportation systems analysis is a single field of study and practice, with a unified theoretical foundation and a diversity of practical applications. As our acknowledgments indicate, in our search for this unified intellectual core we have learned a lot from our colleagues and associates. We see you, the readers of this work, as additional collaborators in our search. The present work is a snapshot of a rapidly evolving body of knowledge and so should evolve rapidly itself. We invite you to contribute to this effort. We look forward to getting your comments and ideas, and especially your reactions, as you test, apply, refine, and accept or reject the concepts presented here.

Acknowledgments

This work has grown out of the teaching and research activities of the transportation systems program at MIT. I have learned much from my colleagues and students.

Some of the material included here has evolved from joint efforts, initially presented in papers and technical reports. Where possible, specific acknowledgments of these debts have been made in the text. In particular, the material on demand draws heavily on the work of Moshe E. Ben-Akiva; that on choice and the role of the professional on joint works with Elizabeth Deakin, Arlee T. Reno, and John Suhrbier; and the case studies on work of George A. Kocur and Earl R. Ruiter. I have also benefited from the insights and comments of Wayne M. Pecknold, Steven R. Lerman, Jorge Barriga, Clint Heimbach, Frank S. Koppelman, Thomas Larson, and Kumares N. Sinha, as they have struggled to teach with this material in its earlier, more primitive forms.

Among those who have contributed substantially to the development of the exercises are Mark Abkowitz, Richard L. Albright, Moshe E. Ben-Akiva, Kiran U. Bhatt, Daniel Brand, Harry Cohen, Mark Daskin, Greig Harvey, George A. Kocur, Steven R. Lerman, Mary McShane, Jacques Nahmias, Wayne M. Pecknold, Leonard Sherman, and William Swan. Earl R. Ruiter developed the original case study in chapter 13, using DODOTRANS. Mark Abkowitz, Greig Harvey, and Steven Lerman were responsible for the development of TTP-1, Mark Abkowitz converted the case study to that format, and Mary McShane made later modifications.

In addition, less tangible but nevertheless important influences have come from Lowell K. Bridwell, Carlos Daganzo, Michael Florian, Ernst G. Frankel, Stuart Hill, Michael Lash, Brian V. Martin, Lance Neumann, C. Kenneth Orski, Paul O. Roberts, Robert W. Simpson, Richard M. Soberman, Joseph H. Stafford, and Martin Wohl.

Particular thanks are extended also to those at MIT and elsewhere who made it possible for me to spend substantial time developing this material and provided other support: at MIT, C. L. Miller, Peter S. Eagleson, Frank Perkins, and Joseph Sussman; at the Institut de Recherche des Transports, Paris, Michel Frybourg and Alain Bieber; at OECD, Paris, C. Kenneth Orski; and at the Israel Ministry of Transport and the Israel Institute for Transportation Planning and Research, Uri Ben-Efraim and Gideon Hashimshony.

Responsible for the production of the many preliminary and final editions over the years have been Carol Walb, Charna Garber, Gilbert High, and Janet Brown, assisted by Steven Kahn, Gary Garrels, Nancy Pfund, and Colleen Keough.

I especially want to acknowledge the guidance and inspiration of A. Scheffer Lang, who over the past twenty years has influenced so significantly not only this work but also the whole direction of our transportation systems activities at MIT.

Needless to say, the author alone is responsible for the imperfections of this material.

Fundamentals of Transportation Systems Analysis

Prologue
The Profession of Transportation Systems Analysis

THE FIELD TODAY

In the last ten years the field of transportation systems analysis has emerged as a recognized profession. More and more government agencies, universities, researchers, consultants, and private industrial groups around the world are becoming truly multimodal in their orientation and are adopting a systematic approach to transportation problems. Specialists in many different disciplines and professions are working together on multidisciplinary approaches to complex issues.

The field of transportation systems analysis has the following characteristics:

It is *multimodal,* covering all modes of transport (air, land, marine) and both passengers and freight.

It is *multisectoral,* encompassing the problems and viewpoints of government, private industry, and the public.

It is *multiproblem,* ranging across a spectrum of issues that includes national and international policy, the planning of regional systems, the location and design of specific facilities, operational issues such as more effective utilization of existing facilities, carrier management issues, and regulatory, institutional, and financial policies. The objectives considered relevant often include national and regional economic development, urban development, environmental quality, and social equity, as well as service to users and financial and economic feasibility.

It is *multidisciplinary,* drawing on the theories and methods of engineering, economics, operations research, political science, psychology, other natural and social sciences, management, and law.

Transportation systems analysts are professionals who endeavor to analyze systematically the choices available to public or private agencies in making changes in the transportation system and services in a particular region. They work on problems in a wide variety of contexts, such as:

• urban transportation planning, producing long-range plans (5–25 years) for multimodal transportation systems in urban areas as well as

short-range programs of action (0–5 years), including operational improvements in existing facilities and services and location and design decisions for new facilities and services;
• regional passenger transportation, dealing primarily with intercity passenger transport by air, rail, and highway and possible new modes (as in the Northeast Corridor Study in the United States or Project 33 in Western Europe; see Grēvsmahl 1978, Wheeler 1978, Wilken 1978);
• national freight transport, in developed countries such as the United States, where issues of truck-rail-water competition are of particular importance, as well as in developing countries, where the magnitude of investments in the transport sector, its spatial distribution, and its allocation among modes are all important components of the overall problem of national economic development planning;
• international transport, where issues such as containerization, competition between sea and air, and intermodal coordination are important for freight shippers and carriers in an era of increasing international trade.

The field of transportation systems analysis began with the application of systems analysis methods to urban transportation studies. Most of these early applications were concerned with long-range planning, were public-sector-oriented, and used similar methodological approaches. Now, many different variations in methodologies are being used in a wide variety of operational, planning, design, and policy applications, in both private and public sectors, and involving short-range as well as long-range perspectives, in all of the contexts indicated above.

Today, transportation systems analysis is a mature profession, with a unified theoretical basis and many and diverse practical applications. It is an exciting field in which the concerns extend from abstract theory and complex models to politically important policy questions and institutional change strategies. Our objective in this volume is to show the unity and the diversity of this field. We also hope to impart some of the excitement and satisfaction of practicing this profession.

UNITY AND DIVERSITY

The field today is characterized by a diversity of problem types, institutional contexts, and technical perspectives. But underlying this tremendous diversity is a central intellectual core: a body of theory and a set of basic principles to be utilized in every analysis of a transportation system. The elements of this core are introduced in chapter 1 and amplified in later chapters.

The intellectual core provides a set of unifying themes. As a consequence of the historical development of the field, however, there is a rich variety of ways in which analysts can draw on this core in performing a practical analysis of a specific set of issues. While the same basic theory and principles apply to each problem, very different types of models and methods of analysis are appropriate in different situations.

THE CHALLENGE

The focus of transportation systems analysis is on the interaction between the transportation and activity systems of a region. *The substantive challenge of transportation systems analysis is to intervene, delicately and deliberately, in the complex fabric of a society to use transport effectively, in coordination with other public and private actions, to achieve the goals of that society.* To know how to intervene, analysts must have substantive understanding of transportation systems and their interactions with activity systems; this requires understanding of the basic theoretical concepts and of available empirical knowledge.

To intervene effectively, and actually bring about change, analysts must also have a proper perspective on their role. *The methodological challenge of transportation systems analysis is to conduct a systematic analysis in a particular situation which is valid, practical, and relevant, and which assists in clarifying the issues to be debated.*

An analyst will often use models and other technical means to assist in developing the analysis. There is a wide spectrum of modeling approaches available, ranging from complex computerized simulation models, to very simple algebraic models, to no formal models at all.

A key task for the analyst is to select a process of analysis, including a choice of model, that will help to produce an analysis that is relevant, valid, and practical, and that helps to clarify the issues. To implement this process effectively may involve the analyst in public participation and even in institutional change. An important element of the design of a process of analysis may be inclusion of activities that stimulate constructive and timely involvement of affected interests in an open, participatory process designed to recognize explicitly potential value conflicts and to promote constructive resolution of those conflicts.

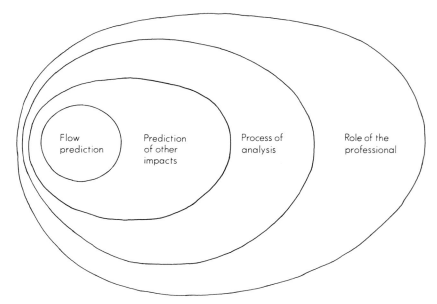

Figure P.1 The scope of transportation systems analysis.

Figure P.1 presents symbolically the image we have been describing. At the core of the field is the prediction of flows, which must be complemented by the prediction of other impacts. Prediction, however, is only a part of the process of analysis; and technical analysis is only a part of the broader problem, namely the role of the professional transportation systems analyst in the process of bringing about change in society.

Today, transportation systems analysis is a field so broad and diverse that few individuals can remain competent in all its aspects; rather, many specialties are emerging, such as demand analysis, evaluation, policy, and the development of new systems. It is an exciting field, spanning the range from abstract theory and sophisticated mathematics to important public policy questions and issues of political strategy.

Within this broad spectrum of intellectual styles and problem applications, each individual, building on the same basic foundations, can develop his or her own unique potential as a transportation systems analyst.

PROFESSIONAL TRAJECTORIES

An education in transportation systems analysis can lead to many different professional careers (figure P.2). Transportation systems analysts

Application specialties

highway engineering
flight transportation
marine transportation
transportation management
traffic engineering
urban transportation planning
developing country transportation
rail transportation
port development and planning
airport planning
transit operations
trucking
transportation regulation
transportation and economic development
transportation engineering
transportation economics
national transportation policy
transportation environmental analysis
and others

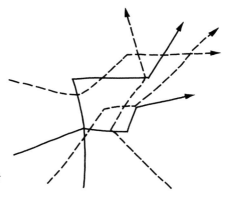

Methodological specialties

demand
transportation system performance
evaluation
policy analysis and implementation
institutional change strategies
urban planning and development
management
systems analysis methods
environmental impacts
economics
activity systems analysis
and others

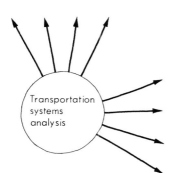

Figure P.2 Careers in transportation systems analysis.

work for private firms and for public agencies; for carriers such as airlines, steamship companies, railroads, or transit agencies and for other operators such as airport or seaport authorities or highway departments; for government agencies at local, state, and federal levels, as analysts, planners, and policy makers, as traffic engineers, highway engineers, transit planners, airport planners, or railroad analysts; and for private firms involved in the design and operation of facilities, in the manufacture of equipment, or in consultation work.

Professionals in the field can take many different roles: technical analysts, working primarily with quantitative methods in any or all of the varied methodologies of the field; project managers, managing groups of technical professionals; community interaction specialists, at the interface of technical analysis and political action; policy analysts, providing technically oriented support to elected officials, legislators, and others; policy makers, such as heads of transportation firms or agencies, or ministers or secretaries of transportation; and, of course, educators and researchers.

Thus transportation systems analysts can follow a wide variety of professional careers. We like to use the term "trajectory" because, as suggested by the upper right-hand corner of figure P.2, an individual's career is rarely a predictable "linear" progression up a well-defined career ladder.

Transportation is a rapidly changing profession in a rapidly changing world. The careers of most transportation systems analysts are likely to resemble the randomness of Brownian motion more than a simple linear progression. Each individual's career will evolve in unpredictable ways: new jobs, new events, changing external forces, development of new personal skills, all contribute to a largely unpredictable professional trajectory.

This uncertainty suggests that an individual must acquire a broad professional base as well as specialized training in particular aspects of the field. From this basic grounding in the fundamentals of transportation systems analysis, one will usually go on to acquire more specialized training through academic coursework and on-the-job experience. As the individual acquires this more specialized training and advances from job to job, he or she becomes more "expert." This is valuable and natural, but it is also a source of concern.

As one acquires more and more technical expertise, one also acquires a set of attitudes, values, and perspectives peculiar to a particular subculture—the community of related specialists. While this has positive features, it also has serious dangers. The dangers arise from the loss of a sense of perspective and increasing rigidity in one's professional approaches—the belief that there is a "right way" to do something, or a "right solution" to a particular problem, or, most dangerous of all, that "the expert knows best."

As one enters into a career in transportation systems analysis, one needs to be conscious of the balance to be achieved between "expertise" and "flexibility." Specialization and increasingly deeper knowledge of one's specialty are important; but personal flexibility, the ability to modify one's capabilities in response to the needs and challenges of new opportunities in one's unpredictable professional trajectory, is equally important. (These themes are taken up in chapters 14 and 15 and in the epilogue.)

1
The Challenge of Transportation
Systems Analysis

1.1 A WORLD OF CHANGE

We live in a world of rapid change. This is particularly significant for transportation systems analysis because of the strong interactions between transportation and the rest of society.

We can identify three critical dimensions of change relevant to transportation. The first is change in the demand for transportation. As the population, income, and land-use patterns of metropolitan areas and states change, so do the patterns of demand for transportation—both the amount of transportation desired and the spatial and temporal distribution of that demand.

The second dimension of change is in technology. For example, in urban transportation, until just a few years ago the only actively considered alternatives were highways and rapid rail transit. Now we are able to consider such alternatives as lanes or even whole expressways restricted to buses; basically new technologies such as "dual-mode" systems, in which vehicles operate under individual control on local streets and automatically on tracked interurban guideways; and a variety of policy options designed to improve the efficiency of use of existing technology, such as incentives for carpools and van pools, "dial-a-ride" small buses, road pricing strategies, disincentives for automobile use, and auto-restricted zones (UMTA 1975, Smith, Maxfield, and Fromovitz 1977, TRANSPORTATION SYSTEM MANAGEMENT 1977). These new technologies provide a rich market basket of alternatives, from which a wide variety of transportation systems for metropolitan areas can be developed.

Change has been rapid in other areas of transportation technology as well, as exemplified by the development of freight containerization, "jumbo" jet aircraft, vertical or short takeoff and landing (V/STOL) aircraft, and air-cushion vehicles for water and land transport.

The third dimension of change is in the values, public and private, that are brought to bear on transportation decision making. It has become clear that many different groups are affected by decisions made about transportation. No longer is it sufficient to design transportation systems simply to serve the "users," in some aggregate sense. Rather, we must identify which groups are served well and which groups poorly by a particular facility or system; and so we have begun to focus on the needs of those who are too poor or too ill or too young or too old to have ready access to automobile transportation. We have also become deeply concerned with the social and environmental effects of transportation: air pollution, noise pollution, community disruption, and ecological effects are given increasing weight in transportation decision making.

These three dimensions of change—in demand, in technology, and in values—form the background against which we shall develop the basic concepts of transportation systems analysis.

1.2 THE SCOPE OF THE PROBLEM

The first step in formulating a systematic analysis of transportation systems is to examine the scope of the analytical task. We shall start by setting out the basic premises of our approach, namely, the explicit treatment of the total transportation system of a region and of the interrelations between transportation and its socioeconomic context. We shall then identify those aspects of the system that can be manipulated —the "options"—and those aspects that are relevant to decision making—the consequences, or "impacts," of the options. Given this framework, we can proceed to discuss the problem of prediction (section 1.3).

1.2.1 Basic Premises

Two basic premises underlie our approach to the analysis of transportation systems:

1. The total transportation system of a region must be viewed as a single, multimodal system.
2. Consideration of the transportation system cannot be separated from consideration of the social, economic, and political system of the region.

THE TOTAL TRANSPORTATION SYSTEM

In approaching the analysis of a transportation systems problem, initially we must consider the total transportation system of the region:

1. All modes of transportation must be considered.
2. All elements of the transportation system must be considered: the persons and things being transported; the vehicles in which they are conveyed; and the network of facilities through which the vehicles,

passengers, and cargoes move, including terminals and transfer points as well as line-haul facilities.

3. All movements through the system must be considered, including passenger and goods flows from all origins to all destinations.

4. For each specific flow, the total trip, from point of origin to final destination, over all modes and facilities must be considered.

For example, in a study of intercity passenger transport in a megalopolitan region, initially we must consider railroads, airplanes, buses, private automobiles, and trucks as well as new and innovative modes such as tracked air-cushion vehicles (TACV) and V/STOL aircraft. We must consider not only the direct intercity line-haul links but also the vehicles that will operate over these links, the terminals, en route stations, and other transfer points, and such means for access to, and egress from, the intercity portion of the system as taxis, limousines, automobiles, local transit, and other means of intracity transport. We must consider the diverse patterns of origins and destination of movements as well as how passenger and goods flows may use the same facilities. In examining each movement, we must consider the service provided on access and egress portions of each trip as well as on the line-haul portion.

After this initial comprehensive definition of the transportation system has been made, the analyst, as he defines more finely the primary objectives of his analysis, can narrow his focus to those elements of the system that are of direct concern. This procedure will force him to consider explicitly the assumptions introduced by eliminating individual elements of a highly complex and interrelated system.

THE INTERRELATION OF TRANSPORTATION AND ACTIVITY SYSTEMS

The transportation system of a region is tightly interrelated with the socioeconomic system. Indeed, the transportation system will usually affect the way in which the socioeconomic system grows and changes. And changes in the socioeconomic system will in turn call forth changes in the transportation system. This interrelationship is fundamental to our view of transportation systems analysis.

The system of interest can be defined by three basic variables: T, the transportation system; A, the activity system, that is, the pattern of social and economic activities; and F, the pattern of flows in the transportation system, that is, the origins, destinations, routes, and volumes of goods and people moving through the system. Three kinds

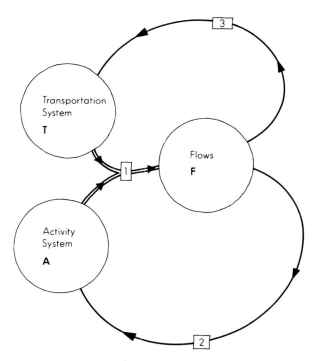

Figure 1.1 Basic relations.

of relationships can be identified among these variables (see figure 1.1):

1. The flow pattern in the transportation system is determined by both the transportation system and the activity system.
2. The current flow pattern will cause changes over time in the activity system: through the pattern of transportation services provided and through the resources consumed in providing that service.
3. The current flow pattern will also cause changes over time in the transportation system: in response to actual or anticipated flows, entrepreneurs and governments will develop new transportation services or modify existing services.

Though we label the activity system with the single symbol **A**, we must not assume that this system is as simple as the symbol suggests. On the contrary, the activity system of a metropolitan area or a megalopolitan region or a developing country consists of many subsystems, overlapping and interrelated—social structures, political institutions, housing markets, and so on. Transportation is only one of these subsystems.

The evolution of the activity system is determined by a large number of forces and pressures. The internal dynamics of this system are very complex, and our understanding of these dynamics is very incomplete.

Transportation plays a role in influencing the evolution of the activity system, but, except in very special situations, it is not the sole determinant of that evolution. The development of automobiles and of extensive systems of freeways does not alone cause suburbanization and dispersal of metropolitan areas, but it does interrelate closely with the dynamics of rising income, changing housing and labor markets, and other subsystems. Even the provision of access roads to a hitherto virgin area of an underdeveloped country will not by itself stimulate agricultural development. There must be a market for the produce, and there must be an array of adequate incentives to development.

The interrelation between transportation and the activity system is fundamental to our approach. *The challenge of transportation systems analysis is to intervene, delicately and deliberately, in the complex fabric of a society to use transport effectively, in coordination with other public and private actions, to achieve the goals of that society.* Responding to this challenge is not easy. We must understand transportation as a technology, a system of physical elements managed by human organizations to move people and goods. We must also understand transportation as a subsystem of the complex of social, economic, political, and other forces we so tersely summarize as "the activity system." Most important of all, we must know how to use this understanding effectively.

1.2.2 The Major Variables

Now that we have defined in broad terms the nature of the system with which we are dealing, we must explore the major variables needed in an analysis. In the last section we characterized the system in terms of three major, interrelated variables—**T**, **A**, and **F**. The questions we now address are: What options are available for influencing the system? What impacts should be considered in evaluating alternative courses of action?

INTERVENING IN THE SYSTEM: OPTIONS

There are many individuals, groups, and institutions whose decisions interact to affect the transportation system, the activity system, and thus the pattern of flows. The *user* of transportation, whether a shipper of goods or a passenger, makes decisions about when, where, how, and whether to travel. The **operator** of particular transportation facilities or services makes decisions about vehicle routes and schedules, prices to be charged and services offered, the kinds and quantities of vehicles to be included in the fleet, the physical facilities to be provided, and so on. **Governments** make decisions on taxes, subsidies, and other financial matters that influence users and operators, on the provision of new or improved facilities, and on legal and administrative devices to influence, encourage, or constrain the decisions of operators or users.

It is often important to identify which groups have control over particular decisions, particularly when it is time to implement a selected course of action. We shall often ignore this question, however, in order to clarify the task of analysis. In other words, we shall attempt to identify all the possible decisions that might be made, without regard to who has the power to make a specific decision in a particular context.

Options, or decision variables, are those aspects of the transportation and activity systems that can be directly changed by the decisions of one or several individuals or institutions. The options available can be divided into two groups: those dealing with the transportation system itself and those dealing with the activity system.

Transportation options

Many aspects of a transportation system can be varied. Not all of these are open to a single decision maker, nor are all open at the same time. This spectrum of options, or "decision variables," may be summarized as follows:

Technology The development and implementation of new combinations of transportation components enable transportation demand to be satisfied in ways not previously available. Examples are containers, container ships, and piggyback trucks and railcars; the supersonic transport; and new urban mass transportation concepts, such as dual-mode and "dial-a-ride" systems.

Options involving technology include fundamental decisions about the means of propulsion, the medium through which the vehicle travels, supporting way and suspension systems, vehicle size and shape characteristics, typical route and network structure, and general mode of operations. Decisions must be made about these options within the constraints of technological feasibility, but there is a wide range of options nevertheless, and we have seen very rapid growth in the variety of specific technologies available for urban, interurban, and developing country contexts.

Networks Options involving networks include their general configurations and the approximate geographical locations of their links. Examples are the grid systems typical of many of our present cities versus radial links and concentric circles.

Link characteristics Networks consist of links and nodes. Links correspond to facilities, such as highways, rail lines, or urban streets. Where it is necessary to model the characteristics of intersection points within a single mode (highway intersections, rail yards) and of transfer points between modes (airports, rail terminals, bus stops), these are also represented as links. Nodes simply express the connectivity relations of links in the network. Options include the detailed physical location of links and nodes and those characteristics of the links that affect flow, such as the number of lanes of highway or tracks of railroad, the grades and curves of the roadway, the type of signaling or traffic control, and the internal layout of terminals.

Generally we shall adopt the convention of most transportation network analysis and assume that all flow properties are represented in links and that nodes create no barriers to flow. Where node properties must be modeled—for example, transfer time at a rail terminal or airport—we shall do so by a subnetwork of links in the model that represents, and has the same properties as, the terminals. Thus nodes serve only to express the topology of the network.

Vehicles Most transportation modes involve vehicles (exceptions: pipelines, conveyors). The major options include the number of vehicles in the system and their characteristics. (Note that the choice of technologies sets a broad range to such options as networks, links, vehicles, and operating policies, but detailed decisions must still be made within the feasible range.)

System operating policies This set of options includes the full spectrum of decisions about how the transportation system is operated. The networks, links, and vehicles establish an envelope of possibilities; within that envelope a large variety of detailed operating decisions must be made. These options include vehicle routes and schedules, types of services to be offered, including services auxiliary to transportation (passenger meals, diversion and reconsignment privileges for freight), prices (both general pricing policy and specific pricing decisions), financing, subsidies, and taxing schemes, and regulatory decisions. Some of these operating policy options can be varied almost on a day-to-day basis; others, such as pricing policy and regulatory decisions governing the entry of new carriers, may be unchanged for decades.

Organizational policies This set of options includes a wide variety of management, organizational, and institutional decisions. Within a single transportation organization, public or private, there are many detailed decisions about functional and geographic structure. Within a region there are decisions about how the transport sector should be organized, including the numbers and types of institutions, the functions to be assigned to each, the relative domains of responsibility, and the channels of communication, coordination, and control.

This set of transportation options fully defines the space of possible transportation plans and policies. However, these options are exercised not in a vacuum but in the context of a system of social and economic activities.

Activity-system options

The activity system is defined as the totality of social, economic, political, and other transactions taking place over space and time in a particular region. These transactions, both actual and potential, determine the demand for transportation; in turn, the levels and spatial patterns of those interactions are affected in part by the transportation services provided. Therefore, in modeling transportation systems, we must clearly identify those options in the activity system that will affect transportation demands.

Travel options These are the options open to every potential user of the transportation system: whether to make a trip at all, where to make it, when, and how—by what mode and route. These options apply to the individual traveler and to the shipper of freight. The decisions actually made by the shipper or traveler will be based in part upon the perceived characteristics of the transportation system and in part upon the actual and potential patterns of transactions in the activity system. The aggregate result of all the individual decisions about travel is expressed as the demand for transportation.

Other activity options Most of the social, economic, and political actors in the activity system have a wide range of options about how, when, and where they will conduct their activities. Over the long term these options profoundly influence the demand for transportation. For example, as major changes in a transportation system are made over time, the spatial pattern of population and economic activity will change, as actors exercise their options for changing the location or scale of their activities. Forces within the economy external to the transportation system, such as national economic policy, rapid social change, housing subsidies, or mortagage policy, may impact on the spatial pattern of activity and thus affect the demand for transportation.

In many transportation analyses most of these activity options— for example, rate of economic growth, sectoral and regional patterns of growth, aggregate population—must be treated as exogenous, completely uncontrollable by the transportation analyst. The exercise of some of these options by various decision makers will be partially influenced by transportation; for example, transportation will affect the detailed distribution of population and employment within a region. Still other options are controllable to some extent in explicit coordination with transportation options—for example, the control of land use through zoning and land-development incentives.

Whether fully controllable or not, however, the full set of transportation and activity system options must be considered in any analysis.

THE CONSEQUENCES OF TRANSPORTATION: IMPACTS

When evaluating alternative transportation systems, one would like to consider all the relevant consequences. Any change in the transportation system can potentially affect a variety of groups and interests. *Impacts* are those aspects of the transportation and activity systems that should be considered in evaluating possible changes to the transportation system.

The prospective impacts can be broken down as follows, in terms of the groups on which the impacts fall:

1. *User impacts:* Impacts on travelers and shippers of goods. Users are differentiated by location within the region, by trip purpose, and by socioeconomic group. Examples: suburban resident commuting to central-city job; low-income non-car-owning resident of center city traveling to health facilities.

2. *Operator impacts:* Impacts on operators of the transport facilities and services. Differentiated by mode, by link, and by route. Examples: air carrier, trucker, highway maintenance agency, port authority, toll-bridge operator.

3. *Physical impacts:* Impacts caused by the "physical presence" of transport facilities or services affect many who are neither users nor operators. These groups can be differentiated by type of impact and by location. Examples: families, jobs, and taxable real estate displaced by new construction; neighbors affected by environmental degradation

through noise, fumes, air pollution, or groundwater changes.

4. *Functional impacts:* The impacts on the activity system as users change travel patterns in response to transport system changes. Differentiated by location within region and by type. Examples: changes in retail sales areas in suburban shopping centers and central business districts; changes in production costs; changes in land values.

5. *Governmental impacts:* Differentiated by location and by level of government or agency type. Examples: municipal, state, or federal agencies; citizen groups; elected representatives.

An essential characteristic of transportation is the differential incidence of its impacts. Some groups will gain from any transportation change; others may lose. Therefore, transportation choices are essentially sociopolitical choices: the interests of different groups must be balanced. This view has profound implications for the evaluation of alternative options.

1.3 PREDICTION OF FLOWS

Any proposed change in a transportation system (or a completely new system) can be expressed in terms of the options identified in section 1.2. The problem of prediction is to anticipate the impacts that a particular proposal will have; that is, we need procedures for predicting the impacts associated with any set of options (figure 1.2). In transportation the impacts depend upon the pattern of flows resulting from the particular set of options.

Consider the present transportation system **T** and activity system **A**. A particular proposed plan will be defined in terms of changes in the transportation options, Δ**T**, and in the activity-system options, Δ**A**. Implementation of the plan will change the transportation system from **T** to **T'** and the activity system from **A** to **A'**. Corresponding to these changes there will be a change in the pattern of flows: **F** will become **F'**.

The core of any transportation systems analysis is the prediction of changes in flows. There will usually be many other significant impacts as well, but predicting the change in flows is always an essential step. (Even if there is no change in flows, this judgment must be reached explicitly.)

Specification of the transportation system **T** at any point in time and of the activity system **A** implies the pattern of flows **F**. The basic hypothesis underlying this statement is that there is a market for transportation which can be separated out from other markets (Beckmann, McGuire,

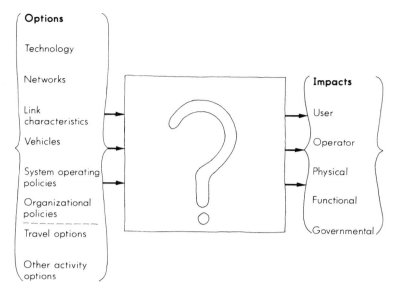

Figure 1.2 The prediction problem.

and Winston 1956, Manheim 1966b, Wohl and Martin 1967). This market is represented by the type 1 relation introduced in section 1.2.1; the hypothesis is that the type 1 relation can be separated from the type 2 and type 3 relations. This hypothesis can be expressed symbolically as follows. First, to our three variables **T**, **A**, and **F** we add two more: **S**, the service characteristics experienced by a particular flow or set of flows (travel times, fares, comfort, and so forth), and **V**, the volume(s) of flow in the network. Each of these variables may be a vector or other array.

We express the hypothesis as follows:

1. Specification of the transportation system **T** establishes ***service functions,*** **J**. These service functions indicate how the level of service varies as a function of the transportation options and the volume of flows; for a particular transportation system **T**, the level of service **S** that a traveler will experience is a function of the volume **V** of travelers using the system:

$$\mathbf{S} = \mathbf{J}(\mathbf{T}, \mathbf{V}).\tag{1.1}$$

2. Specification of the activity-system options, **A**, establishes ***demand functions***, **D**. These demand functions give the volume of flows as a function of the activity-system options and the level of service; for a particular activity system **A**, the volume of travelers **V** that will use

the system is a function of the level of service **S** experienced by those travelers:

$$V = D(A, S). \tag{1.2}$$

3. The flow pattern **F** consists of the volume **V** using the system and the level of service **S** experienced by those travelers:

$$F = (V, S). \tag{1.3}$$

For a particular transportation system **T** and activity system **A**, the flow pattern that will actually occur, $F^0 = F(T, A)$, is the volume V^0 and the level of service S^0 determined as the equilibrium solution to the service and demand relations (1.1) and (1.2):

$$\left.\begin{array}{l} S = J(T, V) \\ V = D(A, S) \end{array}\right\} \longrightarrow (V^0, S^0). \tag{1.4}$$

Thus the specification of **T** and **A** implies particular values of equilibrium volume V^0 and level of service S^0 (if a unique equilibrium exists—see chapters 8 and 12):

$$(T, A) \longrightarrow (J, D) \longrightarrow [F(T, A) = (V^0, S^0)]. \tag{1.5}$$

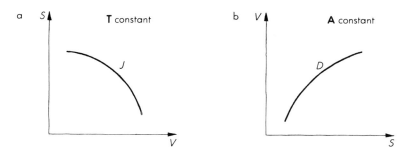

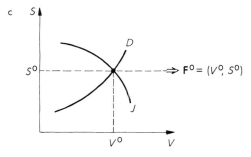

Figure 1.3 Simple equilibrium.

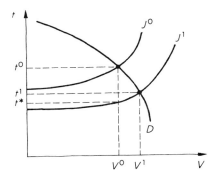

Figure 1.4 Comparing two systems.

The graphical interpretation of this formulation is shown in figure 1.3. In this figure **V** and **S** are assumed one-dimensional. Further, it is assumed that as the volume of flow in the system increases, the level of service decreases, as shown in part a of the figure; and as the level of service increases, the volume desiring to use the service increases, as shown in part b.[1]

To see the implications of this formulation, suppose that we are considering two alternative transportation systems, T^0 and T^1. T^0 is the existing transportation system, for example, a highway between two towns. We are considering replacing the highway by a new, improved facility T^1. Figure 1.4 shows the two service functions, J^0 and J^1, corresponding to T^0 and T^1. Let us assume that there is one service attribute that is important: travel time over the routes, t. (Since improvement in S corresponds to reduction in t, the curves in this figure are opposite in shape to those of the previous figure.)

The equilibrium flow over T^0 is the flow $F^0 = (V^0, t^0)$ determined by the intersection of J^0 and D, the demand curve. Now consider the improved system T^1, represented by J^1. If we assume that the same volume of travel V^0 will occur on the new system as on the old, we

[1]Note that the graphical conventions vary in the figure. In engineering the usual convention is that the independent variable is shown on the horizontal axis and the dependent variable on the vertical axis. This is followed in parts a and b. From the perspective of transportation system performance, V is the independent variable and S the dependent. From the perspective of the activity-system behavior, S is the independent variable and V the dependent variable, as expressed by equations 1.1 and 1.2. In part c the convention is arbitrary, since both variables are interrelated. We have chosen the economist's convention, in which V is on the horizontal axis and S (usually price in the economics literature) is on the vertical axis. The shape of the curves reflects the convention that "service" is positively valued.

would anticipate a service level t^*: that is, if volume remains constant, we expect a lower trip time because of the improved facility.

However, the constant-volume assumption is erroneous, for the travel volume will increase because the increased level of service—the decreased trip time—will attract more users. The extent of this increase in volume is given by the demand function D. Thus the actual flow pattern resulting will be that given by the equilibrium of D and J^1: $F^1 = (V^1, t^1)$. That is, the traffic volume will increase, and the level of service will be intermediate between t^0 and t^*: the new facility will serve more users at a level of service that is better, but not as good as it would be if no new users were attracted.

1.4 APPLYING THE CONCEPTS

1.4.1 Simple Equilibrium: An Example
To illustrate these concepts we consider a highway connecting two towns, Suburb and City. We assume the following characteristics.

SERVICE LEVEL
The level of service **S** will be expressed by the travel time t for a trip between the two towns.

TRANSPORTATION SYSTEM
The road is a two-lane highway divided into two one-lane roadways, one in each direction. It is ten miles long.

SERVICE FUNCTION
We consider each of the roadways separately. The general form of the service function is

$$S = J(T, V) \tag{1.6a}$$

or, in this example,

$$t = m + nV, \tag{1.6b}$$

where options **T** are reflected in the values of the parameters m and n:

$$T = (m, n). \tag{1.7}$$

For this particular highway the parameter values are

$$m = 10 \text{ minutes,}$$
$$n = 0.01 \text{ minute per vehicle/hour.} \tag{1.8}$$

That is,

$$t = 10 + 0.01V. \tag{1.9}$$

The units of t and V are thus minutes and vehicles per hour, respectively.

ACTIVITY SYSTEM

The two towns are characterized by their populations, employment levels, and income levels. The trip-making behavior of the residents reflects these variables.

DEMAND FUNCTION

We consider the one-way demand for travel from City to Suburb only. The general form of the demand function is

$$\mathbf{V} = \mathbf{D}(\mathbf{A}, \mathbf{S}) \tag{1.10a}$$

or

$$V = a + bt, \tag{1.10b}$$

where options **A** are reflected in the values of the parameters a and b:

$$\mathbf{A} = (a, b). \tag{1.11}$$

For travel between the two towns the parameter values are

$$\begin{aligned} a &= 5{,}000 \text{ vehicles/hour,} \\ b &= -100 \text{ vehicles/hour per minute.} \end{aligned} \tag{1.12}$$

Thus

$$V = 5{,}000 - 100t. \tag{1.13}$$

FLOW PATTERN

The flow pattern **F** is defined by the volume V of travelers from City to Suburb, in vehicles per hour, and the level of service they experience, expressed by the travel time t in minutes:

$$\mathbf{F} = (V, t). \tag{1.14}$$

EQUILIBRIUM

The equilibrium flow pattern (V^0, t^0) corresponding to the options $(\mathbf{T}, \mathbf{A})$ will be such that both service and demand relations are satisfied:

$$t^0 = m + nV^0 = 10 + 0.01V^0$$
$$V^0 = a + bt^0 = 5,000 - 100t^0. \tag{1.15}$$

1.4.2 Exercises

INSTRUCTIONS FOR ANSWERING QUESTIONS
Many of the questions that follow are "self-checking" in that their answers immediately follow them. First cover the page with a sheet of paper. Then slide the paper down to the solid square that announces the answer. Now, keeping the answer covered by the paper, read the question. Think through your answer and jot it down on a piece of scratch paper (especially if you are asked to sketch or calculate something). Then uncover the printed answer and compare with your solution. If correct, go on to the next question. If incorrect, go back and review the material until you understand why your answer was wrong.

■ *Question 1.1*   Examine the values of the parameters a, b, m, and n as given in equations (1.8) and (1.12). Discuss briefly the physical significance of these values. What is the significance of their signs ($+$ or $-$)? of their relative magnitudes?

■ *Answer 1.1*   *Parameters a and b:* The demand function describes the number of people or vehicles that will travel at different levels of service (considering travel time as the level of service). The parameter a can be considered as a potential demand, that is, the demand for travel if travel time between the two zones were zero. The equilibrium volume of flow will certainly be less than a. The parameter b represents the change in demand for each unit change of travel time in minutes. Note that $b < 0$, correctly indicating that as travel time increases, demand decreases.

Parameters m and n: The service function describes the level of service that a particular transportation option will provide for various flow volumes. The parameter m measures the free-flow travel time, the travel time over the link for zero volume. The parameter n represents the effects of congestion on travel time. Specifically, for each vehicle on the link, travel time increases by 0.01 minute per mile. Note that $n > 0$ correctly indicates that as V increases, t increases.

■ *Question 1.2*   Find the equilibrium flow pattern graphically. Plot the service and demand functions on the same set of axes. (Place t on the horizontal axis, V on the vertical.) Determine the equilibrium flow pattern F^1 from the intersection of the two functions. (The answer for this question follows the next question.)

■ *Question 1.3* Find the equilbrium flow pattern by solving the equations for F^1 algebraically. Check to see that your results match the graphical solution. (Remember that F^1 is determined by specifying both an equilibrium flow volume and a travel time.)

■ *Answers 1.2 and 1.3* The demand equation is

$$V = 5,000 - 100t,$$

and the service equation is

$$t = 10 + 0.01V.$$

Solving these simultaneous equations, we obtain

$$V = 2,000 \text{ vehicles/hour,}$$

$$t = 30 \text{ minutes.}$$

Thus

$$F^1 = (V, t) = (2,000, 30).$$

This is shown graphically in figure 1.5.

■ *Question 1.4* The highway department is considering building an alternative link connecting zones 1 and 2. This link would be characterized by the following service function:

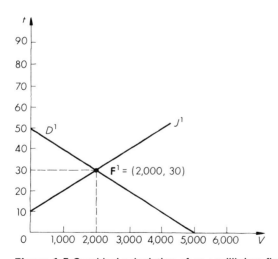

Figure 1.5 Graphical calculation of an equilibrium flow pattern.

$$t = 10 + 0.005V.$$

Plot this function on the same set of axes used in 1.2. Find the new equilibrium volume and travel time, graphically and algebraically. Discuss your results.

■ *Answer 1.4* The new equilibrium flow pattern is $F^2 = (2,666, 23.33)$. Notice that the new link results in decreased travel time and increased volume. Thus the improved facility has "induced," or "generated," $2,666 - 2,000 = 666$ new users on the link. The result is shown graphically in figure 1.6.

1.5 OTHER ELEMENTS OF PREDICTION

While the prediction of flows is an important part of the prediction of transportation impacts, it is not the whole of it. In section 1.2.1 we identified three major types of interrelations among the basic variables **T**, **A**, and **F**. The first relationship is that in which **T** and **A** determine **F**. As we have just seen, this type 1 relation corresponds to the hypothesis that there is a transportation market in which service and demand reach equilibrium, thus establishing the flow pattern $F = (V, S)$.

In addition to the type 1 relation, there are also type 2 and type 3 relations to consider. While the prediction of flow patterns is the core of an analysis, it is rarely the sole element of prediction; many other impacts must usually be predicted as well.

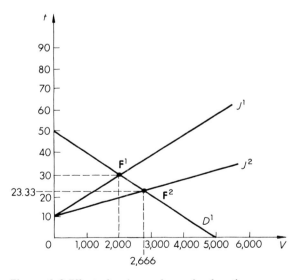

Figure 1.6 Effect of a change in service function on an equilibrium flow pattern.

1.5.1 Activity Shifts

We now explore the type 2 relationship: the effect of the current flow pattern in causing, over time, changes in the activity system. To do this we continue the simple graphical example of section 1.3.

Since it takes time to implement transportation system improvements while population and travel time continue to increase, the demand curve D^0 may shift upward and to the right, yielding a curve D^2, as shown in figure 1.7. The corresponding equilibrium flow $\mathbf{F}^2$ may be such that the improvement in trip time is even less.

This shift in the demand curve is, we assume, independent of any change in the transportation system. The forces influencing this shift are external, or exogenous, events such as population growth or changes in the economy. We designate these as $\mathbf{E}$, for exogenous events; the shift in the demand curve will be a function of $\mathbf{E}$.

The implementation of $\mathbf{T}^1$ may cause further shifts in demand—for example, the development of residential subdivisions and shopping centers may follow the construction of a new highway, or the development of an industrial city may be a consequence of major rail or port development. Thus the demand curve shifts to D^3. (The new equilibrium (V^3, t^3) may actually be such that t^3 is greater than t^0: the level of service over the new system is actually worse than the level of service over the previous system at the initial period. However, it is better than the level of service t^{2*} that would have resulted from the old system $\mathbf{T}^0$ and the shifted demand function D^2.)

This effect takes place, of course, in the context of exogenous

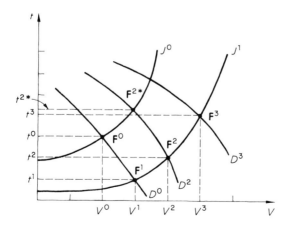

Figure 1.7 Activity shifts.

events **E**. We can represent this chain of effects schematically *(t''* being later than *t')*:

$$(\textbf{T}', \textbf{A}') \longrightarrow [\textbf{F}' = (\textbf{V}', \textbf{S}')] \longrightarrow \textbf{A}''.$$

We call this the activity-shift relation: the pattern of service at time *t'* modifies the activity system at time *t''*. From the point of view of a transportation analysis, the significance is that the demand curve at *t''* is shifted from that at *t'*.

It is often useful to distinguish between these two relationships in the following manner. The type 1 relation involves short-run equilibrium—the pattern of flows that results from a particular activity system. The type 2 relation involves long-run equilibrium—shifts in the activity system itself in response to the flow pattern. We therefore call the type 1 relation ***travel-market equilibration*** and the type 2 relation ***activity-system equilibration.***

1.5.2 Resource Consumption

Transportation systems consume resources such as energy, labor, materials and supplies, and land. Even if no change is made to a system, resources are consumed simply to provide service. If changes are made, especially involving major acquisitions of new vehicles or new guideway facilities, then the resources consumed can be quite substantial. Thus, in addition to predicting flows, we should also predict the resources consumed in providing and operating a particular transportation system.

1.5.3 The Operator Decision Loop

The resources consumed are of interest to a variety of groups, but especially to operators of transportation systems. Here we are concerned with how the operators of particular components of the transportation system decide when and how to adjust the transportation options with which they are concerned.

The structure of this decision is represented by the type 3 relation: the way the actual flows influence decisions concerning transportation options. We do not want to assume away the logic of that decision of what options to implement and thus of what level of service to offer. Rather, we want to isolate the decision variables that are within the control of the operator and include them explicitly in our vector of options. Thus a carrier may determine fares and schedules internally under the criterion of maximizing net revenue, for example. However, a systems analyst would not want to assume that criterion, but would prefer to vary these options—schedules and fares—explicitly. That is, the analyst should deal with the full vector of options explicitly, regardless of which actors have control over particular subsets of options. Then he is in a position to try to identify those options that are within the control of the particular agency or firm for which he is doing the analysis, and to try to anticipate how other options will be manipulated by the actors who have control over them. Since the decisions of other actors may be influenced directly or indirectly, it is important that the decision-making logic of the various actors not be subsumed into the analyst's predictive models.

Therefore, in our approach to analysis we choose to keep all of the transportation decision options external to the prediction process. That is, we "break the loop" on the type 3 relation and do not model it explicitly, as we do with the type 1 and type 2 relations.

Of course, there will be some contexts in which it may be useful and desirable to model the operator's decision processes—for example, when an analyst working for one carrier attempts to develop a strategy in the face of competition from other carriers, or when a regulatory agency attempts to influence, through promotion or restriction, the actions of all carriers. In such cases appropriate models can be developed to predict the decisions of specific transport operators (see section 5.7, where we show how assuming an operator decision logic can lead to development of a "supply" function).

1.5.4 Systems of Models

Thus, to predict all significant impacts, five major types of models are required:

1. *Service models* are needed to determine, for any specified set of options, the levels of service at various flow volumes. Examples: travel time over a rail link as a function of train length, schedule, roadway conditions, and volume of passengers; volume vs. travel time curves as used in traffic assignment procedures.

2. *Resource models* are needed to determine the resources consumed (land, labor, capital, and other direct costs; air, noise, and other environmental impacts; aesthetic and social impacts) in providing a particular level of service with specified options.

3. *Demand models* are needed to determine the volume of travel demanded, and its composition, at various levels of service.

4. *Equilibrium models* are needed to predict the volumes that will

actually flow in a transportation system for a particular set of service and demand functions (short-term equilibrium in the travel market).

5. ***Activity-shift models*** are needed to predict the long-term changes in the spatial distribution and structure of the activity system as a consequence of the short-run equilibrium pattern of flows, that is, the feedback effect of transportation on land use (activity-system equilibration).

These are the five basic components of any system of prediction models in transportation. The interrelationships among them are illustrated in figure 1.8. In addition, it would be desirable also to have models for predicting the changes in organizational and institutional behavior that result from changes in organizational policies. These models, however, are beyond the scope of this volume (see, for example, Allison 1971).

This structuring of the transportation systems analysis problem incorporates five hypotheses. The first hypothesis is that this is a complete and useful summary of the types of options and impacts. The second hypothesis is that it is meaningful to model transportation technology from two perspectives: in terms of the service perceived by prospective users, reflected in the service functions, and in terms of the resources consumed in providing that transportation service, reflected in the resource functions. The third hypothesis is that it is useful to separate short-term and long-term equilibrium: the short-term re-

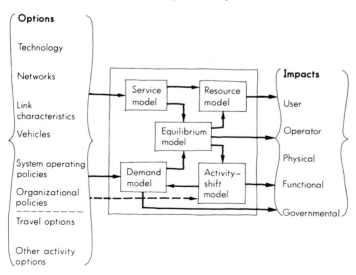

Figure 1.8 Basic prediction models.

sponses of transportation users, in a "transportation market" with the activity system fixed, as represented by the demand functions (the type 1 relation); and the long-term responses of users and others in a larger, more general market, the total economy, as represented by the activity shifts (the type 2 relation). The fourth hypothesis is that a unique equilibrium exists in each of these markets and that it can be found. The fifth hypothesis, which in a sense is the operational test of the second, third, and fourth hypotheses, is that valid predictive models can indeed be constructed.

1.5.5 The Variety of Applications (Optional Reading)

This framework has been applied (implicitly if not explicitly) in a wide variety of analytical activities, including urban transportation planning, intercity passenger transport studies, and national transportation planning in developing countries.

Urban transportation studies began in Detroit and Chicago in the mid-1950s. The prediction portion of the conventional urban transportation planning process consists of variants of the following sequence (Martin, Memmott, and Bone 1961, Hutchinson 1974):

1. Project land use, population, and employment changes.
2. Predict trip ends generated in each zone.
3. Predict interzonal distribution of trip ends (using gravity or opportunity models).
4. Predict modal split.
5. Predict distribution of flows over the proposed network.

These steps implicitly represent a travel-market equilibration (see chapter 11).

There are serious internal inconsistencies in this sequence, from the point of view of an equilibrium analysis (Wohl and Martin 1967, Manheim 1970b, 1973b). For example, the estimation of trip ends assumes implicitly a general level of service in the system, whereas the interzonal distribution calculations require an explicit level of service (derived by means of a gravity model, for example). The last step of the process, traffic assignment, predicts an "actual" level of service, or set of travel times, for flows in the network. However, the initial estimates of level of service used for trip generation and distribution are rarely revised to be consistent with the travel times predicted by the traffic assignment.

In spite of these inconsistencies and other limitations, the structure implicit in conventional urban transportation models is fundamentally that described here. The service functions are represented as volume vs. travel time functions or simply link capacities and travel times. The demand functions are represented by predicting trip ends, interzonal distribution of trips, and then modal split. The travel-market equilibrium model is the "traffic-assignment" process, with the various "capacity-restraint" formulations representing explicit attempts to find equilibrium in the network, given fixed demands. (All-or-nothing assignments are obviously very difficult to justify as a meaningful prediction of "equilibrium" flows.) The resource models are represented in a variety of ad hoc calculations involving such factors as rights-of-way and construction and operating costs. Activity-shift models are sometimes explicit, as when land-use models are used to predict the effects of differential changes in accessibilities on the location of population and economic activities. More often they are left unstated.

While the conventional urban transportation planning models have serious limitations, a new generation of models is now being developed. These models encompass much improved demand functions and a sounder theoretical basis for explicit travel-market equilibrium analysis (see chapter 11).

In intercity passenger transport studies, this equilibrium structure has been more explicit. For example, in the Northeast Corridor Transportation Project—the first major intercity study—the system of models used included explicit demand models for passengers and freight (see section 4.3.2); technology models to produce service and resource functions; a network simulator for travel-market equilibration; and activity-shift models for forecasting changes in inter- and intraregional location and intensities of economic activities as a function of changes in transportation and other factors (Bruck, Manheim, and Shuldiner 1967).

The Harvard-Brookings Model System was designed for use in planning investment in transportation in developing countries (Kresge and Roberts 1971). Several explicit technology models were used for predicting service levels and resource consumption of highways, railways, and other modes and of intermodal transfer points. Demand for travel was derived from a macroeconomic model containing an interregional input-output model; these were also used to predict activity shifts. Network equilibrium was found with a modified traffic-assignment approach.

These examples illustrate some of the applications of the basic concepts. They are very cursory descriptions of highly sophisticated systems of models, and they simply point out how the basic framework outlined above has been applied, implicitly or explicitly, in several major transportation analyses. In each application different practical approximations have been made.

1.5.6 Two Styles of Prediction

The prediction of the future impacts of alternative transportation plans is a difficult task. For plans that involve small changes to an existing system, and impacts in the near future, information about the present system and its effects can play a strong role. In this case it is useful to predict impacts by predicting the magnitudes of the changes from present conditions, leading to a style that we shall term *incremental prediction.*

In incremental prediction the analyst knows the present states of the transportation and activity systems—T^0, A^0—the flow patterns— $F^0 = (V^0, S^0)$—and the resources being consumed—R^0. For any specified change ΔT^i in the transportation system, the impacts to be predicted are the incremental changes in the various elements—ΔV^i, ΔS^i, ΔR^i, ΔA^i. (These symbols generally represent vectors and may represent variations over time.)

In *synthetic prediction,* or simply "prediction," the analyst predicts the new values of V^i, S^i, R^i, and A^i directly.

The major difference is a practical one. Incremental prediction opens the way for application of powerful approximation methods. It is also good discipline for the analyst's judgments about the magnitudes of changes likely to occur from existing conditions.

In later chapters we shall often show how short-cut, simplified analyses can be done using incremental instead of synthetic prediction.

1.5.7 Conclusions: The Elements of Prediction

The same basic theory is applicable to every transportation systems problem. Prediction of the impacts of the range of alternative transport plans requires, in general, the whole system of five models for service, demand, equilibrium, resources, and activity shifts. In actually applying the theory to a particular context, however, very different practical methods may be appropriate in different problems.

The principles presented in section 1.2 and the approach to prediction presented in this section are guidelines, not rigid prescriptions. One element of the art of doing a valid yet pragmatic and relevant analysis is to apply these concepts judiciously. The development of a long-range multimodal plan for an urban region might utilize a set of approximations very different from that of an analysis of next month's schedule changes for a single bus route or the planning of a rail system in a developing country. The practical application of these concepts in a particular context requires understanding of the theoretical basis of the field and of the practical methods available in a specific situation.

This frames *the methodological challenge of transportation systems analysis*, which is to conduct an analysis in a particular situation which is valid, practical, and relevant.

1.5.8 Example (continued)
We continue with the example of section 1.4.

■ *Question 1.5* Often, while new transportation facilities are being planned and constructed, changes occur within the activity system. In our particular case, over the ten-year period of planning and construction of the new link described in question 1.1, the following changes occur in the activity system:

1. Population and job levels in the two zones increase.
2. On the average, people now place a relatively higher value on time.

Assume that the parameters of the new demand function describing the activity system at this future date are

$a' = 7,500$ vehicles/hour,
$b' = -150$ vehicles/hour per minute.

i. Compare these values with those given earlier in this section, for the existing conditions. Are they consistent with the activity-system changes described above? Briefly discuss your reasoning.

ii. Plot the new demand function on the same set of axes as in questions 1.2 and 1.4. Find the new equilibrium graphically or algebraically. Remember which service and demand functions we are now considering.

iii. What would the travel time over the existing link be if the new one had not been built?

■ *Answer 1.5*
i. The two demand functions are

$V = 5,000 - 100t,$
$V = 7,500 - 150t.$

The demand parameters of the second function are consistent with the described changes within the activity system. Increases in population

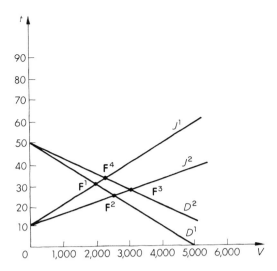

Figure 1.9 Effect of activity-system changes.

and job levels tend to increase the potential demand as expressed by parameter a'. As time is valued more dearly, the unit change in demand (for each unit of travel time) will increase. Thus b, which measures the sensitivity of demand with respect to travel time, becomes more negative as people value time more dearly.

 ii. Solving algebraically:

Demand: $V = 7{,}500 - 150t$,
Supply: $t = 10 + 0.005V$.

Thus

$V = 3{,}430$ vehicles/hour,
$t = 27.15$ minutes,
$F_3 = (V, t) = (3{,}430, 27.15)$.

Comparing this result to those of question 1.1, we see that both travel time and volume have increased. Referring to figure 1.9, we see that our equilibrium point has moved along the service curve because of the shift in demand.

 iii. From the plot or algebra,

$F_4 = (2{,}400, 34)$.

■ *Question 1.6* There are many examples of facilities being out-dated from their very first day of service. For example, the Long Island

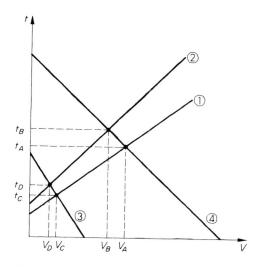

Figure 1.10 Effect of the introduction of a new highway.

Expressway was congested soon after it was opened (Caro 1974, p. 949). In fact, it is observed that travel times can increase on supposedly new, improved facilities. Discuss this phenomenon with reference to figure 1.10.

i. Specifically, identify the functions that represent the old facility (highway), the new, improved facility, the old activity system, and the new activity system.

ii. Describe the relative magnitudes of the equilibrium volumes and travel times for the old and new systems.

iii. An irate traveler was quoted as saying, "Look, since they've built the new highway my trip time is worse than ever. I haven't derived any benefit from this road." Study the figure. Do you agree that the new road has made things worse for society? Ponder seriously, but comment only briefly.

■ *Answer 1.6*

i. The old facility is represented by function 2, the new facility by function 1, the old activity system by function 3, and the new activity system by function 4.

ii. Referring to the figure, it can be seen that the new equilibrium flow is (V_A, t_A). Both travel time and volume are greater than the old equilibrium flow pattern (V_D, t_D).

iii. As paradoxical as it may seem, it must be concluded that users have benefited from the new system. Consider that most trips are made for useful purposes (on urban highways, for example, we find that most trips are for work, shopping, school, or recreation). If a new system induces greatly increased travel, we can only conclude that more people are traveling to work, shopping centers, schools, and social functions. From the viewpoint of users, we see that more people are making more trips and thus deriving more benefits from the new highway than from the old. The increased travel time is an unfortunate by-product of urban growth. Of course, key questions are: What costs were incurred in order to build this new facility? What would have occurred if the facility was not built? Who benefited and who was hurt by the new facility?

It should be stressed that travel demand and changes in land use are not independent of changes in transportation systems. Often new highways spur tremendous growth in residential and industrial land use. For example, the Long Island Expressway brought about a tremendous growth in residential areas of Long Island. And Route 128 in the Boston area precipitated an industrial migration as large firms found it more profitable to locate in suburban areas (served by the new road) than in a downtown business district. Thus new highways can create jobs and spur residential land development. These benefits are often difficult to measure directly but can have great effects on society.

1.6 PUTTING PREDICTION IN CONTEXT

So far, in discussing options, impacts, equilibrium analysis, and model systems, we have been relatively abstract. What implications can we draw from this discussion? What steps should we go through in order to analyze a particular transportation system problem?

1.6.1 The Analysis Cycle

We start with a particular transportation system plan. This plan proposes certain transportation and activity systems described as sets of options. To assess the impacts of this plan, we must predict the flow pattern that will occur if it is implemented, that is, the short-run equilibrium of the transportation market and the long-run equilibrium effects of transportation on the location and character of social and economic activity. These predictions require a system of five models describing service, demand, equilibrium, resources, and activity shifts.

Thus the core of the transportation systems analysis problem is prediction of the impacts of a particular plan using a system of equilibrium models. *Prediction* is concerned with anticipating the consequences of alternative plans: What impacts will each alternative have? On whom will they fall? For a particular pattern of available transportation services, what will be the flows? How will each alternative affect the evolution of the activity system?

But how did we get the plans in the first place? There must have been some kind of process by which a variety of possibilities were quickly examined and discarded, until some reasonably good candidates emerged. This is the *search process*—the generation of alternatives sufficiently well-defined to be tested in prediction. The search process may be algorithmic (a linear-programming procedure, for example) or completely intuitive (an analyst proposing a change in services or prices, or a designer sketching a network on a map) or some mixture of the two extremes. The questions one must ask in this process are: What possibilities for intervention are there? What aspects of the transportation system might be modified or improved? What alternative actions should we examine? What actions are most likely to achieve the objectives desired?

Once one or several alternative plans have been generated through some search procedure, and the impacts have been predicted using the system of prediction models, the next task is to evaluate those impacts, compare the predicted impacts for the various alternatives, and arrive at a judgment as to which alternatives are preferred, and why. *Evaluation* and *choice* are the activities through which the predicted consequences of alternative actions are distilled and weighed, to reach a decision on a course of action. They involve such questions as the following: What impacts would be most desirable? Which of the al-

a Prediction

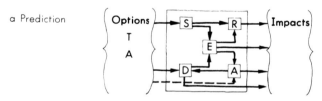

b Analysis cycle

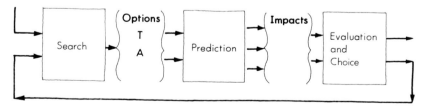

Figure 1.11 Prediction in the larger process.

39   The Challenge of Transportation Systems Analysis

ternative actions would be most desirable? Whose points of view should be considered in reaching a decision? What should be the process of reaching a decision? Which alternative should be implemented?

Figure 1.11 brings out the interrelations of these activities. Part b of the figure emphasizes the iterative nature of the process: after evaluation and choice, there should be the option of recycling to search again, one or more times, generating and evaluating a succession of alternatives. This iterative process may proceed until a desirable alternative is found or until the available resources (dollars, time) are exhausted.

1.6.2 Analysis and Implementation

Of course, even this view of the process of analysis is limited, and we must embed it in a yet larger picture. This is shown in figure 1.12, in which several additional distinctions have been made:

1. A **setup phase** precedes the technical analysis. In order to do the prediction, the system of models must be developed: data must be collected, initial goals formulated, and substantial development activity

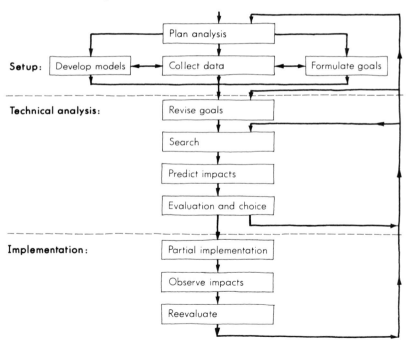

Figure 1.12 The continuing analysis process—Image 1.

must occur in order to produce appropriate service, demand, and other models. The analysis and setup phases must be planned.

2. The ***technical-analysis phase*** includes not only search, prediction, and evaluation and choice, but also a goal formulation and revision task. Initial statements of objectives must be formulated in the setup phase to provide guidance for the development of models and data collection. At the start of analysis these goals are revised to provide guidance for search and a basis for evaluation and choice. However, it is to be expected that, as the transportation analysts learn about the problem by iterating through search, prediction, evaluation, and choice, goals will be revised and refined (Manheim 1970a).

3. Transportation systems analysis is rarely conducted in a vacuum. There is usually a purpose to the analysis: to come to a conclusion as to a desirable course of action to be implemented in the real world. Therefore, we show an ***implementation phase*** following the technical analysis.

The central idea behind this figure is that transportation systems analysis is a dynamic activity. For existing systems, analysis of alternative options is a continuing task. For systems being expanded or built new, it must be recognized that change takes time. It may take many years to implement fully a particular course of action—building a highway or an airport, restructuring the routes and services of a transit system or an airline, building a major new freeway or transit system—even after it has been adopted in principle.

Many transportation analyses are still being set up as "one-shot" activities: do a study, recommend a course of action, and disappear. However, it is now becoming more widely recognized that a truly effective transportation systems analysis must be a continuing activity because of the long time period for implementation. As implementation of the recommended action gets under way, the actual impacts should be observed and compared with the predictions. Simultaneously, changes in technology, in demand, and in values should also be monitored. Based upon this new information, the analysis and even setup phases should be recycled, to adapt the previously recommended action to changing conditions.

1.6.3 The Product of Analysis

To emphasize the continuous nature of the task, the relation of analysis and implementation might be visualized as in figure 1.13. Here we emphasize that actions are implemented periodically, leading to system

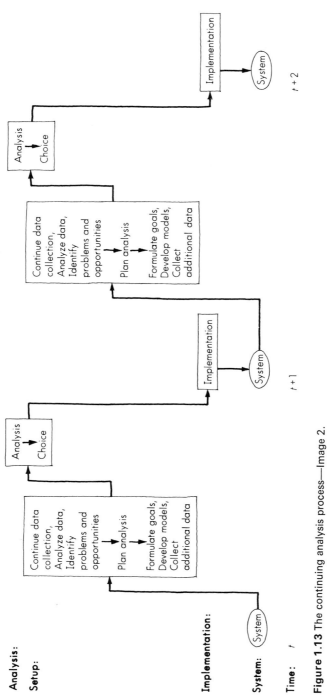

Figure 1.13 The continuing analysis process—Image 2.

changes. The system evolves over time, influenced partly by internal dynamics (the interactions of transportation and activity systems) and partly by actions taken deliberately as a result of analysis.

The synthesis of the images of figures 1.12 and 1.13 can be described in terms of the product of analysis, the **_multiyear program plan_** (MYPP) shown in figure 1.14. The MYPP reflects the view that the product of analysis is a program of actions staged over an extended period, which might range up to perhaps twenty-five years. The outcome of the first period of the plan is firm and detailed: it is the set of specific implementable actions that will be taken in the next period. That is, inclusion of an action in the first period of the MYPP represents a decision to implement that action in the next period. That first period may be a year in the case of a regional or national planning agency, or a quarter (three months) in the case of an operator such as a transit agency or airline. Each succeeding period of the plan is less firm and less detailed. The actions in the first few periods (up to year three or five) of the MYPP constitute the "Short-Range Plan"; those further off (say, in years six to fifteen), the "Midrange Plan"; and later actions (say, in years sixteen to twenty-five) the "Long-Range Plan." These time periods may be shorter or longer in different organizational contexts. For example, for an airline the short range may be three to six months, the midrange six to twenty-four months, and the long range two to five years.

The MYPP contains all significant transportation actions proposed for the system. For a region these would cover all modes and all types of transportation and related options: changes in facilities, in vehicle fleets, in operating policies (routes, schedules, fares, classes of services, restraint and other disincentive policies), in organizations and institutions, and in transportation-related actions (staggered work hours, land-use controls, sewer and water policies). For a private carrier such as a trucker or an airline the actions would be more restricted, such as changes in vehicle fleets, routes, schedules, and services.

The MYPP also includes a listing of studies to be undertaken. These actions are as important as implementation actions because they influence, and sometimes constrain, the implementation actions that can be seriously considered in future years—you cannot consider implementing a major new service strategy *next* year if you didn't do some homework on it *this* year.

The MYPP logically should have different degrees of detail for different types of actions. The MYPP for a region such as a metropolitan area or state may contain component MYPPs for various sub-

Action	Year			
	1 Implement	2 3 4 5 Short range	6 ... 15 Midrange	15 ... 25 or 30 Long range
Implementation				
Facilities: New Improvements				
Vehicles				
System operating policies (including pricing)				
Organization				
Transportation-related activity-system actions				
Studies				
Planning				
Design				
Monitoring				
Evaluation				
Research				
Costs				
Category A				
·				
·				
·				
Category Z				

Figure 1.14 The transportation multiyear program plan (Manheim 1977a).

regions. Different levels of detail would be appropriate for different levels of geographic aggregation. The MYPP for a county or medium-sized city would be more detailed than that for a state. The state MYPP would summarize in a single item what might be a large number of specific actions in a county MYPP. Similarly, the MYPP for an operator's system may contain MYPPs for portions of the system.

A sample MYPP for a particular region is given in figure 1.15.

Where decisions on actions to be taken in future years have not been made yet, or are contingent on alternative outcomes of earlier actions, the MYPP can show these. For example, unresolved issues can be included or explicit contingencies shown, as in figure 1.15.

The MYPP must be reviewed periodically and revised according to an explicit decision process in which progress in implementing actions in the first period of the preceding year's MYPP is reviewed. Obviously, not all elements of the MYPP would be subject to the same degree of scrutiny in each review cycle. For example, the long-range portion of the MYPP might be revised in a major way only once every three or five years, or when a decision is to be taken on implementing a major project in the next year.

In the periodic decision process, some of the actions in the second year of the preceding year's MYPP may be advanced into the first year of the new MYPP, reflecting decisions to implement those actions; others may be deferred for implementation or may be discarded altogether. This reflects the fact that while the MYPP lays out planned future actions, in actuality the only firm decision is an implementable one: how to spend next year's dollars. Since actions indicated in the MYPP are never certain of implementation until they move into the first year of a current MYPP, an important issue in choosing an action for implementation in a given year is its degree of "commitment" versus "flexibility": If this action is implemented, which future options will be foreclosed, and which will remain open for future implementation?

1.6.4 Implications for Analysis

Designing an analysis thus involves more than just developing a prediction model. The analyst must develop a **strategy for analysis** that includes plans for the full range of necessary technical activities:

1. What data should be collected?
2. What models should be developed?
3. How should the tasks of search, prediction, and evaluation and choice be organized into a coherent process?

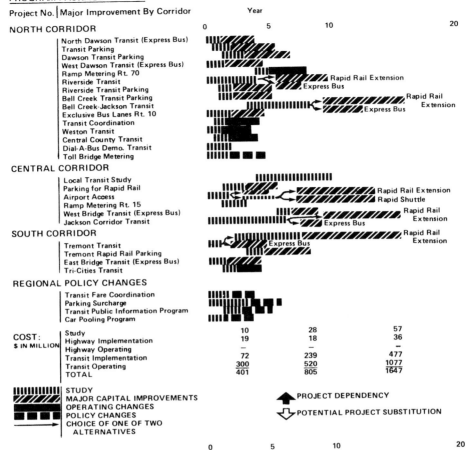

Figure 1.15 A sample multiyear program plan (Manheim et al. 1975b, based on Neumann 1976).

4. How should technical activities interface with the political process?

5. What should be the nature of the continuing analysis and implementation process?

1.6.5 Systematic Analysis

The general structure of a systematic analysis is illustrated metaphorically in figure 1.16: the options **T** are varied systematically over a range, and the impacts on various interests—here, users, operators, and government—are traced out as **T** is varied. For example, it is often especially important to explore trade-offs among various types of options—increasing frequency of service versus reducing fares to increase ridership; changing the relative mix of resources expended on new facilities as opposed to operating expenses and improvements in existing facilities; or changing the relative mix of expenditures on various modes.

Of course, the prediction of impacts for each **T** requires use of the system of prediction models. Practically, therefore, the metaphor may be difficult to apply in some situations. As we shall demonstrate in later chapters, however, a systematic analysis can be achieved in most situations. Practical strategies involve careful design of the iterations of the basic analysis cycle of search-prediction-evaluation to trace out trade-offs.

1.6.6 Analysis and the Political Process

To intervene effectively in the fabric of society and bring about change through the implementation of a transportation system plan, the analyst

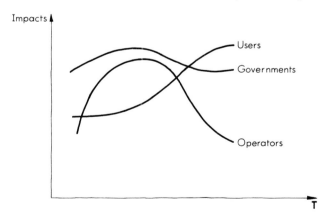

Figure 1.16 The general structure of a systematic analysis.

must have a perspective on the relation between analysis and the political process.

The transportation systems analyst usually operates in a complex institutional environment, whether public or private. In such an environment there are usually many different groups that will have an interest in the outcome of the analyst's work, and they will all have different ideas about what it is desirable to achieve with transportation. Typically, also, there are many different institutions involved.

To be useful, analysis must be relevant to the issues with which these institutions and interest groups are concerned (or are likely to be concerned), and must clarify the issues in ways that contribute to the constructive resolution of potential conflicts and to the making of implementable decisions by responsible decision makers.

With this view, and with the definition of systematic analysis in the preceding section, we see that our definition of the methodological challenge of transportation systems analysis (section 1.5.7) needs to be broadened, by adding the concepts of "systematic analysis" and "clarification of issues": *The methodological challenge of transportation systems analysis is to conduct a systematic analysis in a particular situation which is valid, practical, and relevant, and which assists in clarifying the issues to be debated.*

In responding to this challenge, the analyst must be concerned with many basically different kinds of activities. Our focus in this book will be primarily on prediction, with some attention to evaluation. As a result of this concentration, we shall develop a rather abstract, technical view of transportation systems analysis. This is necessary in order to foster the understanding of fundamentals that is essential to doing good analysis. But it must be kept in mind that transportation systems analysis must be rooted in the complexities of social and political reality. Ultimately we must return from the delights of abstract analytics to the realities of social and political issues and forces.

Successful response to the challenge requires deep understanding, not only of the theory and techniques of prediction, but also of search, evaluation, choice, the structuring of a process of analysis, and, most importantly, the social, economic, and political context in which an analysis is being conducted.

1.7 SUMMARY

We live in a world of rapid change—change in transportation technology, in transportation demand, and in the values, public and private, that will influence decisions about transportation systems. The challenge of transportation systems analysis is to use the transportation system to help a society achieve its goals. Therefore, analysis must be a continuous process. Setup, technical analysis, and implementation must be continuously iterated and adjusted to changing conditions, with the adopted course of action revised appropriately.

At the core of this process is the prediction task: based upon the current understanding of the mechanisms of interaction between transportation and activity systems, a set of models is developed and used to predict the impacts of proposed courses of action. The heart of this prediction of impacts is the prediction of flows in networks, based upon service–demand equilibrium concepts. Although simple in concept, prediction is a major technical task.

It is this task of prediction to which we turn first in the following chapters. Though the discourse will become highly technical and somewhat abstract, it is important that the reader keep in mind the broader context in which these techniques are embedded.

TO READ FURTHER
For further discussion of the interrelation of transportation and activity systems, see S. B. Warner (1962) and Meyer, Kain, and Wohl (1965). The best sources of information on current transportation issues and news are newspapers, news magazines, and industry-oriented publications such as *Railway Age, U.S. Transport, Mass Transit,* and *Aviation Week and Space Technology.*

EXERCISES
1.1(C)   Select a current transportation issue that interests you and that involves the transportation services of a particular region or operator. Identify the key elements you think should be included in an analysis of this issue, such as:

a. major options to be analyzed
b. major impacts to be predicted
c. major flow types
d. service attributes
e. prediction procedures
f. possible search procedures
g. what the choice process might be like.

1.2(P)   Select a transportation study for which you have adequate documentation (a final report, environmental impact statement, or an internal staff study).

a. Summarize concisely the key issues that the study seems designed to address.

b. Identify the key elements of the study:

i. system considered (refer to the system principles in section 1.2)

ii. options and impacts considered

iii. flow types considered (passengers and/or commodities)

iv. service attributes considered

v. prediction procedures used (demand functions, activity-shift functions, service and resource functions, travel-market equilibration, operator and activity-system equilibration procedures)

vi. search procedures and evaluation procedures

vii. choice process

viii. assumptions about exogenous events.

c. Discuss the study elements:

i. Does the system definition seem appropriate to the issues? If not, why not?

ii. Do the options and impacts seem appropriate? If not, why not?

iii. Continue the disscussion with other elements identified in part b.

1.3(P)   Choose two of the following contexts: air carrier, trucking company, shipping company, port authority, national highway agency.

a. What are the major types of options that might be considered by this organization?

b. Sketch out a hypothetical multiyear program plan for this organization.

c. What would be the basic features of the prediction models required to predict the impacts of this MYPP?

1.4(E)   In railroad operations there is substantial debate about train length. In a particular market longer trains reduce crew costs. On the other hand, by operating more frequent, shorter trains, "railroads incur greater crew costs, but obtain better service and improved freight car utilization. Furthermore, short trains can be handled more easily at yards, at sidings, and on the line than long trains. In some instances, however, running more short trains could cause operating delays on congested portions of the system" (Martland, Assarabowski, and Mc-Carren 1977). Consider the situation of a 200-mile segment of rail line on which the present operating policy is to run two trains per day with 90 cars each, or a total capacity of 180 cars per day:

$$\mathbf{T}^0 = (Q^0, L^0) = (2, 90),$$

where

Q = frequency (trains per day),

L = train length (cars per train).

The cost per train in dollars is (after Martland 1977)

$$C_{TRAIN}(Q, L) = 2.40 \frac{L}{Q} + (480 + 1.33L + 0.004L^2)$$

or, for a day's schedule of Q trains,

$$C_{DAY}(Q, L) = QC_{TRAIN} = 2.40L + Q(480 + 1.33L + 0.004L^2).$$

The total capacity available in cars per day, V_C, is

$$V_C = QL.$$

Operating management believes that the following demand function applies in this corridor (V_D is demand volume):

$$V_D(Q, L) = 180 \left(\frac{Q}{Q_0} \right)^\beta;$$

a "best estimate" of β is 0.5.

Management's objective is to increase net revenue, I_{NR}, where

$$I_{NR} = I_{GR} - C_{DAY}$$

and gross revenue, I_{GR}, is a function of equilibrium volume V_E and price P:

$$I_{GR} = V_E P.$$

At present P = \$15 per carload for freight over this segment.

a. Consider the possibility of adding 1, 2, or 3 more trains per day, maintaining the same train lengths. Predict the equilibrium flows and the corresponding costs and revenues for these strategies. Which of these strategies (T^0, T^1, T^2, T^3) would you recommend to management, and why?

b. If your objective were maximum service to users, which would you recommend, and why? Compare with your answer to part a and discuss.

c. For a given frequency, what are the advantages and disadvantages of varying train lengths? If you knew that for a frequency Q^i the demand would be V^i, what train length would you recommend?

d. Consider these alternative strategies: $T^4 = (Q^4 = 3, L^4 = 75)$, $T^5 = (4, 75)$, $T^6 = (5, 75)$, $T^7 = (4, 70)$, $T^8 = (5, 70)$, $T^9 = (5, 60)$. Which of these would you recommend from the operator's perspective? for $Q = 4$? for $Q = 5$? Which of the ten strategies T^0–T^9 would you recommend from the operator's perspective? from the user's perspective? Discuss.

e. Using your result to part c, find the train length L_{OPT} that is best from the operator's perspective for each frequency $Q = 3, 4, 5$, and predict the impacts of the corresponding strategies. Plot the results on axes defined by V_D and I_{NR} and discuss. Which would be best from the operator's perspective? from the user's perspective? Why? Which would you recommend, and why?

f. How might the results change for $\beta = 0.2$? $\beta = 0.8$? (Check only for $L = L_{OPT}$ for this range of frequencies.)

g. Critique the assumptions (implicit and explicit) of this formulation of the problem: Under what conditions, and to what extent, do you think they would be reasonable? (For example, what do you think of the explicit assumption that demand is independent of the train length?)

1.5(E) The country of Freelandia gained independence a few years ago and is mounting a major effort to promote new agricultural development in previously underdeveloped regions. A trucking operator in the town of K has previously been providing only local service. Now that a new major agricultural development program is under way, this operator is considering providing farm-to-market service to carry agricultural and other natural products from their origin in locality M to market at K. The distance is 150 miles (one way), with no intermediate major settlements.

After discussions with the local agents of the producers at M, the trucker estimates that the demand function for shipments from M to K is

$$V = Z + a_0 Q - a_1 P,$$

where V is volume in tons per week, Q is frequency of shipments (per week), P is price charged per ton, and a_0, a_1, and Z are parameters. Based upon an average traveling speed of 30 miles per hour, plus a loading or unloading time of 3 hours at each end, he estimates that he can manage at the most one round trip every two days, so $Q = 3$ per week. He also figures that his costs are related to the mileage he drives per year: his total cost per year is

$$C_T = b_0 + b_1 m_T,$$

where $m_T = 300Q$ is the total round-trip mileage driven and b_0 and b_1 are parameters. The truck carries 15 tons. He is considering offering an initial frequency of 1 or 2 trips per week at a rate of \$25.00 or

$30.00 per ton. Assume $b_0 = \$270$, $b_1 = \$0.50$, $Z = 25$, $a_0 = 13$, $a_1 = 1$.

a. For these four combinations of frequency and price, what would be the tonnage carried, the gross revenues, the total cost, and the net revenue?

b. Which of the four options would be preferred by the operator if his objective where to maximize net revenue? to minimize costs? to maximize volume carried? Which option would be preferred by users (shippers)? Can both interests get their first choice simultaneously? If not, why not?

c. For the proposed service the predominant movement is from M to K; the amount of freight to be carried in the reverse direction is negligible. There is a possibility of picking additional cargo at D to go to M; this would incur a detour of 100 miles additional but could result in an additional load and source of revenue. Would it be profitable for this operator to make the detour? Discuss qualitatively.

1.6(E) A railroad operator utilizes a fleet of 2,000 freight cars for service to a particular group of shippers, who produce grain. At present train schedules are poorly coordinated. Because service is unreliable, shippers take an excessive amount of time to load and unload the cars, with the result that an average car delivers $n = 10$ carloads per year (that is, the cycle time is $t_c = 365/10 = 36.5$ days).

The cost of owning a railroad car is $2,000 per year (equivalent annual cost). At present shippers are charged $p = \$1,200$ per load, and the operating costs (excluding ownership) are $a = \$1,100$ per load.

The service now runs at a loss. Management is considering three options: (A) increase rates; (B) improve schedule coordination and other aspects of operation so that service is more reliable, delivery times are shortened, and shippers load and unload cars more quickly; or (C) do both of the above. The marketing staff has come up with the following approximate demand function showing the effect on total carloads V of a change in rates, in cycle time, or in both:

$$\frac{\Delta V}{V_0} = \alpha \frac{\Delta p}{p_0} + \beta \frac{\Delta t_c}{t_{c0}}.$$

a. Assume $\alpha = -0.4$, $\beta = -1.2$, $V_0 = 2,000 \times 10 = 20,000$. Predict the new volume V' for (A) $\Delta p = +\$100$; (B) $\Delta t_c = -4.5$ days; and (C) both.

b. Assuming that the fleet size stays the same, predict for each option the increase in annual revenues from shippers (Vp), the increase in operating costs ($2,000na$), and the change in net operating revenue ($Vp - 2,000na$). Which option would you recommend?

c. Which option would you recommend if the cost of implementing option B turned out to be equivalent to an increase in operating costs to $a = \$1,200$ per load?

d. Do a sensitivity analysis for the assumed demand parameters, using $\alpha = -0.8$ and -1.2; $\beta = -0.4$ and -0.8. Discuss.

1.7(E) A marine operator presently offers service between ports A and B, 6,000 miles apart, utilizing a single ship. At an equivalent land speed of 20 miles per hour (ship speeds are usually expressed in nautical miles or knots), the total sailing time for a one-way voyage is 300 hours or 12.5 days. The average time spent loading or unloading cargo in either port is two days, so the average one-way trip time for the ocean voyage for a cargo is $12.5 + 0.5(2 + 2) = 14.5$ days. The round-trip time is thus 29 days. For a "working year" of 330 days (allowing time for periodic maintenance), the effective frequency is $330/29 = 11.4$ round trips per year. The ship's capacity is 15,000 tons of cargo; the rate presently charged is $25 per ton. The average cost of a one-way trip is $225,000 per voyage, or $15 per ton of available capacity.

The operator estimates that the demand function in this market is

$$V = Z_0 - \alpha t_{iv} - \beta/Q - \gamma c,$$

where

V = round-trip volume in tons per year
Z_0 = market size factor
t_{iv} = one-way trip time
Q = frequency in round trips per year
c = freight rate in dollars per ton
α, β, γ = parameters.

His estimates of the parameters are $\alpha = 19,500$, $\beta = 3.1 \times 10^6$, $\gamma = 8,000$, and $Z_0 = 982,680$. The average volume per voyage is 20,000 tons.

a. Are his estimates of the parameters consistent with this volume? What fraction of available capacity is utilized per voyage? What is his gross revenue (receipts from rates paid), total cost, and net revenue (gross revenue less total cost) per voyage?

b. The operator is considering replacing the present ship with a newer vessel, which would have a speed of 24 miles per hour, thus cutting the one-way sailing time to 10.4 days. The cost per voyage of this newer, faster ship would be $250,000 per one-way trip. The capacity and loading/unloading times would be the same. Would this ship be more attractive to the operator: (i) if frequency and rate remained the same? (ii) if the frequency were increased to take advantage of the increased speed but the rate remained the same? (iii) if the frequency were increased and the rate increased to $30.00 per ton? Summarize and discuss your results: What consequences can a change in vehicle speed have? Discuss the significance of the parameters α, β, and γ.

c. After doing this analysis, the operator suddenly realizes that he has ignored a fundamental principle: the time that will influence shipper's decisions (that is, the demand function) should be the total door-to-door time, not just the trip time on the ocean leg. He estimates that an average shipment spends about six days in the land portion of the trip, for a total travel time of 20.5 days. How might this affect his estimates? (Discuss qualitatively.)

1.8(E) A railroad runs from A to B, a distance of 500 miles, through mountainous terrain. The present one-way travel time (including time at intermediate yards) is 20 hours, and the rail freight rate is $20 per ton. There is a truck service which competes with the railroad, running over roughly parallel roads for approximately the same distance, at an average speed of 30 miles per hour and at a rate of $30 per ton. A new highway is planned to replace the existing road; while there is some auto traffic, it is expected that most of the traffic will be trucks. The service function of the new facility is $t_T = t_0 + bV_T$, where V_T is the total volume in trucks per hour (the anticipated auto usage is negligible), $t_0 = 10$ hours, $b = 0.08$ hour per truck per hour. The railroad's estimate of the demand function is

$$\frac{V_T}{V_R} = a_0 \left(\frac{t_T}{t_R}\right)^{a_1} \left(\frac{c_T}{c_R}\right)^{a_2},$$

where t_T and t_R are the trip times by truck and rail, respectively, c_T and c_R are the rates, V_T and V_R are the volumes, and a_0, a_1, and a_2 are parameters. The total volume is likely to remain constant at $V_{TOT} = V_T + V_R = 200$ truckloads per hour. The rail system is utilized at only a fraction of capacity, so its service function is flat—travel time is constant independent of volume.

a. If $a_0 = 1$, $a_1 = -1$, and $a_2 = -2$, find the present volumes (mode split) of truck and rail.

b. Make an approximate estimate of the equilibrium flows if the new highway were built. (*Hint:* Try a range of truck volumes in a trial-and-error approach.)

c. What would the equilibrium flow be if the railroad dropped its rates to $15 per ton? if truckers were taxed $5 per ton to help pay for the new highway? if both changes occurred? Discuss.

d. Discuss the advantages and disadvantages of the new highway from the perspectives of each of the major affected interests.

e. A regulatory commission is examining the question of rates. The railroad is arguing for a truck rate of $35 per truckload, while the truckers are arguing for a rate of $30. What would be the corresponding equilibrium volumes? Why is each interest advocating the particular rates indicated?

1.9(E) An urban expressway presently carries a peak traffic volume of 2,200 vehicles per hour over three lanes in the peak direction. A simple, approximate service function for this facility is

$$t = t_0 + b\frac{q}{kq_c},$$

where k is the number of lanes, $q_c = 1,200$ vehicles per hour per lane, q is the total one-way flow volume in vehicles per hour ($q \le 0.95kq_c$), $b = 3$, and $t_0 = 2$ minutes per mile (see section 7.6). One bus is considered equivalent to about 1.6 automobiles, and the flow stream in the peak hour includes about 60 buses. The demand function for bus transit usage in the corridor is

$$V_B = V_0 - at_B,$$

where t_B is bus travel time in minutes, $V_0 = 4,200$ people per hour, and $a = 75$.

a. What is the present travel time for buses and automobiles over the eight-mile expressway? Show that the ridership on the 60 buses is $V_B = 1,982$ persons per hour.

b. It is proposed that one auto lane be replaced by a lane for exclusive use of buses, with semipermanent barriers such as rubber cones between the bus and auto lanes. If the number of buses in the peak hour remained the same, what would their travel time be? (Assume no en route stops and no congestion for buses at exit ramps.) What would be the equilibrium volume of passengers using buses? If the maximum capacity of the buses were 50 passengers, would they be crowded?

c. How would the automobile travel times change if one lane were set aside for the exclusive use of buses?

d. What assumption is made in this model about the influence of automobile travel times on bus ridership? If you relaxed this assumption, how might the results change?

2
The Demand for Transportation

2.1 INTRODUCTION

The basic concern of transportation systems analysts is to be able to anticipate the consequences of any proposed change in a transportation system. In chapter 1 a basic framework for prediction was presented. This framework focused on the interrelationships between transportation and the socioeconomic activity system, and three basic types of interrelations were identified. In this chapter we shall deal with two of these interrelations: first, that between the pattern of social and economic activities and the short-run demand for transportation; and second, the influence of transportation upon the long-run distribution of social and economic activities. Thus our purpose in this chapter is to explore the behavioral aspects of transportation—the activity system and the way we represent it for the analysis of transportation systems.

2.2 THE NEED TO UNDERSTAND HUMAN BEHAVIOR

2.2.1 The Effects of Transportation on Social and Economic Activity

Transportation has always played an important role in influencing the development of societies. In more recent history transportation has played a major role in the development of the modern industrial city.

Cities usually develop at some natural transportation link—an intersection of trade routes, a river junction, a harbor. Then, as they grow in population, they begin to expand geographically. During their early years the major influence on development is that of the local topography. However, as cities begin to reach a scale beyond that of reasonable walking distance, the available transportation technologies play a role in shaping their forms. For example, in the development of American cities during the middle of the nineteenth century, horse-drawn streetcars provided radial spokes along which the development of suburbs took place (S. B. Warner 1962). These spokes radiated outward from the central business district and served to move commuters into and out of the center of the city. As horsedrawn streetcars were replaced by electric-powered "trolley" streetcars, this pattern of development along the radial spokes of the transportation arteries continued. These arteries were replaced and extended by suburban railroads, which stimulated the development of even more extensive commuter suburbs.

With the coming of the automobile, the areas between the radial spokes began to be filled in. Even so, until the end of World War II the level of reliance on public transport was such that cities remained relatively compact.

In America, with the ending of World War II, a combination of public policies and private aspirations resulted in forces that significantly changed the character of most cities. Growth in personal income led to a rapid increase in the number of private automobiles and the fulfillment for many of the dream of a single-family house on a small lot in the suburbs. The explosion of American population into suburbia was accelerated and aided by this growth in auto ownership, by federal housing policies that made mortgage money more easily available, and by the development of extensive systems of express highways. These express, limited-access highways allowed rapid movement for large numbers of automobiles and trucks, radially from the central cities to the suburbs and circumferentially among suburbs. This system of highways accelerated the dispersal of population, businesses, and industry. As suburban shopping centers mushroomed to bring goods and services to the growing suburban populations, the role of central business districts began to change. Industrial parks in the suburbs brought jobs to where people lived.

Of course, as use of the automobile became easier and as population dispersed, there was a corollary effect on public transit. Transit ridership had been declining since the early 1920s as incomes had risen and the number of private automobiles had increased. With the rapid postwar development of highways and acceleration of dispersion, the decline of public transit became calamitous. As transit ridership dropped and labor costs increased, fares were increased and service cut back in order to stabilize deficits. These changes resulted in further declines in use and made automobiles relatively more attractive.

This short sketch of American urban patterns illustrates the extensive interrelationship between transportation and social and economic activity (Meyer, Kain, and Wohl 1965). Similar patterns have begun to emerge in Western Europe.

As another example, consider the growth of air travel since 1945.

The convenience of present-day intercity air travel within North America and within Western Europe has had important effects on the behavior patterns of businessmen on these two continents. One can make a round trip between Boston and Washington or between London and Paris in a single day, and many businessmen and government officials may visit two to four cities each week.

Similarly, air transportation also provides great opportunities for social and recreational travel. Even people with moderate incomes can afford to take vacations, at any season of the year, for a few days or up to a month, almost anywhere in the world. In Boston, weekends in Miami are advertised widely; in Paris, weekends in New York or Tangiers or even Jerusalem.

Similar interrelationships between transportation and social and economic activities can be discerned in other contexts. For example, in a country undergoing rapid development, a proposal for major improvements in the national highway network raises fundamental questions. What impact will such a highway network have on the development pattern? Will it aid the economic development and social viability of small towns and cities in the hinterland? Or will the highway systems and bus services make the one or two major metropolitan areas of the country more attractive and more accessible, so that people migrate in large numbers to the metropolis? Alternatively, what should be the relative roles of rail, truck, and water for freight transport? The provision of transportation in a developing country can have a significant impact on the social and economic development patterns, and transportation planning in this context must therefore quite explicitly be a part of overall national development planning.

2.2.2 What We Are Trying to Predict

As analysts, our goal is to predict the effects of a change in the transportation system on the broader fabric of society. As discussed above, such changes in the transportation system of a region can have significant effects on the patterns of social and economic activity. In the short run a change in the transportation system will be reflected in changes in travel patterns; over a longer period of time the location and even the nature of social and economic activity may change significantly.

To predict how the individuals and firms in a region might respond to these changes and to understand why present conditions have come about—why travel and locational patterns have taken the forms they now have—we must understand human behavior. At present our understanding of human behavior in response to transportation system changes is far from perfect, but substantial progress is being made. This information can be summarized in a *demand function,* which is a representation of human behavior that can be used to predict how an individual or firm, or groups of individuals or firms, will respond to changing conditions.

2.2.3 The Dimensions of Human Behavior

LEVELS OF CHOICE

In most countries an individual's *activity pattern* can be defined by the choices he or she makes about such things as employment, including type of work, income, and location; residence, including location, type of home, type of neighborhood, and such related factors as schools, access to shopping, interactions with neighbors, and rents or mortgage rates; "consumption" patterns; shopping and other personal business activities, including goods and services purchased, shopping areas frequented, prices paid, as well as related activities such as "browsing" or banking; and social and recreational activities, such as visiting friends and relatives and excursions on weekends and holidays.

Each individual has a conception of the activity pattern that would constitute a full and satisfying life. This is the "basic" demand that motivates individual and household decisions: the desire to undertake particular activity patterns.

There are several "levels" of choice that an individual must make (figure 2.1). At the highest, most basic level is the choice of a desired pattern of activity that reflects one's life-style aspirations. Then, in order to undertake a particular activity pattern, the individual must be at particular locations at particular times; this leads to basic locational choices, including the choice of a residential location and of a place of

Figure 2.1 Levels of choice for an individual.

work. Such locational choices form a second level of decisions. Next, in order to undertake the desired activities at the chosen locations, a third level of choices is required: choices about where, when, and how to travel.

DERIVED DEMAND

The travel choices are the ones that lead directly to a "demand" or "desire" for travel. It is clear, then, that the demand for travel is a derived demand, in this sense: travel is desirable not in itself but as a means of being at certain locations at certain times, and this goal is itself derived from the desire to undertake certain patterns of activities. Thus, to understand the demand for travel we need, ideally, to understand the basic human desires for various activity patterns; from this we could derive the demand for locations of activities, especially for locations of residence and workplace, and from this locational demand we could derive the demand for travel.

A similar hierarchy of choices exists in the freight sector. The primary choices made by commercial enterprises include the products to produce, the general markets to pursue, and the magnitude of economic activity (sales, employment, investment) to engage in. In order to achieve a desired pattern of economic activity, the firm must make locational decisions for its production facilities and select specific markets (that is, geographic regions) to be served and sources of raw materials. From these choices are then derived the commodity transportation choices: which commodities to ship, from where, to where, by what means (see figure 2.2).

Clearly, in the cases of both personal travel and freight movements, the choices at each level interact in significant ways. For example, the

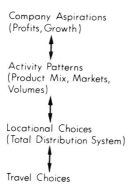

Company Aspirations
(Profits, Growth)

Activity Patterns
(Product Mix, Markets,
Volumes)

Locational Choices
(Total Distribution System)

Travel Choices

Figure 2.2 Levels of choice for a firm.

choice whether or not to produce a particular commodity at X for sale in market Y is determined in part by the available transportation choices.

A WORKING HYPOTHESIS

At the present time we know most about the demand for transportation and least about the desire for certain activity patterns. Therefore, in order to cut through the complexity of the interactions between the transportation and the socioeconomic activity systems, we make the following hypothesis: *It is feasible to separate the long-run shifts in the location and scale of socioeconomic activity from the short-run behavior of the market for transportation.* Under this hypothesis, in considering the demand for transportation, we may assume that the patterns of social and economic activity are fixed. Then we can treat the related problem of the long-run shift in socioeconomic activity separately from that of the demand for travel; this we have called the activity shift. The separation of demand and activity-shift models—the type 1 and type 2 relationships in the analytical framework introduced in chapter 1—reflects this hypothesis.

Thus, recalling our earlier definition of a demand function as a representation of human behavior, we find it convenient to separate the "total" demand function into two parts. The *transportation demand function* is a representation of human behavior which can be used to predict how individuals or firms, or groups of individuals or firms, will change transportation choices in response to changes in future conditions. The *activity-shift function* is a representation of human behavior which can be used to predict how individuals or firms, or groups of individuals or firms, will change activity and location choices in response to changes in future conditions.

In a sense, the basic difference is in the time scale over which decisions take place. Transportation decisions can be made and changed very quickly. Changes in the location and scale of socioeconomic activity take much longer to occur. Therefore, another way of interpreting the hypothesis is that it is useful to distinguish between short-run and long-run decisions.

This hypothesis is one that has often been made in practice, and it is useful for teaching purposes. However, ongoing research suggests that it may be too simple. We shall discuss this further in chapter 11, but for the rest of this chapter we shall assume its validity. For simplicity, whenever we say "demand" we shall mean "demand for transportation" unless explicitly stated otherwise.

2.3 BEHAVIOR AT THE INDIVIDUAL LEVEL

The problem of predicting the demand for transportation can be approached at two levels: that of the individual or that of groups of individuals. By an individual we mean any group that behaves as a single unit in making transportation decisions. Such a unit can be: for goods movements, a firm, a part of a firm, such as the shipping or traffic department, or an individual such as a traffic manager or shipping clerk; for personal travel, a household, consisting of several interacting persons, or a single person. The essential point is that when a unit consists of more than one person, they interact in reaching a decision. For example, in a household where several drivers (parents and teenage children, say) share one automobile, the decisions about use of the automobile in the evening and on weekends may involve a collective decision among competing demands.

For simplicity, we shall use the term *consumer* to denote a single decision-making unit, whether that unit consists of one or several persons.

2.3.1 A Model of Consumer Behavior

Once we recognize that we are dealing with human behavior, we see that we face a tremendous challenge: People are complex; their preferences and decision-making behaviors are very different and are continually changing. In order to predict future travel, we must understand human behavior in a way that can produce operational results. Thus any model for explaining consumer behavior must indicate (1) what alternative choices consumers perceive; (2) what consequences of these alternatives they consider important; and (3) how they make their choices from among the perceived alternatives.

ALTERNATIVE CHOICES

The basic decisions with which the consumer must deal from the point of view of transportation are whether to make a trip, where to make the trip, at what time to make the trip, and which mode and route to take. These decisions are obviously highly interrelated. The extent of this interrelationship depends on, among other things, the purpose of the trip. For example, in an urban area trips between home and work have the "whether" and "where" fixed; the individual generally has a fixed residence and a fixed workplace and is committed to making the home-to-work trip regularly. The time, mode, and route taken are usually determined together and once a pattern is established, the typical consumer rarely changes these decisions. On the other hand, consider another example: where to go on a summer weekend. For this kind of recreational trip, all the options are open and are probably determined simultaneously.

ATTRIBUTES

What factors does the consumer take into account when choosing among these alternatives? In introducing the basic framework of analysis in chapter 1, we defined the concept of service level, **S**: the *service variables* are those attributes of the transportation system that influence the consumer's decisions as to whether, where, when, and how to make a trip. In general, each consumer considers a number of service variables. Therefore, the consequences are expressed as a vector, $\mathbf{S} = (S_1, S_2, \ldots, S_j, \ldots, S_n)$. An illustrative list of service variables is given in table 2.1. As this list shows, consumers may consider many attributes of transportation service. In general, different consumers will consider different service attributes to be important, reflecting differences in their socioeconomic characteristics and preferences. Since it is usually not possible to include explicitly all possible service variables when forecasting travel demand, an important practical problem is to identify those service variables that have the greatest influence on consumer choices. Another important and related practical problem is that some service variables cannot readily be quantified ("comfort," "safety," "perceived security").

Furthermore, even such seemingly simple attributes as "travel time" turn out to be complex in their influence on traveler behavior. In table 2.2 we show some of this complexity by breaking down travel time into some of its major components. These components are perceived differently in different situations; for example, in some travel forecasts "excess time" or "out-of-vehicle time" is defined as "all time components other than in-vehicle travel time."

In addition, "time" is not always synonymous with "distance" from the viewpoint of consumer behavior. For example, numerous surveys have shown that walking distance is a very important determinant of bus ridership—very few people will walk more than a quarter mile to use a bus. Thus walking distance should usually be one of the service parameters used to predict ridership on a bus system.

On the other hand, for a door-to-door system such as the demand-responsive bus—"dial-a-ride"—there is no walking required. ͏
ing distance is obviously not a factor. However, the re͏
trip time for dial-a-ride may be lower than for mo͏
tems, since it is a demand-responsive service, so tl͏

Table 2.1   Illustrative service attributes

Time[a]

total trip time

reliability (variance in trip time)

time spent at transfer points

frequency of service

schedule times

Cost to user

direct transportation charges such as fares, tolls, fuel, and parking

other direct operating costs such as loading and documentation

indirect costs such as the cost of acquiring, maintaining, and insuring an automobile or, for freight, warehousing, interest, and insurance

Safety

probability of fatality or of destruction of cargo

probability of accident of any sort

probability distribution of accident types (shock vibration, water damage, and so on)

perceived security

Comfort and convenience for user

walking distance

number of vehicle changes required

physical comfort (temperature, humidity, cleanliness, ride quality, exposure to weather)

psychological comfort (status, privacy)

other amenities (baggage handling, ticketing, beverage and food service)

enjoyment of trip

aesthetic experiences

Shipper services

division and reconsignment privileges

insurance

[a] Time is often divided into the components shown in table 2.2.

Table 2.2 Major components of travel time

	Out-of-vehicle time	In-vehicle time
Access time	Walk time Wait time	Time in feeder vehicle (for example, in automobile or bus en route to mainline transit)
Line-haul time	Transfer time	Time in line-haul vehicle (mainline transit time or automobile driving time)

should be included in any dial-a-ride analysis. Thus service attributes will have different degrees of importance in influencing consumer behavior for different transportation systems. Therefore the service variables to be included in any analysis will depend to some extent on the systems being analyzed.

In general, travel time, wait time, and fare have been the primary service variables used to predict traveler behavior in urban transportation, especially for conventional transit services. The relationships might simply be described as follows: as the transit travel time, wait time, and fare decrease, the level of usage of transit will increase—more consumers will find the transit mode more attractive.

DECISION PROCESS

The third major feature of a model of consumer behavior must be a description of how the consumer operates on the two preceding sets of information—the perceived alternatives and the attributes of those alternatives—to reach a decision. A part of this description must include some representation of the consumer's preferences or goals as well as some characterization of the consumer in ways that allow us to distinguish among the behavior patterns of different groups of consumers. Various formulations can be proposed for this decision process. We shall next examine two particular formulations.

2.3.2 Consumer Behavior Model I

In this first model it is assumed that the consumer: formulates his preferences explicitly, identifies explicitly all the alternatives open to him, identifies the consequences of each alternative, and evaluates the alternatives and chooses among them using a well-defined decision rule.

REPRESENTING PREFERENCES

A key feature of this model is the approach taken to representing the preferences of the consumer (see, for example, Baumol 1965, Henderson and Quandt 1958).

The preferences of consumers vary not only in which service attributes they consider important, but also in the relative values they place on various attributes. To represent this variation the model uses the concept of an ***indifference curve,*** which is a curve indicating all combinations of choices among which the consumer is indifferent. Figure 2.3 shows a set of indifference curves involving two service attributes, travel time t and out-of-pocket cost c. This set of curves represents the preferences of a particular consumer: the consumer is essentially indifferent to all combinations of time and cost on a single curve but has definite preferences among curves. For example, he is indifferent between the combination of time and cost represented by point A on curve I and that combination represented by point B. On the other hand, both of these points are preferred to point C on curve II, because point C has both a higher travel time and a higher cost than either A or B.

Furthermore, A and B are both preferred to D. Although D has lower cost than B, its time is sufficiently greater than B's so that it is still less desirable. In addition, the consumer is indifferent between C and D, so since B is preferred to C, B must also be preferred to D.

The set of indifference curves can be expressed in functional form as

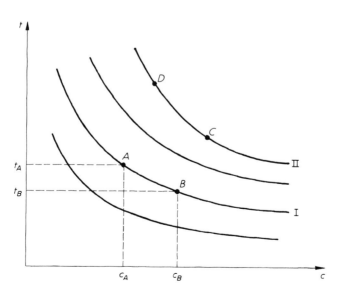

Figure 2.3 Indifference curves.

$$U = f(\mathbf{S}, \theta),\qquad(2.1)$$

where $\mathbf{S}$ is the vector of service attributes and θ is a vector of parameters. Two specific forms of interest are the product form,

$$U = \alpha t^{\beta} c^{\gamma},\qquad(2.2)$$

and the linear form,

$$U = \alpha t + \beta c.\qquad(2.3)$$

In these cases $\mathbf{S} = (t, c)$ and $\theta = (\alpha, \beta)$ or (α, β, γ). Each of these equations defines a family of curves; each curve shows, for a specific value of U, those combinations of t and c that are equally preferred by the consumer. The product form (2.2) would generate a family of indifference curves like figure 2.3; the linear form (2.3), a family of indifference curves like figure 2.4. Different curves correspond to different values of the quantity U.

The value of U can be interpreted as a measure of the degree to which a particular combination (t, c) is desired by the consumer. When it is useful to do this, U is called a **utility** and the functions defining the indifference curves are called **utility functions.** Utility is valued positively; that is, utility is so defined that if $U_A > U_D$, then the consumer prefers A to D. For example, in figure 2.3 $U_I > U_{II}$ because the consumer prefers either A or B to either C or D.

Note that the service attributes of time and cost are negatively valued; that is, the consumer prefers *less* time and/or *less* cost, rather than more. So, as t and/or c increase, the corresponding values of U decrease. The parameters in θ must have corresponding signs. Sometimes the term **disutility** or **negatively valued utility** is used. In this case, instead of maximizing utility, the consumer is assumed to minimize disutility. The result is the same. To prevent confusion, we shall always use the term utility; whether the utility actually reflects a disutility will be clear in a particular context from the definitions of the service attributes used and the values of the parameters in θ.

Utility can be measured in any convenient units: time, monetary units, or, most generally, "utiles." The values of the parameters of these indifference curves explicitly express the preferences of the consumer. For example, one useful property of these curves is represented by the **trade-off ratio,** the slope of the curve. For the linear indifference curve, the trade-off ratio is α/β. This ratio expresses the "value" of time to the consumer, that is, the amount he would be willing to pay to save one unit of travel time. For every minute of time saved, the

a

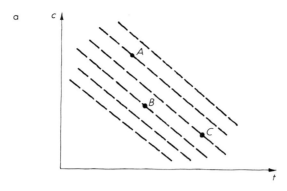

b

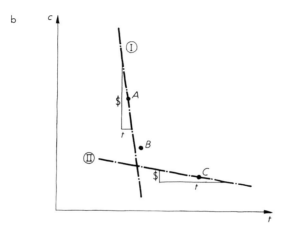

Figure 2.4 Consumer behavior model I.

consumer would be willing to pay α/β additional dollars.

We would expect different consumers to have utility functions with different indifference curves and trade-off ratios. For example, people with high incomes would likely place a high value on travel time and would be willing to pay a relatively high cost to save a minute of travel time; this would be reflected by a high ratio of α to β and thus by the slope of their indifference curves. On the other hand, low-income consumers would probably be willing to spend substantial additional travel time to save on travel costs; this, too, would be reflected in their trade-off ratios and in the shape of their indifference curves.

DECISION PROCESS
The steps in the decision process in this model are as follows:

1. The consumer explicitly formulates his preferences for all possible combinations of attributes.
2. He identifies all the alternatives open to him.
3. He characterizes each alternative in terms of its attributes.
4. He uses his preference information to select an alternative.

Assume that the consumer has expressed the preferences indicated by the set of indifference curves in figure 2.4a (the dashed lines). Each curve shows all combinations of time and cost with equal utility U, that is, all combinations that are equally desirable from the point of view of the consumer. Assume also that he has identified three alternative choices—A, B, and C—and has characterized each by two service attributes, time and cost. Thus each of the available alternatives can be represented by the time and cost that it offers, as shown in figure 2.4a.

The decision process follows from the definition of utility and indifference curves. In line with his expressed preferences, the consumer will pick the alternative (of those available) that has the greatest utility, that is, the one that is on the indifference curve closest to the origin of the axes. In the case of the curves in part a of the figure, this is alternative B.

Consumers with different preferences, and thus different indifference curves, will pick different alternatives. For example, in part b of the figure a consumer who places a high value on time is shown by indifference curve I; this consumer would pick alternative A. On the other hand, a consumer who places a low value on time, with indifference curve II, would pick alternative C.

There are two alternative ways of describing this choice process:
1. Using the consumer's expression of his preferences, construct the indifference curves. Characterize each alternative by its service attributes and determine on which indifference curve it lies. Then pick the alternative that is on the indifference curve with the highest value of utility (in figures 2.3 and 2.4, the curve to the lowest left).
2. Characterize each alternative by its service attributes. Using the information on preferences, calculate the utility for each alternative. Then pick the most preferable alternative (that is, the one with the highest value of utility).

Both methods produce the same results. We have used method 1 so far, but method 2 is a more flexible way of dealing with situations with many alternatives. In future applications of this model, we shall first find the utility for each alternative and then compare alternatives on the basis of their utilities.

2.4 APPLICATIONS OF CONSUMER BEHAVIOR MODEL I

The examples in this section illustrate the use of the foregoing model in predicting consumer responses for passenger and freight transportation. They trace through the effects of changes in the transportation in order to identify how choices may change as a result of such system changes, how consumers may differ in their behavior, and how changes in socioeconomic factors may modify consumer choice.

2.4.1 A Freight Example

THE CHOICE OF A SINGLE CONSUMER

A particular manufacturer has a choice between rail and truck for shipping his goods to market. We assume that the only service attributes that affect his choice are cost c, in-vehicle travel time t, and excess or out-of-vehicle time x, which incorporates such components as waiting times at both ends of the trip and the reliability of service. Cost includes the freight rate for either mode plus ancillary charges such as packaging for shipment and insurance.

The present service characteristics of the two modes are shown in table 2.3. We can try to predict the choice made by this consumer by estimating the relative weights he places on cost, in-vehicle time, and excess time (w_c, w_t, and w_x, respectively). With these weights the three service variables can be collapsed into a single measure of utility:

$$U = w_t t + w_x x + w_c c. \tag{2.4}$$

Note that all the weights take negative values, since an increase in any of the attributes reduces the utility of the mode. Using our model, we then assume that the consumer will select the mode that has the highest value of this utility, that is, the least value of a negative number. We assume that the weights are − $2 per day (per ton) for travel time (w_t) and − $4 per day (per ton) for excess time (w_x) for this particular shipper, relative to a weight of −1 for w_c.

The utilities of the two competing modes are as follows (note that

Table 2.3 Characteristics of two competing freight modes

	Rail	Truck
Cost	$4/ton	$5/ton
In-vehicle time	2.5 days	2.0 days
Excess time	1.0 day	0.3 day

the utilities are negative because the higher the time or cost, the less attractive that choice would be, and thus the lower the utility):

$$U_R = (-2 \times 2.5) + (-4 \times 1.0) + (-1 \times 4) = -\$13, \qquad (2.5)$$

$$U_T = (-2 \times 2.0) + (-4 \times 0.3) + (-1 \times 5) = -\$10.20. \qquad (2.6)$$

In this case, we thus predict that the consumer will select truck as the preferred mode because it has a higher utility (a lower value of a negative number—a lower disutility). Furthermore, as long as the characteristics of the two modes and the values of the consumer do not change, the choice would always be the same for this type of shipment—from day to day and from month to month.

THE CHOICES OF DIFFERENT CONSUMERS
A different consumer faced with exactly the same choice would use different weights on the service attributes to evaluate the modes. Table 2.4 shows the behavior of consumers with different preferences. The resulting choice is shown for each consumer. Some choose rail and others choose truck because of the difference in preferences, reflected in the differences in weights and thus in utility functions.

EFFECT OF A CHANGE IN LEVEL OF SERVICE
This model is very useful for understanding the effects of a potential or actual change in the transportation system. Any such change can be expressed as a change in one or more service attributes for one or more of the alternatives. This would cause a change in the utility a particular consumer places on the affected alternatives.

Consider shipper A in table 2.4. While under present conditions this shipper would choose truck, it is possible that changes in service could alter this. For example, if truck freight rates are increased by $4, then the utility of truck becomes $-\$14.20$, while the utility of rail stays at

Table 2.4 Example of mode choice based on a simple utility model

Shipper	Relative weights			Utilities		Choice
	w_t	w_x	w_c	Rail	Truck	
A	−2	−4	−1	−13	−10.20	Truck
B	−3	−8	−1	−19.50	−13.40	Truck
C	−2	−3	−4	−24	−24.90	Rail
D	−2	−3	−8	−40	−44.90	Rail

— $13. The shipper now shifts to rail. Or if special nonstop trains are introduced ("unit trains"), or other operational improvements are made, such that rail in-vehicle time drops to 1 day, then the utility of rail becomes − $10, relative to a truck utility of − $10.20. The shipper again shifts to rail.

The effects of such variations are shown graphically in figure 2.5. Here the mode choice is shown as a function of a single service attribute, truck freight rate. For rates below $7.80, the shipper chooses truck; above $7.80, he chooses rail.

In these examples the consumer's utility function does not change, only the value that the function takes for a particular alternative. Note also that while utility is a continuous function of freight rate, the choice is discrete: either rail or truck is chosen.

SERVICE LEVEL NECESSARY TO CAUSE A SHIFT IN CHOICE
The utility functions can be used to find, for each shipper type, the truck freight rate that would cause that consumer to shift from truck to rail or from rail to truck. This is the point at which the utilities are just equal:

$$U_R = U_T \tag{2.7}$$

or

$$w_t(t_R - t_T) + w_x(x_R - x_T) + w_c(c_R - c_T) = 0. \tag{2.8}$$

Solving for c_T yields

$$c_T = \frac{w_t}{w_c}(t_R - t_T) + \frac{w_x}{w_c}(x_R - x_T) + c_R \tag{2.9}$$

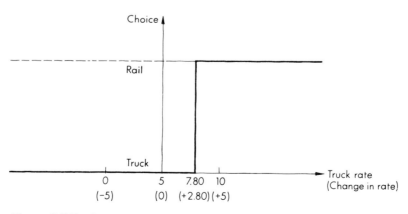

Figure 2.5 Truck rate as a determinant of mode choice.

74   The Demand for Transportation

or, for the given values,

$$c_T = \frac{w_t}{w_c} (0.5 \text{ days}) + \frac{w_x}{w_c} (0.7 \text{ days}) + \$4. \qquad (2.10)$$

For shipper A,

$$c_T = 2(0.5) + 4(0.7) + 4 = \$7.80;$$

for shipper B,

$$c_T = 3(0.5) + 8(0.7) + 4 = \$11.10;$$

for shipper C,

$$c_T = \frac{2}{4} (0.5) + \frac{3}{4} (0.7) + 4 = \$4.78;$$

for shipper D,

$$c_T = \frac{2}{8} (0.5) + \frac{3}{8} (0.7) + 4 = \$4.39.$$

Thus, to get shippers C and D to shift from rail to truck would require truck rates below $4.78 and $4.39, respectively, versus the present rate of $5. On the other hand, since shippers A and B now prefer truck, the truck rates could be increased to as much as $7.80 and $11.10, respectively, before they would shift from truck to rail.

This behavior is shown graphically in figures 2.5 and 2.6. Figure 2.5 shows the behavior of shipper A, with the choice of rail or truck displayed as a function of both the absolute value of the truck rate and the change in rate from the present level. Figure 2.6a shows the behavior of each of the four shippers, separately, for comparison.

TRADE-OFFS AMONG SERVICE ATTRIBUTES

Knowledge of the shippers' utility functions can also be used to explore trade-offs among the various service attributes.

Consider shipper A again. The truck operator, because of external factors (for example, increases in driver wages or fuel prices), knows that he will soon have to increase his rate by $4 per ton, to $9. As shown earlier, this would cause shipper A to shift from truck to rail. If the truck operator wanted to prevent this shift, what in-vehicle time would he have to offer as compensation? Thus what we want to know is what in-vehicle time will give a value of truck utility equal to the rail utility; then, for lower in-vehicle times, truck will be more attractive to this shipper. Using $U_T = U_R = -\$13$, we have, from (2.4),

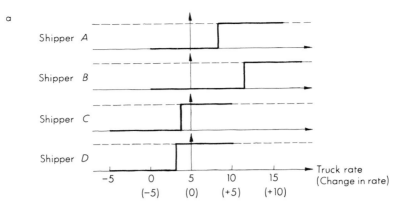

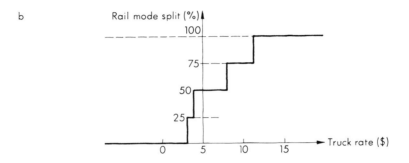

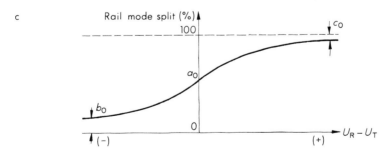

Figure 2.6 Relationship of individual to group choices.

$$-\$13.00 = (-\$2 \times t_T) + (-\$4 \times 0.3) + (-1 \times c_T) \qquad (2.11)$$

or, solving for in-vehicle time,

$$t_T = 5.90 - 0.5c_T. \qquad (2.12)$$

This is, of course, the equation of the indifference curve relating t_T and c_T for this value of utility, as represented in figure 2.4.

For $c_T = \$9$, the corresponding value of t_T is 1.4: if the truck operator intends to increase his rate by $4, he must bring his in-vehicle time down below 1.4 days if he wants to retain the patronage of shipper A.

AGGREGATE BEHAVIOR

So far we have looked at each of our four shippers as an individual consumer. We now examine the behavior of the group as a whole. We shall use the results shown in figure 2.6a.

Each shipper represents 25 percent of the group of four shippers. At the present truck rate ($5), 50 percent of the group choose truck (two shippers) and 50 percent choose rail. We call this a "50 percent rail mode split": the total market "splits" so that 50 percent choose rail. If we increase the truck rate, we change the mode split: shipper A will shift to rail at a truck rate of $7.80, thus increasing the rail mode split to 75 percent. If we increase the truck rate further to $11.10, shipper B will also shift to rail, resulting in a 100 percent rail mode split. Conversely, if we decrease truck rate to $4.78, we will attract shipper C to truck, for a 25 percent rail mode split, and a decrease to $4.39 will yield a 0 percent rail mode split (a 100 percent truck mode split).

We can thus derive the aggregate behavior of the group from the behaviors of each of the individuals in the group. This relationship is shown in figure 2.6b.

Usually a group will be composed of many more than four consumers. In that case the relationship between the service attribute and the fraction of the group making a particular choice will be much smoother and can be approximated by a continuous function, as shown in figure 2.6c.

In general, of course, the modal split of a particular group can be affected by changing one or more of the service attributes. To represent this we might show on the horizontal axis the *differences* in utilities, leading to a function like the one shown in figure 2.6c. The intercept on the vertical axis, a_0, represents the modal split that would result even if both modes had the same utilities (that is, zero difference in utilities).

Then c_0 might represent the magnitude of "captive" truck users, those who do not have the option of using rail—perhaps because they or the firms to which they ship are too remote from rail service. Further, b_0 might represent those shippers who require rail for some particular reason and so will not shift to truck no matter how much the relative attractiveness changes.

Symbolically this curve would represent the demand function

$$\gamma_R = \frac{V_R}{V_T + V_R} = f_D(U_R - U_T), \tag{2.13}$$

where γ_R is the share or fraction choosing rail, V_R and V_T are the volumes choosing rail and truck, respectively, and U_R and U_T are the utilities of rail and truck, respectively.

2.4.2 An Urban Passenger Travel Example

THE CHOICE OF A SINGLE CONSUMER
For the home-to-work trip in a particular city, a commuter has two choices, transit or automobile. Each mode is characterized by three service attributes: in-vehicle travel time t in minutes; out-of-vehicle time x (for automobile, total parking and walk time; for transit, total walk and wait time) in minutes; and out-of-pocket cost c (for automobile, operating cost based on mileage traveled plus parking charges; for transit, fares) in cents. The utility function is similar to (2.4):

$$U = w_t t + w_x x + w_c c. \tag{2.14}$$

Assume that for the commuters residing in a particular area the relative weights are

$w_t = -1.0,$
$w_x = -2.5,$
$w_c = -k/y,$

where y is annual income in dollars and $k = 5{,}000$ \$-min/¢-yr, so that w_c has units of min/¢. Thus

$$U = -t - 2.5x - (5{,}000/y)c. \tag{2.15}$$

Since U takes on negative values, each traveler will pick the option that has the highest value of U.

Note that the utility depends on the consumer's income. The relative values a consumer places on time and cost are given by w_t/w_c. Consumers with higher incomes have smaller values of w_c relative to w_t

and thus place a higher value on time. The value of the coefficient k reflects the premise that consumers value time at about 25 percent of their hourly wage rate. The relative values of w_x and w_t reflect the premise that out-of-vehicle time is 2.5 times as onerous as time spent traveling in a moving vehicle.

The present characteristics of transit and automobile are shown in table 2.5. The out-of-vehicle time for transit is composed of 8 minutes of walking time and an average waiting time of 12 minutes (half the 24-minute interval between trains).

For a consumer with an annual income of $10,000, (2.15) becomes

$$U = -t - 2.5x - 0.5c. \tag{2.16}$$

The resulting utilities are -80 equivalent minutes for automobile and -90 for transit. Thus the consumer would choose the automobile.

The transit authority is proposing a doubling of frequency along this route. Would this affect the consumer's choice? Since a doubling of frequency would yield, on average, a halving of waiting time, x_T would be reduced to 14 minutes. The effect would be an increase in utility from -90 to -75. Now transit would be more attractive than automobile, and the model predicts that the traveler would shift to transit.

EFFECT OF A CHANGE IN SOCIOECONOMIC CHARACTERISTICS

Any model for predicting consumer behavior should reflect the particular socioeconomic characteristics and behavior of the consumer explicitly. In the freight example we simply had different values of the parameters to represent different preferences for each shipper. In this urban example the parameters are explicitly a function of income, allowing us to see how changes in this socioeconomic characteristic would affect the consumer's choice.

For example, consider a consumer with an annual income of $5,000. His utility function would be

$$U = t - 2.5x - c. \tag{2.17}$$

Table 2.5 Characteristics of two competing transportation modes

	Transit	Automobile
In-vehicle time	30 minutes	40 minutes
Out-of-vehicle time	20 minutes	4 minutes
Out-of-pocket cost	20¢	60¢

For him the automobile would have a utility of -110, so transit, having a utility of -100, would be more attractive. As his income increases, the model predicts that his tastes will change. At \$10,000 his choice will be automobile over transit.

EFFECT OF A CHANGE IN SERVICE CHARACTERISTICS

Given the utility functions, we can derive the value, for any service attribute, at which the choice of mode would change. Take, for example, transit in-vehicle time. Let t_E be the value of transit travel time such that if $t_T < t_E$, transit is preferred. Then for $t_T = t_E$,

$$U_T(t_E) = U_A(t_E) \tag{2.18}$$

or

$$w_t t_E + w_x x_T + w_c c_T = w_t t_A + w_x x_A + w_c c_A. \tag{2.19}$$

Thus

$$
\begin{aligned}
t_E &= \frac{w_x}{w_t}(x_A - x_T) + \frac{w_c}{w_t}(c_A - c_T) + t_A \\
&= 2.5(4 - 20) + \frac{5{,}000}{y}(60 - 20) + 40 \\
&= 2 \times 10^5/y. \tag{2.20}
\end{aligned}
$$

Thus the transit travel time at which riders would be indifferent between transit and automobile is a function of income. This demonstrates the effect of socioeconomic characteristics on the choice of mode as a function of level of service.

AGGREGATE BEHAVIOR

In the freight example we saw how the aggregate behavior of a group of shippers was related to the underlying individual preferences of each shipper. For this urban example consider the two groups of travelers shown in table 2.6. Group A is a relatively low-income group: its average income is \$8,200, versus \$11,800 for group B. Each group is divided into three subgroups. The distribution of incomes within each group is different, too; the median of group A is \$7,000, lower than the mean, while the median of group B is \$13,000, higher than the mean. Group C is the combination of groups A and B, with a mean income of \$10,000.

Figure 2.7 shows the aggregate behavior of the three groups, using (2.20). Because mode choice is a function of income as well as travel

Table 2.6 Example of aggregate mode choice

Subgroup	Size	Mean annual income	Number choosing transit for t_T =							
			50	40	30	25	20	15	10	5
A1	500	$4,000	250	500	500	500	500	500	500	500
A2	300	10,000	0	0	0	0	150	300	300	300
A3	200	16,000	0	0	0	0	0	0	200	200
Total A	1,000		250	500	500	500	650	800	1,000	1,000
Average A		8,200	0	0	0	0	1,000	1,000	1,000	1,000
B1	200	4,000	100	200	200	200	200	200	200	200
B2	300	10,000	0	0	0	0	150	300	300	300
B3	500	16,000	0	0	0	0	0	0	500	500
Total B	1,000		100	200	200	200	350	500	1,000	1,000
Average B		11,800	0	0	0	0	0	1,000	1,000	1,000
C1	700	4,000	350	700	700	700	700	700	700	700
C2	600	10,000	0	0	0	0	300	600	600	600
C3	700	16,000	0	0	0	0	0	0	700	700
Total C	2,000		350	700	700	700	1,000	1,300	2,000	2,000
Average C		10,000	0	0	0	0	1,000	2,000	2,000	2,000

Lines labeled "total" give total of those in subgroups choosing transit. Lines labeled "average" give the number of persons choosing transit based on the average income over subgroups. Group C is the combination of groups A and B.

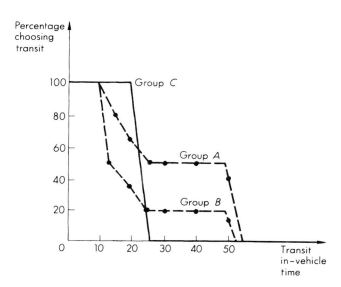

Figure 2.7 Effect of income distribution on aggregate mode choice.

time, and each group has a different composition, the aggregate modal splits of groups A and B differ by as much as 30 percent over the range of transit in-vehicle times from 5 to 50 minutes. Furthermore, the behaviors of the two groups are each different from the aggregate behavior of the combined group C, as predicted on the basis of the average income for group C.

It is important to note that at any given transit time each consumer at the same income level makes the same choice. However, different consumers at different incomes may make different choices at the same service level. Therefore, the aggregate choice of any grouping of consumers depends on the composition of the group.

Thus, as in the freight example, the behavior of a group can, in principle at least, be derived by knowing the behaviors of the individuals in the group. Different groups with different distributions of individual characteristics can be expected to have different aggregate behaviors. Even if two groups have the same average characteristics—for example, the same average income—their behaviors may differ because the distributions of characteristics within the groups are different (see section 4.7).

2.5 A SECOND MODEL OF CONSUMER BEHAVIOR

2.5.1 Appraisal of Consumer Behavior Model I

If we know (1) the set of alternatives each consumer has available to him, (2) the attributes of each alternative, and (3) the consumer's utility function, we have shown that we can use consumer behavior model I to predict the effects of transportation system changes. Clearly this is a useful model. However, it is important to be aware of its limitations. Consider the following:

The alternatives: Do consumers really perceive *all* of the available alternatives? Do they consciously and deliberately consider every one of them? Or do they scan the set of alternatives and only examine carefully a small number? How does past experience influence which alternatives a consumer will consider explicitly?

The consequences: How do consumers perceive consequences? What consequences do they consider important? What kinds of biases in their perceptions of those consequences? How are these ⟩s biased by individual experiences, word of mouth, or other ⟩?

⟩*ion process:* Does the consumer go through a careful calculation of the consequences of each alternative to

Transportation

reach a decision? Does he really formalize his preferences explicitly in the form of an indifference curve? Does he even behave as if he had formalized his preferences in this way? Does he choose among all alternatives in a single step or in a sequence of decisions?

The static nature of the model: Don't consumers change their information, and their preferences, over time? Don't they "learn" from actual experiences and sometimes shift choices?

As an example, consider the introduction of a basically new transportation technology, such as a computer-routed-and-scheduled "dial-a-ride" minibus system. How will people respond to this new technology initially? How will their responses change as they gain experience with the new system? How will they perceive the alternatives? How will their perceptions of the consequences of using this system be biased by their own experiences or the experiences of friends or acquaintances? Model I does not deal with elements of behavior such as these.

The major limitation of the model is that it assumes that the consumer has "perfect" information: he knows all of the alternatives open to him, he knows all of their characteristics, and he knows his own preferences so that he behaves as if he had a well-defined utility function. It is also a static model, in that it does not allow for changes in information over time. What would be more desirable is a behavioral model that explicitly incorporated the biases and limited perceptions of consumers making decisions and allowed for time-varying behavior.

2.5.2 Consumer Behavior Model II

One important way of partially overcoming the limitations described in the preceding section is to recognize that the consumer does not make decisions with "perfect" information. That is, there is a random or probabilistic element that enters into his decision process. This random element can be expressed a number of ways. One useful approach is to introduce a random variable ε, representing the probabilistic error, as an additive term in the utility function for each mode m:

$$U_m = \alpha + \beta t_m + \gamma c_m + \varepsilon. \tag{2.21}$$

The practical result of this addition is that now we do not know precisely which alternative the individual will choose, because we do not know precisely the values of utility he will place on each choice. We must therefore talk about the *probability* that individual i will choose alternative m.

Several factors may contribute to this randomness:

1. There may be service attributes that are important to some consum-

ers but have not been explicitly represented in our estimation of their utilities (for example, comfort, perception of security, or other non-quantifiable attributes).

2. Consumers may not perceive all the alternatives open to them or may not have correct information on the attributes of the alternatives (for example, because of poor marketing, consumers are often not aware of route and schedule information that might influence their decisions).

3. There may be essentially random elements in the consumer's behavior, in that his preferences vary from day to day or are influenced by external events (for example, the weather or the availability of the family car).

Models of individual behavior that include an explicit random element are often termed **stochastic disaggregate models** in the literature. Different assumptions about the form of the utility function and/or the nature of the random elements lead to different specific forms for this consumer behavior model II.

2.5.3 An Example

To illustrate, we shall extend the previous deterministic model to include an explicit random element.

In both the freight example and the urban example the consumers involved had linear utility functions:

$$U_m = \sum_{i=1}^{3} w_i s_{mi}, \tag{2.22}$$

where $\mathbf{s}_m = (s_{m1}, s_{m2}, s_{m3})$ is the vector of service attributes, $\mathbf{w} = (w_1, w_2, w_3)$ is the vector of weights in the consumer's preference function, and there are two choice alternatives ($m = 1, 2$).

We now assume that the utility is composed of two parts, a deterministic part $u_m = \sum w_i s_{mi}$ and a random part ε:

$$U_m = u_m + \varepsilon = \sum_{i=1}^{3} w_i s_{mi} + \varepsilon. \tag{2.23}$$

The probability that the consumer chooses alternative 1, denoted by p_1, is

$$p_1 = \text{prob}(U_1 > U_2). \tag{2.24}$$

Similarly,

$$p_2 = \text{prob}(U_2 > U_1). \tag{2.25}$$

Under certain assumptions about the probability distribution of ε—specifically that ε is Weibull-distributed (Charles River Associates 1972, Ben-Akiva 1973, 1974, McFadden 1975)—the following results are obtained:

$$p_1 = \frac{e^{u_1}}{e^{u_1} + e^{u_2}},\tag{2.26}$$

$$p_2 = \frac{e^{u_2}}{e^{u_1} + e^{u_2}}.\tag{2.27}$$

Equations (2.26) and (2.27) define a particular stochastic disaggregate model, the binomial logit model. This can be generalized to the case where there are M alternative choices to form the **multinomial logit model** (MNL):

$$p(m: M) = \frac{e^{u_m}}{\sum\limits_{m' \in M} e^{u_{m'}}}.\tag{2.28}$$

For the two-choice case it is instructive to define

$$G(\mathbf{S}) = u_1(\mathbf{S}) - u_2(\mathbf{S}),\tag{2.29}$$

so that (2.26) and (2.27) become

$$p_1 = \frac{1}{1 + e^{u_2 - u_1}} = \frac{1}{1 + e^{-G(\mathbf{S})}},\tag{2.30}$$

$$p_2 = \frac{1}{1 + e^{u_1 - u_2}} = \frac{1}{1 + e^{G(\mathbf{S})}}.\tag{2.31}$$

These probabilities are shown as functions of $G(\mathbf{S})$ in figure 2.8. If $u_1 = u_2$, then $G(\mathbf{S}) = 0$ and the probabilities of both choices are the same, 0.5. If, on the other hand, $u_1 = u_2 + A'$, then $G = u_1 - u_2 = A'$ and $p_1 = p_1'$ while $p_2 = 1 - p_1' = p_2'$. (Appendix A gives values of this reciprocal exponential for use in the exercises.)

Finally, it should be noted that alternative assumptions about the probabilistic choice structure lead to other types of stochastic disaggregate models (see McFadden 1974b, Domencich and McFadden 1975, Ben-Akiva 1977). Logit models have been especially important in the early development of practical disaggregate models. Other potentially important models are those that do not have the "independence of irrelevant alternatives" property, such as the multinomial probit (Hausman and Wise 1976, Daganzo, Bouthelier, and Sheffi 1977, Lerman and Manski 1977) and the generalized extreme value model (McFadden 1978).

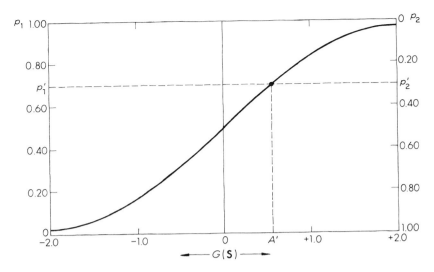

Figure 2.8 Probabilistic choice.

While in this section we have used u and U to distinguish the deterministic and total utilities, respectively, in general we shall not make this distinction.

2.6 NOTE ON DIFFERENCES WITH CLASSICAL TREATMENTS OF CONSUMER THEORY (OPTIONAL READING)

The formulation of the consumer behavior model I presented in this chapter is close to but different from standard presentations of consumer theory (Henderson and Quandt 1958, Baumol 1965, de Neufville and Stafford 1971). The differences, and the reasons for them, are as follows:

1. Choices are considered to be among discrete objects rather than among continuous, infinitely variable combinations of commodities because most transport choices *are* among discrete items or combinations of items: destinations, modes, routes, and auto ownership levels are naturally discrete, and even variables such as trip frequency, shipment size (for freight), and time of trip are often treated as discrete choices (off-peak versus peak hours for the time of day of the trip; carload or less-than-carload for shipment size).

2. Choices are characterized by the values of their attributes rather than by quantities of commodities in a mix of commodities. This is a natural consequence of the first point; the only way to characterize a

set of discrete objects (except by the name of each object) is by its characteristics with respect to a common set of attributes. The intellectual basis of this approach derives from Lancaster (1966) and Quandt (1970a), as articulated for transportation demand by Quandt (1970b) (although the practical applications, such as travel time ratios used for diversion curves, antedated these theoretical concepts): "The crucial modification [in this approach] is that the consumer is now regarded as deriving utility from characteristics or attributes while commodities are regarded as producing attributes in varying amounts and proportions" (p. 5). This is especially important in areas where the number of available commodities may change—for example, by the introduction of a new commodity, such as a new transportation service, to the market.

3. Utility is maximized, constrained only by the set of available choices; no explicit budget constraint is included. Since the set of available choices is discrete, if the set is bounded (finite, or infinite and bounded), there is at least one choice that has the maximum utility of any in the set. Therefore there is no methodological reason why a budget constraint is necessary to yield a choice. Equally important, in the domain of transportation choices there is no reason to continue the emphasis on budget constraints used in standard consumer theory. First, the amount of household or firm monetary resources spent on transportation is usually only a modest portion of the available resources and is therefore almost never constrained by budget limits. Second, attributes other than monetary cost may play more important roles as constraints in many situations (a travel time budget constraint, a maximum walk distance or waiting time constraint, a "maximum probability of loss or damage" constraint). The most general approach is a general utility function that can potentially include all attributes identically. If in a specific situation the levels of one or more attributes become subject to constraints—or, equally, to "satisficing" behavior (see Simon 1960)—a specific formulation of the utility function can be established (for example, maximizing utility subject to a constraint on one or more specific attributes).

2.7 SUMMARY

2.7.1 The Need to Understand Human Behavior

Changes in the transportation system of a region affect the patterns of social and economic activity. Over the long term changes occur in the distribution and intensity of these activities; in the short term many individuals may change decisions about modes and routes of travel and many firms may change the modes and routes they use to ship to particular markets.

To predict how the many individuals and firms in a region will respond to changes in the transportation system, we need to understand human behavior: We need to understand present behavior, and we need a deep enough understanding of the basis of that behavior to be able to predict how individuals and firms will change their behaviors in response to a variety of factors.

This understanding of actual and potential behavior can be represented in the form of a demand function. In transportation it is important to emphasize that the alternatives the consumer considers are, first and foremost, activities. For passenger travel these activity choices are about *what* to do, *where* and *when* to do it. For freight movements the choices are about *what* products to sell *where*. Included in these activity choices are corresponding choices of means of transport (both mode and route). Thus the demand for transport is derived from a demand for activities.

As a useful working hypothesis, the total demand is separated into two parts: a transportation demand function predicts how individuals or firms, or groups of individuals or firms, will change transportation choices; an activity-shift function predicts how they will change locational choices.

2.7.2 Behavior at the Individual Level

A consumer is any individual or group of individuals, such as a household or firm, that behaves as a single unit in making transportation decisions.

A model of consumer behavior must indicate what alternative choices the consumer perceives, what consequences he considers important, and how his choice is made from among the perceived alternatives. For travel demand analysis, the choices are various combinations of transportation decisions. The attributes to be considered form the service vector **S**, which characterizes the various transportation choices. The decision process model then indicates how the consumer operates on these choices and their attributes to reach a decision, based upon his characteristics and preferences.

Two models for describing the behavior of an individual consumer have been described. Consumer behavior model I assumes that the consumer formulates his preferences explicitly, identifies explicitly all the alternatives open to him and the consequences of each alternative, and evaluates and chooses among the alternatives using a well-defined decision rule based upon his expressed preferences. A key feature of this model is that the consumer expresses his preferences as a utility function defined over all combinations of attributes of the alternatives. The decision rule follows: the consumer picks the alternative that has the maximum value of this utility.

This model is useful as a representation of the behavior of consumers of transportation. Once the utility function is known, it can be used to predict how a particular consumer will respond to changes in service attributes of the available choices or will accept trade-offs among different service attributes; how different consumers with different preferences will make different choices; how groups of consumers will behave; and how choices will change as a result of changes in socioeconomic characteristics that are then reflected in changed preferences.

This model is limited, however, in that it assumes that the consumer has perfect information, operates in complete consistency with his well-defined utility function, and does not learn from experience. Consumer behavior model II overcomes some of the limitations of this model by introducing an explicit probabilistic element. This can represent incomplete information on alternatives or their consequences, a poorly defined preference function, or intrinsic randomness in human behavior. Particular assumptions about the mathematical forms of the utility function and of this random element lead to various forms of stochastic disaggregate models.

Stochastic disaggregate models also assume that the consumer maximizes his utility. Since they include an explicit probabilistic element, such models predict the probability of a consumer making a specific choice.

TO READ FURTHER
For basic presentations of the conventional treatment of consumer theory see Henderson and Quandt (1958), Baumol (1965), or de Neufville and Stafford (1971). For a comprehensive but advanced treatment of stochastic disaggregate models see Domencich and McFadden (1975) and also the suggestions in chapters 4 and 11. We shall treat activity-system shifts only briefly in this volume (chapter 8). The reader interested in this area might begin by consulting the following: Isard

(1960, 1975), Alonso (1965), Kresge and Roberts (1971), Edel and Rothenburg (1972), Echenique et al. (1974), James (1974), Senior (1974), and Lerman (1976).

EXERCISES

2.1(E) Consider the urban commuters discussed in section 2.4.2.

a. Consider a commuter with an annual income of $10,000. By how much would a parking lot operator have to reduce the parking charge of 60¢ to attract this consumer back to automobile from transit after the transit frequency has been doubled?

b. If the consumer's annual income were $20,000, by how much would transit waiting time have to be decreased to attract him from automobile to transit?

c. Consider the initial conditions. At what income level will the consumer shift from transit to automobile?

d. Consider the relationship behind figure 2.5:

i. Verify the curve shown in the figure.

ii. How would the in-vehicle time necessary to cause a shift in mode change if frequency were doubled? Develop numbers and sketch curve.

iii. How would the in-vehicle time necessary to cause a shift in mode change if frequency were halved?

2.2(C) In the urban passenger travel example in this chapter, the characteristics of the consumer influence the weight placed on cost. In the freight example different consumers have different weights on all service attributes. Is there any difference between these two approaches?

2.3(P) Using the results of section 2.4.2, show graphically, as a function of income, (a) the transit travel time at which riders are indifferent between auto and transit, and (b) the transit out-of-vehicle time at which riders are indifferent between auto and transit. Compare and discuss.

3
Case Study I: Disaggregate Prediction of Behavior

3.1 INTRODUCTION

In this chapter we consider an example of a stochastic disaggregate demand model and explore its use for predicting responses of different consumers to various conditions. We also demonstrate how demand models can be used for prediction in a simple and direct way, with only pencil-and-paper calculations (after Jessiman and Kocur 1975, Cambridge Systematics 1976b, Kocur, Rushfeldt, and Millican 1977, Kocur et al. 1977).

3.2 AN URBAN MODE-CHOICE MODEL

3.2.1 The Model

Consider the following urban transportation mode-choice model:

$$p(m: M) = \frac{e^{U_m}}{\sum_{m' \in M} e^{U_{m'}}}, \tag{3.1}$$

$$U_m = \theta_m + \theta_1 t_m + \theta_2 \frac{x_m}{d} + \theta_3 \frac{c_m}{y}, \tag{3.2}$$

where

$p(m: M)$ = probability of an individual choosing mode m
t_m = in-vehicle time (minutes, one-way)
x_m = out-of-vehicle time (minutes, one-way)
d = distance (miles, one-way)
c_m = out-of-pocket cost (cents, one-way)
y = annual income (dollars)
m = automobile (A) or transit (T).

The parameters θ_1, θ_2, and θ_3 are the same for both modes; θ_m is specific to each mode. In the case of two modes, one constant can be arbitrarily set to zero (for example, θ_T), since only the difference $\theta_T - \theta_A$ influences the mode choice.

Define $G(\mathbf{S})$ as follows:

$$p(m = \text{T}) = \frac{e^{U_\text{T}}}{e^{U_\text{T}} + e^{U_\text{A}}} = \frac{1}{1 + e^{U_\text{A} - U_\text{T}}} = \frac{1}{1 + e^{G(\text{S})}}, \qquad (3.3)$$

where

$$G(\text{S}) = U_\text{A} - U_\text{T}$$

$$= (\theta_\text{A} - \theta_\text{T}) + \theta_1(t_\text{A} - t_\text{T}) + \frac{\theta_2}{d}(x_\text{A} - x_\text{T}) + \frac{\theta_3}{y}(c_\text{A} - c_\text{T}). \qquad (3.4)$$

Values of the parameters have been determined empirically:

$$\theta_1 = -0.030, \qquad \theta_2 = -0.34, \qquad \theta_3 = -50. \qquad (3.5)$$

The value of the mode-specific constant θ_A reflects the socio-economic characteristics of the worker and the household. We consider two examples: household type A with $y = \$5,000$ and $\theta_\text{A} = -0.13$; and household type B with $y = \$10,000$ and $\theta_\text{A} = 0.32$.

3.2.2 Basic Calculations

Now consider the following situation:

$$\begin{aligned}
t_\text{A} &= 11.3 \text{ min} & t_\text{T} &= 14 \text{ min} & (3.6) \\
x_\text{A} &= 5 \text{ min} & x_\text{T} &= 8 \text{ min} \\
c_\text{A} &= 122.5\text{¢} & c_\text{T} &= 50\text{¢} \\
d &= 7.25 \text{ miles.}
\end{aligned}$$

Then, for household type A,

$$\begin{aligned}
U_\text{A} &= -0.13 - 0.03(11.3) - 0.34(5/7.25) - 50(122.5/5,000) \\
&= -0.13 - 0.34 - 0.23 - 1.23 \\
&= -1.93, \\
U_\text{T} &= -0.03(14) - 0.34(8/7.25) - 50(50/5,000) \\
&= -1.30, \\
e^{U_\text{A}} &= 0.15, \qquad e^{U_\text{T}} = 0.27,
\end{aligned}$$

so the probability of choosing transit is

$$p_\text{T} = \frac{e^{U_\text{T}}}{e^{U_\text{T}} + e^{U_\text{A}}} = \frac{0.27}{0.42} = 0.65. \qquad (3.7)$$

An alternative way to perform these calculations is to use the difference in utilities (3.4):

$$G(\text{S}) = U_\text{A} - U_\text{T} = -1.93 + 1.30 = -0.63, \qquad (3.8)$$

$$p_\text{T} = \frac{e^{U_\text{T}}}{e^{U_\text{T}} + e^{U_\text{A}}} = \frac{1}{1 + e^{U_\text{A} - U_\text{T}}} = \frac{1}{1 + e^{-0.63}} = 0.65, \qquad (3.9)$$

$$p_A = \frac{e^{U_A}}{e^{U_A} + e^{U_T}} = \frac{1}{1 + e^{U_T - U_A}} = \frac{1}{1 + e^{0.63}} = 0.35. \tag{3.10}$$

Thus, for a worker in this household, transit has the highest probability, and we predict that this individual would choose transit. For a group of 100 identical individuals, we would expect that 35 percent would choose automobile and 65 percent would choose transit.

A similar calculation for household type B shows that

$$U_A = -0.87, \qquad U_T = -1.05, \tag{3.11}$$
$$U_A - U_T = +0.18, \qquad p_T = 0.46, \qquad p_A = 0.54.$$

Again we predict that this individual would choose transit over automobile. Correspondingly, out of 100 identical individuals, 54 percent would choose automobile and 46 percent would choose transit. This example shows that differences in socioeconomic characteristics are often reflected in different transportation demands.

3.2.3 Use of Worksheets

Worksheets provide a good means of organizing the calculations involved in prediction, especially when computers are not available or when the computations are to be done on a pocket calculator or by assistants without advanced technical training.

The logic of the worksheet shown in figure 3.1 is directly related to the preceding calculations. First, the levels of service (t, x, c), the model parameters (θ_i), and other data (distance, income) are provided as inputs. Then, in steps 1.1 and 1.2, the automobile and transit utilities are computed. In step 2 the mode-choice probabilities are computed using the exponential functions of utility as required for the logit model. In step 3, if the number of individuals in each group, or "market segment," is known, the expected number making each choice can be calculated. A worked example is given in the figure, repeating the earlier calculations. The market-segment sizes are arbitrarily taken as 100 individuals.

3.3 THE EFFECTS OF VARIATIONS IN SERVICE LEVELS

3.3.1 Parametric Variations

The effects of variations in service levels can be explored with this model. As an example, consider the effects of a variation in transit fare from the present level of 50 cents to values of 0, 25, 75, 100, 125, 150, and 175 cents. The results are graphed in figure 3.2.

Policy: *Base Case*

Market Segment: *Household Type A*

Origin: *Zone I*

Destination: *Zone IV*

Assumptions:

By: *MLM*

Date: *6/21/77*

1. Utility for each mode

1.1 Auto

$(1.1\text{--}1)$

(t)		$(\theta_1 = 0.030)$		
11.3 min	$\times$	-0.03	$=$	-0.34

$(1.1\text{--}2)$ $+$

(x)		(trip length)		$(\theta_2 = -0.34)$		$+$
5	$\div$	7.25	$\times$	-0.34	$=$	-0.23

$(1.1\text{--}3)$ $+$

(c)		(income)		$(\theta_3 = -50)$		$+$
122.5	$\div$	5,000	$\times$	-50	$=$	-1.23

$(1.1\text{--}4)$ $+$

(θ_A)		$+$
-0.13	$=$	-0.13

$(1.1\text{--}5)$ Total utility (U_A) = $\boxed{-1.93}$

1.2 Transit

$(1.2\text{--}1)$

(t)		$(\theta_1 = -0.030)$		
14.0	$\times$	-0.030	$=$	-0.42

$(1.2\text{--}2)$ $+$

(x)		(trip length)		$(\theta_2 = -0.34)$		$+$
8	$\div$	7.25	$\times$	-0.34	$=$	-0.38

$(1.2\text{--}3)$ $+$

(c)		(income)		$(\theta_3 = -50)$		$+$
50	$\div$	5,000	$\times$	-50	$=$	-0.50

$(1.2\text{--}4)$ Total utility (U_T) = $\boxed{-1.30}$

2. Modal Probabilities

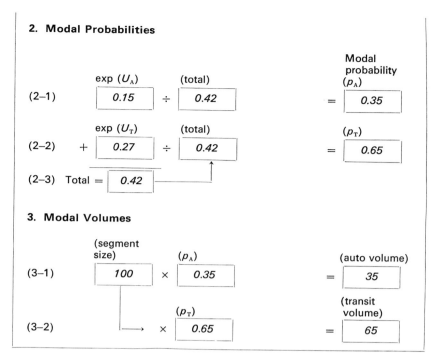

3. Modal Volumes

Figure 3.1 Volume estimation worksheet with a sample calculation for household type *A*.

To perform these calculations a reduced form of the model can be derived and used as follows. From (3.3) and (3.4):

$$p_T = \frac{1}{1 + e^{G(S)}},$$ (3.12)

$$G(S) = U_A - U_T$$

$$= (\theta_A - \theta_T) + \theta_1(t_A - t_T) + \frac{\theta_2}{d}(x_A - x_T) + \frac{\theta_3}{y}(c_A - c_T).$$ (3.13)

Since the only component of **S** that will vary will be c_T,

$$G(S) = \alpha_0 + \alpha_1 c_T,$$ (3.14)

where

$$\alpha_0 = (\theta_A - \theta_T) + \theta_1(t_A - t_T) + \frac{\theta_2}{d}(x_A - x_T) + \frac{\theta_3 c_A}{y}$$

$$= U_A - \theta_T - \theta_1 t_T - \frac{\theta_2}{d} x_T,$$ (3.15)

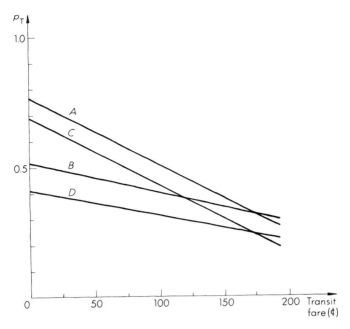

Figure 3.2 Effect of fare variations on the transportation decisions of households at two income levels and facing two different sets of service characteristics.

$$\alpha_1 = -\frac{\theta_3}{y}. \tag{3.16}$$

By reference to figure 3.1, we see that for household type A,

$$\alpha_0 = -1.93 + 0 + 0.42 + 0.38 = -1.13, \tag{3.17}$$

$$\alpha_1 = \frac{50}{5,000} = 0.01. \tag{3.18}$$

Thus the methodology for this calculation is as follows:

Step 1. For the particular household type and basic conditions, calculate α_0 and α_1 as given by (3.15) and (3.16).
Step 2. For each transit fare c_T being considered:
2.1 Calculate $\alpha_1 c_T$.
2.2 Calculate $G(\mathbf{S}) = \alpha_0 + \alpha_1 c_T$.
2.3 Calculate p_T by (3.12).

Figure 3.3 shows a worksheet format for systematic execution of this calculation. Sample numerical results are given in the figure and in table 3.1. (Note that $\alpha_0 = U_A - U_T^*$.) Figure 3.2 shows the results graphically for household types A and B.

**Worksheet 2
Estimation of Volumes
for Transit Fare
Variations**

Policy: *Transit Fare
Variations*
Market Segment: *Household
Type A*
Origin:
Destination:
Assumptions:
By: *MLM*
Date: *6/21/77*

1. Basic constants

1.1 Auto utility

(t) $(\theta_1 = -0.030)$

(1.1–1) 11.3 $\times$ -0.03 $=$ -0.34

(x) (trip length) $(\theta_2 = -0.34)$ $+$

(1.1–2) $+$ 5 $\div$ 7.25 $\times$ -0.34 $=$ -0.23

(c) (income) $(\theta_3 = -50)$ $+$

(1.1–3) $+$ 122.5 $\div$ $5,000$ $\times$ -50 $=$ -1.23

(θ_A) $+$

(1.1–4) $+$ -0.13 $=$ -0.13

(1.1–5)   Total utility (U_A) $=$ -1.93

1.2 Transit utility components

(t) $(\theta_1 = -0.030)$

(1.2–1) 14.0 $\times$ -0.030 $=$ -0.42

(x) (trip length) $(\theta_2 = -0.34)$ $+$

(1.2–2) $+$ 8 $\div$ 7.25 $\times$ -0.34 $=$ -0.38

(1.2–3)   Partial utility (U_T^*) $=$ -0.80

1.3 Constant

(U_A) (U_T^*) (α_0)

(1.3–1) -1.93 $-$ -0.80 $=$ -1.13

1.4 Variable term

$\theta_3 = -50$ (income) (α_1)

(1.4–1) -50 $\div$ $5,000$ $\times (-1)$ $=$ $+0.01$

2. Parametric variations

Transit fare c_T (¢)	$\alpha_1 c_T$	α_0	$G(S) = \alpha_0 + \alpha_1 c_T$	$e^{G(S)}$	$1 + e^{G(S)}$	$p_T = [1 + e^{G(S)}]^{-1}$	$p_A = 1 - p_T$
0	0	−1.13	−1.13	0.32	1.32	0.76	0.24
25	0.25	−1.13	−0.88	0.42	1.42	0.71	0.29
50	0.50	−1.13	−0.63	0.53	1.53	0.65	0.35
75	0.75	−1.13	−0.38	0.68	1.68	0.60	0.40
100	1.00	−1.13	−0.13	0.88	1.88	0.53	0.47
125	1.25	−1.13	+0.12	1.13	2.13	0.47	0.53
150	1.50	−1.13	+0.37	1.45	2.45	0.41	0.59
175	1.75	−1.13	+0.62	1.86	2.86	0.35	0.65

Figure 3.3 Volume estimation worksheet for transit fare variations with a sample calculation for household type *A*.

Table 3.1 Effect of transit fare variations by household type

Transit fare (¢)	Type A (low income, walk distance)		Type B (medium income, walk distance)		Type C (low income, beyond walk distance)		Type D (medium income, beyond walk distance)	
	P_A	P_T	P_A	P_T	P_A	P_T	P_A	P_T
0	0.24	0.76	0.48	0.52	0.31	0.69	0.58	0.42
25	0.29	0.71	0.51	0.49	0.37	0.63	0.61	0.39
50	0.35	0.65	0.54	0.46	0.43	0.57	0.64	0.36
75	0.40	0.60	0.57	0.43	0.49	0.51	0.67	0.33
100	0.47	0.53	0.60	0.40	0.55	0.45	0.69	0.31
125	0.53	0.47	0.63	0.37	0.62	0.38	0.72	0.28
150	0.59	0.41	0.66	0.34	0.67	0.33	0.75	0.25
175	0.65	0.35	0.69	0.31	0.72	0.28	0.77	0.23

3.3.2 Differences in Base Service Levels

We now consider two other household types, C and D, with the same socioeconomic characteristics as A and B, respectively. They differ from A and B in that their base levels of service are different:

$$t_A = 14.2 \text{ min} \qquad t_T = 21.7 \text{ min} \qquad\qquad (3.19)$$
$$x_A = 5 \text{ min} \qquad x_T = 15.5 \text{ min}$$
$$c_A = 131.3¢ \qquad c_T = 75¢$$
$$d = 8.13 \text{ miles.}$$

The base mode splits are, for C, $p_T = 0.57$ and, for D, $p_T = 0.36$. The effects of transit fare variations are shown in table 3.1 and figure 3.2.

Note that the same model is being used to represent the behavior of individuals with different socioeconomic characteristics in the same circumstances, that is, with the same service levels (A vs. B, C vs. D); and individuals with the same socioeconomic characteristics in different situations (A and C, B and D). This is the real power of demand models: they represent behavior in a generalized way such that the different behaviors of individuals in different situations can be predicted.

3.4 SERVICE LEVELS

So far we have used the demand model to predict consumer responses without going into how we actually obtain values of the service attributes. In this section we examine this question and see how differences in service levels arise and how these differences affect behavior.

Figure 3.4 shows an urban corridor, with a rapid transit line and an expressway connecting the centers of the four zones. A network of streets covers the area. There is a rapid-transit station at the center of

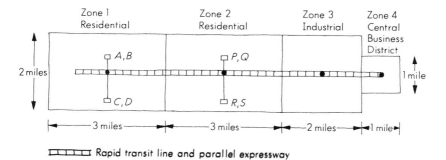

Figure 3.4 Characteristics of an urban corridor.

Table 3.2 Typical speeds of various transportation modes in an urban corridor

Mode	Speed[a]
Walking	3 mph = 0.05 mpm (4.8 kph = 0.08 kpm)
Auto, local streets (peak period)	18 mph = 0.30 mpm (29.0 kph = 0.48 kpm)
Auto, expressway	40 mph = 0.67 mpm (64.4 kph = 1.07 kpm)
Bus-feeder, local streets[b]	8 mph = 0.13 mpm (12.9 kph = 0.21 kpm)
Bus-express, expressway	50 mph = 0.83 mpm (80.5 kph = 1.34 kpm)
Light rail transit (grade-separated)[b]	22 mph = 0.37 mpm (35.4 kph = 0.59 kpm)
Rail rapid transit[b]	30 mph = 0.50 mpm (48.3 kph = 0.81 kpm)

[a]mph = miles per hour; mpm = miles per minute; kph = kilometers per hour; kpm = kilometers per minute.
[b]Average, taking stops into account.
Note: Speeds vary greatly according to specific local conditions.

each zone. Table 3.2 gives the typical speeds of the various transportation facilities in the corridor. In addition, we must know the transit waiting time. Pecknold, Wilson, and Kullman (1972) reported the following empirical function for urban bus operations:

$$\text{waiting time} = \begin{cases} h/2 & \text{for } 0 \leq h \leq 18.3, \\ 5.5 + 0.2h & \text{for } h \geq 18.3, \end{cases} \qquad (3.20)$$

where h is the headway (interval) between vehicles in minutes. The cutoff at $h = 18.3$ simply indicates the tendency of people to know scheduled arrival times on systems with long headways.

3.4.1 Trip Profiles
In a trip from home to work a traveler will generally use a combination

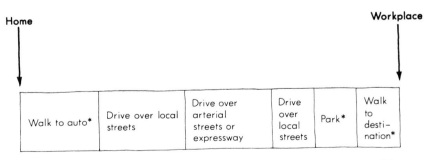

Figure 3.5 Trip profile—auto. * = out-of-vehicle time. After Jessiman and Kocur (1975).

100   Case Study I

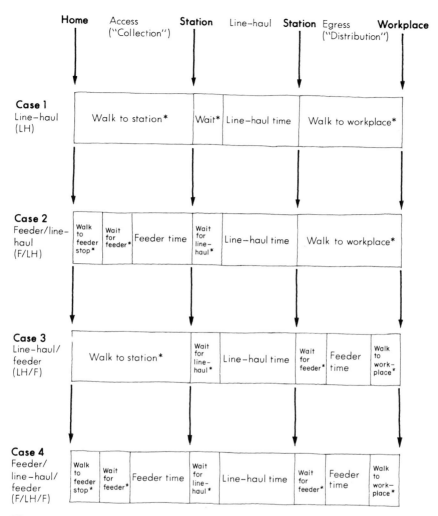

Figure 3.6 Trip profiles—transit. * = out-of-vehicle time. After Jessiman and Kocur (1975).

of transportation means. Figures 3.5 and 3.6 show a sampling of possible combinations. The trip profiles in which transit is used are particularly varied, and only four possible combinations of feeder and line-haul services are shown. (Note that additional complexities could exist, such as one or more transfers within the line-haul system.)

3.4.2 Worksheets
Determining the levels of service over a path for a set of trip profiles is conceptually simple but requires careful attention to detail. To assist in this process it is often helpful to use worksheets similar to those introduced earlier for calculating choice probabilities. Figure 3.7 shows such a worksheet for calculating service levels. (The speeds indicated are those of table 3.2; other assumptions may be appropriate in various contexts.)

3.4.3 Examples

CASE I: WITHIN WALK DISTANCE OF TRANSIT STATION
Two individuals live within walk distance of a transit station, in zone 1, and work in the central business district (CBD), zone 4. (Generally it is assumed that the maximum acceptable walk distance is 0.25 mile or 0.4 kilometer.) One individual is a member of a household of type A; the second, of type B. Both have essentially the same trip profiles open to them for travel between home and work:

1. For automobile:
• Walk to auto, garaged at home: distance essentially negligible.
• Drive over local streets to arterial street: distance about 1/8 mile; in-vehicle time = 0.4 min.
• Drive on expressway to CBD zone: 7 miles; in-vehicle time = 10.5 min.
• Drive over local streets to parking location: about 1/8 mile; in-vehicle time = 0.4 min.
• Time spent parking car: 3 min (parking charge $1.00 per day, or 50¢ each direction); out-of-vehicle time = 3 min; cost = 50¢.
• Walk to workplace: about 0.1 mile; out-of-vehicle time = 2 min.
• Auto operating costs: about 10¢ per vehicle-mile, for 7.25 miles; cost = 72.5¢.
• Totals: in-vehicle time = 11.3 min; out-of-vehicle time = 5 min; cost = 122.5¢.
• Total auto in-vehicle distance = 7.25 miles; total distance = 7.35 miles.

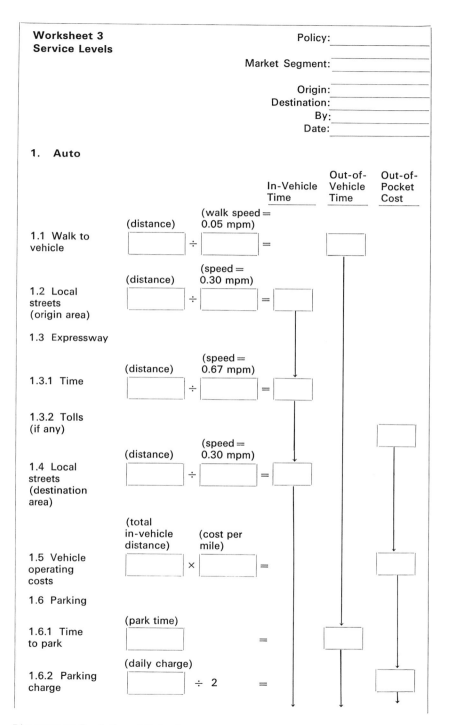

Worksheet 3
Service Levels

Policy: _____

Market Segment: _____

Origin: _____
Destination: _____
By: _____
Date: _____

1. Auto

		In-Vehicle Time	Out-of-Vehicle Time	Out-of-Pocket Cost

1.1 Walk to vehicle
(distance) ÷ (walk speed = 0.05 mpm) =

1.2 Local streets (origin area)
(distance) ÷ (speed = 0.30 mpm) =

1.3 Expressway

1.3.1 Time
(distance) ÷ (speed = 0.67 mpm) =

1.3.2 Tolls (if any)

1.4 Local streets (destination area)
(distance) ÷ (speed = 0.30 mpm) =

1.5 Vehicle operating costs
(total in-vehicle distance) × (cost per mile) =

1.6 Parking

1.6.1 Time to park
(park time) =

1.6.2 Parking charge
(daily charge) ÷ 2 =

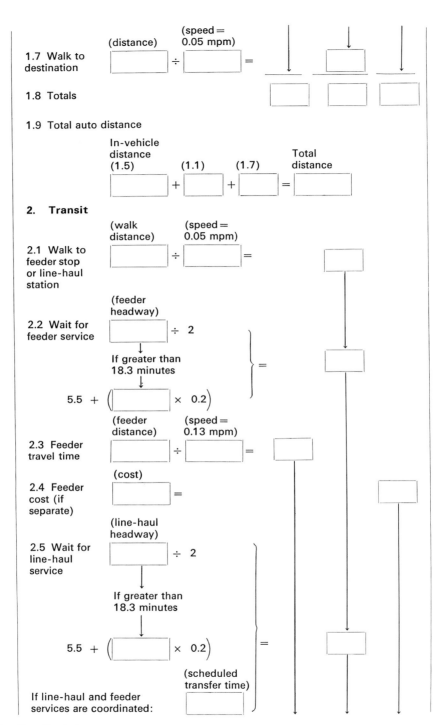

1.7 Walk to destination

(distance) ÷ (speed = 0.05 mpm) =

1.8 Totals

1.9 Total auto distance

In-vehicle distance (1.5) + (1.1) + (1.7) = Total distance

2. Transit

2.1 Walk to feeder stop or line-haul station

(walk distance) ÷ (speed = 0.05 mpm) =

2.2 Wait for feeder service

(feeder headway) ÷ 2

If greater than 18.3 minutes

5.5 + (☐ × 0.2)

2.3 Feeder travel time

(feeder distance) ÷ (speed = 0.13 mpm) =

2.4 Feeder cost (if separate)

(cost) =

2.5 Wait for line-haul service

(line-haul headway) ÷ 2

If greater than 18.3 minutes

5.5 + (☐ × 0.2)

If line-haul and feeder services are coordinated:

(scheduled transfer time)

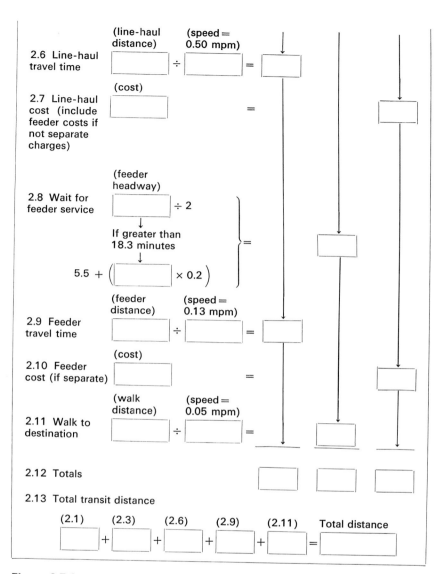

Figure 3.7 Service-level worksheet.

2. For transit:
- Walk to transit station, about 1/8 mile; out-of-vehicle time = 2.5 min.
- Wait for transit vehicle, about half the headway between vehicles, which is 6 min; out-of-vehicle time = 3 min.
- Ride in the line-haul rapid transit vehicle to CBD zone: 7 miles; in-vehicle time = 14 min.
- Transit fare 50¢ in one direction; cost = 50¢.
- Walk from station to workplace, about 1/8 mile; out-of-vehicle time = 2.5 min.
- Totals: in-vehicle time = 14 min; out-of-vehicle time = 8 min; cost = 50¢.
- In-vehicle distance = 7 miles; total distance = 7.25 miles.

Note that, although the two individuals have different socioeconomic characteristics, because they live and work in almost identical geographical locations they both face the same service characteristics in each of the two modes. They do have different responses to these characteristics, however. The levels of service calculated above are those that were used in section 3.2. (Note that the distance used is the total automobile in-vehicle distance.) These led to mode-choice probabilities of (p_T = 0.65, p_A = 0.35) for the individual in household type A and (p_T = 0.46, p_A = 0.54) for the individual in household type B.

CASE II: BEYOND WALK DISTANCE

Many residents of a corridor will live beyond any "reasonable" walking distance of a line-haul transit station. In this case they may have the option of walking to a "station" (such as a bus stop) from which a "feeder" transit vehicle will take them to the line-haul transit station.[1] Consider individuals in household types C and D with the same socioeconomic characteristics as A and B, respectively, but residing beyond walking distance to line-haul transit. Assume that they live 1 mile from the nearest line-haul transit station but within walking distance (1/8 mile) of a feeder transit service. Again, both individuals have the same trip profiles open to them:

[1] A third important case exists: beyond walking distance of either feeder or line-haul transit. In this case the only real alternative is the automobile: for the entire trip, "automobile" mode; or as feeder to transit, in either the "park-and-ride" or the "kiss-and-ride" mode. These alternatives will not be examined in this example, although they are often important in practice.

1. For auto:
- Walk to auto, garaged at home: distance negligible.
- Drive over local streets to arterial street: distance 1 mile; in-vehicle time = 3.3 min.
- Drive on expressway to CBD zone: 7 miles; in-vehicle time = 10.5 min.
- Drive over local streets to parking location: about 1/8 mile; in-vehicle time = 0.4 min.
- Time spent parking car: 3 min, out-of-vehicle time (parking charge $1.00 per day, or 50¢ each direction); out-of-vehicle time = 3 min; cost = 50¢.
- Walk to workplace: about 0.1 mile, out-of-vehicle time = 2 min.
- Auto operating costs: about 10¢ per vehicle-mile, for 8.13 miles = 81.3¢.
- Totals: in-vehicle time = 14.2 min; out-of-vehicle time = 5 min; cost = 131.3¢.
- In-vehicle distance = 8.13 miles, total distance = 8.23 miles.

2. For transit:
- Walk to feeder service station (bus stop), about 1/8 mile; out-of-vehicle time = 2.5 min.
- Wait for feeder transit vehicle, about half the headway of 15 min; out-of-vehicle time = 7.5 min.
- Feeder travel 1 mile, cost 25¢; in-vehicle time = 7.7 min, cost = 25¢.
- Wait for line-haul transit vehicle, about half the headway of 6 min; out-of-vehicle time = 3 min.
- Ride in line-haul rapid transit vehicle, 7 miles; in-vehicle time = 14 min.
- Line-haul fare cost = 50¢.
- Walk from CBD station to workplace, about 1/8 mile; out-of-vehicle time = 2.5 min.
- Totals: in-vehicle time = 21.7 min; out-of-vehicle time = 15.5 min; cost = 75¢.
- In-vehicle distance = 8 miles; total distance = 8.25 miles.

These service-level assumptions result in the values used in section 3.3.2. The corresponding mode-choice probabilities are, for household type C, ($p_T = 0.57$, $p_A = 0.43$) and, for household type D, ($p_T = 0.36$, $p_A = 0.64$). Table 3.1 and figure 3.2 show the responses of these households to transit fare variations.

DISCUSSION

These two cases show that access characteristics have an important effect on choice. Figure 3.8 shows the implications diagrammatically. Part a shows a zone divided into two subzones, based upon the maximum walk distance to a line-haul station. Subzones I and II thus correspond to cases I and II, respectively. We see from the results obtained above that there can be significant variations in choices *within* zones. The choices made by households in a zone can vary by socioeconomic characteristics and by access characteristics (that is, the choices available). This line of reasoning can be extended to the availability of an automobile ("transit-captive") as well as the availability of transit ("auto-captive").

Part b of the figure shows one extension of this line of reasoning. Subzone III consists of households beyond walking distance of line-haul or feeder services.

3.5 A METHODOLOGY FOR INCREMENTAL ANALYSIS

The foregoing examples have demonstrated the basic procedure for predicting choices as a consequence of alternative service levels. For some models, once a prediction has been made for existing "base" conditions, a powerful shortcut exists for analyzing the effects of changes to those base conditions. We consider here the case of the multinomial logit model:

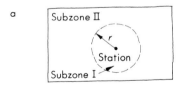

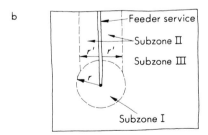

Figure 3.8 Access conditions. *r* and *r'* are maximum walk distances to a station and a feeder service, respectively. After Kocur et al. (1977).

$$p(m) \equiv p(m: M) = \frac{e^{U_m}}{\sum\limits_{m' \in M} e^{U_{m'}}}. \tag{3.21}$$

It can be shown that, given a set of changes ΔU_m for each mode m and base probabilities $p^0(m)$, the new probability $p'(m)$ is

$$p'(m) = \frac{e^{\Delta U_m} p^0(m)}{\sum\limits_{m' \in M} e^{\Delta U_{m'}} p^0(m')}. \tag{3.22}$$

In the case of two modes i and j,

$$p'(i) = \frac{e^{\Delta U_i} p^0(i)}{e^{\Delta U_i} p^0(i) + e^{\Delta U_j} p^0(j)} = \frac{1}{1 + [p^0(j)/p^0(i)] e^{\Delta U_j - \Delta U_i}}. \tag{3.23}$$

Thus, given initial mode-choice probabilities (or shares) $p^0(m)$ and a specific set of changes ΔS_m, the new probabilities $p'(m)$ can be found from the corresponding $\Delta U_m = f(\Delta S_m)$.

3.6 MODE-CHOICE MODEL II

The model introduced in section 3.2.1 is a special case of a more general model. Model II is summarized in table 3.3 and will be used in selected exercises. This model explicitly includes two socioeconomic attributes: income and the ratio of automobiles owned to the number of licensed drivers. We see that the mode-specific constant of model I arises from differences in these attributes.

This model is a composite of several statistically estimated models and was designed primarily for teaching purposes. A number of such multinomial logit models have been estimated using Washington, D.C., data from a conventional home interview survey carried out in 1968. Many of these were estimated as part of a project studying the relationship between automobile ownership and transportation service levels (Lerman and Ben-Akiva 1975, Cambridge Systematics 1976a). Both binary and three-mode models were estimated in this study, the binary models dealing with choices between automobile and transit and the three-mode models with choices among transit, automobile driven alone, and shared-ride automobile ("carpooling," with at least one traveler in addition to the driver). The reported models were estimated with sample sizes on the order of 800–1,200 observations and met appropriate statistical tests for significance satisfactorily (see chapter 11).

3.7 SUMMARY

In this chapter we have used a demand function to predict the re-

Table 3.3 Binary mode-choice model

Variables

Service attributes (**S**) (all one-way, or half the round-trip values):

t_m = in-vehicle time (minutes)

x_m = out-of-vehicle time (walking, waiting, parking) (minutes)

c_m = cost (out-of-pocket: fares, tolls, parking) (cents)

θ_m = mode-specific characteristic

d = distance (miles)

Socioeconomic attributes (**A**):

y = income (household total) (dollars per year)

a_{LD} = autos owned divided by the number of licensed drivers (per household)

Parameters ($\boldsymbol{\theta}$):

θ_i = general parameter value applying to ith characteristic in mode m's utility

θ_{mi} = mode-specific parameter value applying to ith characteristic in mode m's utility

θ_{m0} = mode-specific constant

m = mode (A = auto, T = transit)

Modal utilities

General form:

$$U_m = \theta_m + \theta_1 t_m + \theta_2 \frac{x_m}{d} + \theta_3 \frac{c}{y}$$

$$\theta_m = \theta_{m0} + \theta_{m4}y + \theta_{m5}a_{LD}$$

Coefficient values:

	θ_1	θ_2	θ_3	θ_{m4}	θ_{m5}	θ_{m0}
Automobile	-0.030	-0.34	-50	8.957×10^{-5}	2.84	-2.00
Transit	-0.030	-0.34	-50	0	0	0

sponses of different consumers to changes in transportation service levels. The function used was disaggregate in that it predicted the behavior of individual consumers. It was also stochastic in that it predicted the probabilities of various choices.

Use of the demand functions was organized around worksheets, which helped to systematize the various calculations.

In order to use the demand function, values of service levels were required; these were developed by simple estimating procedures. Simple manual worksheets were also demonstrated for these calculations.

The examples demonstrate that a single demand function can represent the behavior of consumers with different socioeconomic characteristics and/or with different transportation service levels available; consumers with different socioeconomic characteristics will display different behaviors, even at the same service levels; consumers with similar socioeconomic characteristics may behave differently when confronted with different service levels; and any grouping of consumers—such as a geographic grouping into traffic zones—may include consumers with widely varying socioeconomic characteristics and transportation service levels, and thus different choice behaviors.

TO READ FURTHER
Disaggregate models with simple manual worksheets have been applied to a number of practical problems. For applications to energy conservation analysis, see Cambridge Systematics (1976b) and Dunbar (1976). Of course, disaggregate models can also be used in large-scale computer models. For use in regionwide sketch planning as part of an analysis aimed at establishing transportation research and development priorities, see Kocur et al. (1977).

EXERCISES
3.1(E) Select two of the cases examined in section 3.3 (combinations of household type and residence location) and analyze the following (calculate typical values, plot graphs, and discuss):
a. The effect of variations in walk distance (over a range from 0.02 to 1 mile) on the probability of choosing transit.
b. The effect of variations in automobile parking charges (from 0 to $5 per day) on the probability of choosing automobile.
c. The effect of changes in transit line-haul headway (from 1 to 18 minutes).

3.2(E) Design worksheets for the parametric analysis in exercise 3.1 and demonstrate their use.

3.3(E) Using the service-level worksheets, work through the examples in section 3.4.3 and check your understanding of the calculations and results.

3.4(E) In this chapter trip profiles were shown for automobile and for transit. Other profiles occur in urban transportation: passenger in shared-ride automobile (carpool); automobile driven alone to transit station, then transit (park-and-ride); automobile passenger to transit (kiss-and-ride); local bus for access portion of trips, then same bus in express (nonstop) operations along arterial street, expressway, or busway to destination.

a. Construct typical trip profiles for cases other than those presented in this chapter.

b. Make reasonable assumptions about performance characteristics where necessary, and calculate levels of service for typical trips, using households selected from the examples in section 3.3.

c. Make reasonable assumptions, calculate utilities of these profiles, and calculate corresponding mode-choice probabilities.

3.5(E) Consider the following contexts, construct typical trip profiles, make reasonable assumptions about performance characteristics, and compare:

a. Interurban passenger transport, with choices of automobile, airplane, railroad, and bus.

b. Interurban freight transport, with choices of railroad, truck, pipeline, or inland waterway.

c. International freight transport, with choices of ships or airplanes.

3.6(C) The discussion in section 3.4.3 applies to many transportation contexts. Develop examples to illustrate similar influences of access characteristics for the contexts indicated in exercise 3.5. Use the trip profiles developed in your answer to that exercise.

3.7(E) Consider the incremental logic described in section 3.5.

a. Design worksheets for implementing this logic.

b. Use these worksheets to explore the effects of the changes indicated in exercise 3.1.

3.8(E) Discuss the effects of the transit fare variations shown in table 3.1 and figure 3.2.

3.9(E) Consider the binary mode-split model shown in table 3.3.

a. For each of the nine combinations of a_{LD} and y for which values of θ_A are shown in the table, find p_T for the case in which automobile and transit service are identical. (*Check:* for $a_{LD} = 0$ and $y = \$5,000$, $p_T = 0.83$.) Discuss the implications for urban transportation policy: Is a_{LD} exogenous, or can it be affected by policy? If it can be affected, then how?

b. Consider the case $a_{LD} = 0.5$, $y = \$10,000$, with all service attributes except those indicated equal for automobile and transit:

i. What is p_T under this assumption?

ii. What would the difference in automobile and transit in-vehicle times have to be to yield $p_T = 0.5$? 0.6? 0.8?

iii. What would the difference between automobile and transit out-of-vehicle times have to be to yield p_T = 0.5? 0.6? 0.8? (Assume equal in-vehicle times.)

iv. If transit fares were increased by 25 percent, what reduction in transit out-of-vehicle time would be necessary to maintain the same transit share as in part i? What reduction would be necessary to keep the same share of passengers with a_{LD} = 1.0 and y = $15,000?

v. At present automobile congestion is high. Highway improvements are proposed that would reduce automobile in-vehicle time by 15 minutes. How would this affect the value of p_T in part i?

vi. Assume that it is desired to keep p_T constant. If the highway improvement is implemented, what reduction in transit fares would be necessary to maintain the present mode split? Alternatively, transit frequencies can be increased to decrease the transit out-of-vehicle time. How great would this increase in frequency have to be?

vii. Discuss the policy implications of parts iv and v.

c. Consider some other household types (that is, other values of a_{LD} and y), and explore selectively the answers to the questions in part b for these households. Discuss.

3.10(E) In zone 2 of figure 3.4, household types P, Q, R, and S are located the same distance from the transit station as are A, B, C, and D, respectively, in zone 1; members of these households all work in zone 4.

a. Predict the levels of service these four households face.

b. Calculate the corresponding mode-choice probabilities.

c. Compare your results with those for A, B, C, and D and discuss.

d. Parametrically vary transit fares over the range indicated in figure 3.2, plot your results on that figure, and discuss.

e. Consider each of the changes in exercise 3.1 parts a–c. For each change, rank the eight households A, B, C, D, P, Q, R, S in order of increasing sensitivity to the change. Explain how you developed your rankings.

4

Aggregate Prediction of Behavior

4.1 INTRODUCTION

Chapters 2 and 3 examined demand functions that described the behavior of single consumers—individuals, households, or firms (considered as single decision-making units). This disaggregate view proved very useful in analyzing the bases of consumer choice behavior in transportation. For practical predictions of the impacts of transportation strategies, however, it is important to be able to predict the behavior of *groups* of consumers.

We start by making the important distinction between disaggregate and aggregate demand functions. A *disaggregate demand function* predicts the behavior of a single consumer in response to changes in future conditions. An *aggregate demand function* predicts the behavior of a group of consumers (several individuals, households, or firms) in response to changes in future conditions.

Historically the vast bulk of effort in transportation demand analysis has been focused on aggregate demand functions. While research on disaggregate demand functions began at least as early as 1962, only since about 1971 have disaggregate approaches begun to be put into practice (see S. L. Warner 1962, Rassam, Ellis, and Bennett 1971, Charles River Associates 1972, and the historical survey in Domencich and McFadden 1975). For this reason most of the literature simply uses the term "demand functions" to refer to aggregate functions. When a disaggregate function is used, it is labeled "disaggregate" explicitly. For convenience we shall follow this usage in this text, adding the modifier "aggregate" to "demand function" only when it is not clear from the context.

4.2 MARKET SEGMENTS

The potential users of a transportation system can be classified according to many different sets of criteria. Ideally we try to include in each group consumers who are very similar in their preferences and characteristics and thus will respond similarly to changes in transportation, while at the same time we try to make the groups relatively dissimilar one from another. Thus we try to divide the total market—the total population of potential travelers or shippers—into segments each of which is relatively homogeneous but is different from other segments. Typical ways of forming such segments are as follows:

In urban passenger transportation, consumers might be classified by:

1. income
2. automobile availability (cars per household)
3. household size
4. occupation of head of household
5. stage in family life cycle (for example, two-person household with children living at home, two-person household without children, or elderly without children; see Aldana, de Neufville, and Stafford 1974, Cambridge Systematics 1976a)
6. geographic location (for example, through combinations of households or firms into "traffic zones")
7. trip purpose.

In planning access to airports, travelers might be grouped as:

1. air travelers resident in the region
   a. business travelers
   b. other travelers
2. air travelers not resident in the region
   a. business travelers
   b. other travelers
3. airport employees
4. visitors accompanying travelers
5. visitors not accompanying travelers.

In analyzing freight transportation, consumers might be classified by:

1. firm size
2. industry type
3. commodity types being purchased and/or sold.

A particularly important form of aggregation into market segments is by geographic location. In almost all transportation studies the region is divided into geographic zones, with all of the consumers in each zone forming the main market segments (although this is usually not stated explicitly). Then various subsidiary market segments are constructed. For example, in an urban transportation study, once the zones are established, each zone might be characterized by an average income per household and an average automobile ownership per household; alternatively, the households in the zone might be grouped by income and number of automobiles per household.

There are obviously many different ways in which the total travel market in a particular region could be divided into market segments. Particular care must be given to constructing these segments in a way that is useful for anticipating the effects of the transportation changes being considered.

4.3 EXAMPLES OF AGGREGATE DEMAND FUNCTIONS

Once we have established the basic market segments into which we shall group potential users, the next step is to develop a basis for characterizing the behavior of each group.

Aggregate demand functions represent the behavior of a group (or "aggregate") of individuals. These functions are of the form first introduced in chapter 1:

$$V = D(A, S), \tag{4.1}$$

where V is the vector of volumes or numbers of consumers making particular choices, A represents the social, economic, and other characteristics of the activity system and of the individuals in the group, and S the service attributes that characterize the transportation choices open to prospective travelers.

Thus the aggregate demand function D gives the potential volumes and composition of flow between two (or more) points as a function of the service attributes experienced during movement between those points for a particular activity system. The activity-system variables describe the characteristics of the consumers whose behavior is represented by the demand function and of the activity system that influences their choices.

Examples of aggregate demand functions follow. The examples were selected to illustrate the major historical streams of model development.

4.3.1 Gravity Models

The gravity model is perhaps the classic transportation demand model (see the survey in Isard 1960). In its simplest form it was originally developed as a "law of social physics" analogous to Newton's law of gravitation for physical systems. We start with *gravity I:*

$$V_{kd} = Y_k Z_d L_{kd}, \tag{4.2}$$

where Y_k is some measure of the intensity of activity at zone k, such as the population; Z_d is some measure of the intensity of activity at zone d, such as the population or employment level; and L_{kd} represents the effect of transportation service attributes on demand for travel between k and d. One common assumption is that

$$L_{kd} = t_{kd}^{\alpha},$$ (4.3)

where t is travel time and α is a parameter. Originally it was assumed that $\alpha \approx -2$, thus leading to the equivalent of Newton's law of gravitational attraction.

More generally, other service attributes may enter as well. As an example we have **gravity II**, described by (4.2) and the assumption that

$$L_{kd} = t_{kd}^{\alpha_1} c_{kd}^{\alpha_2},$$ (4.4)

where c is out-of-pocket cost and the αs are parameters taking various values.

The widest application of the gravity model in transportation has been to predict, not how many people will travel, but which destination they will choose. Assume that the region is divided into N traffic zones and that, by some separate analysis, we have estimated that V_k trips will originate in zone k. Now the problem is to predict what fraction of these trips will go from k to another zone d. The gravity model used for this purpose is **gravity III:**

$$V_{kd} = V_k \frac{Z_d L_{kd}}{\sum\limits_{d' \neq k} Z_{d'} L_{kd'}}.$$ (4.5)

Alternatively we could write

$$V_{kd} = V_k \gamma_{kd},$$ (4.6)

where

$$\gamma_{kd} \equiv \frac{Z_d L_{kd}}{\sum\limits_{d' \neq k} Z_{d'} L_{kd'}}.$$ (4.7)

(The index in the summation indicates that all values of d' are to be included *except* $d' = k$.) The term $Z_d L_{kd}$ is often called the "potential" (Isard 1960); (4.5) suggests that each destination d competes for the trips originating at k and that the competitive power of d is proportional to its "potential" relative to the "total potential" of all destinations.

If we define V_k as follows, gravity III becomes identical to gravity I:

$$V_k = Y_k \sum\limits_{d' \neq k} Z_{d'} L_{kd'}.$$ (4.8)

This suggests *gravity IV:*

$$V_{kd} = V_k \gamma_{kd},$$ (4.9)

where γ_{kd} and L_{kd} are defined by (4.7) and (4.3), respectively, and

$$V_k = (\beta_k)^\theta,$$ (4.10)

$$\beta_k = Y_k \sum_{d' \neq k} Z_{d'} L_{kd'}.$$ (4.11)

Thus

$$V_{kd} = (Y_k)^\theta \left(\sum_{d' \neq k} Z_{d'} L_{kd'} \right)^\theta \frac{Z_d L_{kd}}{\sum_{d' \neq k} Z_{d'} L_{kd'}}.$$ (4.12)

As in gravity III, the second factor indicates that the total number of trips originating in zone k depends on the "total potential" of travel to various destinations. The last factor reflects the split or distribution of these trips among alternative destinations according to their potentials relative to the total.

4.3.2 Some Intercity Passenger Demand Models

The first important demand models for intercity passenger travel were developed for the Northeast Corridor Project of the U.S. Department of Transportation. These models were used to predict the level of travel between any pair of cities together with the split among the competing modes.

First developed in point of time was the Kraft-SARC model (Kraft 1963). Later a family of models was developed by Quandt and Baumol (1966; see also Crow, Young, and Cooley 1973), and a third type of model was developed by James McLynn (McLynn and Woronka 1969).

For the case of three modes, and considering only time and cost as service variables,[1] these models are:

Kraft-SARC:

$$V_{kdm} = \phi_{m0}(P_k P_d)^{\phi_{m1}}(I_k I_d)^{\phi_{m2}}(t_{kd1}^{\theta_{m11}} c_{kd1}^{\theta_{m12}})(t_{kd2}^{\theta_{m21}} c_{kd2}^{\theta_{m22}})(t_{kd3}^{\theta_{m31}} c_{kd3}^{\theta_{m32}}),$$ (4.13)

McLynn:

[1]In the original formulations of the Baumol-Quandt and McLynn models a third service attribute, frequency, was included as well. In the Kraft-SARC and Baumol-Quandt forms frequency was handled the same way as the other two variables. In the McLynn model frequency was introduced as exp(frequency). The frequency terms have been left out of this discussion for purposes of clarity. For similar models for the urban context see Domencich, Kraft, and Vallette (1968).

$$V_{kdm} = \phi_0 (P_k P_d)^{\phi_1} (I_k I_d)^{\phi_2} \frac{t_{kdm}^{\theta_{m1}} c_{kdm}^{\theta_{m2}}}{\sum_q t_{kdq}^{\theta_{q1}} c_{kdq}^{\theta_{q2}}} \sum_q (t_{kdq}^{\theta_{q1}} c_{kdq}^{\theta_{q2}})^{\delta_1},$$ (4.14)

Baumol-Quandt:

$$V_{kdm} = \phi_0 (P_k P_d)^{\phi_1} (I_k I_d)^{\phi_2} (t_{kdm}^{\theta_1} c_{kdm}^{\theta_2}) (t_{kdb}^{\theta_3} c_{kdb}^{\theta_4}),$$ (4.15)

where

V_{kdm} = volume between k and d by mode m,
P_k = population in zone k,
I_k = median income in zone k,
t_{kdm}, c_{kdm} = travel time and fare between k and d by mode m,
t_{kdb} = travel time by fastest mode,
c_{kdb} = fare by cheapest mode (not necessarily same as fastest mode!),
ϕ, θ, δ = parameters of the model.
Subscripts indicate whether the parameters are mode-dependent (θ_{mj}) or mode-independent (θ_1).

Note that these models assume implicitly in each mode that there is only one path connecting each origin-destination pair of zones. This is often not a bad assumption in the case of intercity passenger travel.

These three models are very similar and yet very different. The reader should compare them carefully after reading the discussions in the following sections.

4.3.3 The Urban Transportation Model System

In urban transportation planning the prediction of travel flows is typically done in four steps. This breaks the demand model down into four submodels, but it also involves some significant assumptions and approximations in the way the submodels are used to compute equilibrium. The submodels are:

1. Trip generation: The total trips made by a particular market segment are estimated for each zone of the region being studied.
2. Distribution: The total trips originating at each zone are distributed among possible destinations.
3. Modal split: The volume of trips going from a particular zone to a particular destination are split among the possible modes.
4. Network assignment: The trips for each origin-destination-mode combination are assigned to paths in the network.

This approach has been widely used in many urban transportation studies since the late 1950s. Because of the importance of understanding this model system, together with its limitations, a detailed discussion is presented in chapter 11.

4.3.4 Stochastic Aggregate Demand Functions (Optional Reading)

We began our discussion of demand at the level of individual behavior with consumer behavior model I. This is a disaggregate model, in that it deals with a single consumer as an entity. It is also deterministic, in that the consumer is assumed to make his choice with perfect information and perfect rationality. After discussing the limitations of this assumption, we introduced the concept of stochastic disaggregate models with consumer behavior model II. In these models the consumer is still treated at the individual level, but a random element is assumed in his behavior to reflect less-than-perfect information. Stochastic disaggregate models yield probabilities of making particular choices rather than a prediction of a specific choice.

In this chapter we have introduced the concept of aggregate demand functions, which represent the behavior of a number of consumers grouped into a single market segment. As we shall see in the next section, such aggregate demand functions can be derived from explicit disaggregate models of individual consumer behavior.

All aggregate models developed to date have been deterministic, in that they predict that a specific number of individuals will make a particular choice. Such models are based, explicitly or implicitly, on consumer behavior model I (Blackburn 1970, Golob and Beckmann 1971). One would expect that, as in the disaggregate case, *stochastic aggregate demand models* would have been developed which would explicitly account for the variability in human behavior. These models would predict a probability distribution over the number of individuals making a particular response to a set of changes in future conditions. Such models have not, in fact, been developed yet, to our knowledge.[2]

Note that we are defining the stochastic nature of a model as describing the form used for prediction. Explicit statistical estimation of the parameters of any demand model involves an underlying probabilistic formulation; for example, linear regression assumes an additive, normally distributed error term. However, even when statistical meth-

[2]Some areas of development that would appear to be aggregate stochastic models are in fact deterministic, in that the resulting models predict only an expected value, not a distribution of behavior. These include "entropy"-derived models (A. G. Wilson 1973, 1974), the intervening-opportunities model, multipath assignment models (Dial 1971), and explicit derivations of aggregate models from disaggregate models (Blackburn 1970).

ods are used to estimate the parameters of demand models such as those described in the preceding section, the model is described and used in prediction as a deterministic model.

4.4 ALTERNATIVE APPROACHES TO THE PREDICTION OF AGGREGATE BEHAVIOR: INTRODUCTION

In practice, one is interested in predicting the responses of groups of individuals to changes in transportation service. The prediction methods used depend in part on the type of demand function with which one begins.

In the preceding chapters and sections we have discussed a two-way classification of demand functions: disaggregate versus aggregate and deterministic versus stochastic. These categories define four major groups of functions.

The present state of development of the four potential groups of demand functions can be summarized as follows:

Group I: disaggregate, deterministic demand functions—development primarily theoretical, used especially for expository purposes.

Group II: disaggregate, stochastic demand functions—extensive development in recent years for both research and practical applications.

Group III: aggregate, deterministic demand functions—the major area of development historically for travel demand analysis.

Group IV: aggregate, stochastic demand functions—no theoretical or practical developments.

At present, the major directions of development and practical use of travel demand models involve models in groups II and III.

If aggregate demand functions have been developed for each market segment, these functions can be used directly to predict the behaviors of the corresponding segments. If disaggregate demand functions have been developed for various segments, prediction is more complex, but there are a number of practical approaches available (see section 4.7). Before turning to a discussion of specific prediction methods, however, we shall first examine some important properties of demand functions.

4.5 PROPERTIES OF DEMAND FUNCTIONS

In developing demand functions and using them for prediction of consumer behavior, the analyst must make many judgments, often involving simplifying assumptions and approximations. To make these thoughtfully the analyst must understand the implications of a particular demand function as a representation of consumer behavior.

When we define a demand function, what we are trying to do is to characterize the activity system **A**—that is, the set of consumers, their characteristics, and the potential activities in which they might engage —and the transportation system **T**—that is, the levels of service **S** of the alternative travel choices available—so that we can predict the volumes **V** that will demand particular transport services. The activity system may be characterized in terms of population, employment, income, family size, cars per household, or any of a wide variety of other variables. The transportation service attributes might include any one or several of the variables identified earlier.

In general we can expect that since different consumers will have different behavior patterns, the demand functions will be different for different social and economic groups, for different trip purposes, and for different time periods. For example, the demand function for home-to-work trips by high-income workers during weekday peak hours might be different from the demand function for shopping and recreational trips by low-income workers on weekends. These differences in behavior of various market segments will be reflected in the values of the parameters of the demand functions, as well as in the forms of the functions.

In the following subsections we shall examine a number of properties of demand functions. Then in section 4.6 we shall explore how knowledge of some of the properties of demand functions can be used for approximate predictions—for example, how incremental analysis can be done with limited information and explicit judgments.

4.5.1 Variables Included

Two basic sets of variables—activity-system variables and service attributes—enter into a demand function. Various choices can be made about what activity-system and service variables are explicitly included in the demand function. The service attributes of the transportation system include travel time (separated into in-vehicle and excess or out-of-vehicle time), time reliability, service schedule, out-of-pocket cost, perceived security, tolls, freight rates, and so on, as described in section 2.3.1. The activity system may be described in terms of such variables as population, employment, income, household size, stage in family life cycle, industrial sector, or commodity code. Some of the activity-system variables will describe the characteristics of the con-sumers included in the market segment, such as income or cars per household (or type of industries for freight demand models). Other activity-system variables will describe characteristics of the choices open to the consumers, such as the attractiveness of alternative destinations for shopping trips as measured by retail sales volume or square feet of retail floor space.

4.5.2 Algebraic Forms of Demand Functions

There are many different forms of demand functions possible. It is useful to distinguish several basic algebraic forms (X represents a single service attribute or activity-system variable):

Linear: for example, $V = \alpha + \beta X$,

Product: for example, $V = \alpha X^\beta$,

Exponential: for example, $V = \alpha e^{\beta X}$,

Logistic: for example, $V = \alpha/(1 + e^{\beta X})$.

These forms are often used because they are simple to handle algebraically, and they are particularly suitable for calibration by standard statistical techniques. For example, for aggregate functions, linear regression techniques can be used to estimate the coefficients of the linear form of the demand model directly, from observations of the form (X, V). To estimate the coefficients of the product and exponential forms, logarithms are taken to transform the equation into a linear form, and then regression techniques are used on this transformed equation. (For disaggregate models alternative techniques are available, such as maximum-likelihood methods for the "logit" form analogous to the logistic.)

Obviously, far more complex forms can be used, and many more activity-system or service variables could be included.

The choice of an algebraic form for a demand function is not simply a question of convenience in calibration. Each functional form represents a somewhat different assumption about the way in which consumers will respond to changes in the choices available. These behavioral differences are seen most clearly by examining the derivatives of the demand function and a related concept, the elasticity.

4.5.3 Behavioral Representations: Directions, Magnitudes, Derivatives, and Elasticities

The behavioral issue is best illustrated by an example. Consider a situation in which firms in one region ship freight to different markets. In market A the freight rate is $5 per ton; in market B, $500 per ton. A rate increase of $5 per ton is imposed. Thus the rate in market A goes from $5 to $10 per ton, a 100 percent increase. The rate in market B goes from $500 to $505 per ton, a 1 percent increase.

What kind of behavior would we expect from these changes? There are two aspects to this question: the *direction* of the change in behavior, and the *magnitude*. First, if we increase the freight rate, would we expect the volume to increase or to decrease? In most situations we would expect any decrease in service quality, such as an increase in travel time or in cost or an increase in probability of loss or damage to the cargo, to result in a decrease in volume. Second, if we increase the rate by 5 percent, would we expect the relative magnitude of the change in volume to be about the same (5 percent) or greater (perhaps 50 percent) or smaller (perhaps 1 percent)? To answer this question we must examine the specific applicable demand model; we shall see that the algebraic form of the demand function and the numerical values of its parameters imply particular patterns of behavior. Several properties of a demand function will be examined to explore the behavior implied by the function.

DERIVATIVES

Consider a demand function $V = D(X)$. The change in volume V, for a change in variable X from X' to X'', equal to ΔX, is given by

$$\Delta V = V'' - V' = D(X'') - D(X'). \tag{4.16}$$

The magnitude of the change in V relative to the change in X is

$$\frac{\Delta V}{\Delta X} = \frac{D(X' + \Delta X) - D(X')}{(X' + \Delta X) - X'}. \tag{4.17}$$

In the limit (as ΔX goes to zero), this is the partial derivative, $\partial V/\partial X$.

Thus, to determine the behavioral pattern represented by a particular demand function, we compute its derivative. The sign of the derivative tells us whether the direction of the response to changed conditions will be the same as or opposite to the direction of change: if the derivative of the demand function with respect to freight rate is negative, then an increase in rate will cause a decrease in volume. The magnitude of the derivative allows us to estimate the magnitude of the response, since

$$\Delta V \approx \frac{\partial V}{\partial X} \Delta X. \tag{4.18}$$

The derivatives of several basic demand functions are given in table 4.1. In some cases, such as the linear form, the derivative is closely related to, or equal to, a particular coefficient, and then it is sufficient to look at the magnitude and sign of that coefficient.

Table 4.1   Derivatives and elasticities of some common functions

	Functional form (V)	Derivative ($\partial V/\partial X$)	Elasticity ($(X/V)(\partial V/\partial X)$)
Linear	$\alpha + \beta X$	β	$\dfrac{\beta X}{V} = \dfrac{1}{1 + (\alpha/\beta X)}$
Product	αX^β	$\alpha\beta X^{\beta-1}$	β
Exponential	$\alpha e^{\beta X}$	$\beta V = \alpha\beta e^{\beta X}$	βX
Logistic	$\dfrac{\alpha}{1 + \gamma e^{\beta X}}$	$-\beta V\left(1 - \dfrac{V}{\alpha}\right) = -\dfrac{\alpha\beta\gamma e^{\beta X}}{(1 + \gamma e^{\beta X})^2}$	$-\beta X\left(1 - \dfrac{V}{\alpha}\right) = -\dfrac{\beta\gamma X e^{\beta X}}{1 + \gamma e^{\beta X}}$
Logistic-product	$\dfrac{\alpha}{1 + \gamma X^\beta}$	$-\dfrac{\beta V}{X}\left(1 - \dfrac{V}{\alpha}\right) = -\dfrac{\alpha\beta\gamma X^{\beta-1}}{(1 + \gamma X^\beta)^2}$	$-\beta\left(1 - \dfrac{V}{\alpha}\right) = -\dfrac{\beta\gamma X^\beta}{1 + \gamma X^\beta}$
Share	$\gamma_i = \dfrac{V_i}{\sum_j V_j} = \dfrac{X_i}{\sum_j X_j}$	$\dfrac{\partial \gamma_i}{\partial X_i} = \dfrac{\sum_j X_j - X_i}{(\sum_j X_j)^2}$	$E_{x_i}(\gamma_i) = 1 - \gamma_i$
		$\dfrac{\partial \gamma_i}{\partial X_j} = \dfrac{-X_i}{(\sum_j X_j)^2}$	$E_{x_j}(\gamma_i) = -\gamma_j$

ELASTICITIES

One problem with the derivative is that its value depends on the units in which V and X are measured. It would be more desirable to have a dimensionless measure of change. Thus we define the *elasticity of V with respect to* X, $E_X(V)$, as the percentage change in V for a 1 percent change in X. The elasticity of volume with respect to a variable X is then

$$E_X(V) = \frac{X}{V}\frac{\partial V}{\partial X},\qquad (4.19)$$

where X is a service or activity-system variable. Note that $E_X(V)$ is the limit, as ΔX tends to zero, of $(\Delta V/V)/(\Delta X/X)$, from which comes the interpretation "percentage change in V for a 1 percent change in X."

The elasticities of several basic demand function forms are shown in table 4.1.

Implications of elasticities

We now consider the demand function forms of section 4.5.2 in the context of the example with which we began this section.

For the linear form we can see from the table that the derivative of V with respect to X is β, a constant. If X is taken as the rate c, we would expect an increase in rate to cause a decrease in volume, so the derivative should be negative. Thus, continuing the example, a \$5 rate increase ($\Delta c = \$5$) would cause the same loss in volume in both markets A and B. This seems highly unlikely: we would certainly expect a 1 percent change in freight rate to cause a much lower loss of volume than a 100 percent change.

For the product form, again with $X = c$, if the derivative is to be negative, β must also be negative (since α and X must be positive to yield positive volumes). Since the derivative is a function of X, the magnitude of ΔV will depend on the magnitude of X. Note that the elasticity of the product form is a constant, β: thus the percentage change in volume for each 1 percent change in cost is a constant. Therefore the \$5 increase from a base rate of \$500 would cause a β percent decrease in volume in market B. In market A, however, the same increase from a base rate of \$5 would have an effect one hundred times greater: a decrease in volume by a *factor* β.

Thus the two function forms represent very different assumptions about behavioral responses. Each function is valid in some cases but not in others. In the case of the linear function, the absolute magnitude of the response is directly proportional to the change. In the case of the product form, the absolute magnitude of the response varies with the level of the initial condition because the percentage change remains constant.

The logistic form is in a sense most general. Over the middle portion of its range the response is roughly linear; at the upper and lower ends of the range the response is more like that of the product form.

Elastic and inelastic behavior

The relative magnitude of the elasticity is often important. When $|E_X(V)| < 1$, V is said to be *inelastic with respect to* X. When $|E_X(V)| > 1$, V is said to be *elastic with respect to* X.

To see one aspect of the significance of this distinction, consider an example. Let

$$V = f(p), \tag{4.20}$$

where p represents price. Then gross revenue to the transportation operator is

$$R = Vp. \tag{4.21}$$

A change in price will produce a change in revenue:

$$\frac{\partial R}{\partial p} = V + p \frac{\partial V}{\partial p} = V[1 + E_p(V)].$$ (4.22)

Obviously since $\partial V/\partial p$ is negative, $E_p(V)$ will be negative. Therefore if V is inelastic with respect to p, an increase in price will yield an increase in gross revenue; if V is elastic with respect to p, an increase in price will yield a decrease in gross revenue.

Arc and point elasticities
A distinction should be drawn between arc and point elasticities. The *point elasticity* is

$$E_X(V) = \frac{X}{V} \frac{\partial V}{\partial X}.$$

The *arc elasticity* is

$$E_{\bar{X}}(V) = \frac{X}{V} \frac{\varDelta V}{\varDelta X}.$$

In the limit as $\varDelta X$ tends to zero, the arc and point elasticities become equal. Occasionally, however, data will only be available for specific values of X and V, so only arc elasticities can be computed. Generally arc and point elasticities are different, the exceptions being special cases such as unit elasticity in a product-form model or situations in which $D(X)$ is a straight line. This is illustrated in figure 4.1, where the point elasticity is proportional to the slope of the tangent to the curve at X_0, C–O–C', whereas the arc elasticity over X_0–X_B is proportional to the slope of the arc cutting the curve, B–O–B'. These are clearly not equal, although the difference becomes smaller as X_B approaches X_0.

Direct and cross-elasticities
Elasticities can also indicate the interrelationships of several variables. Consider, for example, a case in which the demand for travel by a mode k depends on the value of a service variable s in mode k and also on the value of s in a competing mode r:

$$V_k = \alpha s_k^\beta s_r^\gamma.$$ (4.23)

Here we define two elasticities:

$$E_{kk} \equiv \frac{s_k}{V_k} \frac{\partial V_k}{\partial s_k} = \beta,$$ (4.24)

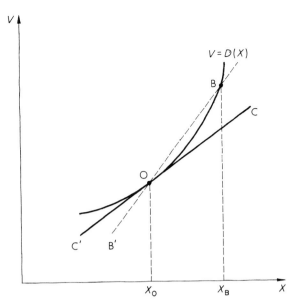

Figure 4.1 Arc and point elasticities.

$$E_{kr} \equiv \frac{s_r}{V_k} \frac{\partial V_k}{\partial s_r} = \gamma. \tag{4.25}$$

The **_direct elasticity_** E_{kk} is the elasticity of the volume choosing mode k with respect to a change in the level of service of mode k. The **_cross-elasticity_** E_{kr} is the elasticity of the volume choosing mode k with respect to a change in the level of service of the competing mode r. The cross-elasticity thus indicates how the volume choosing one alternative is influenced by the characteristics of another alternative.

Properties of elasticities

Table 4.2 lists several important properties of elasticities. Elasticities of complex functions can often be derived by sequential application of these basic formulas. For example, consider the multinomial logit (MNL) model:

$$\gamma_i = \frac{X_i}{\sum_j X_j}, \tag{4.26}$$

where

$$X_i = e^{U_i}, \qquad U_i = \lambda_i \sum_k (a_{ik} Y_{ik}).$$

Table 4.2   Properties of elasticities

Definition

If $y = f(x)$, then

$$E_x(y) \equiv \frac{x}{y} \frac{\partial y}{\partial x}.$$

Property E1

If $y = f(w)$ and $w = g(x)$, then
$$E_x(y) = E_w(y)E_x(w).$$

Property E2

If $y = uw$, where $u = f(x)$ and $w = g(x)$, then
$$E_x(y) = E_x(u) + E_x(w).$$

Property E3

If $y = u/(u + w)$, where $u = f(x)$ and $w = g(x)$, then
$$E_u(y) = 1 - y,$$
$$E_x(y) = (1 - y)E_x(u),$$
$$E_w(y) = y - 1.$$

Property E4

If $y = u + w$, where $u = f(x)$ and $w = g(x)$, then
$$E_x(y) = \frac{u}{y}E_x(u) + \frac{w}{y} E_x(w).$$

Then define f, g, and h as follows:

$$\gamma_i = f(X_i), \qquad X_i = g(U_i), \qquad U_i = h(Y_{ik}).$$

Using property E1, we have

$$E_{Y_{ik}}(\gamma_i) = E_{X_i}(\gamma_i)E_{U_i}(X_i)E_{Y_{ik}}(U_i).$$

Then from table 4.1 we have

$$E_{X_i}(\gamma_i) = 1 - \gamma_i,$$

$$E_{U_i}(X_i) = U_i,$$

$$E_{Y_{ik}}(U_i) = \frac{\lambda_i a_{ik} Y_{ik}}{U_i}.$$

Thus

$$E_{Y_{ik}}(\gamma_i) = (1 - \gamma_i)\lambda_i a_{ik}Y_{ik}. \tag{4.27}$$

Similarly

$$E_{Y_{jk}}(\gamma_i) = -\gamma_j\lambda_j a_{jk}Y_{jk}. \tag{4.28}$$

4.5.4 Prediction Using Demand Elasticities

The elasticities of a demand function provide a convenient shorthand way of summarizing the behavior represented in a particular function.

Therefore it is often useful to compare evidence about the values of particular elasticities that have been observed in various situations— for example, elasticities of time and cost obtained in different cities or different countries. Knowledge of the approximate values of key elasticities can also be useful in making quick, approximate estimates of the consumer responses to particular changes.

In all discussions and practical applications of elasticities, however, the analyst must keep in mind that elasticity is not a constant but a variable. Indeed, as shown in table 4.1, only for product-form relationships is the elasticity constant over the range of variation of a variable. Therefore a numerical value of elasticity can only give an approximate indication of the nature of a relationship. Nevertheless it is often a useful indication.

The following paragraphs illustrate the use of elasticities for judgments about the effects of various policies.

INFERENCES FROM ELASTICITIES

Once a demand model has been obtained, examination of elasticities can lead to useful insights. In an important early study a demand model for urban passenger travel was estimated econometrically as part of a policy study of the effects of possible free (no-fare) transit (Charles River Associates 1968, Domencich, Kraft, and Vallette 1968). The model was analogous in structure to the product form of the Kraft-SARC model. Service attributes and elasticities are shown in table 4.3 for automobile and transit and for work and shopping trips. (Limitations in the data and the estimation methods resulted in (1) some elasticities being constrained to zero by prior hypothesis on signs and (2) an inability to separate out some service attributes, necessitating aggregated estimates.)

■ *Question 4.1* What inferences can be drawn from these results? Discuss. (For example, you might compare fare sensitivities for work and shopping trips, time and fare sensitivities, and sensitivities to in-vehicle and out-of-vehicle times.)

■ *Answer 4.1* There are a number of conclusions one can draw from these results. First, examine transit trips. Note that for both the time and the cost components, demand is relatively inelastic (-0.09 to -0.71). Second, fare elasticities are greater for shopping trips than for work trips. This corresponds to what our intuition tells us: people making shopping trips should be more sensitive to fare changes than people going to work. Third, time changes (on a percentage basis) would

Table 4.3 Some examples of elasticities of urban passenger travel demand

	Travel time			
	Direct elasticities		Cross-elasticities	
Auto trips	Auto IV time	Auto OV time	Transit IV time	Transit OV time
Work	−0.820	−1.437	0	0.373
Shopping	−1.020	−1.440	0.095	0
Transit trips	Transit IV time	Transit OV time	Auto IV time	Auto OV time
Work	−0.390	−0.709	0	0
Shopping	−0.533[a]		0	0

	Travel cost			
	Direct elasticities		Cross-elasticities	
Auto trips	Auto LH cost	Auto OP cost	Transit LH cost	Transit AC cost
Work	−0.494	−0.071	0.138	0
Shopping	−0.878	−1.650	0	0
Transit trips	Transit LH cost	Transit AC cost	Auto LH cost	Auto OP cost
Work	−0.090	−0.100	0	0
Shopping	−0.323[a]		0	0

IV=in-vehicle. OV=out-of-vehicle. LH=line-haul. OP=out-of-pocket. AC=access.
[a]The available shopping transit trip sample was unsuitable for estimating elasticities for the disaggregated time components.

appear to have two to seven times the effect a fare change would have: for shopping trips $E_t(V) = -0.533$ while $E_c(V) = -0.323$. Finally, and perhaps most importantly, changes in out-of-vehicle time (t_{ov}, waiting and walking times at the collection and distribution ends of transit trips) appear to have a much more significant effect on demand than changes in in-vehicle time (t_{iv}): $E_{t_{ov}} = -0.71$ versus $E_{t_{iv}} = -0.39$. Although the cross-elasticities for all terms are extremely low or negligible, the results indicate that there is more likelihood of shifting transit demand to automobile than there is of shifting automobile users to transit (on a percentage basis). For example, a 1 percent increase in transit line-haul cost will cause a 0.138 percent increase in automobile usage by people going to work, the increase coming from shifted transit users, whereas a 1 percent increase in automobile costs causes almost no shift to transit. This result is somewhat to be expected: automobile users have sunk capital costs into their vehicles, but transit users have no sunk costs, as individuals, in the transit system.

PIVOT-POINT METHODS

The preceding discussion has illustrated the policy implications that can be drawn from a simple examination of elasticities. It is also possible to use numerical values of elasticities for incremental prediction by means of "pivot-point" methods.

The basic concept of pivot-point methods derives directly from the definition of elasticity,

$$E_X(V) = \frac{X}{V}\frac{\partial V}{\partial X} \approx \frac{X}{V}\frac{\Delta V}{\Delta X}. \qquad (4.29)$$

Given an initial condition (X^0, V^0) and a change ΔX, the corresponding change in V can be estimated as follows:

$$\Delta V \approx V^0 \frac{\Delta X}{X^0} E_X(V). \qquad (4.30)$$

For example, given an estimate of the transit fare elasticity $E_c(V)$, a simple model for predicting the effect on demand of a fare change would be

$$\Delta V = V \frac{\Delta c}{c} E_c(V). \qquad (4.31)$$

This is applied in the following example.

It should be emphasized that while it is a useful, approximate method, pivot-point analysis assumes a constant elasticity. Further, since it uses the point elasticity, the error increases rapidly with the magnitude of the change.

■ *Question 4.2*
1. If $E_c(V) = -0.3$, the existing fare is 30 cents, and the present volume is 2,000, what change in transit demand will be expected following a fare increase of 10 cents?
2. How sensitive would this result be to alternative elasticity values of -0.2 and -0.4?
■ *Answer 4.2*
1. $\Delta V \approx (2,000)\left(\frac{10}{30}\right)(-0.3) \approx -200.$
2. For $E_c(V) = -0.2$, $\Delta V \approx -133.$
For $E_c(V) = -0.4$, $\Delta V \approx -267.$

LIMITATIONS ON THE USE OF ELASTICITIES

One must be cautious about the use of elasticities. Michael Kemp has stated the difficulty nicely:

An elasticity value is merely an abstraction of a very limited amount of information from one portion of the demand surface (two points on the surface, or at best, a uni-directional point gradient) under a particular set of conditions. What it conveys about the nature and structure of demand is minimal. More importantly, a price [or any other] elasticity measured under one particular set of circumstances need not necessarily have any relevance under a different set of circumstances.

However, as long as one is prepared to talk in very approximate terms, one often finds sufficient pattern or "constancy" in empirically determined values of elasticity to be able at least to distinguish between high and low elasticity commodities. (Kemp 1973, pp. 27–28)

4.5.5 Treatment of Market Segments

In general each market segment (group of prospective users) will have different preferences. For example, the relative weights prospective travelers place on travel time and on fare (or other out-of-pocket costs) will be different for different trip purposes, for groups with different income levels, and at different times of the day or year. Thus the demand function for work trips by high-income travelers will differ from that for shopping and recreational trips, or from that for work trips by low-income travelers.

These differences can be expressed in the demand functions in a variety of ways. Essentially the differences are reflected in the values of activity-system variables, especially those that reflect the relative weights placed on different travel attributes, and of other variables that characterize the consumers. The major means of incorporating these activity-system variables in the demand functions are stratification, explicit inclusion, and a composite of these two methods.

In stratification a separate demand function is established for each market segment, with different parameters for each. For example,

$$V_{em} = a_e c_m + b_e t_m, \tag{4.32}$$

where

V_{em} = volume of market segment e choosing alternative m,
$\mathbf{S}_m = (c_m, t_m)$ = service attributes of m,
$\mathbf{A}_e = (a_e, b_e)$ = parameters reflecting those activity-system characteristics that describe the travel behavior of segment e.

Some activity-system variables, such as income, can be included in the demand function explicitly. For example,

$$V_{em} = gl_e + ac_m + bt_m,$$ (4.33)

where l_e is the median income of market segment e. Thus for work trips originating in different zones the number of trips will vary with the income of the zone, even if (c_m, t_m) is the same from zone to zone.

Finally, the above two approaches can be combined. For example,

$$V_{em} = g_e l_e + a_e c_m + b_e t_m.$$ (4.34)

4.5.6 Composite Variables

Many demand functions include a number of variables. To better understand the behavior represented in a particular function, it is often useful to group these according to their roles and to form composite variables. Three major groups of variables are often distinguished:

1. transportation service attributes, which can often be incorporated into a composite service variable;

2. consumer attributes, the activity-system variables that describe the characteristics and preferences of the customers included in a market segment; and

3. destination attributes, the activity-system variables that describe the characteristics of alternative destinations.

COMPOSITE SERVICE LEVEL

Our discussion of the decision process of the individual consumer was based on the concept of indifference curves among the various transportation service attributes. Each indifference curve indicates those combinations of values of the service attributes for which the consumer has the same utility. In chapter 2 we discussed how the equation of the indifference curve could be used to derive trade-offs among attributes such as the value of time.

There is a direct analogy to the indifference curve at the level of the aggregate demand function representing the behavior of a group of individuals. For example, consider the following demand functions for modes 1 and 2 (similar to the McLynn model, section 4.3):

$$V_1 = A \frac{t_1^\beta c_1^\gamma}{t_1^\beta c_1^\gamma + t_2^\beta c_2^\gamma},$$ (4.35)

$$V_2 = A \frac{t_2^\beta c_2^\gamma}{t_1^\beta c_1^\gamma + t_2^\beta c_2^\gamma}.$$ (4.36)

If we define

$$L_i \equiv t_i^\beta c_i^\gamma,$$ (4.37)

we can rewrite (4.35) and (4.36) as

$$V_1 = A \frac{L_1}{L_1 + L_2}, \tag{4.38}$$

$$V_2 = A \frac{L_2}{L_1 + L_2}. \tag{4.39}$$

The total volume V_T is given by

$$V_T = V_1 + V_2 = A, \tag{4.40}$$

so that

$$\frac{V_1}{V_1 + V_2} = \frac{L_1}{L_1 + L_2} = \frac{1}{1 + (L_2/L_1)}, \tag{4.41}$$

$$\frac{V_2}{V_1 + V_2} = \frac{L_2}{L_1 + L_2} = \frac{1}{1 + (L_1/L_2)}. \tag{4.42}$$

Thus L expresses the composite effect of all the service attributes on demand. Figure 4.2a shows the shares of model 1 and 2 directly as a function of L_2/L_1. Figure 4.2b shows the various combinations of t_i and c_i that will yield the same value of L_i. (Note that L_i increases with decreasing values of c_i and/or t_i, since β and γ are usually negative.)

Part a shows that if we want to introduce an increase in fare for mode i and still keep V_i constant, we must keep the same level of L_i. Part b shows that to keep L_i constant, we must vary t_i as we vary c_i.

We call this variable L, which expresses the composite effect on demand of all of the service attributes, the **composite service level**. Note that L is positively valued: as it increases, the volume increases, reflecting the view that "service" is positively valued. This is shown in part a of the figure, where V_1 is an increasing function of L_1 (relative to L_2).

Since most service attributes are negatively valued by consumers (time, cost), L is often a negative or inverse function of these variables. Therefore, it is often convenient to use the negative of L, defined as the **composite negative worth of service**, W. In the technical literature such terms are used as "impedance," "friction factor," "generalized cost," and "generalized price." These all have roughly the same form as W_i; that is, they are composite service variables that are negatively valued by consumers. In most usages, however, these terms are defined independent of an explicit demand function. The definition used here explicitly recognizes that the composite service level is not arbitrary but is specific to a demand function.

In particular, the definition of L may be different for different market

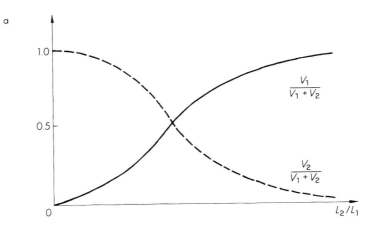

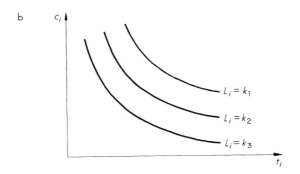

Figure 4.2 Composite service level. a: Shares of modes 1 and 2 as a function of L_2/L_1. b: Graphs of L_i = constant for three constants.

segments. For example, if the population of consumers is stratified into market segments by income and household size, then the parameters β and γ in (4.37) will take different values for different market segments (since, as pointed out in section 2.3.2, the ratio of β to γ represents the value of time relative to cost, and this will vary with income). Therefore the value of the composite service level will be different for each market segment.

COMPOSITE ACTIVITY VARIABLES

It is sometimes convenient to collect the effects of some or all the activity-system variables in a demand function into one or two composite variables. These composite activity variables summarize the effect of the activity system on travel demand in much the same way as the composite service level L summarizes the effects of the transportation service attributes on demand.

Activity-system variables in an aggregate demand function tend to fall into two major groups:

1. destination attributes, which characterize the activities at possible destinations; and

2. consumer attributes, which characterize the specific market segment in terms of its characteristics at the zone of origin and its preferences.

Since part of the consumer preference information is reflected in the parameters of service attributes, clearly not all activity-system characteristics can be brought into the composite activity variables. We therefore define two composite activity variables: The **composite destination-specific activity variable** Z replaces all the activity-system variables characterizing a particular destination. The **composite origin-specific activity variable** Y replaces all the activity-system variables characterizing the consumers at a particular origin. For example, consider the following demand function:

$$V_{kdm} = \alpha_1 P_k^{\alpha_2} I_k^{\alpha_3} E_d^{\alpha_4} L_{kdm}, \tag{4.43}$$

where P, I, and E represent population, income, and employment level, respectively, L is the composite service level, k and d are the origin and destination of transportation, m is the mode, and the α_i are parameters. For this specific demand function we can define

$$Y_k = \alpha_1 P_k^{\alpha_2} I_k^{\alpha_3}, \tag{4.44}$$

$$Z_d = E_d^{\alpha_4}, \tag{4.45}$$

and the demand function can be written

$$V_{kdm} = Y_k Z_d L_{kdm}. \tag{4.46}$$

It is often useful, in comparing demand functions, to construct such composite variables and write the demand functions in terms of them. This helps in isolating similarities and differences among the various models (see exercise 4.1). Composite variables are also useful for analysis of elasticities using the elasticity properties in table 4.2.

■ *Question 4.3*   Consider the demand function

$$V_{12} = P_1^{\alpha_1} P_2^{\alpha_2} t^{\alpha_3} q^{\alpha_4} c^{\alpha_5},$$

where

P_1 = population at zone 1,

P_2 = population at zone 2,

t = travel time between 1 and 2 (hours),

q = frequency of service between 1 and 2 (per day),

c = fare between 1 and 2 (dollars),

$(P_1^{\alpha_1} P_2^{\alpha_2}) = 10{,}000$,

$\alpha_3 = -2$,

$\alpha_4 = +0.8$,

$\alpha_5 = -1$.

The present level of volume is 1,088 trips per day. A fare increase of 20 percent is being contemplated. If the transportation operator wants to keep the same travel volume, what changes in service could he consider ?

■ *Answer 4.3* Examining the demand function, we observe that the composite service level is

$$L_{12} = t^{\alpha_3} q^{\alpha_4} c^{\alpha_5}.$$

As long as L_{12} remains constant, the volume V_{12} will remain constant. Since $E_c(L) = \alpha_5$, $E_t(L) = \alpha_3$, and $E_q(L) = \alpha_4$, if we increase c by 20 percent, this will result in an (approximate) increase in L of 0.20 α_5, or 20 percent. To counter this, we can make changes in frequency of service, in time, or in both. If we choose to increase q, the required percentage change is $0.20\alpha_5/\alpha_4$, or $+25$ percent. This can be derived as follows:

i. $\Delta L_1 \approx E_c(L) \dfrac{L}{c} \Delta c = \alpha_5 \dfrac{L}{c} \Delta c$,

ii. $\Delta L_2 \approx E_q(L) \dfrac{L}{q} \Delta q = \alpha_4 \dfrac{L}{q} \Delta q$,

iii. $\Delta L_1 = \Delta L_2$,

iv. $\Delta q \approx \dfrac{\alpha_5}{\alpha_4} \dfrac{q}{c} \Delta c$,

v. $\dfrac{\Delta q}{q} \approx \dfrac{\alpha_5}{\alpha_4} \dfrac{\Delta c}{c}$.

This is an approximate relationship. For a more precise answer, it would be necessary to integrate along the demand curve or to use the demand function explicitly.

4.5.7 Choice-Specific and Choice-Independent Attributes (Optional Reading)

A DISAGGREGATE VIEW
Consider the following utility functions for two modes, rail (R) and air (A):

$$U_R = \alpha_R t_R + \beta_R c_R, \tag{4.47}$$

$$U_A = \alpha_A t_A + \beta_A c_A. \tag{4.48}$$

The attributes are time t and cost c.

Two cases of parameter values can be identified:

Case I: $\quad \alpha_R = \alpha_A = \alpha, \qquad \beta_R = \beta_A = \beta,$

Case II: $\quad \alpha_R \neq \alpha_A, \qquad \beta_R \neq \beta_A.$

In the first case the two utility functions become identical and independent of the modes:

$$U_m = \alpha t_m + \beta c_m. \tag{4.49}$$

Thus the attributes t and c are not defined specific to the modes, but are common to both modes; the attributes are **choice-independent**. Each mode is characterized by the same attributes and the same utility function, although of course the *levels* of the attributes and of the utilities will usually be different.

In case II the attributes have a different effect on each mode; because $\alpha_R \neq \alpha_A$, a minute of time by rail is, apparently, not worth the same as a minute of time by air.

A common assumption is the **hypothesis of choice-independent utilities**, which states that the utility function U_m over the attributes of a set of choices is independent of the specific choices being compared. When we apply this hypothesis, we are assuming that we can include all the aspects of each choice that may be influencing a consumer's decision in a utility function whose parameters are independent of the choices.

This hypothesis may be invalid in a particular situation for any of several reasons:

1. We have ignored attributes that the consumer considers important.
2. We are not measuring the attributes in the same way he measures them.
3. Our knowledge of the weights he places on the attributes is imperfect.

To accurately predict the consumer's behavior in such a situation, we must incorporate in his utility function one or more elements that are specific to a particular choice and that reflect those attributes of the choice that have been omitted or measured imperfectly or for which information about weights is imperfect. These are called **choice-specific attributes**.

In transportation, particularly at the present state of knowledge, the hypothesis of choice-independent utilities is often not completely realistic. For example, in passenger transportation it is difficult to represent adequately such attributes as privacy or flexibility of route and time of trip, which are important aspects of automobile travel. This hypothesis is therefore particularly critical in attempting to predict which mode the traveler will choose. Because of the significance of the mode-choice problem, a name often given to this hypothesis is the **abstract-mode assumption**: it deals with the question of whether we can characterize each mode by the same attributes—without, in a sense, knowing its name—or whether we must know which mode we are dealing with in order to predict the utility perceived by the consumer.

In the general situation where we must allow for choice-dependent utilities, we might have utility functions that look like

$$U_m = \beta_m + \sum_i \alpha_{mi} X_{mi} \tag{4.50}$$

or

$$U_m = \beta_m \prod_i X_{mi}^{\alpha_{mi}}. \tag{4.51}$$

In these forms the unique characteristics of each alternative are expressed through several means. The weights β_m are given to the modes independent of their explicit attributes. For example, in the linear form β_m may give greater attractiveness to the automobile than to other modes because of its schedule and route flexibility. The weights α_{mi} on attributes X_i depend on the specific alternative. For example, a minute of travel time in an automobile may be more attractive than a minute in a bus if the driver enjoys listening to his own radio or stereo tapes in the car, or it may be less attractive if he enjoys being free to read the newspaper and is annoyed by driving through traffic; and a minute of time waiting in an airport lounge may be weighted differently from a minute of time in an intercity bus terminal.

In the demand model used in chapter 3 the hypothesis of choice-independent utilities was partially met:

$$U_T = \theta_T + \theta_1 t_T + \theta_2 \frac{x_T}{d} + \theta_3 \frac{c_T}{y}, \tag{4.52}$$

$$U_A = \theta_A + \theta_1 t_A + \theta_2 \frac{x_A}{d} + \theta_3 \frac{c_A}{y}. \tag{4.53}$$

Here the coefficients of in-vehicle and out-of-vehicle times and of cost are the same for both automobile and transit. Thus these attributes in the model are choice-independent. However, there is a need to reflect important remaining differences between automobile and transit, resulting in the choice-specific constants, θ_T and θ_A. Thus the utilities are partially choice-independent.

In our development of models for predicting consumer behavior in transportation we shall always strive toward the objective of sufficient understanding of the consumer so that we can utilize the hypothesis of choice-independent utilities. Then we shall be able to predict the response of the consumer to any choice that may be offered him. We shall often fall short of this objective, however, and be forced to employ utility models that are at least partially choice-dependent and that include some attributes that are choice-specific. For example, the automobile as a mode and the central business district as a destination will often enter passenger demand models with choice-specific attributes.

AN AGGREGATE VIEW

If the hypothesis of choice-independent utilities applies at the level of the individual consumer, for all consumers in a group, then the aggregate demand function for the group as a whole will exhibit similar independence of the specific choices.

Operationally this means that the parameters of the demand function are independent of the alternative choices. For example, consider an aggregate analog to (4.47):

$$V_R = \gamma t_R^{\alpha_R} c_R^{\beta_R} \tag{4.54}$$

$$V_A = \gamma t_A^{\alpha_A} c_A^{\beta_A}. \tag{4.55}$$

Again, if $\alpha_R = \alpha_A = \alpha$ and $\beta_R = \beta_A = \beta$, the general model is

$$V_m = \gamma t_m^{\alpha} c_m^{\beta} \tag{4.56}$$

and the attributes are choice-independent; we can also say that the model itself is *choice-abstract*.

There are several significant advantages when the condition of choice independence applies. First, far fewer parameters must be estimated to get the demand function for a particular situation, and so available data can be used more effectively. Second, the analyst can feel more confident in using the demand model to predict consumer response to conditions basically different from those observed so far (for example, when a completely new mode of transport is to be introduced), because it is sufficient to characterize that mode only by its attributes. (If each mode needed different parameters α_{mi}, then the analyst would have to guess their values for the new mode. Is it most like existing mode 1, 2, or 3?)

Analysts have historically striven to develop transportation demand models that are choice-abstract. Their efforts began with simple "diversion curves," in which the volume of traffic in a corridor was assumed to divide between a freeway and parallel arterial streets according to some ratio of the travel times (Martin, Memmott, and Bone 1961, FHWA 1973b). Later the term "abstract mode" was used to designate a group of specific intercity passenger demand models that also reflected this hypothesis of choice-independent utilities (for example, the Baumol-Quandt model in section 4.3). The concepts as defined here apply to all types of travel choices, as will be discussed in chapter 11.

4.6 SIMPLE PREDICTION METHODS

In general the prediction of flows requires explicit consideration of both service and demand models, as indicated in chapter 1. Often, however, it is possible to make useful predictions using only demand functions (for example, when service levels are assumed known—see chapter 8).

When there is available both a complete aggregate demand function, including all the parameter values, and also the necessary data, then the prediction of flows is straightforward. On the other hand, the analyst is often confronted with situations in which there is limited information available and estimates are needed quickly. Particularly common are situations in which there is inadequate time or resources to calibrate a model for a particular situation. In such cases approximate prediction methods using knowledge gained elsewhere can be quite useful. There are several methods available.

4.6.1 The Use of Limited Information: Incremental Analysis

Often the only data an analyst will find available will be present volumes V^0 and service levels S^0. No other demand-related information can be collected. How can the analyst make best use of these data?

One approach is to adapt information developed elsewhere, such as values of demand parameters or elasticities, perhaps modified by judgment. In this section we shall show how such information can be utilized.

There are several possible approaches for utilizing limited information in this context with an incremental-analysis approach based on the observed flows (V^0, S^0): pivot-point analysis using elasticities or model structure assumptions, or "judgmental-model" analysis.

The concept behind pivot-point analysis was described in section 4.5.4. For a single mode and a single service attribute, the change in volume ΔV is estimated as a function of the change in service level and the elasticity $E_S(V)$ (Pecknold, Wilson, and Kullman 1972):

$$\Delta V \approx V^0 \frac{\Delta S}{S^0} E_S(V). \tag{4.57}$$

No judgment about the form of the demand function is required. (Note that this approach is equivalent to assuming a product-form model, in that elasticity is assumed constant, and also a linear-form model, in that the change in V is assumed to be proportional to the change in S. These assumptions, while acceptable for small changes, are inconsistent and not acceptable for large changes.)

To apply the pivot-point approach with elasticities, only the numerical value of the elasticity $E_S(V)$ is required, as indicated by equation (4.57), provided the change ΔS is in only one attribute. If several attributes change simultaneously, a more complex approach is required. In this case it is necessary to assume a functional form of the demand function or at least of the composite service level L, so that a more precise expression can be derived for the change in volume corresponding to the multidimensional service change.

The derivatives and elasticities of common demand function forms were given in table 4.1. The variable X used there can be a single variable or a function of several variables, such as a composite service level that is a function of several service attributes. In the latter case the total elasticity can be computed as a function of the desired variables using the various properties of elasticities given in table 4.2 (see exercise 4.1).

Some types of demand models lend themselves to a variation of pivot-point analysis in which judgments are made about the structural form of a model and about elasticities or (equivalently) the value(s) of key parameter(s). Share-type models are particularly useful in this respect. As will be shown in section 4.6.2, ΔV for a given mode is a function of the existing shares and of a parameter that can be estimated directly or derived from an estimate of a corresponding elasticity. For example, for a multinomial logit model, the new share γ_m' is a function only of the old share γ_m^0 and the change in utility, $U_m' - U_m^0$, so the only parameters required are the coefficients of those service attributes that change (for example, the coefficient of time in the utility function if only time is changed). The value of this coefficient can be estimated on the basis of empirical evidence or from an assumed elasticity.

Finally, in the judgmental-model approach a demand model is estimated by judgment so that it meets two conditions: it fits the observed flows (V^0, S^0), and it is consistent with judgments made about elasticities or other elements (such as the flows for other certain sets of conditions). Many model forms lend themselves to this approach, as shown below in the case of share models such as the multinomial logit. Specific relationships can be derived through which information on observed flows and judgments about elasticities can be used to estimate model parameters. These are described in section 4.6.3.

4.6.2 Pivot-Point Analysis with an Assumed Model Structure (Optional Reading)

To illustrate this approach we shall analyze the class of share-type models. Many demand models are (or can be) expressed as share-type models:

$$\frac{V_i}{V} = \frac{R_i}{R},\qquad (4.58)$$

where

$$V = \sum_i V_i, \qquad R = \sum_i R_i.$$

Here R_i is a function of activity-system and service variables and V_i is the volume of travelers making travel choice i. The **share** of a choice i is

$$\gamma_i \equiv \frac{V_i}{V}. \qquad (4.59)$$

For any change in service (or other) variables, for a single choice i,

$$\rho_i \equiv \frac{R_i'}{R_i^0}, \qquad (4.60)$$

where the superscript zero indicates an initial value, the prime indicates the value following a change, and

$$R_j' = R_j^0 \quad \text{for all} \quad j \neq i \qquad (4.61)$$

(that is, $\rho_j = 1$ for $j \neq i$). Then it can be shown that the new share of mode i is

$$\gamma_i' = \frac{\rho_i \gamma_i^0}{\rho_i \gamma_i^0 + (1 - \gamma_i^0)}$$

$$= \frac{1}{1 + \frac{1}{\rho_i}\left[\frac{1 - \gamma_i^0}{\gamma_i^0}\right]}. \qquad (4.62)$$

For example, for the logistic form (as in the multinomial logit model),

$$R_i = e^{U_i},$$ (4.63)

$$\gamma_i' = \cfrac{1}{1 + e^{-\Delta U_i}\left[\cfrac{1 - \gamma_i^0}{\gamma_i^0}\right]},$$ (4.64)

where

$$\Delta U_i = U_i' - U_i^0,$$

$$\rho_i = e^{\Delta U_i}.$$

Note that (4.64) is an exact relationship, not an approximate one as in the pivot-point approach using elasticities (section 4.5.4).

In the more general case where (4.61) does not hold,

$$\gamma_i' = \frac{\rho_i \gamma_i^0}{\sum_j \rho_j \gamma_j^0}$$

$$= \frac{1}{1 + (\rho_i \gamma_i^0)^{-1} \sum_{j \neq i} \rho_j \gamma_j^0}.$$ (4.65)

The corresponding form when (4.63) applies is

$$\gamma_i' = \frac{\gamma_i^0 \, e^{\Delta U_i}}{\sum_j \gamma_j^0 \, e^{\Delta U_j}}$$

$$= \frac{1}{1 + (\gamma_i^0 \, e^{\Delta U_i})^{-1} \sum_{j \neq i} \gamma_j^0 \, e^{\Delta U_i}}.$$ (4.66)

Thus for models that can be expressed in share form the changes in shares for any change in activity-system or service variables can be estimated directly from the present shares γ_i^0 and the value of ρ for the specific change. An estimate of ρ requires knowledge of, or assumptions about, the form and parameter values of the composite function R only insofar as they concern the variables changing.

As an example consider

$$R_i = e^{U_i}, \qquad U_i = \sum_k a_k Y_{ik}.$$ (4.67)

In the case of a single variable $Y_{ik'}$,

$$\rho_i = e^{\Delta U_i} = e^{a_{k'} \Delta Y_{ik'}}.$$ (4.68)

The only parameter value needed is $a_{k'}$ (along with $\Delta Y_{ik'}$ of course); this can be estimated directly or by estimating the elasticity $E_{Y_{ik'}}(\gamma_i)$

and deriving the corresponding value of $a_{k'}$ from that estimate, using the relationship for elasticity of a multinomial logit model (4.27):

$$E_{Y_{ik'}}(\gamma_i) = (1 - \gamma_i)\, a_{k'} Y_{ik'};$$ (4.69)

thus

$$a_{k'} = \frac{E_{Y_{ik'}}(\gamma_i)}{Y_{ik'}(1 - \gamma_i)}.$$ (4.70)

4.6.3 Incremental Analysis Using a Judgmentally Estimated Model (Optional Reading)

To apply the judgmental-model approach assumptions must be made about the form of the model and about numerical values of elasticities or other parameters. (Alternative sets of assumptions can and usually should be made in order to produce a sensitivity analysis.) For a specific model, and given the observed flows, certain relationships must exist among the parameters, depending on the model form. The second column of table 4.4 shows these relationships for some basic forms: given an observation (V_0, X_0) and an estimate of some parameter(s)

Table 4.4   Relations among parameters and elasticities

	Demand function	Parameter relations at an observed point (V_0, X_0)	Relation to elasticities
Linear	$V = \alpha + \beta X$	$\alpha = V_0 - \beta X_0$	$\alpha = V_0 (1 - E)$
			$\beta = \dfrac{V_0}{X_0} E$
Product	$V = \alpha X^{\beta}$	$\alpha = V_0 X_0^{-\beta}$	$\alpha = V_0 X_0^{-E}$
			$\beta = E$
Exponential	$V = \alpha e^{\beta X}$	$\alpha = V_0\, e^{-\beta X_0}$	$\alpha = V_0\, e^{-E}$
			$\beta = \dfrac{E}{X_0}$
Logistic	$V = \dfrac{\alpha}{1 + \gamma e^{\beta X}}$	$\alpha = V_0(1 + \gamma e^{\beta X_0})$	$\beta = \dfrac{-E/X_0}{1 - (V_0/\alpha)}$
			$\gamma = \dfrac{1 - (V_0/\alpha)}{V_0/\alpha}\, e^{-\beta X_0}$
Logistic-product	$V = \dfrac{\alpha}{1 + \gamma X^{\beta}}$	$\alpha = V_0 (1 + \gamma X_0^{\beta})$	$\beta = \dfrac{-E}{1 - (V_0/\alpha)}$
			$\gamma = \dfrac{\log\left[\dfrac{1 - (V_0/\alpha)}{V_0/\alpha}\right]}{\log X_0}$

$(\beta; \gamma$ where applicable), the remaining parameter α is a function of these data. Thus an observation and a judgment can be used to "fit" a model.

Alternatively judgments can be made about the elasticity, $E_X(V)$. As shown in the third column of the table, for the first three forms, with only two parameters α and β, an estimate of E together with the observation (V_0, X_0) is sufficient to "fit" a model. For the others, an estimate of one additional parameter, α, is required.

4.7 PREDICTION WITH DISAGGREGATE DEMAND FUNCTIONS

As indicated in the preceding section, prediction using aggregate demand functions is relatively straightforward when service levels are assumed known. One can use either the entire demand function or various simple methods.

Prediction with disaggregate demand functions requires a little more care. The methods for predicting the behavior of a group of consumers from disaggregate functions fall into two basic categories:

1. development of an aggregate demand function from the disaggregate function;
2. use of the disaggregate function directly.

4.7.1 Aggregating Individual Preferences into Demand Functions

In principle, an aggregate demand function for a market segment can be derived from the individual utility functions for each member of the group.

Consider a utility function of the form

$$U_{mj} = \alpha_j t_m + (\beta_j / y_j) c_m, \tag{4.71}$$

where

t_m, c_m = service attributes of alternative m,
α_j, β_j = preferences of consumer j,
y_j = yearly income of consumer j.

Assume that the N individuals in the group can be divided into subgroups j, of size n_j, such that all the individuals in a subgroup have the same preferences and income (α_j, β_j, y_j). For a given service level **S**, we can then determine which alternative m the individuals in a given subgroup j will pick: define $r_{mj} = 1$ if subgroup j picks alternative m, and $r_{mj} = 0$ otherwise. Summing over all the subgroups, we can get the aggregate demand for alternative m:

$$V_m = \sum_j r_{mj} n_j. \qquad (4.72)$$

This aggregate demand depends, of course, on the level of service: as **S** changes, so also will the r_{mj} and the V_m. If we explicitly explore a large number of such changes, we can observe how V_m changes as **S** changes. (This was demonstrated in section 2.4.)

Thus, in principle, we can develop the aggregate demand function for the group as a whole by knowing (1) the individual utility functions, (2) the distribution of individuals in the group by subgroups (that is, their characteristics and preferences), and (3) the characteristics of the choices they face.

In practice, it is difficult to derive an aggregate demand function explicitly with either deterministic or stochastic disaggregate functions. The primary source of difficulty is the need to integrate the disaggregate function over the distribution of individual characteristics. If $p(\alpha_j, \beta, y_j)$ is the distribution of individual characteristics, and if r_{mj} is replaced by $D_f(\mathbf{S}, \alpha_j, \beta_j, y_j)$, where D_f is the disaggregate demand function, then (4.72) becomes

$$V_m(\mathbf{S}) = \sum_j n_j \iiint p(\alpha_j, \beta_j, y_j)\, D_f(\mathbf{S}, \alpha_j, \beta_j, y_j) d(\alpha, \beta, y). \qquad (4.73)$$

This integration is impractical except under very special conditions that are of limited practical importance, such as a demand function linear in all variables or probability distributions that degenerate into single values (see Koppelman 1975, 1976b; also Koppelman and Ben-Akiva 1977, Blackburn 1970). However, it indicates the nature of the problem of using disaggregate demand functions: it is necessary to incorporate in some way the distribution of characteristics represented by $p(\alpha, \beta, y)$.

These relationships are illustrated in figure 4.3. Here an **aggregation procedure** is a procedure that uses a disaggregate demand model together with information on the distribution of activity-system and service-level characteristics to produce a prediction of aggregate behavior.

4.7.2 Practical Approaches

While deriving an aggregated demand *function* explicitly is generally impractical, there are many practical aggregation procedures that can be used to predict aggregate *behavior* with a disaggregate demand function (Koppelman 1975, 1976b). In relation to figure 4.3 these aggregation procedures are essentially alternate ways of representing

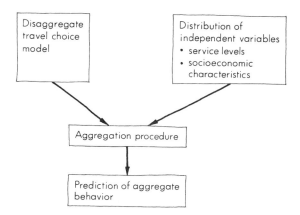

```
┌─────────────────┐          ┌──────────────────────┐
│ Disaggregate    │          │ Distribution of      │
│ travel choice   │          │ independent variables│
│ model           │          │  • service levels    │
│                 │          │  • socioeconomic     │
│                 │          │    characteristics   │
└─────────────────┘          └──────────────────────┘
          ↘                    ↙
          ┌────────────────────────┐
          │ Aggregation procedure  │
          └────────────────────────┘
                    │
                    ↓
          ┌────────────────────────┐
          │ Prediction of aggregate│
          │ behavior               │
          └────────────────────────┘
```

Figure 4.3 Predicting aggregate behavior with a disaggregate model. Adapted from Koppelman (1975).

the distribution of independent variables and operating on them with the disaggregate demand function. In this section we discuss some currently used approaches.

THE NAIVE APPROACH

Each market segment is characterized by its average characteristics (for example, $\bar{\alpha}$, $\bar{\beta}$, $\bar{\gamma}$, and $\bar{S}$), and the disaggregate function D_f is used with these average values:

$$V_m(\mathbf{S}) = ND_f(\bar{\mathbf{S}}, \bar{\alpha}, \bar{\beta}, \bar{\gamma}), \tag{4.74}$$

where

$\bar{\alpha} = \sum_j \alpha_j n_j / N$, and so forth.

CLASSIFICATION

Each market segment is divided into subgroups of size n_j; for each subgroup j mean values of the characteristics ($\bar{\alpha}_j$, $\bar{\beta}_j$, $\bar{\gamma}_j$, and $\bar{S}_j$) are used together with the disaggregate function to predict a response; then the response of the market segment as a whole is obtained as

$$V_m(\mathbf{S}) = \sum_j n_j D_f(\bar{\mathbf{S}}_j, \bar{\alpha}_j, \bar{\beta}_j, \bar{\gamma}_j). \tag{4.75}$$

This approach is particularly useful when the variables that have the greatest influence on an individual's choices are used as a basis of classification. For example, in an urban mode-choice model, if no automobile is available, then the choice "drive alone" is not available. Separating each market segment into those with access to an automo-

149   Aggregate Prediction of Behavior

bile and those without is thus a useful classification. Historically the latter group, called "transit-captive," has been separated out in aggregate modeling. Similarly, whether the individual has his origin (or destination) within walking distance of a transit line-haul or feeder service determines whether transit is a realistically available choice; households can thus be classified as to whether they are "auto-captive" or not. In the first case classification is by automobile ownership level (0; 1 or more); in the second, by transit service level (whether or not the traveler lives beyond a maximum walk distance to transit; see figure 3.8). Income is often also an important variable in classification.

DISTRIBUTIONS
For each market segment the distribution of characteristics $(\alpha, \beta, y, \mathbf{S})$ is represented in one of several ways: by explicit probability density functions characterized by their parameters or their moments, or by an explicit frequency distribution.

SAMPLING
For each market segment a population of M individuals is constructed, either from the original data base used in developing the demand function or from other data sources. Then a sample of k individuals is drawn from this population. To predict an individual's behavior, that person's socioeconomic characteristics (α_i, β_i, y_i) together with the appropriate service levels $(\mathbf{S}_i)$ are used in the disaggregate demand function D_f. The predicted behaviors of the sample of k individuals are then tabulated as in (4.72), and this estimate is expanded (by the ratio M/k) to obtain the predicted behavior of the market segment as a whole. The general methodology is shown in figure 4.4.

A particularly interesting example of the sampling approach appeared in a recent study of the energy consequences of alternative freight transportation policies (Roberts et al. 1976).

These are only a few of the major approaches available. Various combinations of these and other approaches are also useful; for example, sampling or distributions can be combined with classification. Alternatively the sample can be synthesized from aggregate data (Watanatada 1977, Manheim, Furth, and Salomon 1977).

4.7.3 Prediction with Disaggregate Models: An Example
In this section we shall expand the urban transportation example introduced in chapter 3 to demonstrate prediction with a disaggregate

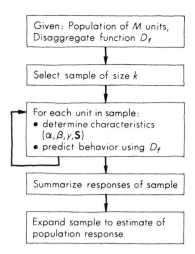

```
┌─────────────────────────────┐
│ Given: Population of M units, │
│ Disaggregate function D_f     │
└─────────────────────────────┘
              │
              ▼
┌─────────────────────────────┐
│ Select sample of size k       │
└─────────────────────────────┘
              │
              ▼
┌─────────────────────────────┐
│ For each unit in sample:      │
│ • determine characteristics   │
│   (α,β,γ,S)                   │
│ • predict behavior using D_f  │
└─────────────────────────────┘
              │
              ▼
┌─────────────────────────────┐
│ Summarize responses of sample │
└─────────────────────────────┘
              │
              ▼
┌─────────────────────────────┐
│ Expand sample to estimate of  │
│ population response           │
└─────────────────────────────┘
```

Figure 4.4 Sampling approach to prediction.

function. This example will also help explain why a disaggregate approach is often more effective than an aggregate one.

THE POPULATION

We consider the corridor shown in figure 3.4. Zones 1 and 2 are residential zones; zones 3 and 4 are locations of workplaces. Thus there are four origin-destination zone pairs: 1–3, 1–4, 2–3, and 2–4.

The households in this corridor have different levels of income and of automobile ownership. The mode-choice model to be used was shown in table 3.3. The model includes income and number of automobiles owned explicitly as variables. Thus choice behavior, as shown by the choice probabilities, varies with socioeconomic characteristics as well as with the service attributes of the available choices.

We shall use the method of classification and shall classify households in the corridor by level of automobile ownership and income, dividing each variable into classes. Further, based on the analyses of chapter 3, we know that it is important to distinguish the different types of trip profiles available, specifically the "access" choices. Thus we consider the following combinations:

I. Origin-destination pairs
- two origins: zones 1 and 2
- two destinations: zones 3 and 4
- total: four origin-destination zone pairs

Table 4.5 Distribution of 1,000 households with origin in zone 1 and destination in zone 4

	Automobiles per licensed driver (a_{LD})											
	0			0.5			1.0			Total		
Income	LH	F–LH	Total	LH	F–LH	Total	LH	F–LH	Total	LH	F–LH	Total
$5,000	0	0	0	150	200	350	0	0	0	150	200	350
				15%	20%	35%				15%	20%	35%
$10,000	0	0	0	100	0	100	0	50	50	100	50	150
				10%		10%		5%	5%	10%	5%	15%
$15,000	0	0	0	0	0	0	350	150	500	350	150	500
							35%	15%	50%	35%	15%	50%
Total	0	0	0	250	200	450	350	200	550	600	400	1,000
				25%	20%	45%	35%	20%	55%	60%	40%	100%

II. Market segments
• three levels of income
• three levels of automobile ownership
• total: nine segments, defined by combinations of income and automobile ownership
III. Level of access choices
• two cases within each origin zone:
Case 1: within walking distance of line-haul transit station
Case 2: within walking distance of feeder transit station but beyond walking distance of line-haul transit
• total: two combinations:[3]
Combination 1: within walking distance at home and workplace zones (line-haul only, LH)
Combination 2: within walking distance at workplace zone but not at home zone (feeder to line-haul, F–LH)

The resulting distribution of households, by classification, for one origin-destination pair and three trip profiles is shown in table 4.5. The levels of service that confront trips from zone 1 to zone 4 are those used in chapter 3 (summarized in table 4.6); the others can be estimated in the same way as in that chapter.

[3]Two access cases could be defined at the destination also, adding two more combinations: within walking distance at home zone but not at workplace zone (line-haul to feeder, LH–F); and not within walking distance of line-haul system at either zone (feeder at both ends, F–LH–F). In addition, "beyond walking distance" could also occur, for which the only modes available are auto-based.

Table 4.6 Levels of service encountered by two classes of travelers

	t_A (min)	x_A (min)	c_A (¢)	t_T (min)	x_T (min)	c_T (¢)	d (miles)
LH	11.3	5	122.5	14	8	50	7.25
F–LH	14.2	5	131.3	21.7	15.5	75	8.13

Groups of individuals differing by origin and destination zones, and by location within those zones (as reflected in the different access conditions and available trip profiles), face different levels of service. Thus two groups with the same socioeconomic attributes may make different choices.

PREDICTION USING CLASSIFICATION

Table 4.7 shows the automobile and transit choice probabilities for various market segments and trip profiles with origin in zone 1 and destination in zone 4. This table, developed using the methods described in chapter 3, shows that mode-choice probabilities vary quite significantly within an origin-destination zone combination.

Using the numbers of individuals falling into each combination of conditions from table 4.5, average (weighted) mode-choice probabilities can be derived:

$$\bar{p}_T = \sum_{i,j,k} p_T(i,j,k) \frac{n_{ijk}}{N}, \tag{4.76}$$

where i indicates income class, j automobile ownership class, k access class, n_{ijk} the number of households in class (i, j, k), $p_T(i,j,k)$ the probability of choosing transit for a household in class (i, j, k), and

N = total number of households = $\sum_{i,j,k} n_{ijk}$.

Table 4.7 Mode-choice probabilities for travelers with origin in zone 1 and destination in zone 4

	Automobiles per licensed driver (a_{LD})					
	0		0.5		1.0	
Income	LH	F–LH	LH	F–LH	LH	F–LH
$5,000	0.89	0.81	0.65	0.51	0.31	0.20
$10,000	0.78	0.67	0.46	0.33	0.17	0.11
$15,000	0.66	0.55	0.32	0.22	0.10	0.07

For origin in zone 1 and destination in zone 4,

$$\bar{p}_T = (0.15)(0.65) + (0.10)(0.46) + (0.20)(0.51) + (0.35)(0.10)$$
$$+ (0.05)(0.11) + (0.15)(0.07)$$
$$= 0.297.$$

PREDICTION USING THE NAIVE METHOD

The mode choices can also be predicted using the naive method. The first step is to determine the mean values of each of the independent variables. If we define

$$n_i \equiv \sum_{j,k} n_{ijk},$$

with n_j and n_k defined similarly, then the weighted averages of the independent variables are

$$\bar{y} = \sum_i \frac{n_i}{N} y_i = \frac{1}{1,000} [(350)(5,000) + (150)(10,000) + (500)(15,000)]$$
$$= 10,750,$$

$$\bar{a}_{LD} = \sum_j \frac{n_j}{N} a_j = \frac{1}{1,000} [(0)(0) + (450)(0.5) + (550)(1.0)] = 0.775,$$

and, for each dimension s_l of $\mathbf{S}$,

$$\bar{s}_l = \sum_k \frac{n_k}{N} \bar{s}_{lk},$$

so that the average service attributes are

$$\bar{t}_A = (0.6)(11.3) + (0.4)(14.2) = 12.46,$$
$$\bar{x}_A = (0.6)(5) + (0.4)(5) = 5,$$
$$\bar{c}_A = (0.6)(122.5) + (0.4)(131.3) = 126,$$
$$\bar{t}_T = (0.6)(14) + (0.4)(21.7) = 17.08,$$
$$\bar{x}_T = (0.6)(8) + (0.4)(15.5) = 11.0,$$
$$\bar{c}_T = (0.6)(50) + (0.4)(75) = 60,$$
$$\bar{d} = (0.6)(7.25) + (0.4)(8.13) = 7.60.$$

With these average values, the mode-choice probability can be determined as $p_T = 0.22$. Comparison with the preceding result demonstrates the differences introduced by using average characteristics rather than detailed distributions.

DISCUSSION

Demand models have traditionally been developed at an aggregate level, with geographically defined zones used as a primary basis for aggregation. For example, trip-generation models in UTMS (see chapter

11) were developed by regression of total trips on zone averages of income, automobile ownership, and so on. We have seen that such zonal averages can be quite misleading. In general, there is more variation in behavior *within* zones than between zones (Fleet and Robertson 1968, McFadden and Reid 1975). Thus if one wants to aggregate, one might prefer to aggregate *across* zones, keeping access conditions and/or market segment characteristics as bases for defining classes, rather than averaging out these important variables.

Similar behavior is observed in most situations. Thus it is usually better to begin with disaggregate models and then develop bases for aggregation appropriate to the issues to be studied (Koppelman 1975, Landau 1976, Watanatada 1977).

4.7.4 Approximate Methods with Disaggregate Functions

All of the methods for simple predictions with aggregate functions identified in section 4.6 can be used with disaggregate functions also. The major difference is that the disaggregate function gives a probability, which must then be multiplied by a market-segment size to give a volume.

As an example, consider the relationship given in section 3.5 for incremental analysis with a multinomial logit model. Similarly, the elasticities of an MNL model can be computed from the relationships in table 4.1; note, however, that this is the elasticity of a probability, that is, the percent change in the probability of choosing a mode for a 1 percent change in some attribute.

4.8 LOOKING AHEAD

This chapter completes a basic introduction to transportation demand. There are many important topics we have not discussed; some of these will be treated later in this volume, while others will not be discussed here at all.

The complexity of consumer decisions in transportation will be examined in chapter 11, where we shall consider the dimensions of consumer choice and how alternative ways of structuring these dimensions lead to different types of demand models.

Developing good demand models for a specific situation is always a difficult task. To be effective, the analyst must understand not only the aspects of consumer behavior and the transportation issues that are most important in a particular situation, but also the statistical methods available for estimating model parameters and their limitations. This subject demands a specialized course in itself; in chapter 16, however, we shall introduce a few basic ideas on general model development strategy.

We have chosen to teach demand from the perspective of disaggregate models estimated by econometric methods. These models represent the third generation of transportation demand modeling. The first generation was that of the Urban Transportation Model System and related intercity models formulated on the basis of physical analogies (such as gravitation) or weak or nonexistent causal theories and estimated on aggregate data (see chapter 11). The second generation was that of models based on explicit economic reasoning and estimated on aggregate data, such as the Kraft-SARC or Baumol-Quandt models. The disaggregate models form a third generation because, while still founded on basically economic theories of behavior (the two consumer behavior models in chapter 2), the formulation and estimation of a model at the disaggregate level allows much more subtle and realistic behavior to be represented and also allows greater efficiency in the use of data (see chapter 11). A fourth, potentially more powerful direction is beginning to emerge. This direction of model development draws on methods from psychology and market research to increase our ability to model the subtleties and complexity of consumer behavior. These methods have not yet been developed to the stage of practical use in transportation systems analysis.

4.9 SUMMARY

For practical purposes it is necessary to predict the behavior of groups of consumers. A *disaggregate* demand function predicts the behavior of individual consumers, whereas an *aggregate* demand function predicts the behavior of a group of consumers. Market segments are groups of consumers whose behavior is represented by a single demand function.

Many types of aggregate demand functions have been used, including gravity models, intercity passenger demand models, and the Urban Transportation Model System.

Like disaggregate models, aggregate models can be either deterministic or stochastic. Thus four major groups of travel demand models can be identified: disaggregate deterministic, disaggregate stochastic, aggregate deterministic, and aggregate stochastic. The major types of travel demand models presently available for practical use are disaggregate stochastic and aggregate deterministic.

A number of important aspects of demand functions can be identified: the variables included, the algebraic form, representation of behavior, the treatment of market segments, the use of composite variables, and the inclusion of choice-specific characteristics. The algebraic form of a demand function, in terms of the specific variables included, implies a particular representation of the behavior of the consumers in the corresponding market segment. The behavior is expressed in the magnitudes and signs of the coefficients, the derivatives of the function, and the elasticities (direct and cross-elasticities). The elasticity of a demand function expresses the relative magnitudes and directions of changes in a dimensionless form that is often quite useful.

When an aggregate demand function has been calibrated for a particular situation, prediction of consumer behavior is relatively straightforward (if service levels can be assumed known). On the other hand, in many situations the analyst may have to do without a calibrated model. In such cases various properties of demand functions can be utilized for simple, approximate predictions. For example, information on elasticities can be used in the pivot-point approach to obtain quick, approximate estimates when no other method is available. A particularly important composite variable is the composite service level, which helps to identify possible trade-offs between transportation service attributes. Several approaches to prediction using demand-model properties and simple judgments have been demonstrated.

When a disaggregate demand function is available, the prediction of group behavior requires use of an aggregation procedure. Numerous practical procedures are available, including the naive procedure, classification, distributions, and sampling. As with aggregate functions. properties of disaggregate functions can be utilized for shortcut predictions.

TO READ FURTHER

There is an abundant literature on transportation demand. For general economic treatments of demand in terms of the economic theory of consumer behavior see Henderson and Quandt (1958), Baumol (1965), or de Neufville and Stafford (1971). For a discussion of aggregate models and their foundations and a historical review see Domencich and McFadden (1975). Ben-Akiva (1977) and Spear (1977) describe a number of urban applications of disaggregate models. For recent models—primarily mode-choice models and their applications—see Liou, Cohen, and Hartgen (1975), Dunbar (1976), and Train (1977). Further suggestions will be found in chapter 11.

For fourth-generation directions see Stopher and Meyburg (1976), Hauser and Koppelman (1976), Brog, Heuwinkel, and Neumann

(1977), Brog and Schwerdtfeger (1977), Dix (1977), Fried, Havens, and Thall (1977), Hautziger and Kessel (1977), Heggie (1977), Hensher and Stopher (1978), and P. M. Jones (1978).

For freight applications see Quandt (1970a), Hartwig and Linton (1974), Terziev (1976), Roberts (1977), and Schneider, Baker, and Waldner (1977). For air travel applications see Damay and de Terra (1974) and Kanafani and Sadoulet (1977).

An important early application of pivot-point methods is reported in Pecknold, Wilson, and Kullman (1972) and also, in extract form, in the more readily available Cambridge Systematics (1974). For a more detailed discussion of directions of development in urban passenger models see Brand and Manheim (1973), especially the paper by Ruiter, and Cambridge Systematics (1974).

For approaches to market segmentation see Aldana, de Neufville, and Stafford (1974) and Cambridge Systematics (1976a).

For recent aggregate models see Crow, Young, and Cooley (1973), Lave, Mehring, and Kuzmyak (1977), and Wilken (1978).

EXERCISES

4.1(C) Consider each of these models discussed in this chapter: Gravity I–IV, Kraft-SARC, McLynn, and Baumol-Quandt.
a. For each, identify the composite service level, L_{kd} or L_{kdm}, and the composite destination-specific and origin-specific activity variables, Z_d and Y_k.
b. Derive relevant elasticities for each model using the composite variables and the properties of elasticities in table 4.2.
c. Identify choice-specific and choice-abstract parameters in each.
d. Discuss. Compare the models critically.

4.2(E, P) In section 4.5.4 we examined inferences from elasticities as utilized in a study of free transit.
a. Compare the elasticities discussed in section 4.5.4 with the elasticities of the model used in chapter 3. Discuss.
b. Numerous demand models have been developed since that early study. Review recent technical literature and analyze the pros and cons of "free transit" in light of contemporary knowledge of traveler behavior. (You may wish to examine the original study: Charles River Associates 1968.)

4.3(E) The classical gravity model is given at (4.2). A disaggregate model of destination choice d might have the form

$$p(d) = \frac{e^{U_d}}{\sum_{d'} e^{U_{d'}}}, \text{ where } U_d = \alpha_0 + \alpha_1 t_d + \alpha_2 c_d + \alpha_3 \gamma_d.$$

Show that the gravity model is a special case of the disaggregate destination-choice model, in aggregated form. Discuss the limiting assumptions of this special case.

4.4(C) In Washington, D.C., aggregate trip-generation models were estimated using regression (Washington, D.C., Council of Governments 1974). A typical equation of this form is

$$V_e = \alpha_0 + \alpha_1(Z_1 Z_2) + \alpha_2(Z_1 L),$$

where the α_i are parameters and

V_e = daily home-based trips per household for purpose e,
Z_1 = total number of persons in the household,
Z_2 = natural logarithm of household annual income (in dollars),
L = transit accessibility (ratio of jobs that can be reached in 45 minutes by transit to total regional employment).

a. What signs would you expect for each parameter? Why?
b. For home-based shopping trips, the following values were found:

$$\alpha_0 = 0.35, \qquad \alpha_1 = 0.029, \qquad \alpha_2 = -0.48.$$

(The magnitudes and signs were similar for other trip purposes.) Discuss the results.

4.5(E) In exercise 1.6 we used the approximate incremental demand function

$$\frac{\Delta V}{V} \approx \alpha \frac{\Delta p}{p} + \beta \frac{\Delta t_c}{t_c}.$$

Using the properties of elasticities, derive this from the following function:

$$V = Y p^\alpha t_c^\beta.$$

4.6(E) In developing table 4.4 the assumption was made that X is a single rather than a composite variable. Now consider the following cases:

1. $X = \mu_1 X_1 + \mu_2 X_2,$
2. $X = \mu_0 X_1^{\mu_1} X_2^{\mu_2},$
3. $X = \mu_0 e^{\mu_1 X_1} e^{\mu_2 X_2}.$

a. Extend the results of table 4.4 to these cases by deriving appropriate relationships.

b. Make appropriate numerical judgments and demonstrate the use of your derived relationships.

4.7(E) Consider question 4.3 in section 4.5.6.

a. What change in travel time would be required to maintain volume in the face of a 20 percent fare increase if there were no change in frequency?

b. If the transportation facility connecting zones 1 and 2 were congested, would the analysis given in answer 4.3 be valid? Discuss.

c. If $t^0 = 2$ hours, $c^0 = \$4$, and $q^0 = 2$ per day, compare the answers you obtain using the approximate relationship v in answer 4.3 and the explicit demand function stated at the start of question 4.3.

4.8(P) We have presented only a few specific demand models in these discussions. The following exercises are meant to broaden the reader's perspective.

a. Select and analyze a transportation demand model reported in the literature:

i. What options and impacts explicitly or implicitly influenced the design of this model?

ii. What are the major service variables? activity-system variables? other variables?

iii. How were the values of model parameters determined (data sources, statistical networks)?

iv. Discuss the behavior represented by the reported model (the magnitudes and signs of coefficients, important elasticities, etc.).

v. Take some typical values of the variables in the model (reported or hypothesized variables), and use the model to predict changes in demand for several possible transportation policies (and changes in exogenous variables). Do the results seem reasonable?

vi. To what extent does the model seem "reasonable," "valid," "relevant," and "useful"?

vii. Any other comments?

b. Select a problem area in transportation systems analysis, do a literature search to identify several possibly useful demand models, and compare them critically using the preceding questions as a guide. Examples of such problem areas are changes in passenger fares on North Atlantic air routes; introduction of a panatransit service in a particular area; or restructuring of rail system operations in a particular region. Include in your analysis discussions of the major options and impacts that should be analyzed in this problem and the service attributes and activity-system variables that should be included.

4.9(P) The following article by Ian McIntyre, an employee of an international chemical company, appeared in *The Sunday Times* of London (October 26, 1975). The author describes a number of features of the commuting lifestyle, some attractive to him and some unattractive.

a. Discuss the implications for demand modeling:

i. What features must demand models have to adequately reflect the types of behavior illustrated by this article?

ii. Critically appraise selected demand models with which you are familiar. How well or poorly do they reflect this type of behavior?

iii. Suggest a research program to develop demand models to adequately reflect this behavior.

b. Discuss the policy issues raised by the article. Assume you are responsible for developing a comprehensive transportation strategy for a major metropolitan region. What issues does this article suggest to you should be explored? What technical analyses would you do to clarify these issues?

Why I Commute: High-Speed Therapy

No one believes me when I say I actually enjoy commuting. But I do. It has always seemed to me a logical way of life.

All married people who have a working life away from their families find they lead two quite separate lives. They have their business life, frequently with its own language and life-style, and circle of friends. You even buy clothes for this half of your life which seldom get worn in the other, domestic sector: your private life.

Commuting, particularly over long distances, provides a valuable buffer period—a kind of therapeutic vacuum—between the two existences.

I can leave the office seething with discontent over some minor skirmish in the eternal warfare of office politics. An hour later it has all been purged from my mind by the homeward journey. I step out on to the platform in the Surrey countryside a new man, with the office sealed away, as it should be, in the appropriate corner of my mind.

It works the other way, too. I can leave home in the morning worried about some childish ailment which kept us awake most of the night, or the arrival of an unusually large bill; but when I get to Waterloo [a London rail station] these problems, too, have worked their way out of my system and I'm ready to tackle anything the world throws at me.

Of course, there are snags. It's infuriating when things go wrong on Southern Region, which is stretched to such limits in the rush hour that one defective signal seems able to cripple the whole system. But most trains are on time, and the annual labour dispute can easily be seen writhing its way over the horizon, and convenient holidays arranged.

You soon learn how to cope with train bores: the men who insist on talking for the whole journey to anyone who will listen. And how to avoid the early cigar smoker, who likes to blow the minds of his fellow travellers by lighting his first Havana at the uncivilised hour of 7:45 A.M. People of like interests seem to congregate by instinct in their own sections of the train.

But what do you *do* with all that spare time, people are apt to say.

One bonus is reading. How many breadwinners, with family, dog, house, garden, and perhaps charity or recreational commitments, can actually find time to read these days? I have a whole two hours a day when I can read books or office papers without that guilty feeling that I should be doing something else.

And yet—I must be realistic—commuting has a bad name. I blame part of this on the shorter Oxford dictionary. Explaining how the word "commuter" came into existence, it quotes an aphorism of 1663: "Perhaps the shame and misery of this life may commute for hell." Then, illogically, "hence commuter, one who commutes."

There's nothing hellish about my kind of commuting. The long distance men (I live 40 miles from London) always get a seat, and a cheaper rate per mile. We can have all the advantages of living in the country while working in the world's greatest city.

I've travelled some 154,000 miles to and from work in the past eight years, with another third of a million miles to go before retirement. You can almost say I'm looking forward to every furlong of the journey.

5
Transportation System Performance

5.1 INTRODUCTION

Transportation involves the movement of people or goods from one location to another. This requires the expenditure of energy by man, animal, or machine. There are many different means of transportation, using a variety of energy sources and possessing widely differing characteristics. In many cases, especially in industrialized countries, transportation is achieved by quite complex processes in which men and machines interact, within institutions that are often large and complex, to deliver transportation services to consumers.

The challenge facing the transportation systems analyst is to intervene effectively in these large, complex systems. To accomplish this the analyst must be able to predict the consequences of alternative actions, and this in turn requires that he be able to abstract from those systems a simplified representation—a "model"—that he can manipulate to analyze the options open to him. The model should be sufficiently close to the real system that it can reasonably be used to draw inferences about that system, should help to illuminate the issues that the analyst thinks should be clarified, and yet should be feasible within the resources available—both the resources required for model development and the resources required for model use. In this process the analyst must understand the system to be modeled, have an explicit model development strategy, and have a deliberate strategy for using the model to clarify the issues.

It is impossible in a single volume, much less a few chapters, to discuss all aspects of all the types of transportation systems that an analyst must understand. In keeping with the introductory nature of this volume, our objectives are limited to identification of some of the key features of transportation systems that are relevant to any analysis, a description of a general approach to analyzing the performance of transportation systems that will provide the analyst with a basic framework useful in many situations, and illustration of this approach with simple examples. The various chapters dealing with transportation system performance try to achieve these limited objectives.

In this chapter we shall first look briefly at transportation systems from several different perspectives in order to identify the major system aspects that should be represented in performance models. Then we define the concept of a transportation performance function and explore how such a function can be used in a systematic analysis. To illustrate this approach we shall develop a simple example of such a function and demonstrate its use through an air transportation example; this enables us to identify a number of issues in the use of performance functions. Finally, we shall discuss some specific principles on which the analyst can draw in developing and using performance functions in specific contexts. These will become the focus of later chapters in this group.

5.2 WHAT IS A TRANSPORTATION SYSTEM?

5.2.1 Alternative Perspectives

There are many different perspectives from which a transportation system can be viewed. In this section we shall explore a few in order to demonstrate the complexity of real systems.

COMPONENTS OF A SYSTEM

A transportation system has many components. Some are physical, others institutional. Table 5.1 displays the major components of most transportation systems, together with some of the major subsystems of these components. This list is not intended to be definitive. Our intent is simply to illustrate the variety of components and functions that interact to influence system performance.

SPATIAL AND TEMPORAL STRUCTURE

A transportation system's components are spread over space and interact over time. The spatial structure of a system, reflected in its network characteristics, is important, as is its temporal structure (how the system's characteristics vary over time).

Consider the example shown in figure 5.1. This system consists of

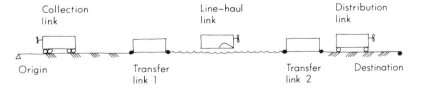

Figure 5.1 A transportation system.

164   Transportation System Performance

Table 5.1 Components of transportation systems

Major components	Subsystems	Examples
Load-carrying system (vehicle, conveyor belt, pipeline)	Load-containing system	Passenger and cargo compartments (truck, rail, air)
	Support system (transmits load from vehicle to guideway or other supporting medium)	Chassis and suspension system including wheels (truck, rail); airframe, wings, and landing gear (air); ship hull (marine)
	Power and propulsion system	Fuel tanks, engines, transmission, drive wheels (truck, rail); fuel tanks, engines, propellors (air, marine)
	Guidance and control system	Driver, steering system, wheel interactions with roadway (truck, rail); pilot, navigation, communication and control equipment (air, marine)
	Crew support	Driver's compartment (truck); cockpit and related areas (air); crew quarters (marine)
	Load support services	Galleys, food and other services (air, rail); hold-cleaning mechanisms (marine, rail)
	Loading/unloading systems	Lifts, doors (truck); doors, ramps (air); hoists, hatches (marine)
Guideway	Support system (transmits load to supporting medium)	Pavement and subgrade (truck); track and subgrade (rail); air medium (air); water medium (marine)
	Power and propulsion system	Railside or overhead power distribution system (rail); fuel storage and distribution systems (truck, air, marine)
	Guidance and control system	Traffic signals, control devices, regulations (truck); navigation control system, enroute air traffic control, airport approach and ground control (air); navigation aids, piloting systems, harbor procedures (marine); signal and communication systems for headway and speed control, dispatching system for movement control (rail)

Table 5.1 (continued)

Major components	Subsystems	Examples
Transfer facilities (intra- and intermodal)	Guidance and control system	Dispatching and train make-up (rail)
	Loading/unloading system	Passenger boarding gates and ramps (air); cargo belts, cranes, other loading equipment (marine, rail, air); internal materials-handling equipment such as conveyors or forklifts
	Vehicle service systems	Fueling, cleaning, maintenance checks
	Storage systems	Cargo storage, short-term and longer-term
	Load support systems	Documentation; passenger waiting areas and services
Maintenance system	Vehicle maintenance system	Facilities, personnel, equipment, spare parts, policies, procedures
	Guideway maintenance system	Facilities, personnel, equipment, spare parts, policies, procedures
	Transfer facility maintenance system	Facilities, personnel, equipment, spare parts, policies, procedures
Management system	Load support services	Fare collection, load processing, documentation, reservations, tracing
	Operating systems	Scheduling, dispatching, resource assignment, emergency procedures
	Marketing system	Load procurement, sales force, advertising, follow-through, incentives
	Communications and control system	System status monitoring, channels for issuing changes to current operations
	Personnel system	Recruiting, training, management, career ladders, incentives
	Financial system	Cash management, billing, internal accounting and analysis
	Planning and analysis system	Corporate planning, short-range planning
	Organizational structure	Internal organization structure for accountability and control

five subsystems or *links*: movement over significant distances occurs by way of a collection link, a line-haul link, and a distribution link; much shorter movements occur within the two transfer links. This figure might represent the movement of cargo from a producer by truck (or rail or inland waterway) to an ocean port or airport, transfer to airplane or ship for a long-distance move to another ocean port or airport, and then movement to a final destination by truck or rail or water. Alternatively the figure could represent an urban passenger trip, by walk or feeder bus to a transfer station, by rail transit or express bus to another transfer station, and then by walk or local bus to a final destination.

For simplicity we shall view each of these subsystems as a single link; in actuality each may represent networks of facilities and services.

LINK TYPES

There are many kinds of links and various ways of classifying them. One useful classification is by function: *movement links* involve movements over distances that are significant (in the particular context) in both line-haul and collection/distribution roles; *transfer links* involve movement over relatively short distances from one movement link to another.

It is also sometimes useful to distinguish links according to the means of transport used: *vehicle links* are subsystems that involve movement in vehicles over facilities (in the case of ships or planes the "facilities" are defined by controlled shipping lanes or airways or uncontrolled sea or airspace); *nonvehicle links* are subsystems other than walk links in which no vehicle is involved (pipelines for solids and fluids, conveyor belts); *walk links* are subsystems in which people move on their own legs.

A movement link can be a vehicle, nonvehicle, or walk link. A transfer link is often assumed to be a walk or other nonvehicle link, but this is not necessarily true. For example, passenger movement through an airport may involve vehicles such as shuttle buses or elevators or nonvehicle links such as conveyors. Also, freight moving through a marine port will often be moved around within the port by trucks, forklift devices, mechanical conveyors, or other devices, so that, while it is a transfer link, a port is not necessarily a nonvehicle link or a link in which no movement takes place.

Clearly these definitions are relative. For one analysis it may be useful to visualize an airport or a marine port as a single transfer, nonvehicle link (for example, in a national or regional analysis). On

168   Transportation System Performance

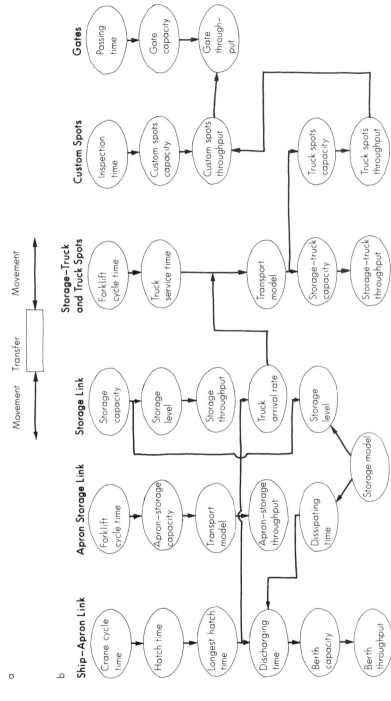

Figure 5.2 Alternative views of a transfer facility. a: A single link. b: A subsystem (from Frankel and Tang 1977).

the other hand, for detailed analysis of changes in physical features or specific operating procedures, a port could be visualized as an elaborate and detailed network of links composed of both movement and transfer links at a much smaller scale (figure 5.2).

In analyzing and modeling a particular system, the characteristics of each type of link must be considered explicitly. In some cases different types of models may be appropriate for different types of links. From a general perspective, however, all types of links are functionally the same. Therefore, for our analyses of system performance in this volume, we shall deal primarily with a single type of link, a vehicle movement link, as a basis for developing fundamental concepts of transportation systems performance.

NETWORKS OF FACILITIES

The idea of links leads naturally to a visualization of a transportation system as a network of facilities, such as might be abstracted from a map (figure 5.3a).

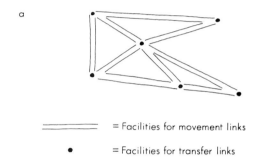

a

$\overline{\qquad\qquad}$ = Facilities for movement links

● = Facilities for transfer links

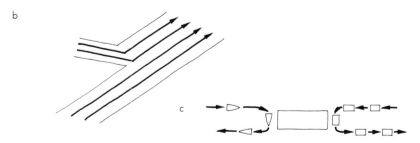

b

c

Figure 5.3 a: A network of facilities. b: Merging of two streams of vehicles within facility channels. c: Interactions of vehicles at a transfer facility.

VEHICLE TRAJECTORIES

Clearly, as suggested by table 5.1, facilities are only parts of a system; the vehicles are also important. The path of a vehicle through a system may be quite complex and, as figure 5.4 indicates, not at all a simple mirror of the network of facilities.

INTERACTIONS OF VEHICLES AND FACILITIES

The vehicles and facilities interact in various ways. Over a movement link, such as a highway or stretch of rail line, vehicles interact in a flow stream and are affected by the characteristics of the facilities over which they move. Over a network of movement links, such as a highway or rail network, the interactions of the vehicle flows are influenced by the properties of a number of links, as when congestion occurs at intersections in a road network (figure 5.3b). At a transfer link the interactions are more complex, in that the performance of the transfer link depends not only on its own facility characteristics, but also on the vehicle and facility characteristics of the movement links leading to and from the transfer link (figure 5.3c).

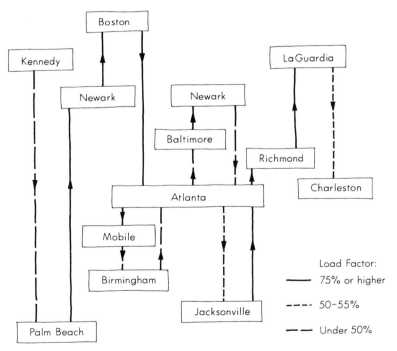

Figure 5.4 Vehicle trajectories: An aircraft routing pattern. From Borman (1977).

A USER PERSPECTIVE

Each major interest has a different perspective on transportation. From the point of view of the user, the service level over the total trip from origin to destination is important: the total trip time, the total waiting time, the total cost, the total probability of loss or damage, the maximum waiting time, the maximum walking distance, and so on. This total service level is composed of the service levels over each of the subsystems or links used in the total trip. In this respect, therefore, the performance of the system as a whole is a function of the performance of each element in the system.

AN OPERATOR PERSPECTIVE

In general, each subsystem of a transportation system is controlled by a different organization (and sometimes by several different organizations). Thus there are usually several operators in a system. Each operator has available a particular set of resources in its subsystem (vehicles, facilities, labor personnel) and exercises directly options that control these resources.

In general, each operator is interested only in the performance of his own subsystem. Resource consumption is an important consideration, particularly insofar as it is reflected in direct monetary costs. Service is considered primarily in terms of its effects on the revenues derived from users whose decisions are influenced by that service. Thus the operator is usually primarily concerned with net monetary revenues and those detailed operational aspects that influence resource consumption, and thus costs, and only secondarily with service levels. (As a further refinement, one often distinguishes the interests of various elements of an operator, such as management and operating labor.)

Building and operating a system require an input of resources. The major areas of resource consumption in transportation are illustrated in table 5.2.

Resource consumption can be categorized in many ways. Resources are consumed in building a system, in maintaining it in operating condition, and in operating it to provide useful services. Some resources are literally consumed, as in the taking of land from other uses or the consumption of fuel or labor. Other forms of consumption are, strictly speaking, degradations of existing quality (for example, air pollution or noise involve the "consumption" of resources in the sense that existing levels of air purity and quiet are degraded).

Table 5.2 Typical resources consumed in building and operating a transportation system

Labor	Vehicle operations
	Fixed facilities operations (guideways, transfer facilities)
	Vehicle maintenance
	Fixed facilities maintenance
	Management system
	Vehicle fabrication
	Fixed facilities fabrication
Materials	Vehicle fabrication (metals, rubber, plastics, etc.)
	Fixed facilities construction (cement, steel, etc.)
	Consumables in system operations other than energy (food, paper, replacement parts, etc.)
Land	Fixed facilities for the system (guideways, transfer facilities, management facilities)
	Fixed facilities for the fabrication of materials
Energy	Power for system operations
	Power for vehicle fabrication
	Power for facilities fabrication
Environmental degradation	Air quality
	Noise level
	Water quality
	Odors
Ecological effects	Effects on animal life
	Effects on plant life
Social effects	System as a physical barrier
	Effects of displacement of homes and businesses
	Effects on community cohesion
	Effects on social stability
Aesthetic effects	View of the system from the outside
	View of the system to users
	View of the environment from the system

PERSPECTIVE OF OTHER INTERESTS

While resource consumption is especially important to the operator, not all of its effects or costs are incident on the operator exclusively. Groups that are neither users nor operators may receive environmental, social, and economic impacts as a consequence of the resources consumed by a particular system or subsystem. These groups were identified in chapter 1 as those receiving physical or functional impacts plus agencies of government.

5.2.2 Implications for Analysis

The preceding discussion demonstrates the complexity of real transportation systems. Clearly the transportation system of a region can be visualized and analyzed in many different ways. The point of view one takes depends on one's objectives. Our objective as analysts is to understand the behavior of a transportation system in ways that allow us to predict the effects of proposed changes in that system. To do this we must focus on those aspects of transportation that are of greatest concern to all those on whom the impacts of transportation fall.

From the perspective of users, we have seen that service is most important: It is the level of service offered by a system that most influences how users will respond to changes in that system. From the perspective of users, operators, and other interest groups, the resources consumed are also important. This is the perspective from which we shall try to understand system performance. When we discuss links, vehicles, facilities, or networks, we shall do so primarily with the aim of understanding how the characteristics of these elements influence the levels of service offered and resources consumed by a system.

5.3 REPRESENTING TRANSPORTATION SYSTEM PERFORMANCE

We can now define what we want in a representation of transportation system performance. What do we want to predict? As we consider changes $\varDelta T$ in the transportation system T, we want to know what impacts they will have. To determine the impacts on users we need to know how service levels will change as we vary T; then using appropriate demand functions we can predict how users will respond. To determine the impacts on operators and others we need to know how the resources consumed in providing the transportation service will change. Then we can identify the actors on whom those impacts are incident: some of the costs of the resources consumed (monetary and nonmonetary) will be borne by operators, some will be borne by physically impacted groups (for example, homeowners on the approach paths to an airport), and some will be borne indirectly by society as a whole through taxes and other fiscal means and through effects on social and economic activity patterns.

Each possible change in T will have a different set of effects, in terms of both service levels and resources consumed. In addition, the magnitudes of these effects may depend not only on T but also on the actual volumes of users (shippers or travelers) of the services.

We can summarize this symbolically as follows. The magnitudes of the various resources consumed by a system (R) will depend on the specific decisions taken about the design and operation of the system, represented by the vector of transportation options (T), the specific geographic and economic environment in which the system exists (**E**), and the volume of users of the system (**V**).

The primary purpose of a transportation system is to provide services to users. The level of service (**S**) offered by a particular system will depend on **T** and also on **E**; moreover, in most cases the service level will also vary with **V** even if **T** is held constant (due, for example, to congestion effects).

Thus from an analyst's perspective we want to characterize transportation systems in terms of **R** and **S**, with both of these variables as functions of **T**, **E**, and **V**.

For our discussions here and in the related chapters on system performance, we shall ignore the diversity of operators and of interests with different points of view. We shall concentrate primarily on the viewpoints of users and operators and shall, furthermore, assume a single operator. The style of analysis thus developed will be extended to a broader context when we take up topics such as evaluation and choice.

5.3.1 The Performance Function

Thus a transportation system can be viewed as a process in which resources are consumed to produce transportation services in a particular environment. We characterize transportation by a performance function of the form $\phi_E(\mathbf{R}, \mathbf{S}, \mathbf{T}, \mathbf{V})$. This function describes a surface in (**R**, **S**, **V**) space for a given **T**, as illustrated in figure 5.5b. This representation indicates that if we specify **T** and **E**, then **R** and **S** both vary as a function of **V**.

Although **R** and **S** are both outputs of the system, we distinguish **S** as that set of characteristics of the system which, when perceived by users, influences their demand for transportation. Further, **R** can in some cases be thought of as a set of inputs to the process of producing transportation (although, strictly speaking, some resources consumed, such as noise, are physically outputs). To emphasize this it is often convenient to view ϕ as composed of a ***service function*** ϕ_S and a ***resource function*** ϕ_R in a particular environment **E**:

$$\mathbf{S} = \phi_S(\mathbf{V}; \mathbf{T}, \mathbf{E}), \qquad \mathbf{R} = \phi_R(\mathbf{V}; \mathbf{T}, \mathbf{E})$$

(see figure 5.5a). We designated these as **J** and **H**, respectively, in chapter 1; we shall use the ϕ notation when we want to emphasize, as here, that **J** and **H** are two facets of the same underlying process.

The interrelationship of **R** and **S** is a fundamental aspect of transportation system performance. As figure 5.5b emphasizes, specification

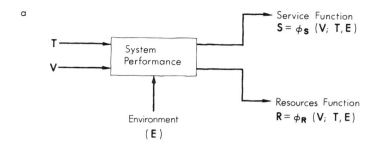

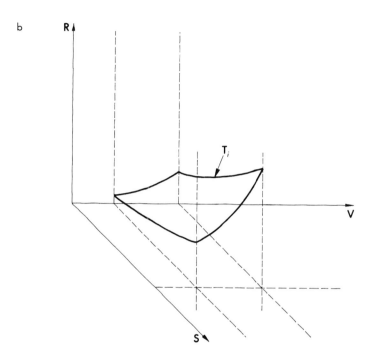

Figure 5.5 a: Service and resource aspects of the performance function. b: A performance function surface in (**R, S, V**) space (after Morlok 1968).

of **T** establishes a specific relationship between **R**, **S**, and **V**; as **T** or **V** varies, in general both **R** and **S** vary.

The actual shapes of these relationships will depend significantly on the environment **E** in which a particular system is being operated, as well as on the characteristics of the system itself. The environment includes the physical environment (distance, geography, climate, and so forth), the economic environment (prices and availabilities of various resources such as labor, rights-of-way, and fuel), and the institutional environment (legal and administrative requirements, the structures of institutions external to the transport operators, the internal organizational structure and relationships of the operators, and related factors).

5.3.2 Using a Performance Function for Analysis

We shall now outline the use of a performance function for analysis. The first step in the process is to interface the performance function with a demand model in order to predict travel-market equilibration. The second step is to use the performance function with the full set of prediction models for a systematic analysis of the options. For simplicity, we suppress the variable **E**.

EQUILIBRIUM ANALYSIS

The key features of an equilibrium analysis are that (1) the actual volume using a system is in general different from the maximum volume the system could handle or any prespecified design volume, and (2) the actual volume depends on the level of service offered, where that dependency is given by an explicit demand function. We use the following definitions (for a single-component volume):

V_E = equilibrium volume (the actual volume that would use the system under the specified conditions),
V_C = the maximum or capacity volume,
V_D = demand volume (volume desiring to use the system at a particular service level **S**).

(The units of volume are usually passengers or tons per hour or month or year.) The demand volume will usually be different from the available volume. It is given by an explicit demand function:

$$V_D = f_D(\mathbf{S}). \tag{5.1}$$

As shown in chapter 1, at equilibrium the volume and service levels must by definition be such that both demand and service conditions are met:

$$V_E = f_D(\mathbf{S}_E),\tag{5.2}$$

$$\mathbf{S}_E = \phi_S(V_E, \mathbf{T}).\tag{5.3}$$

Note that the equilibrium volume cannot exceed capacity, so (5.2) must be modified as follows:

$$V_E = \min[V_C, V_D(\mathbf{S}_E)].\tag{5.4}$$

If capacity is not constraining, then $V_E = V_D$ at the equilibrium service level $\mathbf{S}_E$.

The relationship between V_E and V_C is important. To reflect the differences between the equilibrium volume and capacity, a *load factor* λ is defined by

$$\lambda \equiv \frac{V_E}{V_C}.\tag{5.5}$$

In some modes of transport, where no standees are allowed in the vehicle for safety reasons (airplanes, for example), the load factor for passengers, λ^P, is always less than or equal to one. In other modes (bus or rail transit) λ^P is sometimes allowed to be greater than one; this is called "crush loading" for obvious reasons.

Corresponding to the equilibrium volume in the system is a certain level of resource consumption:

$$\mathbf{R} = \phi_R(V_E, \mathbf{T}).\tag{5.6}$$

SYSTEMATIC ANALYSIS

In section 1.6 we presented the image of systematically exploring variations in $\mathbf{T}$ and tracing out the differential impacts on various interests. To implement this image we shall want to structure a performance function in ways that allow efficient systematic analysis. Specifically, as we vary $\mathbf{T}$, $\mathbf{S}$ will also vary, bringing about changes in $\mathbf{V}$; impacts on users can be represented by $\mathbf{V}$ or $\mathbf{S}$. At the same time users generate revenues to the operator, and monetary and other costs are incurred, resulting in a net revenue to the operator, I_{NR}.

Considering simply these two interests, we would like to use our performance function ϕ in a style of analysis illustrated schematically in figure 5.6. Here we systematically explore a range of options $\mathbf{T}$, tracing out variations in $\mathbf{S}$ and $\mathbf{R}$ as $\mathbf{T}$ varies (parts 1 and 2 of the figure). As $\mathbf{S}$ varies, the demand and thus the equilibrium volume $\mathbf{V}_E$ also vary (part 3). The impacts on users, I_U, thus are also functions of $\mathbf{T}$ (part 4). Similarly the economic and other impacts on the operator, I_O, are also

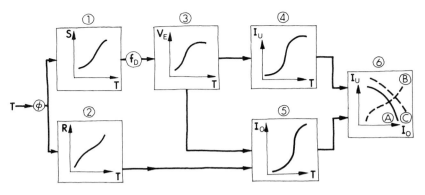

Figure 5.6 Using a performance function for systematic analysis.

varying (part 5). These impacts can be summarized in trade-off curves as in part 6 of the figure. If I_U and I_O both measure desirable impacts (such as an increase in net revenues or a reduction in travel times), curve A illustrates a situation in which users and operators are in conflict (each increase in desirable impacts on users is achievable only by a decrease in desirable impacts on the operator, and vice versa), while curve B illustrates a situation where both users and operator can be made better off simultaneously. To illustrate the generalization of this analysis to multiple interests part 6 shows two different levels of impact of an environmental contaminant as curves A and C.

5.4 A SIMPLE PERFORMANCE MODEL

In this section we shall develop a very simple performance model and demonstrate how it can be used for a systematic analysis.

5.4.1 Defining the Model

BASIC RELATIONSHIPS

We assume a single route running between two points, such that the one-way distance is d and the round-trip distance (A to B and back to A) is $D = 2d$. We assume also that vehicles travel back and forth over this link at an average speed v and cycle continuously at uniform constant headway. Each one-way trip of one vehicle results in the delivery of a payload of w tons (or passengers).

The productivity of a single vehicle can be determined as follows. Each vehicle makes one round trip in a time D/v. Alternatively, in one hour a vehicle makes n round trips, where

$$n = \frac{v}{D};$$

(5.7)

that is, the one-way trip time t is

$$t = \frac{d}{v} = \frac{1}{2n}.$$

(5.8)

In one round trip one vehicle delivers $2w$ tons of freight; therefore, in one hour one vehicle would deliver $2nw$ tons.

Now consider a fleet of vehicles. Let Q be the total number of vehicle round trips scheduled per hour and q the number actually accomplished (which may be different from the number scheduled). Then the maximum total volume that can be delivered by the fleet, the capacity volume, is $2qw$.

The price to be charged per one-way trip per ton, P, is set as an option.

To formalize these relationships we add the following variables: $\mathbf{T}$, the vector of transportation options; $\mathbf{M}$, the vector of options specifying technological characteristics; and V_C, the capacity volume (the maximum payload that can be carried in both directions, per hour, for the options $\mathbf{T}$). For this system

$$\mathbf{T} = (\mathbf{M}, Q, P),$$

(5.9)

where

$$\mathbf{M} = (w, v);$$

(5.10)

the environment $\mathbf{E}$ is

$$\mathbf{E} = (d);$$

(5.11)

and the capacity volume is

$$V_C(\mathbf{T}) = 2wq.$$

(5.12)

In this case we assume also that

$$q = Q.$$

(5.13)

SERVICE-LEVEL RELATIONSHIPS

We now consider the service variables:

t_{iv} = one-way in-vehicle travel time,
t_w = average waiting time for next vehicle,
h = average time interval between successive vehicles (headway),
t_T = total one-way trip time,

c = out-of-pocket price paid by traveler,

$\mathbf{S} = (t_{iv}, t_w, t_T, c)$.

These are related to the options and other parameters as follows. First, $c = P$ is set explicitly as a transportation option. Since each vehicle will cover the round-trip distance in $1/n$ hours, the one-way in-vehicle travel time will be

$$t_{iv} = \frac{d}{v} = \frac{1}{2n}. \tag{5.14}$$

We assume that the vehicles are scheduled to cycle continuously at a uniform rate over the route. The total number of vehicles passing any particular point per hour is q. The headway is thus

$$h = \frac{1}{q}. \tag{5.15}$$

We assume that shipments arrive at random without knowledge of the schedule, so the average wait time experienced by a user is half the headway:

$$t_w = \frac{1}{2} h = \frac{1}{2q} \tag{5.16}$$

or, since $q = Q$,

$$t_w = \frac{1}{2Q}. \tag{5.17}$$

The total trip time is

$$t_T = t_{iv} + t_w$$

$$= \frac{1}{2} \left(\frac{1}{n} + \frac{1}{Q} \right). \tag{5.18}$$

Let us look at the service level as a function of the options $\mathbf{T}$. Specifically, we vary frequency Q over a range of values, holding $\mathbf{M}$ and P fixed; then we can vary $\mathbf{M}$ and P. The components of $\mathbf{S(T)}$ are shown in figure 5.7, parts a–c. Note that only t_w and t_T are actually influenced by Q; c and t_{iv} depend only on P and $\mathbf{M}$.

RESOURCES CONSUMED

Assume for this example that the resources can be expressed wholly in terms of vehicle-hours. The magnitude of resources consumed is then the total vehicle-hours per hour, or

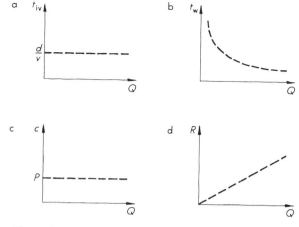

Figure 5.7 Service and resource variations (for a given technology).

$$R = \frac{Q}{n} = Q\,\frac{d}{v}.$$ (5.19)

This is shown in figure 5.7d.

THE TRANSPORTATION PERFORMANCE FUNCTION
Thus this model expresses the performance function explicitly in terms of the options, as shown in table 5.3.

5.4.2 Travel-Market Equilibration
In the general case finding the equilibrium volume V_E that satisfies both service and demand conditions can involve complex calculations. In this performance model, however, the service level is a function of the options **T** only and does not vary as V_E varies (there are no congestion effects). Thus travel-market equilibration is trivial (also because we are dealing with a single link and not a network), and, as in section 5.3.2,

$$V_D = f_D(\mathbf{S}),$$ (5.20)

$$V_E = \min(V_D, V_C).$$ (5.21)

For this performance model

$$V_C = 2wQ,$$ (5.22)

so the load factor is

$$\lambda = \frac{V_E}{V_C} = \frac{V_E}{2wQ}.$$ (5.23)

Table 5.3   Performance model I

Options	$T = (M, Q, P)$
	$M = (w, v)$
Environment	$E = (d)$
Basic relationships	$q(T) = Q$
	$V_c(T) = 2wq$
	$n(T) = \dfrac{v}{2d}$
Service level	$S(T) = (t_{iv}, t_w, t_T, c)$
	$c(T) = P$
	$t_{iv}(T) = \dfrac{d}{v}$
	$t_w(T) = \dfrac{1}{2q}$
	$t_T(T) = \dfrac{1}{2}\left(\dfrac{2d}{v} + \dfrac{1}{q}\right)$
Resources consumed	$R = \dfrac{q}{n}$

Thus λ, V_E, and V_C are all functions of the options **T**. (Note that, consistent with our definition of V_C, V_D and V_E are also the total payloads of one-way trips.)

5.4.3 Evaluation

We now want to trace out impacts on users and operators. The user impacts are expressed in terms of the service levels and volume at equilibrium, S_E and V_E. For our present purposes V_E is a sufficiently good measure of the impact on users. (In chapter 9 various economic formulations for expressing user impacts in terms of both service levels and volumes are considered. Since V_E is a monotonically increasing function of the level of service, we shall use V_E as a proxy for the more elaborate formulations.)

From the operator's perspective, economic measures such as costs and revenues are often important. Users pay fares and thus provide revenues to the operator. The gross revenue from users, I_{GR}, is the product of V_E and the price charged, P:

$$I_{GR} = PV_E. \tag{5.24}$$

The magnitude of the resources consumed can also be expressed in monetary terms. The total cost incurred by the operator, C_T, is

$$C_T = aR, \tag{5.25}$$

where a is the unit cost in dollars per vehicle-hour. (This is a simple assumption; more general formulations will be explored in volume 2.) One useful measure of impact on the operator is the net revenue, I_{NR}:

$$I_{NR} = I_{GR} - C_T. \tag{5.26}$$

Other measures can be defined to reflect other objectives of the operator, but for our present, introductory discussion, this one measure will suffice. (More subtle and realistic evaluation approaches are described in chapter 9.)

5.4.4 Summary: Methodology for Analysis

This gives us all that we need for a systematic exploration of the options open to this transportation operator.

The step-by-step methodology is shown in figure 5.8. The methodology includes three basic activities of analysis: search, prediction, and evaluation. (Choice and implementation are not shown here.) The approach to prediction includes the basic elements defined in chapter 1 (except for activity shifts, in this case). Steps 5, 6, and 9 utilize the performance model defined in section 5.4.1. Travel-market equilibration reflects the assumption that there is no congestion (in chapter 7 we shall relax this assumption and introduce the loop indicated by the dashed line marked 1 in this figure to take into account the effects of volume on levels of service). Loop 2 indicates another step we could add later, in which resource consumption is also influenced by actual volumes. We have added a sensitivity analysis in step 12 and feedback loops to step 4 based on the results of prediction (loop 3) and evaluation (loop 4).

5.5 AN AIR TRANSPORTATION EXAMPLE

To illustrate the use of a transportation performance function in a systematic analysis we consider in this section a simplified air transportation example.

5.5.1 The Situation

The operator serves a single market between two cities with round-trip distance D. The options $\mathbf{T} = (\mathbf{M}, Q, P)$, where $\mathbf{M}$ denotes choice

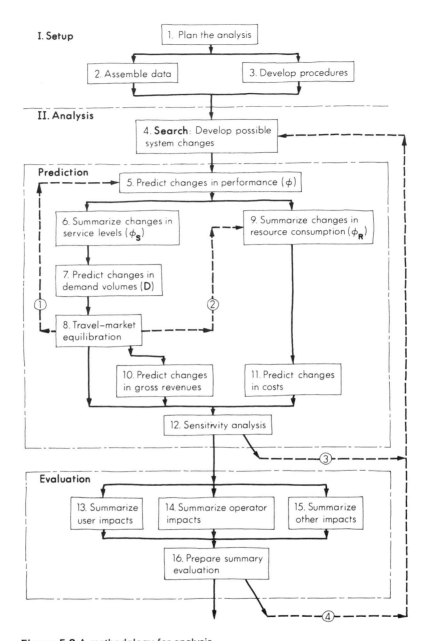

Figure 5.8 A methodology for analysis.

of aircraft type, with corresponding maximum payload w, effective speed v, and cost structure a (in dollars per vehicle-hour). The level of service is, as before, $\mathbf{S} = (t_{iv}, t_w, t_T, c)$.

PERFORMANCE FUNCTION

The performance of the system, including available volume V_C, resources consumed R, and level of service $\mathbf{S}$, is determined as in section 5.4 and summarized in table 5.3.

DEMAND

The demand function is

$$V_D = f_D(\mathbf{S}) = f_D(t_{iv}, t_w, t_T, c) \tag{5.27}$$

or specifically

$$V_D = Z\left(\frac{1}{1 + e^{U_0 - U}}\right), \tag{5.28}$$

where

$$U = \alpha_1 t_{iv} + \alpha_2 t_w + \alpha_3 c, \tag{5.29}$$

$$U_0 = \alpha_0, \tag{5.30}$$

$$t_w = \frac{1}{2q}, \tag{5.31}$$

the αs are empirically determined parameters, and Z is some measure of the activity system's influence on total demand in the market. The behavior of this type of model is similar to that of figure 2.8. We take $\alpha_0 = -1.36$, $\alpha_1 = -0.5$, $\alpha_2 = -1.2$, $\alpha_3 = -0.015$, and $Z = 900$.

For all options (aircraft types and schedule frequencies) being considered, D and v are the same. Therefore t_{iv} is constant. For this section we shall hold P constant also and assume there is no congestion; thus

$$c = P, \qquad q = Q. \tag{5.32}$$

Therefore V_D is a function of schedule frequency only:

$$V_D = f_D(Q) = \frac{Z}{1 + \beta_1 e^{\beta_2/Q}}, \tag{5.33}$$

where

$$\beta_2 = \frac{\alpha_2}{2}, \qquad \beta_1 = e^{\alpha_0 - \alpha_1 t_{iv} - \alpha_3 P}. \tag{5.34}$$

(Note that V_D is the two-way volume in total one-way trips per hour.)
For this example we take

$$d = 800 \text{ miles}, \quad D = 2d = 1{,}600,$$
$$v = 400 \text{ miles per hour}, \quad t_{iv} = 2 \text{ hours}, \quad (5.35)$$
$$P = \$60.$$

Thus in (5.33) we have $\beta_1 = 1.72$ and $\beta_2 = 0.6$.

For any specific set of options $\mathbf{T}^i$, prediction is straightforward, following the equations in table 5.3 and the steps in figure 5.8:

1. The available volume V_C is determined from (5.22).
2. The number of round trips per vehicle per hour is $n = v/D = 0.25$.
3. For $\mathbf{S}$, c and t_{iv} are known, and t_w is found by (5.31) and enters directly into the demand function (5.33).
4. For R, vehicle-hours per hour are determined from (5.19).
5. The demand volume V_D is determined from the demand function (5.33).
6. Since there is no congestion, $V_E = \min(V_D, V_C)$.
7. I_{GR} is determined from (5.24).
8. C_T is determined from (5.25).
9. Evaluation follows directly, too: I_{NR} is determined from I_{GR} and C_T by (5.26).

5.5.2 Systematic Analysis of the Options

To analyze the options we use the approach described in section 5.4: we systematically vary the options $\mathbf{T}$ over a range of values and trace out the impacts on the affected interests (in this case, users and operators), and we examine the predicted impacts and look for trade-offs among the affected interests.

The options available include choice of vehicle type and schedule frequency (for this section we assume that fare is fixed, for example by regulatory policy). The first question is, for a particular vehicle type, What is the best frequency? From the point of view of the operator, we assume that the best frequency is the one that maximizes net revenue. From the point of view of the users, who want the maximum service, the higher the frequency the better. If net revenue increases as frequency increases, users and operator will both benefit; if net revenue decreases, they will clearly be in conflict.

The second question is, What are the impacts of alternative vehicle types? Several alternative choices of vehicle are considered, as shown in table 5.4.

Table 5.4 Three transportation technology options

Aircraft type	Payload (w, seats)	Cost per vehicle-hour (a)	Cost per available seat per hour
M_1	200	$2,800	$14
M_2	140	$2,240	$16
M_3	90	$1,620	$18

VARYING OPERATING POLICY

Figure 5.9 illustrates a systematic analysis of operating policy: holding vehicle type fixed at M_2, frequency Q is varied over a range. The corresponding variations in V_D, V_E, and V_C are shown in part a of the figure. Part b shows the variation in load factor. Part c shows the monetary impacts on the operator, C_T and I_{GR}, and part d the net revenue I_{NR}. For $Q = Q_{OPT}$, net revenue is a maximum. Points B and D have $I_{NR} = 0$; point C, the frequency for maximum I_{NR}, is different from A, the point of maximum load factor. The shaded area in part c has a positive I_{NR}; maximum I_{NR} is achieved at point C, where the slopes of the C_T and I_{GR} functions are equal.

Part e shows the resulting trade-offs between the users and the operator. Note that in the range B to C increases in frequency make both operator and user better off, while in the range C to D a change in frequency increases benefits to one group while decreasing them to the other. The range C to D thus represents an area of potential conflicts.

This figure illustrates a systematic procedure for finding (graphically, numerically, or, under some conditions, analytically) the schedule frequency that gives maximum I_{NR} for a particular market, a particular fare, and a particular vehicle choice.

EFFECT OF A CAPACITY CONSTRAINT

In some cases the capacity constraint may be binding, in that the point of maximum I_{NR} occurs at a load factor of 1.0. This is illustrated schematically in figure 5.10 for vehicle M_3. If there were no capacity constraint, the frequency for maximum net revenue would be Q_2, where the slopes of the C_T and I_{GR} curves are equal. Since the capacity constraint is operative, net revenue is maximized at frequency Q_1.

VARYING VEHICLE TYPE

In figure 5.11 the three alternative vehicle choices are compared. Note that there is one demand and gross revenue curve that applies to all

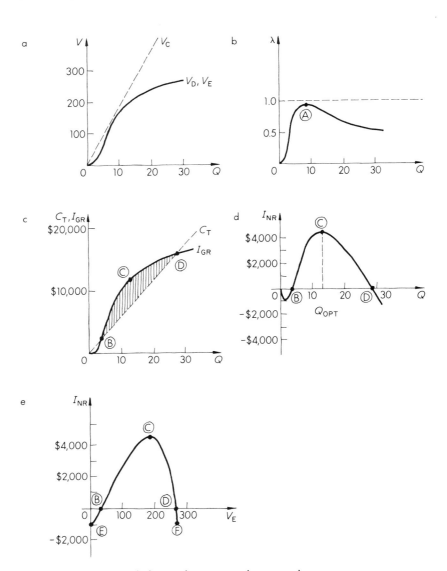

Figure 5.9 Basic analysis for an air transportation example.

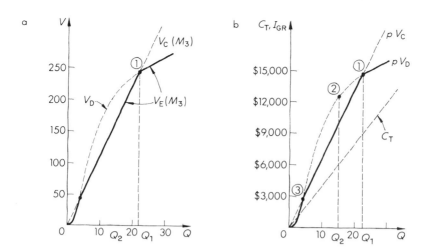

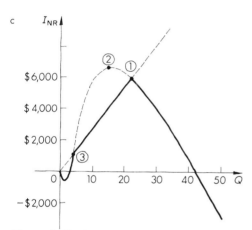

Figure 5.10 Effect of a volume constraint.

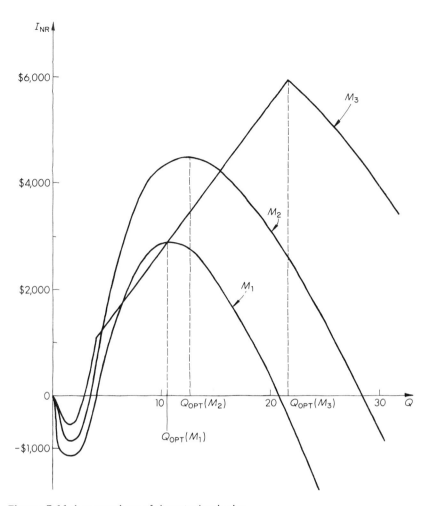

Figure 5.11 A comparison of three technologies.

three technologies, since at any Q they have the same service levels in all respects. However, there are different C_T, V_C, and V_E curves for each of the three technologies. As a consequence the optimal frequency is different for each technology: $Q_{OPT}(M_1) = 10$, $Q_{OPT}(M_2) = 12$, $Q_{OPT}(M_3) = 22$.

TRADE-OFFS BETWEEN USER AND OPERATOR

Clearly there are trade-offs between impacts on operators and on users, as shown in figure 5.9e. These are emphasized in figure 5.12. The frequencies that produce maximum net revenue for the operator are not those that are "best" from the user's perspective. From that perspective, the higher the value of V_E, the more attractive the system (since V_E is monotonically related to the service level and to other measures of user benefits).

Figure 5.12 shows some of the trade-offs available. If point N represents the existing service, both users and operators could be made better off by shift to points A, B, or C. From point A, any point in the range A to R would be an improvement for users but a loss for operators relative to point A. Alternatively a shift to a new technology, M_2 or M_3, would keep the same level of I_{NR} for the operator as A but increase V_E to points D or E.

Again, maximum I_{NR} is not necessarily the operator's sole or even primary decision rule. In addition to the clear trade-off between operator and users, many other issues may enter into the operator's decisions, as well as into decisions from a broader perspective.

5.6 EXTENDING THE ANALYSIS

The simplified air transportation example illustrated a basic style of systematic analysis using a performance function. In this section we show how this analysis can be extended to explore many significant questions.

5.6.1 Effects of Price Variations

Consider the option of varying pricing policy. We assume explicitly that carrier i is free to vary his own price while other carriers stick with their original sets of options. (In practice this is not a valid assumption in most air travel markets. Prices are usually regulated, so there are restrictions on a carrier's ability to vary prices, and competition in the industry is so keen that other carriers will usually respond to changes in carrier i's services by changing their own options.)

Figure 5.13 illustrates schematically the structure of the expanded

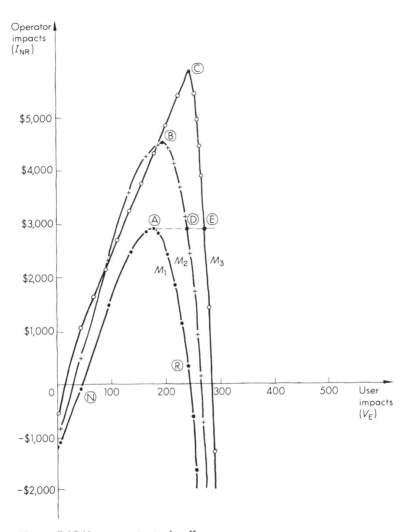

Figure 5.12 User-operator trade-offs.

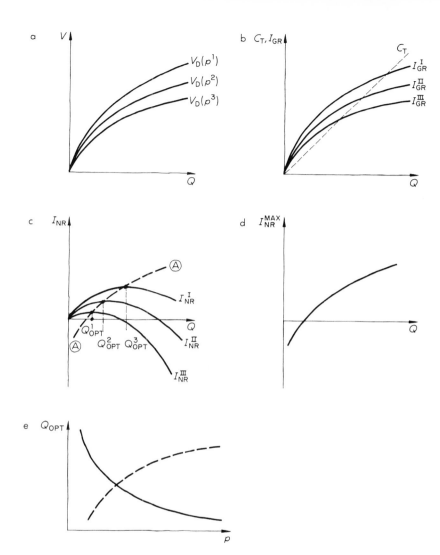

Figure 5.13 The effect of price variations.

analysis. Part a shows that V_D varies as P is varied (we assume that there is no volume constraint, so $V_E = V_D$). Since the elasticity of demand with respect to price is almost always negative, as P increases ($P^3 > P^2 > P^1$), demand will increase. In part b the total cost C_T is compared with the various gross revenue curves corresponding to the different prices. If demand is inelastic with respect to price (elasticity between 0 and -1), an increase in price will cause an increase in gross revenue, so I_{GR}^{III} corresponds to P^1, I_{GR}^{II} to P^2, and so on. If, however, demand is elastic (elasticity less than -1), a price increase causes a decrease in gross revenue, so I_{GR}^{I} corresponds to P^3, I_{GR}^{II} to P^2, and so on.

For each price level a schedule frequency that maximizes I_{NR} can be found, as illustrated in part c. If P is continuously variable, then a curve such as the dashed one can be developed. As shown in part d, this curve gives the maximum I_{NR} that can be achieved for a given Q. (In some cases the value of P that maximizes I_{NR} for a given Q can be derived analytically.) Conversely, for every price there is an optimal frequency, as shown in part e (the dashed line emphasizes that the shape of the curve depends on the characteristics of the specific situation).

This analysis can be repeated for a number of technologies. The result suggested in part d can be generalized to show the maximum net revenue as a function of Q, assuming that the optimum P is used at every Q.

Thus, in general, there will be a different (P, Q) combination that maximizes net revenue for each technology. This fact has important implications for the analysis of alternative transportation options. It is usually difficult or impossible to know beforehand which combination of pricing and operating policies will be optimal for a given technology. Therefore it is usually poor practice to establish a single price or schedule beforehand and compare technologies at that combination. While some technologies will perform better than others at that operating point, it may well be that the relative rankings of the technologies will change significantly at other (P, Q) combinations. For example, one technology may perform well at a low price and a relatively low service level, whereas another system performs well at a high price and a relatively high service level. Thus it is essential that any comparison of transportation options include systematic variations in operating and pricing options in combination.

An alternative way of visualizing this is illustrated in figure 5.14.

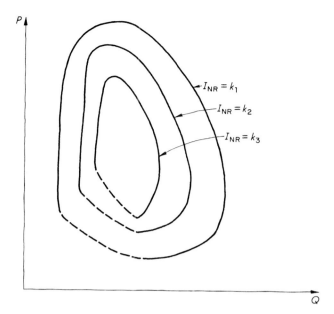

Figure 5.14 Trade-offs among options. $\lambda = 1$ along the dashed portion of the curves.

Here emphasis is placed on showing how options can be explored in (P, Q) space, to trace out isoquants of major impacts—for example, combinations of (P, Q) that give the same levels of I_{GR}, C_T, I_{NR}, or V_E.

Two cautions must be voiced here. First, the actual relationships depend significantly on the demand functions and parameter values. The magnitude of the price elasticity is particularly important— specifically, whether demand is elastic or inelastic with respect to price, that is, whether $E_P(V_D)$ is greater than or less than one in absolute magnitude (see section 4.5.3). Second, most analyses usually encompass several different market segments, and the responses of each segment will be different.

5.6.2 Effects of Parameter Variations

It is important to recognize the degree of uncertainty that may exist in key elements of any analysis. In this type of analysis key elements of uncertainty include the parameter values used in the performance and demand functions. Since uncertainty is always present in any analysis to a greater or lesser degree, it is important to recognize this and to do appropriate sensitivity analyses. A sensitivity analysis simply involves repeating the analysis for several alternative assumptions about the values of specified parameters. (Sometimes analytical relationships can be derived and used to estimate sensitivities.)

In any analysis of transportation options, significant uncertainty may exist about the optimal choice of options due to uncertainty in underlying parameter values. It is essential that appropriate studies be done to explore how sensitive the choice may be to likely variations in key parameters. If the results of a preliminary analysis indicate that the choice of options may be particularly sensitive to the values assumed for one or several parameters, this suggests that in later, more detailed analyses, proportionately greater effort should be devoted to detailed modeling and analysis of these components of the transportation performance function.

The methodology of a sensitivity analysis is particularly important for the planning of new systems.

5.6.3 Example: Setting Transportation Research and Development Priorities

The methodology outlined here can be especially valuable in establishing desired performance levels for new systems, for a specific situation, or for establishing priorities for a national transportation research and development program. The methodology would be applied in the style of a sensitivity analysis. For example, alternative assumptions can be made about design targets for such variables as speed, payload, or unit costs. Then, based on explicit analyses of the type described in this chapter, the impacts associated with alternative design targets can be predicted. Final selection of design targets can then be made with knowledge of their consequences.

Such a methodology was utilized in a study to assist in establishing R&D priorities for a particular class of urban transportation systems (Kocur et al. 1977). "Dual-mode" systems are medium-size buslike vehicles that carry 12–50 passengers and operate in two modes: under automated control on a special guideway, and under the manual control of a driver on local streets. Utilizing Milwaukee as a prototype city, this study explored systematically some 240 different transportation alternatives. Each alternative consisted of a choice of the following options: technology, network characteristics, station locations, link and station characteristics, and operating and pricing policies. Flows were predicted by means of an explicit demand model, a modified version of standard urban transportation planning computer models, and specifically designed performance models. Particular attention was given to systematic exploration of a wide range of operating policies, since dual-mode systems can be operated in a spectrum of ways, ranging from fixed routes and fixed schedules (like conventional buses) to on-demand almost-direct service from a few origins to one or a few destinations (like a shared taxi or carpool).

The style of this type of analysis is illustrated in figure 5.15. Consider aircraft type M_3 as defined in table 5.4. A proposal is under consideration for developing a new aircraft, M_4. This aircraft is expected to have an increased speed such that its productivity over the route studied in section 5.5 is expected to increase by 20 percent, from 0.25 trips per hour to 0.30 (that is, instead of four hours for one trip, the new vehicle

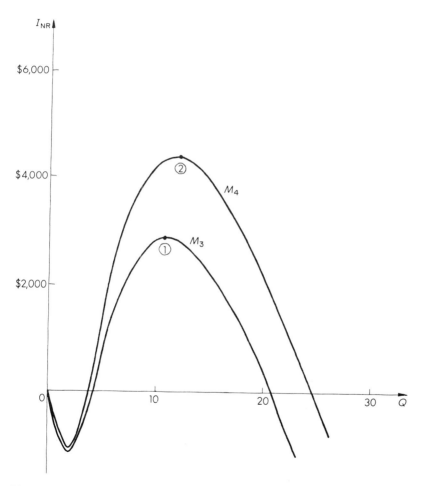

Figure 5.15 Examination of R & D objectives for two technology options.

would do it in 3.3 hours). If the increase in cost were also 20 percent, would this vehicle be an attractive option for the operator, and therefore for the manufacturer? Figure 5.15 compares the net revenue in this market for M_3 and M_4. Clearly M_4 would be attractive: it produces a net revenue about 50 percent higher than that of M_3.

5.6.4 Incremental Analysis

The preceding analyses could be applied to an incremental analysis of variations from an existing, "base-case" condition T^0. Thus, for any changes $\Delta T = (\Delta Q, \Delta P)$, the corresponding changes can be calculated for C_T, V_E, I_{GR}, and I_{NR}. To compute ΔV_E, the methods for incremental analysis of demand described in section 4.6 could be used. This formulation is demonstrated in the exercises and in chapter 10.

5.6.5 General Applicability of Systematic Analysis

The idea of a systematic analysis of a range of options applies at any scale of concern in transportation systems analysis. For example, similar concepts have been applied in the analysis of highway projects in developing countries. In a pioneering work Soberman (1966a, b) demonstrated that there are significant trade-offs among the design elements of a highway. He showed that various combinations of road width and pavement design yield different traffic capacities and different construction and operating costs, and he demonstrated that the relative consumptions of domestic capital, foreign exchange, and labor can be varied by varying these design parameters. (See also Lago 1968.) Roberts and Deweese (1971) extended this type of analysis to explore alternative alignments and demonstrated the trade-offs between user and operator impacts achievable by variations in alignments. More recently Moavenzadeh et al. (1975) and Hide et al. (1975) (see also Robinson 1975) have further extended this type of analysis to the analysis of trade-offs among initial road design, staged construction, and alternative maintenance strategies.

5.7 STYLES OF ANALYSIS

The preceding sections have illustrated an analytical style in which the options are stated explicitly; prediction of impacts is done using a performance function and with an explicit equilibrium analysis; the options are varied systematically over a range; and trade-offs among different interests are explicitly considered.

There are a number of ways in which analyses can be carried out using less explicit procedures. Each such style of analysis has advantages and

198 Transportation System Performance

disadvantages. The analyst should be aware of these in order to make an informed judgment about which style to utilize in a particular application. In this section we shall begin a discussion that will be extended in later chapters.

5.7.1 The Load-Factor Assumption

In some applications it is customary to assume a load factor and use it to estimate impacts. For example, one might assume $\lambda = \lambda^*$ and thereby estimate equilibrium volume:

$$V_{\mathrm{E}} = \lambda^* V_{\mathrm{C}}. \qquad (5.36)$$

Costs and revenues are then predicted as in explicit analysis.

This is a strong assumption, specifically that, over the range of options being explored, $\lambda = V_{\mathrm{D}}/V_{\mathrm{C}}$ is constant (see, for example, figure 5.9b). This may be a reasonable approximation in some situations, especially when the range of variations in $\mathbf{T}$ is small, but it must be carefully examined in each case.

Note that the assumption of a load factor is a shortcut to avoid explicitly stating a demand function and calculating equilibrium. An alternative method would be to utilize an incremental approach: given present demand volume V_{D}^0, estimate the change ΔV_{D} for the change in options and, considering the change in capacity ΔV_{C}, find the new load factor explicitly:

$$\lambda' = \frac{V_{\mathrm{D}}^0 + \Delta V_{\mathrm{D}}}{V_{\mathrm{C}}^0 + \Delta V_{\mathrm{C}}}. \qquad (5.37)$$

5.7.2 Service Level as an Input

In an explicit analysis service levels are predicted as functions of the options $\mathbf{T}$. Alternatively an analysis may begin with an explicit statement of goals in terms of desired service levels $\mathbf{S}^*$ (for example, a maximum waiting time). The performance function can then in principle be used in a search procedure to specify the values of some or all of the options.

For example, consider a desired level of waiting time, t_{w}^*. From performance model I we have

$$t_{\mathrm{w}} = \frac{1}{2q}, \qquad q = Q. \qquad (5.38)$$

The schedule frequency Q^* that achieves this service level is then

$$Q^* = \frac{1}{2t_{\mathrm{w}}^*}. \qquad (5.39)$$

In general, however, a careful distinction must be made between the search and prediction steps. With more complex models, and especially with explicit consideration of congestion and/or network effects, a full prediction of impacts together with explicit equilibration may produce an equilibrium service level different from the desired goal. For example, consider a case in which congestion effects cause q to be different from Q:

$$q = f(Q). \tag{5.40}$$

Then $t_w(Q^*)$ may be significantly different from t_w^*. Thus, while (5.39) produces a good suggestion for an initial schedule frequency, in the general case it does not necessarily specify the value of Q that will achieve the desired service level.

Therefore, while it is often useful to transform an explicit performance model into a form useful for search, it is always important to test the output of search (for example, Q^*) by doing explicit prediction of impacts with the explicit performance function and equilibration.

5.7.3 Desired Capacity as an Input

In explicit analysis available capacity is predicted as a function of the options. Alternatively an analysis may begin with an explicit statement of a desired or "design" capacity V_C^*. Again the performance function can in principle be used in a search procedure.

In performance model I

$$V_C = 2wq, \qquad q = Q, \tag{5.41}$$

so the schedule frequency that achieves this capacity is

$$Q^* = \frac{V_C^*}{2w}. \tag{5.42}$$

The same comments apply to the use of this search procedure as to one with service levels as an input: the values of the options resulting from search must be tested in full-scale prediction to see what impacts they actually achieve.

5.7.4 The Supply Function

In chapter 1 we identified the type 3 relationship as the adjustment of options $\mathbf{T}$ by the operators. We indicated that for most purposes we would not model this relationship, preferring to vary the options $\mathbf{T}$ explicitly. Sometimes, however, it is desirable to model this relationship. In such a case a supply function can be derived.

Table 5.5 Impacts of alternative strategies

Strategy			Impacts[a]			
T^i =	$(P^i,$	$Q^i)$	V_E	I_{GR}	C_T	I_{NR}
11	$1.50	2	4.1	6.2	2.0	4.2
12		4	6.3	9.4	4.0	5.4
13		6	8.0	12.0	6.0	6.0
14		8	9.5	14.2	8.0	6.2
15		10	10.8	16.3	10.0	6.3
16		12	12.1	18.1	12.0	6.1
17		14	13.3	19.9	14.0	5.9
	Q_{OPT} =	9.4	10.4	15.7	9.4	6.3
21	$2.00	2	2.7	5.4	2.0	3.4
22		4	4.1	8.1	4.0	4.1
23		6	5.2	10.4	6.0	4.4
24		8	6.2	12.3	8.0	4.3
25		10	7.1	14.1	10.0	4.1
26		12	7.9	15.7	12.0	3.7
27		14	8.6	17.2	14.0	3.2
	Q_{OPT} =	6.6	5.5	10.9	6.6	4.4
31	$2.50	2	1.9	4.8	2.0	2.8
32		4	2.9	7.3	4.0	3.3
33		6	3.7	9.3	6.0	3.3
34		8	4.4	11.0	8.0	3.0
35		10	5.0	12.6	10.0	2.6
36		12	5.6	14.0	12.0	2.0
	Q_{OPT} =	5.0	3.3	8.3	5.0	3.3
41	$3.00	2	1.5	4.4	2.0	2.2
42		4	2.2	6.6	4.0	2.6
43		6	2.8	8.5	6.0	2.5
44		8	3.4	10.1	8.0	2.1
45		10	2.8	11.5	10.0	1.5
	Q_{OPT} =	4.0	2.2	6.6	4.0	2.6
51	$3.50	2	1.2	4.1	2.0	2.1
52		4	1.8	6.1	4.0	2.1
53		6	2.2	7.8	6.0	1.8
54		8	2.7	9.3	8.0	1.3
55		10	3.0	10.6	10.0	0.6
	Q_{OPT} =	3.3	1.2	5.4	3.3	2.2
61	$4.00	2	0.9	3.8	2.0	1.8
62		4	1.4	5.7	4.0	1.7
63		6	1.8	7.3	6.0	1.3
64		8	2.2	8.7	8.0	0.7
65		10	2.5	10.0	10.0	0
	Q_{OPT} =	2.8	1.1	4.6	2.8	1.8

[a]In units of 1,000, rounded to one decimal place.

To derive a supply function from a performance function it is necessary to have an explicit decision rule $\mathscr{D}$ that describes the objectives of the operator in completely operational terms. Then we can use the following procedure:

1. Select a set of alternative strategies $\mathbf{T}^i$ that the operator is assumed to consider.
2. Using the full set of prediction models (including demand, performance, travel-market equilibration, and activity shifts), predict the impacts $\mathbf{I}^i$ of each strategy $\mathbf{T}^i$.
3. Apply the decision rule $\mathscr{D}$ to predict which strategy $\mathbf{T}^*$ the operator will pick.

As an example, consider the results shown in table 5.5. Assume the operator has the decision rule, "maximize net revenue." Then assume that a regulatory agency is setting price. We might derive from table 5.5 a supply function that predicts the frequency Q_{OPT} the operator would choose to offer as a function of this externally set price, and thus the capacity V_C (proportional to Q_{OPT}) that would be available at each level of price. Figure 5.16 shows Q_{OPT} as a function of price. This is the conventional supply function. Also shown is $I_{\mathrm{NR}}(Q_{\mathrm{OPT}})$, a function of price also.

Note these important points:

1. Travel-market equilibration has to be done in order to develop each point of the supply function.
2. The supply function depends explicitly on the choice of decision rule $\mathscr{D}$.
3. The service-function aspect of the performance function shows service as a function of volume for a fixed choice of $\mathbf{T}$ and always has service levels constant or decreasing (for example, travel time increasing) as volume increases. However, the supply function shows a family of choices of $\mathbf{T}$ and can have service levels increasing as volume increases. (In figure 5.16 service level is decreasing as price is increased. The shape of the relationship depends in a complex way on both demand and performance functions and on parameter values.)

This is important and complex topic; indeed, the difference between a performance function and a supply function is often confused. For further discussion see Manheim (1978a) and also volume 2.

5.8 CONCLUSIONS

We have demonstrated a basic approach to representing transportation system performance and analyzing transportation options. A simplified

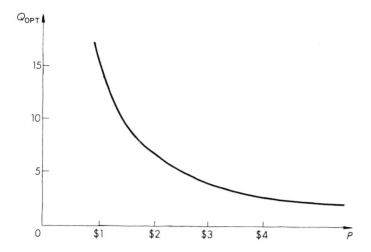

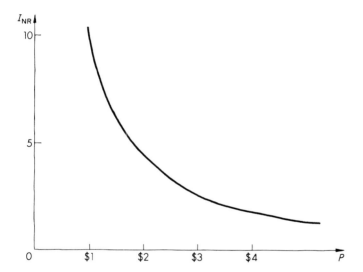

Figure 5.16 The supply function.

formulation of the decisions faced by an air transportation operator was used as an example.

5.8.1 The Basic Approach

The primary elements of this approach are:

1. representing the transportation system explicitly by a performance function so that both service levels and resources consumed are functions of the options and of the volume served;
2. comparison of alternative options by explicit determination of equilibrium volumes with an explicit demand function;
3. evaluation of impacts on operator and user in terms of equilibrium volumes, service levels, resources consumed, and monetary impacts such as costs and revenues; and
4. systematic variation of options to trace out trade-offs among various impacts and various interests.

The example demonstrated several key points:

1. There are significant trade-offs achievable between resources consumed and levels of service; for example, by varying frequency, higher service levels can be achieved at greater costs.
2. Actual volume at equilibrium is often very different from capacity volume; put another way, load factor is a variable and not a constant.
3. Different transportation systems and different ways of operating a system will capture different portions of the market, that is, different values of equilibrium volume.
4. For each system the actual volumes, resources consumed, costs, and gross and net revenues will depend on how the system is operated.
5. The best way to operate a system—for example, the best schedule frequency—will generally be different for each system.
6. The actual volume at which a system performs best will generally be different for each system.
7. There will be different combinations of pricing and operating policies for which each system performs best.
8. There are often important trade-offs between user and operator impacts.
9. Uncertainty about values of performance or demand parameters may significantly affect the choice of options because of the influence of those parameters on costs and revenues.

These observations have the following general implications for the analysis of alternative options and especially of different transportation systems:

1. A range of options should be systematically explored for each system.
2. An explicit equilibrium analysis should be done, with an explicit demand function.
3. A range of actual volumes should be considered.
4. The trade-offs between operators and users should be explicitly considered.
5. Pricing and operating options should be systematically explored in combination.
6. Systematic sensitivity studies should be done to identify effects of uncertainties in key parameters.

While these principles apply generally, in each specific situation enough may be known from prior experience to allow substantial shortcuts in the analysis (such as assuming a load factor or setting a service-level target).

The preceding sections have illustrated an analytical approach that might seem to imply a rigid structure leading invariably to the optimal policy an operator should follow. This is not our intent. We have described a style of analysis, not a rigid prescription. Many issues in a particular situation may cause an analyst to make significant simplifications. These are acceptable, provided the analyst understands the limitations thereby imposed on his results. In taking such shortcuts, however, the analyst must carefully weigh any resulting limitations on the usefulness of his analysis.

The most important aspect of the approach presented here is explicit representation of service levels together with resources consumed. Characterizing a transportation system in terms of its level-of-service and resource-consumption trade-offs is fundamental to understanding system performance.

5.8.2 Looking Ahead

Performance model I, while simple, has helped to establish the types of variables and relationships that must be included in such models and the ways in which performance models can be used in an analysis. In order to analyze service levels and resource consumption in more realistic and complex transportation systems, more detailed performance models will generally be required.

To form a basis for deciding which factors should be included explicitly, which relationships should be modeled in detail, and which can be approximated in specific situations, we must begin to delve more deeply into the various elements of a transportation system. While the core of most performance analyses is the movement of vehicles through space and time, we must also consider a number of other elements: the various transportation options are often interrelated, can have widely varying implementation time scales, and may exhibit indivisibilities; the effective speed of a vehicle is influenced by many factors such as grades and en route stops; vehicle interactions produce congestion, which often significantly affects system performance; and the services provided to different markets in a large system interact in complex ways.

The details of elements such as these significantly affect the performance of particular transportation systems in particular contexts. The actual resource and service relationships may vary greatly from one context to another. The analyst must understand each of these elements, their causes, their effects on service levels and resource consumption, and alternative ways in which they can be modeled.

Chapter 6 will examine the vehicle cycle and some important economic concepts. Chapter 7 will consider the dimensionalities of options, congestion and its effects, and the spatial and temporal structure of services. Detailed examination of these and many other elements influencing system performance will, however, be deferred to volume 2.

To understand these elements fully requires substantial additional background in a number of areas of theory and methods, including statics; kinematics; traffic flow theory; the physics and chemistry of such environmental aspects as air pollution, noise, and energy consumption; simulation, queuing theory, optimization, and other modeling methods that are applied to the analysis of performance of particular types of systems; and other areas of engineering, systems analysis, management, accounting, finance, labor relations, and so on, that bear on the understanding of system performance. These important topics are usually covered in transportation engineering or similar courses. They are not, however, in our view fundamental to understanding system performance, and so are not discussed in this volume. In volume 2, in a more detailed treatment of system performance, the relationships of these traditional areas of study to the concepts laid out in this volume will be discussed.

5.9 SUMMARY

Transportation systems are complex and include many components: vehicles, guideways, stations, control and communication systems, maintenance systems, and management organizations and systems.

The objective of this chapter has been to describe the key features that should be considered in developing an analysis of any particular system.

Many options are available for changing any given transportation system. In general, both service levels (performance) and resources consumed vary as the options are varied and as the actual volume of usage of the system varies. A model of transportation system performance must explicitly represent these relationships.

The actual volume is also a function of the service levels offered, as indicated by the demand function. Thus for any specified options the actual resources consumed and the actual service level can be found only after an equilibration of service level and volume through the demand function.

Varying operating and other options can produce a wide range of variation in resources consumed and services produced for any given transportation system. As a consequence of this range of variation, different combinations of options can have significantly different impacts on various interests. Finding the best operating regime for each technology requires systematic analysis of a range of options and equilibration with explicit demand functions.

Characterizing a transportation system in terms of its service-level and resource-consumption trade-offs is fundamental to understanding system performance.

TO READ FURTHER

The literature of technology is vast, but seminal material is sparse. New texts by Morlok (1978) and Daganzo (1978b) are useful, as is the proceedings volume edited by Florian (1978). See also Hay (1961), Haase and Holden (1964), Soberman (1966a, b, c), DeSalvo and Lave (1968), Morlok (1968), DeSalvo (1969), Bhatt (1971), Rea and Miller (1973), Simpson (1974), and Anderson (1977).

For an example of the policy consequences of the concepts presented in this chapter see UMTA (1976a) and Manheim (1977b).

For some of the practical problems in predicting service levels see, for example, Branston (1973), Johnson (1976), Terziev and Roberts (1976), Chiang and Roberts (1977), Samuelson and Lerman (1977), and Wilson, Roberts, and Kneafsey (1977).

EXERCISES

5.1(E) In exercise 1.4 we introduced the problem of deciding optimal train operating strategies. The capacity volume is $V_C = LQ$, and the general cost function is (after Martland 1977)

$$C_{\text{TRAIN}}(Q, L) = \alpha_1 D + \alpha_2 L \left(\frac{D}{v} + \frac{12}{Q} \right) + \alpha_3 DL^2,$$

$$C_T(Q, L) = QC_{\text{TRAIN}},$$

where

Q = frequency (trains per day),
L = train length (cars per train),
C_{TRAIN} = cost per train,
C_T = total daily cost,
D = round-trip distance,
v = average speed,
α_1 = crew costs per train-mile,
α_2 = car costs per hour per car,
α_3 = train length costs,
P = freight rate (price per car per one-way trip).

The first term represents labor costs for train operation, the second and third terms represent the costs per car for over-the-road travel time (D/v) and for waiting time between trains [$(1/2Q) \times 24$ hours per day], and the last term represents those aspects of operating costs that go up more than proportionately to train length.

The demand function is

$$V_D = \beta_1 \left(\frac{Q}{Q_0} \right)^{\beta_2}.$$

Consider this situation: $D = 200$ miles, $Q^0 = 2$, $L^0 = 90$, $V_D^0 = 180$, $P = \$15$, $\alpha_1 = \$2.40$, $\alpha_2 = \$0.20$, $\alpha_3 = \$2 \times 10^{-5}$, $\beta_1 = 180$, $\beta_2 = 0.5$.
a. Determine C_T, I_{GR}, I_{NR}, V_E, and λ as functions of Q and L. Consider frequencies between 2 and 8 and a reasonable range of train lengths, including those lengths, L_{OPT}, that provide just sufficient capacity to meet the demand. Display useful results in graphs and discuss (include L_{OPT}).
b. What policies would you recommend from the operator's perspective? From the user's perspective?
c. Consider the assumption $\beta_2 = 0$. Predict impacts selectively. What would you recommend, and why?
d. Explore the sensitivity of the results to alternative values of β_2 (use $\beta_2 = 0$, 0.8) and cost (use ± 10 percent on all parameters). Discuss.

e. Expand your previous results by considering a range of freight rates.

f. A search strategy that is often proposed is as follows (see, for example, Martland 1977): Assume that the operator's objective is to minimize costs. For a given Q, C_T is minimized by taking $L = L_{OPT}$, where L_{OPT} is found by setting $V_C = V_D$:

$$L_{OPT} = \frac{V_C}{Q} = \frac{V_D(Q)}{Q}.$$

When $\beta_2 = 0$, so that $V_D = \beta_1$, we can find the Q_{OPT} for minimum total cost by calculus:

$$Q_{OPT} = \sqrt{\frac{\alpha_3}{\alpha_1} V^2 + \frac{12\alpha_2}{\alpha_1 D} V}.$$

Verify this result. Then calculate Q_{OPT}, C_T, I_{GR}, and I_{NR} for a range of values. Compare with previous results, especially for parts a and c. Discuss. What are the implications of using this type of search strategy?

5.2(E)   In the example in section 5.4, the alternative technologies all provided the same level of service at a particular frequency. This happens to be true at the current state of jet aircraft technology but is unlikely to be true in general. What would be the implications if the speeds of the three aircraft were different? Sketch a revised version of Figure 5.11.

5.3(C)   While many transportation studies require much more elaborate approaches than that reflected in performance model I, there is a surprisingly large number of policy-oriented studies in which the methodology employed is not much more detailed. It is useful to examine a particular transportation analysis and reformulate it (if necessary) in terms of the methodology described here, in order to better understand both the methodology and the reported policy analysis. Some suggestions (there are many others in the literature):

1. A choice of shipping system technologies (Gilman 1977).
2. An analysis of the economic potential of specialized wool shipping services (Chudleigh 1975).
3. Comparative analyses of urban transit options (Meyer, Kain, and Wohl 1965, Bhatt 1976, Boyd, Asher, and Wetzler 1976; see also Vuchic 1976, Manheim 1977b).

5.4(P)   Select a transportation performance model for which documentation is available.

a. Identify the key elements of the model:

i. the general class of problems that the model is designed to address,

ii. the options **T**,

iii. the service variables **S**,

iv. the cost variables **C**,

v. the volumes **V**,

vi. the environmental variables **E**,

vii. other key data items (parameters) required,

viii. the inputs required to operate the model,

ix. the outputs produced by the model,

x. the general logic of the model, including key assumptions, major limitations, and how it is related to demand models and equilibration.

b. Discuss the model critically: what are its strengths and its weaknesses?

5.5(P)   Select an area of transportation system performance for potential development of a performance model. Prepare a preliminary design of a model and a User's Manual, that is, a document stating how the model is to be used. Include the following:

a. an overview of the model, clearly spelling out the key elements listed in exercise 5.4a;

b. a critical review of the relevant literature (where appropriate, specific references should be given to indicate where you have followed an approach taken by someone else or have explicitly decided to take a different approach);

c. a general flow chart of the model's logic, a flow chart showing relations to other models, a glossary of variable names and symbols, and a concise list of needed data.

You should, of course, include a clear description of options, parameters, and service, volume, resource, cost, and other impact variables.

The manual should be arranged in a usable form; it should not resemble a stream-of-consciousness "core dump." Some feeling for areas of uncertainty in model structure should be given, and you should also discuss how one might do sensitivity studies of key areas of uncertainty with the model.

5.6(C)   The discussions in this chapter have all assumed that the operator's goal is to maximize net revenue, I_{NR}. Formulate other possible operator goals and discuss how they might affect the results that have been presented. For example, consider the profit ratio I_{NR}/C_T and the return on sales I_{NR}/V_E (see Kneafsey 1974).

5.7(C)   We have limited ourselves to a single market segment in this chapter. How might the analysis be modified by explicit inclusion of two market segments (with different demand-function parameters)? How about five market segments? Five hundred?

5.8(E) Consider the following demand and cost functions:

$$C_T = aQ,$$
$$V_D = \beta_0 P^{\beta_1} Q^{\beta_2}, \qquad \beta_2 > 0, \quad \beta_1 < 0.$$

a. Assume that the operator's decision rule is to maximize net revenue. Show that, for an externally specified price (set by a regulatory agency perhaps), the operator's supply function is, for $\beta_2 < 1$,

$$Q_{\text{OPT}} = \left(\frac{a}{\beta_0 \beta_2 P^{\beta_1 + 1}} \right)^{1/(\beta_2 - 1)}$$

(Ignore possible capacity restraints, congestion effects, and the effects of network structure and travel-market equilibration.) Why must β_2 be less than one for this relationship to hold?

b. We have

$$\frac{\partial Q_{\text{OPT}}}{\partial P} = -Q_{\text{OPT}} \left(\frac{\beta_1 + 1}{P(\beta_2 - 1)} \right).$$

Under what conditions would Q_{OPT} increase and under what conditions would it decrease with increasing P? Discuss the implications for operator behavior.

c. Consider some of the factors that were ignored in part a. What effects do you think each would have on the derived relationship of Q_{OPT} to P?

d. Explore alternative decision rules for the operator and their implications for the supply function $Q_{\text{OPT}}(P)$.

5.9(E) Refer to table 5.6, used in deriving the supply function of section 5.7 on the basis of the decision rule $\mathcal{D}_1 = $ "maximize net revenue."

a. Considering only the strategies shown in that table, sketch supply functions for these alternative decision rules:

i. $\mathcal{D}_2 = $ "maximize capacity" (assume that capacity is proportional to Q, that is, $V_C = 2wQ$);

ii. $\mathcal{D}_3 = $ "maximize the ratio of net revenue to total cost";

iii. $\mathcal{D}_4 = $ "maximize capacity subject to a ratio of net revenue to total cost of at least 0.15";

iv. $\mathcal{D}_5 = $ "maximize volume served subject to a ratio of gross revenue to cost of at least 1.25."

b. Compare the results and discuss.

c. How might the results be different if:

i. congestion effects occurred?

ii. the price elasticity were inelastic?

iii. the demand function were linear or multinomial logit in (P, Q), rather than product-form?

5.10(E) The supply function in section 5.7 was generated from the relationships in exercise 5.8, with the following parameter values:

$$a = 1,000, \quad \beta_0 = 5,000, \quad \beta_1 = -1.5, \quad \beta_2 = +0.6.$$

Develop $Q_{\mathrm{OPT}}(P)$ for P in the range \$1–\$4 for these alternative sets of values of the parameters (all parameters not specifically mentioned stay at base-case values):

a. Case I, $\quad a = 1,200$;
b. Case II, $\beta_0 = 3,789, \quad \beta_1 = -1.1$;
c. Case III, $\beta_0 = 3,078, \quad \beta_1 = -0.8$;
d. Case IV, $\beta_0 = 7,155, \quad \beta_1 = -1.5, \quad \beta_2 = +0.4$;
e. Case V, $\beta_0 = 3,494, \quad \beta_1 = -1.5, \quad \beta_2 = +0.8$.

(Note that the values of β_0 are such that $V_E = 5,180$ at $Q = 6$ and $P = \$2$.) Plot, compare, and discuss.

5.11(E) The treatment of the capacity restraint in this chapter has been relatively simple. A more realistical assumption is that the availability of a seat—that is, the load factor—has an influence on demand given by $x = f(\lambda)$, where λ is the load factor of the flight (average over a particular route) and x is the percentage of available flights over this route that were fully booked and closed to sale prior to departure. How would you modify the analysis of this chapter to incorporate such a function? One air carrier reports data (Borman 1977, Appendix D) that allows estimation of the following relationship:

$$x = \begin{cases} 0, & \lambda < 0.37, \\ 186(\lambda - 0.37), & 0.37 \le \lambda \le 0.91, \\ 100, & \lambda > 0.91. \end{cases}$$

5.12(E) Various relationships can be derived to guide a systematic analysis of the options. For example:

1. for a given frequency, the fare that maximizes net revenue is the P such that $E_P(V) = -1$, if such a fare exists;

2. for a given fare, the frequency that maximizes net revenue is Q such that

$$\frac{\partial V}{\partial Q} = \frac{1}{P} \frac{\partial C_T}{\partial Q}$$

or, alternatively,

$$E_Q(V) = \frac{C_T}{PV} E_Q(C_T);$$

3. for a constant level of I_{NR}, Q and P can be varied together as

$$P = \frac{-Q}{E_Q(V)} [1 + E_P(V)] + \frac{C_T}{V} \frac{E_Q(C_T)}{E_Q(V)}$$

or

$$Q = \frac{(C_T/V)E_Q(C_T) - PE_Q(V)}{1 + E_P(V)}.$$

Although results such as these are useful, they do have important limits: they assume a single market segment and ignore the capacity constraint. (For extensions and examples see Simpson 1974, Lion and Opperman 1977.)

a. Verify these results.

b. Discuss their limitations: How can they be useful? What are the limits and corresponding issues?

c. For the case $C_T = kQ$, the above results 1–3 become:

4. $E_P(V) = -1$;

5. $\dfrac{\partial V}{\partial Q} = \dfrac{k}{P}$;

6. $P = \dfrac{Q}{E_Q(V)}\left[\dfrac{k}{V} - 1 - E_P(V)\right]$

or

$$Q = \frac{PE_Q(V)}{(k/V) - 1 - E_P(V)}.$$

Using these results, develop a plot of constant values of I_{NR} for the example in section 5.5.

5.13(E) One value of the load factor concept is that it is sometimes a useful surrogate for the relative profitability of a system, from the viewpoint of the operator. The revenues are related to the actual volume V_E, whereas the costs are more directly related to the available volume V_C. Thus operators can often establish a desired load factor as a target to achieve profitability.

The concept of the break-even load factor, λ_B, expresses this viewpoint: λ_B is the minimum load factor required for break-even operations.

The value of λ_B can be determined as follows for the example of section 5.5. For a particular price P, the gross revenue I_{GR} from users of the system will be

$$I_{GR} = PV_E.$$

The total costs will be, as previously,

$$C_T = aR = aQ\,\frac{2d}{v}.$$

For break-even operations

$$I_{GR} - C_T = 0.$$

Thus the break-even volume V_{BE} would satisfy

$$PV_{BE} = C_T,$$

and the break-even load factor would be the load factor at this equilibrium volume:

$$\lambda_{BE} = \frac{V_{BE}}{V_C}$$

$$= \frac{C_T}{PV_C}.$$

a. Show that for this case

$$\lambda_{BE} = \frac{k}{Pw},$$

where $k \equiv ad/v$.

b. Discuss the relationship between k and λ_{BE}.

c. Is λ_{BE} a constant or does it vary with Q or with other elements of the options $\mathbf{T}$?

5.14(E)   Consider an operator whose objective is to maximize net revenue. If there is no capacity constraint, then the Q for maximum I_{NR} can be found by elementary calculus, from the cost and demand functions.

Given the cost function $C_T(Q)$ and the demand function $V_D(Q)$, the point of maximum net revenue can be found by setting

$$\frac{\partial I_{NR}}{\partial Q} = 0$$

or

$$\frac{\partial I_{GR}}{\partial Q} = \frac{\partial C_T}{\partial Q},$$

provided the appropriate conditions on the second derivatives are also met:

$$\frac{\partial^2 I_{\text{NR}}}{\partial Q^2} \leq 0$$

or

$$\frac{\partial^2 I_{\text{GR}}}{\partial Q^2} \leq \frac{\partial^2 C_{\text{T}}}{\partial Q^2}.$$

Consider the case where

$$C_{\text{T}} = a_0 + a_1 Q.$$

Then

$$\frac{\partial C_{\text{T}}}{\partial Q} = a_1$$

and

$$\frac{\partial^2 C_{\text{T}}}{\partial Q^2} = 0.$$

Show that the values of Q that maximize net revenue are as follows:

a. Case I: $V = \alpha Q^\beta$:

$$Q_{\text{OPT}} = \left(\frac{a_1}{\alpha \beta P}\right)^{1/(\beta-1)}, \qquad 0 < \beta < 1.$$

b. For Case I, what happens if $\beta > 1$?

c. Case II: $V = \dfrac{\alpha_1}{\alpha_2 + (\alpha_3/Q)}$:

$$Q_{\text{OPT}} = \frac{-\alpha_3 \pm \sqrt{\alpha_1 \alpha_3 P / a_1}}{\alpha_2}.$$

d. Case III: $V = \dfrac{\alpha}{1 + \gamma e^{\beta Q}}$:

$$Q_{\text{OPT}} = \frac{\ln x}{\beta}, \qquad x = \frac{\rho - 1 \pm \sqrt{\rho(\rho - 1)}}{\gamma}, \qquad \rho = \frac{P \alpha \beta}{2 a_1}.$$

6
Understanding Performance Functions I:
The Vehicle Cycle and the Analysis of Cost Functions

6.1 INTRODUCTION

Chapter 5 introduced the basic conceptual structure we shall utilize in trying to understand the performance of transportation systems. That structure begins with the following premises.

1. We are interested in both the service provided to the user and in the resources consumed: service because this is what influences demand and thus the benefits and revenues of a system; resources consumed because these are the costs and other undesirable consequences (air quality degradation, energy consumption) of a system.

2. We are interested in how, for a particular system specification, the service levels provided and resources consumed vary with the volume using the system, especially with respect to the influence of congestion effects.

3. We are also interested in how varying the options—the system specification—can change the performance of a system as reflected in service levels and resources consumed.

To express these concepts symbolically we represent the transportation system by a performance function ϕ in which two sets of "outputs" are important: the resources consumed, R, and the service levels provided, S. Both S and R depend on the set of options T specifying the characteristics of the system, and both are influenced by the actual volumes using the system, V. Thus S and R are interrelated in ways that significantly influence decision making.

Our objective in this chapter and chapter 7 is to begin a more detailed examination of the phenomena that underlie transportation performance functions. As noted in section 5.8.2, there are many topics that might be discussed; we have chosen to explore in these two chapters those concepts that in our view are fundamental to understanding transportation system performance.

A key feature of transportation is the spatial and temporal structure of a system. This structure can affect the service-resource trade-offs in complex ways. From the perspective of the user, the key issue is the service level offered for the possible paths between a particular origin and possible destinations; different users perceive the system differently. From the perspective of the operator, the key issue is the overall performance of a system of services, in terms of revenues received and resources consumed.

A system in general consists of fleets of vehicles moving over networks of facilities. The vehicles can have complex trajectories over space and time, as suggested by figure 5.4, and the vehicles and facilities can interact in several ways, as suggested by figure 5.3. Thus the structure of a transportation system, and especially the patterns of services offered to users and of impacts on the operators, may be quite complex.

To dissect this complexity we shall begin our analysis by looking at the vehicle cycle—the performance of a vehicle over its total annual (or daily) operational pattern (section 6.2). We shall then examine some basic economic concepts that are especially useful in a systematic analysis of performance functions (sections 6.3–6.6). In sections 6.7 and 6.8 we shall apply these concepts to the analysis of vehicle cycles and see the implications in several examples.

Vehicles do not operate in isolation, however, but over networks of facilities. Vehicles affect one another and are affected by facilities and by demand in a set of phenomena we call congestion. Sections 7.2 and 7.3 will explore various types of congestion and their implications for system performance.

In chapter 1 we noted that changes in a number of types of options can be considered: technologies available, fixed facilities and network structure, vehicles, and organizational and operating strategies, including specifically the assignment of vehicles and personnel to routes, schedules, and pricing policies. The performance of a system depends on the system specification in terms of all of these options. Therefore, in any analysis of alternative specifications it is important to systematically explore all dimensions of T and to trace out impacts on different interests. Sections 7.4–7.6 will explore the implications of this dimensionality of options, especially the implications of their different time frames and indivisibilities and their interrelation with congestion.

In section 7.7 we shall return to our basic theme of system performance in space and time and, through the concept of an operating plan, suggest how all of these factors interrelate to determine system performance.

6.2 THE VEHICLE CYCLE AND ITS COMPONENTS

In most transportation systems (except those using continuous media such as pipelines or conveyors) the vehicle plays a major role. For this reason, understanding the anatomy of the vehicle's movements over time and space is very important. We shall look first at the cycle of a single vehicle; then in chapter 7 we shall explore the composite performance of a fleet of vehicles.

6.2.1 A Trucking Example

In their study of truck operators who own their own vehicles ("owner-operators") Wyckoff and Maister (1975) developed the following estimate for a truck operator's cost function (see section 6.5.2):

$$C_T = \$36,000 + 0.24\, m_T, \tag{6.1}$$

$$C_{tmL} = \frac{C_T}{\gamma w m_T}, \tag{6.2}$$

where

m_T = total mileage driven per year,
w = vehicle payload,
γ = fraction of total mileage traveled on a loaded basis,
C_T = total cost per year,
C_{tmL} = average cost per loaded ton-mile (that is, per ton-mile carried).

Taking $w = 20$ tons and $\gamma = 0.8$, we have

$$C_{tmL} = \frac{36,000}{0.8(20)m_T} + \frac{0.24}{(0.8)(20)} = 0.015 + \frac{2,250}{m_T}. \tag{6.3}$$

Consider the following situation. A particular trucker serves two cities 600 miles apart on a regular basis. With two drivers, each round trip, or complete vehicle cycle, takes about 39 hours, including rest time, travel time, and time spent waiting to get into the terminal, loading, and unloading. Of this, about 9 hours per trip (4.5 hours each way) is spent in congested conditions: about 1.5 hours each way in each city moving over congested local streets and 1.5 hours at delivery waiting to get into the overcrowded truck terminals. Thus about 30 hours are spent in over-the-road travel with an average over-the-road speed of 40 mph. (We assume that there are no legal constraints on driver hours. Such constraints exist in most countries for safety reasons but are often violated.)

This operator averages about 60 trips a year, so that $m_T = 72,000$. Thus his cost per ton-mile is $\$0.015 + \$0.0313 = \$0.0463$.

We now ask by how much the trucker would be able to reduce his cost per ton-mile carried if the following changes in the vehicle cycle occurred:

a. New loading docks are built at one terminal, reducing delay time to essentially zero in that city.

b. A new terminal is built nearer the outskirts of city A, and near intercity highways, reducing travel time over local streets to zero and waiting time to 15 minutes at most.

c. A new intercity highway is built, allowing an average over-the-road speed of 50 mph.

d. Both b and c occur.

To analyze these changes we first note that the total time the truck and drivers are in service per year is (39 hours/trip) × (60 trips/year), or 2,340 hours. We assume that this figure remains constant. Then we can calculate the cost savings from the four cases as follows:

a. If delay time were zero at the terminal, then the round-trip time would become 37.5 hours, and the number of round trips per year would increase to 2,340/37.5 = 62.4 with m_T = 74,880 miles and a corresponding cost per ton-mile of $0.015 + $0.030 = $0.045. Thus a time reduction of 3.9 percent leads to a cost reduction of about 2.7 percent.

b. If local travel time and delays were reduced by 4.25 hours by the new terminal in city A (saving 1.5 hours each way in local travel and 1.25 hours in delays), then the round-trip time would be reduced to 34.75 hours, a reduction of 10.9 percent. The resulting number of round trips would be 2,340/34.75 = 67.3 with m_T = 80,805 and an average cost of $0.015 + $0.0278 = $0.0428 per ton-mile. This is a cost reduction of 7.5 percent.

c. If the average speed increased to 50 miles per hour, then over-the-road travel time would be 1,200/50 = 24 hours and the total round-trip time would be 24 + 9 = 33 hours. This corresponds to 70.9 round trips and 85,090 miles per year, for an average cost of $0.015 + $0.0264 = $0.0414 per ton-mile. This is a cost reduction of 10.6 percent.

d. If both b and c occurred, the round-trip time would be 24 + 4.75 = 28.75 hours, corresponding to 81.4 trips and 97,670 miles per year, for an average cost of $0.015 + $0.0230 = $0.0380 per ton-mile, a reduction of 17.9 percent.

This example demonstrates the important influence of the vehicle cycle, as reflected in round-trip time and in total annual mileage. Ima Truck cycle

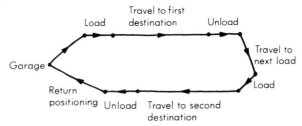

b Railcar cycle

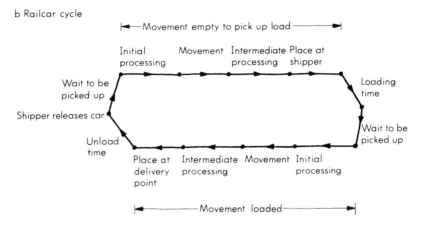

Figure 6.1 Two examples of vehicle cycles.

provements in the vehicle cycle can reduce monetary costs to the operator. Note that the user can benefit too: directly if travel or delay time is reduced or frequency is increased, and indirectly if the operator passes on a portion of his cost savings to the user by reducing prices.

6.2.2 Major Components of the Vehicle Cycle

The typical trajectory of a transport vehicle is illustrated in figure 6.1 (see also figure 5.4). The vehicle cycle has three major components: the operating cycle, the service cycle, and the annual cycle.

The *operating cycle* begins and ends at an operational base, a temporary or permanent terminal where the vehicle rests when not in service. It includes travel time while loaded and unloaded, loading and unloading time, positioning time, operational servicing time, processing time, schedule slack, and other components (these terms are defined below).

The *service cycle* begins and ends at a major maintenance base, where the vehicle is garaged and maintained. Each service cycle is composed of one or more operating cycles. For systems in which a vehicle returns to its maintenance base only after periods of months or years (for example, railcars and tramp ocean vessels), a service cycle can be quite long.

The **annual cycle** consists of the total trajectory of the vehicle over the year. It includes the service cycle plus time spent in periodic (major) maintenance plus idle time.

The relationships among these major components are illustrated in figure 6.2.

6.2.3 Key Relationships in the Operating Cycle[1]

In the operating cycle a number of segments can be identified:

Positioning time (t_P) is time spent moving from the vehicle's maintenance base to its operating base at the beginning of service and back at the end and/or time spent moving from the operating base to the first station on the route and from the last station back to the operating base. It is sometimes useful to distinguish t_{PC}, positioning time in the operating cycle, and t_{PS}, positioning time to and from the maintenance base.

Travel time while loaded (t_{TL}) is time spent actually carrying a productive (revenue-producing) load. As shown in figure 6.2, travel time is composed of acceleration/deceleration times, time at cruise speed, and delays due to congestion and other factors.

Travel time while unloaded (t_{TUL}) is time spent in motion traveling between loads (from a point at which one load is discharged to another point at which a new load will be obtained).

Load/unload time (t_{LULD}) is time spent actually loading and/or unloading passengers or cargo.

Operational servicing time (t_{OS}) is time spent while in operation for fueling, cleaning, maintenance, supply replenishment, crew rests, crew changes, and other servicing. Often some, or even all, operational servicing is accomplished while the vehicle is being loaded or unloaded, so that only a fraction of the total operational servicing time impacts on the operational cycle time.

Station stopped time (t_{STA}) is time spent in operational servicing

---

[1]The definitions and symbols presented in this and the next two subsections are intended to be generally useful in all modes and situations. In a particular situation, however, it may be useful to modify some of the definitions to fit specific operating practices and analytical needs.

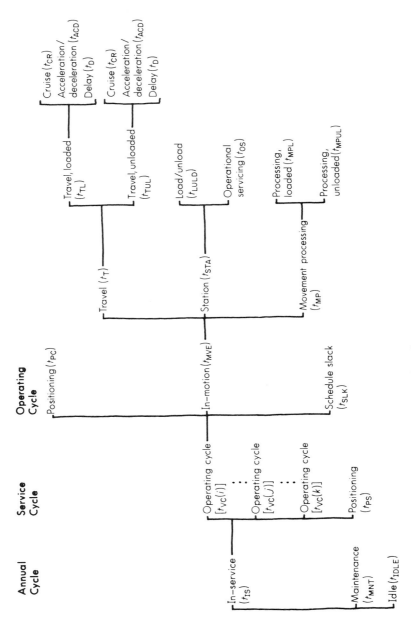

Figure 6.2 The vehicle cycle—variables and relationships.

and in loading or unloading. Station stopped time is a function of t_{OS} and t_{LULD}.

Schedule slack (t_{SLK}) is, for operations according to a schedule (timetable), the time spent idle while in operation to maintain adherence to the schedule. A slack period, or cushion, is often provided between operational cycles, or even between segments of a cycle, to accommodate random delays on one cycle without disrupting the schedule of the next cycle, and/or to provide a rest for the vehicle operator. For operations that are demand-responsive rather than prescheduled, t_{SLK} is the time spent waiting between demands at rest (that is, it does not include travel time unloaded to the point of pickup of a new load).

Movement processing time (t_{MP}) is time spent in motion between two points for processing (for example, rail cars being processed through a classification yard and shifted from one train to another).

Total vehicle operating-cycle time (t_{VC}) is the sum of all of these components:

$$t_{VC} = t_{PC} + t_{TL} + t_{TVL} + t_{SLK} + t_{STA} + t_{MP}, \tag{6.4}$$

where

$$t_{STA} = f(t_{OS}, t_{LULD}). \tag{6.5}$$

If operational servicing is done simultaneously with loading and unloading, then the station stopped time is the maximum of t_{OS} and t_{LULD}; if it is done sequentially, the station stopped time is the sum of the two. Thus

$$\max(t_{OS}, t_{LULD}) \leq t_{STA} \leq t_{OS} + t_{LULD}. \tag{6.6}$$

Other useful characterizations of the vehicle cycle are total travel time (the time the vehicle is moving whether loaded or unloaded), t_T, and total time in motion (the time spent either moving or stopped temporarily at a station for loading, unloading, or operational servicing), t_{MVE}. By definition,

$$t_T = t_{TL} + t_{TUL}, \tag{6.7}$$

$$t_{MVE} = t_T + t_{STA} + t_{MP} = t_{TL} + t_{TUL} + t_{STA} + t_{MP}. \tag{6.8}$$

Thus

$$t_{VC} = t_{MVE} + t_{PC} + t_{SLK}. \tag{6.9}$$

These definitions and relationships are summarized in figure 6.2. It is, of course, possible to refine these definitions further for use in specific analyses. For example, in many traditional transportation engineering analyses, extensive studies are made of travel times, decomposing t_{TUL} and t_{TL} into components such as time spent at vehicle cruise speed, t_{CR}, time spent accelerating or decelerating, t_{ACD}, and delays due to congestion and other factors, t_{D}.

6.2.4 The Service Cycle

In an extended period of time between returns to a major maintenance base a vehicle accomplishes a number n_{C} of operating cycles. The total time spent in these operational cycles, together with the positioning time to and from the maintenance base, is the *in-service time*, t_{IS}:

$$t_{\mathrm{IS}} = t_{\mathrm{PS}} + \sum_{i=1}^{n_c} t_{\mathrm{VC}}(i). \tag{6.10}$$

If t_{V} is the average total vehicle operating-cycle time, so that

$$t_{\mathrm{V}} = \frac{1}{n_{\mathrm{C}}} \sum_{i=1}^{n_c} t_{\mathrm{VC}}(i), \tag{6.11}$$

then

$$t_{\mathrm{IS}} = t_{\mathrm{PS}} + n_{\mathrm{C}} t_{\mathrm{V}}. \tag{6.12}$$

6.2.5 The Annual Cycle

In addition to in-service time, over the course of a year a vehicle typically requires a certain amount of *maintenance time*, t_{MNT}: this consists of scheduled maintenance, which may be required every x hours or y miles to maintain the vehicle in an operational state, and unscheduled major maintenance, such as occurs when the breakdown of a component requires the vehicle to be pulled out of service for a period of days or longer. The rest of the year is made up of *idle time*, t_{IDLE} (though it should be emphasized that there are often substantial periods of time at rest during the in-service time, such as t_{SLK} or t_{STA}).

The basic relationship is, by definition (if times are measured in days),

$$t_{\mathrm{IS}} + t_{\mathrm{MNT}} + t_{\mathrm{IDLE}} = 365. \tag{6.13}$$

Usually t_{MNT} is fixed by the vehicle design and especially by maintenance policy (sometimes it is not a constant but a function of the number of cycles or related variables such as vehicle-hours or vehicle-miles). From an operator's perspective, t_{IS} is established by the assignment of routes and schedules—the operating plan (see chapter 7)—and thus the corresponding cycle times, $t_{VC}(i)$, leading to n_C and t_V and thus t_{IS}. The idle time is then the residual. In general, the operator, in trying to maximize net revenue or pursuing other economic objectives, will also try to minimize t_{IDLE}, but it is important to note that the minimum t_{IDLE} may in fact produce lower net revenue than the optimum value.

6.2.6 Examples of Vehicle Cycles

A BUS CYCLE

For urban buses in public mass transit service, the maintenance base is usually the garage to which the vehicle returns at night (or sometimes more frequently). The operating base is the terminus where the bus rests between scheduled runs and may simply be a street corner. A typical vehicle cycle might have the following components.

Positioning time: 10 minutes in the morning plus 10 minutes in the evening traveling from garage to starting point of route and return; so t_{PS} = 20 minutes for the daily service cycle. (We assume that the bus begins and ends each run at the same point on the route and does not change routes, so t_{PC} = 0; positioning occurs only at the beginning and end of the day.)

Operating cycles: The route is such that the bus makes one round trip per hour. Since there are 16 operating hours (4 peak hours and 12 off-peak hours) in a day, n_C = 16.

Travel time: Each one-way trip takes 25 minutes in peak periods and 20 minutes in off-peak periods. Each one-way trip makes an average of 18 stops, at an average stopped time of 30 seconds for loading and unloading, so t_{STA} is 18 × 0.5 × 2 = 18 minutes per operating cycle, or 16 × 18 = 288 minutes per day. The travel time t_T is 50 − 18 = 32 minutes per round trip for peak hours and 40 − 18 = 22 minutes for off-peak hours, or a total of (4 × 32) + (12 × 22) = 392 minutes per day, all (in general) loaded time (in revenue service, although the vehicle may be partially full or even empty at times).

Operational servicing, processing: There is no requirement for operational servicing or movement processing.

Schedule slack: For user convenience the trips are scheduled to depart from either terminus every half hour. Thus the time allowed for a one-way trip is 30 minutes, versus run times of 20 or 25 minutes, and schedule slack is 10 minutes per round trip in peak hours and 20 minutes in off-peak hours, for a total of $(4 \times 10) + (12 \times 20) = 280$ minutes per day. Note that on the last return trip 10 minutes slack is avoided because the vehicle can proceed directly from the last stop to the garage, so the total is $280 - 10 = 270$.

Total service cycle: The total time the vehicle is in operational service consists of the initial positioning time (10 minutes) plus the 16 hours in the operating cycles (travel, loading, unloading, slack) less the last 10 minutes of schedule slack at the end of the day plus the return positioning time (10 minutes), or 16 hours 10 minutes. (Note that several drivers may be assigned to the vehicle over the day.)

The per-cycle averages of these components are

$t_{TL} = 392/16 = 24.5$ min/cycle,
$t_{STA} = 288/16 = 18.0$ min/cycle,
$t_{SLK} = 270/16 = 16.9$ min/cycle,
$t_P = 20/16 = 1.25$ min/cycle,
$t_V = 970/16 = 60.6$ min/cycle,
$t_T = t_{TL} = 24.5$ min/cycle,
$t_{MVE} = t_T + t_{STA} = 24.5 + 18.0 = 42.5$ min/cycle.

Thus

$t_T/t_V = 24.5/60.6 = 40$ percent,
$t_{MVE}/t_V = 42.5/60.6 = 70$ percent,
$t_{IS} = n_c t_V = 970$ min $= 16$ hr 10 min.

In this situation the vehicle is traveling only 40 percent of the time it is in service and is in motion only 70 percent of the time. Conversely 30 percent of the in-service time is spent in schedule slack or in positioning.

THE RAILCAR CYCLE

The movements of rail freight cars in typical services are quite illuminating (see figure 6.3, which was adapted from a study of freight car movements in the United States). The stages in an average car movement are given in table 6.1. Analysis of these figures yields the following values for the various time components of the cycle:

$t_{VC} = 25.5$ days,
$t_{TL} = 2$ days,
$t_{TUL} = 2$ days,
$t_T = 4$ days,
t_{MPL} (total time spent in processing while loaded) $= 6$ days,
t_{MPUL} (total time spent in processing while unloaded) $= 8.5$ days,

Figure 6.3 Anatomy of the railcar cycle (thick rules indicate times of shipper control). Adapted from Reebie Associates (1972).

$t_{MP} = t_{MPL} + t_{MPUL} = 14.5$ days,

t_{SH} (total time spent under shipper control while being loaded or unloaded) $= 6$ days   [line 7 plus line 13],

t_{RR} (total time spent under railroad control while being loaded or unloaded) $= 1$ day   [line 8 plus line 2],

$t_{LULD} = t_{SH} + t_{RR} = 7$ days,

$t_{VC} = t_T + t_{MP} + t_{LULD} = 25.5$ days.

Thus the fraction of time actually spent traveling is

$$\frac{t_T}{t_{VC}} = \frac{t_{TL} + t_{UL}}{t_{VC}} = \frac{4}{25.5} = 15.7 \text{ percent;}$$

the fraction of time spent loaded is

$$\frac{t_{TL} + t_{MPL}}{t_{VC}} = \frac{14.5}{25} = 56.9 \text{ percent;}$$

the time spent in processing (being switched from one train to another, waiting for the next train) is

Table 6.1 Stages in a railcar cycle (days)

	Elapsed time	Cumulative elapsed time	Component
Empty time			
1. An empty car becomes available to be assigned to pick up a new load (car is released).	0	0	—
2. Empty car waits at point of release to be picked up (pulled) for movement to the terminal.	0.5	0.5	t_{LULD}
3. Empty car is processed at initial terminal (includes switching into outbound train, waiting time).	2	2.5	t_{MPUL}
4. Empty car moves over system to pickup point.	2	4.5	t_{TUL}
5. Empty car is processed at intermediate terminals (switching from one train to another, waiting time).	4.5	9	t_{MPUL}
6. Empty car is processed at final terminal and delivered to point of pickup of load (car is "placed").	2	11	t_{MPUL}
Loaded time			
7. Empty car is loaded and released by the shipper for movement by the railroad.	3	14	t_{LULD}
8. Loaded car waits after release to be picked up for movement.	0.5	14.5	t_{LULD}
9. Loaded car is moved to and processed through initial terminal.	1	15.5	t_{MPL}
10. Loaded car moves to load delivery point.	2	17.5	t_{TL}
11. Loaded car is processed at intermediate terminals.	4	21.5	t_{MPL}
12. Loaded car is processed at final terminal and delivered to point of destination of load.	1	22.5	t_{MPL}
13. Loaded car is placed at delivery point, unloaded, and released by the recipient for pickup.	3	25.5	t_{LULD}

$$\frac{t_{MP}}{t_{VC}} = \frac{10.5}{25.5} = 41.2 \text{ percent};$$

and the fraction of time spent under shipper control being loaded or unloaded is

$$\frac{t_{SH}}{t_{VC}} = \frac{6}{25.5} = 23.5 \text{ percent.}$$

From this we can see the basis for the frequently encountered statement that the average American railcar moves about 70 miles per day: even if the average train speed overall is about 19 mph, since a car is in traveling status only 15.7 percent of the time, its effective speed is $24 \times 0.157 \times 19 = 71.6$ miles per day.

As we shall see shortly, the low fraction of time a vehicle spends in actual productive travel has significant economic implications. In the case of railcars, the U.S. railroads have undertaken a major research program aimed at developing a better understanding of car movement cycles and of how rail economics can be improved by increasing the amount of productive travel time relative to unproductive time. One key target is to reduce the time spent in loading or unloading under shipper control, which as we have seen is 23.5 percent of the vehicle cycle time. We shall return to this example in section 6.7.

6.2.7 Opportunities to Affect the Vehicle Cycle

The following sections will demonstrate the economic importance of the vehicle cycle. There are a wide variety of points of leverage on the vehicle cycle and thus on the economics of system performance:

1. Travel time (t_T) can be affected by changes in the vehicle, enabling higher cruise speeds (lower t_{CR}) and more rapid acceleration or deceleration (lower t_{ACD}), changes in the guideway, enabling higher speeds or shorter distances, or strategies to reduce congestion delays (t_D), such as control system improvements.

2. The travel time while unloaded (t_{TUL}) reflects the need to move from a point of unloading one load to the point of pickup of another load (the backhaul problem). Improvements in t_{TUL} can be achieved through marketing strategies designed to increase demand in nonpeak directions and nonpeak periods and through vehicle-fleet management strategies designed to match the distribution of empty vehicles more closely (in time and space) to the distribution of demands.

3. In modes such as rail, the time required for processing while in motion (t_{MP}) can be quite significant. A wide variety of operational

strategies can be utilized to reduce t_{MP}, such as running more trains over longer distances to provide more direct services, increasing the frequency of service, improving schedule coordination, and improving travel-time reliability.

4. The time required for operational servicing (t_{OS}) can be reduced by more efficient servicing procedures or by changes in vehicle design to reduce operational servicing requirements or to allow more efficient procedures.

5. The time required for loading and unloading (t_{LULD}) can be affected by vehicle design, by terminal design, and by operational procedures. This has been a major aspect of the containerization revolution in marine transportation and is also important in aircraft operations.

6. Since station stopped time (t_{STA}) is a function of both t_{OS} and t_{LULD}, it can be affected by improvements in those components and especially by approaches that allow maximum overlap between them; it can also be affected by changing the number of stops, as by changing from local to express services.

7. For scheduled modes slack time (t_{SLK}) is set by policy but is based in part on expectations of the degree of variability in other elements of cycle time. Thus improvements in time reliability for any vehicle cycle components can lead to decreases in t_{SLK}. For demand-responsive modes t_{SLK} is the time spent waiting between demands; it reflects the variability of cycle time components in that the ability to assign vehicles to new loads is influenced, in part, by the degree of uncertainty in the time when loaded vehicles will be unloaded and available for a new load.

8. The positioning time (t_P) can be affected by the location of vehicle (maintenance) bases, the design of routes, and especially the positioning of starting and terminating points.

Obviously all components of the vehicle cycle are affected in major ways by the design of routes, by scheduling decisions, and by vehicle assignments to operating bases and to routes and schedules. Clearly, too, changes in system strategies that affect the vehicle cycle will potentially impact both users and operators. Thus, in looking at the economics of the vehicle cycle, we must consider both costs and revenues to the operator as well as effects on users. First, however, we need to review some basic concepts of systematic analysis relevant to an economic analysis.

6.3 SOME BASIC CONCEPTS IN SYSTEMATIC ANALYSIS

6.3.1 Average and Marginal Products[2]

In the analysis of change in a function $y = f(x)$, several concepts are of interest, namely the **average product of** y **with respect to** x,

$$\bar{y}_x \equiv \frac{y}{x} = \frac{f(x)}{x}, \tag{6.14}$$

and the **marginal product of** y **with respect to** x,

$$y'_x \equiv \frac{\partial y}{\partial x} = \frac{\partial f(x)}{\partial x}. \tag{6.15}$$

Average and marginal products are particularly useful for analysis of various dimensions of resource consumption, and especially for resources that can be evaluated as monetary costs incurred by the operator. (Recall that there are many different types of resources consumed in producing transportation. Some of these lend themselves to ready evaluation in monetary terms, such as the direct costs borne by the operator; others cannot be so evaluated without the application of value judgments.)

As the options **T** are varied, capacity volume V_C will vary along with the amount of resources consumed. Consider air quality degradation, as measured by the number of milligrams of hydrocarbons emitted, r:

$$\bar{r}_{V_C} \equiv \frac{r}{V_C} \tag{6.16}$$

is the average hydrocarbon emission per unit of capacity;

$$r'_{V_C} \equiv \frac{\partial r}{\partial V_C} \tag{6.17}$$

is the marginal increase in hydrocarbon emissions for each additional unit of capacity.

A particularly useful application of average and marginal products is to the total cost incurred by the operator, C_T:

$$\bar{C}_{V_C} \equiv \frac{C_T(V_C)}{V_C} \tag{6.18}$$

is the average cost per unit of capacity;

$$C'_{V_C} \equiv \frac{\partial C_T(V_C)}{\partial V_C} \tag{6.19}$$

[2]See Henderson and Quandt (1958), section 3-1. Our terminology derives from, but differs from, the concepts of microeconomics.

is the marginal increase in cost for each additional unit of capacity.
For the simple cost function assumed in section 5.4,

$$C_T = \frac{a}{n} Q, \qquad V_C = 2wQ. \tag{6.20}$$

Thus

$$\bar{C}_{V_C} = \frac{C_T}{V_C} = \frac{a}{2wn}, \tag{6.21}$$

$$C'_{V_C} = \frac{\partial C_T}{\partial V_C} = \frac{a}{2wn}. \tag{6.22}$$

In this simple case the average and marginal total operator costs, defined with respect to capacity volume, are equal and constant, independent of V_C. Note, however, that the average and marginal costs with respect to equilibrium volume V_E would not necessarily be equal or constant. For example (assuming that capacity never constrains V_E), with a demand function

$$V_D = \alpha_0 Q^{\alpha_1}, \qquad \alpha_1 > 0, \tag{6.23}$$

and

$$V_E = V_D, \tag{6.24}$$

so that

$$Q = \left(\frac{V_E}{\alpha_0} \right)^{1/\alpha_1}, \tag{6.25}$$

(6.20) becomes

$$C_T = \frac{a}{n} \left(\frac{V_E}{\alpha_0} \right)^{1/\alpha_1}. \tag{6.26}$$

Then

$$\bar{C}_{V_E} \equiv \frac{C_T}{V_E} = \frac{a}{\alpha_0 n} \left(\frac{V_E}{\alpha_0} \right)^{(1/\alpha_1)-1}$$

$$= \left(\frac{a}{\alpha_0 n} \right) Q^{1-\alpha_1}, \tag{6.27}$$

$$C'_{V_E} \equiv \frac{\partial C_T}{\partial V_E}$$

$$= \frac{a}{\alpha_1 n \alpha_0} \left(\frac{V_E}{\alpha_0} \right)^{(1/\alpha_1)-1} = \frac{a}{\alpha_1 n \alpha_0} Q^{1-\alpha_1}$$

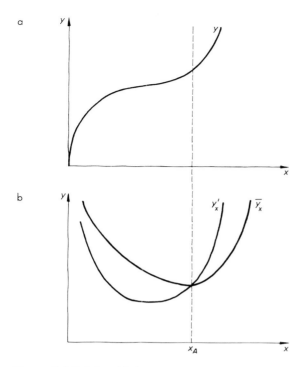

Figure 6.4 Relationship between average and marginal products.

$$= \frac{1}{\alpha_1} \bar{C}_{V_E}.$$
(6.28)

In this case the average and marginal costs with respect to equilibrium volume are unequal and vary with volume and with frequency.

More generally we can define average and marginal products in terms of any of the impacts of interest. In particular, from the perspective of the user, we might examine average or marginal levels of service. From the perspective of the operator, average and marginal net revenues are useful, as well as many other constructs. Historically, particular attention has been paid to average and marginal monetary costs, but these are not by any means the only impacts of interest.

Figure 6.4 illustrates a common functional relationship for $y = f(x)$ and the corresponding relationships of $\bar{y}_x$ and y'_x. The point $x = x_A$ has particular importance (if it exists in a particular case): it is the point at which $\bar{y}_x = y'_x$. In this case, for values of $x > x_A$, $y'_x > \bar{y}_x$: the marginal product of y is greater than the average product. For example, if y is total cost, for $x > x_A$ each additional unit of x increases the total cost at a rate greater than the average total cost of each unit (see section 7.2).

6.3.2 Choice of the Output Dimension: Cost Functions

It is important to understand the relationship between the foregoing concepts and those developed in chapter 5. There we traced out impacts as a function of options; for example, all of the graphical illustrations dealt with schedule frequency Q as the independent variable, representing the options **T**, and showed the variations of volumes, costs, revenues, and so on, as functions of Q.

There are various ways in which the results of a systematic analysis can be displayed. Traditionally transportation analysts have dealt with costs and revenues as functions of "output," using the concepts of average and marginal products.

In the notation of section 5.4, some possible output measures are:

1. scheduled frequency of vehicle trips, Q,
2. available capacity, $V_C = 2Qw$, where w is a payload,
3. "revenue" volume, V_E,
4. available ton-miles per round trip, $V_C D = 2Qwd$, where $D = 2d$ is the round-trip distance,
5. revenue ton-miles per round trip, $V_E D$.

Structurally the analyses would be the same regardless of the output dimension chosen. Following the pattern of the analyses in chapter 5, we vary the options **T** over a range. For each value of **T**, the value of the impact of interest (for example, total cost, net revenue, or volume of air pollutants) and the value of the chosen output dimension (for example, V_C or V_E) are determined. Then the results can be displayed in tabular or graphic form and analyzed.

A particularly common analysis is that of the ***cost function***, in which total cost C_T is expressed as a function of capacity volume V_C. In the next section we shall explore such cost functions and see some of the policy implications that can be developed from their analysis. Here we should note that the choice of output unit can have a significant effect on the outcome of an analysis. For example, while V_C has been a traditional basis of cost function analysis, V_E is often a more appropriate measure because it reflects the actual usage of the system: "average cost per actual user" has more significance than "average cost per seat available." Using V_E does, however, require either explicit equilibration with a demand function or a judgment about the load factor and how it varies with **T**.

It is important to recognize that different choices of measures may lead to different displays and possibly to different conclusions. The analysis in chapter 5 showed that different technologies may have different optimal schedule frequencies. For each technology there will thus be a different equilibrium volume at which that technology performs best, in the sense of maximizing I_{NR} or any other objective. This is demonstrated in exercise 6.1.

There has been substantial debate about which of the various possible output measures is the best measure to use (G. Wilson 1959). From our perspective, each measure has advantages and disadvantages. The analyst should use several measures, choosing the ones that appear to be most useful in a particular context.

6.4 ANALYSIS OF COST FUNCTIONS

While variations in all dimensions of resource consumption are important, special attention is often focused on how costs, and specifically the total monetary cost incurred by the operator, vary as options are varied. The following discussion, while formulated in terms of monetary costs and volumes, could be generalized to include any element of **S**, **R**, or **V**.

In general, the total cost will be a function of the volume, and we shall use V_E for this discussion. Figure 6.5 shows the variety of forms this functional relationship may take. Consider the alternatives A, B, and E. All three express the hypothesis that a large initial cost is re-

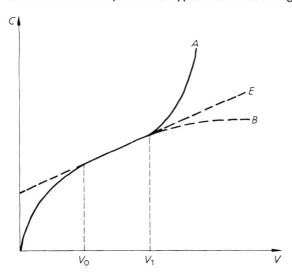

Figure 6.5 General cost function. Adapted from Meyer et al. (1960).

quired to serve any volume at all and that, over a range of moderate volumes V_0–V_1, the cost of serving an additional unit of volume is relatively constant. Curve B assumes that, after a certain point V_1, the system becomes particularly efficient, so that each additional unit of traffic served costs less and less (economies of scale). Curve A assumes that the cost of serving additional units begins to increase rapidly (diseconomies of scale). Curve E assumes that the incremental cost remains constant.

Let us assume that we have the total cost as a function of volume for a particular transportation system: $C_T = f(V)$. Two additional quantities of interest are the average total cost, $\bar{C}_V = C_T/V$, and the marginal cost, $C'_V = \partial C_T/\partial V$. The average total cost is precisely that: the share of the total cost per unit of volume, assuming that all units of volume bear the total cost equally. The marginal cost, on the other hand, reflects the incremental total cost incurred when a single unit of volume is added to the system.

To explore the implications of these concepts we shall look at some general forms of the total cost function and study their properties.

6.4.1 A Linear Cost Function
One simple form is the linear cost function:

$$C_T = a + bV = C_{FC} + C_{VC}. \qquad (6.29)$$

Here an initial cost a must be incurred before the system can begin operation, and the addition of a single unit of volume increases the cost by b. The portion $C_{FC} = a$ is often termed the **fixed cost** because it is independent of volume. The portion $C_{VC} = bV$ is similarly termed the **variable cost**. This cost function has the following properties:

1. average total cost: $\qquad \bar{C}_V = \dfrac{C}{V} = \dfrac{a}{V} + b,$

2. average fixed cost: $\qquad \bar{C}_{FC/V} = \dfrac{C_{FC}}{V} = \dfrac{a}{V},$

3. average variable cost: $\qquad \bar{C}_{VC/V} = \dfrac{C_{VC}}{V} = b$

4. marginal total cost: $\qquad C'_V = \dfrac{\partial C_T}{\partial V} = b,$

5. marginal fixed cost: $\qquad C'_{FC/V} = \dfrac{\partial C_{FC}}{\partial V} = 0,$

6. marginal variable cost: $\qquad C'_{VC/V} = \dfrac{\partial C_{VC}}{\partial V} = b.$

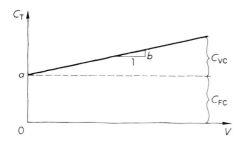

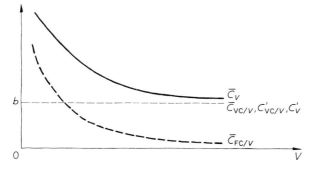

Figure 6.6 Characteristics of a linear cost function.

These properties are illustrated in figure 6.6.

6.4.2 Example: A Penetration Road

In underdeveloped countries a major transportation problem is to provide access to previously inaccessible areas. Often the traffic volumes to be expected are very low—perhaps only a few thousand vehicles per year. In this context there is a range of choices of transport technologies; each technology consists of the specification of the roadway to be provided and the vehicle type(s) to be operated over that roadway.

We consider three alternative technologies (Guenther 1968):

A: off-road tracked vehicles, operating on a "burro-path" or other cross-country track,
B: vehicles with four-wheel drive, operating on a packed-earth roadway,
C: heavy-duty two-axle vehicles, operating on an all-weather gravel road.

The cost functions are shown in figure 6.7. They reflect the following

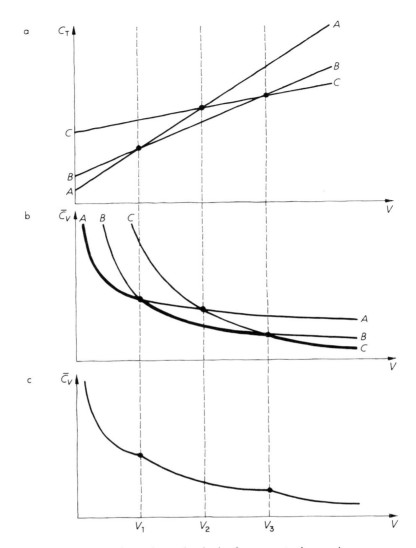

Figure 6.7 Three alternative technologies for a penetration road.

relationships among the alternatives, going in order *A*, *B*, *C*, and for a specified volume level:

1. the initial construction cost of the roadway increases and the roadway maintenance cost decreases,
2. the vehicle procurement and operating costs decrease,
3. speeds increase, trip time decreases, and thus fewer vehicles are required to transport a given volume per time period.

Thus

$$\bar{C}^A_{FC/V} < \bar{C}^B_{FC/V} < \bar{C}^C_{FC/V}$$

and

$$\bar{C}^A_{VC/V} > \bar{C}^B_{VC/V} > \bar{C}^C_{VC/V}.$$

These curves illustrate how the cost advantages of different systems change as the volume varies. For low volumes, between 0 and V_1, system *A* has the lowest total cost and average total cost, because it requires no investment in roadway construction and the lowest level of roadway maintenance. That is, average fixed cost is low. Because the average variable cost for *A* is high, however, for volumes between V_1 and V_3 system *B* has the lowest cost. Above volume V_3 system *C* has the lowest cost; the heavier investment in the roadway (high average fixed cost) is spread over a large volume and is also offset by the lower vehicle costs (low average variable cost).

If total cost or average total cost were the only relevant criterion (for example, if differences in levels of service were negligible, which is unlikely, or if demand were insensitive to service levels over this range), then the cost functions alone could be used as a basis for decision. Otherwise, the more general equilibrium analysis of chapter 5 would be required (see section 6.6).

All of these alternatives are highway alternatives; taken as a family, they could be characterized by the single cost function in part c of the figure, which is the same as the dark boundary line in part b of the figure.

This same curve is shown as *AA'* in figure 6.8; it has been extended to higher volume ranges, with the successive peaks representing additional lanes of highway constructed. Curve *RR'* represents an alternative technology, namely railroad.

The two modal choices are abstracted in part b of the figure, where the relatively minor perturbations of the alternative choices within the spectrum of roadway–vehicle options have been smoothed out. For

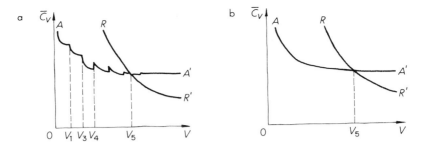

Figure 6.8 Two alternative modes.

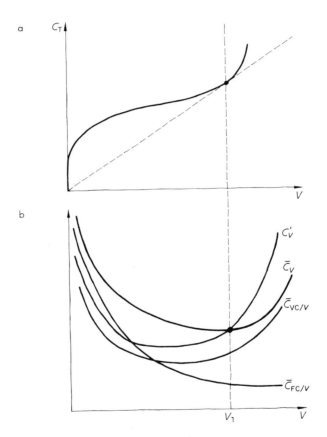

Figure 6.9 A composite cost function.

some purposes, where it is necessary only to understand the major differences between modes, it may be sufficient to determine only the broad trend of the cost function, as in part b. In other instances the choices within modes may become important, in which case the component curves must be determined as in figure 6.7. Occasionally it may be important to reach even more deeply into the detailed options of vehicles, link characteristics, and operating decisions and so to have even more detailed curves within the envelope of a single curve of figure 6.7—for example, different combinations of vehicle size, highway pavement width, and pavement thickness (see Soberman 1966a, Walters 1968, Niebur 1975).

6.4.3 Nonlinear Cost Functions

Many, if not most, transportation systems exhibit cost behavior more complex than that implied by the simple linear cost function. In particular, many systems have the property of diseconomies of scale, as illustrated by curve A in figure 6.5. The general case is illustrated in figure 6.9. This function has the following properties. The average fixed cost decreases as volume increases, since the cost is spread over more units. However, the average variable cost decreases initially, is almost constant over a middle range, and then increases over high volumes.

The phenomenon of increasing average variable cost is called the law of diminishing marginal productivity. The hypothesis underlying this law is that, as higher levels of volume are accommodated, the production process becomes inefficient in its use of resources, so that increasing proportions of some resources are required and/or the cost of the resources increase. For example, in building urban highways, going beyond six lanes of width often requires separated roadways, more median barriers, and more complex interchanges, which may result in diseconomies of scale under some conditions. In transportation one particularly important source of diminishing marginal productivity is the set of phenomena we call congestion (see chapter 7).

As an example of a nonlinear cost function figure 6.10 shows a set of cost functions for pipelines.

6.4.4 Implications: Variations in Transportation Performance Functions

The cost functions of most types of transportation systems have both fixed and variable components, and the variable components usually exhibit a range of diseconomies of scale. However, the relative influences of the fixed and variable components vary significantly among

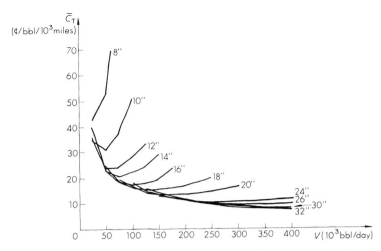

Figure 6.10 An example of cost functions for pipelines of various diameters. bbl = barrel. From Cookenboo (1955).

transportation systems, and such differences can be a major factor in the choice among systems (Heflebower 1965).

As a rough generalization, at one extreme are systems such as water or air transport and bus transit. Although there are significant investments in fixed facilities in each of these modes—port facilities, airports and maintenance facilities, and highways—the institutional structure is usually such that the transport operator—air carrier, ship owner, transit operator—pays for the infrastructure only indirectly. Some of the mechanisms used are port or airport landing fees, facilities rentals, and fuel taxes. Thus from the operator's perspective the fixed costs are basically those of owning or leasing vehicles, and variable costs therefore play a key role in the operator's cost function.

At the other extreme are systems such as railroads. Here major infrastructure investments are borne directly by the operator, and so the fixed-cost component tends to be a high proportion of the average cost.

Again we stress that these are generalizations and that the specifics of particular situations can vary greatly and need to be investigated individually in detail.

6.5 USING COST FUNCTIONS FOR POLICY ANALYSIS

The analysis of cost functions can often lead to useful insights. As an example we shall examine a particular segment of the U.S. trucking industry.

6.5.1 The Nonuniformity of Demand by Direction: Backhaul and Positioning

In almost every situation, in any time period, there are unequal flows in the two opposite directions on the same route. Freight flows are almost always unbalanced: raw materials move in one direction, finished goods in the opposite direction. For passenger movements the flows usually balance over a long enough period of time, such as a day or week (except for the rare situation of migratory movements), but over short periods of time the movements in two directions are unbalanced. For example, in peak periods in most urban areas there is a dominant movement toward the city's central area in the morning and in the reverse direction in the evening.

These directional imbalances in demand lead to the **backhaul problem**—unequal load factors in the two directions, yielding an overall load factor lower than that in the direction of maximum flow.

Closely related to the backhaul problem is that of **positioning**. When a load is dropped at *A*, the empty vehicle may have to move to *B* to pick up its next load. Thus a vehicle must spend time in empty movement. This was illustrated in general terms in section 6.2.

The economics of the backhaul situation can be quite complex. In response to this market condition operators may vary pricing options or even route structures in order to reduce the disparity in demand directions. An analysis of cost functions can show the impact of these imbalances.

6.5.2 Backhaul: A Trucking Example

Wyckoff and Maister (1975) analyzed the cost structure of a particular class of truckers: owner-operators operating on a lease basis, subcontracting to a larger carrier. They established high, medium, and low estimates of cost based on interviews and other data sources. These estimates show costs to be a roughly linear function of total vehicle mileage per year. Thus the cost equation is approximately

$$C_T = \alpha_0 + \alpha_1 m_T, \tag{6.30}$$

where m_T is the total number of vehicle-miles driven per year and α_0 and α_1 are parameters.

From this cost equation can be derived the average cost per mile $c_m \equiv \bar{C}_{T/m}$ and, for an average payload of w tons, the average cost per ton-mile $c_{tm} \equiv \bar{C}_{T/mw}$:

$$c_m = \frac{C_T}{m_T} = \frac{\alpha_0}{m_T} + \alpha_1, \tag{6.31}$$

$$c_{tm} = \frac{C_T}{m_T w} = \frac{1}{w}\left(\frac{\alpha_0}{m_T} + \alpha_1\right). \tag{6.32}$$

Some of the mileage traveled each year is empty mileage. This is referred to as *empty backhaul*—the mileage traveled without a load in the return or backhaul direction. This can also be thought of as positioning mileage: after dropping off one load, an operator may drive several hundred miles to pick up a load that he can carry back to his origin. Thus

$$m_T = m_L + m_E, \tag{6.33}$$

where m_L and m_E are the numbers of miles driven while loaded and empty, respectively.

The ratio of loaded to total mileage is

$$\gamma \equiv \frac{m_L}{m_L + m_E} = \frac{m_L}{m_T}. \tag{6.34}$$

Thus the cost per loaded mile c_{mL} and the cost per ton-mile loaded c_{tmL} are determined by correcting (6.31) and (6.32) by γ (note that empty miles are actually somewhat cheaper to operate than loaded miles, but this difference is small and will be ignored in this discussion):

$$c_{mL} = \frac{C_T}{m_L} = \frac{C_T}{\gamma m_T}, \tag{6.35}$$

$$c_{tmL} = \frac{C_T}{\gamma m_T w}. \tag{6.36}$$

Sometimes an alternative parameter is used: the ratio of empty backhaul to loaded miles,

$$\beta \equiv \frac{m_E}{m_L}. \tag{6.37}$$

Thus

$$m_L = m_T\left(\frac{1}{1 + \beta}\right). \tag{6.38}$$

Both β and γ can be expressed as fractions or as percentages and can range from 0 to 1 (0 to 100 percent). (Wyckoff and Maister use β as an empty backhaul percentage. Sometimes a third parameter is used: the empty backhaul ratio ρ defined as the percentage of the backhaul miles that are empty. If the backhaul miles are assumed to be half the total miles, then $\rho \equiv 2m_E/m_T$.)

The two parameters are related as follows:

$$\gamma = \frac{1}{1 + \beta},$$ (6.39)

$$\beta = \frac{1}{\gamma} - 1.$$ (6.40)

Thus (6.35) and (6.36) can also be expressed in terms of β:

$$c_{\mathrm{mL}} = \frac{C_{\mathrm{T}}}{m_{\mathrm{L}}} = \frac{C_{\mathrm{T}}}{m_{\mathrm{T}}} (1 + \beta),$$ (6.41)

$$c_{\mathrm{tmL}} = \frac{C_{\mathrm{T}}}{m_{\mathrm{L}} w} = \frac{C_{\mathrm{T}}}{m_{\mathrm{T}} w} (1 + \beta).$$ (6.42)

Combining (6.42) and (6.30) yields

$$c_{\mathrm{tmL}} = \frac{1}{w} \left(\frac{\alpha_0}{m_{\mathrm{T}}} + \alpha_1 \right) (1 + \beta).$$ (6.43)

Values of c_{tmL} are shown in table 6.2 for a range of values of β and for three sets of parameter values. The results are displayed in figures 6.11 and 6.12, with the average payload w taken as 20 tons.

These results show that owner-operator costs are sensitive to assumptions about m_{T} and β as well as to alternative cost assumptions. While precise data are not available about any of these elements, the numerical results, together with informed judgments, do provide a basis for important policy conclusions.

For example, in figure 6.12 the lines RR-1 and RR-2 correspond, respectively, to the estimated average rail rate for grain, coal, and canned goods and to the estimated average rail rate for iron and steel. An owner-operator who records 100,000 miles per year, a commonly occurring figure according to Wyckoff and Maister, and incurs approximately 10 percent empty backhaul or less can compete with rail for coal, grain, and canned goods if he is an efficient, low-cost-estimate operator. If he is very productive, covering 150,000 miles per year, he can still be competitive with 25 percent empty backhaul. Competing for steel traffic, even a medium-cost operator can be competitive with only 100,000 miles per year and a 30 percent empty backhaul (Wyckoff and Maister 1975, pp. 110–112).

Wyckoff and Maister undertook this analysis "to examine the long-term viability of the owner-operator as a competitor to the railroads and other bulk-volume carriers" (p. 23). They concluded that "the owner-operator is able to provide transportation at costs that are directly

Table 6.2 Owner-operator trucking cost as a function of major parameters

Cost estimate	α_0 ($)	α_1 ($/mile)	Total annual mileage (m_T)	c_{tmL} (¢/ton-mile) for $\beta =$			
				0%	25%	50%	100%
Low	28,100	0.197	75,000	2.86	3.57	4.29	5.72
			100,000	2.39	2.99	3.59	4.77
			150,000	1.92	2.40	2.88	3.84
Medium	36,200	0.242	75,000	3.62	4.53	5.44	7.25
			100,000	3.02	3.78	4.53	6.04
			150,000	2.42	3.02	3.63	4.83
High	50,300	0.260	75,000	4.65	5.82	6.98	9.31
			100,000	3.82	4.77	5.72	7.63
			150,000	2.98	3.72	4.47	5.95

Source: Developed by linear regression on the results of Wyckoff and Maister (1975), table 3-3. Some numbers differ slightly because of approximations due to the linear cost function equation assumed here. Figures are for owner-operators operating on a lease basis. Costs are estimated for mid-1974. An average payload of 20 tons is assumed.

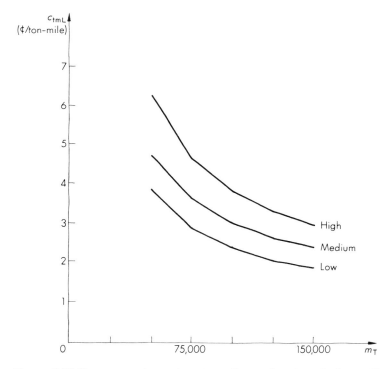

Figure 6.11 Owner-operator cost per ton-mile as a function of mileage ($\beta = 0$, $w = 20$ tons).

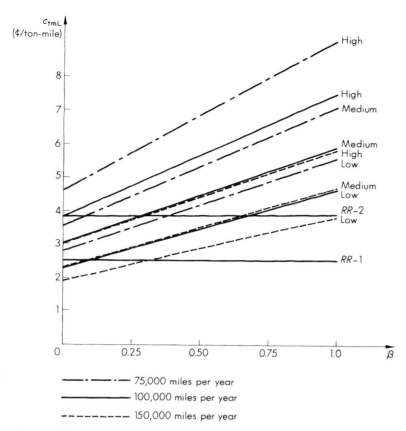

Figure 6.12 A comparison of railroad and truck costs.

competitive with rates of rail-secure traffic" (p. 37). That is, since an owner-operator running 100,000 miles per year can offer his services at a rate of 2.5–3.0 ¢/ton-mile, he can compete effectively with railroads for such traffic as canned goods, for which the rate is 3.5 ¢/ton-mile for moves of 500–700 miles; steel moving at 3.7 ¢/ton-mile for moves up to 1,100 miles; and grain moving at 2.6 ¢/ton-mile up to 1,200 miles.

It is a common assumption that trucking is an inherently more expensive mode of transportation than rail. In contrast to this conventional wisdom the Wyckoff-Maister analysis showed that certain types of truckers can, under certain conditions, become "price-competitive as well as service-competitive with railroads" (p. xviii).

This example demonstrates the type of policy conclusion that can sometimes be drawn from an analysis of cost functions. Note also that the analysis is an approximation of an equilibrium analysis, in that β is very similar to a load factor, reflecting what can be achieved in the market.

6.6 THE LIMITS OF COST FUNCTION ANALYSIS

Analysis of cost functions, and particularly analysis of the marginal and average costs and the fixed and variable components of costs, can assist one in understanding how and why selected impacts vary as options are varied. The analyst should, however, keep in mind several cautions that have been raised throughout this discussion:

1. Monetary costs are only a portion of the relevant impacts. It is useful to look at many other dimensions of resource consumption (grams of air pollutants, acres of land) with the same methodology.

2. Various measures of output may be useful. In particular, use of equilibrium measures such as V_E may give conclusions different from capacity measures such as V_C.

3. A cost function is not an acceptable basis for making a decision; that is, even if technology A has the least total monetary cost to the operator at volumes less than V, this does not mean that it is the optimal choice. A complete equilibrium analysis is necessary to take into account, for example, variations in service levels and their effect on actual volumes and thus net revenues.

As an example figure 6.13 shows the net revenues of two technologies, A and B. If they both have the same service levels at all volumes, then they will have the same gross revenue curve I_{GR}^1 and the same net revenues at V_1, where their costs are equal (and only at V_1); the points of maximum net revenue will be V_2 and V_3, respectively. In this case the technology with the lowest average cost at any volume V will also have the lowest net revenue; for values less than V_1 technology B has lower total and average cost and higher net revenue than A. If, on the other hand, there are differences in service levels, then the volumes at which net revenues are equal will necessarily be different from the volumes at which costs are equal. For example, let the service levels be such that technology A produces I_{GR}^1 while B produces I_{GR}^2. Then the point of equal net revenues shifts to V_5, different from V_1. (Note that the point of maximum net revenue shifts from V_2 to V_4.)

Thus, since in general no two technologies can have precisely the same service levels, analysis on the basis of cost functions alone can often be misleading.

To overcome this limitation an important early comparison of urban transportation options (Meyer, Kain, and Wohl 1965) used what might be called an equivalent-service approach. In this approach all options

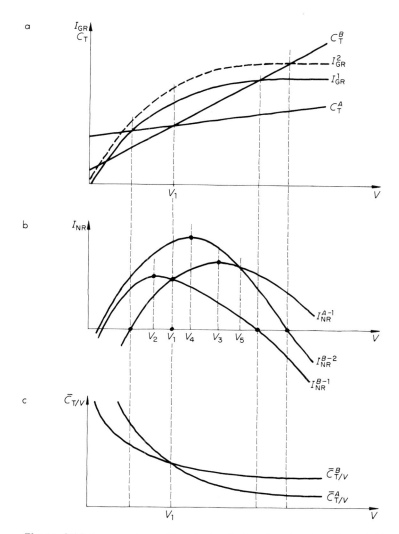

Figure 6.13 A comparison of two technologies, showing the effect of differences in service levels and thus the limitations of an analysis on the basis of cost functions alone.

are tailored to provide the same or equivalent levels of service. Then the options can be compared strictly on the basis of cost. For example, in the cited study various forms of bus rapid transit, rail rapid transit, and automobile were compared by developing the total cost as a function of volume for various geographic and demographic configurations:

The reported costs of specific travel modes were computed while observing certain service constraints which, it was hypothesized, put all modes at about the same advantage or disadvantage and therefore permitted a determination of the "best" mode on the basis of cost considerations alone. This analytic approach is sound enough so long as we can assume that all travelers attach about the same values to travel time savings, avoidance of transfers, schedule frequency, and the like, and that the service standards established accord with these values. It is more realistic, however, to take human differences into account. Some travelers would pay dearly to save time on the work-trip; others would not. Some travelers highly value privacy, personal comfort, and convenience; others are relatively unconcerned. . . . In sum, aspects of cost, price, service, and the specific demand characteristics of the traveling public *are vitally important and must be integrated and synthesized* to arrive at the most effective and economic choice or combination of choices in any particular application. (Meyer, Kain, and Wohl 1965, pp. 305–306; emphasis added)

This same approach has been used in a number of recent studies (Boyd, Asher, and Wetzler 1976, Bhatt 1976, Deen, Kulash, and Baker 1976).

This approach can be useful under some highly specialized conditions, but it ignores the basic fact that each mode provides relatively unique service characteristics. This can lead to serious errors; the different service attributes offered by each option should be considered explicitly as they are perceived by users and reflected in the demand functions (Vuchic 1976, Manheim 1977b). The most generally valid approach remains that described in chapter 5, based on explicit options, systematic analysis, explicit travel-market equilibration, and explicit prediction of impacts on different interests and display of trade-offs.

6.7 AN OVERVIEW OF VEHICLE CYCLE ECONOMICS

We now return to the vehicle cycle and apply the concepts developed in preceding sections.

The characteristics of the vehicle cycle in a particular situation can profoundly influence the impacts on users and on operators, especially in terms of economics. The basic logic of this influence is straightforward, though it takes different forms in different contexts. In this section we shall explore the economics of the vehicle cycle and derive some basic relationships. These will be illustrated and extended in later sections.

6.7.1 A Cost Perspective

First, we consider the cost to the vehicle operator. Let

C_{VA} = equivalent annual ownership cost of a vehicle, taking into account useful life, salvage value, and the cost of capital,

a = all other costs per unit of available capacity,

X = units of available capacity per year (for example, vehicle cycles, vehicle-miles, or ton-miles).

Then the total annual cost per vehicle, including ownership and other costs (but excluding nonvehicle costs), is

$$C_T = C_{VA} + aX, \tag{6.44}$$

and the average total cost per unit of available capacity is

$$\bar{C}_T = \frac{C_{VA}}{X} + a. \tag{6.45}$$

Thus, as in all cases of fixed costs, the average cost per unit drops as the number of units of available capacity increases.

The available capacity X is often called the **utilization**, especially when the sense is that available capacity is utilized for productive (revenue) service. As the examples will show, it is common in the analysis of rail systems to talk of the utilization of a freight car as the number of cycles or "turns" that can be accomplished per year; in the analysis of air systems the utilization is usually defined as the number of revenue flight hours per year (though sometimes total flight or "block" hours are used also). We see no reason to fix on a single definition of utilization. Different definitions will be useful in different analyses. Further, any simple definition can be misleading for some analytical needs. We shall use utilization as a generic concept, as in "the utilization of the available resources," and shall employ more precise definitions as appropriate.

A RAIL EXAMPLE

Consider a railcar for which the annual cost of ownership is C_{VA} = $1,600. Rail analysts often use the number of car cycles as a measure of the number of loads that can be delivered in a year (implicitly, one full load is delivered for each cycle). Let X_{CC} be the number of car cycles (or loads delivered) per year and assume that other costs of

Table 6.3 Effects of railcar utilization

Utilization (cycles per year)	Total cost ($/year)	Average cost ($/cycle)	Vehicle ownership cost fraction (C_{VA}/C_T)
12	8,800	733.33	0.18
15	10,600	706.67	0.15
18	12,400	688.89	0.13
21	14,200	676.19	0.11
24	16,000	666.67	0.10
27	17,800	659.26	0.09
30	19,600	653.33	0.08
33	21,400	648.48	0.07
36	23,200	644.44	0.01

operation amount to $a = \$600$ per cycle. Then the total cost and average cost per cycle are

$$C_T = 1{,}600 + 600X_{CC}, \tag{6.46}$$

$$\bar{C}_{X_{CC}} = 600 + \frac{1{,}600}{X_{CC}} \tag{6.47}$$

Table 6.3 shows the effects of changes in the number of productive car cycles per year. The table also shows the ratio C_{VA}/C_T, which demonstrates the importance of utilization in the relative composition of costs.

Consider a situation in which the utilization is 15 cycles per year and the average revenue is $700 per cycle, resulting in a loss of $6.67 per cycle. As the table shows, if the number of cycles were increased to 18 and if the average revenue per cycle remained the same, the operator would gain a net revenue of $700.00 − $688.89 = $11.11 per cycle. This illustrates the profound effect of the vehicle cycle on the economics of a system.

AN AIR EXAMPLE

Consider an aircraft for which the annual cost of ownership is $C_{VA} = \$500{,}000$ per year. Typically airline planners are interested in the number of hours per year an aircraft can be utilized in productive service ("airborne revenue hours"). Let X_{HU} be the number of useful vehicle-hours per year and assume that other costs of operation amount to

Table 6.4 Characteristics of three types of jet aircraft

Type	Seats	Costs C_{VA} ($\$ \times 10^6$)	a ($\$$ per useful vehicle-hour)	Typical utilization (revenue hours per year)
A	140	0.50	950	2,832
B	234	1.32	1,300	2,538
C	342	2.00	1,780	2,969

Source: Civil Aeronautics Board (1975).

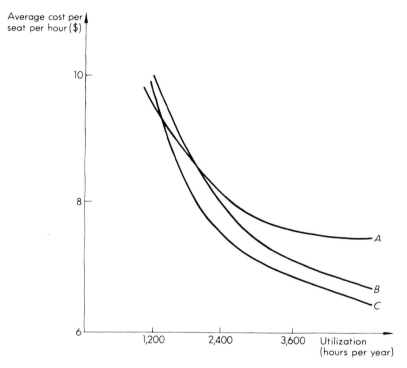

Figure 6.14 The effect of the utilization on the relative costs of three types of jet aircraft.

$a = \$950$ per useful vehicle-hour. Then the total cost and average total cost per useful vehicle-hour are

$$C_T = 500{,}000 + 950 X_{HU}, \tag{6.48}$$

$$\bar{C}_{X_{HU}} = 950 + \frac{500{,}000}{X_{HU}}. \tag{6.49}$$

For example, at $X_{HU} = 2{,}500$ hours per year, $\bar{C}_{X_{HU}} = \$1{,}150$ and $C_T = \$2{,}880{,}000$.

Table 6.4 gives the characteristics of three types of jet aircraft. The average costs per seat per hour are shown for a range of utilizations in figure 6.14. Note that at low utilizations A has a lower cost per available seat per hour, but this is reversed at high utilizations. (A and B have the same cost per available seat per hour at a utilization of 1,682 hours.)

6.7.2 A Net Revenue Perspective

As noted in chapter 5 and in section 6.6, a focus on costs and available capacity can be quite misleading. What is most important to the operator—and to the user too—is the actual usage (the equilibrium volume) and the implications of both costs and usage for net revenue (or similar measures from the operator's perspective).

To extend the preceding discussion we define the following variables (note that we distinguish capacity available by subscripts C and capacity utilized or revenue units by subscripts E, denoting equilibrium volumes):

I_{NR} = net revenue per year for a fleet of vehicles,
N = number of vehicles in the fleet,
X_C = number of units of available capacity per vehicle per year (cycles, flying hours, vehicle-miles),
X_E = number of revenue units (units of capacity actually utilized per vehicle per year),
λ = load factor (fraction of available capacity actually utilized),
r_{VE} = net revenue per vehicle per revenue unit,
r_{VC} = net revenue per vehicle per unit of available capacity,
p = price charged per unit of utilized capacity,
a = operating cost per unit of available capacity,
C_{VA} = equivalent annual vehicle ownership cost,
$C_{T/V}$ = total cost per vehicle,
$I_{GR/V}$ = gross revenue per vehicle,
$I_{NR/V}$ = net revenue per vehicle.

Then, as before, we have

$$C_{T/V} = C_{VA} + aX_C,$$ (6.50)

$$I_{GR/V} = X_E\, p,$$ (6.51)

$$I_{NR/V} \equiv I_{GR/V} - C_{T/V} = X_E p - aX_C - C_{VA}.$$ (6.52)

Since

$$\lambda \equiv \frac{X_E}{X_C},$$ (6.53)

$$I_{NR/V} = X_C(\lambda p - a) - C_{VA},$$ (6.54)

and, for the fleet as a whole,

$$I_{NR} = NI_{NR/V} = N[X_C(\lambda p - a) - C_{VA}].$$ (6.55)

It is useful to write this differently. We take

$$
\begin{aligned}
r_{VE} \equiv \frac{I_{NR/V}}{X_E} &= p - a\,\frac{X_C}{X_E} - \frac{C_{VA}}{X_E} \\
&= p - \frac{a}{\lambda} - \frac{C_{VA}}{\lambda X_C},
\end{aligned}
$$ (6.56)

$$
\begin{aligned}
r_{VC} \equiv \frac{I_{NR/V}}{X_C} &= \lambda p - a - \frac{C_{VA}}{X_C} \\
&= \lambda r_{VE}.
\end{aligned}
$$ (6.57)

Since

$$I_{NR/V} = r_{VE}X_E = r_{VE}X_C\lambda,$$ (6.58)

for the fleet as a whole we have

$$I_{NR} = Nr_{VE}X_C\lambda$$ (6.59)

and, comparing two alternative strategies T^0 and T^1,

$$\frac{I_{NR}^1}{I_{NR}^0} = \frac{N^1}{N^0}\,\frac{r_{VE}^1}{r_{VE}^0}\,\frac{X_C^1}{X_C^0}\,\frac{\lambda^1}{\lambda^0}.$$ (6.60)

These relationships will be used in the following discussions.

6.7.3 Influence of the Vehicle Cycle on Costs and Revenues

The relationship presented above relates costs and revenues to general measures of available capacity and units of utilized capacity. We now focus specifically on the vehicle cycle, as illustrated by the railcar example of section 6.7.1, where the utilization is X_{CC}, the number of vehicle cycles per year.

Consider a possible change in transportation strategy from T^0 to T^1, which will affect the vehicle cycle in one or more ways, resulting in changes in the total vehicle cycle time t_{VC}. Changes in t_{VC} can have several important effects:

1. A decrease in cycle time can mean an increase in X_{CC}.
2. An increase in X_{CC} can reduce the average cost per cycle by spreading the vehicle ownership cost C_{VA} over a larger number of cycles.
3. A reduction in average cost per cycle can result in an increase in net revenue per vehicle per cycle r_{VC} if the average cost per cycle is decreased and/or if the additional cycles made available can be utilized for revenue service.
4. An increase in demand (or more precisely equilibrium volume)—the number of cycles utilized in revenue service—can result from (i) the direct effect of the change in cycle time on service as perceived by users; (ii) changes in price made feasible or necessary by changes resulting from changes in cycle time; or (iii) the effect on other aspects of service quality of actions taken to implement the change in cycle time.
5. Changes in demand, or in the cycles available per vehicle, can affect required fleet size N.

Equation (6.60) demonstrates this. A change in t_{VC} can bring about an increase in I_{NR} if there is an increase in r_{VE}, X_{CC}, N, or λ. These relationships are illustrated in figure 6.15.

It should be emphasized that these relationships leave out factors that may be significant in a particular situation. For example, there may be costs incurred in implementing the change in vehicle cycles, such as a guideway improvement, that are not shown in the above formulas; moreover vehicle life, maintenance costs, and depreciation considerations may change.

6.8 A RAIL SYSTEM CASE STUDY

6.8.1 The Burlington Northern Experience
In section 6.2.6 we examined the cycle of the typical U.S. railcar and showed the very small fraction of time the vehicle is actually in motion. One of many possible points of leverage on the railcar cycle is the amount of time during which a car is under control of the shipper or the receiver, waiting to be loaded or unloaded. A recent attempt to influence shipper behavior is illuminating.

In December 1971 the Burlington Northern Railroad introduced

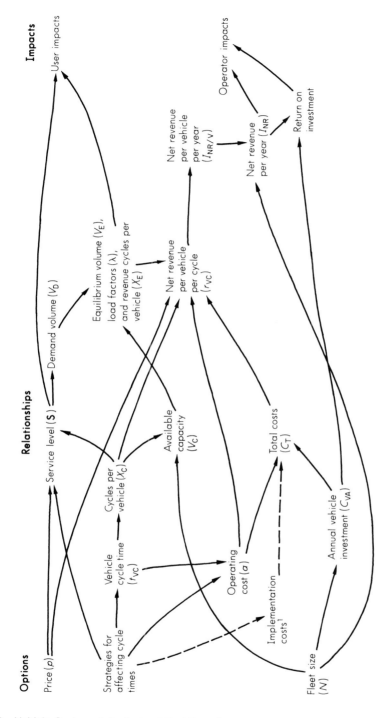

Options

Relationships

Impacts

Price (p)

Strategies for affecting cycle times

Service level (**S**)

Demand volume (V_D)

Vehicle cycle time (t_{VC})

Cycles per vehicle (X_C)

Equilibrium volume (V_E), load factors (λ), and revenue cycles per vehicle (X_E)

Available capacity (V_C)

Net revenue per vehicle per cycle (r_{VC})

Net revenue per vehicle per year (I_{NR}/v)

User impacts

Operator impacts

Return on investment

Net revenue per year (I_{NR})

Operating cost (a)

Implementation costs[1]

Total costs (C_T)

Annual vehicle investment (C_{VA})

Fleet size (N)

[1] Omitted from explicit consideration in this chapter

Figure 6.15 Economics of the vehicle cycle.

Table 6.5 Effect of incentive rate

	Average time before incentive rate	Average time after incentive rate	Average time savings
Time at origin			
1. Daylight loading hours from placement to release	20:02 [a] (0.83)	6:64 (0.24)	13:1 (0.55)
2. Total loading hours from placement to release	41:38 (1.73)	11:38 (0.48)	30:10 (1.26)
3. Total hours from placement to departure from origin station (removal from shipper location)	68:17 (2.85)	32:24 (1.35)	35:53 (1.50)
Time in transit			
4. Time from origin to destination terminal	89:29 (3.73)	76:34 (3.19)	12:56 (0.54)
Time at destination			
5. Time from arrival at destination terminal to placement at receiver[b]	94:09 (3.92)	44:10 (1.84)	49:59 (2.08)
6. Time from placement at receiver until unloaded and released	85:26 (3.56)	47:02 (1.96)	38:24 (1.60)
Total movement time[c]			
(3 + 4 + 5 + 6)	337:26 (14.06)	200:09 (8.34)	137:16 (5.72)

[a]Hours:minutes (days in decimal fractions in parentheses).
[b]Or until placement at interchange to connecting carrier.
[c]Excluding time spent for return move empty or times moving loaded over other carriers. Total cycle times went from 25 to 19 days, based on estimates from other sources.
Source: Burress (1975). Data two months after the introduction of rates.

incentive rates for the movement of grain in covered hopper cars (Burress 1975). These incentive rates offered shippers a substantially reduced price per load (with some reduced ancillary services by the railroad), if an empty car was loaded within 10 daylight hours after delivery to the shipper and the loaded car was unloaded within 48 hours after delivery to the receiver. The penalties for violating these time limits (called demurrage charges) were severe—$80 per day versus $5–$10 per day under then-current rates.

These changed incentives did lead to changed behavior on the part of customers (see table 6.5). Average total loaded movement time was decreased by 5.72 days out of an original time of 17 days, a reduction of 40.7 percent. This can be translated into a savings in the number of car-days required to move a given volume of grain. In 1971 Burlington Northern moved approximately 30,000 carloads of grain over the routes covered by these new rates. A saving of 5.72 days per load released more than 170,000 additional car-days during that period. These could have been used to carry other traffic, or alternatively Burlington Northern could have reduced its investment in this type of car.

On first glance this seems like a very attractive move. But we must be careful: What steps were taken to implement this strategy? What were the overall impacts on costs and revenues? After all, the incentive rate offered was a reduction of 25 percent. Although the increased time savings resulted in a decrease in costs, did the net revenue increase or decrease with this drop in price? To answer these questions we need a more detailed analysis.

It was reported that, after introduction of the incentive rates, the railroad's volume doubled (market share went from 40 to 80 percent) and the cycle time went from about 25 to 19 days, so

$$\frac{V_E^1}{V_E^0} = \frac{X_E^1}{X_E^0} = 2, \tag{6.61}$$

$$\frac{p^1}{p^0} = \frac{1 - 0.25}{1} = \frac{3}{4}. \tag{6.62}$$

Since $X_{CC} = 365/t_{VC}$, we have $\hspace{4cm}$ (6.63)

$$\frac{X_{CC}^1}{X_{CC}^0} = \frac{t_{VC}^0}{t_{VC}^1} = \frac{25}{19} = 1.32. \tag{6.64}$$

If we assume that the fleet was fully utilized in both cases ($\lambda^1 = \lambda^0 = 1$) and was expanded to meet the demand, then

$$N = \frac{V_E}{w X_{CC} \lambda}, \tag{6.65}$$

$$\frac{N^1}{N^0} = \frac{V_E^1/V_E^0}{X_{CC}^1/X_{CC}^0} = \frac{2}{1.32} = 1.52. \tag{6.66}$$

Suppose the following unit values were applicable. (The numbers are hypothesized to illustrate the possible consequences of the reported relative changes in volumes, prices, and cycle times.) For the initial conditions,

$t_{VC}^0 = 25$ days,
$p^0 = \$1,500/\text{carload}$,
$a^0 = \$600/\text{cycle}$,

$V_E^0 = 30{,}000$ carloads/year,
$C_{VA} = \$1{,}600$/vehicle.

After the change,

$t_{VC}^1 = 19$ days,

$p^1 = \dfrac{3}{4}p^0 = \$1{,}125$/carload,

$a^1 = \$625$/cycle,
$V_E^1 = 2V_E^0 = 60{,}000$ carloads/year.

Then, with $\lambda = 1$ and $w = 1$ carload (1 cycle $= 1$ carload),

$$X_{CC}^0 = \frac{365}{25} = 14.6 \text{ cycles/year,} \tag{6.67}$$

$$N^0 = \frac{V_E^0}{wX_{CC}^0} = \frac{30{,}000}{14.6} = 2{,}055, \tag{6.68}$$

$$r_{VE}^0 = p^0 - \frac{a^0}{\lambda} - \frac{C_{VA}}{\lambda X_{CC}^0} = (1{,}500 - 600) - \frac{1{,}600}{14.6} = 900 - 109.59$$
$$= \$790.41\text{/cycle,} \tag{6.69}$$

$$I_{NR/V}^0 = X_{CC}^0 r_{VE}^0 = (14.6)(790.41) = \$11{,}540\text{/vehicle.} \tag{6.70}$$

$$I_{NR}^0 = N^0 X_{CC}^0 r_{VE}^0 = 2{,}055(11{,}540) = \$23.71 \text{ million.} \tag{6.71}$$

For the new conditions,

$$X_{CC}^1 = \frac{365}{19} = 19.21 \text{ cycles/year,} \tag{6.72}$$

$$N^1 = \frac{V_E^1}{wX_{CC}^1 \lambda} = \frac{60{,}000}{19.21} = 3{,}123, \tag{6.73}$$

$$\Delta N = N^1 - N^0 = 3{,}123 - 2{,}055 = 1{,}068, \tag{6.74}$$

$$r_{VE}^1 = \left(p^1 - \frac{a^1}{\lambda}\right) - \frac{C_{VA}}{\lambda X_{CC}^1} = (1{,}125 - 625) - \frac{1{,}600}{19.21} \tag{6.75}$$
$$= 500 - 83.29 = \$416.71\text{/cycle,}$$

$$I_{NR/V}^1 = X_{CC}^1 r_{VE}^1 = (19.21)(416.71) = \$8{,}005\text{/vehicle.} \tag{6.76}$$

Thus

$$\frac{r_{VE}^1}{r_{VE}^0} = \frac{416.71}{790.41} = 0.53, \tag{6.77}$$

$$\frac{X_{CC}^1}{X_{CC}^0} = \frac{19.21}{14.6} = 1.32, \tag{6.78}$$

$$\frac{N^1}{N^0} = \frac{3,123}{2,055} = 1.52, \tag{6.79}$$

and, by (6.60),

$$\frac{I^1_{NR}}{I^0_{NR}} = (1.52)(0.53)(1.32) = 1.05. \tag{6.80}$$

We also have

$$\frac{I^1_{NR/V}}{I^0_{NR/V}} = \frac{8,005}{11,540} = 0.69. \tag{6.81}$$

Thus, in this case:

1. Net revenue increases.
2. Net revenue per car per cycle decreases by a factor of 0.53, primarily because of the substantial price decrease.
3. Even though cycles per car per year increase by a factor of 1.32, net revenue per car per year still decreases by a factor of 0.69 because of the substantial decrease in net revenue per car per cycle.
4. The volume of cars that can be productively utilized increases by a factor of 1.52; net revenue of the fleet therefore increases even though net revenue per car decreases.

This example demonstrates that improvements in cycle time can have significant economic effects. Whether or not these effects result in an increase in net revenue (or an improvement in other pertinent economic measures) can depend on some relatively subtle interactions (see, for example, Martland, Assarabowski, and McCarren 1977, sec. 2.3).

The example also demonstrates that while the performance of a single vehicle is important, our primary concern should be the performance of the fleet as a whole, since net revenue for the fleet can increase even when net revenue per car decreases. We shall explore this idea further in chapter 7.

6.8.2 Implications of Vehicle-Cycle Considerations for Railroad System Policy

We have now developed the relationship of the vehicle cycle to the economic issues relevant to the operator (and ultimately to the user) as reflected in costs and revenues. For most modes and most situations these relationships are of great importance. To illustrate we shall examine some current policy-oriented transportation systems research in the U.S. railroad industry. This research is a joint effort of the industry, the federal government, and a university research team (Industry Task Force 1975).

In the United States the utilization of railcars has become a major political and economic issue. In some regions and for some seasons of the year, shippers have difficulty obtaining enough railcars to ship their commodities to market:

Over the years, depending on the economic level of activity, shippers have not received the number of cars requested for certain commodities during peak loading periods of the year. Their expressions of concern have created a widespread conviction that there have indeed been extensive car shortages. Further, inflationary trends in the costs of purchasing new equipment and the debt financing associated with such purchases have added to the concern of the industry about replacing existing fleets of equipment. (Industry Task Force 1975, p. iv)

Rapidly escalating freight car costs and interest rates have pushed the problem of car utilization to the fore in recent years. Given the current average turnaround times and rates, the return on new freight cars barely covers their capital costs. Many roads, not only the bankrupt roads, are no longer able to profitably finance even their minimum freight car needs. As a result, these roads are forced to rely heavily on foreign cars and the industry as a whole fails to satisfy the demand for cars during peak loading seasons. Although the problem of car supply has lessened during the current recession, there is no reason to believe it will not once again be common after the economy starts to recover. Further, the financial aspects relating to return on investment have worsened. When economic recovery does occur, the industry must decide whether to invest heavily in equipment, which at best is marginally profitable, or to attempt a comprehensive program for improving car utilization, which would have the same effective impact on car supply. (pp. 1–2)

Utilization has at least four aspects important to shippers and rail operator management (p. 7):

1. cycle time, or the average time between successive car loadings;
2. capacity utilization, or the average degree to which a load fills a car;
3. serviceability, or the fraction of time that a car is available for service;
4. life time.

The Industry Task Force notes that

an improvement in car utilization could be achieved by reduction in the percent of time a car is unserviceable, a reduction in car cycle time, a decrease in empty line-haul miles, and an increase in the percentage of volume or weight capacity used by shippers. A quantitative assessment of the potential for improvement can be made when an adequate data base on car cycles is available. Analysis of these car cycles from load to load would reveal the fraction of time a car spends being moved by the railroad and being unloaded. These car cycles would also identify the time a car spends after unloading until it is spotted for loading at a shipper's dock. In each of these segments of the car cycle, a different set of changes in practice may be required to improve utilization. (p. iv)

In response to this identification of a problem and realization of the importance of improving vehicle utilization as one approach to resolving the problem, a major research program is under way, focusing particularly on reliability of service and its impact on the car cycle. Reliability is "the amount of variability in rail trip times." The reliability of rail system operations can have a significant impact on utilization, especially the cycle time. As illustrated in figure 6.16, an improvement in reliability

will have both direct and indirect impacts leading to an increase in the level of car utilization. . . . Most actions that improve reliability will also reduce average trip times as well; this results in a shorter trip time for loads and allows the railroad to distribute empty cars more rapidly and effectively. These changes in rail performance, once they are perceived by shippers, should in turn lead to the indirect impacts noted in the [figure]. As a result of the shorter trip times and the higher degree of reliability, shippers and receivers will perhaps be able to plan loading and unloading operations more effectively, thereby shortening the time that cars remain in their control. If the service improvements persist, the railroad should also begin to capture a larger share of the traffic moving over the corridors affected by the change. With higher traffic levels, the railroad may be able to increase the frequency of some trains or to add new blocks to existing trains, thereby further reducing average trip times. Together, the direct and indirect impacts that promote better car utilization should lead to a reduced need for new freight cars or, if traffic conditions are favorable, to an ability to move more traffic with the same number of cars. Finally, the change in capital costs and in net railway operating income will, for a successful strategy, raise profitability. (pp. 9–11)

This relationship between reliability and utilization has important implications for research strategy. Particular attention has been given to assessing rail system reliability in order to predict the effects of possible strategies that might lead to improvements in both mean trip time and trip time reliability: "The conceptual framework suggests the kinds of models that are needed to evaluate alternatives for improving reliability and car utilization. Models are needed to predict:

• Reliability and trip time improvements as a function of changes in operations, investments, and institutional arrangements.

• The impacts of service improvements on empty car distribution, shippers' detention of cars, and traffic levels.

• Freight car utilization as a function of railroad and shipper policies.

• Profitability as a function of the changes in capital costs, operating costs, and revenues" (pp. 9–11).

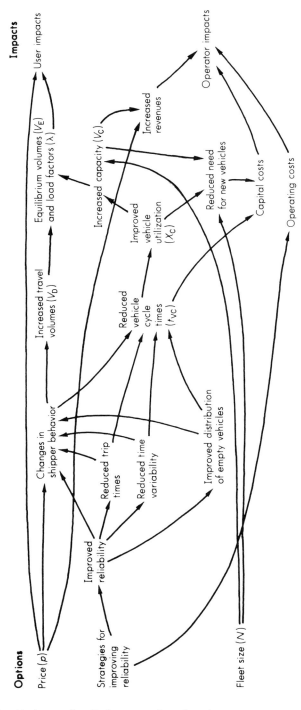

Figure 6.16 Influence of reliability on utilization. Adapted from Industry Task Force (1975).

Table 6.6 Possible mechanisms for improving reliability

Operating Alternatives

Runthrough trains
More frequent trains
Faster trains
Revised train schedules
Schedule adherence
Extra train policy
Blocking policy
Priorities
Local and interchange operations
Inspection policies
Revised power cycles

Capital Investment Alternatives

Additional power
Consolidation and modernization of yards
Construction of new yards
Right-of-way improvements
Better equipment design
Freight car control systems

Institutional and Commercial Alternatives

Work rule modifications
Hourly per diem system
New methods of local distribution such as unit trains or trailer or container on flatcar.
New operations control systems or procedures

Source: Industry Task Force (1975).

As a result of analysis along these lines, the authors conclude that "numerous operating, investment, and institutional strategies will lead to more reliable railroad service. In fact, any railroad decision or action offers some potential for improving reliability, if, directly or indirectly, it:

a. reduces the number of times cars are handled;
b. improves the reliability of train connections at intermediate yards;
c. improves the consistency of routing between origin and destination;
d. improves the reliability of local service at the origin or destination;
e. reduces the number of delays caused by unusual circumstances such as lost waybills, misroutes, and mechanical failures" (p. 17).

Some of the possible mechanisms for improving reliability are shown in table 6.6 (see also Martland, Sussman, and Philip 1977).

Focusing on the vehicle cycle and its implications has thus led to recognition of a very important area for policy influence on the rail transport system, namely strategies to improve reliability, and particularly operating strategies.

6.9 SUMMARY

The vehicle cycle has three major components: the operating cycle, the service cycle, and the annual cycle. The operating cycle begins and ends at the operational base and includes positioning time, travel time while loaded and unloaded, load/unload time, operational servicing time, schedule slack, and movement processing time. The service cycle begins and ends at a major maintenance base and includes one or more operating cycles as well as positioning time from and to the maintenance base. The annual cycle includes the service cycle, time spent in periodic maintenance, and time spent in idle status. The total vehicle cycle time includes all of these components. Numerous points of leverage on the vehicle cycle can be identified.

A number of basic concepts have been introduced: marginal and average products, marginal and average costs, and cost functions. The cost function is a useful way of displaying the results of a systematic analysis, although analysis of the cost function alone can be quite misleading. The only generally valid approach is an explicit analysis of the type described in chapter 5.

These concepts were used to examine the economics of the vehicle cycle. The characteristics of the cycle in a particular situation can profoundly influence the behavior of users and operators, especially as they are reflected in monetary impacts.

Changes in any of the components of the vehicle cycle can increase the utilization of a vehicle. In particular, changes in total vehicle cycle time can change the average cost per cycle, the net revenue per vehicle per cycle, the number of cycles available per vehicle, and the equilibrium volume; it can also allow productive changes in vehicle fleet size. All of these factors are interrelated and will affect net revenue to the operator and other economic measures.

Improvements in the vehicle cycle create opportunities for economic gains. (Whether or not these gains are achieved depends, of course, on whether and how the opportunities are utilized.) Recognition of these relationships can be an essential factor in policy and planning decisions.

TO READ FURTHER

Whatever one's modal interests, the directions of contemporary rail systems research are quite illuminating: see Industry Task Force (1975), RAILROAD RESEARCH STUDY BACKGROUND PAPERS (1975), Martland, Sussman, and Philip (1977), C. E. Taylor (1977), and Williamson (1977). There are similar examples from other modes: see

Frankel and Marcus (1973), Borman (1977), and Gilman (1977).

For an analysis of transportation cost functions see Meyer et al. (1960), Heflebower (1965), Soberman (1966a, b), and Thomson (1974).

EXERCISES

6.1(E) Section 6.3.2 discussed alternative dimensions of output. Consider the results of sections 5.5 and 5.6 and the descriptions of three alternative technologies offered in table 5.4.

a. Plot total cost and net revenue for each of the technologies as a function of:
i. equilibrium volume V_E,
ii. capacity volume V_C,
iii. available seat-miles,
iv. revenue seat-miles.

b. Compare and discuss.

6.2(E) Compare the explicit analysis in chapter 5 with the analysis on the basis of cost functions in exercise 6.1:
a. Use the data of sections 5.5 and 5.6 (table 5.4). Discuss.
b. Use the data of section 5.7 (table 5.5). Discuss.

6.3(C) Review the discussions of cost function analysis by Vuchic (1976) and Manheim (1977b) and the analyses of Meyer, Kain, and Wohl (1965), Bhatt (1976), Boyd, Asher, and Wetzler (1976), and Deen, Kulash, and Baker (1976).
a. Critically appraise the various analyses.
b. Discuss critically the U.S. Department of Transportation's policy as expressed in UMTA (1976b). Draw on your answers to part a.

6.4(P) Select a transportation operation for which data are available to you (for example, local bus transit, an air carrier, a shipping line). Describe typical vehicle cycles for this operator, making estimates of the times for each component. Analyze the possibilities for changes in the cycle. Estimate the cost and revenue consequences of alternative changes (indicate clearly any cost assumptions that you have to make).

7

Understanding Performance Functions II: Congestion, Dimensionalities, and the Spatial Structure of Services

7.1 INTRODUCTION

In this chapter we shall examine a number of basic characteristics of transport technologies and explore their implications for system performance. We start with a consideration of the phenomenon of congestion. Section 7.2 introduces the basic concept and several types of congestion, and section 7.3 describes the effects of congestion, using an extension of the performance model developed in chapter 5. Section 7.4 discusses the dimensionality of options, especially the implications of their different time frames and their indivisibilities, and section 7.5 introduces a performance model that includes these factors. Section 7.6 examines the combination of dimensionality of options and congestion, using the case of vehicle-facility congestion. Finally, section 7.7 explores system performance in space and time, returning again to the concept of vehicle cycles introduced in chapter 6.

7.2 CONGESTION AND CAPACITY

7.2.1 Basic Concepts

We begin with the concept of capacity. For any system component the *capacity* is the maximum number of items, per unit of time, that can be processed through the component. In this definition capacity is a firm, "hard" number.

Congestion arises out of the conjunction of two factors. The first is that every process has a finite capacity. The second is that every process has a stochastic character: there is some degree of randomness in both the demands placed on a process and the ability of the process to service those demands.

Consider a system component with a capacity of μ units per unit of time. That is, each unit takes an average time $t_P = 1/\mu$ to be serviced. Units arrive at the component at a rate λ per unit of time. If μ and λ are both fixed, then the total time each arriving unit spends being processed is

$$t_\tau = \begin{cases} t_P, & \lambda \le \mu, \\ \infty, & \lambda > \mu. \end{cases} \tag{7.1}$$

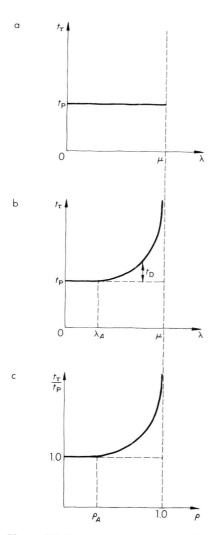

Figure 7.1 Capacity and congestion. Part a shows a deterministic case; parts b and c show a more realistic case with congestion.

This is shown in figure 7.1a.

If $\lambda > \mu$, several alternative conditions can occur: (1) the system breaks down, in that there is a complete jam-up and no units are processed ($t_\tau = \infty$); (2) a waiting queue is formed and grows ever longer (so that $t_\tau \to \infty$); or (3) under non-steady-state conditions, when $\lambda > \mu$ only for a finite period of time, the queue that builds up is eventually dissipated (see Yagar 1977).

If either λ or μ or both are random variables, then even when $\lambda < \mu$, queues will occasionally build up. The time t_τ then depends on the nature of the probabilistic process controlling λ and μ.

The total processing time, per unit, is the processing time t_P plus a delay time t_D:

$$t_\tau = t_P + t_D. \tag{7.2}$$

In general, for probabilistic processes t_D is an increasing function of λ relative to μ:

$$t_D = f(\lambda/\mu). \tag{7.3}$$

It is often useful to characterize processes by the ratio λ/μ and to normalize by defining

$$\rho \equiv \frac{\lambda}{\mu}, \tag{7.4}$$

so that

$$\frac{t_\tau}{t_P} = 1 + \frac{t_D}{t_P} = 1 + g(\lambda, \mu) = 1 + g(\rho). \tag{7.5}$$

The practical significance of congestion is shown in parts b and c of figure 7.1. The range of arrival rates between 0 and λ_A (corresponding to ρ between 0 and ρ_A) is the "uncongested" area: $t_\tau = t_P$ over this range, since $t_D = 0$. Above λ_A, however, $t_D > 0$ and there is congestion. Thus **congestion** occurs when the average processing time per unit increases because of demand for service. That is, congestion occurs when $t_D > 0$ or, equivalently, $t_\tau > t_P$.

The capacity of a system is best understood by reference to figure 7.1. As the level of demand λ rises, approaching the average service rate μ, the delay increases. The maximum throughput rate is a number infinitesimally smaller than μ: any level of demand greater than μ cannot be handled, and the queue will build up to infinity if the demand level stays constant (if it varies, then the queue will begin to dissipate when λ drops below μ).

The problem with defining μ as *the* capacity is that, except in perfectly deterministic systems, the average delay per unit is very large at λ very close to μ. Thus μ is sometimes called the ***physical capacity*** to emphasize that it is physically the maximum number of units that can be squeezed through the system per unit of time. In contrast, a ***practical capacity*** is usually chosen at a lower level such that the delays are still in some sense tolerable.

For example, in a recent railroad simulation study the following comments were made on the estimation of capacity of a rail line:

A number of definitions of capacity were considered in attempting to develop the most useful definition. ***Ultimate capacity***, where absolutely no more trains can be forced through the line, is too unstable and dependent upon precisely how trains are scheduled and what failures occur. An ***economic capacity***, where an optimal balance between operating and capital costs would occur, is not within the scope of the project and would probably be too site specific for a general analysis such as this. Other possible definitions, such as an arbitrary percent delay of total running time or an ***operationally stable capacity*** where a line could recover from a disruption in service of moderate length (e.g., 4 hours) and return to normal service levels, were also rejected as too arbitrary or unstable. The most useful and stable definition appears to be one based on the maximum allowable time for the most delayed train to traverse the line. It was discovered that maximum time could be related to average delay and would allow the user to define capacity constraints based on either minimum level of service (maximum acceptable trip time) or minimizing the need to recrew trains because of the 12 hour on-duty time limitation imposed by the Hours of Service Law. It should be noted that since the parametric runs were designed to represent "typical day" operations, this approach would not eliminate all trains that exceed the time limit. Unusual delays or catastrophic failures could still result in some trains exceeding the time limit. (Prokopy and Rubin 1975; emphasis added)

In highway studies the approach has been to define six levels of service, designated *A–F*. Each level of service reflects a range of a number of factors, including not only travel time (or its inverse, speed) but also "traffic interruptions, freedom to maneuver, safety, driving comfort and convenience, and operating costs" (HIGHWAY CAPACITY MANUAL 1965, p. 7). Thus, while physical capacity corresponds to $\lambda \approx \mu$, highway designers are encouraged to think in terms of essentially different levels of t_D: this procedure "offers a choice of four [service] levels [*A–D*] below capacity [*E, F*], each of which is related to an operating speed [*t*]; these levels offer more freedom to the local administrator or engineer to select that type of operation most suitable for his local conditions" (p. 87).

Although physical capacity is usually a well-defined concept, work-

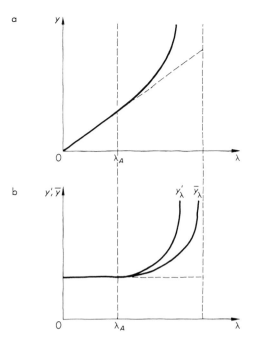

Figure 7.2 a: Total service time as a function of arrival rate. b: Average and marginal total service times as functions of arrival rate.

able, practical definitions of capacity must be related explicitly to levels of delay.

SIGNIFICANCE OF CONGESTION

Figure 7.2 shows the significance of congestion effects. Part a shows the total processing time y (for all units) as a function of arrival rate λ:

$$y = \lambda \bar{t}_\tau,$$ (7.6)

where $\bar{t}_\tau$ is the average value of t_τ for all units being serviced. Part b shows the average and marginal total processing times $\bar{y}_\lambda$ and y'_λ (note that $\bar{y}_\lambda = y/\lambda = \bar{t}_\tau$). For arrival rates less than λ_A, the marginal and average processing times are equal. For arrival rates greater than λ_A, however, the marginal total processing time is greater than the average total processing time.

This has great significance. Above λ_A each additional arrival per unit of time will experience a processing time equal to the average processing time $\bar{y}_\lambda$. However, such additional arrivals increase the total pro-

272 Understanding Performance Functions II

cessing time of all other users of the system by an amount equal to y'_λ—an average increase of y'_λ/λ. Thus such additional arrivals may receive benefits, but they cause disbenefits to all other users of the system.

This difference between average and marginal times (or, more generally, between average and marginal costs or composite service levels) leads to the important concept of adding an additional charge p so that the average cost plus p equals the marginal cost at equilibrium volume. In urban transportation, for example, it has often been proposed that automobiles entering the congested central area of a city be charged a "congestion toll" (see, for example, Walters 1961, Thomson 1974, URBAN TRANSPORTATION PRICING ALTERNATIVES 1976, Arrillaga 1978, McGillivray, Neels, and Beesley 1978).

TRANSIENT CONDITIONS

So far we have dealt only with the steady state, where λ and μ are constant over time, and with $\lambda < \mu$. In many practical situations λ is a function of time, and sometimes μ is also.

Consider the case where μ is constant but λ is a function of time and $\lambda(t) > \mu$ for some period Δt. Even while $\lambda(t) < \mu$, congestion can occur due to the probabilistic nature of λ and μ, but although queues build up, they also dissipate. Once $\lambda(t)$ becomes greater than μ, the queue continues to build at a rate faster than it dissipates, until such times as $\lambda(t)$ drops below μ again. At that time there still is a queue, or backlog, to be dissipated. In the discussion that follows we shall assume that such transient saturated systems ($\lambda > \mu$) can be represented approximately by an equivalent unsaturated system ($\lambda < \mu$) if we take a long enough time interval that the transient effect is averaged out. (This is not necessarily a good assumption in a practical analysis. In some cases it is very important to take into account the time dynamics; see Odoni and Kivestu 1976, May and Orthlieb 1976, Yagar 1977.)

7.2.2 Models of Congestion

It will be useful to have some simple models of congestion. One useful class of models for these processes is provided by queuing theory; we shall use this theory here for expository purposes, but the reader should be aware that other probabilistic models may be more appropriate in particular applications.

When the arrival rate or the service rate or both are randomly distributed, there is a certain probability that an arriving unit will have to wait before being serviced. As a standard result of queuing theory (Wohl and Martin 1967, Wagner 1969), the expected or average delay t_D is (under the assumptions of a Poisson arrival distribution, exponential service-time distribution, and a single channel):

$$t_D = \frac{1}{\mu} \frac{1}{(\mu/\lambda) - 1} = \frac{1}{\mu} \frac{\lambda/\mu}{1 - (\lambda/\mu)}. \tag{7.7}$$

Since the average service time without congestion is $t_P = 1/\mu$, the average total processing time is

$$t_\tau = t_P + t_D = \frac{1}{\mu}\left(1 + \frac{\lambda/\mu}{1 - (\lambda/\mu)}\right), \tag{7.8}$$

and

$$\frac{t_\tau}{t_P} = 1 + \frac{t_D}{t_P} = 1 + \frac{\lambda/\mu}{1 - (\lambda/\mu)} = 1 + \frac{\rho}{1 - \rho}, \tag{7.9}$$

where $\rho \equiv \lambda/\mu$. The behavior of this function is shown in figure 7.3.

More general models can also be formulated. Following Davidson (as described in Hutchinson 1974, p. 128), we can write

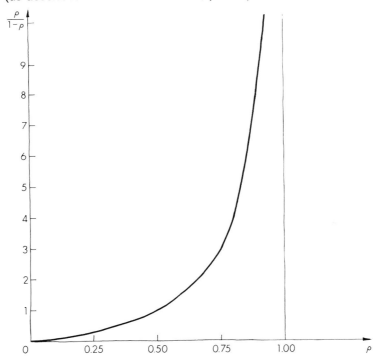

Figure 7.3 Basic queuing model. After Wohl and Martin (1967).

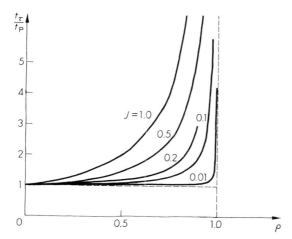

Figure 7.4 A general congestion model. After Hutchinson (1974).

$$\frac{t_\tau}{t_P} = 1 + J \frac{\lambda/\mu}{1 - (\lambda/\mu)}$$

$$= 1 + J \frac{\rho}{1 - \rho}. \tag{7.10}$$

This function is shown in figure 7.4 for various values of J.

The value of the parameter J is derived from theoretical or empirical arguments to characterize a particular process. For example, for the case of Poisson arrivals and Erlang service times (Wohl and Martin 1967, p. 372; Wagner 1969),

$$J = \frac{k + 1}{2k}, \tag{7.11}$$

so that

$$t_D = t_P J \frac{\rho}{1 - \rho} = t_P \frac{k + 1}{2k} \frac{\rho}{1 - \rho}. \tag{7.12}$$

Here the parameter $k = 1, 2, 3, \ldots$ characterizes the variability of the servicing time; as k increases, the variance of service time decreases, and the times become more regular. Correspondingly the average delay t_D becomes smaller.

We emphasize that, while the queuing model is a useful one for our present purposes, it is not necessarily the most appropriate model for every practical application. The roots of this model lie in a particular formulation of delay processes. Many other probabilistic formulations of delay processes are possible. In each application the analyst must carefully examine the probabilistic mechanisms in the congestion phenomena under study to determine which of the many alternative types of models is most appropriate. See, for example, Rallis (1967) for a variety of transportation applications of this class of models. For highway traffic applications see Drew (1968), chapter 10.

7.2.3 Types of Congestion

Many types of congestion occur in transportation systems, but it is especially important to distinguish two major categories:

1. *Load-independent congestion* occurs when system performance is degraded by the interactions of system components, even if the system is not utilized. For example, vehicles moving along guideways can experience congestion even if there are no passengers or cargo on the vehicles. In this case the demand that causes congestion is that of system components such as vehicles rather than passengers or cargo.

2. *Load-dependent congestion* occurs when system performance is degraded by the volume of flow of loads (passengers or cargo). If the flow volume of passengers or cargo is zero, no degradation occurs.

Within these categories there are a number of specific types of congestion that can occur in transportation systems, and we list below two examples from each category.

LOAD-INDEPENDENT CONGESTION

Vehicle-facility congestion

Every facility, whether guideway or terminal, exhibits congestion effects. A terminal has a service rate at which it can handle arriving or departing vehicles. A guideway has a service rate at which vehicles can move over the facility. (The mechanism controlling congestion on guideways is the headway spacing–speed distribution.) As the volume of vehicles scheduled or otherwise attempting to move through a guideway approaches capacity, vehicle interactions cause speed reductions and thus delays.

In this case $\lambda = q$, the actual frequency (flow rate) of vehicles, while $\mu = q_C$, the flow capacity of the facility. Note that vehicle-facility congestion can occur whether the vehicles are empty or full; the demand is not loads but vehicles. (For further discussion see section 7.6.)

Vehicle-schedule congestion

This type of congestion arises when the number of scheduled trips is large relative to the number that can be produced by the available fleet. Here the service rate is a function of the number of vehicle round trips that can be produced by a fleet of size N: $\mu = Nn$, where n is the number of round trips per vehicle per time period. The demand rate is the number of round trips required to meet the schedule: $\lambda = Q$, where Q is the scheduled frequency.

LOAD-DEPENDENT CONGESTION

Load-vehicle congestion

This type of congestion arises when a stream of vehicles moves over a route past a terminal at which loads are waiting to board. The waiting time experienced by a passenger (or cargo load) at the terminal has two components: waiting time until the first vehicle arrives (after arrival of the passenger at the terminal) and the additional time (if any) until a vehicle with an empty space arrives. In this case, if q is the frequency at which vehicles move past the terminal and each vehicle has a payload capacity w, then the number of seats (or tons) available per unit of time is wq, and the service rate is $\mu = wq$. (This is a crude model; a more realistic one would model the arrival of batches of seats of size w at a rate q.) The arrival rate λ is the number of passengers (or tons) at the terminal ready to board (per unit of time). That is, the delay time reflects the probability of finding a seat. In the case of a grain shipper waiting for an empty railcar to be made available to him for loading by the rail carrier, the delay may be due to competing demands for the available vehicle capacity.[1]

Load-schedule congestion

A key element of a schedule is the time allowed for each detailed element of a vehicle's movement—for example, the time allowed for loading and unloading cargo or passengers at each stop. Congestion occurs when the actual volumes to be loaded require more time than originally scheduled. In this case the service rate is the quantity of passengers or cargo that can be loaded per unit time, and the arrival rate is the actual volume requiring loading.

DISCUSSION

We emphasize again that both vehicle-facility and vehicle-schedule

[1]See the treatment of vehicle availability in the Harvard-Brookings model (Kresge and Roberts 1971); see also Philip (1978).

congestion can occur even when there is no load—no passengers or cargo using the system. These two types of congestion arise solely from the performance interactions of vehicles and facilities; the demands for service that cause congestion are established by the operating schedules of the system. On the other hand, load-vehicle and load-schedule congestion can arise even when there is no vehicle-facility or vehicle-schedule congestion.

This distinction has important practical implications. Load-dependent congestion effects enter directly into the process of travel-market equilibration. Load-independent congestion effects, on the other hand, can often be analyzed separately from, and prior to, travel-market equilibration.

7.3 EFFECTS OF CONGESTION

Congestion can have significant effects on the performance and especially on the economics of a system, and each type of congestion has different effects. To illustrate these effects we shall examine load-vehicle congestion with a simple model. Then in section 7.6 we shall examine vehicle-facility congestion. We start by introducing a modification of performance model I, developed in chapter 5.

For a schedule frequency Q, if we assume random arrivals of loads at a terminal, the average waiting time for the first vehicle to arrive after the load arrives is $t_{w1} = 1/2Q$. The average waiting time t_w for an empty seat (or empty unit of cargo capacity) may be greater than this, by t_{w2}, since some arriving vehicles may be fully loaded.

To represent this phenomenon we take as a first approximation to t_w a queuing model with arrival rate equal to the demand volume V_D. For the service rate we use the arrival rate of seats, $2Qw$, where w is the vehicle payload capacity (alternatively we could treat each direction separately, taking into account such factors as load imbalances: see section 6.5). Thus

$$\rho \equiv \frac{V_D}{2Qw} = \frac{V_D}{V_C}, \tag{7.13}$$

$$\frac{t_D}{t_P} = \frac{t_{w2}}{t_P} = \frac{J\rho}{1 - \rho}, \tag{7.14}$$

$$t_P = t_{w1} = \frac{1}{2Q}, \tag{7.15}$$

and, combining terms,

$$t_\tau \equiv t_w = t_{w1} + t_{w2} = \frac{1}{2Q}\left(1 + \frac{JV_D/2Qw}{1 - V_D/2Qw}\right) \quad \text{for } V_D < 2Qw. \tag{7.16}$$

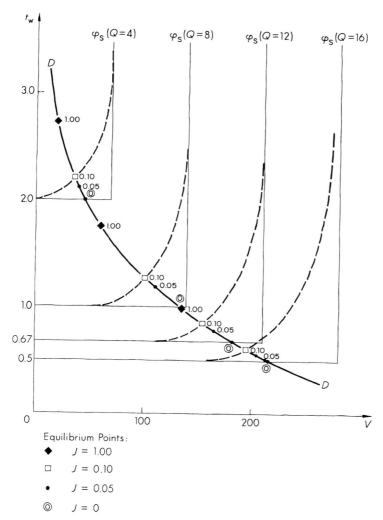

Figure 7.5 Effects of congestion. *D–D* is the demand function. The solid lines are service functions for the indicated *Q* and *J* = 0. The dashed curves are service functions for the indicated *Q* and *J* = 0.10. Some equilibrium flows are also shown for *J* = 0.05 and *J* = 1.00.

Table 7.1 Performance model II

Options	$T = (M, Q, P)$
	$M = (w, v)$
Environment	$E = (d)$
Basic relationships	$q(T) = Q$
	$V_C(T) = 2wq$
	$n(T) = \dfrac{v}{2d}$
Service level	$S(T) = (t_{iv}, t_w, t_T, c)$
	$c(T) = P$
	$t_{iv}(T) = \dfrac{d}{v}$
	$t_w(T) = \dfrac{1}{2q}\left(1 + \dfrac{J\rho}{1-\rho}\right)$
	$\rho = \dfrac{V_D}{2qw}$
	$t_T(T) = t_{iv} + t_w$
Resources consumed	$R = \dfrac{q}{n}$

This function is shown by the dashed curves in figure 7.5 for $J = 0.10$. Each curve is the service function for the indicated values of Q.

Our definition of performance model II is summarized in table 7.1. Referring back to the air transportation example in chapter 5, we can take the demand function

$$V_D = \frac{Z}{1 + e^{U_0 - U_A}}, \qquad U_0 - U_A = \alpha_0 - \alpha_1 t_{iv} - \alpha_2 t_w - \alpha_3 c, \qquad (7.17)$$

and reduce it, for purposes of travel-market equilibration, to a function of t_w:

$$V_D = \frac{Z}{1 + \beta_1 e^{-\alpha_2 t_w}}, \qquad \beta_1 = e^{\alpha_0 - \alpha_1 t_{iv} - \alpha_3 c}. \qquad (7.18)$$

Now we can apply the methodology of figure 5.8. Note that for a specific set of options $T^i = (M, Q, P)$ we must do an explicit travel-market equilibration to find equilibrium flows before we can compute the remaining impacts. The conditions to be met at equilibrium are (7.16) and (7.18). Numerical methods can be used to find the solution to these two simultaneous equations (this example was solved on a programmable pocket calculator using a general routine for finding the roots of an arbitrary function).

Table 7.2 Effects of congestion on equilibrium

Q	V_C	$J = 0$			$J = 0.01$		
		V_E	t_w^E	I_{NR}	V_E	t_w^E	I_{NR}
4	70	45	2	471	43.4	2.03	364
		(1.00)	(1.00)	(1.00)	(0.96)	(1.02)	(0.77)
8	140	134	1	3,583	123.9	1.08	2,954
		(1.00)	(1.00)	(1.00)	(0.92)	(1.08)	(0.82)
12	210	187	0.67	4,485	179.5	0.71	4,050
		(1.00)	(1.00)	(1.00)	(0.96)	(1.06)	(0.90)
16	280	218	0.50	4,125	214.6	0.52	3,916
		(1.00)	(1.00)	(1.00)	(0.98)	(1.04)	(0.95)

$J = 0.05$			$J = 0.10$			$J = 1$		
V_E	t_w^E	I_{NR}	V_E	t_w^E	I_{NR}	V_E	t_w^E	I_{NR}
39.0	2.13	100	35.6	2.21	−104	19.0	2.75	−1,100
(0.87)	(1.07)	(0.21)	(0.79)	(1.11)	(0.22)	(0.42)	(1.38)	(−2.34)
110.5	1.19	2,150	101.7	1.27	1,622	59.9	1.75	−886
(0.82)	(1.19)	(0.60)	(0.76)	(1.27)	(0.45)	(0.45)	(1.75)	(−0.25)
165.5	0.79	3,204	155.0	0.86	2,580	100.4	1.28	−696
(0.89)	(1.18)	(0.71)	(0.83)	(1.28)	(0.58)	(0.54)	(1.92)	(−0.16)
204.6	0.57	3,316	195.6	0.62	2,776	137.0	0.98	−740
(0.94)	(1.14)	(0.80)	(0.90)	(1.24)	(0.67)	(0.49)	(1.96)	(−0.18)

Note: Numbers in parentheses are ratios relative to values at $J=0$.

We can take the example of chapter 5, use performance model II, and solve for equilibrium at each alternative frequency. Table 7.2 and figure 7.5 show the results for $J = 0$ (no congestion), 0.01, 0.05, 0.1, and 1. The shifts in equilibrium flows can be quite significant.

The economic significance of congestion is clear from the table. The presence of congestion causes significant losses to both user and operator over the uncongested conditions.

7.4 DIMENSIONALITY, TIME FRAMES, AND INDIVISIBILITIES IN OPTIONS

Performance model I was very simple in many respects. Congestion effects were not included, and the number of types of options explicitly represented was artificially small. In general, in transportation there is a wide range of options, including fixed facilities, vehicle fleet size and mix, and operating, pricing, and organizational policies; different options are variable over different time frames, ranging from years for construction of new fixed facilities to weeks or days for schedule and route changes; and many of the options exhibit "lumpiness" or indivisibilities. In this section we shall explore the implications of these multiple dimensions of options.

7.4.1 Time Frames

The transportation analyst is often interested in examining the extent to which changes can be implemented at various points in time. For convenience we separate options into three groups according to the time it takes to implement a change in the system (Heflebower 1965):

1. Long-run options: Changes in many aspects of a transportation system can occur only slowly because they require extensive planning, construction, and investment. These long-run options, T_{LR}, generally involve the fixed facilities, such as links and terminals (rail tracks, highway lanes, airports), which take significant amounts of time to plan, design, and construct—often on the order of 7–12 years or more.

2. Short-run options: Some aspects of a transportation system can be changed fairly quickly. These short-run options, T_{SR}, generally involve changes in the operations of specific services in the system—for example, changes in routes, schedules, prices charged and ancillary services offered, and taxes and subsidies (although in many contexts some of these options may be so constrained by institutional procedures, such as regulatory commissions, that the short run becomes several years).

3. Intermediate-run options: Some changes to a transportation system fall between the short and long run and are worth distinguishing as "intermediate" in degree of rigidity. These options, T_{IR}, generally involve changes in the vehicle fleet such as procurement of new or replacement vehicles or changes in vehicle characteristics, fleet mix, or fleet size.

These groupings of options are general; in particular contexts very different groupings may be appropriate. Further, what is short-run in one analysis may be long-run in another, and vice versa.

To explore the implications of these time frames we examine the cost function for a particular system. In part a of figure 7.6 we assume that long-run, intermediate-run, and short-run options are fixed at T'_{LR}, T'_{IR}, and T'_{SR}, respectively, and show how average total cost $\bar{C}$ might vary as a function of volume. (We assume the general case of

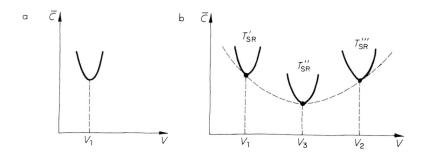

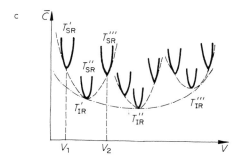

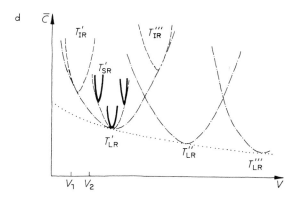

Figure 7.6 Effect of differing time frames of options.

both economies and diseconomies of scale.) In part b, we let the short-run options take three different values, T'_{SR}, T''_{SR}, and T'''_{SR}, while holding long- and intermediate-run options fixed. For each a different curve of $\bar{C}$ is generated. If T_{SR} is varied over a wide enough range, we can consider each level of V and find the T_{SR} for which $\bar{C}$ is lowest for that volume. We thus generate the envelope of $\bar{C}$ shown by the dashed line in the figure. This envelope gives the curve of lowest values of $\bar{C}$ achievable for the particular values of the (fixed) T_{LR} and T_{IR}.

In part c we continue to hold the long-run options fixed but now let the intermediate-run options take the values T'_{IR}, T''_{IR}, and T'''_{IR}; for each of these we let the short-run options vary over a range. For each setting of T_{IR}, the variation of T_{SR} again generates an envelope of $\bar{C}$; this envelope results from taking the setting of T_{SR} for each volume level which yields the lowest $\bar{C}$ for that volume, conditional on the level of T_{IR} and T_{LR}. If we now consider the variability of T_{IR} as well as T_{SR}, we generate the $\bar{C}$ envelope shown by the dot-and-dash curve. (Note that the scales of parts c and d are different from those of a and b, for clarity, as emphasized by the spacing of V_1 and V_2.)

In part d we consider T_{LR} to be variable as well. The dashed curves mark the envelopes generated by varying T_{SR} for T_{IR} and T_{LR} fixed. The dot-and-dash curves mark the envelopes generated by varying both T_{SR} and T_{IR} for T_{LR} fixed. The dotted curve marks the envelope generated by varying T_{LR} as well.

Thus the distinction of long-, intermediate-, and short-run options allows us to distinguish a corresponding hierarchy of $\bar{C}(V)$ curves. In the technical literature, one often sees reference to long-, intermediate-, and short-run cost functions, corresponding to the outer envelopes in parts d, c, and b, respectively.

This distinction is a relative one: what is long-run in one context may be short-run in another. The key issue is to determine, over any prespecified time frame, which options are variable and which must be considered fixed.

The practical implications follow in a straightforward way. Part b of the figure gives the short-run average total cost function. The cost function can be shifted to match demand only over a range; to change the intermediate- and long-run options (from T'_{IR} and T'_{LR}) takes time. Therefore, if a volume V_3 occurs, the operator is in relatively good position, since he can vary the short-run options to T''_{SR} to produce the lowest average total cost for T'_{IR} and T'_{LR}. If, on the other hand, volume turns out to be substantially greater than expected, say V_2

(or, alternatively, substantially lower), then the operator's average total cost even with the best choice of short-run options (T_{SR}''', say) may be much greater than what it might have been if T_{IR} or T_{LR} could have been varied. If the operator has competitors, they may have a lower $\bar{C}$, having made wiser past decisions, and may be able to offer a lower price and thus capture a larger share of the market. If the operator is a public agency and does not have competitors, then operator net revenues and/or user service suffer because higher costs are incurred than might otherwise be achievable.

Thus the interrelationship of options with different time frames has a significant effect in reducing the effectiveness of transport, because with the time lags required to change intermediate- and long-run options, and with imperfect information about future demand, it is often difficult to choose the combination of options that is "best" (in the limited sense of minimum average total cost). For example, in the mid-1970s many air carriers had excess vehicle capacity and higher costs because demand was less than had been forecast at the time in the early 1970s when the decision was made to invest heavily in jumbo aircraft.

We note that this type of analysis can be done with any measure of impact: resource consumption, service level, net revenue, and so forth.

7.4.2 Indivisibilities

Most types of transportation systems are characterized by indivisibilities; that is, some options cannot be varied continuously over a range but must take discrete values. For example:

1. Fixed facilities: The number of runways at an airport, the number of boarding gates or apron positions at a terminal, and the number of airports in a metropolitan area must be integers; the number of lanes in a highway or tracks in a railroad or transit stations can only take integral values.
2. Vehicles: The number of aircraft, ships, trucks, railcars, locomotives, etc., owned or operated by a particular carrier must be integral. (When there is the option of short-term charters or of sharing of vehicles with another carrier, this is no longer strictly true.)
3. Operating policy is not necessarily discrete and usually is continuously variable (frequency, price, taxes, subsidies). One exception occurs when a vehicle must return to its home base at fixed intervals; then the number of round trips per interval over a particular route must be integral.

The indivisibility of options is an important aspect of transport costs. The major implication is that, for many transport technologies, the options cannot be varied so as to have precisely the right amount of capacity to serve a particular volume of demand. Rather, there is usually either too much capacity or too little. For example, if each lane of highway can carry 1,600 vehicles per hour, then a demand volume of 3,500 vehicles per hour must be served by more than two lanes; two is too little and three is more than sufficient.

Thus the presence of indivisibilities, together with the different time frames of various options, usually make it impossible to tailor the choice of options to provide just that capacity which is "best."

7.5 AN EXPANDED PERFORMANCE MODEL

In this section we shall expand the simple performance model introduced in chapter 5 to take account of the multiple dimensions of options, their interrelations and varying time frames, and the presence of indivisibilities. Then we shall examine this expanded performance model and draw some conclusions.

7.5.1 Defining the Model

As before, we assume that service is provided over a single route connecting two points, such that the round-trip distance (A to B and back to A) is $D = 2d$, with vehicles traveling at an average speed v at uniform constant headway h. Each one-way trip of one vehicle results in the delivery of a payload of w tons. In one hour a vehicle makes $n = v/D$ round trips and delivers $2nw$ tons.

We consider a fleet of vehicles. Let Q be the total number of vehicle round trips scheduled per hour and q the number accomplished. Then the total volume delivered by the fleet is a function of q, namely $2qw$.

CONSTRAINTS

Two kinds of constraints may apply. First, the vehicles operate over fixed facilities whose capacities may limit the number of round trips they can accomplish. Second, the size of the vehicle fleet may not be sufficient to implement the Q scheduled trips.

To explore the first constraint we let K indicate the number of units of fixed facilities, such that each unit can accommodate q_C round trips per hour. (For example, K might be the number of highway lanes or airport runways.) Then Kq_C is the maximum number of round trips per hour that can be accommodated.

As for the second constraint, if there are N vehicles in the fleet, each of which can make at most n round trips per hour, then the maximum number of round trips N vehicles can make per hour is Nn.

The transportation options $\mathbf{T}$ are now the expanded set $(\mathbf{M}, K, N, Q, P)$, where $\mathbf{M} = (w, v, q_C)$. Here $\mathbf{M}$ specifies the basic characteristics of the technology chosen, K indicates the amount of investment in fixed facilities, N the amount of investment in vehicles, Q the frequency at which the vehicles are scheduled to operate over the route, and P the price to be charged.

We now consider q, the actual frequency at which vehicles are able to operate over the route. We know from the foregoing arguments that the maximum frequency is constrained by two factors, the capacity of the fixed facilities, set by K, and the size of the vehicle fleet, N:

$$q \leq Kq_C, \tag{7.19}$$

$$q \leq Nn. \tag{7.20}$$

The actual frequency is thus

$$q = \min(Q; Kq_C; Nn). \tag{7.21}$$

The total volume that can be delivered per hour is then

$$V_C(\mathbf{M}, K, N, Q, P) = 2qw. \tag{7.22}$$

Defining

$$Q_{max}^i = \min(Kq_C; Nn), \tag{7.23}$$

we can rewrite (7.21) as

$$q = \begin{cases} Q, & Q \leq Q_{max}^i, \\ \text{undefined}, & Q > Q_{max}^i. \end{cases} \tag{7.24}$$

SERVICE RELATIONSHIPS

The service relationships were given in section 5.4:

$$c(\mathbf{T}) = P, \tag{7.25}$$

$$t_{iv}(\mathbf{T}) = \frac{d}{v} = \frac{1}{2n}, \tag{7.26}$$

$$t_w(\mathbf{T}) = \frac{1}{2q}, \tag{7.27}$$

$$t_T(\mathbf{T}) = \frac{1}{2}\left(\frac{1}{n} + \frac{1}{q}\right). \tag{7.28}$$

RESOURCES CONSUMED

The resources consumed can be assumed to fall into the following categories:

R_F (fixed facilities): resources required to build and operate the fixed facilities; proportional to the number of units of fixed facilities (for example, lane-miles), that is, to K (for given d);

R_V (vehicles): resources required to acquire a vehicle fleet and maintain it in operating condition; proportional to N;

R_O (operations): resources required to operate the scheduled service; proportional to the number of vehicle-hours, per hour, that is, to Q/n.

Thus we can write

$$R_F = b_F K, \qquad\qquad (7.29)$$

$$R_V = b_V N, \qquad\qquad (7.30)$$

$$R_O = b_O \frac{Q}{n}, \qquad\qquad (7.31)$$

where the bs are appropriate constants.

COST RELATIONSHIPS

The monetary costs incurred by the operator in providing transportation are assumed to fall into three groups and are, in general, functions of the technology, **M**:

c'_{FK} = cost of fixed facilities per unit of capacity (for example, per lane-mile)
  $= f(q_C, v, d)$,
c'_{VN} = cost to procure one vehicle
  $= g(w, v)$,
c'_{OQ} = operating cost of one vehicle (per vehicle-hour)
  $= k(w, v, d)$.

In other words, the investment in fixed facilities depends on the design standards that determine q_C, the average speed, and the distance; the cost of a vehicle depends on its characteristics, and the operating cost depends on the characteristics of both the vehicle and the fixed facilities.

The total cost is given by

$$C_T = C_{TF} + C_{TV} + C_{TO}, \qquad\qquad (7.32)$$

where

Table 7.3 Performance model III

Options	$\mathbf{T} = (\mathbf{M}, K, N, Q, P)$
	$\mathbf{M} = (w, v, q^c)$
Environment	$\mathbf{E} = (d)$
Basic relationships	$n(\mathbf{T}) = \dfrac{v}{2d}$
	$q(\mathbf{T}) = \min(Q;\ nN;\ q_c K)$
	$V_c(\mathbf{T}) = 2wq$
Service levels	$\mathbf{S}(\mathbf{T}) = (t_{iv}, t_w, t_T, c)$
	$c(\mathbf{T}) = P$
	$t_{iv}(\mathbf{T}) = \dfrac{d}{v}$
	$t_w(\mathbf{T}) = \dfrac{1}{2q}$
	$t_T(\mathbf{T}) = \dfrac{1}{2}\left(\dfrac{2d}{v} + \dfrac{1}{q}\right)$
Resources consumed	$\mathbf{R} = (R_F, R_V, R_O)$
	$R_F = b_F K$
	$R_V = b_V N$
	$R_O = b_O \dfrac{Q}{n}$
Evaluation component	$C_T(\mathbf{T}) = C_{TF}(\mathbf{T}) + C_{TV}(\mathbf{T}) + C_{TO}(\mathbf{T})$
(monetary costs incurred by operator)	$C_{TF}(\mathbf{T}) = c_{FK} K$
	$C_{TV}(\mathbf{T}) = c_{VN} N$
	$C_{TO}(\mathbf{T}) = c_{OQ}\dfrac{Q}{n}$

$C_{TF}(\mathbf{T})$ = total cost of fixed facilities
$\qquad = c'_{FK} R_F$
$\qquad = c_{FK} K \qquad (c_{FK} = c'_{FK} b_F),$ \hfill (7.33)

$C_{TV}(\mathbf{T})$ = total cost of vehicles
$\qquad = c'_{VN} R_N$
$\qquad = c_{VN} N \qquad (c_{VN} = c'_{VN} b_V),$ \hfill (7.34)

$C_{TO}(\mathbf{T})$ = total cost of operations
$\qquad = c'_{OQ} R_O$
$\qquad = c_{OQ} Q/n \qquad (c_{OQ} = c'_{OQ} b_O).$ \hfill (7.35)

Thus the total cost is

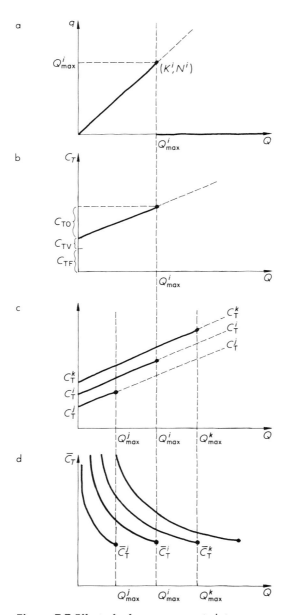

Figure 7.7 Effect of a frequency constraint.

$$C_T(T) = c_{FK}K + c_{VN}N + c_{OQ}Q/n. \tag{7.36}$$

This performance model III is summarized in table 7.3.

7.5.2 Implications: Indivisibilities and Interrelations of Options

The implications of this model are shown in figure 7.7. Part a shows actual schedule frequency q, as a function of planned schedule frequency Q, for a particular set of options (K^i, N^i) and a particular vehicle type. This capacity constraint has the effect on total cost C_T shown in part b: C_T is a function of Q for $Q \leq Q^i_{max}$. As the options are varied, both the costs and the capacities shift, generating the family of cost curves shown in part c. From these total cost curves can be derived the average cost curves shown in part d.

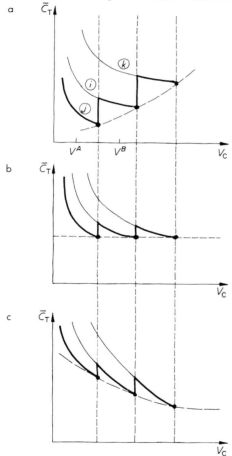

Figure 7.8 Effects of variations in interrelated options.

Figure 7.8 shows three possibilities for three alternative sets of options $\mathbf{T}^i$, $\mathbf{T}^j$, and $\mathbf{T}^k$. In part b the average total costs at each $V_C^{\max}$ are equal, in part a they increase, and in part c they decrease.

Consider part a of the figure, where curves i, j, k correspond to different choices of the options K and/or N. Assume for the moment that levels of service are equal or demand is inelastic, and thus that the operator's objective is to minimize average cost. If the volume anticipated is V^B, then to achieve a minimum average total cost, the options (K^i, N^i) would be chosen. If several years later the volume V^A were actually observed, rather than V^B, the average total cost $\bar{C}_T^i(V^A)$ would be greater than the average total cost $\bar{C}_T^j(V^A)$ that would have been incurred if the more desirable options (K^j, N^j) had been chosen. Because K and N are relatively long-term options, the operator would have no choice but to live with this higher cost until such time as these options could be adjusted. (This is in fact what happened in the international air travel market in the mid-1970s, when airlines collectively bought too much capacity.)

Thus the fact that K, N and Q have different time frames means that the options cannot usually be precisely tailored to the volume demanded. This problem is further compounded by the lumpiness of the options—the fact that K and N can, in general, take only integral values.

7.5.3 Service-Oriented Analysis

So far we have varied the options explicitly and found that sometimes target values of Q are infeasible because they exceed the capacity set by K and/or N. An alternative approach is to set Q and then choose whatever values of K and N are required to allow sufficient guideway capacity and a sufficient number of vehicles to meet the desired level of service. This approach is found in many types of models in the literature. To demonstrate the implications of this approach we shall reformulate the model defined in section 7.5.1.

Service-oriented analysis begins with the specification of a desired service policy, reflected in the schedule frequency Q and fare P, together with the technology $\mathbf{M} = (w, q_C, v)$. Then the required values of K and N, K_R and N_R, are found.

The logic of this type of analysis is as follows:

1. Specify service policy (Q, P) and technology $(\mathbf{M})$ to establish $\mathbf{T} = (\mathbf{M}, Q, P)$.

2. Determine design requirements for K and N to provide enough physical capacity to satisfy Q:

$$K_R(\mathbf{T}) = \left\langle \frac{Q}{q_C} \right\rangle, \qquad\qquad (7.37)$$

$$N_R(\mathbf{T}) = \left\langle \frac{Q}{n} \right\rangle. \qquad\qquad (7.38)$$

The brackets indicate "next-highest-integer value"; that is, K_R equals the quantity in brackets rounded up to the next highest integer.

3. Predict the available volume capacity:

$$V_C(\mathbf{T}) = 2Qw. \qquad\qquad (7.39)$$

4. Predict the level of service.

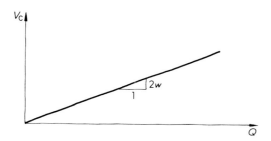

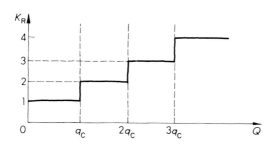

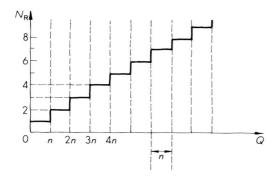

Figure 7.9 A service-oriented analysis.

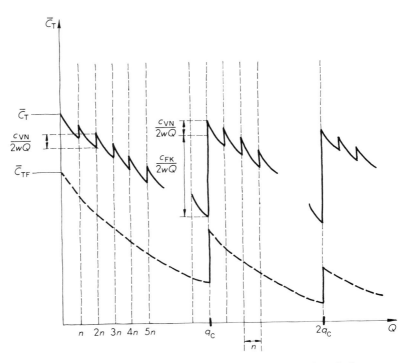

Figure 7.10 Average total cost function for a service-oriented analysis.

5. Predict the resources consumed.
6. Predict the total cost.

The significance of this formulation can be seen in figure 7.9. Here the indivisibilities of K and N show up clearly—for example, to achieve a service frequency of $Q = 3.5n$, $N_R = 4$ since N_R can take only integral values.

The implications for the average total cost function are shown in figure 7.10. These curves demonstrate the effects of long-, intermediate-, and short-run options and of indivisibilities on total cost. Further, we can see that very different kinds of technologies can be represented by this model; by varying the magnitudes of w, q_C, and v, and of c_{FK}, c_{VN}, and c_{OQ}, we can greatly affect the shape of the $\bar{C}_T$ curve.

The indivisibility of components is reflected by discontinuities in the cost curves. The costs suddenly jump when an additional fixed facility or vehicle is acquired (figure 7.11). Jump J_1 represents the acquisi-

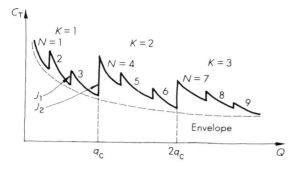

Figure 7.11 Effect of indivisibilities on average total cost. Jump J_1 represents acquisition of a vehicle; J_2 represents construction of a unit of fixed facilities. After Bhatt (1971).

tion of an additional vehicle; J_2 represents an additional unit of capacity of fixed facilities. Jump J_2 is much larger in magnitude because the unit vehicle acquisition cost is small compared to the unit cost of a fixed facility.

The magnitudes of the discontinuities depend on the technological and cost characteristics of the particular system. In some cases the envelope of the cost curve (dashed line) is a satisfactory approximation to the true cost curve. For example, if vehicle acquisition cost is a small percentage of the total cost, J_1 will be small. Systems with high fixed facility costs relative to vehicle costs show such characteristics. If the vehicle acquisition cost accounts for a large percentage of the total cost and is large compared to the unit cost of the fixed facility, then the jumps will be prominent and the envelope will not approximate true costs very closely.

It is important to recognize that this formulation represents a specific premise about the objectives to be achieved. These objectives are sufficient capacity in fixed facilities and in vehicle fleet to fully accommodate the desired schedule frequency Q. Many other objectives can be considered, such as choosing K and N to maximize net revenue for a given Q. The results will, in general, be different.

7.6 VEHICLE-FACILITY CONGESTION

So far we have examined the dimensionality of options without considering the congestion effects introduced in section 7.2. To illustrate the interactions of these characteristics of transportation performance functions we shall consider vehicle-facility congestion.

295   Congestion, Dimensionalities, Spatial Structure of Services

7.6.1 A Simple Model

Using the queuing analogy, which was a useful modeling approach in the early development of traffic flow theory (see Baerwald 1976), we take for the service rate

$$\mu = Kq_C, \tag{7.40}$$

where q_C is the capacity in vehicles per unit of time per unit of fixed facilities and K is the number of fixed facilities, and for the arrival rate

$$\lambda = q. \tag{7.41}$$

Thus

$$\rho \equiv \frac{\lambda}{\mu} = \frac{q}{Kq_C}, \tag{7.42}$$

$$\frac{t_\tau}{t_P} = 1 + J\frac{\lambda/\mu}{1 - \lambda/\mu} = 1 + J\frac{q/Kq_C}{1 - q/Kq_C}, \tag{7.43}$$

$$\frac{t_\tau}{t_P} = 1 + J\frac{1}{(Kq_C/q) - 1}. \tag{7.44}$$

In the highway engineering field relationships of this type are widely studied (Wohl and Martin 1967, Drew 1968, Pignataro 1973); an example, in the form of a speed-volume curve, is shown in figure 7.12. (Speed is, of course, proportional to $1/t_\tau$.) The quantity ρ is called the **volume-capacity ratio**. Empirically determined variations on (7.44) have included, for highways (FHWA 1973b),

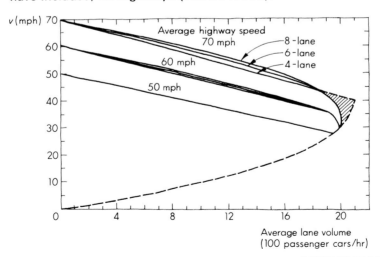

Figure 7.12 Typical highway congestion function. From HIGHWAY CAPACITY MANUAL (1965).

$$\frac{t_\tau}{t_P} = 1 + 0.15 \left(\frac{q}{Kq_C}\right)^4 \tag{7.45}$$

and, for arterial streets (prevailing speed 30 mph, three intersections with signals per mile, $t_P = 3.05$ minutes per mile) (Davidson as cited in Hutchinson 1974),

$$\frac{t_\tau}{t_P} = 1 + 0.1711 \frac{q/841}{1 - q/841}, \tag{7.46}$$

where in both cases q is in passenger-cars per hour and t_τ is in minutes per mile. Similar relationships have been developed for other modes for vehicle and nonvehicle links (Rallis 1967, Hengsbach and Odoni 1975).

7.6.2 Effects of Congestion on Costs and Revenues

The effect of vehicle-facility congestion is shown in figure 7.13. Part a shows how t_τ/t_P increases as q approaches the capacity, Kq_C, for each value of K. Part b shows the effect of the congestion on speed relative to the free speed, v_τ/v_P, where $v_i = d/t_i$. Part c shows the effect of the reductions in speed on relative productivity, where $n_i = v_i/2d$ and n_P is the productivity in trips per vehicle per time period at uncongested conditions:

$$\frac{n_\tau}{n_P} = \frac{t_P}{t_\tau}. \tag{7.47}$$

From (7.36) we have

$$C_T(T) = c_{FK} K + c_{VN} N + c_{OQ} \frac{Q}{n_\tau}. \tag{7.48}$$

For simplicity we assume that the vehicle fleet size is adequate at all times.

Figure 7.14a shows the cost function for $q = Q$ and different values of K. As n decreases, cost increases. Because n decreases as q approaches capacity for a given K, the total cost increases (as shown by the solid curves) faster than in the previous, uncongested case (shown by the dashed lines). As a result, crossover points for the different cost functions for various options K shift: for example, for values of q between q_1^* and q_C, $K = 2$ has a lower C_T than $K = 1$. This is demonstrated more clearly by part b, which shows the average total cost $\bar{C}_T$. The congestion effect causes the average cost functions to become U-shaped.

In the general case we would consider more than just the cost func-

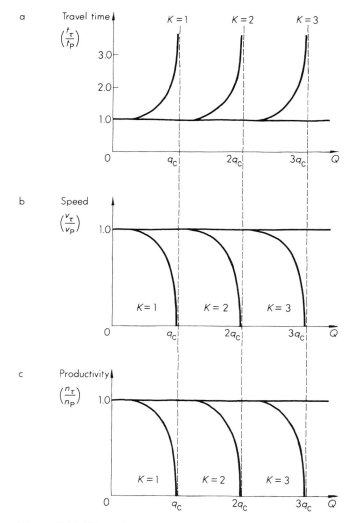

Figure 7.13 Effect of vehicle-facility congestion on travel time, speed, and productivity.

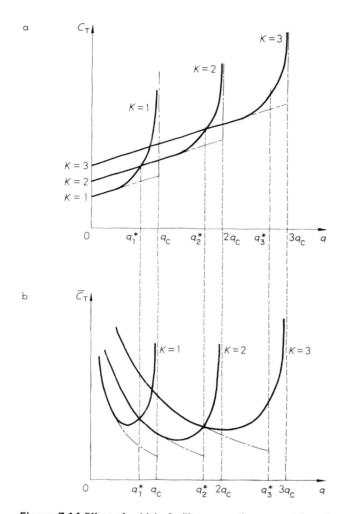

Figure 7.14 Effect of vehicle-facility congestion on cost functions.

tion: we would examine the effects of congestion and of variations in the options on service levels, equilibrium volumes, gross revenues, and user and operator impacts such as net revenues. Congestion affects not only the costs but also the service levels and thus the equilibrium volume, thereby reducing net revenues below those at uncongested conditions. Thus we would expect that from a net revenue perspective, the frequency at which an additional increment of capacity (in this case, fixed facilities) is desirable may be substantially lower than it would be from a cost perspective alone.

From the perspective of capacity alone, in designing a system one wishes ideally to match all of the options so that there is just the right amount of capacity to meet the projected demand. This leads to the service-oriented formulation of a performance function. This is not always practical or desirable for several reasons: the lumpiness of the options, their different time frames, the influence of congestion effects, and the difference between design and actual (equilibrium) volumes. Because of congestion effects (even ignoring demand equilibration), the most attractive options may be different from the ones that just provide sufficient capacity to meet a specified demand level. Further, when demand functions are explicitly considered, the choices may be even more significantly different, since actual volumes may be significantly different from design volumes or capacities (see sections 5.7 and 6.6).

7.7 SYSTEM PERFORMANCE IN SPACE AND TIME

In chapter 6 we explored the basic economics of the vehicle cycle. In this chapter we have examined congestion effects and the dimensionality of options. We shall now look at the full system of services offered in a network and suggest how all of these elements interact.

7.7.1 Some Basic Concepts and Definitions

We start by introducing some basic definitions that are essential in understanding the structure of transportation services over space and time.

AN EXAMPLE

Consider the transportation system shown in figure 7.15. Services can be provided, potentially, at three locations, designated A, B, and C in part a. The services would use the network of facilities shown in part b, consisting of seven links. Links 1-3, 3-5, and 1-5 are movement links; links 1-2, 3-4, and 5-6 are transfer links. Link 4-7 connects the

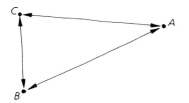

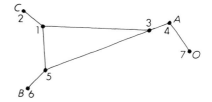

Figure 7.15 A simple transportation system.

Table 7.4   Characteristics of five options for the transportation system of figure 7.15

		T^0	T^1	T^2	T^3	T^4
Routes						
R_0 : A-B-A		x		x	x	x
R_1 : A-B-C-B-A			x			
R_2 : B-C-B				x		x
R_3 : A-C-A					x	x
Markets	**Paths**					
A-B	Direct nonstop	x	x	x	x	x
	Direct one-stop					
	Connecting, one transfer					x
B-C	Direct nonstop		x	x		x
	Direct one-stop					
	Connecting, one-transfer				x	x
A-C	Direct nonstop				x	x
	Direct one-stop		x			
	Connecting, one-transfer			x		x

301   Congestion, Dimensionalities, Spatial Structure of Services

terminal at *A* with the operating base at *O*. If this were an airline network, the movement links would represent the controlled airways among cities and the transfer links would represent the airports (including the controlled approach zones, runways, and so forth). For a rail network, the movement links would represent the intercity rail lines, and the transfer links would represent the stations and associated rail yards.

At present service is being offered between *A* and *B*, designated as option T^0. This service has the characteristics shown in table 7.4.

The possibility of extending service to *C* is being raised. Several alternatives are available:

Plan T^0: Maintain present service.

Plan T^1: Extend service from terminal *B* to *C*, operating vehicles from *A* through *B* to *C* and return.

Plan T^2: Operate present service between *A* and *B*, and operate a sep-

a A single route $(O-A-B-C-A-O)$

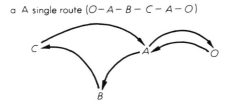

b Multiple routes (movements to operating base not shown)

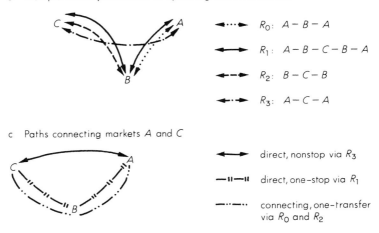

R_0: $A-B-A$

R_1: $A-B-C-B-A$

R_2: $B-C-B$

R_3: $A-C-A$

c Paths connecting markets *A* and *C*

direct, nonstop via R_3

direct, one-stop via R_1

connecting, one-transfer via R_0 and R_2

Figure 7.16 Relation of definitions.

arate service with different vehicles between B and C; thus passengers going between A and C would have to change vehicles at B.

Plan T^3: Operate present service between A and B, and operate a service between C and A.

Plan T^4: Combination of T^0, T^2, and T^3.

The general logic of the basic analysis introduced in chapter 5 applies here, but we must add significantly to the detail.

DEFINITIONS

The following concepts must be distinguished (the relationships among these definitions are shown in figure 7.16).

A *market* is a potential set of flows that might be served, specified in terms of their origins and destinations. In the example there are three potential markets (for two-directional flows): B-A, A-C, B-C.

A *route* is the path followed by one or several vehicles as each moves from its origin station through one or more way stations and back to the origin. In the example the four routes shown in table 7.4 are under consideration.

A *link* is a facility over which vehicles may move. In the example the possible links are 1-2, 3-4, 5-6, 1-3, 3-5, 1-5, and 4-7. Note that, in general, the links are not the same as the markets.

A *path* is the route or routes used by a passenger in moving from an initial origin to a final destination. The possible paths in the example are shown in table 7.4.

For convenience we shall assume that passengers follow the same path in both directions. In general, there will be several paths available in each market, and some paths may require transfers between routes. In the example the available paths depend on which options are implemented. This is shown in the table.

THE USER'S PERSPECTIVE

Each user has a different view of the system. Each sees a set of alternative paths p_{kdp} from an origin k to each destination d; and each path p_{kdp} is characterized by a service vector $\mathbf{S}_{kdp}$. Some of the paths may involve direct nonstop services, some direct one- or multistop services, and some one- or multiple-transfer services; further, these paths may use routes of one or several modes. The service attributes characterizing the paths reflect the differences in these services (for example, the effects of en route stops or transfers).

Any of the demand functions discussed in chapters 2–4 can be

used to represent user behavior. The essential point is that the probability of an individual choosing path p should be a function of the
service attributes of that path relative to those of alternative paths (see
chapter 12).

There are a variety of ways in which the differences between one-
and multistop or between direct and transfer services could be included. At the simplest level the increments of in-vehicle and waiting
time due to a stop or transfer could be added to those for other trip
components, without any special treatment. More realistic formulations
might include the number of en route stops or the number of transfers
as explicit service attributes, or might even try to distinguish qualitative
aspects of these attributes (for example, in international air travel a
three-hour transfer time at a modest tropical airport with minimum
facilities might influence traveler behavior differently from a three-hour
transfer time at a major international center with extensive tax-free
tourist shops and related services).

THE OPERATOR'S PERSPECTIVE
Users view the system primarily (perhaps exclusively) from a disaggregate perspective: what matters to them is the services available
in the markets in which they are interested. Operators, on the other
hand, are interested almost solely in the aggregate performance of
their portions of the system. For a private-sector operator the total net
revenue and other measures of profitability are of primary interest.
Even a public-sector operator is mainly concerned with maintaining
maximum effectiveness. (Both obviously do pay some attention to
the degree of service in disaggregated markets, if for no other reason
than to understand which parts of the system are relatively weak or
strong contributors to profitability.)

From the operator's perspective the basic question is, What are the
alternative strategies for implementing and/or operating the system
and what are the costs and revenues associated with these strategies?
A fully specified strategy includes the fixed facilities and their characteristics; the types and numbers of vehicles and their characteristics;
the structure of routes on which services will be offered; for each
route, the schedule (or frequency of service), the vehicle(s) to be
assigned, the fixed facilities to be traversed; and for each path in each
market, the price to be charged. Thus the operator must specify a
complex and detailed pattern of services over space and time. (Figure
5.4 illustrates just how complex the route of a single vehicle can be.)
At the core of this specification is the assignment of vehicles to

routes, since each assigned vehicle operates according to the prescribed schedule. Correspondingly, for each vehicle there is a vehicle cycle, or pattern of use, involving operational cycles, service cycles, and the annual cycle. The economics of each vehicle cycle can be viewed in isolation, but that can be misleading. In the context of operations in space and time, the economic performance of a strategy is likely to be significantly different from the simple addition of independent vehicle cycles. This happens because of the ways in which the parts of the system are interrelated and the ways in which the system operates to deliver different services to different markets (Taylor 1977). Figure 7.16 shows just how different the views of users and operators are; indeed the paths taken by users are often very different from the routes of vehicles (for example, compare the one-transfer path in part c with the vehicle movement over routes R_0 and R_2, which may be only portions of the routes flown by the respective vehicles).

In order to understand the economics of vehicle performance we must therefore understand the ways in which several vehicles on several routes perform as a system, delivering different services in different markets. To develop this understanding in this introductory discussion we shall build on our previous analysis of the vehicle cycle and its economic implications.

7.7.2 The Operating Plan
An operator typically utilizes a fleet of vehicles over a number of routes. In the simplest cases each vehicle is assigned to a specific route and shuttles back and forth over that route at regular intervals. In general, however, the efficient utilization of a fleet of vehicles will involve the integrated use of a number of vehicles on a number of routes. The specification of an operating plan includes:

1. a list of the vehicles to be utilized;
2. a list of the routes to be served;
3. a timetable of services over each route;
4. an assignment of each vehicle to a schedule such that the set of routes is covered and the timetable is met; and
5. an assignment of operating labor (crews) to vehicles and services.

AN AIRFREIGHT EXAMPLE
Figure 7.17 shows an operating plan for a London-based fleet of seven freighter aircraft. These are European short-haul services to 24 cities

Aircraft
cycle

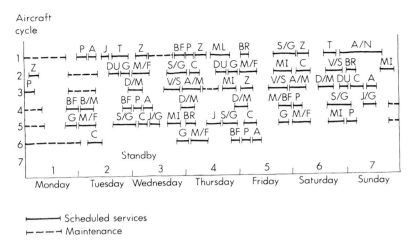

├───┤ Scheduled services

├───┤ Maintenance

Figure 7.17 An airfreight operating plan. Letters represent cities. From P. S. Smith (1974), p. 88.

over 19 routes. The following features of this plan should be noted (P. S. Smith 1974, p. 88ff.):

1. Six aircraft are assigned to operational cycles and the seventh is retained on standby reserve in case of unexpected problems with the other aircraft or weather problems.

2. Each operational cycle covers the seven-day week and is unique.

3. The assignment of specific aircraft to the seven operational cycles is changed each week.

4. Service to any given market is provided by a different aircraft on different days.

5. Much of the maintenance is scheduled early in the week, since the bulk of the flying time occurs in the evening, at night, and late in the week when demand is greatest.

6. Operational servicing occurs during the operational cycles, generally at the periods of lowest demand.

7. Some services are provided at the same time throughout the week to provide regularity to shippers.

8. There appears to be spare capacity in the fleet (see cycle 6) in that there do not seem to be any opportunities for sufficiently productive use of this capacity.

In discussing the vehicle cycle in chapter 6, we noted that one measure of productive utilization of a vehicle is the number of hours it is utilized. The utilization achieved by this particular operating plan varies by operational cycle, as shown in table 7.5. The average utili-

Table 7.5 Variations in utilization by operating cycle

| | Utilization in hours | |
Cycle	Per week	Per year
1	64.2	3,371
2	51.0	2,678
3	49.8	2,615
4	36.5	1,916
5	54.8	2,874
6	18.8	987
7	0	0

Source: P. S. Smith (1974).

zations are 45.8 hours for the first six aircraft and 39.3 hours for the fleet of seven (corresponding to annual utilizations of 2,407 and 2,063 hours, respectively). Note that the average for the fleet as a whole is significantly lower than the maximum achievable by a single vehicle on a single cycle.

This example demonstrates the complexity that can enter into an operational plan. It also demonstrates that the effective utilizations of specific vehicles can vary widely, so that the estimation of the effective utilization of a fleet, or of an "average" vehicle, is often difficult if one does not actually construct a detailed operating plan. Since the economics of the system depend significantly on the utilization achieved, as illustrated in section 6.7.1, it is clearly important to examine the utilization of the fleet rather than that of a single vehicle.

OTHER RESOURCES

In the foregoing example we explicitly mentioned only vehicles. In general, there are several types of resources that are assigned in the process of developing an operating plan:

1. vehicles;
2. vehicle crews (the driver or pilot and other personnel traveling with the vehicle);
3. other labor (for example, at terminals or maintenance facilities); and
4. facilities.

Since the capacities of fixed facilities are limited, in many contexts the scheduling of these facilities is an important part of the operating plan, as in the case of boarding gates at airports.

The treatment of operating labor (vehicle crews) is often particularly complex. In many contexts historical practices and negotiated agreements on work rules result in quite detailed and complex constraints on how crews can be utilized. For example, there may be limits on maximum working hours per shift, maximum in-travel hours, maximum distance traveled, minimum time between successive shifts, and so forth. As a result, the development of an operating plan with an efficient utilization of personnel resources is a difficult task, usually requiring intimate knowledge of specific working practices in a particular system. As we have seen, the influence of fixed facilities and various types of congestion effects can also be important.

Various mathematical models and computer programs have been developed for use in preparing portions of an operating plan (Simpson 1969, 1977, Ehrlich 1977; see especially the journal *Transportation Science* and the operations research literature).

7.8 SUMMARY

In this chapter we have examined three sets of factors that can significantly influence the performance of a system.

Congestion in a transportation system occurs when the average processing time per unit increases as demand for service increases. The level of demand at which congestion becomes important is determined by the capacity of the system. The physical capacity is the maximum number of units that can be processed by a system under any circumstances, but this may well involve very long delays. In contrast, various definitions of practical capacity can be chosen such that delays are within more tolerable limits.

The significance of congestion is that the marginal time (or cost) is greater than the average time (or cost).

Many types of congestion occur in transportation systems. It is especially important to distinguish load-dependent and load-independent congestion. The first category includes load-vehicle and load-schedule congestion. The second category includes vehicle-facility and vehicle-schedule congestion, which can occur regardless of the load (passengers or freight) moving through the system.

Using simple models of congestion, we modified performance model I to demonstrate the effects of congestion on user and operator impacts.

In general, transportation system planners are faced with a wide variety of options that offer a range of implementation time frames and show various forms of indivisibilities. These interrelationships among options have a significant effect on user and operator impacts in that it often becomes difficult to choose a precise combination of options that is "best" for a particular situation. A third performance model was used to demonstrate these effects.

As an example of the combined effects of congestion and the dimensionality of options, vehicle-facility congestion was explored through traditional highway facility models. The effect of congestion was shown in the cost functions, which became U-shaped.

The spatial structure of a transportation system can be quite complex. A wide variety of different service strategies can be implemented in the same network. Each user sees a set of alternative paths from an origin to a set of possible destinations. Some paths may involve non-stop or one- or multiple-stop direct services; other paths may require one or more transfers. User choice of alternative paths is a function of the service levels of the paths.

While users see the system from a disaggregate perspective, operators are interested primarily in the aggregate performance of a total system, as reflected in economic and other measures.

Complete specification of a system from the operator's perspective requires identification of the fixed facilities, the vehicles, the set of routes; for each route, the vehicles assigned and the schedule; and for each path, the prices. The assignment of vehicles to routes is at the heart of this specification; the economics of a system are related to the characteristics of each vehicle cycle over each route. The relationships are not simply additive. Because of the interrelations of vehicle routes and markets, evaluation of the economic performance of a system strategy is likely to be significantly different from a simple addition of independent vehicle cycles.

The operating plan of a system is the description of how vehicles are utilized to provide services. The detailed specification of an operating plan includes the vehicles to be used, the routes to be served, the timetable of services over each route, and the assignment of vehicles, facilities, and operating labor to the scheduled services.

In the working out of a practical operating plan, numerous deviations from a nominal optimum may be required. For example, the utilizations in a fleet of vehicles in international airfreight service may range from 64 to 19 hours per week, with one aircraft kept in reserve (0 hours per week). Thus the average effective utilization for the fleet as a whole is 40 hours.

TO READ FURTHER

The various formulations and models of congestion comprise a large body of material: see, for example, Rallis (1967), Gazis (1974), and Daganzo (1978b). For applications to port and airport planning see De Weille and Ray (1974), Robinson and Tognetti (1974), Wilmes and Frankel (1974), and Hengsbach and Odoni (1975). For models of systems interrelations see Simpson (1969, 1977), Pollack (1974), Ehrlich (1977), and the large body of literature in operations research on optimization and simulation applications.

EXERCISES

7.1(E) At present, a regularly scheduled shipping route is operated by operator *A* with direct service to both ports *X* and *Y*, on the same coast, from port *Z*, 5,000 miles across the ocean. Operator *A* thinks it might be financially advantageous to eliminate port *Y* from the route; then cargo from *Y* would be transshipped to *X*, either by truck or by other water carrier, and loaded there for shipment to *Z*. Thus the ship from *Z* would no longer call at port *Y*. The carrier is prepared to absorb the cost of the inland transportation between *X* and *Y* if the savings are great enough.

Will the elimination of the separate port call at *Y* be profitable if demand is constant? if demand varies?

Define the necessary variables and relationships and indicate the analysis you would do to answer these questions.

7.2(E) In exercises 1.6 and 5.1 we considered the issue of optimal train operating strategies under the assumption that service levels were independent of demand. In fact, the time a car spends waiting at a railyard to be placed on an outgoing train is an example of vehicle-load congestion. Let

$$\mathbf{S} = (t_{iv}, t_w),$$

$$t_{iv} = \frac{D}{v},$$

$$t_w = \frac{24}{2Q}\left(1 + \frac{J\rho}{1-\rho}\right), \quad \text{where } \rho = \frac{V_D}{V_C} \text{ and } V_C = QL.$$

Incorporate this service function with congestion into exercise 5.1. Assume $J = 0.1$ and then 0.001 and discuss the results.

7.3(C) The relationships developed in this chapter ignore a number of elements that are sometimes important:
1. fixed facilities costs and utilization

2. general overhead and administrative costs

3. relationships of vehicle usage (for example, miles per year) to serviceable life, maintenance requirements, depreciation, and salvage values (see De Weille 1966, Annex I).

a. Extend the relationships developed in this chapter to include consideration of elements 1, 2, and 3, separately and together.

b. Take a particular mode or context and develop specific relationships and numerical examples for that situation, incorporating elements 1, 2, and 3 separately and together.

7.4(C) Compare the "fundamental diagram" of traffic flow theory (Drew 1968, Pignataro 1973, or Baerwald 1976) with figure 7.13 and discuss.

7.5(C) The Bay Area Rapid Transit System (BART) was heralded as a major innovation in rail rapid transit. Soon after the system opened, however, it became clear that innovation involves many problems. One of the key problem areas turned out to be vehicle reliability.

Planners of BART anticipated that in due course at least 80 percent of the cars in the fleet would be available for service at any given time. Instead, for a number of reasons that are still the subject of active investigation and litigation, car availability for revenue service during 1974 and 1975 varied between 45 and 60 percent (Ellis and Sherrett 1976). What impact would this have on system performance? How would you incorporate this factor in a performance model?

8
Equilibration

8.1 THE SCOPE OF EQUILIBRATION

In the prediction step of transportation analysis we consider both human behavior and system performance. We represent human behavior (primarily as consumer behavior) by means of demand and activity-shift models. We represent the performance of the transportation system through resource and service models.

Equilibration involves creating an interface between these two factors. The interactions between human behavior and system performance are resolved over several different time frames and through several different mechanisms. Three major groupings of these interactions were identified in chapter 1: travel-market equilibrium, activity-system equilibrium, and transportation-operator equilibrium.

In the short range the transportation-system options **T** and the activity-system options **A** are fixed. Thus the service function **S** can be interfaced with the travel demand function **D** to determine an equilibrium flow pattern. This is the type 1 relationship. There are two key methodological issues in this travel-market equilibration. The first is how to take into account the service function, and especially the congestion effects introduced in chapter 7. The second involves the spatial distribution of services, the topological structure of networks, and the behavioral bases of choice of travel routes.

In the long range the activity system will, in general, change. The nature of the change in any period will be affected in part by the equilibrium flow patterns that have existed in each prior period and in part by forces internal to the activity system, such as economic and social changes in a society. The time lags are an important part of this process, and it may be more correct to describe long-run activity-system equilibrium as a direction toward which the system is continually adjusting rather than as a state that is ever reached. Metaphorically the travel demand function **D** can be described as shifting over time, thus causing shifts in travel-market equilibrium which then bring about further activity shifts, and so on. This is the type 2 relationship. Because of the time lags and the complex interrelationships, developing good models of this activity-system equilibration process is very difficult.

In the long range also, each transportation operator can, in principle, adjust the options within his control to achieve a travel-market equilibrium at each point in time that maximizes the achievement of his own objectives. In principle, one could construct models for predicting the behavior of operators under various conditions if a number of special conditions are met. As demonstrated in section 5.7, the result would be the supply function of classical economics. Then one could also predict the equilibrium conditions of the transportation operators. In practice, however, these conditions are not met, and for many additional practical reasons it is difficult to model the process of transportation-operator equilibration except under special and usually highly idealized conditions. (In volume 2 we shall analyze in greater detail operator equilibration and the relationship between the classical supply function and the transportation system performance function.)

In this chapter we shall explore the concept of travel-market equilibration, with particular emphasis on alternative computational approximations, and the implications of actions defined over time for the relationships between travel-market and activity-system equilibration. In chapter 12 we shall expand our consideration of travel-market equilibration to include the spatial structure of networks.

8.2 TRAVEL-MARKET EQUILIBRATION

Given a demand function, one is tempted to use it for predicting flows by assuming that the transportation-system service levels are known at the outset of the analysis and do not change. In general this is not the case; at least some of the service attributes will vary according to the number of users of the system. For example, travel time over a highway or bus route, or processing time through a rail classification yard, will depend on a level of usage. This often makes prediction of an actual level of usage difficult even if the demand function is known. The level of usage will be a function of the service provided, as specified by the demand function; but the service will be affected in turn by the level of usage. This second dependency is reflected by a service function S of the form

$$S = J(V, T), \tag{8.1}$$

where T represents the characteristics and V the volumes of the transportation system.

8.2.1 Equilibrium Conditions

In general, both service and demand functions must be used, and the volume is determined by the equilibrium of service and demand. Prediction of flows requires consideration of the interactions of demand (consumer behavior) and service (technology) through finding the equilibrum flow pattern in the travel market.

In the general case travel-market equilibration requires a computational process that explicitly determines a flow pattern—volumes and levels of service—that meets both service and demand conditions. Specifically, at equilibrium, the service levels S_i on each facility i in the system are those that would occur at the predicted volumes,

$$S_i = J_i(V_i) \quad \text{for all } i; \tag{8.2}$$

and the volumes V_i on all facilities i are those that would occur at the predicted service levels,

$$V_i = D(S_i) \quad \text{for all } i. \tag{8.3}$$

This approach of explicit equilibration is the most general one. Prediction of volumes and service levels under a new set of transportation system options using the demand function alone generally leads to errors, because the service level assumed may be inconsistent with the volume predicted by the demand function alone. The service function, if taken into account, will ensure this consistency. The importance of these effects is shown in the following example.

8.2.2 An Example

Consider travel by air between two cities in a densely populated region. The volume of travel in the base year, 1960, is 6,000 persons per day. The demand is forecast to increase by 1,000 per year each year (about 15 percent per year, not compounded). (In the mid-1960s typical forecasts envisioned 14–17 percent per year increases in air passenger travel, compounded annually.) We consider three ways in which demand could be forecast.

In the first approach demand is simply assumed to grow by 1,000 per year.

In the second approach we recognize that demand depends on travel time and formulate an explicit demand function:

$$V = a - bt. \tag{8.4}$$

In 1960 a is 10,000, and it increases by 1,000 each year. Also in 1960, t is 2 hours. The coefficient b equals 2,000 persons per day per hour

Table 8.1 Comparison of forecasts

Year	(a) Volume for constant travel time	(b) Volume with congestion considered	(c) Overestimate of volume	(d) Time with congestion
1960	6,000	6,000	0	2.00
1962	8,000	8,000	0	2.00
1964	10,000	9,000	1,000	2.50
1966	12,000	10,000	2,000	3.00
1968	14,000	11,000	3,000	3.50
1970	16,000	12,000	4,000	4.00
1972	18,000	12,400	5,600	4.80

of travel time. If we assume that travel time remains constant, independent of volume, we get the same forecasts as in the first approach.

In the third approach we recognize that travel time is affected by volume; that is, after a certain volume congestion builds up in the system. This is reflected in the service function. We assume an explicit function made up of three linear segments:

$$t = \begin{cases} 2, & 0 \leq V \leq 8,000, \\ \dfrac{V}{2,000} - 2, & 8,000 \leq V \leq 12,000, \\ \dfrac{V}{500} - 20, & V \leq 12,000. \end{cases} \qquad (8.5)$$

At $V = 12,000$ the time has doubled to four hours; from this point on the system is very close to capacity, and travel time increases at the rate of two hours for every additional 1,000 passengers per day.

The effects of congestion are shown in table 8.1. Column a indicates the results with constant travel times, and column b the results when congestion effects are considered. The amount of overestimation due to neglect of the service effects is shown in column c. Column d shows how the equilibrium travel time changes from the initial value $t = 2$ hours. The results are shown graphically in figure 8.1.

The implications are clear: service effects can be ignored only under special conditions. In general, omitting the service effects results in serious errors in forecasting flows. For example, consider the year 1966. If congestion is not considered, the estimate of flows would be a volume of 12,000 persons per day and a travel time of 2 hours—point A in the figure. When congestion effects, reflected in the service

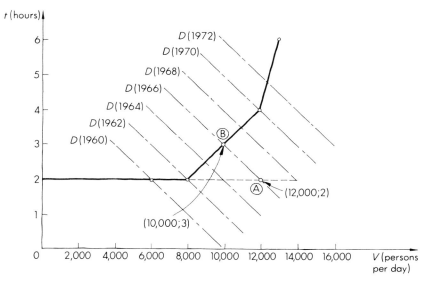

Figure 8.1 Effects of congestion on demand.

function, are considered, the estimate would be 10,000 persons
per day and 3 hours, as shown by point *B* (see also section 7.3).

8.3 SOME PRACTICAL APPROXIMATIONS TO TRAVEL-MARKET EQUILIBRATION

The preceding discussion has indicated why an explicit treatment of the
interaction of service and demand is important in an equilibration
procedure. By "explicit" we mean that the analyst explicitly considers
alternative approaches and the implications of simplifying assumptions.
In particular situations approximations may well be desirable.

8.3.1 Alternative Assumptions

Sometimes it may be acceptable, practical, or even essential to reduce
the complexity of the general problem by making one of several assumptions. Either of the assumptions we shall now describe may be
appropriate in a particular context. The analyst must, however, carefully
weigh the limitations introduced by making such assumptions, as
illustrated in section 8.2.2. If the assumptions are acceptable, equilibration is greatly simplified.

KNOWN-SERVICE-LEVEL ASSUMPTION

Sometimes the analyst may feel that congestion effects are sufficiently insignificant that the level of service resulting from an equilibrium analysis can be estimated beforehand, either because it is essentially the same as that assumed prior to equilibration (as when operating in the flat portion of the service function) or because there is a good basis for an estimate of the change.

KNOWN-VOLUME ASSUMPTION

Sometimes demand effects are sufficiently insignificant that the volume predicted by an equilibrium analysis can be estimated beforehand, either because it is essentially the same as that for a prior condition (as when demand elasticities are close to zero) or because there is a good basis for estimating the magnitude of the demand without an elaborate analysis.

8.3.2 Using the Known-Service-Level Assumption

If the service levels can be easily estimated, then equilibration is simplified, and priority is placed on the demand function:

Step 1: Estimate new service levels, S_i'.
Step 2: Using the demand function, find $V_i' = D(S_i')$.
Step 3: Check against the service functions:

$$S_i'' = J_i(V_i'),$$

$$\Delta S_i \equiv S_i'' - S_i'.$$

If the ΔS_i are sufficiently small, terminate; if not, revise estimates of S_i' and repeat step 2.

This approach is especially useful when it is believed that congestion or other volume-related influences on service levels are minimal or insignificant and that the major effects are changes in the level of demand. It was used in the demand chapters (2, 3, and 4) and in much of the technology chapters (5 and 6), and its limitations were illustrated in section 8.2.2.

This assumption is often made in practice. For example, in assessing urban transportation systems, analysts often assume that transit travel times are constant and independent of volumes. In many freight system analyses in which a demand function is used, this assumption has also been made.

The approach is illustrated in figure 8.2b, where J^0 is the initial service function and J' the new service function. Both are constant and independent of volume over the range of volume of interest. (J' is shown dashed to indicate that it may be the same as J^0.)

a General case

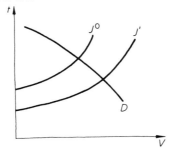

b Known-service-level assumption

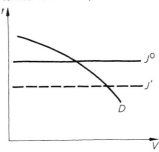

c Known-volume assumption

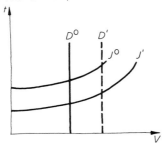

Figure 8.2 Two simplifying equilibration assumptions.

8.3.3 Using the Known-Volume Assumption

If the volume of demand can be easily estimated, then once again equilibration is simplified, and priority is now placed on the performance function:

Step 1: Estimate new volumes V_i'. These may be assumed the same as the prior volumes V_i^0 or set by a load-factor assumption $(V_i' = \lambda V_C')$ or set as a design goal (see section 5.7).

Step 2: Using the service function, find service levels $S_i' = J_i(V_i')$.

Step 3: Check against the demand function:

$$V_i'' = D_i(S_i'),$$

$$\Delta V_i \equiv V_i - V_i''.$$

If the ΔV_i are acceptable, terminate; if not, repeat step 2 with some appropriate revised estimate of V_i'.

This approach is especially useful when it is believed that demand is relatively insensitive to the changes being analyzed. It is often used (implicitly) where the primary emphasis is on appraising the operational performance of a given system under various operating policies, for example, when a stochastic simulation model is used for port or terminal analysis. Often the only check against demand is whether the system has sufficient capacity to serve the estimated (assumed) volumes V_i. As shown in figure 8.2c, this amounts to assuming constant demand over the range of service levels being examined. (D' is shown dashed to indicate that it may be the same as D^0.)

8.4 INFLUENCE OF MARKET STRUCTURE

Several features of demand influence how a set of options performs in an equilibrium context.

Demand is not uniform in several key respects (see, for example, Hill, Tittemore, and Gendell 1973, Campbell 1977, Taylor 1977). First, the actual volume using a particular service will vary with time: time of day, day of the week, and week of the year. Second, volumes in the two opposite directions on the same route will usually be unequal during a given time period. Third, performance of a system is a composite of performance over many different routes. Fourth, demand is often random; that is, it is a stochastic variable distributed with means exhibiting the properties of temporal and directional variation indicated above. Stochastic variation in demand also affects the average conditions achieved and the economic impacts on the operator. In this section we shall examine the first two elements; the third and fourth will be explored in volume 2.

The cumulative result of all of these market factors is an average or overall economic picture (costs, operator revenues, user benefits) substantially different, in many situations, from "typical" or peak conditions. Further, the overall economic viability of a particular operator may be substantially dependent on the responses it makes to these variations, especially to the off-peak and backhaul conditions.

In general, the demand functions at different times and in different directions are interdependent. For example, peak-period congestion may influence some users to shift their travel to other time periods. Ideally, in a complete analysis all of these effects would be included in the demand functions and in the travel-market equilibration procedures. However, this is not often feasible. For approximate analyses specific parameters can be defined to summarize these effects, such as the backhaul ratio or a peaking factor.

8.4.1 The Nonuniformity of Demand over Space

The nonuniformity of demand over space was discussed in section 6.5.1. There we showed how a backhaul ratio could be defined to approximate the effect of directional imbalances. This parameter was used in a manner analogous to a load-factor estimate as an approximation to equilibrium. In that analysis we showed that the ability of owner-operator truckers to compete for rail traffic depended in part on the value of this parameter.

8.4.2 The Nonuniformity of Demand over Time:
The Peaking Problem

The demand for transportation varies with time and with direction. If we take any fixed period of time as a base, we find that throughout the period the magnitude of demand varies even if the same level of service is offered at all times. For example, in an urban transportation situation the volume traveling inbound to the central business district in the peak morning rush hour will usually be much greater than the volume at midday in the middle of the week.

Because of this variation, the equilibrium volume varies. Thus the average load factor achieved is a composite of varying load factors achieved for different time periods. For example, there are peak and off-peak periods in almost all transportation contexts. All other impacts—costs, revenues, and so on—also vary with time.

A major factor influencing these variations is the fact that the transportation operator usually adjusts the options to provide different levels of service in different time periods. For example, peak-period service frequencies may be greater than off-peak frequencies. Thus the net economic effect of time variations can be quite complex, particularly when labor rules or other factors introduce cross-linkages among costs in different time periods or when demand cross-elasticities produce complex equilibration effects.

To take these variations into account one can explicitly formulate different demand functions for different time periods and directions. For example, to represent these variations in an urban situation we might distinguish the following categories:

1. trip purpose, p: work, school, other (shopping, social, recreational);
2. market segment categorized, for example, by income group, i: high, medium, low;
3. time period, t: weekday peak (A.M. or P.M.), weekday off-peak, evening or weekend;
4. direction, d: inbound, outbound;
5. day of week and season of year, h.

In principle, a set of demand functions can be defined corresponding to the various possible combinations (i, p, t, d, h). Thus there would be a specific demand function for trips from home to work by high-income travelers in the A.M. peak period inbound to the central area on spring weekdays. This would lead to a large number of demand functions. (It is important to realize that since time of trip is a traveler choice, there should ideally be linkages among the time-of-day models such that there is a cross-elasticity among time periods; see chapter 11 and the discussion in Kraft and Wohl 1967.) This approach is often taken in large-scale regional studies, although some of the effects may be represented by factors rather than separate models. Travel-market equilibration would then have to include all of these.

For small-scale studies it is often reasonable to simplify the analysis quite a bit. In the simplest approach one or a few demand functions are formulated explicitly. Travel-market equilibration is done with this function, and the volumes for other combinations of the set are derived from the resulting equilibrium flow. This is illustrated in case study II, chapter 10, where the approach used is to predict peak and off-peak trips in the dominant direction of flow and then to predict trips in the reverse direction as a fixed fraction of these trips. Even more simply, many transportation studies predict explicitly only peak-period flows and then estimate off-peak flows as a fixed ratio to peak volumes.

In predicting impacts from user and operator perspectives, one must consider the different services offered and impacts achieved in each time period. The overall evaluation of a transportation plan must often include consideration of these different impacts in different time periods. The relation between peak and nonpeak periods is particularly important; when sufficient capacity is provided for peak periods, there is excess capacity for other periods. This leads to questions of allocation of costs, differential pricing by time of day, and related issues.

8.5 ACTIVITY-SYSTEM EQUILIBRATION AND THE DYNAMICS OF PREDICTION (OPTIONAL READING)

We start with some definitions:

$\mathbf{T}^t$ = the state of the transportation system at time t,

$\mathbf{A}^t$ = the state of the activity system at time t,

$\mathcal{T}^t$ = a set of actions taken at time t to change the transportation system (defined in terms of the transportation options),

$\mathcal{A}^t$ = a set of actions taken at time t to change the activity system (defined in terms of the activity options),

$\mathbf{E}^t$ = the exogenous events that occur during time period t.

Then a particular **plan** (or policy or program) $\mathscr{P}$ consists of a sequence of actions implemented over n time periods:

$$\mathscr{P} = (\mathcal{T}^1, \mathcal{A}^1; \mathcal{T}^2, \mathcal{A}^2; \ldots ; \mathcal{T}^n, \mathcal{A}^n). \tag{8.6}$$

To predict the impacts associated with this plan requires the explicit interrelationship of travel-market equilibration and activity-system equilibration over time.

8.5.1 Scenarios

The evolution of the activity system over time will be a function of that system's own internal dynamics (including factors such as population growth and the changing structure of the economy), the influences of transportation (as reflected in changing service levels over time), and the influences of exogenous events. A **scenario** $\mathscr{E}$ is a statement of the set of exogenous events that occur over n time periods:

$$\mathscr{E} = (\mathbf{E}^1, \mathbf{E}^2, \ldots , \mathbf{E}^n). \tag{8.7}$$

An explicit scenario is required for every model system; there are always some exogenous variables that must be defined as inputs, such as population growth rate or energy prices.

8.5.2 Linkages

Potentially a model system can incorporate all three types of equilibration. Initially we shall assume the general case in which travel-
market and activity-system equilibration are explicitly included, but
with no operator equilibration. Then we shall consider the special case
where operator equilibration is included.

An activity-shift model represents the type 2 relationship and is
used to predict the changes in the activity system that will occur as a
consequence of activity-system actions, the flow patterns in the transportation system, and the resource consumption by transportation.
Given the activity system A^{t-1}, the flow pattern F^{t-1}, and the resource
consumption R^{t-1} at time $t - 1$ and the actions $\mathscr{A}^t$ to be taken in time
period t, the activity-shift model predicts the state of the activity system at time t, as indicated in figure 8.3. This prediction also includes
the effects of exogenous changes in environmental variables, E^{t-1};
this might represent international commodity prices external to the
country being simulated, or the influence of the national economy on
employment levels and distribution by industry type.

For expository purposes we combine the other four basic types of
prediction models (service, resource, demand, and travel-market equilibration) into a single block called the ***transport model.*** This ter-

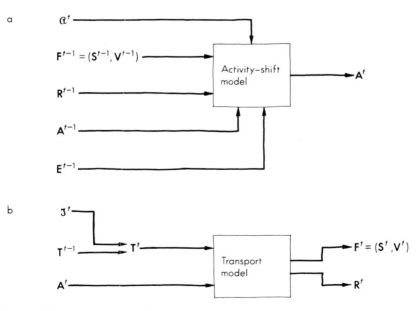

Figure 8.3 Flow charts showing inputs and outputs of (a) an activity-shift model
and (b) a transport model.

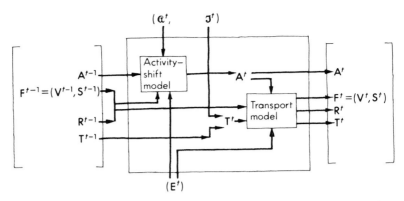

Figure 8.4 Time-dependent forecasts, showing the linkage of activity-shift and transport models.

minology was used in the Harvard-Brookings Model System (Kresge and Roberts 1971). Given an activity system $\mathbf{A}^t$ and transportation system $\mathbf{T}^t$ at time t—or alternatively the transportation system $\mathbf{T}^{t-1}$ at time $t - 1$ and the actions $\mathscr{T}^t$ to be taken in time period t, resulting in a changed system $\mathbf{T}^t$—the transport model predicts the flow pattern $\mathbf{F}^t$ during time period t—that is, service levels $\mathbf{S}^t$ and volumes $\mathbf{V}^t$— and the resources $\mathbf{R}^t$ consumed by transport during that period, as indicated in figure 8.3.

The linkage of the two blocks of models is shown in figure 8.4. The activity-system actions in time period t are assumed to influence the activity system and thus to affect the demand for travel in the transport model in that time period. This is the approach used in the Harvard-Brookings Model System (HBMS). Alternatively activity-system actions in time period t are assumed to affect the activity system in the following time period, and thus the demand for travel in time period t is based on the activity-system changes since the last time period. This approach is often used in urban transportation land-use models.

The integrated combination of transport and activity-shift models allows simulation of the evolution of the transportation and activity systems over time. This is especially important in representing the time lags in transportation impacts on the activity system; an action at time t may take several time periods to impact fully on the activity system. Further, such a time-staged simulation model is essential for testing alternative sequences and timings for implementation of a set of transportation actions. This is illustrated in figure 8.5, where I^t represents all of the impacts predicted to occur in time period t (flows, user impacts, operator impacts, etc.).

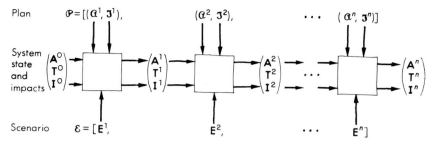

Plan $\mathscr{P} = [(\mathbf{a}^1, \mathfrak{I}^1),$ $(\mathbf{a}^2, \mathfrak{I}^2),$ $\cdots$ $(\mathbf{a}^n, \mathfrak{I}^n)]$

System state and impacts $\begin{pmatrix} \mathbf{A}^0 \\ \mathbf{T}^0 \\ \mathbf{I}^0 \end{pmatrix}$ $\begin{pmatrix} \mathbf{A}^1 \\ \mathbf{T}^1 \\ \mathbf{I}^1 \end{pmatrix}$ $\begin{pmatrix} \mathbf{A}^2 \\ \mathbf{T}^2 \\ \mathbf{I}^2 \end{pmatrix}$ $\cdots$ $\begin{pmatrix} \mathbf{A}^n \\ \mathbf{T}^n \\ \mathbf{I}^n \end{pmatrix}$

Scenario $\mathcal{E} = [\mathbf{E}^1,$ $\mathbf{E}^2,$ $\cdots$ $\mathbf{E}^n]$

Figure 8.5 Prediction of time-staged strategies over n time periods.

Operator equilibration is sometimes included in the process. For this an operator decision logic is assumed, and the transportation system actions in period t are divided into two groups. Some of the actions are established as part of the specification of the plan being tested; these are external to the model and are denoted by $\mathscr{T}^{te}$. Other actions are determined internally, by logic within the model reflecting the operator decision logic assumed, and are denoted by $\mathscr{T}^{ti}$. (This internal selection of transportation actions represents the type 3 relationship in the models.)

For example, in the HBMS the internally determined decisions are primarily decisions on transport prices and on vehicle-fleet sizes and service frequencies. The decisions on investment in facilities are external. Functionally the operator logic is often an integral part of the transport-model block. For example, the required fleet size and schedule frequency may well be calculated after equilibrium flow volumes have been predicted, using design logic as described in section 5.7.

8.5.3 Models versus Scenarios

There is an interesting controversy over the relative importance of scenarios and models (see, for example, Luchtenberg 1976). In most situations the emphasis of an analysis will be on utilizing a set of models to predict impacts over time, conditional on one or more alternative scenarios. In this case scenarios represent alternative assumptions about the future course of exogenous events. In other situations, however, the range of uncertainty about exogenous events may be considered so great that priority is placed on the development and analysis of alternative scenarios. In this case a set of predictive models may be used primarily to test the internal consistency of each scenario. There may even be situations where so much attention is given to the scenarios that no formal predictive models are used at all, other than informal judgment.

8.6 OPERATOR EQUILIBRATION

The analyst usually wants to explore explicitly variations in the transportation options **T**. This means that the type 1 and type 2 relationships must be modeled explicitly in order to predict the impacts of the options. On the other hand, no attempt is made to model the type 3 (operator-equilibration) relationship.

There are several conditions under which an analyst may wish to depart from this general practice:

1. when there are operators that control some options that are *not* in the control of the analyst's agency or firm, and the analyst wishes to predict the response of those other operators to actions under consideration by his organization (for example, one airline wishing to predict the competitive response of another airline to a new service, or a government agency wishing to predict the responses of trucking companies to new taxes or to deregulation of entry into the market);
2. when the analyst wishes to determine which options would be most attractive from his organization's perspective under a hypothesized decision rule;
3. when the analyst wants to employ mathematical optimization methods as search procedures.

In such cases explicit assumptions can be made about the operator's decision rule, and then powerful tools such as mathematical programming can be exploited as search methods. There is an extensive literature on these approaches.

As pointed out in section 5.7, travel-market equilibration always involves service functions in which the level of service either is constant or decreases as volume increases; there does not appear to be any type of transportation facility or service for which the service level improves with increasing volume when the options remain fixed. However, for applications in which it is desirable to assume an operator decision rule and perform operator equilibration to derive the corresponding supply function—so that options are allowed to vary—the service level may be increasing, constant, or decreasing as volume increases.

8.7 SUMMARY

Three basic types of equilibrium relationships are important in transportation systems analysis.

Travel-market equilibration is central to the prediction of flows. In general, both service and demand conditions must be met to find equilibrium flows. In special cases simplifying assumptions can be made, such as assuming that demand is known or that service levels are known.

Activity-system equilibration reflects the long-term interactions of transportation and activity systems. A full set of prediction models would simulate the evolution of transportation and activity systems over time.

To model operator equilibration requires explicit assumptions about the behavior of the operator. When such assumptions are made, a classical supply function can be derived.

TO READ FURTHER
See chapters 11 and 12 and also Ruiter and Kocur (1976). For examples of simplified equilibrium models see Lerman and Wilson (1974), Manski and Wright (1976), and Talvitie and Hasan (1978). A useful discussion of operator decision rules can be found in Kneafsey (1974), p. 102ff. On time-staging see Manheim (1969), Pecknold (1970), Neumann and Pecknold (1973), and UMTA (1976b).

EXERCISES
8.1(E) What kind of equilibration procedure was used in case study I (chapter 3)?

8.2(C) Consider the following five options and four conditions. How reasonable is the approximation in exercise 8.1 for each option or condition? (Classify simply as "reasonable," "likely to produce serious error," or "intermediate.") Discuss your answers.
Options
1 = change in automobile parking price
2 = change in transit service frequency
3 = rerouting of transit over an exclusive lane on a freeway formerly used by automobiles
4 = rerouting of transit over a new transit-only expressway
5 = construction of an extensive new transit network in the region
Conditions
A = next month
B = a few years from now, in a rapidly changing society
C = a few years from now, in a stable society
D = 25 years from now

8.3(C) Review a model system from the technical literature and describe its equilibrium structure in terms of the concepts introduced in this chapter. Examples include the Harvard-Brookings Model System (Kresge and Roberts 1971) and various model systems used in particular urban or regional transportation studies (Kocur et al. 1977, Tober 1977, Morlok 1978).

8.4(C) Manhattan Island is the core of New York City. Long Island lies east of Manhattan; it is 116 miles long and about 12 miles wide. Two boroughs of New York City (Brooklyn and Queens) occupy the west tip of Long Island and are densely populated; the rest of the island is relatively sparsely developed, especially the easternmost portion. The following extracts discuss the effects of two major transportation projects in the New York area:

1. The Triborough Bridge was the fifth bridge constructed over the East River to connect Manhattan to Brooklyn and Queens. It opened on 11 July 1936. Before it opened the man who got it built, Robert Moses,

had estimated that eight million vehicles would use the bridge during its first year of operation. Within four months, the estimate was increased to nine million. Three months later it was ten million. . . . But traffic on the four other East River bridges was not falling off at anything near a comparable rate. The eight million cars and trucks that Moses had forecast would use the Triborough each year were supposed to be cars and trucks that had previously used the other bridges. . . . Otherwise where would these cars and trucks come from? Yet traffic on the other bridges, down about 15 percent immediately following Triborough's opening, was creeping higher again month by month—back, within two years, almost to the pre-Triborough level. Traffic between Long Island and New York had, before Triborough's opening, flooded the twenty-two lanes available on the four old bridges; suddenly the traffic between Long Island and New York had become so heavy that it was also flooding eight new lanes, the new lanes of the Triborough Bridge . . . and it was hardly any lighter than before on the old bridges. (Caro 1974, p. 518)

2. In 1955 Long Island's population was 6.2 million, concentrated mostly in the western quarter of the island. Under the direction of Robert Moses, construction of the Long Island Expressway (LIE) began in 1955; by 1970 it had reached Riverhead near the eastern tip of the island.

As each section of the superhighway opened, it was jammed—with traffic jams of immense dimensions. . . . Year by year, the huge road bulled its way eastward. . . . As each section opened . . . the congestion grew worse. The Long Island Expressway's designed daily capacity was 80,000 vehicles. By 1963, it was carrying 132,000 vehicles per day, a load that jammed the expressway even at "off" hours —during rush hours, the expressway was solid with cars, congested with them, chaos solidified. The drivers trapped on it nicknamed Moses' longest road "the world's longest parking lot." (Caro 1974, p. 949)

a. Summarize the effects described in these extracts in terms of the concepts presented in this chapter. Sketch service and demand curves at several points in time and describe the shifts in these curves in terms of the type 1, 2, and 3 relations as appropriate. Relate your description to figure 8.5. Do figures 8.1 and 8.2 have any relevance to these questions?

b. If you were designing a system of models to be used in planning projects such as these, what features would you want to be sure to include?

c. Discuss the policy implications of these examples. What considerations developed in this chapter did the planners of the projects not consider adequately? How did this affect their planning?

d(P). Assume simple functions and construct a simulation of the phenomena discussed in part a.

9
Evaluation

9.1 THE PURPOSE OF EVALUATION

9.1.1 The Objective of Analysis

Like transportation itself, analysis is a means, not an end. Significant changes in transportation will occur only when conscious decisions are taken by organizations and individuals with the responsibility, authority, and capability for taking action. These decisions may be to make specific changes in the transportation system and services to be offered—for example, to introduce new technologies; to change routes, schedules, or prices; or to make infrastructure changes. The decisions may also be to take no action, to defer a decision.

Analysis is successful only if the results of analysis are useful in the process of reaching these decisions concerning the implementation of change. Thus *the objective of analysis is to clarify the issues that should be considered by decision makers, to assist them in reaching a decision on a course of action.* This definition is in direct and explicit contrast to the cynical view of analysis, which sees the purpose of analysis as being to justify and explain a previously reached decision.

9.1.2 The Role of Evaluation in the Process of Analysis

The major steps in the process of analysis were described in section 1.6. There we defined *search* as the activity in which alternative actions are generated, described in terms of the various transportation and activity-system options. *Prediction* is the activity in which estimates are developed of the likely impacts of each of the actions generated in search; the preceding chapters have introduced the basic concepts used in prediction. The activity of *goal formulation and revision* involves the formulation of critical statements of goals and revision of these goals as the analysis evolves.

Evaluation begins with the outputs of prediction (the actions and their impacts) and of goal formulation and revision (the statements of goals).

Since the objective of analysis is to clarify the issues that should be considered, at some point in analysis the potential actions must be evaluated with respect to the goals to be achieved by transportation. Evaluation is that point. *Evaluation* is the activity of examining the available alternative actions in light of the possible goals, assessing the relative desirability of each action, and summarizing the key issues to be considered by interested parties in reaching a decision. *Choice* is the activity of reaching a conscious decision as to which of the alternative actions (if any) to implement; choice takes as input the results of evaluation. The actions available should include no action—the "null" or "status quo" alternative—as well as various forms of deferring the decision (for example, "continue analysis").

9.1.3 Relationship between Evaluation and Choice

In general, the distinction between evaluation and choice is clear: evaluation is performed by analysts, usually interacting with various interested parties, while choice is performed by one or more decision makers, often interacting in complex institutional environments. Sometimes, however, the interaction of evaluation and choice may be sufficiently complex that they are difficult to separate—for example, when a decision maker looks at the data on the predicted impacts of several actions and reaches an immediate decision on which to implement, or when the decision maker is the analyst. Often, too, the analyst and decision makers interact intensively and frequently so that the choice and evaluation activities are closely intertwined and the decision maker has already reached a decision by the time the analyst has completed a formal evaluation. Even in these cases, however, the distinction between evaluation and choice is a useful one.

One assumption that is often made is that evaluation is an objective technical activity whereas choice is basically political, in that it involves value judgments. This is not true: evaluation is more technical than choice, but it is not value-free; value judgments are inescapable in evaluation, as we shall discuss shortly.

There is also a close interaction between evaluation and the activity we call goal formulation and revision. In general, the initial formulation of goals will change as a result of analysis. The activity of evaluation in particular will often stimulate a reappraisal and revision of the goals initially posed.

9.1.4 The Product of Evaluation

The evaluation activity plays a key role in the process of analysis. It is in this activity that the analyst must pull together all of the information developed through the various activities of the analysis, examine it to increase his understanding of the issues, and then summarize the insights gained in this examination: *The primary product of evaluation should be a summary of the key issues to be considered by interested parties in reaching a decision on a course of action; this summary should be in a form that can be readily understood by laymen such as elected officials, managers, and the general public.*

The summary can be written or verbal, formal or informal. For convenience we shall call this summary an *evaluation report* and describe it as if it were a written document. Written documents are required in many situations, in public or in private agencies, to gain approval for funding, to document for the record the bases of decision, and to meet the requirements of environmental legislation (see section 9.2.5).

We shall place great stress on the readability and understandability of the evaluation report. Most participants in most decision processes are not technically trained or analytically oriented; nor are they comfortable reading lengthy technical documents. They want to know the key issues about which they should be concerned, and they want to find this out quickly. They want documents that are concise and understandable. An evaluation report might also include technical appendixes that provide the details necessary to understand the facts and judgments presented in the summary; but the summary should be able to stand alone as a concise, readable statement of the major issues.

9.1.5 The Issues to Be Clarified

In deciding which change (if any) to implement, the responsible decision makers will wish to have before them a summary of the key issues they should consider in reaching a decision. (While the decision makers will often be interested in the personal and professional views of the analyst as to the most attractive course of action, they will almost always wish to reserve the final choice to themselves.) In reaching this decision, they will be concerned with such issues as these:

1. What are the major alternatives that should be considered?
2. What are the major interests that are benefited or adversely affected by each alternative?
3. What are the views of those interests?

4. What are the most important uncertainties that should be considered?

5. Consequently, what are the major advantages and disadvantages of each course of action?

This list of issues places particular stress on the incidence of impacts. Generally changes in a transportation system will have many different impacts on different groups and interests. Some interests will benefit from a particular change, whereas others will be adversely affected. Different groups will have different views as to the relative desirability of particular alternatives. Thus the problem of evaluation is difficult not only technically but ethically as well. How should gains to one group be balanced against losses to others?

Consider, for example, the construction of a new highway in a densely developed urban area. A highway provides many benefits: it improves service for traffic and relieves some of the congestion on local streets. A highway can create greater accessibility for some areas, thereby stimulating development. On the other hand, this development might otherwise have occurred elsewhere, and so areas that are now relatively less accessible may suffer. Location of a highway along one particular route may serve some groups of travelers well, but at the same time, because it might have been located elsewhere, other groups are served not as well as they might have been. The choice of a mass transit link rather than a highway can result in greater accessibility for still other groups, such as those who do not have access to an automobile for some or all of their trips. The construction of a highway can be, at least in the short run, a disruptive force in the community; it can cause the displacement of families or jobs, form a physical barrier separating people from parks or schools or churches, create a visual barrier or despoil a scenic area, or take parkland or other community facilities out of public use. Construction of highways can change the pattern of air pollution and groundwater flow and can affect land values in a variety of ways. Construction of a highway along one alignment can cause a loss of tax base for some communities while bringing development potential and thus an increased tax base to other communities; construction along an alternate alignment might have reverse effects.

Highways are not unique in this respect. Consider these other examples:

I. Several sites are being considered for a new airport in a metropolitan area. Sites close in to the core of the city will be very convenient for access by air travelers but will subject local communities to aircraft noise and increased road congestion. Sites farther out either are quite distant for air traveler access or destroy a portion of a major wildlife refuge.

II. A federal agency is reviewing its budget for transportation research and development. There are three major programs being considered. Program A, development of a new supersonic air transport, would provide a 30 percent reduction in air travel times for international air travelers, although only a 10 percent reduction in overall door-to-door time; the effects of the sonic booms and the extent of possible depletion of atmospheric ozone are largely unknown, in that even experts do not agree on the magnitudes of effects. Program B, development of a railroad subsidy program, would preserve intercity rail passenger service in some metropolitan corridors and suburban commuter services in a few urban regions. Program C, provision of operating subsidies to urban transit agencies, would support special services for inner-city residents and a revision of routes to better serve the young, the elderly, and the handicapped who need access to health centers and recreational facilities. If only one of these programs can be funded, which one should be selected?

III. A shipping company is planning to introduce major changes in service on its routes, utilizing a new type of ship and new techniques for loading, stowing, and unloading freight. This will result in economies of operation, thus allowing lower costs to shippers and/or higher profits for the ship operator. Because of certain characteristics of the new technology, changes will be made in the service over many routes: some ports will receive much lower frequency of service than before or even get no service at all, while other ports will receive higher frequency of service than before and some new ports will be served. Thus the relative economic growth rates of certain areas will be affected. There will also be some changes in labor requirements: fewer personnel of certain skills will be required, and changes in seniority, work rules, and other labor practices appear likely; these will be of great concern to the workers affected.

Thus every decision about transportation potentially involves a need to balance gains to some interests against losses to others. A major change in any of the transportation facilities, services, or policies of a region can have far-reaching effects and can constitute a major intervention in the fabric of society. Many different people and interests are affected. The total set of effects on all groups and interests must be considered, with particular attention paid to the differential effects (which groups gain, which lose).

In almost every transportation analysis a key issue will be, Whose interests should be served? Which groups should gain and which should lose?

It is essential that the processes of planning, designing, implementing, and operating transportation systems explicitly recognize such issues and take them into account. The planning and design of transportation systems is as much a sociopolitical as a technical and economic problem.

This is true in the private as well as in the public sector. Management of a private firm such as a shipping company or airline may wish to consider only its own financial benefits in reaching a decision, but as a practical political matter it cannot ignore issues such as those in example III above. Public-spirited management would not wish to; pragmatic management cannot afford to.

It is very tempting to ignore these problems by assuming that evaluation is basically a technical problem or that somehow the political process will deal with these issues. In transportation, however, one cannot make this assumption because the great majority of transportation decisions must in the end be political decisions in which the conflicting goals of different groups must be balanced. As analysts, if we wish to be effective in bringing about change, our analyses must be relevant to these sociopolitical issues, and our evaluation reports must address these issues of who gains and who loses.

9.1.6 Evaluation as a Management Tool

Evaluation reports can be produced periodically throughout the process of analysis as well as at the conclusion, to summarize the key issues as they are understood at key points in the analysis. These interim evaluation reports are especially useful in reviewing and revising the relative priorities for further technical work and in focusing public involvement in a constructive way during the analysis process.

This use of evaluation reports suggests the addition of a sixth issue to the above list:

6. Should further analyses be done? If so, what are the relative priorities for further analysis?

9.2 THE EVALUATION METHOD

Producing an evaluation report is a difficult task. The analyst must clarify the issues in a manner that is concise, relevant, clear, and understandable to laymen. To do this he must first organize and ex-

amine the available data in ways that help him to isolate and understand the most important issues.

There is no algorithm or formula that produces the evaluation report
automatically from the data. There are, however, heuristic procedures
that the analyst can use as an aid in understanding the issues. There
are also some technical procedures, such as economic analysis, that
can be useful in supporting the heuristic procedures.

In this section we shall describe the basic structure of the evaluation method; we shall start with some definitions.

9.2.1 Basic Definitions

An *actor* is a group of one or more individuals who are essentially
similar in their relationship to the issues under study. The major types of
actors we shall be concerned with include the *technical team,* the
group of professionals entrusted with the responsibility for analyzing a
transportation problem; the *decision makers,* the individual or group
of individuals that has the final authority for making a decision (for
example, a mayor, a city council, a governor, a president of a transportation company such as an airline or shipline, a minister or secretary
of transportation, a port authority, a state highway commission); and
the *community,* the set of all other individuals and interest groups
affected by the transportation decisions under consideration.

The actors relevant to a particular transportation issue may be fairly
numerous. For example, the Los Angeles, California, metropolitan area
has been considering major investments in a regional rapid transit
system for many years. Debate about regional choices reached a
climax with a referendum in November 1974 about financing such a
system. (It was defeated.) During the months preceding the referendum,
a list of key actors was put together, extracts from which are shown in
table 9.1. This list demonstrates the variety of actors and interests that
may be important in a transportation decision. Note that, as extensive
as it is, the list excludes many important interests, such as local and
state elected officials, businessmen, and citizens' groups formed for
purposes other than transportation, such as neighborhood and environmental groups.

The *impacts* of a set of decisions are those aspects of the consequences of the decisions that may be of concern to one or more
actors (that is, there is at least one actor who has some preference
about the level and kind of impact that might occur). Table 9.2
shows an illustrative list of impacts of alternative urban transportation
systems that might be important issues in a particular situation. Im-

Table 9.1 Some of the agencies, organizations, and committees concerned with the planning and development of transportation in the Los Angeles region (1974)

I. Summary

A. City of Los Angeles
1. City Council Ad Hoc Committee on Rapid Transit
2. Technical Advisory Committee to Ad Hoc Committee on Rapid Transit (TAC AD HOC)
3. City Council Industry and Transportation Committee
4. City Council Planning Committee
5. City Council Traffic and Off-Street Parking Committee
6. Mayor's Ad Hoc City Employee Transportation System Committee
7. General Plan Advisory Board
8. Transportation Committee

B. County of Los Angeles
1. Regional Planning Commission (RPC)
2. General Plan Policy Review Board (GPPRB)
3. Transportation Sub-Committee
4. Interdepartmental Engineering Committee (IEC)
5. Los Angeles County Bicycle Route Sub-Committee (IEC Bicycle Sub-Committee)
6. Citizens Planning Council (CPC)
7. Transportation Committee
8. Aviation Commission

C. Interagency: Southern California Association of Governments (SCAG)
1. General Assembly
2. Executive Committee
3. Comprehensive Transportation Planning Committee (CTPC)
4. Transportation Technical Advisory Committee (TTAC)
5. Los Angeles Regional Transportation Study (LARTS)
6. Transit Advisory Committee (TAC)
7. Metropolitan Transportation Engineering Board (MTEB)
8. Critical Decisions Task Forces
9. Systems Task Force
10. Impact Task Force
11. Modeling Task Force
12. Implementation and Finance Task Force
13. Airport Authority
14. Council of Airport Administrators

D. Southern California Rapid Transit District
1. Board of Directors
2. Board of Control for Alternative Transit Corridors and Systems Technical Study
3. Technical Advisory Committee (TAC)

E. Local Agency Transportation Advisory Committee (LATAC)

F. Los Angeles County Association of Planning Officials (LACAPO)

G. Citizens' Advisory Committee on Rapid Transit (CACORT)

H. Southern California Aviation Council Inc. (SCACI)

II. Memberships and affiliations (selected examples)

A. City of Los Angeles
1. City Council Ad Hoc Committee on Rapid Transit: Created by the city council for review of the SCRTD Alternative Transit Corridor and Systems Technical Study and related matters. Membership: 6 council members.
2. Technical Advisory Committee to Ad Hoc Committee on Rapid Transit (TAC AD HOC): Created by the City Council to advise the Council Ad Hoc Committee on the SCRTD Alternative Transit Corridors and Systems Technical Study and related matters. Reports to the Council Ad Hoc Committee on Rapid Transit. Membership: Chairman, Planning Department representative; Representatives of Harbor Department, Police Department,

Table 9.1 (continued)

Department of Airports, City Administration Officer, Department of Public Utilities and Transportation, Chief Legislative Analyst, City Traffic Engineer, City Engineer.

...

4. City Council Planning Committee: Hears items concerning the Planning Department including transportation planning, and makes recommendations to the full Council. Membership: 3 council members.

5. City Council Traffic and Off-Street Parking Committee: Hears items concerning the Traffic Department and Off-Street Parking Agency. Membership: 3 council members.

...

7. General Plan Advisory Board: Advises the Director of Planning in matters relating to the City General Plan. Membership: Chairman, Planning Department; Mayor; Councilman; City Administrative Officer; City Engineer; Housing Authority; Community Redevelopment Agency; Building and Safety; Department of Environmental Quality; Fire Department; Police Department; Public Utilities and Transportation; Recreation and Parks; Traffic Department; Department of Water and Power; Harbor Department; Department of Airports; Mayoral Appointees (2).

8. Transportation Committee: Considers transportation matters affecting the City General Plan and advises the General Plan Advisory Board. Membership: Planning Department; Traffic Department; City Administrative Office; Public Utilities and Transportation; Bureau of Engineering; Department of Transportation of California; Southern California Rapid Transit District.

B. County of Los Angeles

1. Regional Planning Commission (RPC): Functions as an official hearing body and recommends county-wide comprehensive, general planning policies to the Board of Supervisors. Also responsible for highway protection through subdivision and zoning administration.

2. General Plan Policy Review Board (GPPRB): Advises the RPC on development policies and priorities and coordinates the goals, policies, programs, and projects of individual County Departments which affect the General Plan. Membership: Agricultural Commissioner, Air Pollution Control Officer, Assessor, Director of Beaches, Chief Administrative Officer, County Engineer, Chief Engineer of the Flood Control District, Forester and Fire Warden, Director of Health Services, Executive Director of the Human Relations Commission, Director of Parks and Recreation, Director of Planning, Director of Public Social Service, Director of Real Estate Management, Road Commission, Director of Urban Affairs.

3. Transportation Sub-Committee: Develops policy recommendations to the GPPRB on the Transportation Element and provides departmental input pertinent to development of the Element. Membership: Air Pollution Control District, County Engineer, Human Relations Commission, Regional Planning Commission, Road Department, Department of Senior Citizens Affairs (not on GPPRB).

4. Interdepartmental Engineering Committee (IEC): Advisory technical body responsible for recommending to the Regional Planning Commission changes to the County Highway Master Plan. It also reviews and approves precise alignments for these highways as well as resolving problems encountered by any involved parties. Membership: Road Department, Regional Planning Commission, County Engineer, other departments when affected.

...

6. Citizens Planning Council (CPC): Comprised of 50 members appointed by the County Board of Supervisors for three-year terms. The primary function of the Council is to help determine content of the County General Plan with respect to goals, policies, plans, and programs. This Committee of private, interested citizens is advisory to the RPC.

7. Transportation Committee of the CPC: Provides citizen input to aid the Road Department in the formulation of the Transportation Element of the Los Angeles County General Plan.

...

C. Interagency: Southern California Association of Governments (SCAG)

1. General Assembly: The policy body of SCAG, comprised of an elected delegate from each member county and city plus three additional delegates from the City of Los Angeles (the Mayor and 2 Councilmen).

2. Executive Committee: The official day-to-day policy-making and supervisory body of SCAG as designated in the SCAG bylaws. The committee meets on the second Thursday of

each month. Membership: 18 total. Three from the City of Los Angeles are the same as the delegates to the General Assembly (Mayor and 2 Councilmen); one from each of the 6 member counties (Imperial County, Los Angeles County, Orange County, Riverside County, San Bernardino County, Ventura County); one from each of the collective member cities within each county (Camarillo, Burbank, San Bernardino, Torrance, Santa Anna, Riverside, Brawley, Long Beach, and Fullerton and 3 members at-large).

3. Comprehensive Transportation Planning Committee (CTPC): One of 9 policy committees established by the Executive Committee of SCAG on different aspects of urban planning The CTPC advises the Executive Committee on all transportation matters. Membership: representatives of Orange, Riverside, San Bernardino, and Los Angeles counties; cities of Ontario, Torrance, Palmdale, Baldwin Park, Arcadi, Cypress, San Bernardino, Los Angeles, Oxnard, La Habra, Montebello; and California Department of Transportation

4. Transportation Technical Advisory Committee (TTAC); Members of the committee are appointed by the President of SCAG and represent city and county road and traffic departments, airports, transit operations, state highways, and planning departments.

5. Los Angeles Regional Transportation Study (LARTS): Staff is provided by the State Division of Highways under the direction of TTAC; functions as an arm of SCAG and also performs the work on the Los Angeles Regional Transportation Study, a continuous program of comprehensive transportation planning.

6. Transit Advisory Committee (TAC): Meets on call of the chair at least bimonthly. TAC was established by SCAG in July 1971 to coordinate the planning and operations of transit systems in the region in accordance with the Mass Transportation Planning Guide of 1966 and the California Transportation Development Act of 1971, as amended. The committee is composed of representatives of public transit operating agencies in the region and helps to prepare, update, and review progress on the SCAG Transit Development Program.

7. Metropolitan Transportation Engineering Board (MTEB): The MTEB acts as technical reviewers in street, highway, and freeway transportation planning. This committee, consisting of city and county engineers, the Director of RPC, Los Angeles City Planning, Small City Planning, SCAG, and Division of Highways representatives, acts as advisor to the SCAG CTPC

8. Critical Decisions Task Forces: Review and coordinate investigations by the SCAG staff required to place the region in a position to adopt critical transportation decisions. The task forces function as advisory units to the SCAG staff.
...

12. Implementation and Finance Task Force: Coordinates the preparation of implementation analysis and recommendations for the alternative transportation proposals and systems. The task force provides guidance and reviews analysis of fiscal capabilities and proposed fiscal actions associated with the above proposals and systems. Membership: representatives of Orange County Transit District (OCTD), Los Angeles City Planning, Los Angeles City Mayor's Office, Los Angeles County Road Department, CALTRANS, Los Angeles County, and Southern California Rapid Transit District.

D. Southern California Rapid Transit District (SCRTD)

1. Board of Directors: The policy body of SCRTD. Conducts the affairs of the district in accordance with the laws established by the State of California. Membership: 11, including appointees by each of 5 County Supervisors; 2 appointees of Los Angeles City Mayor; and 4 representatives of corridors elected by City Selection Commission.

3. Technical Advisory Committee (TAC): Created at the request of SCRTD to meet UMTA requirements for a technical liaison and review of their Alternative Transit Corridors and Systems Technical Study with affected agencies. Membership: representatives of SCRTD, City Mayor's Office, L.A. City Planning, L.A. City Administration Office, L.A. City Airports. L.A. Public Utilities and Transportation, L.A. City Legislation Analysis, L.A. City Traffic, L.A. City Engineering, L.A. County Planning, L.A. County Road Department, L.A. County Administration Office, League of California Cities, California Transportation Department, City of Burbank, Southern California Transportation Department, Southern California Association of Governments, Orange County Transit Department, Commission for Central City Planning, Community Redevelopment Agency, UMTA Regional Office, and consultants doing the study.
...

Table 9.1 (continued)

F. Los Angeles County Association of Planning Officials (LACAPO): Encourages cooperation between local governmental jurisdictions in the development of a countywide General
Plan, reasonable uniformity in standards, and joint studies. Membership: members of the
Board of Supervisors, the City Councils, planning commissions, and each of the planning
directors (or officials responsible for planning).

G. Citizens' Advisory Committee on Rapid Transit: Immediate goal is to help SCRTD determine a final rapid transit proposal to present to the voters at the general election in
November 1974. The committee will conduct a campaign effort and fund raising to achieve
voter approval of taxes to fund the rapid transit proposal. Membership: Presidents of
major local industry; Mayoral Appointees, County Supervisor Appointees, City Council
Appointees, and representatives of the community at-large; expected to reach 150 members.

Table 9.2 Possible impacts of urban transportation actions

Community development and growth
Neighborhood cohesion
Neighborhood stability
Community aspirations
Transportation facilities as barriers in the community
School districts disrupted
Parish districts disrupted
Other impacts on religious institutions
Parkland taken
Vacant land taken
Access to employment opportunities
Access to educational opportunities
Access to recreational opportunities
Access to areas of natural beauty
Local land development
Community facilities
Preservation of historic and cultural sites
Displacement of persons and businesses
Effect on welfare and unemployment expenditure
Effect on commercial property values and sales
Effect on residential property values
Tax loss through displacements
Tax gain through increase in land values
Conduct and financing of governments
Creation of unpleasant visual effects
Fiscal efficiency
Maintenance and other nonvehicle operating costs
Right-of-way costs
Facility construction costs
Vehicle costs
Fuel consumption
System operating costs: labor
System operating costs: materials
Maintenance of design standards
Weather reliability
User trip time
User trip cost

Comfort and convenience of users
Vehicle wear and tear
Multiple use of space
Access to and egress from roadways
Congestion on neighboring streets
Regional growth and development
Effect on distribution of economic activity
Changes in retail market area
Effect of construction on the economy
Public health and safety
Noise pollution
Air pollution
Conservation of natural resources
Accident rate
Complexity of demands on drivers
Flow congestion
System efficiency
Accessibility
Serving maximum population
Consistency with local land-use planning objectives
Consideration for future transportation needs
Coordination with other transportation facilities during and after construction
Disruption caused by construction
Integration with existing transportation facilities
Access to recreational and cultural sites
Access to fire and police services
Sequence of perceptions
Aesthetic experience of movement over highway
Aesthetic value of the view of the road
Ease of orientation of drivers
User monotony
Equity

---

pacts can be described operationally by defining corresponding *goal variables;* such goal variables express the level of one or more impacts of a particular action on one or more actors. Goal variables may be defined qualitatively or quantitatively. The types of impacts can also be described in terms of the actors on whom those impacts are incident; in chapter 1 we grouped the impacts of transportation generally in terms of several groups: user, operator, physical, functional, and governmental impacts.

The *actions* are the alternative transportation plans being considered. These are defined in terms of a set of options, which consist of choices of technologies, networks, links, vehicles, and operating and organizational policies. The actions may be simple or complex. Examples include alternative highway route locations; alternative bus or airline routes; comprehensive development plans for a transportation corridor,

Table 9.3 Sample impact tableau: nine alternative alignments for the California Route 42 freeway

	1
Length (miles)	9.5
Cost (10^6 $)	
Construction	51.1
Right of way	57.6
Total	108.7
Traffic impact: 20-year user benefit (10^6 $)	340
Benefit/cost ratio	3.1

Land-use impacts

Number of parcels affected:

Single family	1,588
Multiple family	309
Industrial	43
Commercial	66
Vacant	69
Parks, churches, schools	4
Miscellaneous	9
Total	2,088

Living units displaced, by community:

Compton	Single family	0
(23,190)	Multiple family	0
	Total	0
Downey	Single family	615
(31,220)	Multiple family	368
	Total	983
Lynwood	Single family	75
(16,530)	Multiple family	7
	Total	82
Norwalk	Single family	32
(24,140)	Multiple family	0
	Total	32
Paramount	Single family	0
(11,000)	Multiple family	0
	Total	0
South Gate	Single family	515
(23,360)	Multiple family	217
	Total	732

2	3	4	5	6	7	8	9
9.6	9.2	9.3	9.3	8.8	8.9	8.9	8.9
52.5	53.6	54.8	49.5	42.3	46.0	48.7	50.8
55.2	59.6	57.0	57.7	55.6	54.6	53.2	51.9
107.7	113.2	111.8	107.2	97.9	100.6	101.9	102.7
330	370	360	275	280	275	275	275
3.1	3.3	3.2	2.6	2.9	2.7	2.7	2.7
1,464	1,873	1,760	1,899	1,685	1,475	1,997	1,579
296	293	284	330	294	329	230	311
57	35	49	34	44	58	23	30
50	72	57	72	52	46	39	42
74	54	60	55	32	43	36	47
4	7	7	6	5	7	7	5
8	5	5	6	9	10	2	8
1,953	2,339	2,222	2,121	1,968	2,334	2,334	2,022
0	0	0	0	0	0	183	0
0	0	0	0	0	0	94	0
0	0	0	0	0	0	277	0
439	613	433	411	413	413	412	412
540	315	496	236	236	236	236	236
979	928	929	647	649	649	648	648
75	75	75	361	529	427	462	452
7	7	7	239	323	595	292	663
82	82	82	600	852	1,022	754	1,115
99	32	99	201	201	201	201	201
0	0	0	5	5	5	5	5
99	32	99	206	206	206	206	206
0	0	0	16	78	78	274	274
0	0	0	91	162	162	162	165
0	0	0	107	240	240	436	439
515	776	776	537	151	151	8	8
217	285	285	152	36	36	68	68
732	1,061	1,061	689	187	187	76	76

Table 9.3 (continued)

		1
City of Los Angeles (Watts)	Single family	114
(8,160)	Multiple family	244
	Total	358
County of Los Angeles	Single family	129
(Willowbrook)	Multiple family	254
(8,710)	Total	383

Effect on local tax base of land acquired
(10^6 \$ and % of city total)

Compton	—
($87 million)	
Downey	3.8
($157 million)	(2.4%)
Norwalk	0.5
($85 million)	(0.6%)
Paramount	—
($46 million)	
South Gate	3.2
($117 million)	(2.7%)
City of Los Angeles	0.4
County of Los Angeles	0.7
Total	8.9

Source: Adapted from California Division of Highways data, April 1968.
City totals in parentheses.

including highway location and design, transit facility location and design, a relocation housing program, and a recreational and community facilities program; or regional transportation programs such as the railroad reorganization plan in the northeastern United States. The set of actions must always include the null action.

An *impact tableau* shows, for each of the actions that have been developed, the consequences for each actor, by type of impact. Both beneficial and adverse consequences are shown. The impact tableau may contain some quantitative information such as construction costs, travel times, and numbers of families displaced, but it can also contain qualitative information such as verbal or even graphical descriptions of certain impacts (for example, a description of the ability of a particular community to adjust to social disruption caused by alternative facility locations). The impact tableau presented in table 9.3 shows the

2	3	4	5	6	7	8	9
114	114	114	114	2	2	2	2
244	244	244	244	13	13	13	13
358	358	358	358	15	15	15	15
129	129	129	129	244	167	333	167
254	254	254	254	180	183	355	183
383	383	383	383	424	350	688	350

2	3	4	5	6	7	8	9
—	—	—	—	—	—	0.9 (1.0%)	—
3.6 (2.3%)	3.9 (2.5%)	3.7 (2.4%)	2.2 (1.4%)	2.2 (1.4%)	2.2 (1.4%)	2.2 (1.4%)	2.2 (1.4%)
0.5 (0.6%)	1.2 (1.5%)	1.2 (1.5%)	3.0 (3.7%)	4.2 (5.1%)	4.2 (5.1%)	2.2 (3.5%)	4.1 (5.0%)
—	—	—	0.4 (0.9%)	0.8 (1.7%)	0.8 (1.7%)	1.2 (2.6%)	1.2 (2.6%)
3.2 (2.7%)	3.8 (3.3%)	3.8 (3.3%)	2.4 (2.1%)	0.7 (0.6%)	0.7 (0.6%)	0.2 (0.2%)	0.2 (0.2%)
0.4	0.4	0.4	0.4	—	—	—	—
0.7	0.7	0.7	0.7	0.9	0.9	1.2	0.9
8.7	10.3	10.1	9.8	9.5	9.5	9.3	9.3

effects of alternative alignments for a freeway in the Los Angeles metropolitan area (this particular tableau shows only quantitative impacts).

Goals are the values or preferences or desires of any actor. Goals may be **manifest** (expressed explicitly in some way) or **latent** (not yet expressed). Goals may be expressed in terms of impacts or in terms of specific actions. For example, an actor may prefer that the number of families displaced be minimized or, alternatively, that a particular highway route be chosen. A **goal statement** is an expression of the goals of an individual or group of individuals. Such goal statements may or may not be internally **consistent** (observing such conditions as transitivity) and may be **partial** or **complete,** depending upon whether a statement of goals is clearly formulated over every possible combination of impacts. A **ranking** or preference order over a specific set of actions indicates the relative desirability of the various actions.

Just as information on impacts can be organized into an impact tableau, information about the goals of various actors can be organized as a *value information file.* This file can contain for each actor and impact type what is known by the technical team about the manifest and latent goals of that actor.

With these definitions we can reformulate the definition of an actor. An *actor* is any individual or group of individuals who for all practical purposes are homogeneous with respect to the impacts on them of any actions and their values concerning those impacts and actions. The term *affected interest* is used synonymously with actor; an affected interest is an individual, group of individuals, institution, or resource valued by society which is actually or potentially affected by any of the actions being considered. It is also often useful to distinguish *spokesmen* from the groups or interests they represent (since the question of who represents whom is often an issue).

9.2.2 Evaluation: The Technical Problem

Evaluation operates on two sets of information—information about actions and information about values. The information about actions is summarized in the impact tableau, in which, for each of the available actions, the impacts on each affected interest are displayed. These data may be quantitative or qualitative, and there may be uncertainty about some impacts of some of the actions. Information about values is represented by the manifest preferences that have been expressed by spokesmen for various affected interests and by additional inferences that may be made about latent preferences. This information is assembled in a value information file.

The task of evaluation is to operate on these two sets of information—the impact tableau and the value information file—to assess the relative desirability of alternative actions and to summarize the key issues (figure 9.1).

Several features make this a difficult problem:

1. There are generally many alternative actions.
2. Each action has many impacts on many interests.
3. The information on impacts is rarely complete or known with certainty.
4. While there is available to the technical team some information about the goals of various interests, as expressed by spokesmen for those interests, this information is almost never complete and is rarely totally consistent.
5. Most important of all, beneficial and adverse impacts typically fall

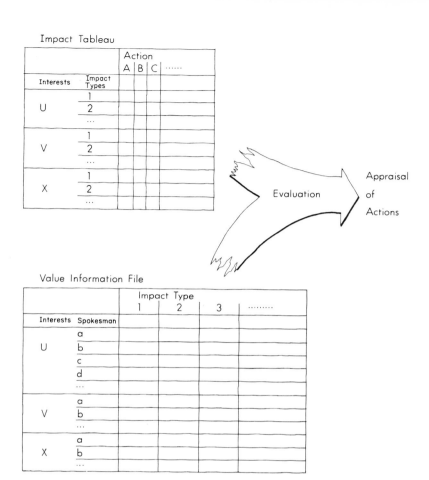

Impact Tableau

		Action			......
Interests	Impact Types	A	B	C	
U	1				
	2				
	...				
V	1				
	2				
	...				
X	1				
	2				
	...				

Evaluation → Appraisal of Actions

Value Information File

		Impact Type			
Interests	Spokesman	1	2	3	....
U	a				
	b				
	c				
	d				
	...				
V	a				
	b				
	...				
X	a				
	b				
	...				

Figure 9.1 Evaluation.

onto different groups: some interests gain and some lose for each alternative action.

These differences in impacts are illustrated in the impact tableau in table 9.3. Note, for example, the differences in dwelling units displaced and in tax-base losses among the various communities affected by the alternative alignments for the Route 42 freeway. These differences in the incidence of beneficial and adverse effects cannot be ignored. It is morally unacceptable to ignore such distributional issues; and it is politically impractical to do so.

Recognition of these five factors has strongly influenced the design of the evaluation method to be laid out in section 9.2.3. The rationale behind the method will be described in detail in section 9.3.

The steps of the method are designed to assist the analyst in distilling out of the data an understanding of the issues and in communicating this understanding to laymen in terms they can understand. One way for the analyst to visualize this objective is to ask himself these questions: If I were limited to ten pages of text and five pages of figures, what would I say, and how would I say it, to communicate to lay readers my understanding of the issues? What are the key issues they must consider, in order to reach a decision about which alternative should be chosen? How can I express these issues in ways that they can understand and that bring out the importance of the decisions to be made?

To prepare such a statement the analyst must understand not only the technical issues—the alternatives and their effects—but also the value issues—the interests that will be affected and how each is likely to feel about the technical issues.

The detailed evaluation procedure laid out in the next section begins with the information on alternatives and their effects and on potential

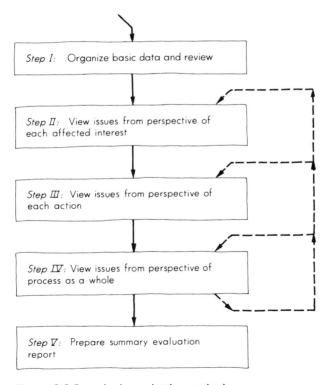

Figure 9.2 Steps in the evaluation method.

value issues. This procedure is one approach by which the analyst can work toward producing the kind of summary statement we have described. (For more detailed discussions see Manheim et al. 1975b, Cohen 1975.) Section 9.5 will describe additional concepts and techniques that are useful in expanding the basic procedure for application to the evaluation of complex system plans.

9.2.3 Steps of the Evaluation Method

The evaluation method can be described as a series of steps. As suggested by the dotted line in figure 9.2, it is likely that the activities in the various steps will be iterated several times in producing an evaluation report.

The first step involves assembling the basic data in a form appropriate for analysis. The next steps deal with the data in its disaggregated form. In step II the current alternative actions are viewed from the perspective of each affected interest in turn, in order to anticipate the likely preferences of each interest. In step III each alternative action is viewed as a whole, to assess its strengths and its weak points.

Since it is rare that any single action will appear to be preferred to all others by all affected interests, further analyses are usually necessary. In step IV the data are treated in more aggregated form. The objective in this step is to develop a further understanding of the issues by searching for various patterns in the data. In step V the analyst sets down his understanding of the issues in the form of a summary evaluation report.

STEP I: ORGANIZE BASIC DATA AND REVIEW

Two basic sets of data are required as inputs to evaluation: the impact tableau and the value information file. Much of the necessary information is developed in the course of the technical team's various activities. However, the data are usually scattered among the many individuals on the team and in various physical locations, and some of it is stored only in people's heads. Thus it is often a major task to assemble the data in one place for use in evaluation (for a discussion of some of the practical problems see Cohen 1975). Often, too, simply organizing a large volume of data physically in an efficient way requires thought.

The first and most difficult task is to develop a list of all parties that might be affected by any of the alternatives being considered. Each such party, or interest, should be relatively homogeneous with respect to values and likely impacts. In many projects the sheer number of such interests will make this task difficult.

The value information file should be organized with a separate record for each interest—one or more pages, or sections of a standard file system. This record should contain all the relevant data collected by the technical team: the obvious economic, demographic, and land-use data for such interests as neighborhoods or communities; and other appropriate background information on commercial and business interests. The file should also contain relevant expressions of attitudes or opinions that may be useful in understanding the needs or values of an interest: newspaper articles, public expressions of positions on transportation or other issues, and especially records of direct communications with the technical team, such as correspondence and memoranda by staff summarizing meetings with representatives of the affected interest.

In short, this file should contain any information that will assist the analysts in understanding the affected interests. The best source of such understanding is direct and extensive communication with the interest, but indirect information is a partial substitute and a useful supplement.

The impact tableau can be visualized as a table in which each row represents a particular type of impact on a particular interest: for example, number of residences displaced, traffic noise level, and accessibility are among the important impacts alternative highway locations can have on a neighborhood, so there would be a row for each impact type for each neighborhood. The columns represent the actions that have been developed. Thus the impact tableau is simply a format for displaying all of the data available to the analysts about the alternative actions being considered and their potential impacts on the various affected interests.

Some of these data would come from the prediction models discussed in previous chapters—data on such impacts as travel times, volumes, noise levels, and accessibility. Other data would come from other types of models or expert judgment—such as the effects of disruption during construction on the viability of local retail stores, the effects of alternative facility locations on community social structure, and aesthetic impacts. While some of the data would be numerical, especially those produced by computer models, other data would be available only in verbal or perhaps in graphical form, such as effects on community cohesion or the visual impact of a facility as seen in the neighborhood. All such data should be included, because some of the impacts most important to some groups, such as social or aesthetic impacts, are those most resistant to quantification.

The impact tableau should be cast in whatever physical form is most usable. While conceptually it is a single table, in almost all situations the numbers of rows and columns will be too great to fit on a single page or even a display board on the wall of a conference room. For working purposes it may be useful to organize the impact tableau as a series of pages in a loose-leaf notebook, perhaps with one page for each affected interest.

Data derived as output from computer models can be organized by alternatives instead of by interests (for example, the matrices of inter-zonal travel times and volumes for a particular network); but care must be taken to put these data into proper perspective. Computer-generated data should not overshadow other less quantitative data, and the analyst should be careful to examine those data from the point of view of each interest affected, not simply from that of the system as a whole.

The following steps may be useful in the initial development of these two sets of data (see also Manheim et al. 1975b, pp. 64–77):

1. Develop a checklist of interests potentially affected, including all of the groups, institutions (public agencies, private businesses, organizations), and resources valued by society (air quality, cultural and historical sites, and so forth) that might be affected, positively or negatively, by the various alternatives under consideration (it is often useful to identify these by location on a map).

2. Develop a checklist of types of impacts, that is, the effects (both positive and negative) about which the various interests might be concerned (see table 9.2).

3. For each interest, assemble available data and establish a value information file.

4. For each interest, identify which types of impacts will be matters of concern, using information in the file and judgment where necessary.

5. Review the alternative actions developed to date. Consider each interest in turn: Are all the impacts of each alternative that are likely to be of concern to that interest on the list of step 4? If not, add the missing impact types to the list. Consider each action in turn. Are there interests potentially affected by any action that are not on the list developed in step 1? If so, add them to the lists of steps 1 and 4.

6. Construct an impact tableau. Be sure to include in the set of actions the null alternative.

7. Assemble and review all available data on the impacts of the alternatives—from travel prediction models, from other models, and from expert judgment.

8. Place these data in the impact tableau. Show for each prediction the range of uncertainty in the level of impact.

STEP II: VIEW THE ISSUES FROM THE PERSPECTIVE OF EACH AFFECTED INTEREST

In this step the analyst attempts to view the issues from the perspective of each affected interest.

1. Examine each affected interest, in turn, by going through the following steps.

2. Review the data in the impact tableau. Consider each action in turn. How is the interest affected by the action? Does it benefit? Is it adversely affected in any way? If there are adverse effects, does the action include steps that will adequately compensate the interest for the adverse effects?

3. Review the data in the value information file and the results of step 2. Consider each action in turn. What would be the attitude of the interest toward this action? Has the interest expressed any opinions on this action? Would the interest support the action? Oppose it? Be neutral? Why? Is there uncertainty about the likely attitude of the interest toward this action? If so, is this because the interest really consists of several interests with different values (so that it should be separated into several different interests)?

4. Appraise the actions in the impact tableau from this interest's perspective. Which actions would the interest support? Oppose? Be neutral toward? How would the interest rank the actions?

5. Explore possible new actions. Are there modifications of any particular action in the impact tableau that would make it much more attractive to the interest? Are there other actions, not in the impact tableau, that the interest has proposed or might propose that would be more attractive to it?

6. Review the uncertainties in the impact data. Consider the data in the impact tableau and their ranges of uncertainty. Are there impacts for which the interest would want more, or more accurate, information? Are there additional types of impacts not yet included in the tableau that the interest is likely to consider important?

STEP III: VIEW THE ISSUES FROM THE PERSPECTIVE OF EACH ACTION

In this step the analyst appraises in a preliminary way the major strengths and weaknesses of each action.

1. Examine each alternative action, in turn, by going through the following steps.

2. Issues of community concern: How does the proposed alternative respond to people's concerns? To transportation issues? To related issues? How can an alternative be changed to make it more responsive to such concerns? Do other agencies or governmental bodies have jurisdiction over some issues being raised?

3. Issues of feasibility: Is the action feasible technically? Legally? Administratively? Financially? If not feasible in some respect, why not? What steps might be considered to make it feasible? Not only changes in the action but also changes in administrative decisions or laws or other constraints should be carefully considered.

4. Issues of equity: Compare this action with the null alternative. Review the results of step II. Which affected interests would receive benefits from this action relative to the null alternative? Which would receive adverse effects? Are any of these adverse effects inadequately compensated? Why? Which interests would not be affected significantly? Which would receive both beneficial and adverse effects?

5. Issues of potential acceptability:

i. Which interests would be likely to support the action? To oppose it? To be neutral?

ii. For which interests is there uncertainty as to their likely attitudes? Why? Does the uncertainty arise because the information about impacts is uncertain, or because the attitudes of the interest are uncertain, or for some other reason?

iii. Would additional information on the effects of this action be desirable or useful? Which effects? What are the relative priorities for impact prediction?

iv. Would additional information on the feelings or reactions of any interests be desirable or useful? Which interests? What are the relative priorities for learning more about the values of various interests?

v. Are there modifications of the action that would increase its desirability from the point of view of particular interests? What are they? What are the relative priorities?

6. Summarize the major assets and liabilities of the action as revealed by this preliminary analysis.

STEP IV: VIEW THE ISSUES FROM THE PERSPECTIVE OF THE PROCESS AS A WHOLE

In steps II and III two different views are taken of the process: how each interest would view the process (as reflected in its views on each of the actions), and how each action compares to the null alternative. Each of these views provides important insights. In this step, in order to gain further insights, the analyst considers all the actions together in a search for patterns or relationships extending across several, many, or all actions and/or interests.

1. Review the results of the preceding steps.

2. Issues of undesirability: Are there actions for which the disadvantages are sufficiently great that they should be removed from further active consideration (for example, because they are infeasible and there is little potential for modifying them to make them feasible, or because they have significant adverse effects on some interests that are unacceptable to those interests and cannot be compensated)?

3. Issues of potential acceptability: Examine the results of steps II and III.

i. Are there groups of affected interests that share similar views (support, opposition, neutrality) about each of a group of several actions? All actions?

ii. Are there affected interests that have opposing views about a single action? Some groups of actions?

iii. For interests in conflict over some actions, are there other actions on which they would not conflict, but which they would support or at least not actively oppose? (If so, these actions are potential compromises.) Is there any way in which compromises among the affected interests might be reached through modification of available actions to change some impacts (or to provide compensation for adverse impacts) or through development of new actions?

iv. Are there any actions that would have or do have substantial acceptance by all affected interests? Which actions have the greatest potential for such acceptance?

STEP V: PREPARE SUMMARY EVALUATION REPORT

1. Review results of previous steps.

2. Summarize the major alternative actions and the most important issues:

i. What are the major advantages and disadvantages of each of the major alternatives, with particular emphasis on the issues as viewed by specific interests?

ii. What are the major issues that have been identified, especially the areas of conflict among interests and among alternative goals?

iii. What are the major priorities for further work on development of additional alternative actions? On development of additional information on impacts? On development of additional information about the views or attitudes of specific interests?

3. Write, review, and edit the evaluation report to ensure that it can be understood by the audience for whom it is intended.

9.2.4 Features of the Method

The key features of this evaluation method are as follows:

1. an emphasis on the differential incidence of adverse and beneficial impacts on different interests;

2. explicit recognition of the fact that different interests place different relative values on various objectives and impacts;

3. explicit emphasis on comparing differences among alternative actions to identify trade-offs (especially differences between the null action and others);

4. recognition of the need to consider qualitative information as thoroughly as quantitative information;

5. recognition of the need to identify uncertainties explicitly;

6. explicit concern for using evaluation as a management tool to assist in establishing work priorities for the technical team.

Basically the method consists of a systematic examination of each alternative action, in light of the available information on impacts and values, to determine whether each affected interest becomes better or worse off. The method explicitly considers the views of each interest separately. It stimulates the technical team to explore possible modifications of specific actions to shift the incidence of gains and losses by modifying actions; and it also encourages the team to think carefully about other priorities for further analysis.

The emphasis throughout the method is on creating a style of analysis in which the analyst ponders questions and confronts the actual data instead of a formal mathematical algorithm. (For an application of this method see Manheim et al. 1975b.)

9.2.5 Relation of the Evaluation Report to Environmental Impact Statements

In many countries legislation requires the preparation of a statement of the environmental impacts of proposed projects. In the United States section 102(2)(c) of the National Environmental Policy Act of 1969 requires that, before decisions are made on major federal actions (such as transportation projects with federal financial assistance), a statement be prepared and circulated to other agencies and to the public summarizing the environmental impacts of the proposed action. This environmental impact statement (EIS) must describe

1. the environmental impact of the proposed action;
2. any adverse environmental effects which cannot be avoided should the proposal be implemented;
3. alternatives to the proposed action;
4. the relationship between local short-term uses of man's environment and the maintenance and enhancement of long-term productivity; and
5. any irreversible and irretrievable commitments of resources which would be involved in the proposed action should it be implemented.

In our view the evaluation report produced by the method described above would be identical with the EIS and would meet the corresponding legal requirements. Both formats are concerned with identifying all significant impacts and discussing trade-offs among alternatives, especially relative to the null alternative. Both reports should be circulated in draft form so that interested parties can comment on them.

Where substantial detail is required for a full and comprehensive treatment of impacts, the report may reach hundreds or, for very large projects such as the Alaska oil pipeline, thousands of pages. The logical structure should be the same, however, in that the summary section should be concise and readable and identify the key issues. The summary section should be produced by the recommended evaluation method. To meet any specific format requirements for an EIS (see, for example, Council on Environmental Quality 1973) there are several approaches possible: either the combination of the evaluation report plus the associated technical appendixes can follow the specific format requirements, or alternatively the evaluation report section itself can be written to meet the format requirements. An example of this second approach may be found in Manheim et al. (1975b), pp. 40–48, where the summary section within the evaluation report fulfills the EIS requirements.

9.3 WHY THIS METHOD?

The evaluation method described in this chapter differs from the evaluation procedures recommended in other transportation-related textbooks. In this section we shall explain the view of evaluation that led to the formulation of this approach and examine the techniques usually recommended.

9.3.1 Evaluation: A Broader View

Our objective in this section is to step back from the technical details of evaluation and examine the kinds of issues with which the evaluation of transportation alternatives must deal.

To do this we shall return to one of the themes of chapter 1, namely, the fact of rapid change in demand, in technology, and in values. We do not turn to this theme lightly: the pressures of a changing world pose a great challenge to the analyst who would work openly and professionally to use transportation to improve society.

The rapidity of change is particularly critical in the area of public and private values. In many countries, and particularly in the United States, recent years have brought rapid changes in the desires and values of many groups. The evolution in values has been particularly important in transportation and has had many implications for the problem of evaluation.

First of all, the issues that must be considered in transportation decisions have changed. In the past the major issues considered for public decisions about transportation were the impacts on users and on operators. For example, in evaluations of highway, airport, or waterway investments, the impacts on operators were considered to be the costs of construction or acquisition of the new facilities, the operating and maintenance costs, and the revenues from fares, tolls, or other sources. The impacts on users were considered to be measured by improvements in travel time, travel costs, and other aspects of the level of service (American Association of State Highway Officials 1960, Department of the Environment 1972, De Weille 1966). (Occasionally the transfer of user benefits to the economy in so-called indirect benefits were also considered.)

This view of the issues to be considered is no longer adequate. For example, no longer is it sufficient to design transportation systems simply to serve "users" or operators. Instead we must identify which groups are served well and which groups poorly by a particular transportation system proposal. Thus we have begun to focus on the needs for transportation of those who are too poor or too ill or too young or too old to have ready access to automobile transportation. We have also become deeply concerned with the social, aesthetic, and environmental effects of transportation, particularly in built-up areas (Bridwell

1969, Organization for Economic Cooperation and Development 1969, Webber and Angel 1969).

A second critical change in values is the increased recognition of the diversity of values that exists in our society. This diversity has probably always existed; what is new is the increased degree to which these differences are actively expressed. Public attitudes have changed, shifting from apathy and indifference to concern and political activism; with greater public awareness has come more effective articulation of values. While most evident in the United States and in Great Britain, such changes are occurring in many other countries as well, particularly as the public interest in environmental issues increases (see, for example, Okita 1972, Simcock 1972, Mauch 1973). The result has been, in many instances, polarization and conflict. These changes in the political realities of transportation are reflected in the term "the freeway revolt" and the image it conjures in some minds: conflict between those who want highways for the greater mobility they provide, and those who oppose highways because of their effects on the quality of life in the communities they traverse. Opposition has also emerged in many countries to major new airports and to other kinds of transportation projects. The increased emphasis on such issues as air and noise pollution and better public transportation is, in part, a reflection of rapid change in the values held by some, if not all, sectors of the public.

A third change in values is a belated recognition that the effects of transportation are pervasive in a society:

Depending on the skill with which we exploit its potential, transportation can be either an instrument of desirable social change or a disruptive force against human development. It can both enhance and damage the quality of the environment. It can either act as a stimulus or act as a brake on urban growth and development. Thus, the ability to make enlightened transportation decisions may to a large extent determine government's success in achieving wider policy objectives. (Organization for Economic Cooperation and Development 1969)

Professionals concerned with transportation decision making have usually been cognizant of these effects of transportation in a general sort of way. These effects were not, however, considered critical by the professionals or by others until recently, and so these perceptions did not influence the actual decisions being made. Now they can no longer be treated superficially or ignored altogether.

A fourth change in values has been a change in the way the public views the professionals to whom it has previously turned for advice and guidance. This is a consequence of the other changes and of the failure of the professionals to respond to these changes in values quickly enough.

The highway engineer and the urban planner provide good examples. The urban planner, once seen as a somewhat utopian dreamer struggling to create a habitable urban environment, is now seen by some groups as the instrument of established interests, destroying viable social communities of low-income residents to erect office towers and luxury housing. Similarly the highway engineer is now seen by many as the servant of the automobile, pushing highways across the country without regard for preservation of urban community or rural amenities. Whether or not these views of the motives and values of planners and engineers are valid is not as important as the fact that a large segment of the public no longer feels confidence in professionals or in their judgments and is no longer willing to follow their recommendations without question.

As a consequence of these changes in values, the traditional approaches to transportation decision making are no longer adequate. For example, an international panel recently concluded that, in urban transportation planning,

a new conceptual approach . . . is emerging—one which gives increased emphasis to human values and to the social and economic goals of urban development. In this approach economic and engineering efficiency, "demand" for transportation and profitability no longer serve as the only guiding principles for investment decisions. These conventional criteria are weighed against the social, economic, environmental, and aesthetic needs of urban residents: personal mobility, accessibility to urban opportunities, comfort and convenience, clean air, open spaces, pleasing surroundings, the preservation of neighborhoods and urban diversity. Underlying this shifting emphasis is the growing conviction that transportation is not an end in itself but a tool for bettering the total condition of urban life; that its objective is not just to move people but to enhance the quality of cities and to improve the social well-being of their residents; and that planning concerned only with the effects on transportation itself has too often resulted in transportation systems that have failed to contribute effectively to these objectives.

. . . There is a need for a methodology which is more sensitive to the important issues facing urban society and more effective in helping to reach socially responsive decisions. . . . (Organization for Economic Cooperation and Development 1969)

Several conclusions can be drawn from this discussion of changing values:

1. There are many different kinds of impacts of transportation systems —not only on the users and operators but also on nonusers. Many of

these are difficult to describe precisely, much less to quantify in numerical terms. Yet impacts that can be treated only qualitatively must nevertheless be fully considered. All of these effects must be considered in evaluating and choosing among transportation alternatives.

2. Alternative actions for transportation system change differ not only in the kinds and magnitudes of their impacts but also in the incidence of those impacts. Each alternative action bestows beneficial effects on some groups and interests and causes adverse effects on others. These differences in incidence must be explicitly considered in evaluation and choice.

3. Society is not homogeneous but is composed of a variety of different groups with different needs, desires, and values. This, together with the fact of the differences in incidence, makes decisions about most transportation system changes essentially political issues. Conflict is almost inevitable: some groups will favor actions that others oppose. This makes progress very difficult unless the analyst explicitly recognizes and addresses the probability of conflict.

4. We can expect values to continue to change. We should never presume that values are static. As the options available change, as the political system and process evolves, and as our knowledge of the effects of various actions grows, values will continue to change. The issues that seem important today may or may not be the issues that seem important tomorrow.

9.3.2 Classical Approaches to Evaluation

The evaluation techniques that have been used in the past fall into three major groups: pure judgment, economic analysis, and rating schemes.

In the first approach the basic method of evaluation is judgment. In some cases the judgment is that of a professional engineer, planner, or economist, using technical data on the costs and feasibility of a project. In other cases the judgment is that of a political decision maker (or manager of a private firm), perhaps with some attention to technical data, perhaps weighing only the political or financial advantages and disadvantages of a project. Our stress on "pure" judgment reflects the fact that, while some judgment enters into all evaluation methods, this method relies solely on judgment. Another way of putting this is that evaluation and choice are tightly intermingled; as the issues are weighed, the decision is made.

In the second approach the evaluation of projects is based upon an economic analysis. For public-sector decisions the basic approach has often been that of benefit/cost analysis, considering primarily user benefits. For example, in the highway field in the United States and many other countries the methods are largely those outlined originally in the "AASHO Red Book" (American Association of State Highway Officials 1960, Wohl and Martin 1967). In this approach the impacts of a highway project are divided into two groups. The costs are the capital costs of investment (land acquisition, construction) and the operating costs (maintenance, administration). The benefits are those received by users of the facility (further reductions in travel times or in vehicle operating cost); using dollar prices, such as a value of travel time in dollars per hours, all the benefits to users are measured in economic (dollar) terms. Through the use of appropriate interest rates and other factors (see section 9.4.2), costs and benefits at different times are made comparable (for example, by evaluating them on an equivalent annual basis). Then each alternative project is evaluated by determining the total costs and the total benefits for the project and computing a benefit/cost ratio; projects are compared on the basis of these ratios. This approach, with numerous variations and modifications, has been used in highway planning, in the United States and elsewhere, and for other kinds of public-sector transportation investments as well (Dawson 1968, Wohl and Martin 1967, De Wielle 1966).

For private-sector decisions (that is, investment by a private firm) economic concepts are also applied. Costs are handled in much the same way as in the public-sector context (except that tax and financing considerations may significantly change the details of the analysis). The benefits are obviously the gross revenues to the firm from increases in traffic, higher charges, and so forth. The total gross revenues are then compared with the total costs, and net revenue, a rate of return on investment, or other economic criteria are computed. Alternative projects are evaluated on the basis of the relative values of these criteria.

In the third type of approach procedures are established for weighing the various impacts of a project and computing a score for each alternative. The various alternatives are then compared on the basis of their scores. One special case illustrating the approach is the linear scoring function (LSF) (M. D. Hill 1967, Riedesel and Cook 1970). In this approach the total score for alternative i is

$$S_i = \sum_{j,k} w_{jk} x_{ijk'}$$

where x_{ijk} is the level of impact type k on affected interest j for alternative i and w_{jk} is the weight placed on impact type k by interest j. The values of x_{ijk} are the data in the impact tableau. Once we have these data, the LSF approach requires us to establish a set of weights, which are then used to compute the total score S_i for each alternative. Alternatives are then compared on the basis of the relative values of their scores.

It is instructive to review the evolution of these three techniques and to put them in perspective. The pure-judgment approach has been used throughout history. In the mid-1950s the economic-analysis approach was first applied to public-sector projects in transportation, beginning with highway projects, as a result of its previous successful use for water-resource projects. Particularly popular was the variation termed benefit/cost analysis. (The use of economic analysis for private-sector transport investment decisions has a longer history. See, for example, Wellington 1891.)

The economic-analysis approach should be seen in historical perspective. When benefit/cost analysis was introduced, it represented a professional approach to the evaluation of alternatives. Because this approach appeared to be an objective technical procedure, decisions about transportation projects could be removed from the domain of "political" judgments: arguments for particular alternatives on political grounds could (at least in principle) be countered by the results of an economic analysis, and a more rational basis for decision established. In the highway and urban transportation fields especially, the economic-analysis approach became the prescribed evaluation procedure in the 1950s and 1960s (see, for example, Department of the Environment 1972).

In some ways the emphasis on economic analysis as an evaluation procedure went too far. To see why, it is useful to examine the rating-scheme approach represented by the linear scoring functions. (The economic-analysis approach is a special case of the LSF approach in which the weights used are the unit prices of benefits and costs.) We shall consider five issues. (These are useful questions to ask of any evaluation method, including the ones recommended in this volume!)

1. What impacts are considered explicitly and what are omitted?
2. What alternative actions are evaluated and what are omitted?
3. Whose values do the weights represent?
4. How are the weights determined?
5. What is the significance of the total score as a basis for choosing among alternative actions?

The impacts considered. To use the LSF all impacts must be expressed in numerical terms. This is obviously a strict requirement. Many significant social, aesthetic, and environmental impacts are difficult, if not impossible, to quantify and so must be omitted from the analysis. In economic analysis the restrictions are even more severe: only those impacts can be considered for which dollar prices can be obtained as weights (see Mishan 1970). In light of present values, omission of qualitative impacts is not acceptable.

The alternative actions considered. Typically, when the LSF or the economic-analysis approach is used, evaluation comes at the end of the process of analysis, after the alternative actions to be considered have been developed. There is then a danger that the choice will be among equally unattractive alternatives. As indicated by the model of the process of analysis in chapter 1, evaluation should be an integral part of the cycle of analysis. It is particularly important that evaluation stimulate search; for example, it should suggest priorities for finding alternatives that modify or shift specific types of impacts on specific affected interests. (In a highway location study this might involve identification of an adverse effect such as displacement of a number of families in a specific neighborhood, thereby focusing effort on developing modifications of the location to reduce the displacement and developing a replacement housing program to ameliorate the adverse effects.) While nothing in the LSF or economic-analysis approaches prevents their being used in a manner more integrated with the process of analysis, they have conventionally not been so used and are not particularly effective (without modification) in this role.

Whose weights? From our discussion of changing values, it should be clear that many different groups, with very different values, are affected by and concerned about transportation alternatives, and that most often there will be conflict and disagreement among these groups as to which alternatives are most desirable. In the LSF approach it is assumed that a single set of weights will be obtained and used. The presumption is that this set of weights represents the values of society. But recent experience indicates that different groups *cannot* agree on values because their values are different (at least at the operational level, though they may well share common values of a more abstract sort). The location for a new airport preferred by air travelers would be different from that preferred by residents of adjacent communities; the attitudes of management and of workers will differ on a proposed change in the structure of a transportation carrier such as a trucking or shipping company. Therefore the basic presumption of a single set of weights in the LSF approach avoids the very important question of whose weights—which group's values—should be used.

The same presumption is made in the economic-analysis approach. It is further presumed in this case that the weights to be placed on various impacts should be the prevailing market prices (except when shadow prices are used: see Little and Mirrlees 1974). This involves a number of critical assumptions, including the assumption that people know the consequences of their present choices and approve of the present distribution of income, and that the action being considered would not significantly alter present conditions (see de Neufville and Stafford 1971, chapters 8–11).

Determination of weights. Even if the problem of whose weights to use could be resolved, there would still remain the practical problem of determining those weights. Assume that we want to obtain values for a particular group with relatively homogeneous interests (air travelers or a residential neighborhood directly adjacent to a potential transportation project). To use the LSF approach we need to know what impacts are likely to be important to this group, and what their preferences are for various combinations of levels of different impacts. Some practical techniques have been developed for use in determining preferences. For example, multidimensional utility functions establishing weights over various impacts can be determined by asking a number of questions of an individual (see, for example, Keeney 1972).

Such an effort is time-consuming for a single individual, however, and would be prohibitive for many individuals representing many groups—not only because of the cost in analyst time but also because of reluctance to expend the necessary effort by the affected individuals. Further, there are many critical assumptions in such an approach: that the individual's values are static and will not be changed by any information presented to him; that all relevant impacts are included in the questions and that no new ones will surface later; that the individual's preferences are independent of external conditions; and that the preferences expressed in such an introspective exercise with abstract, hypothetical alternatives are those he would express when actually making a choice among real alternatives.

An evaluation technique that makes such assumptions is of limited value. Moreover, the number of impacts to be considered and the number of groups with different values are sufficiently large that such techniques would have limited practical use.

The most practical way to determine a group's values is not by constructing abstract functions or weights but by asking members of the group to choose among specific real alternatives. People can express their values best when they are confronted with real alternatives whose impacts they can perceive and understand, when they understand the range of feasible options that are available, and when they are stimulated to clarify their own values through the process of learning about the alternatives and their consequences.

Significance of the total score. Finally, and perhaps most important of all, there is the issue of using a single score as a measure for making a decision. When this is done, the presumption is that only the overall score of the alternative is important; the distributional effects— the incidence of adverse and beneficial impacts—is unimportant. For example, when a benefit/cost ratio is used as a basis for decision, the assumption is made that only the net benefits and the net costs, to whomsoever they might accrue, are relevant to the decision. Thus the benefit/cost ratio measures the efficiency of the investment but ignores the distributional aspects (see Walsh and Williams 1969, Nwaneri 1970, Pearce 1971). As our discussion of changing values stressed, however, it is the incidence of effects with which society has become concerned. Therefore, the use of a single score in evaluation as a basis of decision is directly opposed to the concerns of society today. The use of a single score hides the differential incidence of effects, whereas evaluation should strive to bring out the differences in incidence among various alternatives.

Thus the LSF and economic-analysis approaches involve a number of serious assumptions. Clearly such technical approaches should not be abandoned completely in favor of a return to the pure-judgment approach. Neither extreme is appropriate today. A more subtle approach to evaluation is required, one that combines the positive attributes of both judgment and technical analysis (see Heymann 1965).

We do not reject the LSF and economic-analysis approaches completely: these techniques can have useful, if somewhat minor, roles in a broader, more desirable evaluation process, provided their assumptions and limitations are clearly understood and counterbalanced. Economic analysis in particular can be an important tool for evaluation, so long as it is put in perspective and used in the context of the method outlined in this chapter.

9.4 EXTENDING THE BASIC EVALUATION METHOD
The basic procedure of section 9.2 is generally applicable to all types of transportation problems. As described, however, it is most effective with project-scale issues, that is, the location and design of specific

projects such as highways, transit lines, airports, or changes in operations over a single route. In these projects the alternative actions are relatively few and easy to understand and the number of affected interests and impact types is also relatively small. Thus the basic approach can be used, as outlined, with manual procedures—that is, the analyst can work almost solely with pencil and paper.

For systems planning problems such as a metropolitan or national transportation plan, or the total network of a rail or air carrier, the inherent complexity demands additional techniques. The numbers of affected interests, impact types, and alternatives are much greater than they are at the scale of a single project. The alternative actions themselves are much more complex, since they consist of various combinations of specific projects and thus overlap to a considerable extent (that is, the alternatives are not mutually exclusive) and since differences in the time-stagings of the projects are often important features of the alternative plans. Furthermore, the impacts often extend over much longer time periods than do the impacts of a single project, are more uncertain, and in many respects are more difficult for laymen to understand.

The same basic method is still applicable for large complex actions such as systems plans, but additional techniques become important in applying the approach efficiently (some of these techniques would also be required for the traditional evaluation approaches). These techniques are useful for steps II and III of the basic method but are especially valuable at step IV.

In this section we shall describe briefly two specific techniques: the use of economic constructs to define goal variables and trade-off analysis. We shall assume some familiarity with the basic economic concepts of project appraisal (see McKean 1968, de Neufville and Stafford 1971, Mishan 1971, or any basic text in engineering or managerial economics).

9.4.1 Economic Concepts as Goal Variables

A variety of procedures can be used to develop a set of goal variables for any given analysis. One important method uses economic concepts to construct aggregate measures summarizing some of the impacts important to particular interests, from the perspectives of those interests.

Economic concepts can be used to develop a number of different goal variables. Several principles are common to all economic goal variables. First, impacts are described in terms of monetary values (prices); thus only impacts that can be quantified and for which monetary prices can be established are included in economic goal variables. Second, impacts incurred at different points in time are made commensurable by means of appropriate discount or interest rates. Third, it is possible to construct economic goal variables that combine positively valued impacts (benefits or revenues) with negatively valued impacts (costs or disbenefits) in additive or ratio forms.

In constructing economic goal variables, several points should be kept in mind.

1. Each actor has a different point of view, with different goals and values. Thus one or more goal variables should be constructed to represent the viewpoint of each actor, even in purely economic terms.
2. The impacts of a particular alternative will be different on each actor, and each actor will have different values with respect to the desirability of various impacts. Thus the prices and definitions of economic goal variables may appropriately be different for different actors.
3. Mechanisms for shifting the distribution of impacts among actors can and should be considered. Thus the economic goal variables should be defined in such ways that economic measures to shift the incidence of impacts can be explored—for example, through pricing policies, taxes, subsidies, or compensation payments.

9.4.2 Some Basic Concepts

THE TIME DIMENSION

Significant impacts occur at different points in time. For example, when a transportation operator builds a new facility or acquires a new vehicle, an initial investment of capital is made and then this cost is recovered by revenues that accrue in later time periods. One important issue in evaluation is how to balance the values of impacts that occur at different points in time. Economic methods provide one approach.

The basic concept is that of the time value of money. A sum of money H can earn interest at some rate r, either by deposit in a bank account or by being loaned out in some other manner. Thus at the end of one year, if r is the annual interest rate, the sum H would grow to

$$G = H(1 + r). \tag{9.1}$$

Conversely, if someone were to ask us how much we would pay now for a contract that offered a sure payment of G dollars at the end of one year, then we should be willing to pay H dollars. From this reasoning can be developed the following relationships: The value at end of year n of a present amount H is

$$G_n = H(1 + r)^n. \tag{9.2}$$

The value at present of a future amount G_n to be received at end of year n is

$$H = G_n(1 + r)^{-n}. \tag{9.3}$$

The value at present of a series of future amounts G_n that would be received at the end of the year in years $n = 1, 2, \ldots, N$ is

$$H = \sum_{n=1}^{N} G_n(1 + r)^{-n}. \tag{9.4}$$

The value at present of a series of future equal amounts G that would be received at the end of the year in years $n = 1, 2, \ldots, N$ is

$$H = G \sum_{n=1}^{N} (1 + r)^{-n} \tag{9.5}$$

or, using properties of geometric series,

$$H = \frac{G}{\mathrm{CRF}(r, N)}, \tag{9.6}$$

where the **capital recovery factor** is defined by

$$\mathrm{CRF}(r, N) = \frac{r(1 + r)^N}{(1 + r)^N - 1}. \tag{9.7}$$

The value of equal payments G, paid at the end of the year in years $n = 1, 2, \ldots, N$, that would be received from an amount H invested at present is

$$G = H \times \mathrm{CRF}(r, N). \tag{9.8}$$

These relationships can be used to establish various kinds of economic goal variables. For example, if an operator invests an amount C at the beginning of year 1 and receives revenue each year for N years in the amount B at the end of each year, then his net return can be computed in either of two ways. In the **equivalent-annual-cost method** all costs and revenues are put on an equivalent annual basis. Given the annual revenue payment B and the initial investment C transformed by (9.8) into an equivalent annual payment of

$$c_a = C \times \mathrm{CRF}(r, N), \tag{9.9}$$

the equivalent annual cost EAC is

$$EAC = -B + c_a = -B + [C \times CRF(r, N)]. \qquad (9.10)$$

In the **_net-present-value method_** all costs and revenues are represented by their values at the beginning of year 1. Given that the present value of the investment cost is C and the net present value of the revenue stream of B each year is, by (9.6),

$$b = \frac{B}{CRF(r, N)}, \qquad (9.11)$$

the net present value NPV of the total stream of benefits and costs is

$$NPV = \frac{B}{CRF(r, N)} - C. \qquad (9.12)$$

A comparison of (9.10) and (9.12) indicates that the EAC and NPV are directly related:

$$EAC = -CRF(r, N) \times NPV. \qquad (9.13)$$

Thus either measure can be used as a basis for comparing economic impacts at different points in time. (These are examples; many other types of measures are possible.)

CHOOSING A DISCOUNT RATE
An interest rate r can thus be used to establish equivalencies of economic impacts at different points in time, and the choice of a specific value for r can greatly influence the relative weights of present versus future costs and revenues. Table 9.4 shows this effect.

There are a number of possible bases for the selection of an appropriate discount rate:

Table 9.4   CRF factors

| Year (N) | Interest rate (r) | | | | |
	1%	5%	10%	15%	20%
1	1.01	1.05	1.10	1.15	1.20
2	0.51	0.54	0.58	0.62	0.65
5	0.21	0.23	0.26	0.30	0.33
10	0.11	0.13	0.16	0.20	0.24
20	0.06	0.08	0.12	0.16	0.25
30	0.04	0.07	0.11	0.15	0.20

Note: These figures are approximate; for detailed analyses the appropriate tables in standard references should be consulted.

1. the actual current cost of borrowing money;
2. the "opportunity cost" of capital, based upon the return that could be achieved from alternative investments of the resources;
3. the "risk" in the proposed project, that is, the degree of uncertainty in future revenues and costs; or
4. an explicit value judgment as to the relative desirability of impacts at different points in time, based on the values and preferences of those responsible for making the decision.

There is a substantial literature on the choice of an appropriate discount rate, with the various views expressed depending, in part, on the context (see the discussion in de Neufville and Stafford 1971).

It is our belief that the relative weighting given to present versus future impacts should be an explicit value judgment, as should the relative weights placed on any other types of impacts. These relative values would vary with the viewpoints of most if not all actors. The interest rates operating in the capital market at a given time are not necessarily the values that every interest group would place on impacts at that time. A choice of a discount rate should be made only in the context of the specific action alternatives available, with an awareness of their implications. Therefore, when economic goal variables are used, several alternative values for the discount rate should be established reflecting the perspectives of different interests, and a sensitivity analysis should be done to determine the effect on the economic goal variables (such as NPV) of these alternative values.

9.4.3 Some Useful Economic Constructs

A number of types of economic goal variables can be constructed for comparison of alternative courses of action. Consider courses of action i, j, k, characterized by:

1. initial investment costs I_i, I_j, I_k;
2. annual costs to operate the system A_i, A_j, A_k (all costs except that of the capital in the initial investment); and
3. annual gross revenues from the system R_i, R_j, R_k.

For simplicity we assume that these are the only major categories of costs and revenues and that annual costs and revenues are constant over the life of each system. In actual applications these conditions would not be met; different items would have different useful lives, different salvage values, and perhaps different applicable interest rates, different rates of growth in annual costs and revenues, and so forth.

We consider five categories of economic goal variables:

1. *Equivalent annual cost:*

$$EAC_i = [I_i \times CRF(r, N)] + A_i - R_i. \tag{9.14}$$

2. *Annual net operating revenue:*

$$ANOR_i = R_i - A_i. \tag{9.15}$$

3. *Annual net revenue:*

$$ANR_i = R_i - A_i - [I_i \times CRF(r, N)] = -EAC_i. \tag{9.16}$$

4. *Net present value of costs and revenues:*

$$NPV_i = -I_i + \frac{R_i - A_i}{CRF(r, N)} = \frac{ANR_i}{CRF(r, N)}. \tag{9.17}$$

5. *Ratio of annual net revenue to investment:* In this case the payoff of the investment is measured in terms of increasing annual net revenue, that is, the gain in gross revenue less the operating costs. For a single project one way of defining this is as annual net return on investment:

$$ANRI_i = \frac{R_i - A_i}{I_i} \tag{9.18}$$

or, for comparison of two projects i and j:

$$ANRI_{i,j} = \frac{\Delta ANOR}{\Delta I} = \frac{(R_i - R_j) - (A_i - A_j)}{I_i - I_j}. \tag{9.19}$$

This type of incremental measure is particularly useful when projects are ranked in order of increasing investment cost. It can then be used to answer the question, Is an increment of investment ΔI above the level I_j worthwhile in terms of the increment of return?

It is important to realize that much judgment goes into the choice of items to be included in the various terms of these measures. The actual financing mechanisms, taxes, and subsidies have significant implications. For example, if the investment the operator is considering involves buying an additional vehicle, it is quite likely that that investment will be financed by a mortgage or a similar mechanism through a bank or other source of capital. In this case the operator's investment may be only a down payment d_i, and the major cost of the investment will be an annual charge c_i to pay off the interest and principal on the mortgage. Thus I would be replaced by d_i in the above relationships.

Therefore, for each actor, a mix of measures with practical definitions should be developed which most effectively reflect the viewpoint
of that actor. To illustrate we shall examine some specific forms of
measures useful to various actors.

9.4.4 Economic Goal Variables to Reflect the Viewpoints of Operators

Economic goal variables are especially useful in summarizing impacts
from the viewpoints of transportation operators. For most private
operators, and many public or semipublic operators, such economic
measures directly reflect the impacts that are of greatest concern.
Even in these circumstances, however, it will often be necessary to
define several economic measures to reflect fully the different issues
important to an operator, and there may be some important impacts
that cannot be subsumed into any economic variables.

The gross benefits to operators are the gross revenues from fares
(or other user charges) and other sources, such as advertising, parking facilities, or concessions such as restaurants and other facilities in
terminals. The costs to operate the system include direct operating
costs such as fuel, labor, and spare parts and indirect operating costs
such as management and administration (exclusive of the cost of
capital investment).

Some of the goal variables most often used are functions of these
gross revenues R_i and total direct and indirect operating costs A_i;
these include the ones defined in section 9.4.3. The specific form used
in chapters 5–7 was the annual net revenue:

$$ANR_i \equiv R_i - A_i - [I \times CRF(r, N)] = I_{GR} - C_T \equiv I_{NR}, \qquad (9.20)$$

where

$$C_T \equiv A_i + [I \times CRF(r, N)], \qquad (9.21)$$

$$I_{GR} \equiv R_i. \qquad (9.22)$$

Many different measures are used in particular sectors of the transportation industry, reflecting the variety of financing, tax, and organizational situations of decision makers (see, for example, Frankel
1977).

9.4.5 Economic Goal Variables to Reflect the Viewpoints of Users

The major impacts of system changes on users are through changes in
the levels of service, which may be reflected in changes in the volumes

of freight shipped or the numbers of users making particular travel choices. (For simplicity we consider a one-dimensional volume representing passengers.) While users do incur monetary costs, such as fares or operating costs of a private vehicle, these are just a portion of the impacts important to them. The basic premise underlying the use of economic variables to reflect impacts on users is that the demand function for a group of users shows the values they place on different levels of service. Thus the demand function expresses the users' relative "willingness to pay" for different service levels.

WILLINGNESS TO PAY

The argument for this is as follows (see figure 9.3) in the case of a single service variable, price. Based on the demand function D, a change in price from p_i to $p_i + \Delta p$ will cause a change in volume from V_i to $V_i + \Delta V$ (ΔV will in general be negative for positive p, and vice versa). The ΔV users who leave the system are the ones who got just enough "benefit" or "value" out of using the system at price p_i to make it attractive to them; at the higher price $p_i + \Delta p$, the benefits are no longer sufficient to attract them. Therefore the benefit of using the system for these ΔV users lies between p_i and $p_i + \Delta p$, or for small Δp, the benefit is approximately p_i. Thus if we rewrite the demand function

$$V = D(p) \tag{9.23}$$

as

$$p = g(V), \tag{9.24}$$

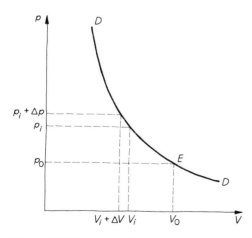

Figure 9.3 The demand function as a measure of users' willingness to pay.

where g is the inverse function of D, we can measure the benefit to a small volume of users between V_i and $V_i + \Delta V$ as

$$B_i \approx g(V_i). \tag{9.25}$$

More generally, if p_0 is the actual price charged uniformly to all users, with a resulting volume V_0, then integration over all volumes between 0 and V_0 gives the total benefit or value to users of that level of price. This **gross user benefit** is

$$UBG(p_0) \equiv \int_0^{V_0} g(V) \, dV, \quad \text{where } V_0 = D(p_0). \tag{9.26}$$

On a graph this is the area under the demand curve from the vertical axis to the line $V_0 = E$. It is finite if the demand curve intersects the axis; if not, while the integral itself may not be bounded, the difference in UBG between two prices p_0 and p_i is finite and can still be found.

APPLYING THE WILLINGNESS-TO-PAY CONCEPT

Now consider a change from p_0 to p_1. We shall discuss three cases. First, assume there is only one service attribute, price, and that volume is a constant, V_0. For a price change from p_0 to p_1, from (9.26),

$$\Delta UBG_{01} \equiv UBG_0 - UBG_1 = (p_0 - p_1)V_0. \tag{9.27}$$

There is an improvement in service that is received wholly by the users V_0. The magnitude of UBG_{01} corresponds to the shaded area in figure 9.4.

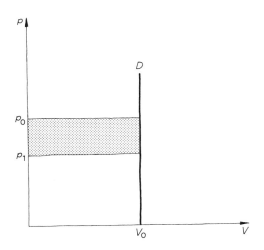

Figure 9.4 User benefit under constant volume.

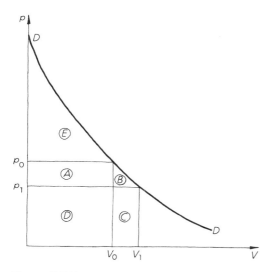

Figure 9.5 User benefit under changing volume.

The price p may be an explicit charge such as a railroad or air fare or bridge or highway toll, an expense such as automobile operating costs (oil, maintenance, and so forth), or the sum of a number of such items. In any of these cases the user benefit can be interpreted as the total cost savings to all users.

Now let service volume vary with price according to a demand function D, as in (9.23). The problem is more difficult in this case for both conceptual and practical reasons. The conceptual issues can be illustrated by reference to figure 9.5. When price changes from p_0 to p_1, volume changes from V_0 to V_1. The original V_0 users benefit from the price decrease, but there are also benefits accruing to the $V_1 - V_0$ new users of the system. There are three alternative views on how to measure benefit to users.

i. *Gross-benefit view.* In this view, corresponding to the willingness-to-pay argument, the total benefit to users is given by the area under the demand curve. In the figure, for price p_0 and corresponding volume V_0 this integral corresponds to the area $E + A + D$. The difference in gross user benefit between two actions would be

$$\Delta UBG_{01} = UBG(p_1) - UBG(p_0) = \int_{V_0}^{V_1} g(V)\, dV \tag{9.28}$$

or, in the figure, the area $B + C$.

ii. *Consumer-surplus view.* A second point of view is that the benefits should exclude the amount actually paid out. The amount paid out is the total *user cost*,

$$UC(p_0) = p_0 V_0. \qquad (9.29)$$

The *consumer surplus* is that amount of benefit received by users beyond what they actually pay:

$$\begin{aligned} UBCS(p_0) &\equiv UBG(p_0) - UC(p_0) \\ &= \int_0^{V_0} g(V)\, dV - p_0 V_0. \end{aligned} \qquad (9.30)$$

In the figure this is area E (which may not be finite if the demand curve does not intersect the vertical axis).

In comparing two alternative actions, the difference in consumer surplus would be used as a measure of user benefits:

$$\begin{aligned} \varDelta UBCS_{01} &= UBCS(p_1) - UBCS(p_0) \\ &= UBG(p_1) - UBG(p_0) - UC(p_1) + UC(p_0) \qquad (9.31) \\ &= \int_{V_0}^{V_1} g(V)\, dV - p_1 V_1 + p_0 V_0. \end{aligned}$$

In the figure this is the area $A + B$.

iii. *User-cost view.* A third point of view is expressed in either of two ways, each leading to the same result. From one perspective the benefit to users should reflect only the reduction in actual prices paid, that is, the reduction in user cost. This *user-cost benefit* is given by

$$\begin{aligned} \varDelta UBUC &\equiv \varDelta UC \\ &= p_0 V_0 - p_1 V_1. \end{aligned} \qquad (9.32)$$

From another perspective the argument is made that the user benefit should be the gross benefit less the consumer surplus (Wohl and Martin 1967):

$$\begin{aligned} UBY &\equiv UBG - UBCS \\ &= UBG - (UBG - UC) \qquad (9.33) \\ &= UC. \end{aligned}$$

The result is the same. In comparing two alternatives, the difference in total user cost (9.32) would be used as a measure of user benefits. This corresponds to the difference between areas A and C in the figure.

iv. *Trapezoidal approximations.* To visualize the differences among these measures, it is useful to assume that the demand function can be approximated by a linear relation in the region of interest. Then

Table 9.5 Three measures of user benefit: comparison of differences in benefit for a change from (p_0, V_0) to (p_1, V_1)

Measure	Differential areas in figure 9.5	Value of trapezoidal approximation
Gross benefit	$B + C$	$\frac{1}{2}(p_0 + p_1)(V_1 - V_0)$
Consumer surplus	$A + B$	$\frac{1}{2}(p_0 - p_1)(V_1 + V_0)$
User cost	$A - C$	$V_0 p_0 - V_1 p_1$

Source: Based on Wohl and Martin (1967).

the integrals can be replaced by explicit areas. These are summarized in table 9.5.

A comparison of the various measures shows that, except under very special conditions, each offers a different description of user benefit, and they may give different results on an incremental comparison of two actions.

In the special case of constant volume

$$\Delta UBG = 0, \tag{9.34}$$

$$\Delta UBCS = \Delta UBUC, \tag{9.35}$$

so that at least two of the measures give the same result.

The conceptual difficulties in developing measures of user benefit involve arguments over appropriateness. At present the consumer-surplus and user-cost measures are the most commonly used (Wohl and Martin 1967, de Neufville and Stafford 1971, McIntosh and Quarmby 1972).

The practical difficulties lie, in this case, in the measurement of areas under the demand curve. The linear assumption leading to the trapezoidal approximation to the areas must be used with caution; for significant changes in p, the approximation may introduce large errors.

The units of these areas are the product of volume and price (for example, dollars per hour if volume is in passengers per hour and price is in dollars per passenger).

In the third case we shall consider, the level of service is a vector **S** and volume varies according to a demand function D:

$$V = D(\mathbf{S}). \tag{9.36}$$

The problems in measuring user benefit in this situation are compounded from those in the case of a single service attribute. In addition to the conceptual and practical problems noted already (different views on which measures to use and the practical problem of computing areas for nonlinear demand functions), there arises the important problem that the units of consumer surplus become complex and specific to the form of the demand functions.

RELATED ISSUES

The value of time

In much of the literature of transportation engineering, a "user-cost" approach is recommended; as pointed out by Wohl and Martin, however, this is actually a consumer-surplus approach (when generated traffic is considered correctly). In this literature substantial effort is often devoted to establishing a "value of time"—a dollar value to be used to convert user travel time savings into equivalent monetary benefits (standard values of $1.375 per hour and, later, $1.75 per hour have been advocated). It should be clear from the preceding discussion that the value of time should be determined explicitly from the demand function; more directly, the demand function itself, together with all service attributes included in that function, should be used explicitly in determining the magnitude of user benefits, rather than a monetary valuation of time savings calculated from some standard independent of the demand function. (Only in the case of a linear demand function will the two approaches give the same result.) Further, since different market segments will have different demand functions, their values of time will be different.

Willingness to accept willingness to pay

Another important limitation of these measures of user benefit is that, if used carelessly, they are biased toward upper-income travelers.

To see this, consider two market segments, one high-income and the other low-income, and assume that a linear demand function applies to each group. The high-income group will place a higher value on travel time than the low-income group; a ten-minute reduction in travel time would therefore result in a greater increase in volume of high-income travelers (all else being equal) than of low-income travelers. Two projects, A and B, are being considered, and each has the same investment cost: A provides a travel time reduction of 10 minutes only for high-income travelers; B provides a reduction of 10 minutes only for low-income travelers. Project A would have a higher value of $\Delta UBGB$ or $\Delta UBCS$ (though a lower value of $\Delta UBUC$). From

either a gross-benefit or a consumer-surplus point of view, then, project A, benefiting high-income travelers, would be preferred. Conversely, from a user-cost viewpoint, project B, benefiting low-income
travelers, would be preferred.

Of course, in real situations the distinctions among beneficiaries of
actions would be far less clear-cut. However, the same general effects
would occur: projects benefiting high-income travelers would show
greater user benefits (UBGB or UBCS) than those benefiting low-
income users.

This is undesirable. To avoid this bias (either way) the impacts on
different market segments should be disaggregated and clearly displayed. In this way the relative emphasis to be given to benefits to
different user groups can be determined explicitly in terms of the trade-
offs involved. Practically this means that user benefits should be determined for each market segment for which there is an explicit demand
function. (For a user benefit measure for multinomial logit demand
functions see Ben-Akiva and Lerman 1978.) Furthermore, where
feasible, user benefits for each market segment should be determined
at the lowest level of detail—by origin, by destination, and by time of
day, income, purpose, and so forth (to the extent these distinctions
are relevant). Figure 9.6 presents one way in which the benefits to
users can be displayed by origin zone for a particular region (see also
Harvey 1972, Syrnick and Harvey 1977).

Values of user benefit may also be shown for various aggregations
of market segments. Clearly, however, any aggregation is a value judgment. Therefore, variations in the weightings of the various groups
should be explored, so that the sensitivity of the rankings of alternative
actions can be determined.

System effects

Clearly changes in user benefits should be computed for all elements
of the transportation system for which volumes and/or levels of service
are changed. For example, a travel time reduction on one route—route
A, say—will benefit travelers already using that route and also travelers
who previously used other routes but now shift to A. This shift will, of
course, reduce the volumes on the other routes, thus attracting additional travelers to those routes, with corresponding gains in benefits to
them.

User benefits accruing to all groups of travelers should be identified
and determined throughout the system. See Neuburger (1971) for the
extension to land-use changes. If a simultaneous-choice demand

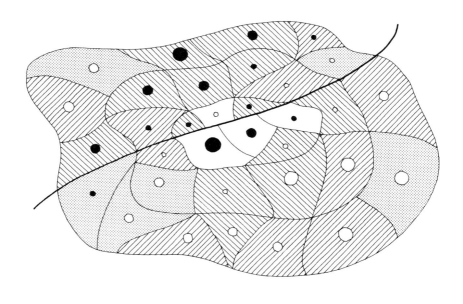

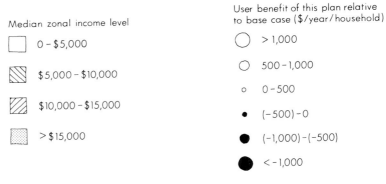

Median zonal income level

☐ 0 – $5,000

▨ $5,000 – $10,000

▨ $10,000 – $15,000

▨ > $15,000

User benefit of this plan relative
to base case ($/year/household)

○ > 1,000

○ 500 – 1,000

∘ 0 – 500

• (–500) – 0

● (–1,000) – (–500)

● < – 1,000

Figure 9.6 Geographic display of user benefit. After a concept suggested by
Harvey (1972).

function is used, then the benefit measures include benefits through new trips, changes in destination, changes in mode, and changes in route.

CONCLUSIONS

Economic variables measuring user benefits are useful in summarizing the service-level impacts on users at a disaggregate level. For example, it is often appropriate to estimate benefits for a single market segment— defined to be relatively homogeneous with respect to income, preferences, geographic origin, and possibly destination patterns—by means of the demand function for that segment. When user benefits are calculated and displayed at this disaggregate level, the differential incidence of user impacts can be clearly displayed.

Economic variables can also be used for various aggregations of market segments, including the total for all users, that is, the total user benefit. Such aggregate measures have biases, however, and unless great care is taken, they tend to focus attention on net effects rather than on the distribution of benefits and adverse effects. Thus, although aggregate measures of user benefits may yield useful insights during the preparation of an evaluation report, the analyst should focus most effort on understanding the *patterns* of user benefits at the disaggregate level.

Since we prefer to resist aggregating as much as possible, we often find it useful to summarize impacts on users in the manner illustrated in chapter 5 and the case studies: that is, we use either equilibrium service level (composite service level, as defined in section 4.5.6, or specific component attributes) or equilibrium volume. Consumer surplus and gross user benefit are both monotonic functions of volume or service level; as service level and volume increase, consumer surplus and gross user benefit will increase. The attraction of using service level or volume directly is that they are intuitively meaningful measures (whereas the others are not) and are transparent to laymen (even with multidimensional service vectors).

9.4.6 Economic Variables to Reflect the Viewpoints of Governments

Economic variables have often been used to construct goal variables that purport to reflect the total worth of an action to society as a whole. Most commonly used are benefit/cost ratios and various measures of total user and operator cost. Some of these measures are now required by national and international agencies that finance transportation projects.

In the ***total-user-and-operator-cost approach*** the benefits to users are assumed to be reflected in either a user-cost measure (UBUC) or a consumer-surplus measure (UBCS) on an annual basis. The costs and revenues to operators are assumed to be fully represented by an equivalent-annual-cost measure, or operator cost (OC), which includes the investment cost (on an annual basis) as well as annual costs and revenues. Then the total cost to society is presumed to be the sum of user and operator costs:

$$\text{TUOC} = \text{OC} + \text{UBUC} \tag{9.37}$$

or, in the case of consumer surplus,

$$\text{TUOC} = \text{OC} - \text{UBUC}. \tag{9.38}$$

Alternatively these can be transformed into the equivalent net-present-value forms.

In the ***benefit/cost approach*** the benefits to users are assumed to be reflected in one of the three measures of user benefit. The costs and revenues to operators are segregated into two categories: (1) investment costs I, and (2) all other costs A and revenues R. Then, a benefit/cost ratio BCR is constructed:

$$\text{BCR} = \frac{\text{UB}}{\text{OC}}, \tag{9.39}$$

where

$$\text{OC} = [I \times \text{CRF}(r, N)] + (A - R). \tag{9.40}$$

Other forms are also found, such as

$$\text{BCR} = \frac{\text{UB} + R - A}{I \times \text{CRF}}. \tag{9.41}$$

Usual practice is to array projects in order of increasing investment cost I and compute incremental benefit/cost ratios (relative to the null action, and pairwise for all successively increasing levels of investment).

Use of such aggregate economic variables in an attempt to reflect the "total" worth of a project to society is highly dubious for the following reasons:

1. Such measures include only impacts that are quantifiable and for which monetary values can be determined, either in the marketplace or by other methods; they thus ignore many significant social, environmental, ecological, historical, cultural, aesthetic, and other effects.

2. They ignore the distribution of beneficial and adverse effects among various interests.

3. They implicitly assume the weights to be placed on various interest groups, as determined by the present distribution of income.

4. They assume that society is homogeneous and has agreed on its goals in a consistent, operational form.

5. They hide many significant issues that decision makers and affected interests should be concerned about.

Thus no economic variable is acceptable, in our view, as the single or even dominant goal variable that can summarize the total desirability to society of a particular transportation system change.

9.4.7 The Role of Economic Goal Variables

The uses of economic goal variables are limited for the reasons indicated above. Economic goal variables are clearly not acceptable as the sole or even the dominant goal variables to be used in making transportation decisions.

Economic concepts are useful, however, in limited but important ways. Economic goal variables can be constructed to represent the viewpoints of various interests and various aspects of the consequences of system changes of interest to each viewpoint.

Thus economic concepts can be useful in constructing some goal variables in the set of goal variables to be used by the analyst, provided the limitations of these economic goal variables are recognized, there is no attempt to subsume all significant consequences into a single goal variable, economic or otherwise, and the goal variables are used sensitively and intelligently—as aids in the distillation of issues but not as substitutes for informed political judgment by responsible decision makers.

The danger of using economic constructs as goal variables are:

1. the natural tendency to place greater emphasis on quantified goal variables, with the risk that other goal variables and impacts (social, environmental, aesthetic) are ignored or deemphasized because they appear to be "soft" and less certain;

2. the common failure to recognize the difference between the values now placed on various impacts by the marketplace—as reflected in current prices and interest rates and in the demand function—and the values different segments of society would place on these impacts if they were given the opportunity to make an explicit choice;

3. the tendency to reduce many issues to a single aggregate goal

variable, with resultant deemphasis of the information contained in the disaggregate data;

4. the common failure to do enough sensitivity analyses—to prices, to interest rates, to impacts, to modeling assumptions (especially model parameters) to give a feeling for just how much confidence can be placed in the numerical values of the economic goal variables (Manheim 1961, F. Miller 1975); and

5. the tendency to rank-order the alternative actions in terms of one or a few goal variables, rather than looking explicitly for trade-offs.

All of these dangers and limitations can be overcome if the analyst recognizes and continually guards against them by placing economic goal variables in the context of the broader, more flexible evaluation method described in this chapter.

9.4.8 Other Methods of Defining Goal Variables

Goal variables can be defined using constructs based in many disciplines other than economics and using many other methods. (For the use of social indicators see Lee, Covault, and Willeke 1972, Peat, Marwick, Mitchell and Co. 1973.) Although we make use only of economic goal variables in this volume, the reader should keep in mind that there are many other useful ways of formulating operational goal variables. (See also Hall and Manheim 1967.)

9.5 TRADE-OFF ANALYSIS

The basic concept of a trade-off is intuitive: A *trade-off* shows what has to be sacrificed of *A* in order to gain something of *B*. As simple as the concept is, it is of fundamental importance in the evaluation of alternative transportation systems. Consider the following questions:

• By how much will ridership decrease if fares are increased?

• How much more will it cost to add sufficient additional capacity to reduce delays to travelers by 10 percent?

• By how much can the number of families displaced in community *X* be reduced, and by how much is the construction cost increased, if the projected highway route is shifted a half mile east?

• How much will it cost the operator in operating losses if a fare increase is delayed six months?

The notion of trading off a reduction of one attribute of a design in order to gain something in another attribute is familiar to most analysts and designers. [In recent years the microeconomic theory of the firm has been extended and interpreted as a theoretical basis for trade-off analysis under the label "cost-effectiveness analysis" (Hitch and McKean 1965, Thomas and Schofer 1970, de Neufville and Stafford 1971); see also discussions of "multiobjective analysis" (Major 1974, 1977).] Essentially all that is required to apply the concept of trade-offs is simply to look for trade-offs in the data: trade-offs among impacts, among interests, among alternatives. This is a style of thinking rather than an algorithm: look for trade-offs (instead of trying to "optimize"!).

We introduced the idea of trade-offs in describing systematic analysis in chapter 1 (figure 1.16), and we have already demonstrated several types of trade-offs, especially in chapter 5: trade-offs among impacts on different interests (as when we showed how net revenue to the operator varies with equilibrium volume, which is a measure of user benefit) and trade-offs among options (as when fare and frequency were varied simultaneously).

It is especially useful to combine trade-off analysis with economic goal variables. For example, although we reject adding operator and user benefits to get a "total worth" to society, we do find it useful to explore trade-offs between users and operators, as demonstrated in chapter 5 and in the case studies in chapters 10 and 13.

9.6 SUMMARY

9.6.1 Role of Evaluation

The ultimate objective of analysis is action—implementation in the real world. To achieve this objective requires a conscious decision by those with responsibility for taking such decisions. The objective of analysis must be to clarify the issues that should be considered by decision makers and thus to assist them in reaching a decision on a course of action.

Evaluation plays an important role in achieving this objective, since it involves examining the available alternative actions in the light of possible goals, assessing the relative desirability of each action, and summarizing key issues.

The primary product of evaluation should be a summary of the key issues that should be considered by interested parties in the course of deciding on a course of action. This summary, called an evaluation report, should be in a form that can be readily understood by all interested parties. These issues include the major alternative actions that should be considered, the major interests that are benefited or adversely affected by each alternative, the views of these interests, the most important uncertainties that should be considered, the major advantages and disadvantages of each course of action, and the relative priorities for further analysis.

9.6.2 The Evaluation Method

The basic steps of the evaluation method advocated here are shown in figure 9.1. The input to this evaluation method can be described in terms of two basic sets of data. The impact tableau contains the available data on the effects of each alternative action being considered; the tableau should present both quantitative and qualitative impacts and should indicate areas of uncertainty in the impacts. The value information file contains the available information on each of the interests potentially affected by the alternatives being considered.

The objective of the evaluation method is to distill out of these data an understanding of the major issues. Throughout the method emphasis is placed on the incidence of impacts (which affected interests benefit and which are harmed by each of the actions being considered) and the diversity of points of view (the fact that each interest will have objectives and desires that differ from, and possibly conflict with, those of other interests, which is to say that there is no agreement on a complete, consistent, and operational statement of goals acceptable to all interests).

The evaluation report should summarize the major positive and negative features of each major alternative action, as viewed by the various affected interests, and the most important issues to be addressed in reaching a decision. It should also identify priorities for further work by the technical team.

9.6.3 Comparison with Classical Approaches to Evaluation

Classical approaches to evaluation include pure judgment, rating schemes such as linear scoring functions or multiattribute utility functions, and economic analysis. None of these is acceptable as a comprehensive evaluation method, but if employed with thought and care, they are all useful supporting techniques for the evaluation method described here.

Economic concepts can be used to develop a number of different goal variables. Some of the most frequently encountered are equivalent annual cost, annual net revenue, ratio of annual net revenue to investment, and net present value. Economic goal variables are especially helpful in summarizing impacts from the viewpoints of particular transportation operators.

Economic variables can also be defined to reflect impacts on users if we assume that the demand function for a group of users shows the values placed on different levels of service by those users; that is, the demand function expresses the users' relative willingness to pay for different service levels. Economic variables measuring user benefits are helpful in summarizing the service-level impacts on users at a disaggregate level. (Instead of measures of user benefits based on willingness to pay, we prefer to use more direct and transparent measures such as level of service, composite service level, or equilibrium volume.)

It is also useful to explore trade-offs among goal variables as an aid to evaluation. Particularly useful are trade-offs among economic goal variables.

TO READ FURTHER

For the broader implications of the views expressed here see chapters 14 and 15 and the epilogue, the references given in those chapters, and Manheim et al. (1975b). See also Braybrooke and Lindblom (1963), Organization for Economic Cooperation and Development (1969), Webber and Angel (1969), and Report to Congress . . . (1972).

For the classical view more substantially developed see United Nations (1958), de Neufville and Stafford (1971), Mishan (1971), Dasgupta, Sen, and Marglin (1972), and Little and Mirrlees (1974). For applications to transportation see Walters (1961, 1968), Wohl and Martin (1967), Dawson (1968), Munby (1968), Department of the Environment (1972), Heggie (1972), Beasley (1973), Harrison (1974), Thomson (1974), Hutchinson (1974), or Foster (1975). For specific techniques see Beimborn (1976).

For examples of trade-off analysis with economic goal variables see Ben-Akiva (1971), Cohon and Marks (1974), and Major (1974); for hierarchically structured goal variable sets see Hall and Manheim (1967), Raiffa (1968), and Peat, Marwick, Mitchell and Co. (1973).

Useful comments on economic evaluation methods may be found in Heymann (1965), p. 22ff., Mishan (1970), Nwaneri (1970), Pearce (1971), and Committee on Principles of Decision-Making for Regulating Chemicals in the Environment (1975).

EXERCISES

9.1(C) Consider the impact tableau in table 9.3.

a. Develop a list of affected interests, including interests identified either explicitly or implicitly in the tableau.

b. How is this list deficient? What other interests might you want to identify and include? Review the list and ask yourself if these interests are really homogeneous. (For example, are the same people in Compton likely to be interested in tax-base losses as in displacements of multi-family households?)

c. Take an illustrative set of interests from your list: make judgments about their likely values with respect to the impacts identified in the tableau and construct a value information file.

d. Write an evaluation report for this example (you may choose to consider only alternatives 1, 2, 3, 7, and 8, or the whole set of alternatives).

9.2(C) Develop lists of impacts and of the interests concerned with each impact for the following issues. You may wish to review newspaper and other records of specific controversies.

a. SST: Should new supersonic transports be developed? If developed, should they be allowed to fly over populated land areas? (Consider, for example, the issues surrounding U.S. Secretary of Transportation William S. Coleman's decisions in the spring of 1976 concerning landing rights at Dulles Airport for the British-French Concorde SST.)

b. Rail reorganization: Should unprofitable branch lines be kept in operation because of public needs? (Consider, for example, the controversy surrounding U.S. railroad reorganization in the northeastern states in 1974–1976.)

c. New container ports: should large-scale ports for container ships be built at locations outside existing ports and urbanized areas?

d. Urban transit: should major investments be made to develop a new rail transit system (or a major extension to an existing system) in a particular urban area?

e. Pick a transportation decision that has been a major issue in your country or city.

9.3(E) Examine the capital recovery factors in table 9.4. What interest rate would you advocate, and why, if you:

a. believed that government investment decisions should be based upon the same rate of interest as private decisions? (*Hint:* What is the current prime rate of interest in your country?)

b. were an advocate of major public investment in new transportation facilities?

c. were an advocate of maximum use of existing facilities and limited or no new investments?

9.4(E) In exercise 1.4 we dealt with the following cost per train function:

$$C_T(Q, L) = Q\left(\alpha_1 D + \alpha_2 L \frac{D}{v} + \alpha_3 DL^2\right) + 12\alpha_2 L,$$

where Q represents frequency, L train length, D distance, and v speed. The coefficient α_1 reflects the crew (operating labor) costs:

$$\alpha_1 = n_T r,$$

where there are n_T persons per train crew and r is the average wage rate (including indirect costs) per person per train-mile.

In the base case $\mathbf{T}^0$ we have taken $n_T = 4$ and $r = \$0.60$. From the viewpoint of operating labor, two issues are important (Martland 1977):

I_{PAY} = total pay per man per day
$\quad = rm,$
I_{EMP} = total number of persons employed
$\quad = Qn_T,$

where m is the mileage per man per day. If D is long enough, each man can make only one trip per day, so

$m = D.$

a. Use the data for exercise 1.4. Explore the trade-offs among operator (I_{NR}), user ($I_{USER} = V_E$), and operating labor (reflected in I_{PAY} and I_{EMP}). If $\beta = 0.8$, are there conditions under which all parties can be better off (relative to $\mathbf{T}^0 = (Q, L) = (2, 90)$)? Discuss; display interesting trade-offs and other results graphically.
b. Repeat for $\beta = 0.5$ and $\beta = 0$. Discuss differences.

9.5(P) Consider the following simultaneous-choice model (Manheim 1973b):

$$V_{kdm} = D(\mathbf{A}, \mathbf{S}) = \alpha\beta_k\gamma_{kd}\delta_{kdm}.$$

Derive a formula for consumer surplus with this demand function and see if you can isolate terms that measure the following elements of user benefit: benefits of new trips; benefits of changing destinations; benefits of changing modes to a given destination. Discuss.

10
Case Study II: Carrier Operations Planning

10.1 PURPOSE OF THE CASE STUDY

In this chapter we shall apply the basic concepts developed in previous chapters to an analysis of a bus transit system. This analysis will demonstrate:

1. prediction of impacts using demand, service, and resource functions;
2. evaluation (considering the differential incidence of impacts on operators and users) and the preparation of an evaluation report;
3. search (the development of possible actions to analyze in detail);
4. systematic analysis (including the exploration of a range of options, the identification of trade-offs among impacts, and sensitivity analyses);
5. a sequentially structured process of analysis with several cycles;
6. the usefulness of simple analyses with limited data; and
7. the role of prediction in the operations planning process.

This case study will use limited data and a number of assumptions in order to simplify the analysis and to demonstrate what can be done even in situations of limited data and limited resources for analysis.

10.2 CONTEXT OF THE METHODOLOGY

The methodology described here was originally developed as part of a project to improve the planning of bus transit operations in medium-sized cities in France (Bien, Bourgin, and Manheim 1976, Bien et al. 1977). The approach envisioned development of a planning methodology based on (1) explicit analysis of the options open to operator management, and (2) collection of information in a centralized management information system. Both the new procedures for analysis and the new information system were to be designed in such a way that they could be implemented in stages (compare Ehrlich 1977, Tober 1977).

10.2.1 Implementation Strategy

The strategy of step-by-step implementation was a key element. It reflected a particular philosophy of organizational change, namely, to build on existing skills and procedures and to observe effects and rethink strategy at many intermediate points during the implementation of the change. To guide this process a conceptual plan for the overall operations planning system was developed. Then a plan for staged implementation of this system was prepared, starting from existing information and management planning procedures. Thus the strategy was to develop and implement the system in stages by using it to analyze specific decision problems as they arose.

A key aspect of this strategy was that initial analyses would utilize only readily available data and simple manual (that is, pencil-and-paper, not computer) methods; this led to the methods illustrated in this chapter.

10.2.2 Conceptual Plan for the Operations Planning Process

The basic steps of the operations planning process are shown in figure 1.13. Operations planning is a periodic process, with some steps taken weekly or monthly and others every three or six months, as indicated in the following descriptions. Here system operations encompass all the activities involved in producing transportation: vehicles and drivers providing specific services over particular routes and all of the support organization (including maintenance, marketing, personnel, and finance functions).

DATA COLLECTION

Certain types of data are collected on a routine basis. Such data come from a variety of sources, including users, local officials, drivers, supervisors, management and the general public. Data types include:

1. regularly collected system operating data at basic levels of detail (line or depot), such as fares collected, riders, vehicle-hours and vehicle-kilometers, driver-hours or driver-shifts, fuel consumed, spare parts consumed, and schedule performance (delays, on-time runs, cancellations);

2. data collected in special surveys conducted on an irregular basis; and

3. qualitative observations, including suggestions, complaints, comments, and ideas from all sources, both external and internal.

Data collection is a continuous process. Suggestions and complaints are analyzed and filed as they are received. Routine system operating data are collected on a regular basis; some are recorded for every trip, others are recorded daily by each driver or for each line.

DATA ANALYSIS

The basic data can be tabulated and summarized in various ways. For qualititative observations summaries can be prepared showing, for example, suggestions for new services, tabulated by geographic area, or complaints about excessive waiting times, tabulated by line. For quantitative data statistical tabulations and analyses can be prepared involving, for example, scheduled vehicle-trips versus actual vehicle-trips by line, driver-hours per line or per depot, or average numbers of passengers per trip by line.

Data analysis is done periodically. For some routine system operating data such as total passengers per line, analysis may be done weekly or monthly; other data analyses may be done only quarterly, such as seasonally adjusted trends in ridership per line.

IDENTIFICATION OF PROBLEMS AND OPPORTUNITIES

In this very important step the results of the data analysis are reviewed to identify existing or potential problem areas and opportunities for major improvements in system services and/or revenues. For example, a high number of complaints about long waiting times on a particular line would immediately suggest a problem area; or requests for increased service to a residential area would suggest an opportunity. Similarly a significant increase in average running time per trip on a particular line would suggest a problem area.

Informal identification of problems and opportunities occurs each time a summary data analysis report is prepared (weekly for some items, monthly for others).

PLAN ANALYSIS

Based on the results of the preceding steps, decisions are made about the most important issues to be confronted, including additional data to be collected, models to be used or developed, objectives to be achieved, and major types of alternative actions to be explored. A key element is the level of personnel and other resources to be used.

FORMULATE GOALS, DEVELOP MODELS, COLLECT ADDITIONAL DATA

Once the analysis plan is developed, the other activities of the setup phase (as defined in chapter 1) are conducted. In some situations these will be major activities; in others, such as when pencil-and-paper methods are utilized, they will be simple.

ANALYSIS
In this step analyses are conducted of the various issues—problems or opportunities—that have been identified. Some analyses may be very simple, requiring perhaps an hour; others may require several man-weeks, or occasionally several man-months, of effort.

EVALUATION REPORT
The evaluation report is a management document that is prepared periodically: monthly, quarterly, or perhaps semiannually (for example, before the decisions on each change in schedules). It can be a relatively brief memorandum or a more elaborate document. In this context the report should have two parts: the first part summarizes major problem areas and opportunities; the second presents and discusses management options. The first part can be prepared after the identification of problems and opportunities. Preparation of the second part may require detailed analyses. The evaluation report includes options for which no analysis is required and options that have been analyzed in the period since the last evaluation report was prepared.

CHOICE
Clearly management decisions will be taken whenever an urgent problem arises. (In a local transit operation a political event such as the intervention of local officials often catalyzes consideration of specific actions.) However, most decisions about changes in schedules, frequencies, fares, or route extensions should be taken on an orderly, regular basis. It is likely that major changes will be implemented at the times of major schedule changes (every three or six months); other changes may be considered at monthly or other intervals. The evaluation reports provide essential background information for these periodic management decisions.

IMPLEMENTATION
Once decisions on matters such as schedule changes, fare changes, or marketing programs have been made, implementation begins.

10.3 METHODOLOGY
The basic methodology will be similar to that employed in chapter 5

for the air transport analysis (see figure 5.8), but the details will vary in some significant respects.

The methodology will involve incremental analysis (section 4.6), manual worksheets to develop the analysis and summarize the results (chapter 3), an evaluation report (chapter 9), a sequence of several cycles of analysis, and more detail on several important aspects that were simplified in chapter 5 (such as the spatial and temporal patterns of demand and service discussed in section 8.4).

To be developed are procedures for estimating changes in service (travel times, headways), in ridership, in costs, in gross revenues, and in measures of economic benefit (such as cash flow or net revenue). As will be seen in the following sections, procedures for estimating changes in ridership are a major requirement. When satisfactory demand models are not available—as occurred in this situation (Bien et al. 1977)—approximations are required.

Several levels of analysis are possible. At the most basic level estimates of demand elasticities or the coefficients of service attributes in a demand model can be used to predict changes in ridership due to changes in fares, in service frequencies, or in trip times. At the next level some estimates of trip generation rates for various purposes (peak-period work and school trips, off-peak non-work trips) are required, to allow prediction of the effects of line extensions and/or new station locations; a complete demand model, if available, might also be used.

Demand models can be used to treat a route (a bus line) as a whole. Alternatively procedures might be developed whereby counts of boarding and alighting passengers yield a station-to-station origin-destination matrix; then demand models would be used to estimate changes in each origin-destination volume. At a third level these procedures could be expanded to include readily available socio-economic data describing the areas served by each station. Later stages would use small interview samples at stations, on board vehicles, or at major attractors or generators to obtain origin-destination and socioeconomic data.

In the development of this methodology maximum use was made of procedures that did not require a fully calibrated set of demand models for estimating changes in ridership. Of course, the availability of such models would have made the task much simpler.

Table 10.1 presents a summary form for an incremental analysis of a single bus route. The major blocks of the table correspond to the steps in figure 5.8.

Table 10.1 An analysis summary form (P = peak; OP = off-peak)

1 Present Conditions

1.1 Description

1.1.1 Line no. _____

1.1.2 Length of route: _____

1.1.3 Cycle time   P: _____   OP: _____

1.1.4 Major features: _____

1.1.5 Service area: _____

1.2 Service levels

1.2.1 Travel time   P: _____   OP: _____

1.2.2 Headways   P: _____   OP: _____

1.2.3 Regularity   P: _____   OP: _____

1.2.4 Fare (average): _____

1.3 Ridership

1.3.1 Volume (hourly)   P: _____   OP: _____

1.3.2 Load factor (hourly) P: _____   OP: _____

1.3.3 Volume (annual)   P: _____   OP: _____

1.3.4 Load factor (annual) P: _____   OP: _____

1.4 Resources

1.4.1 Crews assigned   P: _____   OP: _____

1.4.2 Crews per week: _____

1.4.3 Man-years per year: _____

1.4.4 Vehicles assigned   P: _____   OP: _____

1.4.5 Vehicle-hours per week: _____   per year: _____

1.4.6 Vehicle-km per week: _____   per year: _____

2 Proposed change

2.1 General description: _____

2.2 Specific description: _____

3 Changes in Performance

3.1 Running-time change   P: _____   OP: _____

3.2 Round trips/vehicle/hour   P: _____   OP: _____

3.3 Capacity   P: _____   OP: _____

4 Changes in Service Levels

4.1 Travel-time change   P: _____   OP: _____

                         % P: _____   OP: _____

4.2 Headway change   P: _____   OP: _____

                         % P: _____   OP: _____

4.3 Fare change   P: _____   OP: _____

                         % P: _____   OP: _____

4.4 Regularity   P: _____   OP: _____

5 Changes in Ridership

	Peak		Off-peak		Total	
	Absolute	%	Absolute	%	Absolute	%
5.1 Hourly	_____	_____	_____	_____	_____	_____
5.2 Weekly	_____	_____	_____	_____	_____	_____
5.3 Annual total	_____	_____	_____	_____	_____	_____

6 Performance Checks

6.1 Schedule regularity?

6.2 Local traffic?

6.3 Load factors   P: _____   OP: _____

7 Changes in Resources Consumed

7.1 $\varDelta$Crews per week: _____

7.2 $\varDelta$Man-years per year: _____

7.3 $\varDelta$Vehicles: _____

7.4 $\varDelta$Vehicle-hours per week: _____   per year: _____

7.5 $\varDelta$Vehicle-km per week: _____   per year: _____

8 Changes in Costs (per Year)

8.1 $\varDelta$Labor cost: _____

8.2 $\varDelta$Vehicle operation costs: _____

8.3 $\varDelta$Total operating costs: _____

8.4 $\varDelta$Vehicle ownership costs: _____

8.5 ΔTotal costs: _____

9 Changes in Revenues (per Year)

9.1 ΔGross revenue   P: _____   OP: _____   Total: _____

9.2 ΔNet operating revenue: _____   9.3 ΔNet revenue: _____

10 Ranges of Uncertainty in Estimates of Changes

10.1 Ridership: _____ $\pm$ _____ % _____

10.2 Resources: _____ $\pm$ _____ % _____

10.3 Total operating costs: _____ $\pm$ _____ % _____

10.4 Total costs: _____ $\pm$ _____ % _____

10.5 Gross revenue: _____ $\pm$ _____ % _____

10.6 Net revenue: _____ $\pm$ _____ % _____

10.7 Sources of major uncertainties: _____

_____

10.8 Significance of uncertainties: _____

_____

11 Major User Impacts: _____

_____

12 Major Operator Impacts: _____

_____

13 Other Significant Impacts: _____

_____

_____

14 Other Alternatives Considered and Their Impacts: _____

_____

_____

_____

15 Summary Evaluation: _____

_____

_____

_____

_____

_____

16 Prepared by: _____   Date: _____

Table 10.2 Possible annexes to the analysis summary form

A.1 Details of present conditions

A.2 Details of proposed change(s)

A.3 Detailed analysis of changes in performance

A.4 Detailed calculations of changes in service levels

A.5 Detailed calculations of changes in ridership

A.6 Calculations for performance checks

A.7 Detailed calculations of changes in resources consumed

A.8 Cost calculations

A.9 Revenue calculations

A.10 Details of sensitivity analyses

A.11 Analysis of user impacts

A.12 Analysis of operator impacts

A.13 Analysis of other significant impacts

A.14 Analysis of other alternatives

A.15 Analysis for overall evaluation

Table 10.3 Summary form for a detailed calculation of ridership changes

	Peak hour	Off-peak
1 Judgmental Estimate		
Likely:		
Upper:		
Lower:		
2 Estimate by Formal Method (see worksheet _____)		
Likely:		
Upper:		
Lower:		
3 Final Estimate		
Likely:		
Upper:		
Lower:		

Detailed analyses are necessary to develop the estimates presented in the summary. These analyses can be done on worksheets that are included as annexes to the analysis summary form (see table 10.2). Examples of such worksheets were given in chapter 3.

Formats similar to that of table 10.1 will be useful in many different situations. The specific methods used to produce this information will depend on factors such as the context of the analysis, data and previously calibrated models available, and levels of detail required.

The philosophy of analysis is illustrated by the summary form shown as table 10.3. The first block records judgmental estimates by the analyst, with explicit identification of ranges of uncertainty for likely and upper- and lower-bound estimates. This is followed by ridership estimates developed by a more formal method, which can be complex or simplified, such as a pivot-point analysis using elasticities. The third block records final estimates, which might be the values predicted by the models, the judgmental estimates, or some subjectively developed composite.

This structure reflects the following philosophy: A formal analysis using models is a means of assisting the analyst in making informed judgments. The results of the models are but an approximation to reality, and they should be explicitly compared with the analyst's own judgments and insights developed through training and experience. In the end the analyst alone is responsible for his judgments; decision makers do not really care whether or not a formal model was used, but they do care whether or not the analyst stands behind the estimates of likely impacts.

Table 10.3 would be augmented by a ridership worksheet like the ones described in chapter 3. Worksheets could be developed using other approaches—for example, the pivot-point method of section 4.6, with an elasticity estimate applied to volumes for the bus line as a whole or with each pair of origin and destination stations (bus stops) along the line considered separately (so that the pivot-point method is applied to each origin-destination pair), or any of the other methods described in section 4.6.

Note that the analysis summary can also serve as an evaluation report (see sections 11–15 of table 10.1). This is useful if the decisions are going to be made primarily within the operator organization. If decisions are to be made by a board of elected and/or appointed officials, with opportunity for public involvement, then a concise (one- or two-page) evaluation report would be prepared and this analysis summary would be one of the supporting technical appendixes.

10.4 DEVELOPING AN ANALYSIS: THE SETUP PHASE

Following the methodology indicated in section 10.2.2, the setup phase begins with data collection and analysis and the identification of problems and opportunities. We shall assume that these steps have been completed and that the conclusions are that changes in frequencies and fares should be explored in order to increase ridership and net revenues.

The next step is to plan the analysis. We shall first explore frequency and fare changes separately and in combination, and then we shall explore route changes.

10.4.1 Data Collection and the Base Case

Data are required for describing the present states of the transportation and activity systems and the present flow patterns; for developing models for predicting the impacts of alternative transportation- and activity-system actions; and for developing alternative assumptions or scenarios for major exogenous events. In this case study we shall initially use only available data. We may have data collected at a later stage in the course of the study, from a station-to-station origin-destination survey perhaps, or even a before-after study.

In order to do an analysis it is important to have a description of the situation at a single point in time. Generally this is taken to be the present, but sometimes the available data will suggest a time in the recent past (for example, a year in which a major survey was conducted). In the latter case it is important to check models against selected current data.

The existing situation for the line under study is as follows (a subscript P will be used to indicate peak-period values and a subscript O to indicate off-peak values):

1. The distance of the run d is 4 miles, one-way.
2. The average round-trip cycle time is 60 minutes (including stops, slack time between runs, and so forth), so the average speed v is $2 \times 4/1 = 8$ mph.
3. The present vehicle has a payload capacity w of 50 passengers (seated plus standees).
4. At present the frequency of service Q is 4 vehicle round trips per hour (a vehicle every 15 minutes in each direction) in the 4 peak hours (0800–1000, 1600–1800) and 2 round trips per hour in the 12 off-peak hours (0600–0800, 1000–1600, 1800–2200).
5. In a sample of peak hours total ridership averages $V_P^0 = 151$, in

both directions, with an average of 121 (80 percent) in the dominant direction. In a sample of off-peak hours total ridership averages $V_0^0 = 7$, with an average of 4.2 (66.7 percent) in the dominant direction.

6. Activity-system characteristics:
- The average income y of users, from available census data, is $8,000.
- The route passes through mixed residential and commercial land uses.
- The population within walking distance of the stops on the line (taken as 0.25 mile) is about 9,400 persons.

7. Present service level:
- The average one-way running time along the total length of the route is about 26 minutes and 40 seconds, or 0.44 hour. Thus the average running speed is $4/0.44 = 9$ mph.
- Based on observation of ridership patterns, it is estimated that the average trip length is about 3/4 of the route, or 3 miles, which corresponds to an in-vehicle time t_{iv} of about 20 minutes.
- No information is presently available on the differences between peak period and off-peak speeds, so they will be assumed the same.
- Based on the schedule frequency, it is assumed that the average waiting time for a vehicle is half the interval between vehicles.
- Because of congestion, vehicles tend to be irregular in keeping schedules, but no data are available, so this will be ignored.
- The present fare is a flat 30¢ per one-way trip.

8. No cost data are available on a line-by-line basis. Analysis of aggregate annual statistics over the last few years suggests an approximate cost of $16 per vehicle-hour.

Clearly the amount of directly usable data is limited. Yet useful analyses can be done even with these data.

The general strategy will be to make judgments and assumptions where necessary in order to proceed with the analysis. Then sensitivity studies will be done to explore the effects of some of the key assumptions. If additional data become available in the future, they can be utilized to revise assumptions and refine the analysis.

Based on the available data, the user and operator impacts associated with the present operations of this line can be summarized as shown in table 10.4.

10.4.2 Model Development

To predict resource consumption and service levels we shall use the simple performance model developed in chapter 5. Our primary con-

Table 10.4 Base-case user and operator impacts

	Peak periods (per hour)	Off-peak hours (per hour)	Daily totals
Volume (V_E)	151	7	688
Capacity (V_C)	400	200	4,000
Load factor (λ)	0.38	0.04	0.17
Resource requirements (R in vehicle-hours)	4	2	40
Cost (C_T)	$64.00	$32.00	$640.00
Gross revenue (I_{GR})	$45.30	$2.10	$206.00
Net revenue (I_{NR})	− $18.70	− $29.90	− $433.60
Revenue ratio	0.71	0.07	0.32
Cost/available capacity	$0.16	$0.16	$0.16
Cost/rider	$0.42	$4.57	$0.93
Gross revenue/capacity	$0.11	$0.01	$0.05
Net revenue/capacity	− $0.05	− $0.15	− $0.11
Net revenue/rider	− $0.12	− $4.27	− $0.63

cern here will therefore be the development of a workable demand model. (Alternatively we could simply use elasticities in a pivot-point approach.)

PERFORMANCE AND OPERATOR IMPACT MODELS
The available capacity is

$$V_C = 2wQ. \tag{10.1}$$

We shall estimate in-vehicle time directly by judgment and assume that headways are regular, so that out-of-vehicle time is half the average headway (see section 3.4).

Resource consumption R will be expressed in vehicle-hours per hour:

$$R = \frac{Q}{n} = \frac{2Qd}{v}, \tag{10.2}$$

where $n = v/2d$ is the productivity (round trips per vehicle per hour).

Operator impacts will include total cost C_T, gross revenues from fares I_{GR}, net revenue I_{NR}, and load factor λ:

$$C_T = aR, \tag{10.3}$$

Table 10.5   Temporal variations in demand

Variables

$V_{P,D}$ = volume in the peak period in the dominant direction of flow

$V_{P,R}$ = volume in the peak period in the reverse direction of flow (that is, opposite to the dominant direction)

V_P = total two-directional volume in the peak period

$V_{O,D}$ = volume in the off-peak period in the dominant direction

$V_{O,R}$ = volume in the off-peak period in the reverse direction

V_O = total two-directional volume in the off-peak period

V_Y = total annual volume

$V_{\bar{H}}$ = average hourly volume

$V_{\bar{D}}$ = average daily volume

n_P = number of peak periods per year

n_O = number of off-peak periods per year

n_D = number of days of service per year

n_H = number of hours of service per average day

n_T = total number of time periods of service per year

δ_P = directionality: ratio of volume in peak period in reverse direction of flow to volume in the same period in dominant direction ($0 \leq \delta_P \leq 1$)

δ_O = directionality of off-peak period ($0 \leq \delta_O \leq 1$)

ν = peaking factor: ratio of volume in off-peak period in dominant direction to peak-period volume in dominant direction ($0 \leq \nu \leq 1$)

μ_H = equivalent-hour volume factor: ratio of average annual hourly volume to peak volume in peak direction

μ_D = equivalent-day volume factor: ratio of average annual daily volume to peak volume in peak direction

Basic Relationships

(1) $V_{O,D} = \nu V_{P,D}$

(2) $V_{P,R} = \delta_P V_{P,D}$

(3) $V_{O,R} = \delta_O V_{O,D}$

(4) $V_P = V_{P,D} + V_{P,R}$

(5) $V_O = V_{O,D} + V_{O,R}$

(6) $V_Y = n_P V_P + n_O V_O$

(7) $V_{\bar{D}} = \dfrac{V_Y}{n_D}$

(8) $V_{\bar{H}} = \dfrac{V_{\bar{D}}}{n_H} = \dfrac{V_Y}{n_T}$

(9) $n_T = n_H n_D = n_P + n_O$

(10) $\mu_D = \dfrac{V_{\bar{D}}}{V_{P,D}}$

Table 10.5 (continued)

(11) $\mu_{\text{H}} = \dfrac{V_{\hat{\text{H}}}}{V_{\text{P,D}}}$

Summary Relationships

(12) $V_{\text{P}} = (1 + \delta_{\text{P}})V_{\text{P,D}}$

(13) $V_{\text{O}} = (1 + \delta_{\text{O}})V_{\text{O,D}}$

(14) $V_{\text{O}} = (1 + \delta_{\text{O}})\nu V_{\text{P,D}}$

(15) $V_{\text{Y}} = V_{\text{P,D}}[n_{\text{P}}(1 + \delta_{\text{P}}) + n_{\text{O}}\nu(1 + \delta_{\text{O}})]$

(16) $V_{\bar{\text{D}}} = V_{\text{P,D}}\left[\dfrac{n_{\text{P}}}{n_{\text{D}}}(1 + \delta_{\text{P}}) + \dfrac{n_{\text{O}}}{n_{\text{D}}}\nu(1 + \delta_{\text{O}})\right]$

(17) $V_{\hat{\text{H}}} = V_{\text{P,D}}\left[\dfrac{n_{\text{P}}}{n_{\text{D}}n_{\text{H}}}(1 + \delta_{\text{P}}) + \dfrac{n_{\text{O}}}{n_{\text{D}}n_{\text{H}}}\nu(1 + \delta_{\text{O}})\right]$

(18) $\mu_{\text{H}} = \left[\dfrac{n_{\text{P}}}{n_{\text{D}}n_{\text{H}}}(1 + \delta_{\text{P}}) + \dfrac{n_{\text{O}}}{n_{\text{D}}n_{\text{H}}}\nu(1 + \delta_{\text{O}})\right]$

(19) $\mu_{\text{D}} = \left[\dfrac{n_{\text{P}}}{n_{\text{D}}}(1 + \delta_{\text{P}}) + \dfrac{n_{\text{O}}}{n_{\text{D}}}\nu(1 + \delta_{\text{O}})\right]$

$$I_{\text{GR}} = V_{\text{E}}c, \tag{10.4}$$

$$I_{\text{NR}} = I_{\text{GR}} - C_{\text{T}}, \tag{10.5}$$

$$\lambda = V_{\text{E}}/V_{\text{C}}, \tag{10.6}$$

where c is the user fare ($/trip), V_{E} the equilibrium volume, and a the unit cost ($/vehicle-hour).

TEMPORAL AND DIRECTIONAL VARIATIONS IN DEMAND

As pointed out in section 8.4, demand varies with direction and with time. Different demand functions are generally required to represent different behaviors by time period and direction, especially for peak and off-peak periods.

We shall treat these variations simply (see table 10.5 for definitions of variables). We shall predict explicitly peak and off-peak volumes in the dominant direction of flow. Then, using estimates of peaking factors ν and directionality factors δ, we shall estimate total volumes for peak and off-peak periods, average daily volume and so forth, using the relationships defined in table 10.5.

THE DEMAND MODEL

From the data on present ridership levels given above we have $V_{\text{P,D}}^{0} = 0.8\,V_{\text{P}}$, $V_{\text{P,R}}^{0} = 0.2\,V_{\text{P}}$, and $\delta_{\text{P}} = V_{\text{P,R}}/V_{\text{P,D}} = 0.25$. Similarly $V_{\text{O,D}}^{0} = (4.2/7)V_{\text{O}}$, so $\delta_{\text{O}} = V_{\text{O,R}}/V_{\text{O,P}} = 2.8/4.2 = 0.67$.

Recent survey data indicate that in areas with similar transit service, over the present hours of service, trips are generated at the following rates (per person, totals for all modes): in the four peak hours, 1.28 one-way person-trips (0.32 per hour); in the twelve off-peak hours, 1.92 one-way person-trips (0.16 per hour).

It will be assumed that trip making in this corridor occurs at these same generation rates. Thus the total trips by all modes in the peak and off-peak periods are estimated to be

$$N_P = b_P A = 3{,}008, \tag{10.7}$$

$$N_O = b_O A = 1{,}504, \tag{10.8}$$

where the bs are trip generation rates and A is the population within walking distance of transit stops. In the dominant directions, under the assumption that the directionalities are the same for all modes,

$$N_{P,D} = \left(\frac{1}{1+\delta_P}\right) N_P = \frac{4}{5} N_P = 2{,}406, \tag{10.9}$$

$$N_{O,D} = \left(\frac{1}{1+\delta_O}\right) N_O = \frac{3}{5} N_O = 902. \tag{10.10}$$

The present peak-period volume in the dominant direction thus represents a transit mode share of

$$\gamma_{P,D} = \frac{V_{P,D}}{N_{P,D}} = \frac{121}{2{,}406} = 5 \text{ percent.} \tag{10.11}$$

The total mode share in both directions is

$$\gamma_P = \frac{V_P}{N_P} = \frac{151}{3{,}008} = 5 \text{ percent.} \tag{10.12}$$

Similarly, the present off-peak volume in the dominant direction represents a transit mode share of

$$\gamma_{O,D} = \frac{V_{O,D}}{N_{O,D}} = \frac{4.2}{902} = 0.47 \text{ percent} \tag{10.13}$$

and a total two-direction mode share of

$$\gamma_O = \frac{V_O}{N_O} = \frac{7}{1{,}504} = 0.47 \text{ percent.} \tag{10.14}$$

For our demand model we shall use the logit form introduced in chapter 2. In section 4.6 we showed that the incremental form of the binary logit is

$$\gamma_T' = \frac{\gamma_T^0 \, e^{\Delta U_T}}{\gamma_T^0 \, e^{\Delta U_T} + \gamma_A^0 \, e^{\Delta U_A}}, \tag{10.15}$$

$$\gamma_A + \gamma_T = 1, \tag{10.16}$$

where subscripts A and T refer to automobile and transit modes, respectively. When only transit service levels are changing,

$$\gamma_T' = \frac{\gamma_T^0\, e^{\Delta U_T}}{\gamma_T^0\, e^{\Delta U_T} + (1 - \gamma_T^0)} = \frac{1}{1 + e^{-\Delta U_T}\left(\dfrac{1}{\gamma_T^0} - 1\right)}. \tag{10.17}$$

We shall take as a first estimate of the parameters to use in this situation the model described in table 3.3. Since we shall be examining changes from a base case, only the parameters of the service attributes will be important:

$$\Delta U_m = -0.3\,\Delta t_m - \frac{0.34}{d}\,\Delta x_m - \frac{50}{y}\,\Delta c_m, \tag{10.18}$$

where t and x are in-vehicle and out-of-vehicle times in minutes, respectively, and c is out-of-pocket cost in cents. Using the average trip length of 3 miles for d and $y = \$8,000$ per year, we have

$$\Delta U_m = -0.03\,\Delta t_m - 0.11\,\Delta x_m - 0.0625\,\Delta c_m. \tag{10.19}$$

Now we must ask, Does the model as calibrated give reasonable predictions? For example, if peak-period frequency goes from 4 to 8 round trips per hour, what new mode split does the model predict? For $Q_P = 4$,

$$x_T = \frac{1}{2}\,(60/4) = 7.5 \text{ minutes.} \tag{10.20}$$

For $Q_P' = 8$,

$$\tag{10.21}$$

$$x_T' = \frac{1}{2}\,(60/8) = 3.75 \text{ minutes.}$$

Thus

$$\Delta x_T = -3.75 \text{ minutes,} \tag{10.22}$$

$$\Delta U_T = -0.11\,\Delta x_T = 0.413, \tag{10.23}$$

$$\gamma_{P,D}' = \frac{1}{1 + e^{-0.41}(0.95/0.05)} = 0.074. \tag{10.24}$$

Thus in this case a doubling of frequency leads to a 50 percent increase in ridership. The analyst must decide whether this is reasonable. If not, the model should be modified.

A further check that might be made is to calculate the elasticities.

Since for a multinomial logit model these vary with the share, this is a more difficult basis for comparison.

Clearly we have made a number of assumptions in fitting our model to the situation. This sort of strategy is acceptable only when no additional data are available, as we have assumed here. Models developed in this way should be used cautiously. In most circumstances they are a useful support, but the analyst should be alert to their limitations and try to compensate by doing sensitivity analyses and exploring variations in the model.

When more data become available, more rigorous approaches should be used to estimate the model.

10.4.3 Worksheets

The actual analysis can be performed in a number of ways: by manual calculations, perhaps using worksheets similar to those in chapter 3; by use of portable calculators (Manheim, Furth, and Salomon 1977); or by simple computer programs (in FORTRAN or similar languages).

■ *Question 10.1* Design a set of manual worksheets for use in analyzing changes in frequencies and fares, to develop data for the analysis summary. *Caution:* Remember to take into account temporal and directional variations in demand.

■ *Question 10.2* Discuss the advantages and disadvantages for this scale of problem of manual calculations, portable calculators, and computers.

10.5 ANALYSIS CYCLES I–V

The first actions to be analyzed will be operating-policy options— changes in schedule frequencies and base fares. The following combinations will be explored:

Policy set 1: Exploration of peak and off-peak frequencies ranging from two round trips per hour (two vehicles in each direction each hour) to thirty, with the fare constant at its present level of 30¢.

Policy set 2: The same range of frequencies as in policy set 1 plus a fare increase to 40¢.

Policy set 3: Exploration of fares ranging from 0 to $1, with peak and off-peak frequencies both constant at six round trips per hour.

■ *Question 10.3* (analysis cycle I) Analyze policy set 1 by predict-

ing impacts and answering the following basic analysis cycle questions
(to be repeated each cycle):

a. Which actions would be most desirable from the perspective of
the operator? From that of the users? What are the key trade-offs?

b. To assist your analysis, sketch the following graphs: user volume as
a function of frequency and fare; operator net revenue as a function
of frequency and fare; operator net revenue as a function of the user
volume (equilibrium). Add any other graphs you think might be
useful.

c. Which action would you choose? Why?

d. What actions would you propose analyzing next if the time and
resources were available? Why?

e. Write an evaluation report, modifying the format of table 10.1 as
necessary.

■   *Question 10.4* (analysis cycle II)   Analyze policy set 2. Considering the results of cycles I and II, answer questions 10.3a–10.3e.
Have your conclusions changed?

■   *Question 10.5* (analysis cycle III)   Analyze policy set 3. Answer
the same questions again, considering the results of all three cycles.

■   *Question 10.6*   Apply some of the conventional evaluation methods
described in section 9.4 (benefit/cost, net present value, total user plus
operator cost). Make any necessary assumptions. Which action would
each method prescribe? Compare with each other and with your
answers to question 10.5 and discuss.

■   *Question 10.7*   The demand model plays a key role in these
analyses, so it is useful to have an alternative model. One alternative
way to estimate the model coefficients is to draw upon evidence of
recent service changes on other lines. For example, on several lines
the peak-period frequency was changed from $Q^1 = 4$ round trips per
hour to $Q^2 = 8$. The waiting time is assumed to be, on average,
half the interval between vehicles, which is 7.5 minutes for Q^1 and
3.75 minutes for Q^2. Thus $x^1 = 7.5$ minutes, $x^2 = 3.75$ minutes,
and $\Delta x = -3.75$ minutes. Corresponding to this change, there were
significant changes in transit ridership, involving in some cases a
doubling, and in others a tripling, of peak-period ridership—so that
transit shares increased from 5 to 15 percent in some corridors. It is
important to note that these changes were accompanied by well-
designed marketing campaigns, so there was a widespread increase in
public awareness of the service changes both before and after the
changes.

Although 15 percent seems high, it can be used as an upper bound for initial analyses. As a lower bound, a change in mode share to 7 percent might be assumed (see equation 10.24).

Based upon these judgments concerning the relative changes in share (γ) corresponding to changes in $\mathbf{S}$, the value of λ can be estimated (given the values of μ_1, μ_2, and μ_3) for a binary logit model:

$$\gamma = \frac{1}{1 + e^{U_A - U_T}},$$

$$U_T = \lambda(\mu_1 t_T + \mu_2 x_T + \mu_3 c_T).$$

a. Show that for given γ^1, γ^2, and Δx_T

$$\lambda\mu_2 = \frac{\Delta U_T}{\Delta x_T},$$

where

$$\Delta U_T = U_T^2 - U_T^1 = \ln \frac{(1/\gamma^1) - 1}{(1/\gamma^2) - 1}.$$

b. Using $\gamma^1 = 5$ percent and $\gamma^2 = 15$ percent, find $\lambda\mu_2$.

c. Assume that the coefficients have the same ratios as the model of section 10.4.2:

$$\mu_1 : \mu_2 : \mu_3 = (-0.03) : (-0.11) : (-0.0625).$$

Find $\lambda\mu_1$ and $\lambda\mu_3$.

d. Compare this model with the one developed in section 10.4.2. What would be the differences in predicted demand volumes under each of the following conditions:

i. $x_T = 1.75$ minutes
ii. $c = 50¢$
iii. $t = 10$ minutes
iv. all of the above.

e. Take $\mu_1 = -0.03$; find λ. Discuss. Interpret your results to part d in terms of the role played by λ.

■ *Question 10.8* (analysis cycle IV) Select an alternative demand model (either your answer to 10.7 or another). Redo portions of the previous analysis cycles with the alternative model, doing just enough calculations to get a feel for the differences. Repeat questions 10.3a–10.3e, including all the results so far. Have your conclusions changed? Why or why not?

■ *Question 10.9* (analysis cycle V) Perform sensitivity analyses to aspects you feel are important sources of uncertainty. Discuss.

■ *Question 10.10* Consider the following key assumptions made in this analysis: (1) off-peak and peak demand functions are the same (except for generation rate differences); (2) only a single market segment is modeled; (3) only average volumes over the line are considered.

a. What effects does each of these assumptions have on the analysis?
b. What steps might be taken to modify the analysis to eliminate the need for each assumption?
c. What differences in results might you expect?

10.6 ANALYSIS CYCLES VI–VII

Recently a new expressway was opened. One action that has been proposed is to reroute a portion of the bus line along the expressway. This is shown in figure 10.1. The rerouting would reduce travel times for residents of zones *W*, *X*, and *Y*, but the line would no longer serve *Z*. Table 10.6 shows the average speeds over each segment,

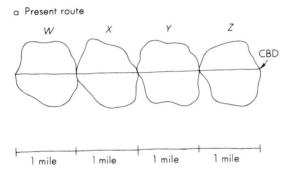

a Present route

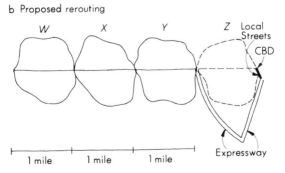

b Proposed rerouting

Figure 10.1 A bus rerouting proposal.

Table 10.6 Speed by segment for the corridor in figure 10.1

Segment	Distance (miles)	Average speed (mph)
W	1	14
X	1	14
Y	1	10
Z via existing route: local streets	1	5
Z via proposed route: expressway local streets	1 0.2	20 5

Table 10.7 Average running times for the present route

Segment	Average running time (min:sec)
W	4:20
X	4:20
Y	6:00
Z	12:00
Total running time	26:40
Schedule slack	3:20
Total schedule time	30:00
Cycle time (round trip)	60:00

Overall distance = 4 miles.
Overall average running speed = 9 mph.

and table 10.7 shows the average running times (present ridership levels were given in section 10.4.1).

To analyze the effects of this possible action we must have some information on the relative populations of the major zones and the average trip lengths of individuals orginating in and destined for each zone. The following estimates have been made, using available data and judgments:

1. Zone W has 5,640 people, about 60 percent of the corridor population; most of them travel to the CBD, an average trip length of about 3.5 miles.

2. Zone X has 1,880 people, about 20 percent of the corridor population; most of them travel to the CBD, an average trip length of 2.5 miles.

3. Zone Y has 940 people, about 10 percent of the corridor population; about 40 percent of them travel an average of 1.5 miles to the CBD and about 60 percent travel outward an average of 2 miles to zones W and X, resulting in an overall average trip length of 1.8 miles.

4. Zone Z also has 940 people, about 10 percent of the corridor population; about 20 percent of them travel an average of 0.5 mile to the CBD, while about 80 percent travel an average of 2.5 miles to zones W and X; the overall average trip length is 2.1 miles.

The results of the analysis of this service change are shown in tables 10.8 and 10.9. The approach taken is straightforward: the change in routing leads to changes in performance (table 10.8) and changes in service levels (table 10.9). The changes in service levels are estimated for each zone and are used to derive an in-vehicle time average for the whole route. To reflect the fact that zone Z is no longer served, the zonal population is subtracted from the corridor population.

This differs from the preceding analysis cycles in that an explicit analysis of performance changes has been done.

Bus service is generally offered along a route with multiple stops. This has several practical ramifications:

1. A single route serves several markets (each combination of origin station and destination station defines a separate market). The service attributes in each market are different, and the response of users in

Table 10.8 Average running times for the proposed route

Segment	Average running time (min:sec)
W	4:20
X	4:20
Y	6:00
Z expressway	3:00
local streets	2:20
Total running time	20:00
Schedule slack	4:00
Total schedule time	24:00
Cycle time (round trip)	48:00

Overall distance = 4.2 miles.
Overall average running speed = 12.6 mph.

Table 10.9 Changes in service levels

Zone of origin	Percentage of total trips	Average trip length (miles)	Initial in-vehicle time[a] (min: sec)	New in-vehicle time[b] (min: sec)	Change (min: sec)
W	60	3.5	23:20	16:40	6:40
X	20	2.5	16:40	11:54	4:46
Y	10	1.8	12:00	8:34	3:26
Z	10	2.1	14:00	10:00[c]	4:00[c]
Weighted average	100	3.0	20:00	14:17	5:43

[a]Based on an average running speed of 9 mph.
[b]Based on an average running speed of 12.6 mph.
[c]No service.

each market to a change in service may be different. The total volume along the route is the total of the volumes served in each market.
2. The effective speed of the vehicle over the route is reduced by the time required to stop at each station along the route.
3. The productivity of the vehicle in round trips per time period depends also on scheduling and vehicle positioning considerations.

In this case the change in route has two major effects. First, by reducing running times, in-vehicle times are reduced, and this increased level of service causes increased ridership and thus increased gross revenues. Second, by reducing running times, vehicle productivity in trips per hour is increased, thus reducing the effective cost of a single round trip (from $16 to $12.80). Both changes contribute to increased net revenues.

■ *Question 10.11* (analysis cycle VI)   Using the weighted average in-vehicle time for the corridor, predict impacts of selected policies. Prepare an evaluation report discussing impacts on users and operators. Be sure to recommend a course of action and discuss your reasoning. How did you treat the loss of service to residents of zone Z in reaching your decision?

■ *Question 10.12* (analysis cycle VII)   An on-board count was done on a sample of vehicles in order to get a preliminary estimate of origin-destination patterns. The results are shown in table 10.10. Using these results, predict changes for each origin-destination pair. prepare an evaluation report and discuss. Compare with the re   ᴼf question 10.11.

Table 10.10 An origin-destination matrix for the four zones in figure 10.1

		Destination				
		W	X	Y	Z	
	W	5	10	15	25	60
	X	3	2	5	10	20
Origin	Y	1	1	1	7	10
	Z	1	1	5	3	10
		10	14	26	45	100

All figures are percentages of the total number of trips.

TO READ FURTHER
See Lee (1976), Shortreed (1976), Ehrlich (1977), Manheim, Furth, and Salomon (1977), Tober (1977), and N. H. M. Wilson (1978); also Bien, Bourgin, and Manheim (1976), Bien et al. (1977).

EXERCISES
10.1(P) Select a bus transit line in your area. Collect the necessary data and do an analysis like the one in this chapter. Alternatively, if you can get cooperation from an operator, do a similar analysis for an airline route, a shipping route, or other services.

10.2(C) Some transit operators would argue that service reliability— the variance in headways—is a key issue. For example, on some routes a scheduled headway of 10 minutes may be unreliable: actual headways may range from 2 to 25 or 30 minutes because of traffic congestion, vehicle bunching, and other factors. If this is true, how would you modify the analysis suggested in this chapter?

11
The Dimensions of Consumer Choice

11.1 INTRODUCTION

In chapters 2–4 we introduced the concept of a demand function as a representation of consumer behavior. We examined four major types of demand functions: disaggregate deterministic, disaggregate stochastic, aggregate deterministic, and aggregate stochastic. From this point on we shall restrict our attention primarily to the two types in which there is now significant practical work in travel demand modeling: aggregate deterministic and disaggregate stochastic.

Our discussion of demand has so far been relatively general; most of the concepts presented have been relevant to many other contexts in addition to travel behavior. In this chapter, however, we introduce a complexity that, while present in other applications of consumer theory, is of particular importance for transportation. This new theme is the multiple dimensions open for consumer choices in transportation.

The basic concept is relatively simple: *The product that a consumer of transportation purchases is not a simple commodity; it is a bundle of choices.* For example, a consumer may choose to make a trip to a particular workplace by automobile over a particular route at a particular time, and a trip home over another route, stopping at a grocery store along the way. Thus the bundle of choices includes a variety of travel-related decisions to achieve a particular pattern of activities.

These bundles of choices are complex, and no practically manageable demand function can represent consumer behavior in all of these dimensions at once. It is usually necessary to make simplifying assumptions about the choice process in order to develop practical travel demand models. When such simplifying assumptions are made, however, they must be examined critically before the models are used for practical transportation prediction.

One particular set of simplifying assumptions has been dominant throughout the last twenty years of evolution of the field of travel demand analysis. Originally developed for urban passenger transportatation analysis, this set of assumptions has been applied to interurban passenger and freight demand analysis as well (see Kresge and Roberts 1971). It is therefore important to understand these particular asumptions and their implications, as well as alternative assumptions that might be made, in order to clarify the major issues in travel demand analysis. We start our discussion of the complexities of consumer choice with an analysis of urban passenger transportation demand.

11.2 CHOICE DIMENSIONS AND THEIR IMPLICATIONS

11.2.1 The Dimensions

The potential consumer of transportation faces a vast array of choices. For example, the activity of "shopping" might involve a pattern of several different trips during a typical week. In North America this might include a major and several supplementary food shopping excursions by automobile, personal business and browsing trips by foot or public transit during workday lunch hours, afterwork errands by some combination of foot, automobile, and public transit, and evening or weekend trips by automobile for purposes such as "comparison shopping" for a major item such as an appliance or a piece of furniture.

Thus a pattern of activity involves many choices: the frequency with which trips are made, the destinations chosen, the modes and routes used, and the times (of day and week) at which trips are made. Moreover, to characterize the consumer's overall pattern of transportation use we must include his choices of location of residence and workplace and the number of automobiles in the household, as well as the patterns of such activities as work, shopping, and recreation.

The basic choices made by the consumer comprise a vector with many components. Some of these choices are made often and change repeatedly (for example, the choice of destination and mode for shopping trips); other choices are made infrequently and remain stable over long periods of time (for example, choices of residence location, place of employment, and mode to work).

11.2.2 The Issue for Demand Functions

If they are to represent consumer behavior adequately, demand functions should be able to predict how consumers will change their patterns of choices in response to changing conditions.

At first glance it would seem that we need a single demand function covering all of these dimensions. This is not practical, however, because of the many elements that go into the full pattern of locational and travel choices of a single consumer, so that incorporation in a single function would be unwieldy, in terms both of estimating and of using the function. It is also not necessary. Some dimensions of choices change very slowly, over long periods of time, while others change quickly and often. In any particular transportation analysis, not all dimensions of choice will be affected to the same extent by the options the analyst is studying.

It is therefore possible, and necessary, to establish a set of demand functions, rather than a single overall function, to represent consumer behavior in all the choice dimensions. Each function can then deal with a subset of the set of choices.

The central issues, from the perspective of demand analysis, are these: How are the dimensions of choice grouped in the various demand functions? Which dimensions of choice are represented in a single demand function? Which are represented in separate demand functions? And when more than one demand function is used, how are the several separate functions to be related?

11.3 SIMULTANEOUS AND SEQUENTIAL CHOICE STRUCTURES

11.3.1 An Example

Consumers residing at location k have three choices of destination for shopping trips: local stores in their general neighborhood (d_1), the central business district of the metropolitan area (d_2), or a suburban shopping center (d_3). There are two choices of transport mode to each destination: automobile $(m_1 = A)$ or transit $(m_2 = T)$. Each mode is characterized by a single service attribute: the travel time by that mode to each destination (t_{dm}). The relative attractiveness of each destination is reflected in a single variable r_d, "retail attractiveness," which might be measured by square feet of retail floor space, number of retail employees, or dollar volume of retail sales. Finally, the total number of shopping trips (per day or per week) made by residents of k is represented by N, and the preferences of the consumers by α, a vector of parameters.

The demand function(s) give us V_{dm}, the number of shopping trips made (per day or per week) from k to each of the destinations (d_1, d_2, d_3) and by each of the modes (m_1, m_2) for every (d, m) combination. By definition,

$$\sum_{d', m'} V_{d'm'} = N, \tag{11.1}$$

where the summation is over all destinations and modes.

The demand will be a function of the service attributes, the attractions of the various destinations, and the total number of trips. For simplicity we denote all these variables by $\mathbf{X}$:

$$\mathbf{X} \equiv [\alpha, \{t_{dm}\}, \{r_d\}]. \tag{11.2}$$

11.3.2 An Aggregate Approach

The choices to be represented in a demand function involve destination and mode. At the aggregate level we could construct either of two representations of consumer behavior. First, we could include all of the choices in a single demand function:

Simultaneous: $V_{dm} \equiv Nf(\mathbf{X})$. $\tag{11.3}$

Alternatively we could divide the choices into groups and form a sequence of demand functions, $g_1(\mathbf{X})$ and $g_2(\mathbf{X})$. For example, we first use $g_1(\mathbf{X})$ to find V_d, the number of consumers going from k to d. We then use $g_2(\mathbf{X})$ to find $V_{m|d}$, the fraction of those going from k to d who choose mode m. Finally we find V_{dm} by combining the two functions:

Sequential I: $V_d \equiv Ng_1(\mathbf{X}),$
$$V_{m|d} \equiv g_2(V_d, \mathbf{X}), \tag{11.4}$$
$$V_{dm} \equiv V_d V_{m|d} = Ng_1(\mathbf{X})g_2[g_1(\mathbf{X}), \mathbf{X}].$$

Other sequences are possible. For example, letting $V_{d|m}$ be the fraction of those leaving k by mode m who choose destination d, we have:

Sequential II: $V_m \equiv Nh_1(\mathbf{X}),$
$$V_{d|m} \equiv h_2(V_m, \mathbf{X}), \tag{11.5}$$
$$V_{dm} \equiv V_m V_{d|m} = Nh_1(\mathbf{X})h_2[h_1(\mathbf{X}), \mathbf{X}].$$

For this example we shall take

$$V_{dm} \equiv \frac{Nr_d^{\alpha_1} t_{dm}^{\alpha_2}}{\sum\limits_{d', m'} r_{d'}^{\alpha_1} t_{d'm'}^{\alpha_2}}. \tag{11.6}$$

The corresponding forms are displayed in table 11.1, where the first line shows the various forms in terms of composite activity and service variables (see section 4.5.6) and the second line shows the forms for the specific example. In this case the composite variables are

$$Z_d = r_d^{\alpha_1}, \qquad L_{dm} = t_{dm}^{\alpha_2} \qquad \text{(generally} \quad \alpha_1 > 0, \quad \alpha_2 < 0). \tag{11.7}$$

Several features of these forms should be noted:

Table 11.1 Three forms of demand models

	Aggregate		Disaggregate	
	General	Example	General	Example
Simultaneous	$V_{dm} =$ $$\frac{NZ_d L_{dm}}{\sum_{d',m'} Z_{d'} L_{d'm'}}$$	$V_{dm} =$ $$\frac{Nr_d^{\alpha_1} t_{dm}^{\alpha_2}}{\sum_{d',m'} r_{d'}^{\alpha_1} t_{d'm'}^{\alpha_2}}$$	$p(m, d) =$ $$\frac{Z_d L_{dm}}{\sum_{d',m'} Z_{d'} L_{d'm'}}$$	$p(m, d) =$ $$\frac{r_d^{\alpha_1} t_{dm}^{\alpha_2}}{\sum_{d',m'} r_{d'}^{\alpha_1} t_{d'm'}^{\alpha_2}}$$
Sequential I (d) form	$V_d =$ $$\frac{NZ_d \sum_{m'} L_{dm'}}{\sum_{d'} Z_{d'} \sum_{m'} L_{d'm'}}$$	$V_d =$ $$\frac{Nr_d^{\alpha_1} \sum_{m'} t_{dm'}^{\alpha_2}}{\sum_{d'} r_{d'}^{\alpha_1} \sum_{m'} t_{d'm'}^{\alpha_2}}$$	$p(d) =$ $$\frac{Z_d \sum_{m'} L_{dm'}}{\sum_{d'} Z_{d'} \sum_{m'} L_{d'm'}}$$	$p(d) =$ $$\frac{r_d^{\alpha_1} \sum_{m'} t_{dm'}^{\alpha_2}}{\sum_{d'} r_{d'}^{\alpha_1} \sum_{m'} t_{d'm'}^{\alpha_2}}$$
$(m\mid d)$ form	$V_{m\mid d} =$ $$\frac{L_{dm}}{\sum_{m'} L_{dm'}}$$	$V_{m\mid d} =$ $$\frac{t_{dm}^{\alpha_2}}{\sum_{m'} t_{dm'}^{\alpha_2}}$$	$p(m\mid d) =$ $$\frac{L_{dm}}{\sum_{m'} L_{dm'}}$$	$p(m\mid d) =$ $$\frac{t_{dm}^{\alpha_2}}{\sum_{m'} t_{dm'}^{\alpha_2}}$$
Sequential II (m) form	$V_m =$ $$\frac{N \sum_{d'} Z_{d'} L_{d'm}}{\sum_{d',m'} Z_{d'm'} L_{d'm'}}$$	$V_m =$ $$\frac{N \sum_{d'} r_{d'}^{\alpha_1} t_{d'm}^{\alpha_2}}{\sum_{d',m'} r_{d'}^{\alpha_1} t_{d'm'}^{\alpha_2}}$$	$p(m) =$ $$\frac{\sum_{d'} Z_{d'} L_{d'm}}{\sum_{m'} \sum_{d'} Z_{d'} L_{d'm'}}$$	$p(m) =$ $$\frac{\sum_{d'} r_{d'}^{\alpha_1} t_{d'm}^{\alpha_2}}{\sum_{m'} \sum_{d'} r_{d'}^{\alpha_1} t_{d'm'}^{\alpha_2}}$$
$(d\mid m)$ form	$V_{d\mid m} =$ $$\frac{Z_d L_{dm}}{\sum_{d'} Z_{d'} L_{d'm}}$$	$V_{d\mid m} =$ $$\frac{r_d^{\alpha_1} t_{dm}^{\alpha_2}}{\sum_{d'} r_{d'}^{\alpha_1} t_{d'm}^{\alpha_2}}$$	$p(d\mid m) =$ $$\frac{Z_d L_{dm}}{\sum_{d'} Z_{d'} L_{d'm}}$$	$p(d\mid m) =$ $$\frac{r_d^{\alpha_1} t_{dm}^{\alpha_2}}{\sum_{d'} r_{d'}^{\alpha_1} t_{d'm}^{\alpha_2}}$$

1. All of the forms take values between 0 and 1.
2. For each of the sequential forms, if the two equations are multiplied as in (11.4) and (11.5), the simultaneous form results. This will hold for any values of the variables (r, t, α_1, α_2) (except the meaningless values of zero for r or t).
3. The three forms give the same result for any given set of values of (r, t). This is not fortuitous; they have been constructed to do this, and this property follows from observation 2. It is possible to show what conditions, in general, must hold for sequential and simultaneous forms to give the same results (see section 11.3.4).

The intuitive meaning of the conditional forms can be seen by examining the sequential I conditional form for our two-mode example. Let $\alpha_2 = 1$; then

$$V_{m_1\mid d} = \frac{1/t_1}{(1/t_1) + (1/t_2)} = \frac{1}{1 + (t_1/t_2)}, \tag{11.8a}$$

$$V_{m_2|d} = \frac{1}{1 + (t_2/t_1)}.$$ (11.8b)

This is a simple "mode-split" model: the relative split of volumes between the two modes is a logistic function of the ratio of their travel times.

Similarly examination of the V_d function in table 11.1 suggests the following interpretation: The composite level of transportation service to any destination d—composite over all modes—is given by the sum over m'. The attractiveness of any destination d relative to all other destinations is proportional to the product of this composite level of service (by all modes) and the inherent attractiveness of the destination (reflected in $r_d^{\alpha_1}$).

11.3.3 A Disaggregate Approach

At the disaggregate level we shall use a stochastic formulation. (A brief review of basic relationships of probability theory is presented in appendix B.) We define the probability that a particular individual chooses to go to destination d by mode m, out of the sets of destinations D and modes M, as $p(d, m : D, M)$, a simultaneous form:

Simultaneous: $p(d, m : D, M) = p_f(\mathbf{X})$. (11.9)

Again, we could divide the choices into two groups and form a sequence of demand functions. One alternative is:

Sequential I: $p(d : D) \equiv p_{g_1}(\mathbf{X})$, (11.10)
$$p(m : M|d : D) \equiv p_{g_2}[p(d : D), \mathbf{X}],$$

where $p(d : D)$ is the probability that an individual chooses to go to destination d and $p(m : M|d : D)$ is the probability that he chooses to go by mode m (given that he has chosen to go to d). A second alternative is:

Sequential II: $p(m : M) \equiv p_{h_1}(\mathbf{X})$,
$$p(d : D|m : M) \equiv p_{h_2}[p(m : M), \mathbf{X}].$$ (11.11)

In both cases a joint probability can be constructed from the two component functions; by definition (see appendix B),

$$p(d, m : D, M) \equiv p(d : D)p(m : M|d : D) = p_{g_1}(\mathbf{X})p_{g_2}[p_{g_1}(\mathbf{X}), \mathbf{X}]$$ (11.12)

or

$$p(d, m : D, M) \equiv p(m : M)p(d : D|m : M) = p_{h_1}(\mathbf{X})p_{h_2}[p_{h_1}(\mathbf{X}), \mathbf{X}].$$ (11.13)

For this example, to allow comparisons with the aggregate form, we shall take

$$p(d, m : D, M) = \frac{r_d^{\alpha_1} t_{dm}^{\alpha_2}}{\sum_{d', m'} r_{d'}^{\alpha_1} t_{d'm'}^{\alpha_2}}.$$

(11.14)

A set of corresponding sequential forms is shown in table 11.1. Several features of these forms should be noted:

1. All of the disaggregate forms are fractions. This is to be expected, since all forms are probabilities, which must take values between 0 and 1 for any values of (r, t).

2. For each of the sequential forms, if the two equations are multiplied as in (11.12) or (11.13) above, the simultaneous form results. This will hold for any nontrivial values of the variables $(r, t, \alpha_1, \alpha_2)$.

3. As in the aggregate forms, as a consequence of the last point, each of the three forms will give the same probability values for any values of (r, t). This is again not fortuitous: the forms have been constructed to have this property.

11.3.4 Consistency

We have seen that whenever the consumer must deal with a bundle of choices, we can represent his behavior either by a single simultaneous demand function that includes all the choice dimensions or by a set of sequential demand functions. Further, several alternative sequences are possible for the sequential functions.

Two alternative demand functions are **consistent** if they give the same values of demand for all values of the independent variables **X**. As noted, the above examples were constructed so that all three forms in each case (aggregate and disaggregate) were consistent. This is, of course, not true of arbitrarily chosen functions.

Ideally a single simultaneous-choice model incorporating all relevant choice dimensions would be utilized. This is impractical because of the large number of dimensions in real situations (section 11.5.2). In practice, some sequential models must be utilized. A key question then becomes how to design such sequential models so that they are consistent with the corresponding simultaneous models. The method used is to link successive models in the sequential form in particular ways that lead to a property called **internal consistency.**

11.3.5 Conditions for Consistency (Optional Reading)

We now examine the conditions that must be met by the sequential

forms for the simultaneous and sequential forms to give the same results for all values of the independent variables (Manheim 1970c,
1973b, Ben-Akiva 1973, 1974).

A DISAGGREGATE EXAMPLE

Continuing the example, we use some basic relations of probability
theory. Consider a joint probability function such as (11.9). For the
simultaneous and sequential forms to give identical results, we see from
(11.9), (11.12), and (11.13) that we should choose the functions
p_f, p_{g_1}, p_{g_2} so that

$$p(d, m : D, M) = p_f(\mathbf{X}) = p_{g_1}(\mathbf{X}) p_{g_2}[p_{g_1}(\mathbf{X}), \mathbf{X}]. \tag{11.15}$$

This can be done by choosing the functions consistent with probability
theory, as follows.

The probability of choosing a destination d, regardless of the mode
chosen, is the marginal probability of d, denoted by $p(d : D)$. By the
laws of probability,

$$p(d : D) = \sum_{m'} p(d, m' : D, M). \tag{11.16}$$

In the specific case given by (11.14),

$$p(d : D) = \sum_{m''} \frac{r_d^{\alpha_1} t_{dm''}^{\alpha_2}}{\sum_{d', m'} r_{d'}^{\alpha_1} t_{d'm'}^{\alpha_2}} = \frac{r_d^{\alpha_1} \sum_{m'} t_{dm'}^{\alpha_2}}{\sum_{d'} r_{d'}^{\alpha_1} \sum_{m'} t_{d'm'}^{\alpha_2}}, \tag{11.17}$$

as indicated in table 11.1.

Also by the laws of probability, the conditional probability of choosing a mode m, given a destination d,

$$p(m : M|d : D) = \frac{p(m, d : M, D)}{p(d : D)}. \tag{11.18}$$

Using (11.11)–(11.14) and (11.16), this becomes

$$p(m : M|d : D) = \frac{t_{dm}^{\alpha_2}}{\sum_{m'} t_{dm'}^{\alpha_2}}. \tag{11.19}$$

Now let $p_{g_1}(\mathbf{X})$ be the marginal (11.17) and $p_{g_2}(\mathbf{X})$ be the conditional
(11.19):

$$p_{g_1}(\mathbf{X}) = p(d : D) = \frac{r_d^{\alpha_1} \sum_{m'} t_{dm'}^{\alpha_2}}{\sum_{d'} r_{d'}^{\alpha_1} \sum_{m'} t_{d'm'}^{\alpha_2}}, \tag{11.20}$$

$$p_{g_2}(\mathbf{X}) = p(m : M|d : D) = \frac{t_{dm}^{\alpha_2}}{\sum_{m'} t_{dm'}^{\alpha_2}}. \tag{11.21}$$

If we compute the joint probability from (11.15), we get

$$p(d, m : D, M) = p_f(\mathbf{X}) = p_{g_1} p_{g_2} = \frac{r_d^{\alpha_1} t_{dm}^{\alpha_2}}{\sum_{d'} r_{d'}^{\alpha_1} \sum_{m'} t_{d'm'}^{\alpha_2}},$$ (11.22)

which is identical to (11.14).

Thus if the several terms of a sequential disaggregate form are to give the same result as a simultaneous form, the terms must be consistent with the basic relations of probability theory. The simultaneous-choice form must equal the product of the parts of the sequential form, for all values of the independent variables, and conversely the parts of the sequential form must equal marginal and conditional probabilities derived from the simultaneous form. This has several practical consequences, as shown by the following example.

A DISAGGREGATE MULTINOMIAL LOGIT MODEL

Consider the example of an MNL model:

$$p(i : I) = \frac{e^{U_i}}{\sum_{i'} e^{U_{i'}}}.$$ (11.23)

For a given choice of destination and mode, U_i can be divided into three components:

$$U_i = U_d(\mathbf{X}) + U_m(\mathbf{X}) + U_{dm}(\mathbf{X}),$$ (11.24)

where $U_d(\mathbf{X})$ and $U_m(\mathbf{X})$ represent the terms that vary only with destination or mode choices, respectively, and $U_{dm}(\mathbf{X})$ represents terms that vary with both destination and mode (for example, t_{dm}). Then the simultaneous-choice MNL model is

$$p(d, m : D, M) = \frac{e^{U_d + U_m + U_{dm}}}{\sum_{d'} \sum_{m'} e^{U_{d'} + U_{m'} + U_{d'm'}}}.$$ (11.25)

From (11.16) (simplifying the notation by dropping D and M):

$$p(d) = \sum_{m'} p(d, m') = \frac{e^{U_d} \sum_{m'} e^{U_{m'} + U_{dm'}}}{\sum_{d'} e^{U_{d'}} \sum_{m'} e^{U_{m'} + U_{d'm'}}}.$$ (11.26)

To simplify we define a general composite variable Λ such that

$$\Lambda_d \equiv \ln\left(\sum_{m'} e^{U_{m'} + U_{dm'}}\right)$$ (11.27)

(this is often referred to as the LOGSUM variable; see Ben-Akiva 1973, Ruiter and Ben-Akiva 1977). Then

$$p(d) = \frac{e^{U_d + \Lambda_d}}{\sum\limits_{d'} e^{U_{d'} + \Lambda_{d'}}} . \qquad (11.28)$$

Similarly, from (11.18), using (11.25) and (11.28):

$$p(m|d) = \left[\frac{e^{U_d + U_m + U_{dm}}}{\sum\limits_{d'}\sum\limits_{m'} e^{U_{d'} + U_{m'} + U_{d'm'}}} \right] \left[\frac{\sum\limits_{d'} e^{U_{d'} + \Lambda_{d'}}}{e^{U_d + \Lambda_d}} \right]$$

$$= \frac{e^{U_m + U_{dm}}}{e^{\Lambda_d}} = \frac{e^{U_m + U_{dm}}}{\sum\limits_{m'} e^{U_{m'} + U_{dm'}}} . \qquad (11.29)$$

Constructed in this way, the sequential models (11.28) and (11.29) are consistent with the simultaneous model (11.25); further, each of the sequential models is a multinomial logit in form. To achieve this, however, the destination-choice model must have in the utility of each destination a term—the Λ variable—that reflects a composite service level over all modes to each destination. (For estimation implications see Ruiter and Ben-Akiva 1977.)

In the case of models other than MNL, consistency among models in a sequential form can be achieved by defining appropriate composite variables similar to Λ_d. Such variables can be defined in many different ways. A definition consistent with utility maximization is proposed in Williams (1977) and Ben-Akiva and Lerman (1978).

AT THE AGGREGATE LEVEL

With aggregate functions the properties a sequential form must have if it is to give the same results as a simultaneous form are directly analogous to those of disaggregate functions. At the disaggregate level, multiplying the two parts of a sequential form should yield a joint probability function,

$$p(d, m : D, M) = p(d : D|m : M)\, p(m : M) = p(d : D)p(m : M|d : D), \quad (11.30)$$

and this condition should be valid over all values of the variables. At the aggregate level the parts of the sequential form should behave just like the corresponding disaggregate probability functions (Manheim 1970c, 1973b):

$$V_{dm} = V_d V_{m|d} \qquad (11.31)$$

or, from (11.3) and (11.4),

$$V_{dm} = f(\mathbf{X}) = g_1(\mathbf{X})g_2[g_1(\mathbf{X}), \mathbf{X}], \qquad (11.32)$$

and, analogous to the marginal and conditional probabilities,

$$V_d = g_1(\mathbf{X}) = \sum_{m'} V_{dm'} = \sum_{m'} f(\mathbf{X}), \tag{11.33}$$

$$V_{m|d} = g_2[g_1(\mathbf{X}), \mathbf{X}] = \frac{V_{dm}}{V_d} = \frac{f(\mathbf{X})}{g_1(\mathbf{X})} = \frac{f(\mathbf{X})}{\sum_{m'} f(\mathbf{X})}. \tag{11.34}$$

Thus the conditional choice functions such as $V_{m|d}$ must be fractions, or share models, and must behave like probability functions. This leads to the concept of a general share model (see Manheim 1973b).

DISCUSSION

If the several terms of a sequential form are to give the same result as a simultaneous form, at either the aggregate or the disaggregate level, certain relationships must exist. For the disaggregate level the relationship is that shown in (11.30): the product of the marginal and conditional probabilities must equal the joint probability. For the aggregate level the requirement is a generalization of this relationship. The practical implication is that when sequential and simultaneous forms are defined consistently, composite variables analogous to (11.27) will be used to link the models of the sequential form. Defined in this way, a sequential form is *internally consistent* (Manheim 1970c, 1973b).

The consequence is that each variable in $\mathbf{X}$ potentially enters into each equation of the sequential form. To see the behavioral implications of this, consider the disaggregate version of sequential I in table 11.1. Given that the consumer has decided to go to destination d, any change in travel time by mode m_1 to that destination will affect the probability of his choosing that mode and thus all other modes. On the other hand, a change in the attractiveness of the destination will not influence the probability of mode choice to that destination, $p(m|d)$, although it will certainly influence the probability of choosing that destination, $p(d)$. Furthermore, the unconditional probability of mode choice, $p(m)$, will be affected by the change in destination attractiveness. These interrelationships could be spelled out more precisely by deriving the various direct elasticities and cross-elasticities for the models.

11.3.6 Conclusions

This section has demonstrated how a demand function can represent consumer behavior when there are several dimensions of choice open to the consumer. At the aggregate and disaggregate levels it is possible to define a simultaneous-choice demand function in which all choices are dealt with in a single step. It is also possible to define various sequential-choice demand functions that deal with the several choice dimensions in a series of steps. Sequential functions can be designed for any sequence of choices in such a way that they will represent the same behavioral pattern as the simultaneous-choice form, provided they are formulated and applied consistently.

The first direction of development of the concepts presented in this section involved aggregate sequential models, which will be described in the next section; but, as we shall see, these were not defined consistently. Aggregate simultaneous models were then developed, primarily for intercity passenger travel (see chapter 4). When disaggregate models were first developed, they were applied within a sequential structure to mode split (S. L. Warner 1962, Quarmby 1967). The development of simultaneous-choice disaggregate models is a recent occurrence (Ben-Akiva 1973).

11.4 UTMS-1, THE FIRST MAJOR TRANSPORTATION MODEL

The Urban Transportation Model System (UTMS) represents the first large-scale use of modern systems analysis methods in transportation. The set of models and procedures that we shall call, for convenience, UTMS-1 took shape in a series of urban transportation studies in the United States and has undergone relatively minor changes as it has been applied in more than 350 metropolitan areas around the world. (Although there have been many minor refinements during the 15 or 20 years in which the UTMS has been in use, the basic structure has stayed constant. The name UTMS-1 indicates our hope that a substantially new approach will soon evolve, to be called UTMS-2.)

11.4.1 The Conceptual Structure of UTMS-1

Because of its long history and widespread use, there is an extensive literature on the methods of UTMS-1 (see, for example, FHWA 1972, UMTA 1976b). To grasp the essential elements of this important modeling approach one must understand its basic conceptual structure. Only then can the analyst put into proper perspective the various alternative ways in which particular details are handled.

DIMENSIONS OF CHOICE

The central feature of the conceptual structure of UTMS-1 is the way in which it deals with the multiple dimensions of consumer choice.

Historically the set of consumer choices considered in UTMS-1 applications has included location choices for residence (*res*) and place of employment (*emp*), automobile ownership level (*ao*), and travel choices for various activities, involving frequency (*f*), destination (*d*), mode (*m*), route (*r*), and time of day (*h*) of trips. That is, the set of alternatives among which consumers choose is assumed to consist of (*f, d, m, r, h; ao, res, emp*), where *f* is usually measured as trips per day but sometimes as trips per peak period. A particular segmentation and sequencing of these choices has typically been assumed. Location choices are predicted first, often independently of transportation service levels. Then automobile ownership levels are predicted, usually independently of transportation service levels. Then, within the set of travel choices, frequencies are predicted first, primarily as functions of income and independently of transportation service levels. Destination choice is predicted next, followed by modal choice and then path choice. Time of day is predicted last, generally by applying a peak-hour factor to daily trips.

Thus UTMS-1 deals primarily with choices of (*f, d, m, r*), and secondarily with (*h, ao*). In most applications residential and employment locations have been assumed fixed; in a few studies these are predicted, separately from the travel choices, by activity-shift models (specifically land-use models). We shall focus here on the treatment of the basic travel choices (*f, d, m, r*).

SEQUENTIAL STRUCTURE

In UTMS-1 individuals are grouped into market segments based primarily on a division of the region being studied into **traffic zones**, which we shall denote by the index k.

From an aggregate perspective the demand function for the consumers in market segment e (a group of individuals or households with similar travel behavior) who originate in zone k would be

$$V^e_{kdmrh;ao} = f^e(\mathbf{A}, \mathbf{S}),\tag{11.35}$$

where **A** and **S** are the relevant activity-system and service variables describing the choices available and the characteristics of the consumers and $V^e_{kdmrh;ao}$ is the total number of trips made, by members of market segment e who own ao automobiles, from origin zone k to destination zone d by mode m and route r at time h.

In the typical situation where it is assumed that choices of time of travel and of automobile ownership are made separately from the others, this becomes

$$V^e_{kdmr} = f^e(\mathbf{A}, \mathbf{S}).\tag{11.36}$$

Historically this demand function has been broken into four components in UTMS-1:

$$V_{kdmr}^e = g_1^e(\mathbf{A}, \mathbf{S})g_2^e(\mathbf{A}, \mathbf{S})g_3^e(\mathbf{A}, \mathbf{S})g_4^e(\mathbf{A}, \mathbf{S}), \tag{11.37}$$

where g_1 is the trip-generation submodel, g_2 the distribution submodel, g_3 the mode-split submodel, and g_4 the route-choice or network-assignment submodel.

By breaking the demand function into four submodels, it is possible to break the forecasting of future travel into a sequence of four steps:

1. *Trip generation:*

$V_k^e \equiv$ total volume of trips generated in zone k by market segment e
$$= g_1^e(\mathbf{A}, \mathbf{S}). \tag{11.38}$$

2. *Trip distribution:*

$V_{kd}^e \equiv$ total volume of trips from zone k to zone d by market segment e
$$= g_2^e(\mathbf{A}, \mathbf{S})V_k^e. \tag{11.39}$$

3. *Mode split:*

$V_{kdm}^e \equiv$ total volume of trips by mode m from zone k to zone d by market segment e
$$= g_3^e(\mathbf{A}, \mathbf{S})V_{kd}^e. \tag{11.40}$$

4. *Network assignment:*

$V_{kdmr}^e \equiv$ total volume of trips by route r and mode m from zone k to zone d by market segment e
$$= g_4^e(\mathbf{A}, \mathbf{S})V_{kdm}^e. \tag{11.41}$$

The functions g_2, g_3, and g_4 are *share functions:* they serve to split a fixed trip total into a number of components (Manheim 1973b). For example, g_3^e is applied to the total volume of trips from k to d by segment e to obtain the fraction, or share, of these trips that go by each of the available modes.

The interrelationships of the functions can be seen by comparing the simultaneous form (11.37) with the sequential forms (11.38)–(11.41). In actually predicting flows, each of the steps (11.38)–(11.41) is applied in sequence, as discussed below.

MARKET SEGMENTS IN UTMS-1

In most applications of UTMS-1 the basic segmentation is by trip purpose and whether or not trips have one base at the home. This leads to classification of trips as home-based work trips, home-based nonwork trips (shopping, social-recreational, school, and miscellaneous), and non-home-based trips (FHWA 1972). Trips by taxi are sometimes treated as a separate purpose (rather than a mode), and truck trips (that is, the movement of goods) form a separate category.

Additional segmentation is sometimes added. For example, households may be stratified by income, number of members, or number of automobiles owned; and transit users may be classified as "captive" or "choice" (which is really a proxy for whether the individuals have a driver's license and a car available). Different market segmentation schemes may be used in the different steps.

It is important to point out the definition used for a trip in UTMS-1. Many trips involve just a single link: home-work-home, home-shop-home, and so forth. Many other trips, however, are multilink chains: home-work-shop-home, home-shop-shop-social-home, work-business-shop-work, and so forth. These multilink trips can be quite significant: in a sample of 1,259 shopping trips in Washington, D.C., Adler found that only 501 were simple home-shop-home trips; the rest were part of multilink chains (Adler and Ben-Akiva 1975, Adler 1976).

For all UTMS-1 applications the chains are broken into simple single-link trips. For example, the chain home-work-shop-work-home would be broken into one home-based work trip (home-work-home) and one non-home-based trip (work-shop-work).

11.4.2 Key Features of the Submodels

Trip generation, the first sequential step, involves the prediction of total trips from an origin or to a destination by trip purpose. Each zone k is described by such activity-system variables as average annual income, average number of automobiles owned, average number of workers per household, percentage of households having an income greater than a specified value, zonal total population, acres of land in various land categories, and zonal total employment. Until very recently generation models have not included any service attributes, so that zonal trips are predicted to remain constant no matter what level of transportation service is provided.

The volume of trips originating in zone k, V_{k}^{e}, is termed the **trip production** or the **total trip ends** of that zone. Often a prediction is also made of the total trips destined for each zone; this is termed the **trip attraction** of that zone. The models for attraction are similar to those for trip production, except that measures of attractiveness are used, such as number of jobs or square feet of retail floor space.

The second step is trip distribution, the prediction of trips from each origin to each destination. The independent variables are the trip productions resulting from the previous step, the service attributes, and, in many formulations, the trip attractions.

The most common functional form is the gravity model introduced in chapter 4. In the United States and Canada travel time by a single mode (usually highway) is typically the only service attribute used. In the United Kingdom a composite service level (termed a *generalized cost*), which is a linear combination of travel time, distance, and out-of-pocket costs, is often used (A. G. Wilson 1973).

In most applications of the gravity model the predictions of trip productions and attractions from the generation stage are treated as first approximations. These are then adjusted in an iterative process to balance with the gravity-model predictions. Although there is a large literature on these balancing procedures, the behavioral basis of this practice is questionable.

The third step in the UTMS-1 approach is the mode split, the prediction of trips by mode from origin to destination. The independent variables are the trip distributions from the previous step and the modal service attributes. Many approaches have been used to develop mode-split models. Most commonly used until recently were models to which curves were fit by hand or by regression. Typically origin zones were classified by income level and automobile ownership, and for each class of zones relations were developed between the fractions of trips by automobile and by transit and the time and cost ratios or differences for the two modes.

The final step in the UTMS-1 approach is network assignment, the prediction of trips by route. The mathematical logic and alternative computational procedures are sufficiently complex as to merit separate discussion (see chapter 12). In current practice the problem is simplified by assigning flows separately to the highway and transit networks, using the mode splits from the preceding step. It is often assumed that transit travel times are constant, independent of volume, so that simplified procedures can be used (that is, no capacity restraint or other equilibrating logic is required for the transit mode). For the highway mode, however, it is usually necessary to take the effects of congestion into account, as reflected in the service functions for each highway link, in which travel times increase as volumes increase. Various methods of adjusting travel times and volumes have been developed.

An important step in this process is the conversion of passenger flows to vehicle flows, especially for the automobile mode. The mode-split prediction in the preceding step gives the volume of passengers choosing the automobile mode; these are converted to vehicles by using an auto-occupancy factor of so many persons per automobile. This enables link travel times to be derived on the basis of volumes in vehicles per hour.

11.4.3 Equilibration

In the computer software packages that implement UTMS-1 (FHWA 1972, Dial 1976, UMTA 1976) the process of finding the equilibrium flow volumes follows the four-step sequence outlined above (see figure 11.1).

The inputs to this process are the specifications of transportation- and activity-system options for a specific year. Using appropriate activity-shift models or, more often, judgment, the distribution of ac- tivities (residential and employment locations) is predicted. If activity-

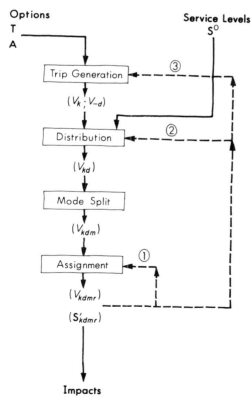

Figure 11.1 Equilibration in UTMS-1.

shift models are used, assumed transportation service levels provide the necessary inputs to the models (which predict locational patterns as functions of transportation service levels and other variables). Based on the characteristics of the households in each zone, automobile ownership levels are predicted, generally as a function of household income, household size, or other demographic characteristics (but not transportation service levels). Thus (*ao, res, emp*) have been predicted to this point, and we are ready to start the basic steps that have been the primary focus of UTMS-1.

The first step is to predict trip generation. This is usually a function only of the average characteristics of each zone: household characteristics for trip productions and, if attractions are used, nonhousehold characteristics (employment, retail sales, and so forth) for destination zones. Transportation service levels rarely enter into this step.

The next step is to use the estimated productions and attractions in the distribution model to predict the trip distributions (origin-destination volumes). This step has usually used only highway travel times; these are estimated or developed from minimum-path trees in the highway network. The estimated origin-destination volumes may be reestimated several times in the process of iterating the attractions and (in some cases) the productions to ensure consistency. The same values of travel times (and other service attributes) are used throughout this iteration process.

The next step is the mode split. This is generally the first point at which transit service levels enter into the predictions. Highway and transit service levels are estimated or developed from minimum-path trees in the separate highway and transit networks.

In the last step the origin-destination-mode volumes are assigned to the networks. Typically the transit trips are assigned to the transit network, and the highway trips are assigned separately to the highway network. In the highway network assignment process a capacity restraint may be applied so that the volumes assigned to various paths are approximately consistent with the travel times over those paths. This iterative process is the first point at which initial estimates of service levels (used for distribution and mode split as well as implicitly or explicitly for steps earlier in the process) are checked for consistency with flow volumes. The only adjustment in volumes made at this step, however, is in the assignment to paths, shown as loop 1 in the figure; the number of trips generated in each zone, the distribution of trips among possible destinations, and the mode splits for each origin-destination pair remain the same as the inputs to the assignment phase.

In a few urban transportation studies (see Hill and Dodd 1962) the results from the assignment phase were fed back to iterate generation, distribution, and mode split in an attempt to make the results of those steps consistent with the levels of service found in the assignment phase (loops 2 and 3).

In sum, then, the approach to equilibration in UTMS-1 is broken into four steps corresponding to the four components of the sequential demand function; different service attributes are used in the various steps; and the values of the service attributes that are used are different in each step because of the lack of iteration in the process.

There have been a number of minor variations in the use of UTMS-1 around the world. For example, sometimes mode split has been done before distribution; recently disaggregate models for mode split have come into use; and there are a few instances in which service attributes have been incorporated in trip-generation equations. In addition, various theoretical approaches have been used to evolve sets of models from perspectives other than that described, such as entropy methods (A. G. Wilson 1977).

Ad hoc procedures have typically been used to develop the parameter values. Each model is calibrated separately, and there is no calibration of the path-choice model. For generation, regression methods, cross-classification, or a tabulation approach called category analysis have been used, separately or in combination. For distribution the basic approach has been adjustment of various parameters in an iterative, trial-and-error approach to get the predicted distribution of trip lengths into approximate agreement with that observed. Statistical estimation methods have been used only for mode split, and that only relatively recently.

11.4.4 Appraisal of UTMS-1

The development and institutionalization of the UTMS-1 approach over the last fifteen years is a major accomplishment: it is one of the first large-scale applications of modern systems analysis techniques to problems of the civil sector. One result of the widespread use of this approach has been the development of a new cadre of transportation professionals who are experienced in the application of computer-based methods to the analysis of urban transportation problems. The basic concepts of UTMS-1 have also been adapted to contexts other than urban passenger transportation (see, for example, Kresge and Roberts 1971). For these reasons the transportation analyst should understand UTMS-1, even though it is rapidly becoming obsolete. It is important to appraise the achievements and failures of the approach in a balanced way.

On the positive side, UTMS-1 has helped transportation planners in many metropolitan areas gain a feeling for the major consequences of alternative transportation plans, especially those consequences dependent on volumes and levels of service. It made important contributions during the 1960s when many major investments in urban highways were being considered. These ideas and methods have also contributed to the rapid development in many countries of systematic approaches to appraising transportation investments.

On the negative side, the criticisms of UTMS-1 deal with either its implementation or its conceptual structure, which is our primary concern in this discussion (Manheim 1969, 1970b, 1973b, Boyce, Day, and McDonald 1970, Roberts 1970, Binder 1973, Bouchard 1973, Cambridge Systematics 1974, World Bank 1975 [Annex 7]).

The following criticisms have been made concerning implementation limitations of UTMS-1:

1. The set of models is difficult to use. Because each step in the process is implemented in several different computer programs, it takes weeks (and sometimes months) to get predicted flows for a single transportation- or activity-system alternative. Therefore, not enough alternatives are studied. (This criticism could be countered by more effective software design.)

2. The set of models is not developed on a rigorous scientific basis. Our brief discussion of calibration showed that many judgmental adjustments must be made on the various models to get them to behave correctly. The level of statistical understanding and treatment in calibrating the models has typically been poor and certainly not up to the standards of modern statistical or econometric methods.

3. The set of models deals only with transportation flows and not with other significant impacts. For example, residential displacements, tax-base effects, air quality, and energy consumption are all issues that have become politically important in transportation; UTMS-1 does not predict any of these effects. (In the $3.5 million Boston Transportation Planning Review, UTMS-1 was used only in a minor and peripheral way; it just was not considered responsive to the issues that were politically important. See Gakenheimer 1976.) Although this criticism was somewhat valid in the past, additional models now being developed complement the flow predictions. For example, given valid predictions of flows, air-quality and energy-consumption impacts can be

predicted using appropriate models that take the flow volumes as inputs. Other impacts, such as displacements of households and tax-base losses, are not related to flow volumes at all and can be predicted by specific procedures external to the flow prediction process.

The most important criticisms of UTMS-1 concern the way it treats the dimensions of consumer choice. From a political perspective, questions such as the following are raised, reflecting the changed political climate of transportation in the 1970s (concern for air quality and the reduction of air pollution; for energy conservation; for increasing the mobility of low-income, elderly, handicapped, and other persons who do not drive their own automobiles; for upgrading transportation services without displacing large numbers of residents and businesses; and for making better operational use of existing highway and transit facilities):

• Aren't the predictions biased toward highways, since automobile ownership and total trips are independent of transportation policy (in that they are independent of service levels)?

• What increase in parking charges in the central business district will influence workers to form carpools or use public transit?

• Will a bus priority scheme—taking street lanes away from automobile traffic (or parking) for exclusive use of buses and possibly carpools—significantly reduce automobile vehicle-miles of travel?

• Will increased automobile congestion in the central business district cause people to shift to transit, or will it cause them to shift their destinations to competing suburban office centers and industrial parks (for work trips) and shopping centers (for social and recreational purposes)? Can a major transit improvement maintain the role of the central business district as a regional center?

From a theoretical perspective, questions such as these can be raised:

• Shouldn't all aspects of service—transit and highway, times and costs—affect generation and distribution as well as mode split and path choice?

• Shouldn't highway congestion affect bus travel times, and vice versa?

• Shouldn't automobile ownership and occupancy (that is, whether an individual driver rides alone or shares the vehicle in a carpool) be sensitive to transit and highway service levels?

• Shouldn't all these aspects of traveler behavior be interrelated?

The resolution of these questions requires a clearer articulation of the dimensions of consumer choice and the structure assumed for those dimensions in the demand functions and use of the consistency conditions introduced in section 11.3.

Further indications of the limitations of UTMS-1, and possible directions for modifications, can be gathered from consideration of the following list of desiderata for such a set of demand models and submodels and equilibrium calculating procedures:

1. Transportation service, **S**, should enter into every step, including trip generation (unless data analysis for a specific situation indicates that trip generation is, in fact, independent of level of service for all market segments over the full range of service levels to be studied).

2. The service attributes used should be sufficiently complete as to allow adequate predictions of traveler behavior. For example, in-vehicle and out-of-vehicle times, out-of-pocket cost, and other attributes such as number of transfers should be included if empirical evidence indicates that these are important.

3. The same attributes of service should influence each step (unless the data indicate otherwise). For example, transit fares, parking charges, walking distances, and service frequencies should influence not only mode split but also assignment, generation, and distribution.

4. The same parameters on the attributes should be used in each step and should vary with market segment. For example, the same relative weights should be used for in-vehicle and out-of-vehicle times and for costs in each step; and if these weights are varied as a function of income and automobile ownership in one step, they should be varied over market segments in all steps.

5. The process should calculate a valid equilibrium of service and demand; the same values of each of the service variables should influence each step. For example, the travel times that are used as inputs for mode split, distribution, and even generation should be the same as the outputs resulting from assignment. If necessary, iteration from assignment back to generation, distribution, and mode split should be done to get this equilibrium.

6. The levels of service of every mode should influence demand. Congestion on highway or transit networks, limited capacity (as in parking lots), fares, and other characteristics of each mode should (in general) affect not only its own demand but also the demand for other modes at all steps.

7. The estimation procedures should be statistically valid and reproducible.

Careful examination of the UTMS-1 approach indicates that it violates each of these conditions (Manheim 1970c, 1973b; see also Manheim 1970b, World Bank 1975 [Annex 7], Ben-Akiva et al. 1977). (Conditions 1–6 are aspects of the consistency conditions discussed in section 11.3.) As a consequence, serious questions can be raised about the biases and limitations of the flow predictions resulting from use of the models in their traditional forms.

Once these limitations have been recognized, positive changes can begin.

11.5 DIRECTIONS FOR IMPROVED MODELS
The concepts developed in this and preceding demand chapters suggest clear directions for developing improved demand models. (This section has been adapted in part from Ben-Akiva, Lerman, and Manheim 1976 and Ben-Akiva 1977.)

11.5.1 General Directions
Three themes underlie the directions we shall explore:

1. Explicit behavioral theory: Beginning in chapter 2, we have stressed the formulation of an explicit theory about how the consumer makes travel and related choices.
2. Explicit treatment of the multiple dimensions of choice: Part of the behavioral theory behind a model must deal explicitly with the structure of multidimensional consumer choices—that is, whether they are simultaneous or sequential and, if sequential, whether they are structured consistently.
3. Use of valid estimation methods: Modern econometrics provides powerful tools for estimating the values of parameters of models in an efficient and valid manner. In particular, we saw in chapters 2–4 that aggregate demand functions tend to hide a lot of the variability in behavior (by grouping observations at the zonal level) that disaggregate functions explicitly bring out. For this reason it is most efficient to estimate disaggregate models on small samples of individual observations (consisting perhaps of a thousand observations), rather than estimate aggregate models on large samples (see Richards and Ben-Akiva 1975, Ben-Akiva 1977). Thus disaggregate estimation methods have become very efficient and economical to use.

These themes suggest the following steps in developing and using improved demand models. First, formulate explicit behavioral hypotheses:

1. Make explicit assumptions about the choice dimensions that should

be included. At a minimum these are frequency, destination, mode, and route. Mode should include (in urban transportation) a distinction of single-person automobile (only the driver) versus carpool (passengers sharing the automobile with the driver). In most situations, even in highly motorized North America, automobile ownership (the number of automobiles owned per household, and the general types of automobiles) should be included as a dimension of consumer choice that can be affected by transportation service levels. Ideally the time of day should be included for all purposes, including work (especially if staggering of work hours is an important policy option).

2. Make explicit assumptions about the choice structure: which dimensions are structured simultaneously and which sequentially.

3. Make explicit which activity and service-level variables are assumed to influence consumer choices, and treat these variables consistently throughout the assumed choice structure (as discussed in section 11.3).

Second, estimate (calibrate) the demand functions using sound statistical methods, in either aggregate or disaggregate form. Disaggregate methods are usually more efficient, and there are several practical approaches to aggregation (see chapter 4).

Third, predict flow impacts using the estimated demand functions with a valid computational approach to equilibrium. If it is desirable to use the demand functions in sequential rather than simultaneous form, the functions in the sequential form should be derived from the simultaneous form in a consistent way (see section 11.3).

These concepts have already become a part of current practice. Several surveys of recent developments are listed at the end of the chapter. We shall not do a comprehensive survey here but shall review briefly some particular model systems that have been developed. First, however, we shall expand the concept of sequential and simultaneous structures to the more general concept of choice hierarchies.

11.5.2 Choice Hierarchies and Systems of Models

The successful development of multidimensional disaggregate choice models (Charles River Associates 1972, Ben-Akiva 1973, 1974) opened the door to serious appraisal of underlying assumptions about traveler behavior. As a result, the concepts of simultaneous and sequential structures have been incorporated in a more inclusive, more general concept, that of choice hierarchies. This concept, first introduced in section 2.2, has been an extremely fruitful one.

Again, we use urban travel demand as an example. In general, a travel demand model is concerned with those household and individual decisions that result in trips being made. However, it is clear that some other choices are so interrelated with actual trip making that it is impossible to separate them from such decisions. For example, while the choice of residential location is not in itself a trip-making decision, the combination of employment and residential location decisions has as its consequence a trip choice, that is, a daily work trip.

BEHAVIORAL HYPOTHESES

It is therefore important to enumerate the dimensions of choice and to give an explicit structure to their interrelationships. We begin with a partition of all possible decisions by household members into two sets: those relevant to transportation analysis, including but not limited to travel choices, and those that can, for practical purposes, be ignored. This partition produces the following sample set of relevant household choice dimensions:

1. employment location (for all workers)
2. residential location
3. housing type
4. automobile ownership
5. mode to work (for all workers)
6. frequency (for each type of nonwork trip)
7. destination (for each type of nonwork trip)
8. mode (for each type of nonwork trip)
10. route (for all trips)
11. time of day (for all trips).

For most situations this vector describes the decisions that a complete model system must consider. (There are possible exceptions. Frequency and time of day for work trips may be distinct choices for some households, unconstrained by the work situation. Some decisions may be constrained by lack of income or lack of a driver's license, though the latter may well be part of some decision vectors.) In theory each decision may be dependent on the rest. For example, there are obvious links among residential location, housing type, and automobile owner ship. Similarly shopping trip destination and mode are likely to be closely linked.

A single simultaneous-choice model that included all these dimensions would be unmanageable since the vector of possible choices would, for practical purposes, be limitless. Fortunately there are some

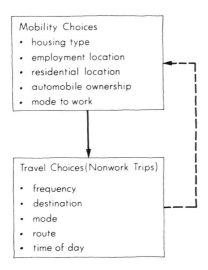

Figure 11.2 A simple choice hierarchy. Based on Ben-Akiva, Lerman, and Manheim (1976).

interrelationships among the components of this vector that are of a distinct character. Some decisions, such as residential location choice, have high transaction costs and are consequently stable over fairly long intervals; other choices, such as social trip frequency, are altered on a daily basis. Some decisions are more logically represented as being made collectively by the household, whereas others can be approximated as individual choices. Thus it is possible to formulate explicit behavioral hypotheses and thereby to establish a structure of the total vector of choices as a logical working hypothesis.

Such an explicit structure greatly simplifies model development. This structure is termed a ***choice hierarchy*** (Ben-Akiva 1973). Figure 11.2 illustrates one possible choice hierarchy. It defines two distinct sets of choices: the long-run ***mobility choices*** of location, housing, automobile ownership, and mode to work; and the short-run ***travel choices*** of frequency, destination, mode, route, and time of day for nonwork trips. These decisions are assumed to be structured hierarchically; that is, location and related decisions in the mobility block are made with travel choices indeterminate, and the travel choices for nonwork trips are made conditional on the outcome of the mobility choice process.

Within each group of simultaneous choices, decisions are assumed to be made by a joint process in which the full range of possible trade-offs is considered by the household. Thus within each block a simultaneous-choice model is used to represent joint choice of the relevant dimensions. Two different simultaneous-choice models are then necessary, one for mobility choices and one for travel choices.

This set of models can be termed **block-conditional,** in that the travel choices (as a group) are conditional on, or sequential to, the mobility decisions (as shown by the solid arrow in the figure). On the other hand, expectations of travel choices feed back to and influence the mobility choices, as shown by the dashed arrow. This feedback is incorporated through composite variables of the Λ type defined in section 11.3.5. In this way a consistent set of sequential models can be developed. (In practice some simplifications and approximations may be made.)

Any hierarchical decision structure is based on explicit behavioral hypotheses about household or individual behavior. Different choice hierarchies might be proposed to represent different decision makers; since each is an approximation of a complex behavior pattern, some hierarchies may prove useful in some situations but inappropriate in others.

Consider, for example, the hierarchy depicted in figure 11.3. In this

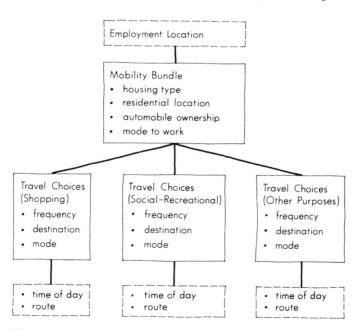

Figure 11.3 A four-stage choice hierarchy. Based on Ben-Akiva, Lerman, and Manheim (1976).

case employment location has been separated from the remaining mobility choices, which for convenience are termed the *mobility bundle.* This hierarchy, which has been invoked in most empirical and theoretical studies of residential location, might be appropriate for skilled workers, since their employment locations are relatively fixed (a skilled employee must generally switch his employer in order to shift his job location).

Thus the formulation of a specific choice hierarchy is dependent on the behavioral patterns being modeled. Different hypotheses might be appropriate, for example, for urban-fringe squatter settlements in developing countries.

INTERRELATIONSHIPS (OPTIONAL READING)

The use of explicit hierarchies of choice has important implications for developing behavioral models of the entire vector of decisions. The assumption of a specific choice hierarchy then leads to a specific structure of simultaneous and sequential-choice models. To illustrate these it is useful to divide the set of factors that could affect the bundle of mobility choices into four classes (Ben-Akiva, Lerman, and Manheim 1976):

1. those entering into the decision process because they are the result of choices made "higher up" in the hierarchy (for example, variables resulting from decisions about employment location);
2. those that directly affect the choice of the mobility bundle;
3. those that arise because of expectations from decisions "lower" in the hierarchy (for example, variables describing decisions made conditional on the mobility choice); and
4. those that directly affect the choice of mobility bundle as well as higher- or lower-level choices.

A brief example will make this distinction clearer. Consider the following four variables with respect to their influence on choices in the mobility bundle:

1. whether a worker in the household is employed in the central business district (CBD);
2. rent (or housing price);
3. level of transit service for shopping trips; and
4. level of transit service to work.

The first of these variables is determined by employment location. Hence it is predetermined when the household makes its mobility choice and does not vary among alternative mobility bundles; for those choices it can be treated as an attribute of the household. The second variable, rent, is an attribute of the alternative location and housing combinations; hence it has a different value for each alternative.

The third variable, shopping level of service, depends on how the household chooses to travel for shopping, a decision that is conditional on the household's mobility choices. Thus shopping level of service is said to be *indeterminate* in the mobility decision. This does not imply that it does not enter into the household's evaluation of mobility alternatives. Rather it means that, although the household does not know the specific shopping trips it will make, it does have some composite picture of the overall shopping level of service it will obtain for various mobility bundles. For example, if the household chooses to own two or more automobiles in its mobility bundle, it will generally have a high composite level of service for shopping in suburban locations because it will typically travel by car. If the household chooses not to own an automobile, it will have a poor composite level of service for suburban locations because it will have to shop exclusively by transit.

The last variable, transit level of service for the work trip, is an attribute of the mobility bundle as well as an attribute of alternative employment location choices.

For a block-conditional model system to be logically consistent, each of these types of variables must be appropriately represented (in the manner indicated in section 11.3.5). Specific models must have appropriate linkages to other models in the choice hierarchy, so that variables influencing travel-related decisions affect the whole range of relevant choices (Ben-Akiva and Lerman 1978). The models discussed in the following section each have appropriate linkages to other components of a choice hierarchy and therefore reflect the full impact of transportation policy decisions on the whole range of relevant choices.

11.5.3 Example: A Set of Urban Travel Models

The initial applications of disaggregate choice modeling techniques for urban travel demand considered a single dimension: the choice of travel mode (see the survey in Domencich and McFadden 1975). The first extension of disaggregate models to include multiple dimensions of choice was by Charles River Associates (1972). In this study a logit model was applied with reasonable results to the choices of frequency, destination, and mode for shopping travel. However, each choice was modeled separately and in an arbitrarily assumed sequence, thereby imposing a strong and statistically unsupported structure on travel decisions.

Ben-Akiva (1973, 1974) demonstrated differences in behavioral assumptions and statistical estimation properties among alternative model structures. For this reason models were developed that included the set of travel choices in a joint structure. The first models included the choice of destination simultaneously with mode and frequency of travel (Ben-Akiva 1973, Richards and Ben-Akiva 1974, Adler and Ben-Akiva 1975). This work was also extended to the joint modeling of mobility choices (Lerman 1975, Lerman and Ben-Akiva 1975).

A BASIC SET OF MODELS

The resulting set of travel models has the behavioral structure shown in figure 11.3. The basic models that have been estimated (solid blocks in figure) are multinomial logit in form and include:

1 Mobility choices:
1.1 Simultaneous choice of automobile ownership and mode to work (Lerman and Ben-Akiva 1975, Cambridge Systematics 1976a).
1.2 Simultaneous choice of residential location and housing type, automobile ownership, and mode to work (Lerman 1975; incorporates 1.1).
2 Travel choices (nonwork):
2.1 Simultaneous choice of frequency, destination, and mode for shopping trips (Adler and Ben-Akiva 1975).
2.2 Simultaneous choice of frequency, destination, and mode for social-recreational trips (Ben-Akiva et al. 1977).

The models were estimated using home-interview survey data collected in 1968 for the Washington, D.C., Metropolitan Area Council of Governments. (The basic survey records were augmented with land-use and transportation service level data.) No special data collection was undertaken to allow use of the disaggregate approach, and so model specifications were constrained to use of variables for which data had been collected. The number of valid records used for estimation of these models was in the range of 800–1,400 households (varying with the model). All statistical tests were satisfactory.

This set of models, or components, has been used in several policy and planning studies, as summarized below. Three of the models are shown as tables: a work mode-choice model with an explicit carpool mode (table 11.2), derived from model 1.1 above; a simultaneous-

Table 11.2 A work mode-choice model

Variable	Symbol	Definition	Coefficient	t-statistic
1. Drive-alone constant	D_c	1 for drive-alone; 0 otherwise	− 3.24	−6.86
2. Shared-ride constant	D_s	1 for shared-ride; 0 otherwise	− 2.24	−5.60
3. Out-of-pocket travel cost divided by income	OPTC/INC	round-trip out-of-pocket travel cost (in cents)/household annual income (in dollars)	−28.8	−2.26
4. In-vehicle travel time	IVTT	round-trip in-vehicle travel time (in minutes)	− 0.0154	−2.67
5. Out-of-vehicle travel time divided by distance	OVTT/DIST	round-trip out-of-vehicle travel time (in minutes)/one-way distance (in miles)	− 0.160	−4.08
6. Auto availability (drive-alone only)	$AALD_c$	# of autos/licensed drivers for drive alone; 0 otherwise	3.99	10.08
7. Auto availability (shared-ride only)	$AALD_s$	# of autos/licensed drivers for shared-ride; 0 otherwise	1.62	5.31
8. Breadwinner (drive-alone only)	BW_c	1 for breadwinner and drive-alone; 0 otherwise	0.890	4.79
9. Government worker (shared-ride only)	GW_s	1 for civilian employees of the federal government and shared-ride; 0 otherwise	0.287	1.78
10. CBD workplace (drive-alone only)	$DCITY_c$	1 for workplace in CBD and drive-alone; 0 otherwise	−0.854	−2.75
11. CBD workplace (shared-ride only)	$DCITY_s$	1 for workplace in CBD and shared-ride; 0 otherwise	−0.404	−1.36
12. Disposable income (drive-alone and shared-ride only)	$DINC_{c,s}$	(household annual income) − (800 × # of persons in household) (in $) for drive-alone and shared-ride; 0 otherwise	−0.0000706	3.46

Table 11.2 (continued)

Variable	Symbol	Definition	Coefficient	*t*-statistic
13. Number of workers (shared-ride only)	NWORK$_s$	# of workers in household for shared-ride; 0 otherwise	0.0983	1.03
14. Employment density (shared-ride only)	DTECA$_s$	employment density at the work zone (employees per commercial acre) × one-way distance (in miles) for shared-ride; 0 otherwise	0.000653	1.34

Sample: No. of observations = 1,114. No. of alternatives = 2,924. Alternatives: c = drive-alone, s = shared-ride (carpool), t = transit.
Source: Cambridge Systematics (1976a).

Table 11.3 A shopping joint-choice model

Variable	Symbol	Definition	Coefficient	*t*-statistic
1. Car constant	DC	1 for auto mode; 0 otherwise	−0.571	−2.22
2. Out-of-vehicle travel time divided by distance	OVTT/DIST	round-trip out-of-vehicle travel time (in minutes)/one-way distance (in miles)	−0.051	−3.31
3. Total travel time	ln (IVTT + OVTT)	round-trip in-vehicle travel time + round-trip out-of-vehicle travel time (in minutes) (natural log)	−2.42	−16.63
4. Out-of-pocket travel cost divided by income	OPTC/INC	round-trip out-of-pocket travel cost (in cents)/household annual income (in code)[a]	−0.0191	−3.39
5. Autos available for nonwork trips (auto mode only)	AAC	# of autos available to household − # of autos used for work trips by workers in the household for auto mode; 0 otherwise	0.663	2.94

Variable	Symbol	Definition	Coefficient	t-statistic
6. Autos available to household (auto mode only)	AOC	# of autos available to household for auto mode; 0 otherwise	0.854	5.14
7. Total land use	ln (AREA)	total land area (acres) (natural log)	1.00	
8. Retail employment at destination/total land area	ln (REMP/AREA)	retail employment at shopping destination (in # of employees)/ total land area (acres) (natural log)	0.296	—
9. CBD destination constant	DCBD	1 for CBD shopping destination; 0 otherwise	0.808	6.99
10. Frequency-zero constant	DF	1 for zero frequency; 0 otherwise	2.52	2.83
11. Household size (frequency-zero only)	HHSF	# of persons in household for zero frequency; 0 otherwise	−0.183	−4.38
12. Retail employment density at origin (frequency-zero only)	DENF	retail employment density in residence zone (employees per acre) for zero frequency; 0 otherwise	0.000068	0.16
13. Household income (frequency-zero only)	INCF	household annual income (in code)[a] for zero frequency; 0 otherwise	0.047	1.27

[a]Income code (in 1968$)

1 = 0 − 2,999	6 = 10,000 − 11,999
2 = 3,000 − 3,999	7 = 12,000 − 14,999
3 = 4,000 − 5,999	8 = 15,000 − 19,999
4 = 6,000 − 7,999	9 = 20,000 − 24,999
5 = 8,000 − 9,999	10 = 25,000 +

Sample: No. of observations = 1,313. No. of alternatives = 44,718.

Alternatives: Trips to shopping destination d and by mode m, for all relevant shopping destinations (including the CBD) and for car and transit modes; for no trip (zero frequency), variables 1–8 equal to zero.

Source: Adler and Ben-Akiva (1975), with modifications reported in Ben-Akiva and Atherton (1977).

Table 11.4 Joint model for automobile ownership and primary worker's mode choice

Variable	Symbol	Definition	Coefficient	t-statistic
1. Zero autos; shared-ride constant	D_{0s}	1 for zero autos and shared-ride; 0 otherwise	−1.62	−4.70
2. One auto; drive-alone constant	D_{1c}	1 for one auto and drive-alone; 0 otherwise	5.22	7.91
3. One auto; shared-ride constant	D_{1s}	1 for one auto and shared-ride; 0 otherwise	5.18	7.64
4. One auto; transit constant	D_{1t}	1 for one auto and transit; 0 otherwise	5.66	8.76
5. Two autos; drive-alone constant	D_{2c}	1 for two autos and drive-alone; 0 otherwise	6.61	7.68
6. Two autos; shared-ride constant	D_{2s}	1 for two autos and shared-ride; 0 otherwise	6.47	7.37
7. Two autos; transit constant	D_{2t}	1 for two autos and transit; 0 otherwise	6.50	7.21
8. Auto availability (drive-alone mode only)	$AALD_c$	♯ of autos/licensed driver for drive-alone; 0 otherwise	3.22	6.22
9. Auto availability (shared-ride mode only)	$AALD_s$	♯ of autos/licensed driver for shared-ride; 0 otherwise	0.472	0.90
10. Remaining income	Z	(household annual income) − (800 × ♯ of persons in household) − (1,000 × ♯ of autos) − (250 × daily round-trip travel cost) (in $)	1.55	5.33
11. Housing type (two autos only)	HT_2	1 for single-family house and two autos; 0 otherwise	1.04	6.18
12. In-vehicle travel time	IVTT	daily round-trip in-vehicle travel time (in minutes)	−0.0129	−2.41
13. Out-of-vehicle travel time divided by distance	OVTT/ DIST	daily round-trip out-of-vehicle travel time (in minutes)/ one-way distance (in miles)	−0.0795	−2.33

Variable	Symbol	Definition	Coefficient	t-Statistic
14. Auto availability	AALD	# of autos/licensed drivers	−4.49	−6.60
15. Shopping relative accessibility (one auto only)	R_1	car generalized shopping travel cost/ transit generalized shopping travel cost for one auto; 0 otherwise	−1.99	−2.42
16. Shopping relative accessibility (two autos only)	R_2	car generalized shopping travel cost/ transit generalized shopping travel cost for two autos; 0 otherwise	−2.80	−3.24
17. CBD workplace (drive-alone only)	$DCITY_c$	1 for workplace in CBD and drive-alone; 0 otherwise	−0.704	−2.21
18. CBD workplace (shared-ride only)	$DCITY_s$	1 for workplace in CBD and shared-ride; 0 otherwise	−0.549	−1.91
19. Out-of-pocket travel cost	TOPTC	250 × daily round-trip out-of-pocket travel cost (in $)	−0.00267	−3.81
20. Government worker (shared-ride only)	GW_s	1 for civilian employees of federal government and shared ride; 0 otherwise	0.347	2.49
21. Number of workers (shared-ride only)	$NWORK_s$	# of workers in household for shared-ride; 0 otherwise	0.322	3.14
22. Employment density (shared-ride only)	$DTECA_s$	employment density at the work zone (employees per commercial acre) × one-way distance (in miles) for shared ride; 0 otherwise	−0.000131	−0.30

Sample: No. of observations = 1,240. No. of alternatives = 7,528.
Alternatives: 0s = zero autos, shared-ride to work; 0t = zero autos, transit to work; 1c = one auto, drive-alone to work; 1s = one auto, shared-ride to work; 1t = one auto, transit to work; 2c = two or more autos, drive-alone to work; 2s = two or more autos, shared-ride to work; 2t = two or more autos, transit to work.
Source: Cambridge Systematics (1976a).

choice model for shopping trips, including choices of travel frequency, trip destination, and mode of travel (table 11.3); and a household automobile-ownership model (table 11.4), also derived from model 1.1. The tables show the variables that enter into the utility functions of various alternatives. The alternatives are listed below the tables. Variables without subscripts enter the utility functions of every alternative listed but take values specific to each alternative; variables with subscripts enter only the utility of the indicated alternative. These models are discussed in Ben-Akiva and Atherton (1977 [appendix]).

FEATURES OF THE MODELS
These models have several major advantages over other urban passenger travel demand models that have been developed.

Policy relevance and sensitivity
Clearly one of the most important advantages of this model system is its sensitivity to a wide range of transportation policies, urban area types, and population characteristics. The sensitivity of the models to market segments, geographical location, and city type is evident from examination of the explanatory variables included in the models. This demonstrated sensitivity represents a substantial improvement on previously developed (empirically estimated and validated) travel forecasting model systems. For example, the model system has these features:

1. Carpooling: The work mode-choice model includes a carpool mode in addition to drive-alone and transit modes. Other existing work mode-choice models consider automobile drivers and passengers as two separate modes, so that one cannot isolate automobiles with several passengers from those with a driver only. Analysis of special incentives to multiple-occupancy vehicles can only be performed using a model with an explicit carpool mode.

2. Automobile ownership: The automobile-ownership model is sensitive to the important transportation policy variables, whereas automobile ownership is assumed as an exogenous (independent) variable in other travel demand models. The importance of this model for the analysis of current policy thrusts is obvious: automobile ownership can be influenced by transportation policies, and these models include this effect (Lerman and Ben-Akiva 1975, Burns, Golob, and Nicolaidis 1976).

3. Trip frequency: The frequency of travel for shopping trips is not assumed constant as it is in the UTMS-1 trip-generation models.

4. Linkage of purposes: For example, the work mode choice influences nonwork travel (see table 11.3, variable 5). Thus policies that decrease automobile use for work trips increase automobile use for nonwork trips because of the increased availability of the car for nonwork trips. (For an example of the policy consequences of this interrelation see Atherton and Ben-Akiva 1977.)

5. Market segments: The automobile-ownership model was originally estimated using a number of market segments: (i) single-person households without children, blue collar; (ii) same, white collar; (iii) young married households without children, both blue and white collar; (iv) households with children, blue collar; (v) same, white collar; (vi) older married households without children, both white and blue collar; (vii) households without workers. The other models also use a richer set of socioeconomic variables than previous UTMS-1 models. Such segmentation allows for a better understanding of how various population groups will respond to a given policy option.

Explicit behavioral theory

The models are based on explicit hypotheses about individual choice behavior in which travel demand is seen as a process arising directly from individual decision makers' choices. Every observed trip is the result of a selection made by either a household or an individual traveler from some set of feasible choices.

Explicit treatment of multiple dimensions of choice

The models are based on an explicit theory of choice that includes the entire set of relevant decisions as well as explicit hypotheses about the hierarchical structure of these decisions (unlike simple mode-choice models). This theory, while still not entirely implemented, has provided a basic working hypothesis within which the various models operate.

Valid and efficient estimation methods

The models are based on the state of the art in econometric theory; each uses the multinomial logit model and is calibrated from disaggregate data. This reduces the amount of data needed to develop the models and fully exploits the information available from a given survey data set. In contrast, more aggregate modeling approaches lose a great deal of the variability inherent in existing data by grouping observations at the zone level. (As pointed out above, most models were estimated from 800–1,400 observations.)

In estimating disaggregate models in the Netherlands, an analysis of the effect of sample size on the reliability of the estimated coefficients was performed (Richards and Ben-Akiva 1975). For an MNL mode-choice model with ten coefficients, it was found that while samples of less than 250 observations resulted in very unstable coefficients, the standard errors of the estimated coefficients were decreased sharply by increasing the sample size gradually from 100–150 to 250–300 observations. Beyond 300 the incremental reductions in standard errors with increasing sample size were much smaller and gradually diminishing. Disaggregate models are clearly very attractive from the perspective of data-collection economics.

Practicality
The set of models is designed to be integrated into a coherent forecasting system for use in "production" travel forecasting, and it has been used in a variety of applications. The independent variables describing the attributes of the alternatives faced by decision makers are all measurable rather than perceived quantities, and the variables describing the decision makers themselves are observable socioeconomic characteristics.

Explanatory power
These models employ a greater variety of explanatory behavioral variables than other available models. The improved specifications, based on the explicit behavioral theory and the treatment of choice dimensions, and the use of valid estimation methods have resulted in a high degree of transferability between quite distinct urban areas. It had been hypothesized that because disaggregate models are based on household or individual information and do not depend on specific zone systems, their coefficients should be transferable among urban areas. A disaggregate mode-choice model sensitive to several key socioeconomic factors has yielded statistically equivalent estimates of coefficients of the level-of-service variables from quite different urban areas (Atherton and Ben-Akiva 1976).

APPLICATIONS
This set of models has been used in a number of policy and planning studies, directly or with various degrees of modification. Our purpose in summarizing these applications is to emphasize that disaggregate models developed with explicit choice hierarchies are practical tools for analysis. They are no longer the research frontier but are production methods (Ben-Akiva 1977, Ben-Akiva, Lerman, and Manheim 1976).

The models have been applied in a range of aggregate forecasting procedures, including manual calculations, sampling, and classification (see section 4.7).

Manual calculations have been done using the models directly or using the incremental logit form or simply elasticities for approximate predictions (section 4.6; see also Cambridge Systematics 1976c, Ben-Akiva and Atherton 1977).

The method of applying the models to a sample of households and expanding the results to obtain an aggregate forecast has been used in several studies concerned primarily with low-capital options such as pricing policies (Cambridge Systematics 1976b, Small 1977). There are procedures for updating an existing sample on the basis of available or forecasted aggregate socioeconomic data, such as might be obtained from a census (Duguay, Jung, and McFadden 1976). To develop a model to be used for a national transportation policy analysis in which a number of urban areas were to be represented in simplified fashion, Watanatada and Ben-Akiva (1978) utilized a Monte Carlo simulation to synthesize a sample from available aggregate data. Manheim, Furth, and Salomon (1977) used a similar procedure in developing pocket-calculator methods for bus-route planning.

Classification based on market segmentation has been used in conjunction with such network-analysis software as the Urban Transportation Planning System (UTPS) (UMTA 1976b, Ben-Akiva et al. 1977; see also section 11.6).

The models have been applied in several major studies:

1. A policy study for the U.S. Federal Energy Administration examined the effects of alternative programs of carpooling incentives. Washington, D.C., and Birmingham, Alabama, were used as prototype cities. The sampling method of aggregation was used (Cambridge Systematics 1976b).

2. Another policy study for the Federal Energy Administration examined the effects of various types of parking restrictions (Cambridge Systematics 1976d).

3. Several planning studies of auto-restricted zones have been carried out for the U.S. Urban Mass Transportation Administration (UMTA). The models were used to predict the effects of various auto-restricted zone concepts in selected cities, as part of the process of selecting sites and implementation strategies for a federally sponsored demonstration program (Sherman, Atherton, and Pecknold 1976).

4. A study of research and development priorities for urban travel

modeling was done for the U.S. Department of Transportation. The models were implemented in the UTPS software, together with versions of the conventional UTMS-1 models. Using Washington, D.C., as a case study, forecasts were made of the effects on travel of a variety of automobile and transit policies (Ben-Akiva et al. 1977).

Models similar to the Washington models have been developed and used in a variety of applications for both detailed analyses and simpler sketch-planning analyses:

5. For assessing alternative transit strategies for Regina, Saskatchewan, models were used in a manual sketch-planning mode (Kocur, Rushfeldt, and Millican 1977).

6. To assist UMTA in establishing research and development priorities, a planning study of automated guideway transit strategies was done for Milwaukee. The models were used in conjunction with UTPS in both sketch-planning and detailed network-analysis approaches (Kocur et al. 1977).

7. Models for predicting the demand for demand-responsive transit were developed using data from Haddonfield, New Jersey, and Rochester, New York (Lerman et al. 1977).

8. For an agency planning a "people-mover" system for internal circulation within the Los Angeles CBD, models were developed for predicting, for peak-period trips, choice of parking lot and egress mode (travel from parking to destination) for arrival by automobile and egress mode for arrival by transit, and for noon-hour trips, frequency, destination, and mode of within-CBD trips (modes include walking, minibus, and people-mover systems) (Barton-Aschman Associates and Cambridge Systematics 1976, Cambridge Systematics 1978).

9. For the Federal Energy Administration, many of these models were synthesized into a variety of simple procedures to be used by local officials in planning energy conservation measures; these procedures involved simple pencil-and-paper methods as well as computerized methods (Cambridge Systematics 1976c).

10. The government of the Netherlands also sponsored development of disaggregate models (Ben-Akiva and Richards 1975), followed by application to a conventional urban transportation study (Richards and Ben-Akiva 1975).

11.6 TOWARD NEW MODEL SYSTEMS

11.6.1 The MTC System

A complete regional model system has been developed for the San

Francisco Bay Area's Metropolitan Transportation Commission (MTC) for use in areawide planning studies (Cambridge Systematics 1977a, Ruiter and Ben-Akiva 1977). This system is the first of a new generation of urban travel forecasting model systems that will be more flexible and more sensitive to human behavior and current policy issues than the first-generation models, UTMS-1. Similar systems are under development for Amsterdam and other regions in the Netherlands.

The models in the MTC system were developed from home-interview survey data collected in the Bay Area in 1965. For forecasting purposes two alternative approaches are used: For regional analyses the estimated models typical of areawide long-range planning were incorporated in the U.S. Department of Transportation's UTPS software (UMTA 1976b), forming a new system, MTCFCST. For short-range, quick-response analyses of a wide range of transportation policies an alternative analysis system was also developed.

The structure of the demand models is shown in figure 11.4. The input to the travel forecasting process comes from a previously developed regional land-use allocation model, the PLUM system, which predicts the locations of jobs, housing stock, and residential location choices. In MTCFCST the demand models shown in the figure interface with the network-equilibration (traffic-assignment) procedures of UTPS and are used in conjunction with appropriate aggregation procedures.

The design of the MTC system builds on the previously described concepts but incorporates a number of features and approximations that were necessary to produce a practical regional forecasting system within tight budget and time constraints. The following excerpts from the paper by Ruiter and Ben-Akiva (1977) describe the basic system:

There are two mobility blocks, one for households with workers and one for households without workers; and the residential location and housing type choices are external to the present model development effort, as they are predicted by the previously developed PLUM system (which also predicts income distributions and work force by zone).

The first mobility choice block distinguishes between primary and secondary workers in a household. Each household with workers has only one primary worker, or breadwinner. All additional workers are termed secondary.

The modelling system deals separately with home-based and non-home-based trips. This simplifies the representation of trip chains (a trip from home, followed by one or more non-home-based trips, followed finally by a trip to home), an area in which basic conceptual development is continuing (Adler 1976). Also, it allows the model system to deal with one-way trips, in accordance with practice, rather

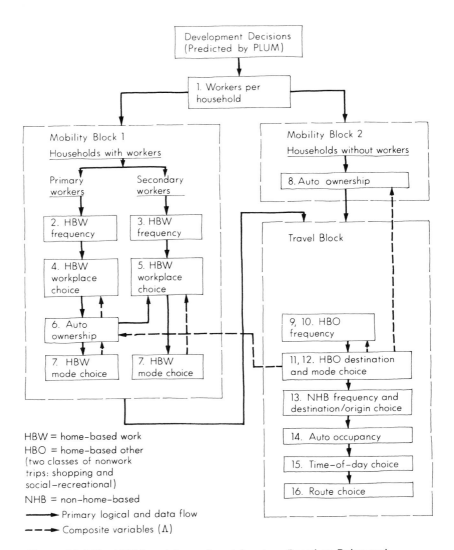

Figure 11.4 The MTC travel demand model system. Based on Ruiter and Ben-Akiva (1977).

than with the round trips more commonly considered in disaggregate modelling.

For a number of closely related travel decisions for which joint models have been previously predicted [*sic*], a series of sequential, rather than joint, models has been developed. Examples are auto ownership and mode choice for primary workers, and nonwork trip frequency, destination, and mode choice. However, due to the structures of these sequential models [see next paragraph], joint effects are not ignored.

There are exceptions to the hierarchy indicated by the solid arrows connecting the models [in figure 11.4]. These are shown by the [dashed] arrows. Each of these represents an accessibility-like [composite] variable in the higher-level model (auto ownership for households without workers, for example) which is obtained from a lower-level model (home-based other destination and mode choice). Each of these variables is based on the full set of variables of the lower-level model. [These are the A composite variables defined in section 11.3.4.] An example of such a variable is the natural logarithm of the denominator of the work mode choice model, which is used as a variable in the work destination choice models. These variables allow consistent representation of level-of-service effects in spite of the sequential structure of the separate models.

The time-of-day decision is modelled using historical peaking characteristics rather than a choice model based on the relationship between peak and off-peak transportation system characteristics.

The vehicle occupancy choice decision for nonwork travel is made using historically observed rates rather than disaggregate choice models.

The route choice decision is modelled using conventional capacity restraint assignment techniques. . . .

The trip purposes used in model development are:

• Home-based work trips (HBW): All trips between home and work are included.
• Home-based shopping trips (HBSH): Shopping is used in a generalized sense to include also medical-dental, business-related, and serve-passenger purposes. All trips between home and any of these purposes are included.
• Home-based social-recreational trips (HBSR): Social-recreational trips include [outside meals,] visiting, and recreational purposes. All trips between home and any of these purposes are included.
• Non-home-based trips (NHB): All trips which do not begin or end at home are included.

These four purpose groups include all surveyed trips except school trips.

The modes considered in the models include auto and pickup drivers and passengers, as well as all bus, streetcar, railroad, and jitney trips.

Trips by truckers and taxi drivers and passengers, and walkers, are not represented by models.

In addition to the basic system, a computerized procedure that applies a subset of MTC travel demand models was developed (called

SRGP for short-range generalized policy analysis). The sampling approach to aggregation described in section 4.7 was used:

The procedure is designed to produce rapid turnaround estimates of the consequences of broadly defined transportation policy options. SRGP processing and outputs are based on an input sample of home interview survey households. The program estimates the travel behavior of the individual households subject to user-controlled facilities for expanding the results in whatever manner is appropriate for the problem universe. This approach takes full advantage of the disaggregate nature of the demand models. Aggregation does not take place until the expansion, after all estimation is complete, and can be straightforward and without bias. (Ruiter and Ben-Akiva 1977)

The MTC system is an important new direction:

[It] represents the first production-oriented system developed for use by a metropolitan planning organization which is based on a consistent theory of traveller behavior and disaggregate model estimation. These models represent a workable compromise between behavioral theory, ability to calibrate, and ability to obtain aggregate travel estimates, given reasonable time and computer cost constraints. Validation of the models has been performed at the disaggregate level for the component models, and at the aggregate level for the entire model system. Application procedures have also been developed both for detailed network analyses and for short-range generalized policy analysis. (Ruiter and Ben-Akiva 1977)

11.6.2 Freight Policy Analysis System

Modeling approaches in freight transportation analysis were also strongly influenced by the concepts of UTMS-1. For example, the first major model system for national transportation planning in a developing country, the Harvard-Brookings model system (HBMS), incorporated a UTMS-1 type of structure, although with many important and insightful changes (Kresge and Roberts 1971).

As new approaches to urban passenger travel analysis have evolved, so also have new approaches to freight analysis. A particularly enlightening example is the use of disaggregate models together with structured sample aggregation for analysis of national policies in the freight sector; this is directly related to the SRGP system summarized above. This system was used to analyze national freight transportation policies designed to reduce energy consumption (Roberts et al. 1976; see also volume 2).

11.7 SUMMARY

Travel demand is the result of a complex behavioral process. To produce valid, credible, policy-sensitive forecasts requires behavioral models based on sound theories and valid statistical estimation procedures. Only such causally structured and carefully estimated models can be used to trace out the impacts a change in transportation service has on a population composed of individual travelers, households, shippers, and firms, each characterized by a unique set of circumstances.

11.7.1 Choice Dimensions and Their Implications

The basic choices open to the consumer comprise a vector with many components. Some of the choices are made often and change repeatedly; others are made infrequently and remain stable over long periods of time. To represent consumer behavior adequately transportation demand functions should be able to predict how consumers will change their choices, over these multiple dimensions, in response to changing conditions. There may be several demand functions to deal with the full set of choices. Important issues are how the dimensions of choice are grouped in the various demand functions and, when more than one demand function is used, how the several separate functions are related so that they are consistent in the ways they represent consumer behavior.

11.7.2 Simultaneous versus Sequential Choice Structures

At both aggregate and disaggregate levels it is possible to define a demand function in which all choices are dealt with simultaneously. Alternatively a set of functions can be defined that deals with the several choice dimensions sequentially.

The example of choice of destination and mode was used to illustrate these functions. At the aggregate level a simultaneous demand function would show the number of consumers choosing each combination of destination and mode. A sequential demand function would consist of two functions. The first would predict the number choosing each destination; the second would predict, for each destination, the fraction of those choosing the destination who would choose each mode. The two functions could then be combined to give the number choosing each mode and destination combination. The opposite sequence could also be used, with the number choosing each mode predicted first, then the fraction of those using a particular mode who would choose each destination. The two sets of sequential functions in the example are such that they give the same results as the simultaneous-choice functions.

At the disaggregate level sample stochastic models indicated the conditions under which the parts of a sequential form would give the same result as a simultaneous form: multiplying the two parts of the sequential form should yield a joint probability function for all values of the variables of interest. Ideally a single simultaneous demand function would be developed which included all relevant choice dimensions. Because this is impractical, a set of demand functions must be used. Such a sequential demand function, either aggregate or disaggregate, can be constructed to be consistent with the equivalent simultaneous form by meeting the requirement that multiplying the parts of the sequential form should yield a joint probability function. As a practical consequence, conditional models are required to be fractions, or share forms, and composite variables are required to link the models.

11.7.3 UTMS-1

The basic feature of the conceptual structure of UTMS-1, the first major transportation model, is that it deals primarily with four major dimensions of choice—frequency, destination, mode, and route—and takes a sequential form. First, trip generation predicts the numbers of consumers choosing to make trips. Second, distribution predicts the number of trips to each destination. Third, mode split predicts the number of trips to each destination by each available mode. Finally, network assignment predicts the choices of paths.

While historically these have been viewed as four separate steps, they can also be visualized as corresponding to four terms in a single simultaneous-choice demand function.

Equilibration in UTMS-1 follows the four-step sequence of the demand functions. A real equilibrium is rarely computed, however, since in only a small number of transportation studies are consistent values of the same transportation service attributes used in all steps. Calibration procedures involve a mixture of simple statistical methods and manual adjustments.

Numerous variations on UTMS-1 have been developed in several countries, but none has altered the basic conceptual structure or resolved its fundamental limitations.

The discussion suggested numerous specific directions for improvement, focusing primarily on making the choice structure explicit and consistent.

11.7.4 New Directions

Substantial progress is being made on the development and implementation of practical travel demand forecasting procedures that are behaviorally sound and policy-relevant. This chapter has illustrated some major directions of production model development. Particular attention has been given to disaggregate models with explicit behavioral assumptions about choice hierarchies.

Such models share a common set of characteristics, both in their theoretical underpinnings and in their implementation:

1. policy relevance and sensitivity;
2. an explicit behavioral theory;
3. an explicit treatment of the multiple dimensions of choice;
4. valid and efficient estimation methods;
5. practicality; and
6. explanatory power.

TO READ FURTHER

For surveys of recent developments see Domencich and McFadden (1975), which also has a good historical review, Ben-Akiva, Lerman, and Manheim (1976), McFadden (1976), Ben-Akiva (1977), or Spear (1977). On UTMS-1 see Hutchinson (1974), Stopher and Meyburg (1975), and UMTA (1976b). For a critical appraisal of the implications of UTMS-1 assumptions see Brand and Manheim (1973) and Ben-Akiva et al. (1977). For approaches in the United Kingdom see A. G. Wilson (1973). On consistency see Manheim (1970c, 1973b), Ben-Akiva (1973, 1974), Ben-Akiva and Lerman (1977), and Williams (1977). For current progress in this rapidly developing area see the following serial publications: *Transportation Research Record, Transportation Research, Transportation,* and the *Journal of Transportation Economics and Policy.*

EXERCISES

11.1(E) Compare the forms in table 11.1 with the several gravity models presented in section 4.3.1. Discuss.

11.2(C) You have been asked by the Minister of Transport of Freelandia to prepare a quick (three-month) appraisal of alternative transportation policies for the capital city Praysopolis. At present the country and especially the capital are undergoing rapid economic development, with incomes rising and a large middle class emerging as workers' real incomes rise and the service sector grows.

The staff of the ministry has established a transport network with data base and conventional UTMS-type models. The minister is especially concerned about the influence of rising incomes on automobile ownership and use. He believes that as incomes rise, each family will want to acquire an automobile as soon as it can afford to do so. This is a symbol of economic achievement and status, and the national government does not want to block the widespread distribution of this symbolic good, important politically as a symbol of achievement by all economic classes. Besides, only the most heavy fiscal disincentives could significantly retard the rate of acquisition of automobiles, and these would not be politically feasible. In addition, the automobile does provide dramatically increased mobility for social and recreational purposes, especially for holiday and weekend travel to the countryside, which contributes symbolically and actually to the increasing "quality of life." Potentially realistic policy objectives might therefore be to try to maintain the present high level of public transport use for home-to-work trips and/or to reduce as much as possible the incentives to acquire more than one automobile per household.

a. What specific policies and plans might be considered and tested as possible means of achieving these objectives?
i. Identify component actions (transportation and activity system).
ii. Identify major strategy alternatives.
iii. Identify six most promising alternatives for detailed analysis. Describe why you believe them to be "most promising."

b. Obviously the demand models required to test such strategies must be more responsive than the conventional UTMS-1 models. Why would the UTMS-1 models be unsatisfactory for testing such policies? (*Hint:* What assumptions do conventional UTMS models make about the influence of transportation- and activity-system policies on automobile ownership? On the use of automobiles for work trips? on the differences between the decision to purchase the first automobile per household and the decision to purchase the second? on the influence of automobile ownership decisions on residential location and job location decisions? What modes would be relevant in a rapidly developing country?)

c. Sketch out a system of models that would be sensitive to the policies and behavior you think would occur.
i. Identify all significant variables and specify in equation form the relationships among variables.
ii. Indicate which variables are likely to be available from relatively conventional data sources such as home interview surveys.
iii. Eliminate all other variables and display the new set of relationships in equation form.

iv. Since you have only three months, there is no time for data collection and analysis. Establish a set of models for specific production use, making judgments about magnitudes and signs of relevant parameters and showing interrelationships of models (if any).

12
Travel-Market Equilibration in Networks

12.1 INTRODUCTION

Transportation deals with space; a person or thing is transported because there is more value received in one location than in another. As a practical matter, transportation is not ubiquitous; some areas are served well by transportation, others poorly or not at all. In developing a transportation strategy, decisions about the spatial aspects of transportation are of fundamental importance: where to locate what types of facilities, and what services to operate over those facilities.

As described in section 7.7, a transportation network consists of a set of fixed facilities and services operated over those facilities. Such a network can be described as a set of links, routes, paths, and nodes. A link is a facility over which vehicles may move; a route is the path followed by one or several vehicles; a path is the route or routes used by a passenger in moving from an initial origin to a final destination; and a node is a point at which two or more links and/or routes come together. In this chapter we shall use the term link in a general sense: if a service exists, over appropriate routes and facilities, between two nodes, we shall represent that service by a link.

The structure of the network in a region influences the way in which the equilibrium of service and demand is reached, as illustrated by the following examples:

1. Does the traveler or shipper have a direct path available from origin to destination, or is only a circuitous path available? For example, in many regions of the world the road network is very sparse, so that there is only one possible path between two cities.

2. Is there direct service between two points, without stops or deviations of route, or must the traveler stop at several intermediate points, or perhaps even transfer? For example, is there direct nonstop air service between cities A and B, or must the passenger traveling from A to B stop also at C and D; or when he reaches C, must he change to another aircraft to fly on to B?

3. Similarly, does an ocean freighter carry freight directly from A to B, or does it stop at many ports on the way, picking up and discharging

cargo at each, before eventually delivering a shipment to B?

In preceding chapters (except chapter 7) we have ignored such issues. In essence, we have assumed there is one origin and one destination between which travel flows, and that this flow moves over a single facility—a highway, rail line, transit line, air route, inland waterway, or shipping route. That is, we have assumed that the transportation system of a region consists of one link.

Real transportation systems will amost always consist of a number of links, connecting various combinations of possible origins and destinations of flow. In general, the transportation system of any particular region is a complex network of facilities, with many origin and destination nodes and many links. (There may be 5,000–10,000 links in the transportation system of a single urban area.) It may at times be reasonable to ignore the complexity of that network and to assume for the purposes of analysis that the system can be represented by a single link. However, in a large number of situations this assumption will not be acceptable, and it will be important to include the complexity of the network in some detail in the analysis.

When there is more than one link in the system, or more than one possible pair of origins and destinations between which flows will occur, the following conditions arise:

1. In moving between a particular origin A and a particular destination B, a flow will generally use a path between A and B with more than one link.

2. There will generally be more than one possible path between origin A and destination B.

3. The volume over any specific link will generally be composed of flows from several origins to several destinations; thus these flows compete for the link's capacity.

Therefore, in considering real transportation systems in a region, the concepts of service, demand, and equilibrium must be extended to take into account the multiple links traversed by a flow along a single path, the multiplicity of paths connecting origins to destinations, and the way in which flows from different origins to various destinations compete for the capacities of the same links in the network. The result is that the travel-market equilibrium reached depends significantly on the structure of the network.

As we shall see in section 12.5, these conditions lead to relatively complex computational problems. Thus, as a practical matter, it is often necessary to make simplifying assumptions in order to incorporate the spatial structure of the transportation system of a region into the analysis at a reasonable cost in computational resources. When one begins exploring the approximations that might be made, one is often forced to consider as well the degree of emphasis that should be given to the various types of interrelationships between the transportation and activity systems.

In chapter 1 three basic types of relationships were identified: (1) travel-market equilibration, (2) activity-system equilibration, and (3) operator equilibration. As part of the process of weighing the simplifying assumptions and approximations that will be made in a particular transportation analysis, the analyst must consider not only the problem of modeling the travel-market equilibrium within the structure of the network, but also the relative importance of including explicitly the type 2 and type 3 relationships.

Thus, although the basic concepts of equilibrium between service and demand developed in preceding chapters are relatively simple, significant approximations and assumptions are required to model a transportation system realistically. In this chapter we shall introduce the issues involved in finding travel-market equilibrium in networks.

12.2 BASIC ISSUES

There are two central conceptual issues in finding equilibrium flows in networks. First, there is **consumer behavior:** Each consumer (passenger or shipper of freight) has a choice of a number of paths through the network; each path is characterized by a vector of service attributes. It is necessary to describe the behavioral basis by which consumers choose one path from out of all the many paths available.

Second, there is the **influence of network structure:** In general, there are many consumers going from many different origins to many destinations. These users compete for the services available on the various links. If service functions for the links in a system were such that travel times and other service attributes were constant regardless of the volume of users of each facility, this competition would not be a problem; the decisions made by any single consumer would have no effect on other consumers. As we saw in chapters 5–7, however, the service functions are such that service levels generally decrease with increasing volumes. Therefore the service attributes that influence consumer A's choice of a path depend on the choices made by other consumers, and vice versa. Thus consumers compete for the services available from different links, and these competitive interactions are influenced by the structure of the network.

These two conceptual issues must be dealt with explicitly in formulating a travel-market equilibrium flow pattern.

12.3 THE BEHAVIORAL BASIS OF PATH CHOICE

In chapter 11 we emphasized the fact that any given consumer must deal with a complex multidimensional bundle of choices; the choice of a route may be quite closely related to choice of mode and destination, and even of whether to make a trip.

12.3.1 An Individual Stochastic View

We shall start by taking the stochastic disaggregate view. The probability that a consumer will choose alternative i is

$$p(i : I) = g(\mathbf{X}^1, \mathbf{X}^2, ..., \mathbf{X}^i, ...), \tag{12.1}$$

where $\mathbf{X}^i$ is a vector of attributes of both alternative i and the consumer, or, considering alternative combinations of frequency f, destination d, mode m, and path r out of the set (F, D, M, R) (Manheim 1970c, 1973d),

$$p(f, d, m, r : F, D, M, R) = g(\{\mathbf{X}^{f,d,m,r}\} \text{ for every } f, d, m, r \in F, D, M, R). \tag{12.2}$$

The probability of choosing a path r, given that a decision has been made to make a trip ($f^0 = 1$) to a particular destination d^0 by a particular mode m^0, is the conditional probability given by

$$p(r \mid f^0, d^0, m^0) = \frac{p(r, f^0, d^0, m^0)}{p(f^0, d^0, m^0)}, \tag{12.3}$$

where $p(r, f^0, d^0, m^0)$ is given by (12.2) and

$$p(f^0, d^0, m^0) = \sum_{r'} p(f^0, d^0, m^0, r') \tag{12.4}$$

(see appendix B). Thus the path-choice behavior of consumers is a facet of the general multidimensional choice behavior discussed in chapter 11.

If each alternative i in (12.1) is characterized by a utility that includes a random component ε (see section 2.5.2),

$$U_i = U_i(\mathbf{X}^1, \mathbf{X}^2, ..., \mathbf{X}^i, ...) = u_i + \varepsilon, \tag{12.5}$$

then

$$p(i : I) = p\{U_i > U_j \quad \text{for all } j \in I\}. \tag{12.6}$$

We noted in chapter 2 that particular assumptions on the form of the random utility function (12.5) lead to specific probability models.

In this chapter we consider the multinomial logit model and restrict our attention to choice of destination and path; generalization is straightforward. (Because of its property of independence of irrelevant alternatives, the MNL model appears less appropriate for path choice than more complex models such as multinomial probit. See section 12.4.1.) Assume that the deterministic part of the utility is

$$u_{dr} = \alpha_0 + \alpha_1 t_{dr} + \alpha_2 a_d, \tag{12.7}$$

where t_{dr} is the travel time to d by path r, a_d is the attractiveness associated with destination d (for example, retail floor space), and the α_i are parameters. Then we have the MNL form:

$$p(r, d) = \frac{e^{u_{dr}}}{\sum\limits_{d', r'} e^{u_{d'r'}}}. \tag{12.8}$$

By basic probability theory

$$p(r \mid d) = \frac{p(r, d)}{p(d)} \tag{12.9}$$

and

$$p(d) = \sum_{r'} p(r', d) = \frac{\sum\limits_{r'} e^{u_{dr'}}}{\sum\limits_{d'} \sum\limits_{r'} e^{u_{d'r'}}}, \tag{12.10}$$

so that

$$p(r \mid d) = \frac{e^{u_{dr}}}{\sum\limits_{r'} e^{u_{dr'}}} = \frac{e^{\alpha_0} e^{\alpha_2 a_d} e^{\alpha_1 t_{dr}}}{\sum\limits_{r'} e^{\alpha_0} e^{\alpha_2 a_d} e^{\alpha_1 t_{dr'}}} \tag{12.11}$$

and

$$p(r \mid d) = \frac{e^{\alpha_1 t_{dr}}}{\sum\limits_{r'} e^{\alpha_1 t_{dr'}}}. \tag{12.12}$$

In this way path-choice behavior can be derived from multidimensional choice behavior.

12.3.2 An Individual Deterministic View
A particularly important case of (12.6) is that in which u_i is deterministic; then

$$p(i : I) = \begin{cases} 1 & \text{if } U_i > U_j \text{ for all } j, \\ 0 & \text{otherwise.} \end{cases} \tag{12.13}$$

That is, only one alternative is chosen and that with certainty. This is consumer behavior model I of chapter 2: the consumer picks the alternative that has the maximum value of utility. If there are m alternatives in subset I_m with the same value of the maximum utility U^*, then

$$p(i:I) \begin{cases} > 0 & \text{if } U_i = U^*, U^* > U_j \text{ for all } j \text{ not in } I_m, \\ = 0 & \text{if } U_i < U^*, \end{cases} \qquad (12.14)$$

$$\sum_{i' \in I_m} p(i' : I) = 1.$$

If there are N consumers with the same deterministic utility function and the volume choosing path i is V_i, then (12.14) becomes

$$V_i \begin{cases} > 0 & \text{if } U_i = U^*, U^* > U_j \text{ for all } j \text{ not in } I_m, \\ = 0 & \text{if } U_i < U^*, \end{cases} \qquad (12.15)$$

$$\sum_{i' \in I} V_{i'} = N,$$

or, equivalently,

$$\frac{V_i}{N} = p(i : I). \qquad (12.16)$$

Equations (12.15) can also be written in terms of the utilities:

$$U_i \begin{cases} = U^* & \text{if } V_i > 0, \\ < U^* & \text{if } V_i = 0. \end{cases} \qquad (12.17)$$

Applied to path choice, (12.17) is a form of **Wardrop's first principle,** a famous model in transportation systems analysis. Wardrop orginally formulated the principle in terms of a single service variable: "The journey times on all routes actually used are equal, and less than those which would be experienced by a single vehicle on an unused route" (Wardrop 1952, as quoted by Florian 1976, p. vii; Florian also quotes an earlier equivalent formulation by Knight 1924). A more precise formulation says that, "at equilibrium, no user can improve his travel time by unilaterally changing routes" (Daganzo and Sheffi 1977). (Potts and Oliver [1972] point out that this is not strictly true if some links on the routes used have a finite capacity, in which case some volume will spill over onto routes with greater times. We ignore this qualification in the following discussion.) This is sometimes called the criterion of selfishness: each user chooses the path that is best from his own perspective.

This principle corresponds to a special case of (12.14) in which utility is taken as a function of time, such as

$$U_i = -\alpha_1 t_i. \qquad (12.18)$$

Then if t^* is the time over the best (that is, least-time) path, (12.15) becomes

$$V_i \begin{cases} > 0 & \text{if } t_i = t^*, \; t^* < t_j \text{ for all } j \text{ not used,} \\ = 0 & \text{if } t_i > t^*, \end{cases} \tag{12.19}$$

which, analogously to (12.17), can be written

$$t_i \begin{cases} = t^* & \text{if } V_i > 0, \\ > t^* & \text{if } V_i = 0. \end{cases} \tag{12.20}$$

Thus users are assumed to choose only minimum-time paths; all paths with times greater than the minimum are unused.

More generally Wardrop's first principle could be formulated in terms of a general utility function, corresponding to (12.15).

Returning to the MNL model (12.12) and using t^* for the time over the best path, we have (with d suppressed)

$$
\begin{aligned}
p(r : R) &= \frac{e^{-\alpha_1 t_r}}{\sum_{r'} e^{-\alpha_1 t_{r'}}} \\
&= \frac{e^{\alpha_1 t^*}}{e^{\alpha_1 t^*}} \frac{e^{-\alpha_1 t_r}}{\sum_{r'} e^{-\alpha_1 t_{r'}}} \\
&= \frac{e^{-\alpha_1 (t_r - t^*)}}{\sum_{r'} e^{-\alpha_1 (t_{r'} - t^*)}}.
\end{aligned}
\tag{12.21}
$$

This formulation, called **multipath stochastic assignment,** was developed by Dial (1971) and has been implemented in standard urban transportation models (UMTA 1976b). In contrast to (12.19), (12.21) has the consequence that paths with times greater than t^* do have nonzero volumes.

Equations (12.21) are a special case of individual stochastic choice models. Again, in the general case utility can be a function of several service attributes. Thus a variety of stochastic and deterministic path-choice models can be formulated as special cases of the general models of consumer behavior introduced in chapter 2.

12.3.3 Network Structure: Definitions

The second key element of the travel-market equilibration problem is the influence of network structure. In this section we shall introduce some basic definitions that will help us demonstrate this influence.

Geographically a region can be considered as divided into mutually exclusive (that is, nonoverlapping) zones that cover the entire region (figure 12.1a). The activity system is then described by reference to

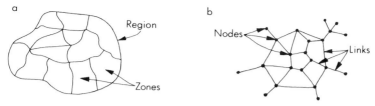

Figure 12.1 Transportation network definitions.

these zones: for example, the population (total or broken down by factors such as income class or family size) and other socioeconomic data are given on a zone-by-zone basis. Zones may be large or small, homogeneous or heterogeneous, according to the purposes of the analysis. (As discussed in section 4.7.3, zones are thus a means of constructing geographic aggregations of individual consumers.)

We have seen that the transportation system can be represented as a network consisting of links that connect nodes (figure 12.1b). (Obviously data such as fares and schedule frequencies are required in addition to the network to fully describe the transportation system of a region.) A link might be a service (a particular nonstop or multistop route), a single transportation facility (a stretch of highway, a parking lot, the facilities over which an automobile driver walks from parking lot to office door, or an aircraft loading gate at an airport terminal), or a group of such facilities or services (an airport link might represent the combination of a landing runway, a taxiway, an aircraft gate, the walkway from the gate to a baggage claim area, the wait for baggage, the path to the parking lot, and the road from the parking stall to the airport exit). Again, as with zones, the degree of detail and disaggregation depends on the purpose of the analysis. Various kinds of information useful in characterizing each link are associated with that link. The links may be uni- or bidirectional.

Two kinds of nodes can be distinguished. Some nodes simply represent the junctions of several links and have no properties associated with them. (As the above examples indicate, we assume that where a node such as a highway intersection or freight transshipment terminal does have characteristics that influence flow, that facility is represented not as a node but explicitly as a link. Thus nodes are purely geometric constructs.) However, some nodes represent the points at which flows enter or leave the network. These are called *zone centroids,* since there must be at least one such node in each zone for flow to enter or leave the zone. (These nodes may or may not be at the geographic centroid of the zones; the term is historical.)

Immediately upon introducing these concepts, we can begin to see the complexities that follow. First of all, we no longer have a single demand function to consider in the equilibrium calculation. Instead we must have a demand function for every possible combination of zone pairs. Thus if there are N zones, there are $N(N-1)$ possible combinations of zone pairs and thus the same number of demand functions. If intrazonal trips are to be considered as well, this becomes N^2; and if various time periods of flows must be considered (for example, in a metropolitan area, morning peak-period flows from residential areas to employment locations will be different from afternoon peak-period flows or flows in off-peak periods), then the number of combinations is PN^2, where P is the number of such periods. If some differentiation is to be made among the various segments of the travel market—perhaps by distinguishing M market segments (according to socioeconomic class and trip purpose for person trips, or commodity type for freight, or time of day for either), the number of combinations is PMN^2 (see section 8.4 and table 10.5). Further, the demand for transportation between each pair of zones is, of course, a function of the vector of service attributes, not just a single attribute.

Second, we can no longer assume a single service function. Each link of the network must be represented by a different service function.

Third, the problem of finding the equilibrium pattern of flows obviously becomes much more complex in a network than in the case of a single link. The large number of demand and service functions is only part of the problem; the major difficulties arise because of the way the structure of the network influences the equilibrium of service and demand.

12.3.4 The Influence of Network Structure

To illustrate the influence of network structure we shall first consider several simple examples (figure 12.2). We shall discuss multimodal networks, so that paths may include links of several modes and the choice of a path is, to some extent, also a choice of mode.

LINKS IN A PATH

Almost every trip in a transportation system passes over more than one link. Consider an urban situation in which link B is the rail transit line from a suburban station to the central business district (CBD). To get to the station the traveler must take some feeder mode from his origin to the station: automobile (as driver or as passenger), local bus, or walk. His decision about whether or not to make this trip, and whether

a Links in a path

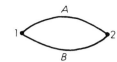
b Alternative paths

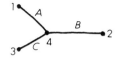
c Multiple flows sharing the same link

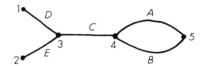
d Composite network

Figure 12.2 Some simple networks.

or not to use transit, is influenced by the level of service he experiences over the total trip, both on the access link A and the line-haul link B (see chapter 3).

Alternatively, consider an intercity air transport system in which link B represents the whole landing cycle at the destination airport (holding, approach, landing, taxiing, passenger debarking, walking from the airplane gate to the terminal, and waiting for baggage). Link A represents the line-haul portion of the trip, the airplane flight from the general area of the origin airport to the general neighborhood of the destination airport. If there is congestion at the destination airport, although the line-haul trip over link A may take only one hour, we must add to this the delays due to congestion on link B, which may in some situations amount to an hour or even more.

Thus when a path consists of two or more links in sequence, the level of service for the path as a whole will be a function of the levels of service over each of the links in the path.

From the behavioral perspective introduced in section 12.3.1, we see that we must include in any model of path-choice behavior a description of how users perceive the level of service of a path. For example, users may make choices among alternative airline paths between two cities based on the following service attributes of each path: total travel time, number of transfers, number of intermediate stops, and maximum waiting time at any transfer point. Then the total travel time over a path may be perceived as the sum of travel times over each link in the path, while the maximum waiting time is the argest of the waiting times at each transfer point.

From a policy perspective, this means that an improvement in any one link in a path may not necessarily significantly improve the level of service for the total trip, as perceived by consumers. Again referring to the intercity air transport example, if it takes one hour to go from origin to originating airport, one hour to fly from origin airport to destination airport, and one hour to go from destination airport to final destination, an increase in aircraft speed resulting in a 20 percent decrease in airport-to-airport time will yield only about a 7 percent decrease in total door-to-door trip time.

ALTERNATIVE PATHS

Almost every trip in a transportation system has a choice of several alternative paths over which to travel. For example, a passenger traveling between two cities may have a choice of going by air, rail, bus, or automobile. Each represents a separate and distinct path through the system (and there may well be several paths for each of these mode choices). Similarly a shipper of freight may choose among paths utilizing truck or rail and, in some cases, air and/or water.

In general, the level of service over each of the available paths will be different. Thus the level of service experienced on a trip from some origin 1 to a destination 2 will depend on which path is chosen through the network (*A* or *B* in figure 12.2).

From a behavioral perspective, this means that the path-choice model must explicitly indicate how alternative paths will be compared, and how the differences in path service levels will influence the choice, as illustrated in sections 12.3.1 and 12.3.2.

Practically this means that a change made in one path of a transportation system may affect not only the volume flowing over that path, but also the volume flowing over other paths. Consider an urban situation in which a new highway is constructed. The highway may attract trips over parallel paths through the public transit system. Similarly a change in transit fares or other service attributes of transit may affect the flows not only over the transit path but also over the parallel automobile paths as well.

MULTIPLE FLOWS SHARING THE SAME LINK

Almost every link in a transportation system carries flows moving along several paths and may carry flows moving among several origin-destination combinations. In figure 12.2c link B carries flows moving between 1 and 2 as well as flows moving between 3 and 2.

For example, a link representing a marine port may carry flows from many origins within a region to any of a number of destinations in other regions. And a railroad line between two points will generally carry shipments traveling between many combinations of origins and destinations.

Since the level of service over such a link is a function of the total volume over that link, and since flows from many origins to many destinations can use any given link, the level of service over a link may be a function of the volumes of flows from many origins to many destinations.

Operationally this means that a change in the characteristics of a link can influence the many different flows that use the link. For example, a single exit ramp on an expressway will be used by vehicles moving from many origins to many destinations; congestion at that ramp, or conversely steps taken to alleviate that congestion, will generally affect many of these flows. Or consider the road A-B in figure 12.2c, which provides access to an airport in the suburbs of a large city: here 1 is the airport, 2 the CBD, and 3 the nearby suburban shopping center, industrial park, and office complex. The facility is presently congested, so that air travelers coming by automobile or bus often miss their flights, because during weekday rush hours, morning and evening, link B is also used for trips between the CBD and the suburban shopping center. There is a plan to double the capacity of the present road A-B. At first glance we might think that this additional capacity should be more than adequate to handle the traffic to the airport. However, when we consider the fact that link B is shared by local trips to the suburban center, we see that the effect of the proposed addition will be very much dependent on the interactions of both sets of movements—the local trips between 2 and 3 and the airport access trips between 2 and 1.

COMPOSITE NETWORK

In almost every real transportation network all of the following features will be present: (i) a single path will traverse several links; (ii) for any origin-destination combination there will be multiple paths available; and (iii) multiple flows will share the same links. This is illustrated, in a simple case, in figure 12.2d.

In this case a change anywhere in the system can have wide-ranging effects on flows through many other elements of the system. The extent of these effects will depend on many factors: the demand functions, the service functions, the structure of the network, and the magnitude of the change that is made. To determine these effects accurately it is necessary to explicitly incorporate these elements into a framework for predicting equilibrium in networks.

12.3.5 Network Equilibrium Relationships: The Gap

In this section we shall describe the basic concepts needed to account for the spatial structure of transportation in the prediction of flows. To do this we must expand the formulation of the equilibrium problem given in chapter 1 to include explicitly the network structure and its effects. The following features must be incorporated in this expanded formulation:

1. Multiple demand functions: The area to be studied is divided into zones; there is a different demand function for each market segment, that is, for each pair of zones (an origin zone and a destination zone) as well as for different groups of consumers and for different trip purposes (passengers) or commodity types (freight). Further, the demand for transportation between each zone pair is a function of the vector of service attributes, S.

2. Multiple service functions: The transportation system is represented by a network of links and nodes. Each link of the network is represented by a different service function. Because the vector S generally has many components, both the service and demand functions are potentially very complex.

3. A procedure for finding the equilibrium pattern of flows: The calculation of the equilibrium flows is a difficult problem because the level of service perceived on a trip between two zones depends on the path taken through the network; the level of service over any path is a function of the levels of service over each of the links in that path (for example, trip time equals the sum of the times over each link in the path); the level of service over a link is a function of the total volume over that link (as given by that link's service function); and the total volume over a link is composed, in general, of flows between many different zone pairs.

As a consequence of these features, the equilibrium flow pattern is not unique; a mechanism of trip behavior must be known or assumed in order to determine a unique equilibrium. Further, the actual computational procedures may be difficult and expensive for large networks.

To take these elements into account we must begin with the service and demand functions. We shall use the following notational conventions:

V^{kd} = volume from k to d (or between k and d if flows go both ways),
V_y = flow volume moving over link y,
V_y^{kd} = volume over link y going from k to d,

and similarly for other variables such as S.

The demand function will relate the volume of flow from origin zone k to destination zone d to the level of service experienced by that flow and also to the levels of activity at k (Y_k) and at d (Z_d) and some appropriate parameters β. In an analysis covering several market segments, the parameters will be different for each segment e. The total demand V^{kd} will be determined by the demand functions of the various market segments:

$$V_e^{kd} = D(\{S^{k'd'}\}, \{Y_{k'}\}, \{Z_{d'}\} \text{ for every } k', d'; \beta_e),$$ (12.22)

$$V^{kd} = \sum_{e'} V_{e'}^{kd}.$$ (12.23)

We shall write

$$V^{kd} = D(S^{kd})$$ (12.24)

for simplicity, assuming that the function D has taken into account the characteristics of k and d relative to all other zones, the market segments, and so forth. Of course, we need relationships (12.22) or (12.23) for every combination of origin and destination zones in the region.

The service function will relate the level of service experienced by flows over a particular link y to the volume of flow over that link, V_y, and to the options T_y and parameters α_y that characterize the link:

$$S_y = J(V_y; T_y, \alpha_y)$$ (12.25)

or

$$S_y = J_y(V_y),$$ (12.26)

which we will write as

$$S_y = J(V_y).$$ (12.27)

(Note that in the most generalized formulation the entire flow pattern may influence the level of service over a particular link. See Dafermos 1976.) Obviously we need a service function (12.25) or (12.27) for every link y in the network.

These two sets of relationships define the basic service and demand portions of the prediction problem. However, they are not sufficient by themselves, since the demand relationship is expressed only in terms of interzonal flows, $F^{kd} = (V^{kd}, S^{kd})$, and the service relationship is expressed only in terms of link flows, $F_y = (V_y, S_y)$. The problem is to relate these, as shown in figure 12.3: the link volumes and interzonal volumes must be related, and also the link and interzonal levels of service.

To build these relations we start from our definition of a path from k to d as the series of links traversed by a flow from origin node k to destination node d, so that a trip from k to d can generally take any of a number of paths. To indicate what use will be made of these various alternative paths we must also define a **_flow distribution rule_** Ψ, which is a description of path-choice behavior and thus a part of the demand function. Many alternative flow distribution rules are possible (see section 12.4). Such a rule has three components:

Ψ_1: a description of how the service level of a path is related to the service levels of links in that path;

Ψ_2: a description of how the service level between each origin-destination pair of zones is related to the service levels of each path; and

Ψ_3: a description of how the volume choosing each path, and the total volume from k to d, is affected by the service levels of all the available paths.

As an example we shall return to the simple networks introduced in section 12.3.4 and assume a particular flow distribution rule. Then in section 12.5.1 we shall introduce the formal structure of the full equilibrium formulation.

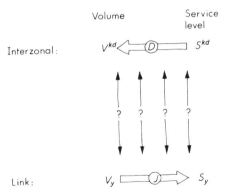

Figure 12.3 Network equilibrium relationships: The gap. Based on a 1971 lecture presentation by A. Scheffer Lang.

478 Travel-Market Equilibration in Networks

12.3.6 Equilibrium Formulations for Some Simple Networks

In the following examples flow is assumed to be two-way. The networks are those discussed in section 12.3.4. As a flow distribution rule $\mathcal{V}$ we shall use Wardrop's first principle (section 12.3.2). We shall assume that all flows are the total two-directional volumes by all market segments: V^{kd} is the total flow from k to d plus the flow from d to k. Further, we shall hold V^{kd} constant, exogenous to the analysis.

We shall use flow variables—times and volumes—defined for links, for paths, and for zone pairs. Then the components of $\mathcal{V}$ are:

$\mathcal{V}_1$: the travel time over a path is the sum of travel times over all links in the path (this is implicit in Wardrop's first principle);

$\mathcal{V}_2$: the travel time for an origin-destination pair (k, d) is the minimum travel time of all the paths between k and d; and

$\mathcal{V}_3$: the flow volume V^{kd} is distributed over the various paths in such a way that nonzero volumes move over paths with the minimum travel time, and volumes over all other paths are zero (see equations (12.15) and (12.17)); link capacities are assumed infinite.

LINKS IN A PATH

This case illustrates how the total travel time t_p along a path from origin k to destination d will be the sum of the times over each of the links in that path (figure 12.2a).

i. Basic variables:
link flow patterns: t_A, t_B, V_A, V_B,
interzonal flow patterns: t^{12}, V^{12} ($V^{13} = V^{23} = 0$),
path flow patterns: t_1^{12}, V_1^{12}.
(We assume that no flow enters or leaves the network at node 3.)

ii. Demand: $V^{12} = D(t^{12})$.

iii. Service: $t_A = J_A(V_A)$,
$\qquad\qquad t_B = J_B(V_B)$.

iv. Path service level ($\mathcal{V}_1$): We first note that there is only one path from 1 to 2: $p = 1$. We then find the total level of service over this path, t_1^{12}, by summing the travel times over the links in the path:
$t_1^{12} = t_A + t_B$.

v. Origin-destination service level ($\mathcal{V}_2$): Since there is only one path, the service level for (k, d) is the service level of that path:
$t^{12} = t_1^{12}$.

vi. Distribution over paths ($\mathcal{V}_3$): Again, because there is only one path, all the flow is on that path: $V_1^{12} = V^{12}$.

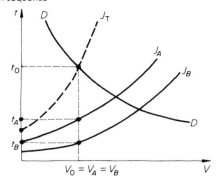

a Links in sequence

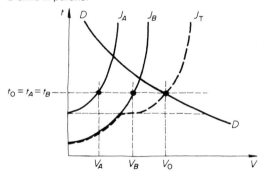

b Links in parallel

Figure 12.4 Graphical solutions of simple networks.

vii. Link volumes: $V_A = V_1^{12}$,
$$V_B = V_1^{12}.$$

There are eight equations in eight unknowns; these can be solved analytically or graphically (see figure 12.4a) for the equilibrium flows V_0^{12} and t_0^{12}. The graphical solution shows how the two service functions, for links in sequence, add along the time axis to yield a composite service function J_T (composite in the sense that it represents the combined effects of the two link service functions).

The interrelations are shown more clearly when we take advantage of the fact that

$$V_A = V_B = V_1^{12} \equiv V_0$$

and reduce the set of equations to the following:

$$V_0 = D(t_A + t_B),$$
$$t_A = J_A(V_0),$$
$$t_B = J_B(V_0).$$

ALTERNATIVE PATHS

This case illustrates how Ψ operates to distribute flow among alternative paths; here the distribution is such that the travel times over all paths used are equal (figure 12.2b).

i. Basic variables:

link flow patterns: t_A, t_B, V_A, V_B,

interzonal flow patterns: t^{12}, V^{12}.

There are two paths between 1 and 2: $p = 1, 2$, for links A and B, respectively, so:

path flow patterns: t_1^{12}, t_2^{12}, V_1^{12}, V_2^{12}.

ii. Demand: $V^{12} = D(t^{12})$.

iii. Service: $t_A = J_A(V_A),$
$$t_B = J_B(V_B).$$

iv. Path service levels (Ψ_1): $t_1^{12} = t_A,$
$$t_2^{12} = t_B.$$

v. Origin-destination service levels and distribution over paths (Ψ_2, Ψ_3): Flow is distributed such that the levels of service over all paths used are equal. That is, the path travel time equals the origin-destination time if that path is used; if not, it is greater:

$$t_1^{12} \begin{cases} = t^{12} & \text{if } V_1^{12} > 0, \\ > t^{12} & \text{if } V_1^{12} = 0, \end{cases}$$

$$t_2^{12} \begin{cases} = t^{12} & \text{if } V_2^{12} > 0, \\ > t^{12} & \text{if } V_2^{12} = 0, \end{cases}$$

$$V_1^{12} + V_2^{12} = V^{12}.$$

vi. Link volumes: $V_A = V_1^{12},$
$$V_B = V_2^{12}.$$

There are ten equations in ten unknowns; they can be solved analytically or graphically (by trying various assumptions about which path combinations are used; see figure 12.4b). In this case the graphical solution shows how the two service functions add along the volume axis to form a composite function J_T.

The interrelations are shown more clearly when the equations are simplified to the following:

$$V_A + V_B = D(t^{12}),$$
$$t_A = J_A(V_A),$$
$$t_B = J_B(V_B),$$
$$t_A = t^{12} \text{ if } V_A > 0,$$
$$t_B = t^{12} \text{ if } V_B > 0.$$

MULTIPLE FLOWS SHARING THE SAME LINK

This case illustrates how the volume of flow over a single link (B) is built up from flows between several origin-destination pairs (figure 12.2c).

i. Basic variables:

link flow patterns: t_A, t_B, t_C, V_A, V_B, V_C,

interzonal flow patterns: t^{12}, t^{23}, V^{12}, V^{23} ($V^{13} = 0$ by assumption),

path flow patterns: t_1^{12}, t_1^{23}, V_1^{12}, V_1^{23}.

(We assume that no flow enters or leaves the network at node 4.)

ii. Demand: $V^{12} = D_{12}(t^{12})$,
$$V^{23} = D_{23}(t^{23}).$$

iii. Service: $t_A = J_A(V_A)$
$$t_B = J_B(V_B)$$
$$t_C = J_C(V_C)$$

iv. Path service levels $(\mathscr{V}_1)$: We note that there is only one path for each origin-destination pair:
$$t_1^{12} = t_A + t_B,$$
$$t_1^{23} = t_C + t_B.$$

v. Origin-destination service levels $(\mathscr{V}_2)$:
$$t^{12} = t_1^{12},$$
$$t^{23} = t_1^{23}.$$

vi. Distribution over paths $(\mathscr{V}_3)$:
$$V_1^{12} = V^{12},$$
$$V_1^{23} = V^{23}.$$

vii. Link volumes:
$$V_A = V_1^{12},$$
$$V_B = V_1^{12} + V_1^{23},$$
$$V_C = V_1^{23}.$$

There are fourteen equations in fourteen unknowns. The set of equations can in principle be solved algebraically, though not graphically. The form of the interrelationships can be seen from the following simplified set of equations:
$$V_A = D_{12}(t_A + t_B),$$
$$V_C = D_{23}(t_C + t_B),$$

$$t_A = J_A(V_A),$$
$$t_B = J_B(V_A + V_C),$$
$$t_C = J_C(V_C).$$

COMPOSITE NETWORK

This case demonstrates how all of the above phenomena interrelate (figure 12.2d).

i. Basic variables:

link flow patterns: $t_A,\ t_B,\ t_C,\ t_D,\ t_E,$
$$V_A,\ V_B,\ V_C,\ V_D,\ V_E,$$
interzonal flow patterns: $t^{15},\ t^{25};\ V^{15},\ V^{25}\ (V^{12} = 0$ by assumption),
path flow patterns: $t_1^{15},\ t_2^{15};\ V_1^{15},\ V_2^{15},$
$$t_1^{25},\ t_2^{25};\ V_1^{25},\ V_2^{25}.$$

(We assume that no flow enters or leaves the network at nodes 3 or 4.)

ii. Demand: $V^{15} = D_{15}(t^{15}),$
$$V^{25} = D_{25}(t^{25}).$$

iii. Service: $t_A = J_A(V_A),$
$$t_B = J_B(V_B),$$
$$t_C = J_C(V_C),$$
$$t_D = J_D(V_D),$$
$$t_E = J_E(V_E).$$

iv. Path service levels (Ψ_1): There are two paths for each origin-destination pair. For (1,5), $p_1^{15} = (D, C, A)$, $p_2^{15} = (D, C, B)$; for (2,5), $p_1^{25} = (E, C, A)$, $p_2^{25} = (E, C, B)$. Thus

$$t_1^{15} = t_D + t_C + t_A,$$
$$t_2^{15} = t_D + t_C + t_B,$$
$$t_1^{25} = t_E + t_C + t_A,$$
$$t_2^{25} = t_E + t_C + t_B.$$

v. Origin-destination service levels and distribution over paths ($\Psi_2,\ \Psi_3$):

$$t_1^{15} \begin{cases} = t^{15} \text{ if } V_1^{15} > 0, \\ > t^{15} \text{ if } V_1^{15} = 0, \end{cases}$$

$$t_2^{15} \begin{cases} = t^{15} \text{ if } V_2^{15} > 0, \\ > t^{15} \text{ if } V_2^{15} = 0, \end{cases}$$

$$t_1^{25} \begin{cases} = t^{25} \text{ if } V_2^{25} > 0, \\ > t^{25} \text{ if } V_2^{25} = 0, \end{cases}$$

$$t_2^{25} \begin{cases} = t^{25} \text{ if } V_2^{25} > 0, \\ > t^{25} \text{ if } V_2^{25} = 0, \end{cases}$$

$$V^{15} = V_1^{15} + V_2^{15},$$

$$V^{25} = V_1^{25} + V_2^{25}.$$

vi. Link volumes: $V_A = V_1^{15} + V_1^{25},$
$$V_B = V_2^{15} + V_2^{25},$$
$$V_C = V_1^{15} + V_2^{15} + V_1^{25} + V_2^{25},$$
$$V_D = V_1^{15} + V_2^{15},$$
$$V_E = V_1^{25} + V_2^{25}.$$

There are 22 equations in 22 unknowns; in principle they can be solved analytically, though the inequalities may make the solution quite difficult.

DISCUSSION

These examples illustrate how network structure and consumer behavior (reflected in the flow distribution rule) combine to affect the flow pattern. The interactions are, of course, even more complex in real networks. Any change in transportation or activity-system options will be reflected in changes in the service and demand functions, and potentially in the network structure as well, thus shifting the equilibrium flow pattern in sometimes complex ways. The consequences of these interactions are illustrated in the case study presented in chapter 13.

12.3.7 An Alternative Behavioral Logic (Optional Reading)

The examples in the last section were based on one flow distribution rule. As noted in section 12.3.2, this rule reflects the behavioral premise of deterministic utility maximization and the special case in which utility is a single variable, time.

For comparison, it is interesting to formulate the composite-network example from the perspective of stochastic behavior, using the MNL formulation given in section 12.3.1. The basic variables and service and path service level relationships would remain the same; but the other elements would be different. In this case, for simplicity, we assume that origin-destination demand is constant:

i. Basic variables:

link flow patterns: $t_A, t_B, t_C, t_D, t_E,$

interzonal flow patterns: $t^{15}, t^{25}, V^{15}, V^{25}$ $(V^{12} = 0),$

path flow patterns: $t_1^{15}, t_2^{15}, V_1^{15}, V_2^{15},$
$$t_1^{25}, t_2^{25}, V_1^{25}, V_2^{25}.$$

ii. Demand: $V^{15} = D_{15}(t^{15}) = k^{15},$
$$V^{25} = D_{25}(t^{25}) = k^{25}.$$

iii. Service: $t_A = J_A(V_A),$

$$t_B = J_B(V_B),$$
$$t_C = J_C(V_C),$$
$$t_D = J_D(V_D),$$
$$t_E = J_E(V_E).$$

iv. Path service levels (Ψ_1): $t_1^{15} = t_D + t_C + t_A,$
$$t_2^{15} = t_D + t_C + t_B,$$
$$t_1^{25} = t_E + t_C + t_A,$$
$$t_2^{25} = t_E + t_C + t_B.$$

v. Origin-destination service levels and distribution over paths (Ψ_2, Ψ_3): Since

$$p(r : R) = \frac{e^{-\alpha t_r}}{\sum_{r'} e^{-\alpha t_{r'}}},$$

we have

$$V^{15} = V_1^{15} + V_2^{15},$$
$$V^{25} = V_1^{25} + V_2^{25},$$

$$\frac{V_1^{15}}{V^{15}} = \frac{e^{-\alpha t_1^{15}}}{e^{-\alpha t_1^{15}} + e^{-\alpha t_2^{15}}},$$

$$\frac{V_2^{15}}{V^{15}} = \frac{e^{-\alpha t_2^{15}}}{e^{-\alpha t_1^{25}} + e^{-\alpha t_2^{25}}},$$

$$\frac{V_1^{25}}{V^{25}} = \frac{e^{-\alpha t_1^{25}}}{e^{-\alpha t_1^{25}} + e^{-\alpha t_2^{25}}},$$

$$\frac{V_2^{25}}{V^{25}} = \frac{e^{-\alpha t_2^{25}}}{e^{-\alpha t_1^{25}} + e^{-\alpha t_2^{25}}}.$$

Note that in this formulation path service levels are used directly, and no definition of a composite (over all paths) origin-destination service level is obvious. It is possible to define such a composite depending on the total origin-destination demand function: for example,

$$V_1^{15} = \frac{e^{-\alpha t_1^{15}}}{\beta_0 + e^{-\alpha t_1^{15}} + e^{-\alpha t_2^{15}}}, \tag{12.28}$$

$$V_2^{15} = \frac{e^{-\alpha t_2^{15}}}{\beta_0 + e^{-\alpha t_1^{15}} + e^{-\alpha t_2^{15}}}. \tag{12.29}$$

It is desired to express the total demand as

$$V^{15} = \frac{e^{-\alpha_1 t^{15}}}{\alpha_0 + e^{-\alpha_1 t^{15}}}. \tag{12.30}$$

Then, from (12.28) and (12.29),

$$V^{15} = \frac{e^{-\alpha t_1^{15}} + e^{-\alpha t_2^{15}}}{\beta_0 + e^{-\alpha t_1^{15}} + e^{-\alpha t_2^{15}}}, \tag{12.31}$$

which can be made equivalent to (12.30) by setting

$$\alpha_0 = \beta_0, \tag{12.32}$$

$$e^{-\alpha_1 t^{15}} = e^{-\alpha t_1^{15}} + e^{-\alpha t_2^{15}}, \tag{12.33}$$

or

$$t^{15} = -\frac{1}{\alpha_1} \ln(e^{-\alpha t_1^{15}} + e^{-\alpha t_2^{15}}) \tag{12.34}$$

(see the disscussion of Λ variables in section 11.3.4).

Thus alternative assumptions about consumer path-choice behavior lead to alternative equilibrium formulations. It is particularly interesting to extend this formulation. The choice alternatives i can be combinations of f, d, m, and r. Thus the above formulation can be expanded to include simultaneous choice of frequency, destination, and mode as well as path by expanding the definition of the network to include nodes (zone centroids) representing all feasible combinations f, d, m, and r (Manheim 1973d, Dafermos 1976, Sheffi and Daganzo 1978).

12.4 POSSIBLE FLOW DISTRIBUTION RULES

Specification of the basis on which flow is distributed among alternative paths is, as shown in the previous sections, a very important element in the definition of a flow prediction problem. The assumption of a flow distribution rule ψ can have a very significant effect on the equilibrium. (Computational issues are discussed in section 12.5.4.)

12.4.1 Major Types of Rules

Three major types of flow distribution rules can be identified. Two of these were originally identified by Wardrop (1952) and have come to be known as Wardrop's first and second principles. Wardrop originally described these rules in terms of highway traffic and considered only a single service attribute, travel time. We shall adopt a more generalized formulation in terms of a set of service attributes **S** and labels for the rules that are more indicative of their nature. Every flow distribution rule involves, explicitly or implicitly, a behavioral assumption.

TYPE I: USER-OPTIMIZING DETERMINISTIC

This is the case, introduced in section 12.3.2, where each consumer has a utility function defined over the attributes of paths and chooses the path that has the maximum utility to him. Equivalently each path can be characterized by its utility, for that consumer (or at the aggregate level, that market segment e),

$$U_p = f(S_p). \tag{12.35}$$

The corresponding condition is that, at equilibrium, all consumers make choices such that no single consumer would be better off by switching his choice (that is, by changing paths). This condition is satisfied when the flow is distributed in such a way that for every origin-destination pair $w = (k, d)$ the utilities as measured by U_p over all paths used for that pair are equal and are not less than the utilities over unused paths. This can be expressed formally as follows (Beckmann 1967, Dafermos 1971): At equilibrium, for every $w = (k, d)$ connected by the allowable paths $p_1, \ldots, p_m$, these paths can be so numbered that

$$U_{p_1} = U_{p_2} = \ldots = U_{p_s} \geq U_{p_{s+1}} \geq U_{p_{s+2}} \geq \ldots > U_{p_m} \tag{12.36}$$

and

$$V_{p_r} \begin{cases} > 0 & \text{for } r = 1, \ldots, S, \\ = 0 & \text{for } r = S + 1, \ldots, m. \end{cases} \tag{12.37}$$

For example, if $U_p = -t_p$, where t is travel time, then the flow distribution rule is that flow is distributed over the available paths in such a way that the travel times are equal over all the paths used (for any w) and less than or equal to the times over all other paths. (This is illustrated in section 12.3.6.)

As a second example let $S_p = (t, c, f)$, where t is travel time, c fare or out-of-pocket cost, and f frequency of service. Further, define

$$U_p = \alpha_1 t_p + \alpha_2 c_p + \alpha_3/f_p. \tag{12.38}$$

Then flow is distributed over the allowable paths in such a way that the values of U_p are equal over all paths used. Thus while different paths may have different travel times, fares, and service frequencies (for example, if in an intercity context one path corresponds to rail, another to air, a third to bus, and a fourth to automobile), the user is assumed to make his decision on the basis of an equivalent composite service level $L_p = U_p$ that characterizes each path.

A similar approach was used in the Harvard-Brookings model system (Kresge and Roberts 1971) with five service attributes: travel time, waiting time, time variability, probability of shipment loss or damage, and cost.

As a third example let $\mathbf{S}_p = (t, d, n, c)$, where t is total trip time, d total walk distance, n number of transfers, and c fare or out-of-pocket cost. Further, define

$$U_p = \begin{cases} -K & \text{if } n_p > 2 \text{ or } d_p > 800 \text{ feet,} \\ (t_p^{\alpha_1})(d_p^{\alpha_2})(n_p^{\alpha_3})(c_p^{\alpha_4}) & \text{otherwise,} \end{cases} \tag{12.39}$$

where K is an arbitrary large number, essentially equal to infinity, and the α_i are behavioral parameters. Thus the path utility U_p again results in a composite service level, but paths with more than two transfers or a walk distance greater than 800 feet are essentially ruled out through their very high disutility. This would correspond to an urban situation in which various paths involve combinations of walk, automobile (as driver or passenger), bus, and rail transit modes and there is a maximum walk distance and a maximum number of transfers that people are willing to accept.

Strictly speaking, the first example is Wardrop's first principle; more generally any utility-optimizing deterministic choice behavior corresponds to this principle: *At equilibrium, the volumes and service levels over all paths are such that no user would increase his utility by shifting paths.* Note that this condition excludes the possibility of large groups changing their choices simultaneously, leading to an increase in utility for several consumers (Hershdorfer 1966, Dafermos 1976). Note also that these conditions for an equilibrium do not necessarily imply the existence of a unique equilibrium.

TYPE II: USER-OPTIMIZING STOCHASTIC

In this case, introduced in section 12.3.1, each consumer has a utility function defined over attributes of paths, but choice is probabilistic. The basis of this randomness can be a random component of the utilities or randomness in the service levels experienced or both. The corresponding equilibrium condition is: *At equilibrium the volumes over all paths are equal to the expected number of consumers choosing each path at the equilibrium service levels.* This is very general; the nature of the equilibrium depends on the specific probabilistic choice model used and the distribution of consumer characteristics.

If there is a single homogeneous market segment, the volume over each path will be proportional to the path-choice probability (this is an example of naive aggregation, discussed in section 4.7.2):

$$\frac{V_p}{\sum\limits_{p'} V_{p'}} = p(U^p > U^j \text{ for all paths } j \neq p). \qquad (12.40)$$

Specific formulations have been proposed by several authors. The assumption of an MNL model for path choice with fixed demand leads to the formulation of Dial (1971), as shown in (12.21), and is readily extended to cases of multidimensional choice (Manheim 1973d). The fact that the MNL model has the property of independence of irrelevant alternatives (IIA) causes particular problems in path choice (Schneider 1973, Florian and Fox 1976, Daganzo and Sheffi 1977). A more general formulation would allow nonzero correlations among attributes of alternatives and thereby avoid the IIA property (McFadden 1978). One such formulation is multinomial probit (MNP). Recent research has significantly increased our ability to deal with MNP (Lerman and Manski 1976, Daganzo, Bouthelier, and Sheffi 1977, Hausman and Wise 1976). Daganzo and Sheffi (1977) have explored the use of MNP as a path-choice model, shown its relation to an earlier heuristic formulation (Burrell 1968), and discussed its application to the multidimensional choice problem (Sheffi and Daganzo 1978).

TYPE III: SYSTEM-OPTIMIZING
The two preceding types of flow distribution rules are based on behavioral formulations that assume that each consumer seeks to maximize his own utility. There are, in contrast, some transportation system contexts where the choices of paths are made not by a large number of individual users but by a single decision-making entity controlling flows in the system. Examples are a single firm controlling shipments in its own logistics system or a military entity controlling movements of its units over its own network of facilities and services.

In this case the decision-making entity can choose which paths will be utilized by various movements in ways that optimize its own objectives. For example, we might take as a measure of the overall quality of a flow pattern

$$\lambda \equiv \sum_{y \in Y} V_y f(S_y), \qquad (12.41)$$

where

$$S_y = J_y(V_y). \qquad (12.42)$$

Then the flow distribution rule is that flow is distributed over the network (subject to the demand, service, and other relationships in section 12.5) such that this measure λ is optimized.

For example, if $S_y = t_y$, the travel time over link y, then Ψ is "minimize λ," where

$$\lambda = \sum_{y \in Y} V_y t_y. \tag{12.43}$$

The flow distribution rule is "minimize total vehicle-hours of travel in the network," or "minimize total passenger-hours," depending on the units of V.

If $S_y = C_y$, the fixed cost per unit of flow shipped over link y, then Ψ is "minimize λ," where

$$\lambda = \sum_{y \in Y} V_y C_y. \tag{12.44}$$

The flow distribution rule is "minimize total cost of shipments (travel) through the network."

There is a large literature dealing with formulations of this type: see *Transportation Science, Operations Research*, and similar journals.

Originally this class of flow distribution rules was formulated by Wardrop (1952) as a second principle in terms of travel time; "average journey time is a minimum" over all users of the system.

12.4.2 Discussion

These are the three major types of flow distribution rules that have influenced the development of practical procedures to date. The system-optimizing rules lead naturally to the use of various mathematical optimization formulations, especially linear programming and a special class of network flow models. The user-optimizing rules lead to a different set of procedures that have been developed primarily in the urban transportation framework. We shall discuss the computational implications of alternative rules in section 12.5.4.

We have stressed a behavioral perspective on flow distribution rules. It should be apparent that the choice of a rule should not be an arbitrary decision, since this choice has profound implications. First, of course, are the implications for computational feasibility. But much more important is the question of the basic validity of the approach used.

The choice of a flow distribution rule is a behavioral assumption—an assumption about how the users of a system will behave. Thus the flow distribution rule should be seen as a component of the demand model, as discussed in section 12.3. For the user-optimizing rules, do users behave as if they chose their paths such that some utility (or composite service level) U_p was equal over all paths used? If so, this presumes that, as in consumer behavior model I introduced in chapter 2, each traveler has full and accurate information about all the paths available to him and about their characteristics, and that the pattern of network flows is so stable over time that his past experience (such as the times over particular routes no longer used by him) is still valid. Obviously such assumptions need to be tested empirically. Even though this type of distribution rule is the basis for most passenger travel models, especially in urban transportation studies, the empirical evidence is not convincing (see Wachs 1967, Chu 1971, Freeman, Fox, Wilbur Smith and Associates 1971, Ratcliffe 1972, Tagliacozzi and Pirzio 1973).

The major alternative, the system-optimizing rule, involves assumptions of a similar magnitude. We have emphasized the assumption that there is a single decision-making entity. There are some transportation systems, particularly those in which there is a centralized control over trip-making decisions, for which this will seem a reasonable assumption. For example, in an industrial logistics system, goods shipments from factories to warehouses and distribution centers may well be made in such a way as to minimize total distribution cost or simply total transportation cost or to maximize profit. However, when there is no single decision-making entity, these system-optimizing rules seem less appropriate. Do users generally behave as if they chose their paths in order to optimize some overall measure of system performance? It is unlikely that individuals in a passenger travel situation behave in this way, or that individual shippers make their decisions in a way that reduces total system cost.

Clearly, then, a distribution rule is an assumption to be weighed carefully and tested if feasible. Ideally there should be some effort at determining empirically to what extent a particular flow distribution mechanism does apply to the problem being analyzed. This question should receive the same kind of attention as the development of a demand model.

Even if it is not possible to test alternative flow distribution rules empirically in a given situation, it is essential that the analyst consider his choice of a general type of rule, and a specific form, very carefully. An inappropriate rule may lead to erroneous results. For example, because linear programming methods are so useful in the search step in an analysis (for example, for capacity additions to a network), analysts sometimes propose using a system-optimizing distribution rule to model an urban transportation or other passenger travel market. (This permits the use of a linear programming formulation to determine "optimal" capacity increases in the network.) It seems quite likely, however, that this will give erroneous results: although we cannot yet verify the precise form of flow distribution rule used by urban travelers, it is unlikely that individual travelers, in their personal trip decisions, behave in such a way that an overall measure of flow quality is optimized. Rather, some form of user-optimizing rule would seem more appropriate for explaining urban travel behavior.

The analyst must be very careful not to destroy the validity of his analysis by choosing an inappropriate flow distribution rule in establishing his procedures for travel-market equilibration.

12.5 A GENERAL FORMULATION: EQUILIBRIUM IN NETWORKS (OPTIONAL READING)

The simple networks in earlier sections illustrated the formulation of the equilibrium problem in networks for one particular flow distribution rule. In this section we shall present a general formulation of the equilibrium problem (Beckmann 1967, Dafermos 1971, Ruiter 1973b, Florian 1976).

12.5.1 Basic Formulation

We start with some definitions. The **network topology** G can be described by giving the list of **nodes** Z and the list of **links** Y. Each link y is described by giving its **initial and terminal nodes** i_y and j_y and by indicating the **options** T_y and **parameters** α_y that apply to the link.

Nodes of the network at which flows may originate and/or terminate are termed **zone centroids;** the set K of all zone centroids is included in the list of nodes $Z (K \subset Z)$. Each zone centroid k is described by indicating the levels of the activity system A_k corresponding to that zone and the parameters β_k describing the trip-making behavior of the zone.

The set of possible interzonal movements W includes every directed pair w of origin-zone centroids k and destination-zone centroids d: $w = (k, d)$, $w \in W$, $k \in K$, $d \in K$. In the general case we allow the possibility of intrazonal flows: $w = (k, k)$. We call w an **origin-destination pair** of zones.

A **path** p connecting the zone pair $w = (k, d)$ is a sequence of links $(z_1, z_2), (z_2, z_3), \ldots, (z_{n-1}, z_n)$, where $z_1, z_2, \ldots, z_n$ are distinct nodes, $z_1 = k$, and $z_n = d$. P is the set of allowable paths of the network G ("allowable" by whatever reasonable criteria). The set of all allowable paths that connect a specific $w \in W$ will be denoted P_w. The path can also be described by listing the labels y for each link in the path; Y_p is the list of links y contained in path p.

The basic relationships in the network equilibrium problem are as follows:

- **Link level of service:** For each link y in the network ($y \in Y$) there is a link service function $\mathbf{J}_y$ such that the link level of service $\mathbf{S}_y$ (a vector) is a function of the link volumes $V_{y'}$ for all links y' in the network:

$$\mathbf{S}_y = \mathbf{J}_y(\{V_{y'}\}). \tag{12.45}$$

- **Path level of service:** For each path p ($p \in p$), the level of service $\mathbf{S}_p$ is some function Ψ_1 of the levels of service over all links in that path:

$$\mathbf{S}_p = \Psi_1(\{\mathbf{S}_y\}, y \in Y_p). \tag{12.46}$$

- **Interzonal level of service:** The level of service experienced on trips from k to d is some function Ψ_2 of the levels of service over all paths $p \in P_w$, $w = (k, d)$:

$$\mathbf{S}^{kd} = \Psi_2(\{\mathbf{S}_p\}, p \in P_w). \tag{12.47}$$

- **Interzonal volume:** The volume of trips from k to d is given by the demand function D_{kd}:

$$V^{kd} = f_D(A_k, \{Z_{d'}\}, \{S^{k'd'}\} \text{ for all } k', d') \equiv D_{kd}(\{S_{k'd'}\}). \tag{12.48}$$

- **Path volumes:** The way in which the interzonal volume V^{kd} is distributed over paths $p \in P_w$ connecting that zone pair $w = (k, d)$ is some function Ψ_3 of the levels of service over those paths:

$$V_p^{kd} = \Psi_3(V^{kd}; \{\mathbf{S}_p\}, p \in P_w), \tag{12.49}$$

$$V^{kd} = \sum_{p \in P_w} V_p^{kd}. \tag{12.50}$$

- **Link volumes:** The total volume flowing over any link y is composed of the volumes flowing over all paths p in which that link is included. If we define

$$\delta_{yp} \equiv \begin{cases} 1 & \text{if } y \in Y_p, \\ 0 & \text{otherwise,} \end{cases} \tag{12.51}$$

then

$$V_y = \sum_{p \in P} \delta_{yp} V_p. \tag{12.52}$$

The way these relationships interconnect is shown in figure 12.5.

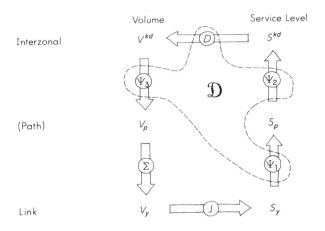

D = demand function (in the narrow sense)

$\mathfrak{D}$ = demand function (in the general sense)

J = service function

Ψ = (Ψ_1, Ψ_2, Ψ_3) = flow distribution rule

Figure 12.5 General network equilibrium relationships.

Note that the flow distribution rule Ψ is reflected in three ways: in Ψ_1, which expresses how path service level is related to link service levels; in Ψ_2, which expresses how origin-destination level of service is related to path level of service; and in Ψ_3, which indicates how the volume of flow for a particular origin-destination pair is distributed over the available paths.

For expository purposes we have defined the demand function D relatively narrowly, as producing V^{kd}, and we have left path-choice behavior to be expressed by the flow distribution rule Ψ. We want to stress again that, conceptually, ***the flow distribution rule is a facet of the demand function.*** This is emphasized by the inclusion of the more general demand function $\mathscr{D}$ in the figure. It is part of the conceptual heritage of UTMS (see chapter 11) that predicting the origin-destination matrix V^{kd} plays a separate role from network assignment, the path-choice prediction. From a more general perspective, path choice is simultaneous with other dimensions of travel choices, as described in section 12.3.

This formulation is very general. There are many particular assumptions that can result in special cases. These will be described further below, but some discusssion of three particular simplifying assumptions is useful in helping to understand these relations.

Often the level of service used is simply travel time or cost; in such a case the functional form of $\mathscr{U}_1$ in equation (12.46) can be a simple summation, so that, for example,

$$S_p = t_p = \sum_{y \in Y_p} t_y;$$

that is, the total travel time over a path is simply the sum of the times over each link in the path.

Often, too, the level of service over a link is a function only of the volume over that link and does not depend on the volumes over other links. Thus equation (12.45) becomes

$$S_y = J_y(V_y). \tag{12.53}$$

As Dafermos (1971) points out, however, this is not always true. For example, travel time through a highway intersection depends on the volume of flow on the cross-street; the travel time experienced by transit riders due to the time spent stopped at an intermediate station may be a function of the volume of boarding and alighting passengers, not just the volume on the train; for some types of centrally dispatched demand-responsive systems, such as a dial-a-ride demand-activated bus system or a PRT (personal rapid transit) system, the travel time from k to d may depend on the volumes of flows elsewhere in the system.

Finally, the most common assumption is that the total demand is independent of the level of service—that is, V^{kd} is given, independent of S^{kd}. Thus (12.48) becomes

$$V^{kd} = V_0^{kd}, \tag{12.54}$$

where V_0^{kd} is a constant provided as data. This leads to several very common special cases, such as the traffic-assignment formulation in urban transportation models or the Hitchcock-Koopmans transportation problem of linear programming.

12.5.2 All-or-Nothing Assignment without Capacity Restraint
To illustrate this general formulation we shall make the three simplifying assumptions discussed in the preceding section:

$$V^{kd} = V_0^{kd}, \tag{12.55}$$

$$S_y = J_y(V_y), \tag{12.56}$$

$$S_p = \sum_{y \in Y_p} S_y. \tag{12.57}$$

The procedure called ***all-or-nothing assignment*** in the urban transportation field takes as its flow distribution rule the following: "All of the volume of flow V is assigned to the path $p \in P_w$, $w = (k, d)$, that has the least total travel time." Hence the term "all-or-nothing": either all of the volume V^{kd} is assigned to a path p or nothing is assigned. (Various arbitrary conditions are set up for the case of a tie among two or more paths, such as "pick one path at random" or "divide flow equally among the tied paths.")

Further, the service functions are assumed to be such that

$$S_y = t_y = a_y; \tag{12.58}$$

that is, the level of service over a link is simply the travel time t_y, and this is assumed to be a constant a_y independent of volume V_y. Thus there is no capacity to the link—that is, the flow pattern need not be restrained by the link capacities. Hence the term "without capacity restraint."

Because of these simplifying assumptions and the simplicity of the flow distribution rule, the basic relationships identified in the preceding section lead directly to a procedure for finding the equilibrium flow pattern, as follows:

● ***Link service functions:*** By (12.56) and (12.58) the travel time of each link is given as part of the input data:

$$t_y = a_y. \tag{12.59}$$

● ***Path level of service:*** By (12.57) the level of service of any path is simply the total travel time over that path, obtained by summing the times over the links in the path:

$$t_p = \sum_{y \in Y_p} t_y. \tag{12.60}$$

● ***Interzonal level of service:*** The level of service for any $w = (k, d)$ is the travel time over that path from k to d that has the least total travel time:

$$t^w = \min_{p \in P_w} \{t_p\}. \tag{12.61}$$

Denote by p_w^* that path. Then

$$t_{p_w^*} = \min_{p \in P_w} \{t_p\},$$

and

$$t^w = t_{p_w^*}.$$

- **Interzonal volume:** By assumption (12.55) the volumes are given, as part of the input data, as the "trip matrix" V_0^{kd} for all k and d:

$$V^{kd} = V_0^{kd}. \tag{12.62}$$

- **Path volumes:** In accordance with the all-or-nothing distribution rule, all of the volume V_0^w is assumed to flow over (be assigned to) the path with the minimum travel time:

$$V_p = \begin{cases} V_0^w & \text{if } p = p_w^*, \\ 0 & \text{otherwise.} \end{cases} \tag{12.63}$$

- **Link volumes:**

$$V_y = \sum_{p \in P} \delta_{yp} V_p, \tag{12.64}$$

where

$$\delta_{yp} = \begin{cases} 1 & \text{if } y \in Y_p, \\ 0 & \text{otherwise.} \end{cases} \tag{12.65}$$

In this case, of course, V_p will be zero for all paths except one for each w, by (12.63).

The logic for actually computing the equilibrium flows under these assumptions follows directly:

1. The input data consist of link travel times t_y, network topology G, and trip matrix V_0^w.
2. For each origin-destination pair w, find the minimum-time path, p_w^*. (Numerous algorithms exist for finding the minimum path between two points in a network: see Dreyfus 1969, Potts and Oliver 1972. Alternatively the minimum-path tree from k to all destinations d can be found at the same time.)
3. Assign the volumes V_0^{kd} to the minimum-time paths p_w^*: for each link $y \in Y_{p_w^*}$, add the volume V_0^w to the volume already assigned. (This is simply a bookkeeping procedure: for each path p_w^* the volume V_0^w given by the trip matrix is added to the link volume for every link on the minimum-time path p_w^*.)
4. Summarize the results: link volumes V_y, best paths p_w^*, and corresponding trip times t^w.

This is one of the simplest equilibrium formulations in use, and one of the earliest developed. However, it has serious limitations. Most important, the all-or-nothing assumption is rarely realistic. Often the results are unrealistically high volumes and times on some links and unrealistically low volumes and times on others.

12.5.3 An Equivalent Simultaneous-Choice Formulation

For completeness and to emphasize the fact that the distribution rule is part of the demand function, we present briefly a modification of the formulation of section 12.5.1:

- *Link level of service:*

$$\mathbf{S}_y = \mathbf{J}_y(\{V_y\}). \tag{12.66}$$

- *Path level of service:*

$$\mathbf{S}_p = \Psi_1(\{\mathbf{S}_y\}, y \in Y_p). \tag{12.67}$$

- *Path volume:*

$$V_p^{kd} = f_D(A_k; \{Z_{d'}\}, \{\mathbf{S}_{p'}^{k'd'}\} \text{ for all } k', d', p'). \tag{12.68}$$

- *Link volumes:*

$$V_y = \sum_k \sum_d \sum_{p \in P_w} \delta_{yp} V_p^{kd}. \tag{12.69}$$

The relationship f_D in (12.68) can be a general demand function reflecting simultaneous choice of frequency, destination, mode, and path, as for example an extension of (12.8).

12.5.4 Computational Approaches

Travel-market equilibration methods have been evolving very rapidly in the last few years. This means that any comments offered here are likely to be outdated very quickly, so we shall not attempt to give a comprehensive state-of-the-art review. Rather, we shall make a few brief observations on current directions and results.

Different computational methods are useful for each of the three major groups of flow distribution rules. Some of these methods work with simplified service functions, as in the all-or-nothing method, where travel time or costs are assumed constant independent of volume. Moreover, historically path choice has been separated from other choice dimensions, so that, from the point of view of travel-market equilibration, the interzonal demands have been treated as fixed (that is, there is a fixed trip matrix) independent of service levels or paths:

$$V^{kd} = D_{kd}(S^{kd}) = V_0^{kd}. \tag{12.70}$$

This results in the traffic-assignment problem.

The first major division is that between system-optimizing and user-optimizing flow distribution rules. One of the major advantages of the system-optimizing rules is that this formulation lends itself to efficient search procedures that utilize mathematical programming. For example, given a fixed investment budget, one can find the optimum amount of capacity to build into each link of the network; or given a fleet of aircraft, one might find the optimum assignment of aircraft to routes. A very rich variety of models of these types has been developed, and some have been used in practical applications. Until recently the bulk of mathematical programming formulations used a fixed trip matrix as in (12.70). This assumption has been replaced by more realistic explicit demand functions in, for example, airline vehicle assignment models (Simpson 1969, 1977).

The system-optimizing formulations are most useful in supporting management decision making for a transportation operator when the assumptions of the flow distribution mechanism are met. They are also useful as search procedures when the resulting solution is treated as a possible action to be tested in more detail in a prediction model with user-optimizing flow distribution rules (since system-optimization per se does not provide a valid prediction of behavior).

User-optimizing formulations are most generally useful because of their stronger behavioral bases. Until recently, however, the computational approaches were quite ad hoc and not very satisfactory from a theoretical perspective. Basically there were a number of pragmatic approaches to the traffic-assignment problem (that is, fixed demand) that were used widely in urban transporation studies (FHWA 1973b). Heuristic approaches to variable demand were also developed, such as the incremental-assignment approach initially implemented in the DODOTRANS system (Manheim and Ruiter 1970), which was the first multimodal equilibrium formulation with variable demand (see also Wigan 1976). However, as with all of these ad hoc approaches, little was known theoretically about the uniqueness of the solutions or about the convergence properties, other than what was acquired through practical experience (see the critique in Ferland, Florian, and Achion 1975).

More soundly based theoretical and practical innovations have been developed recently. The basic stimulus was rediscovery of the results of Beckmann, McGuire, and Winston (1956), who showed that the user-optimizing deterministic problem with variable demand could be formulated as an equivalent system-optimizing problem, for which the solution is unique and stable (Murchland 1969, Ruiter 1973b,

Florian 1976). A number of researchers have developed and tested computational algorithms, both conceptually and practically, building on these results (Nguyen 1974, LeBlanc, Morlok, and Pierskalla 1975, Dafermos 1976, Ruiter 1976a,b, Florian et al. 1977).

In appraising this rapidly changing state of the art, the reader should examine each proposed problem formulation and resulting algorithm carefully: Is the flow distribution rule user-optimizing? What are its behavioral assumptions? Can there be more than one market segment with different demand function parameters? If demand is variable, what choice dimensions are included, and are there any restrictions on the form of the demand functions? Are link service levels variable with volume?

Development of stochastic user-optimizing approaches has been less rapid. The initial formulations were for the fixed-demand traffic-assignment problem (Burrell 1968, Dial 1971) with link service levels constant independent of volume and with relatively simple probability models. Particularly interesting are recent advances in the formulation of more realistic probability models—for example, models in which path service levels are correlated (Daganzo and Sheffi 1977). So far, however, these more realistic models still assume a single market segment and constant link service levels (see section 12.4.1).

12.6 INFLUENCE OF NETWORK REPRESENTATION AND OTHER APPROXIMATIONS

Real-world transportation networks are usually very complex. Any network model necessarily involves some simplification and abstraction from the real-world network. Under certain conditions particular forms of network representation can be accepted by the analyst which then enable significant simplification of the travel-market equilibration process.

Some examples of alternative forms of network representation are:

• a complete network, at a high degree of detail;

• a "spider" network, in which each origin is connected to all adjacent origins (zone centroids);

• a "corridor" network, in which each origin is connected to each destination by several paths (while flows interact for some origin-destination pairs, they are completely independent of flows on paths connecting other pairs);

• a "direct" network, in which there is only one link for each origin-destination pair;

- a single link representing the entire network; and
- a single point (no attempt to model spatial structure).

Selective simplification is often possible. In this approach a subarea of a network is modeled in detail, with the rest of the network simplified. For example, in an airport access study the travel times in the local highway network might be assumed constant independent of volumes of airport access flows, except on certain critical facilities in the neighborhood of the airport.

In addition to network simplification, other forms of approximation and simplification can be adopted. Service functions can be simplified by assuming that congestion effects are negligible for some facilities, so that the level of service is known. In a transit study, for example, one might explicitly model only the transit network; alternative assumptions would be made about the degree of congestion in the highway network and the resultant highway travel times, and these would be used to estimate mode splits and path choices. In highway-transit corridor studies it is often assumed that the transit network operates far below capacity, so that there are no congestion effects. Where buses are affected by highway congestion, bus travel times are assumed known, so only the highway network is modeled explicitly.

In general, the analyst should start out with the premise that a full travel-market equilibration procedure is required, using a single multimodal network with reasonable detail and a complete demand function (that is, one that includes more than just route choice). Then alternative simplifying assumptions should be explored and, in light of the issues to be studied and the resources available for the study, decisions made about accepting or rejecting particular simplifying assumptions.

12.7 SUMMARY

The equilibrium of service and demand in a transportation system is influenced by its spatial structure. There are two central conceptual issues in finding equilibrium flows in networks: consumer behavior (the behavioral basis by which consumers choose one path from the many available) and the influence of network structure (the way consumers interact under the influence of the spatial structure of a network).

From a behavioral perspective, path choice should be seen as part of the overall process of consumer choice among a number of dimensions. Then a conditional model for path choice can be derived. An example was given of a MNL model. Individual choice models can be formulated from both deterministic and stochastic perspectives. Wardrop's first principle is a special case of a disaggregate deterministic model, and Dial's multipath model is a special case of a stochastic disaggregate model.

The formulation of the general network equilibrium problem includes demand functions for each origin-destination pair, service functions for each link, and a flow distribution rule $\mathscr{V}$ with three components:

$\mathscr{V}_1$: a description of how the service level of a path is related to the service levels of links in that path;

$\mathscr{V}_2$: a description of how the service level between each origin-destination pair of zones is related to the service levels of each path; and

$\mathscr{V}_3$: a description of how the volume choosing each path, and the total volume from k to d, is affected by the service levels of all the available paths.

Flow distribution rules fall into three major groups: user-optimizing deterministic, user-optimizing stochastic, and system-optimizing.

TO READ FURTHER
Good bibliographies and summaries of the state of the art can be found in Ruiter (1973a) and Florian (1976, 1978). Daganzo and Sheffi (1977) present an alternative formulation of stochastic disaggregate path-choice models. The current state of the art in user-optimizing models is represented in LeBlanc, Morlok, and Pierskalla (1975), Ruiter (1976a,b), and Florian et al. (1977). The logic of TTP-1, the program used in chapter 13, is that of incremental assignment: see Martin and Manheim (1965), Manheim and Ruiter (1970), Ferland, Florian, and Achion (1975), and Van Vliet (1976). On network representation see Chan et al. (1968), Mowll and Chang (1973), Chan (1976), Talvitie and Hasan (1978), and Watanatada and Ben-Akiva (1978).

EXERCISES
12.1(C) Discuss the approach of all-or-nothing assignment without capacity restraint. Does this seem a reasonable and useful special case of general network equilibrium? For what situations do the assumptions seem reasonable? Can you identify any situations in which this formulation might give absurd results?

12.2(P) Consider the simple networks discussed in section 12.3.4.

Use the service and demand functions presented in section 7.3 (performance model II: for each link a different $\mathbf{T} = (\mathbf{M}, Q, P)$) and section 5.5 (for each origin-destination pair a different set of parameter values in the demand model). Assume a set of numerical values for the necessary parameters.

a. Develop an appropriate computational procedure. Use TTP or any other "direct-search" package that will search systematically for the solutions to the various equation sets.

b. Design and execute a set of runs that explore alternative parameter values. Discuss the resulting equilibrium flow patterns. (For example, in network b in figure 12.2, systematically vary the price of route A and/or the congestion factor J of route B over a range.)

12.3(E) Equilibrium flows have been found for the network in figure 12.6 using each of Wardrop's two principles (section 12.4.1). The demand is assumed to be perfectly inelastic with respect to travel time, so that

$V^{14} = 2{,}000$ vehicles/hour,
$V^{24} = 1{,}000$ vehicles/hour.

(V_{14} is total flow along link 14; V^{14} is total interzonal flow from 1 to 4, which may use a number of links.) The service functions are

$t_{13} = 0.5 + 0.001 V_{13}$,
$t_{23} = 0.5 + 0.001 V_{23}$,
$t_{14} = 1.0 + 0.005 V_{14}$,
$t_{24} = 1.0 + 0.001 V_{24}$,
$t_{34} = 1.0 + 0.002 V_{34}$.

The equilibrium flows using two principles are given in table 12.1.
a. Interpret these results and discuss (briefly). Which principle cor-

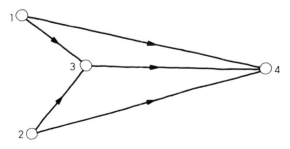

Figure 12.6

Table 12.1 Equilibrium flow volumes for the demand and service functions of exercise 12.3 according to two alternative principles

Link	Principle A	Principle B
14	1,850	1,900
13	150	100
34	262.5	175
23	112.5	75
24	887.5	925
Total travel time	5,803 min	5,825 min

Source: After Overgaard (n.d.).

responds to the system-optimizing rule? the user-optimizing deterministic rule?

b. Describe a transportation case (the actors, their location on the network, their objectives, the facilities making up the links, a description of the nodes) for the sample case above when (i) principle A and not principle B is the appropriate assumption, and (ii) principle B and not principle A is the appropriate assumption. In constructing these cases, assume that the cost of the trip to the traveler plus the valuation of travel time is minimized (rather than travel time alone as in the example). In each case discuss why you believe that the equilibrium flows predicted with the selected principle will be closer to the actual flows than those obtained with the other principle.

12.4(C) Critically appraise the incremental-assignment logic used in TTP in chapter 13 (see the references listed in the section "To Read Further" above).

12.5(P) Review some of the presently available algorithms (see the references in section 12.5.4 and current journals).

a. Critically compare some of these algorithms. What problems are addressed? What critical assumptions are made? What are the relative computational efficiencies?

b. Select one algorithm and prepare a preliminary design of its logic sufficient for FORTRAN-level programming.

13
Case Study III: A Network Analysis

13.1 INTRODUCTION

The basic framework presented in preceding chapters introduced a number of fundamental concepts:

1. There are a variety of transportation- and activity-system options potentially available.

2. Many impacts on many different groups must be considered in choosing among the available options.

3. To predict the impacts of a particular set of options, the resulting flows in the transportation system must be predicted.

4. The theory underlying the prediction of flows is that of equilibrium between service and demand in the (short-run) travel market.

5. While flow prediction is the core of the prediction problem, it is not the whole of it; a full set of transportation prediction models consists of service, demand, equilibrium, resource, and activity-shift models.

6. In addition to prediction, the analyst must also be concerned with search (the generation of alternatives), evaluation and choice, and also the setup phase that must precede analysis and the implementation that follows, in a continuing process of analysis.

The objective of this chapter is to illustrate the steps involved in applying the basic framework to a realistic problem. Although simple, the example is still sufficiently realistic to illustrate many of the directions in which the basic theory must be expanded. Even with this simplicity, a computer model is required to compute equilibrium. (Alternative ways of using this chapter will be found in the teacher's manual.)

13.2 THE SETTING FOR THE CASE STUDY

Nearly all of the workers living in the suburb of Hometown work in the central business district of the metropolitan region, in Loop City. They all journey to work between the hours of 7 and 9 A.M. For their work trips they must choose among three alternatives:

1. Walk to the local commuter railroad station, ride to the downtown station, and then walk to the workplace.

2. Drive to a nearby commuter railroad station, which has a large parking facility, ride a shorter distance on the railroad, and again walk to the workplace.

3. Drive all the way downtown, making use of a radial expressway for part of the trip, park downtown, and walk a much shorter distance to the workplace.

The transportation system that provides these alternatives is shown in figure 13.1. We wish to investigate the effects of various improvements in this transportation system on work-trip travel patterns in the corridor from Hometown to Loop City. We shall be concerned with the impacts of these changes both on the trip makers and on the operators, those who provide transportation in the corridor.

To predict the impacts of alternative improvements we shall model the transportation system of the Hometown–Loop City corridor using the concepts developed in the preceding chapters.

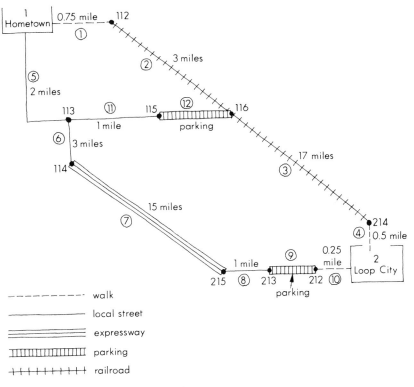

Figure 13.1 The case study network.

13.3 STRUCTURING THE ANALYSIS

We begin with the setup phase, developing the models to be used for analysis. We shall need service, demand, equilibrium, resource, and activity-shift models. Before describing the models, however, let us first review some basic characteristics of this corridor problem.

13.3.1 The Network Context

Compare the transportation system in figure 13.1 with that in section 1.4. The suburb-city system was there represented as a single link: there was one origin for flows, one destination, and only one possible path between origin and destination. That, of course, is a simplified representation of the situation; in most real problems the actual transportation system is a network of many links, as in figure 13.1. Even this is probably a simplified representation of the real network, but it is certainly more realistic than a single link between Hometown and Loop City would be.

We buy this increased realism at a price, however, for now our analysis becomes substantially more complex. We must have a separate service function for each individual link in the network, corresponding to that link's characteristics. We must identify the points in the network at which travelers enter or leave the system; these become the origin and destination nodes for particular groups of travelers. If we have several origins and/or destinations, we must have at least one demand function for each combination of origin and destination.

Most important of all, finding the equilibrium between service and demand becomes much more complex in a network. One reason for this is obvious from figure 13.1: there are several paths possible from Hometown to Loop City. Thus finding the equilibrium flows in a network requires determining, not only the volumes and levels of service at equilibrium, but also which of the many available paths will be used from each origin to each destination (in fact, under most situations many paths will be used, and part of the problem of finding the equilibrium flows involves finding how much of the volume uses each path).

In addition to the complexities introduced by having to deal with a network instead of a single link, there is one other important way in which realistic problems differ from the simple single-link example of chapter 1. This is the complexity of the demand function. The first aspect of this complexity is that, in general, the level of service of

507 A Network Analysis

the transportation system is reflected in several variables, not just one. For example, in the Hometown–Loop City corridor we shall deal with three service variables: fare (or out-of-pocket cost), out-of-vehicle time, and in-vehicle travel time. The second major aspect of demand function complexity is the multiplicity of alternative modes; in our example we shall distinguish rail, park-and-ride, and automobile modes.

The logic for computing equilibrium flows under these conditions can become very complex, as described in chapter 12, and computer programs are usually required to perform the necessary calculations. In this case study the numerical results have been obtained by use of a computer program called TTP.

TTP (Transportation Teaching Package) is specifically designed for teaching the analysis of multimodal transportation systems. The systems might represent a local commuting corridor, as in this case study; a metropolitan area; or a statewide, regional, national, or international network for intercity passenger or freight trips. TTP contains service, demand, equilibrium, and resource models. Future developments of TTP will include activity-shift models, impact calculation and comparison models, aids for the analyst in the search for new alternatives, and aids for monitoring the process of analysis itself. In many cases there are alternative models to perform the same function, thereby allowing the user to adapt the program to his particular needs. The system can be used by transportation analysts who are not computer programmers because the TTP run is controlled by a command-structured, problem-oriented language.

13.3.2 Setup: Preliminaries

We shall now prepare to set up the analysis. To do this we shall apply the basic concepts developed in earlier chapters. The transportation system will be represented by service and resource functions, for whose development we need service and resource models and a specification of the transportation options. The activity system will be represented by demand functions, for whose development we need a demand model and a specification of the activity-system options. (Activity shifts will be external to the models.) To complete the system of prediction models we must also specify the equilibrium model. In addition to these prediction tools, we must also specify the search and evaluation and choice procedures to be used.

First, however, we must make some basic decisions about key elements of the system of models. These will be described in sections

13.3.3–13.3.11. Then in section 13.4 we shall actually set up the base-case set of data and models.

13.3.3 Service Variables

Prior to defining the demand and service functions, we must decide what service variables to use. For this case study we shall use IVTT, the total in-vehicle time from origin to destination; OVTT, the out-of-vehicle time, including walk time, parking time, other components of access to and egress from the line-haul mode, and waiting time, reflecting frequency of service; and OPTC, the total out-of-pocket cost for a trip including fares, tolls, parking charges, and so forth. (Since we are setting up the case study for the computer, we use computer-language variables such as IVTT in this chapter where in previous chapters we used algebraic variables such as t_{iv}.)

13.3.4 Technologies

The transportation system is represented by a single multimodal network, with links of different technologies grouped into modes. There are just two fundamentally different technologies: commuter railroad and private automobiles on local streets and highways. To fully reflect the characteristics of the various alternatives, however, it is useful to specify a number of different types of links and to separate the possible paths through the network into modes. The various transportation technologies in the system are reflected in six types of links and three modes:

Link types
1. walk links, suburban
2. walk links, CBD
3. automobile links, local streets
4. automobile links, expressway
5. automobile links, parking
6. rail links.

Modes
1. automobile (uses local streets, expressway, parking, and CBD walk links)
2. rail (uses suburban walk links, rail, and CBD walk links)
3. park-and-ride (uses local streets, parking, rail, and CBD walk links).

Park-and-ride is distinguished as a mode because it has basically different service characteristics from the other two.

13.3.5 Flow Dimensions

Since we are dealing only with home-to-work travel, we shall measure flow in passengers per time period. We shall treat one-way trips inbound to the CBD in the morning peak period and take as our basic unit of time the two-hour peak period 7–9 A.M. Thus flow will be measured in units of passengers per peak period. (We shall treat this as an average uniform flow over the two-hour period and ignore fluctuations during the period.) We assume that the volume of trips made for other purposes during this time period is negligible compared to the volume of work trips.

13.3.6 Impacts

Since our objective in this case study is to apply the equilibrium approach to a multimodal network context, we shall focus only on user and operator impacts. Although physical, functional, and governmental impacts will be very important in many real situations, we shall neglect them here (for clarity only). To reflect user impacts we shall consider the level of service experienced by users of each mode. To reflect operator impacts we shall consider the total cost, gross revenue, and net revenue (gross revenue less total cost) for the operator of each mode.

13.3.7 Activity System

For this case study we shall assume that the population growth of Hometown and the number of jobs in Loop City are essentially independent of the quality of the transportation system between the two points (over the range of alternative systems that we are likely to consider). Therefore we do not need an activity-shift model.

To get the demand functions we shall need both a demand model and a specific set of activity-system options.

DEMAND MODEL

The demand model selected is the multinomial logit model. Hence the demand can be expressed as a set of six equations giving the service levels offered by each of the available modes and the volume using each mode (as a fraction of the total number of trips):

$$U_R = C_R + a_{R1}\text{IVTT}_R + a_{R2}\text{OVTT}_R + a_{R3}\text{OPTC}_R, \tag{13.1}$$

$$U_P = C_P + a_{P1}\text{IVTT}_P + a_{P2}\text{OVTT}_P + a_{P3}\text{OPTC}_P, \tag{13.2}$$

$$U_A = C_A + a_{A1}\text{IVTT}_A + a_{A2}\text{OVTT}_A + a_{A3}\text{OPTC}_A, \tag{13.3}$$

$$V_R = \frac{e^{U_R} V_T}{e^{U_R} + e^{U_P} + e^{U_A}},$$

(13.4)

$$V_P = \frac{e^{U_P} V_T}{e^{U_R} + e^{U_P} + e^{U_A}},$$

(13.5)

$$V_A = \frac{e^{U_A} V_T}{e^{U_R} + e^{U_P} + e^{U_A}},$$

(13.6)

where R, P, and A represent rail, park-and-ride, and automobile modes, respectively, U_m is the utility of mode m, V_m is the volume of passengers per peak period using mode m, V_T is the total number of peak-period trips from Hometown to Loop City, and the C_m and a_{mi} are parameters reflecting travel behavior. The total volume of passengers over all three modes is

$$V_T = V_R + V_P + V_A.$$

(13.7)

In the general case the region being studied is divided into a number of zones, each of which can be both an origin and a destination zone. For N zones there are $N(N - 1)$ possible combinations of origins and destinations; this requires $N(N - 1)$ specific demand functions V^{kd} describing flows from each possible origin zone k to each possible destination zone d. Further, there may be a separate equation for each mode. In our case there are two zones but we are considering flow in one direction only, so we have one demand function expressed as three modal equations.

ACTIVITY-SYSTEM OPTIONS

Two components of the activity system need to be specified: the level of intensity of the system and the travel behavior. The first component involves the total trips V_T (or alternatively the population of Hometown and a trip generation rate or function), and the second the parameters C_m and a_{mi}. Specific values for the parameters will be offered in a later section, but a general observation can be made about the signs of the parameters: we would expect an increase in the travel time or cost of mode m to decrease volume using that mode and probably to increase volume using the other modes; therefore all a_{mi} should be negative.

13.3.8 Transportation System

The transportation system enters the analysis through the service and resource functions. To get these functions we need to separate the service and resource models from the specification of a particular set of transportation-system options. While the models will remain constant throughout the analysis, the options will vary to reflect the different courses of action being considered. The service and resource functions will also vary as the options are varied.

In the single-link example of chapter 1 these distinctions were easy to make. The service model was

$$\mathbf{S} = \mathbf{J}(\mathbf{V}, \mathbf{T}): \qquad t = m + nV,$$

where the options $\mathbf{T} = (m, n)$. For the particular specification of options $\mathbf{T} = (10, 0.01)$, we get the specific service function

$$t = 10 + 0.01V.$$

In a multimodal network the service function cannot be represented so simply and concisely. For example, the options $\mathbf{T}$ will specify, among other elements, the network structure and link characteristics, including for each link a function relating travel time over the link to the volume using the link. However, the service level perceived by the traveler is the total travel time, cost, and so forth, from Hometown to Loop City; these measures are the sums of the measures over each link in the path used from the origin to the destination. The service function must reflect this fact and also the fact that in a network there are generally many possible paths between two points. Therefore the service function depends in a quite complex way on the network structure, on the characteristics of specific links, and on other transportation options as well.

TRANSPORTATION OPTIONS
The following options will be represented in this case study.

I. Technologies
A. Volume–travel time functions: For each of the six types of links we specify a service function giving the travel time (in seconds per mile) over the link as a function of volume (in persons per hour per lane) (the maximum capacity of the link is part of the function where applicable). The length of the link in miles and the number of lanes are used to get total travel time as a function of the total volume over the link during the peak period. In TTP this form of volume–travel time function is termed a volume-delay function: by convention it is expressed as a piecewise linear function.
B. Cost structure: for each of the three modes we specify the unit costs necessary to compute resource costs as (1) a lump-sum fixed cost in dollars per year and (2) a variable cost in dollars per passenger-mile.

II. The multimodal network is specified by listing the origin and destination nodes for each link.

III. Link characteristics include length (in miles), number of lanes, and specification of technology type (volume-delay function); as indicated above, the number of lanes and the length of a given link are used to convert the volume-delay function to a volume–travel time function for the link. Two volume–travel time functions are associated with each link, one for OVTT and one for IVTT, so that the service offered by various link types can be represented more accurately. (For instance, walking and parking contribute to out-of-vehicle time, while riding in an automobile or transit vehicle contributes to in-vehicle time.) The technology specification also includes the link cost. One must be very careful in formulating link costs because two costs are defined in TTP: path costs (entered in path information) and link costs. Link costs can be directly attributed to the link (parking fees, tolls), whereas path costs are incurred over the course of a trip and cannot be directly attributed to one link (bus fare on a bus line that covers more than one link). (The reader is encouraged to consult the TTP documentation for additional information.)

IV. Operating policies

A. Line (route) information: For modes other than automobile, vehicles operate over routes or lines. All information about lines is entered in the line information, specifically the line number, the headway, and the links over which the line operates. Thus for each mode, origin-destination pair, and path the frequency of service is derived from the headways of the lines in that path.

B. Fare: For each mode and origin-destination pair the fare is specified, in cents per passenger, on two bases: costs that can be attributed to a specific link are specified for that link; costs that are not link-specific are attributed to a path.

C. Path information: There are alternative paths through the network for each origin-destination pair. Paths can be multimodal and can use a number of different lines in sequence. The description of a path includes any path cost and the lines and links traversed by the path.

SERVICE MODEL

The three service variables IVTT, OVTT, and OPTC must be outputs from the service function. The service function indicates the values of the variables for a trip from a particular origin to a particular destination by a particular path. In the corridor from Hometown to Loop City there are only three possible paths, one each for the rail, automobile, and park-and-ride modes, and only one origin-destination combination. Therefore the service model can be specified as follows:

1. OPTC: The out-of-pocket cost is either entered directly as a path cost or computed as the sum of link costs or both. This value is preset as a policy option and is assumed to be independent of volume.
2. IVTT: The in-vehicle time from Hometown to Loop City is computed for each path as the sum of the in-vehicle times over each link in the path from Hometown to Loop City. Each link in-vehicle time is, in general, dependent on the total volume using the link, given by the volume-delay function of the technology and made specific to the particular link through use of the link's length and number of lanes.
3. OVTT: The out-of-vehicle time is computed for each path as the sum of all link out-of-vehicle times along a path (as with in-vehicle time) plus the wait times for each transit line used. Wait time is assumed to be half the headway specified for the line.

Thus while out-of-pocket cost and frequency remain constant as input, the travel times vary as a function of the flow volumes in the network. Since T = (costs, frequencies, volume-time functions, link distances and number of lanes, network structure, cost units) and S = (out-of-pocket costs, in-vehicle and out-of-vehicle travel times), the service function $S = J(V, T)$ is composed of three functions:

J_1: out-of-pocket cost = $\sum$(path and link costs);
J_2: in-vehicle time = f(link distances, lanes, in-vehicle volume-time functions, network structure, volume);
J_3: out-of-vehicle time = g(link distances, lanes, headways, out-of-vehicle time functions, network structure, volume).

The actual calculation of travel times in the service function takes place as part of the equilibrium computations because of the dependence on flow volume, which must come from the demand function.

RESOURCE MODEL

The resource model has two basic components: total cost and gross revenue for each mode.

The total cost for each mode is computed as the fixed cost (dollars per year) plus the variable cost, based on the input unit variable cost (dollars per passenger-mile) and the appropriate conversion factors (from per peak period to per year). All costs calculated for this analysis are annual peak-period costs, assuming 265 working days per year.

All improvements associated with new alternatives are included as half the total improvement cost of the project, in order to isolate improvement costs allocated to the A.M. peak period. The formula used to determine total annual cost (A.M. peak) to the operator of a given mode is

$$C_T = \text{fixed cost per year} + \frac{\text{discounted improvement cost per year}}{2} +$$
$$[(\text{variable cost per passenger-mile}) \times (\text{peak-period volume})$$
$$\times (\text{no. of working days per year}) \times (\text{distance of trip to which}$$
$$\text{variable cost applies})].$$

A more detailed illustration of the method of calculating discounted improvement cost and allocation of costs to different modal operators is presented in section 13.9.

The gross revenue for each mode is based on the computed equilibrium flow volume and the fare per passenger input as an operating policy option. Gross revenue per year for the A.M. peak period is

$$I_{GR} = (\text{no. of working days per year}) \times (\text{fare})$$
$$\times (\text{volume per peak period}).$$

13.3.9 Equilibrium Model

The last component of the system of prediction models is that used to compute the equilibrium flow pattern, the volumes and travel times that will satisfy both the service and the demand conditions. In a multimodal network the procedure for calculating this equilibrium can be quite complex. The theory and techniques for calculating equilibrium flows in networks were discussed in chapter 12. For our present purposes we shall use the procedure implemented in TTP.

The output of the equilibrium calculation will consist of information on flow volumes and service levels. Flow information includes, for the two-hour peak period, interzonal flow volumes (number of passenger trips for each mode, origin, and destination, by market segment) and link flow volumes (total passenger flow for each link). The service levels consist of interzonal trip times (by mode, by origin, and by destination), interzonal composite service level (by mode, by origin, and by destination), interzonal out-of-pocket costs (total by mode, by origin, and by destination), and link speeds and travel times for each link.

13.3.10 Evaluation

Evaluation involves analysis of the impacts of an alternative to determine its acceptability relative to previously analyzed alternatives and absolutely as a candidate for implementation. There are two major interest groups affected directly by the alternatives: users and operators, as described in section 13.3.6.

The impacts described by the prediction models will be, for users, total volume of passengers served, total trip time, and total out-of-pocket costs, all by mode, by origin, and by destination; and for operators, total cost (C_T), gross revenue (I_{GR}), and net revenue $(I_{NR} = I_{GR} - C_T)$, by mode.

To evaluate this information for each alternative we shall first display it in an impact tableau. Then we shall compute several aggregate measures as a way of summarizing the overall impacts. These measures will be operator net revenue over all three modes, obtained by summing gross revenues for all modes and subtracting the total of costs for all modes, and the composite service level, a measure of the overall degree of service provided users. This composite service level will be computed for each mode and as an average for all modes (weighted by the equilibrium volumes).

A fundamental characteristic of transportation systems is the differential incidence of impacts: for many changes in the transportation system, some groups gain while others lose. In our evaluation we shall focus on the differential incidence of impacts by looking at the trade-offs between operators and users. To show this we shall display the effects of various alternatives on a graph with two axes: total operator net revenue and average composite service level (both over all modes; see figure 5.12). In this way we shall isolate the conflict between users and operators, but we shall be underemphasizing the differential incidence of impacts *among* the three modal operators and *among* the users of the three modes. (To emphasize these conflicts we would want to distinguish several market segments.)

13.3.11 Search

No formal search techniques will be used. The judgment, insight, and inventive imagination of the analyst will be the technique for generating good alternatives. We shall use the evaluation information generated for previously tested alternatives as an aid in developing new and better alternatives.

13.4 SETUP: THE BASE CASE

In setting up the models for prediction it is useful to establish a base-case set of options. Typically in a transportation analysis the base case is chosen to be the existing system. This case then serves as a reference point for calibration of the models when necessary and for comparison of alternative transportation options. We shall assume that the models have been calibrated to reflect present conditions sufficiently accurately.

13.4.1 Specification of Transportation Options

The transportation options listed in section 13.3.8 are specified in this section, along with the definition of these options in TTP.

TECHNOLOGIES

We consider three modes and six network link types. The three modes are rail, park-and-ride, and automobile. The characteristics of the six network link types are listed below.

The volume–travel time functions for the six link types are shown in figure 13.2. The cost structures of the three modes are shown in table 13.1. In each case the operator is an agency or business offering transportation services to the general public. This definition of operator eliminates automobile drivers, who only provide transportation services for themselves. For the automobile mode the operator is considered to be the group of agencies that built and operate the highway and the CBD parking lot.

THE MULTIMODAL NETWORK

Our network consists of two districts, Hometown and Loop City, and three modes. The network links correspond to the routes shown in figure 13.1. Each link is described by specifying its origin and destination nodes, its distance, and its capacity (the volume–travel time function to be applied).

LINK CHARACTERISTICS

1. Suburban walk links: Hometown's sidewalks have so much more capacity than walkers that they can handle any foreseeable amount of travel with no change in travel time.
2. CBD walk links: As with a number of link types in this problem, CBD walk links are used by many people in addition to the Hometown workers. Since we shall predict equilibrium flows for only one portion of the total number of actual users, we consider the number of other users to be fixed and deal with the travel-time data for Hometown users only. When this is done, we obtain a function with a definite capacity point, above which travel delays increase moderately.

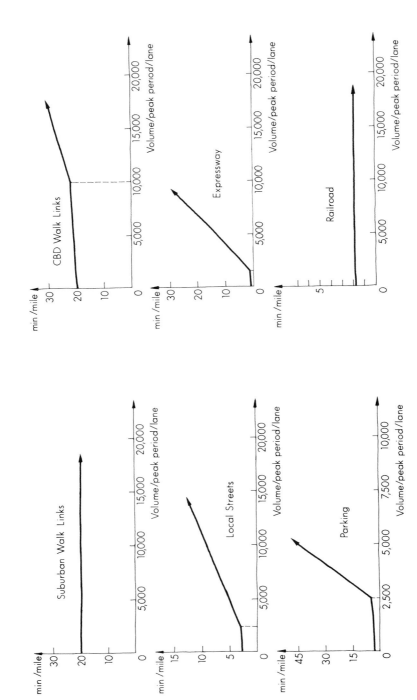

Figure 13.2 Volume–travel time functions for the six link types in the network.

Table 13.1 Base-case modal cost structure

Mode	Annual fixed costs ($/year)	Variable costs ($/passenger-mile)
Rail (total)	871,000	0.01
Park-and-ride		
Total	1,155,000	
Parking lot		0
Rail line		0.01
Automobile (parking lot)	945,000	0

3. Local street links: Both suburban and CBD local streets can be represented by a single volume–travel time relationship similar to that for CBD walk links.

4. Expressway links: The expressway between Hometown and Loop City is very heavily used. Each Hometown user has a significant effect on the expressway travel time. When there are no Hometown users, the speed is 60 mph. When there are 1,700 Hometown users per peak period per lane, the speed is 45 mph. Above 1,700 users the travel time increases 3.6 minutes per mile for each 1,000 additional trips.

5. Parking facilities: Both in Loop City and in Hometown, the parking facilities have a fixed capacity for Hometown users. Parking times increase very rapidly when these capacities are exceeded.

6. Railroad links: Even though the commuter railroad into Loop City is very popular, its capacity compared with present flows is so large that it need not be stated. Slight delays are experienced when larger numbers of riders must board and alight.

OPERATING POLICIES

During the two-hour peak period there are twelve trains, each of which stops at both stations being modeled. This implies that the frequency between districts 1 and 2 will be 12 departures/time period for both rail and park-and-ride modes (10 minutes headway).

Fares for the problem can be derived from the following unit costs:

Automobile operating costs	5¢/mile
Walk costs	0
Parking costs	
suburb	25¢
CBD	50¢

Rail fares
station closest to CBD   50¢
station farthest from CBD   60¢

These unit costs result in the one-way fares shown in table 13.2.

13.4.2 Specification of Activity-System Options

The following parameters will be used in the travel-demand equations defined in section 13.3.7:

$$U_R = -0.000167 \text{ IVTT}_R - 0.000417 \text{ OVTT}_R - 0.0024 \text{ OPTC}_R, \quad (13.8)$$

$$U_P = 0.2 - 0.000167 \text{ IVTT}_P - 0.000417 \text{ OVTT}_P - 0.0024 \text{ OPTC}_P, \quad (13.9)$$

$$U_A = 0.45 - 0.000167 \text{ IVTT}_A - 0.000417 \text{ OVTT}_A - 0.0024 \text{ OPTC}_A. \quad (13.10)$$

Note that this demand model is a mode-split model only. When the service levels (IVTT, OVTT, OPTC) change, there is no change in the total number of trips from Hometown to Loop City ($V_R + V_P + V_A$), only in the mode shares. This is consistent with the assumption that only work trips are being predicted.

Because of the system of demand models chosen, only one activity-system characteristic—the total number of trips from Hometown to Loop City—must be known. For the base year this figure is approximately 15,000.

13.4.3 Flow-Pattern Prediction

Using all of the foregoing data on transportation- and activity-system options, we can calculate link travel times and volumes, interdistrict travel times, and total modal volumes. The link volumes and travel times are shown on a map of the network in figure 13.3, and the total base-case modal volumes and travel times are displayed in table 13.3.

Table 13.2 Base-case one-way fares

Mode	Fare ($/trip)	Representation
Rail	0.60	0.60 path
Park-and-ride	0.90	0.40 link, 0.50 path
Automobile	1.55	1.55 link

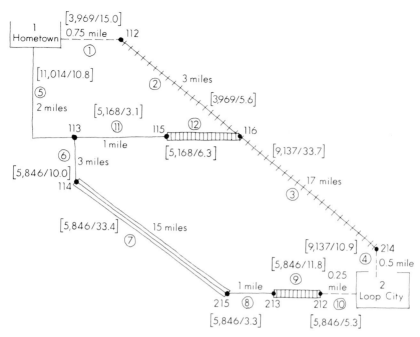

KEY: [volume / travel time (minutes)]

Figure 13.3 Base-case volumes and travel times.

Table 13.3 Base-case total trips and travel time

Mode	Total trips	Travel time (minutes)
Rail	3,969	70.2
Park-and-ride	5,168	69.8
Automobile	5,846	74.6
Total	14,983	

13.5 THE FUTURE CASE

In our first attempt to predict transportation flows in the corridor we shall assume that no transportation options are changed from the base case. This first prediction is therefore the null case. The target for prediction is taken to be fifteen years in the future, or about 1995.

Hometown–Loop City travel is expected to increase from 15,000 to 22,500 trips per peak period over the next fifteen years. The trip-making characteristics for both old and new residents are expected to remain unchanged.

The resulting future flow pattern is summarized in table 13.4 and figure 13.4. Without even considering the cost impacts of this alternative, we can see that a major decrease in the level of service has occurred to accommodate the 50 percent increase in travel volume. Travel time by park-and-ride is over 1.5 hours, by automobile almost 2 hours. Investigation of the network indicates that the major delays are caused by the parking lots and by the CBD walk link from the train station.

■ *Question 13.1* Review the predicted flow patterns for the base and future cases.

a. Where are the points of congestion? Where is there no congestion?
b. Explain the differences in flow patterns for the base and future cases. How have the mode splits changed? Why?
c. What kinds of options would you consider as alternatives?

13.6 SEARCH FOR BETTER ALTERNATIVES

Based on the results in the previous section for the null case, a number of proposals have been made to prevent deterioration in the level of service between Hometown and Loop City. We list five of

Table 13.4 Predicted future year total trips and travel time

Mode	Total trips	Travel time (minutes)
Rail	8,149	75.2
Park-and-ride	7,054	93.1
Automobile	7,266	116.5
Total	22,462	

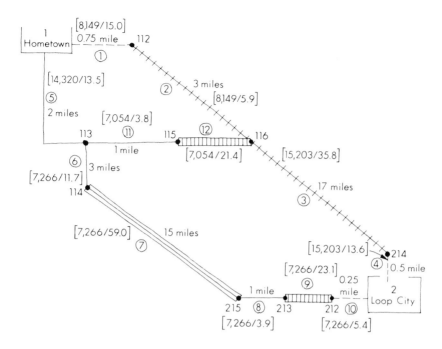

KEY: [volume/travel time (minutes)]

Figure 13.4 Predicted future year volumes and travel times for the null alternative.

these alternatives along with their annual capital costs to the transportation operators:

1. Adding two reversible express lanes to the expressway (annual capital cost: $1,050,390 to be paid by the highway operator).
2. Adding 2,500 new parking spaces to the suburban parking facility (annual capital cost: $578,000 to be paid by the park-and-ride operators).
3. Adding 2,500 new parking spaces to the CBD parking lot (annual capital cost: $964,180 to be paid by the highway operator).
4. Increasing the CBD parking fee to $1 (no capital cost).
5. Reducing rail fares by one-half to 25¢ and 30¢ (no capital cost).

■ *Question 13.2* Examine the proposals that have been made for improvement in the system.

a. What effects do you think each will have on the flows in the network?

b. Which alternative do you think would be the most desirable? Why?

13.7 PREDICTED FLOW PATTERNS

TTP has been used to predict the flow patterns for each of the five alternatives proposed in section 13.6. The results are summarized in table 13.5.

■ *Question 13.3* Study the predicted flow patterns for each of the alternatives. Explain why each alternative has the effects predicted. Do these seem reasonable? Why, or why not? Note that minor differences shown in the tables are due to the approximation procedure utilized (incremental assignment); see Martin and Manheim (1965) and Manheim and Ruiter (1970, 1973).

Table 13.5 Flow patterns

Link	OVTT or IVTT	Base		Future		Alt. 1	
		V	t	V	t	V	t
1	OV	3,969	15.0	8,149	15.0	7,540	15.0
2	IV	3,969	5.6	8,419	5.9	7,540	5.9
3	IV	9,137	33.7	15,203	35.8	14,354	35.5
4	OV	9,137	10.9	15,203	13.6	14,354	13.2
5	IV	11,014	10.8	14,320	13.5	14,934	13.9
6	IV	5,846	10.0	7,266	11.7	8,120	12.7
7	IV	5,846	33.4	7,266	59.0	8,120	19.8
8	IV	5,846	3.3	7,266	3.9	8,120	4.2
9	OV	5,846	11.8	7,266	23.1	8,120	30.0
10	OV	5,846	5.3	7,266	5.4	8,120	5.4
11	IV	5,168	3.1	7,054	3.8	6,814	3.7
12	OV	5,168	6.3	7,054	21.4	6,814	19.5
Rail		3,969	70.2	8,149	75.2	7,540	74.5
Park-and-Ride		5,168	69.8	7,054	93.1	6,814	90.8
Automobile		5,846	74.6	7,266	116.5	8,120	86.0
Total Value		14,983	—	22,469	—	22,474	—
Average Time		—	71.8	—	94.2	—	83.6

All times are in minutes. Alt. 1: Add two expressway lanes. Alt. 2: Expand suburban parking capacity. Alt. 3: Expand CBD parking capacity. Alt. 4: Increase CBD parking fee to $1. Alt. 5: Cut rail fares in half.

13.8 PREDICTED IMPACTS

The user and operator impacts of the base and future cases and alternatives 1 through 5 are indicated in tables 13.6 and 13.7. The trade-off between a single user impact (average composite service level) and a single operator impact (total net revenue) is shown in figure 13.5. Note that the average composite service level is plotted as a negative number so that both axes represent a "benefit"—an impact for which increasing levels represent increasing desirability. (Compare this with figure 5.12.)

■ *Question 13.4* Compare the impacts of the alternative actions. Which action would be preferred? Why?

■ *Question 13.5* What new alternative actions would you suggest be analyzed? Why?

Alt. 2		Alt. 3		Alt. 4		Alt. 5	
V	*t*	*V*	*t*	*V*	*t*	*V*	*t*
7,164	15.0	7,547	15.0	8,282	15.0	8,282	15.0
7,164	5.8	7,547	5.9	8,282	5.9	8,282	5.9
15,457	35.9	14,363	35.5	15,385	35.8	15,385	35.8
15,457	13.7	14,363	13.2	15,385	13.7	15,385	13.7
15,310	14.2	14,926	13.9	14,183	13.3	14,183	13.4
7,017	11.4	8,110	12.7	7,080	11.5	7,080	11.6
7,017	54.5	8,110	74.2	7,080	55.6	7,080	57.0
7,017	3.8	8,110	4.2	7,080	3.8	7,080	3.9
7,017	21.1	8,110	8.2	7,080	21.6	7,080	22.3
7,017	5.4	8,110	5.4	7,080	5.4	7,080	5.4
8,293	4.3	6,816	3.7	7,103	3.8	7,103	3.8
8,293	9.2	6,816	19.5	7,103	21.8	7,103	21.4
7,164	75.4	7,547	74.5	8,282	75.4	8,252	75.3
8,293	82.3	6,816	90.8	7,103	93.5	7,057	93.1
7,017	110.4	8,110	118.7	7,080	111.3	7,159	113.4
22,474	—	22,473	—	22,465	—	22,468	—
—	88.9	—	95.4	—	92.4	—	93.0

Table 13.6 Operator impacts

	Base	Future	Alt. 1	Alt. 2	Alt. 3	Alt. 4	Alt. 5
Trips/Peak Period							
Rail	3,969	8,149	7,540	7,164	7,547	8,282	8,252
Park-and-Ride	5,168	7,054	6,814	8,293	6,816	7,103	7,057
Automobile	5,846	7,266	8,120	7,017	8,110	7,080	7,159
Total	14,983	22,469	22,474	22,474	22,473	22,465	22,468
Improvement Costs (10^6 \$/year)							
Rail	—	—	—	—	—	—	—
Park-and-Ride	—	—	—	0.58	—	—	—
Automobile	—	—	1.05	—	0.96	—	—
Total	—	—	1.05	0.58	0.96	—	—
Operator Net Revenue (10^6 \$/year)							
Rail	−0.45	−0.01	−0.07	−0.11	−0.07	+0.01	−0.65
Park-and-Ride	−0.36	−0.07	−0.11	−0.46	−0.11	−0.06	−0.54
Automobile	−0.17	+0.02	−0.92	−0.02	−0.83	+0.93	0.0
Total	−0.98	−0.06	−1.10	−0.59	−1.01	+0.98	−0.72

Alt. 1: Add two expressway lanes. Alt. 2: Expand suburban parking capacity. Alt. 3: Expand CBD parking capacity. Alt. 4: Increase CBD parking fee to \$1. Alt. 5: Cut rail fares in half.

13.9 NEW ALTERNATIVES

13.9.1 Formulating the Alternatives

Analysis of the results presented in sections 13.7 and 13.8 led to the conclusion that a piecemeal approach to improving the transportation system in the case-study area is not sufficient. Clearing up a single bottleneck only causes another bottleneck to appear. The strategy of removing a single bottleneck in each alternative was therefore changed before a second round of alternatives was generated. The new strategy was to concentrate on each mode in turn, improving all the existing and potential bottlenecks for the mode. This led to the specification of three new alternatives:

Table 13.7 User impacts

	Base	Future	Alt. 1	Alt. 2	Alt. 3	Alt. 4	Alt. 5
Rail							
Volume	3,969	8,149	7,540	7,164	7,547	8,282	8,252
IVTT (min)	39.3	41.7	41.3	41.7	41.3	41.7	41.7
OVTT (min)	30.9	33.6	33.2	33.7	33.2	33.7	33.7
OPTC ($)	0.60	0.60	0.60	0.60	0.60	0.60	0.30
CSL ($)	−1.31	−1.40	−1.39	−1.41	−1.39	−1.40	−1.33
Park-and-Ride							
Volume	5,168	7,054	6,814	8,293	6,816	7,103	7,057
IVTT (min)	47.6	53.0	53.1	54.4	53.1	53.0	53.0
OVTT (min)	22.2	40.0	37.7	27.9	37.7	40.5	40.1
OPTC ($)	0.90	0.90	0.90	0.90	0.90	0.90	0.65
CSL ($)	−1.05	−1.55	−1.49	−1.26	−1.49	−1.56	−1.49
Automobile							
Volume	5,846	7,266	8,120	7,017	8,110	7,080	7,159
IVTT (min)	57.5	88.1	50.7	84.0	105.0	84.3	85.8
OVTT (min)	17.05	28.5	35.4	26.5	13.6	27.0	27.6
OPTC ($)	1.55	1.55	1.55	1.55	1.55	2.05	1.55
CSL ($)	−0.92	−1.52	−1.31	−1.42	−1.32	−1.56	−1.47
Total							
Volume	14,983	22,469	22,474	22,474	22,473	22,465	22,468
Mode Shares							
Rail	0.26	0.36	0.34	0.32	0.34	0.37	0.37
Park-and-Ride	0.34	0.31	0.30	0.37	0.30	0.32	0.31
Automobile	0.39	0.32	0.36	0.31	0.36	0.32	0.32
Average Service Levels							
IVTT (min)	49.3	60.3	48.3	59.6	67.9	58.7	59.3
OVTT (min)	22.5	34.0	35.4	29.3	27.5	33.7	33.8
Time (min)	71.8	94.3	83.7	88.9	95.4	92.4	93.1
OPTC ($)	1.03	1.00	1.03	1.01	1.03	1.15	0.81
CSL ($)	−1.09	−1.49	−1.39	−1.36	−1.40	−1.50	−1.42

Alt. 1: Add two expressway lanes. Alt. 2: Expand suburban parking capacity. Alt. 3: Expand CBD parking capacity. Alt. 4: Increase CBD parking fee to $1. Alt. 5: Cut rail fares in half.

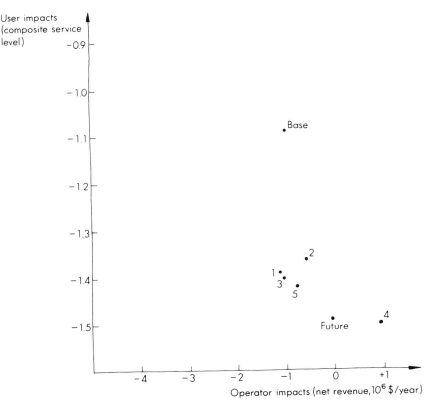

Figure 13.5 Trade-offs between user and operator impacts for the base case, the future case (the null alternative), and five alternatives for improving the system.

A. Rail improvements
1. Double the capacity of the entire rail line.
2. Run twice as many trains from both train stations to the CBD.
3. Replace the existing engines with new engines capable of average speeds of 55 mph.

B. Park-and-ride improvements
1. Double the capacity of the rail line to the park-and-ride station only.
2. Run twice as many trains from the park-and-ride station to the CBD.
3. Add 2,500 new spaces to the suburban parking lot.
4. Replace all existing engines with new engines capable of average speeds of 55 mph.

C. Automobile improvements
1. Add two reversible express lanes to the expressway.
2. Add 2,500 new spaces to the CBD parking lot.
3. Increase the capacity of the local suburban streets by 50 percent.
4. Increase the capacity of the local CBD streets by 50 percent.

A fourth alternative, D, combines all of the improvements listed above for alternatives A, B, and C. Two additional alternatives were developed to investigate the effects of pricing policy on the transportation system:

B1. Reduce park-and-ride and rail fares
1. Eliminate the suburban parking fee.
2. Reduce all rail fares by half to 25¢ and 30¢.

B2. Increase the rail fare to $1 and the park-and-ride fare to $1.20 ($0.15 driving cost, $0.25 parking cost, and $0.80 rail fare).

13.9.2 Development of Annual Costs for Typical Projects

The annual costs for the alternatives described in the previous section were developed using the unit construction or acquisition costs listed in table 13.8. These costs and the associated unit lives and capital recovery factors can be used to calculate the annual costs of a wide range of transportation-system alternatives. The calculations for the projects making up the new alternatives are presented in the following sections. All calculations assume that the entire cost of improvements must be borne by peak-hour travelers, half by the A.M. peak travelers with whom we are concerned. The standard calculations will be described in detail for the first project and then summarized for the remaining projects.

1. DOUBLING RAIL CAPACITY FROM HOMETOWN

Rail capacity can be increased by constructing a second inbound track for the entire distance from Hometown to Loop City (20 miles). This track can be built on the existing right-of-way and roadbed at a cost of $700,000 per mile ($14,000,000 total). Track life is assumed to be 30 years, resulting in a capital recovery factor of 0.1061 at 10 percent interest. The annual cost is therefore

$$\$700{,}000 \times 20 \times 0.1061 = \$1{,}485{,}000,$$

and half of this amount, $742,700, must be allocated to the A.M. peak period.

Both stations must be expanded to take advantage of the new track. The expansion cost per station is $400,000. Using the same capital

Table 13.8 Unit costs of proposed improvements in the transportation system

	Total acquisition cost ($)	Project life (years)	CRF[a]
Rail			
1. Conventional engines, per engine	250,000	30	0.1061
2. Higher-speed engines (55 mph ave.), per engine	350,000	30	0.1061
3. Very-high-speed engines (80 mph ave.), per engine	400,000	30	0.1061
4. Passenger cars (100 passengers), per car	220,000	30	0.1061
5. Track construction on existing right-of-way and roadbed, per track-mile	700,000	30	0.1061
6. Station expansion, per track	400,000	30	0.1061
Highway			
1. Addition of express lanes to existing expressway, per lane-mile	660,000	30	0.1061
2. Widening of suburban arterials, per lane-mile	470,000	30	0.1061
3. Widening of CBD arterials, per lane-mile	750,000	30	0.1061
Parking			
1. Suburban parking structure, per parking space	4,520	40	0.1023
2. CBD parking structure, per parking space	7,540	40	0.1023
Other			
1. Buses for feeder or express service (50 passengers), per bus plus 50¢ per vehicle-mile for labor	32,000	12	0.1468
2. Moving sidewalk from the CBD rail station to the CBD (capacity: 10,000 per hour), total cost	10,000,000	40	0.1023

[a]All capital recovery factors are for an interest rate of 10 percent.

recovery and peak allocation factors, the annual cost for station construction allocated to the A.M. peak period is

$400,000 \times 2 \times 0.1061 \times 0.5 = \$42,440.$

The total annual cost is therefore $785,140.

2. FASTER TRAINS WITH FREQUENCY DOUBLED, BOTH STATIONS

New, faster engines must be purchased. The number needed is a function of the round-trip distance, frequency, and speed. The following formula can be used to calculate the number of trains needed (compare equation 7.38):

$$T = N_R = \left\langle \frac{QD}{2v} \right\rangle, \tag{13.11}$$

where T is the number of trains needed, D the round-trip distance in miles, Q the frequency in departures per peak period ($Q/2$ per hour), v the average train speed in miles per hour, and the brackets indicate "next-highest whole number."

In this case the round-trip distance is 40 miles, the desired frequency is 24 departures, and the new average speed is 55 miles per hour. The number of trains needed is therefore

$$T = \left\langle \frac{40 \times 24}{2 \times 55} \right\rangle = 9.$$

The A.M. peak annual cost can be found from the following data:

Cost per engine = $350,000,
Engines required = 9,
Engine life(CRF) = 30 years (0.1061),
A.M. peak allocation = 0.5,
Annual cost = $350,000 × 9 × 0.1061 × 0.5
 = $167,100.

Since the existing passenger cars can be used with the faster engines, there is no cost for passenger cars.

3. DOUBLING RAIL CAPACITY FROM THE PARK-AND-RIDE STATION

This project is very similar to the first one discussed, with the distance changed to 17 miles and only a single station to be expanded. The annual cost of track construction can be found as follows:

Construction cost per mile = $700,000,
Distance = 17 miles,
Track life (CRF) = 50 years (0.1061),
A.M. peak allocation = 0.5,
Annual cost = $700,000 × 17 × 0.1061 × 0.5
 = $631,300.

The annual cost of station construction is given by:

Construction cost per station = $400,000,
Number of stations = 1,
Station life (CRF) = 30 years (0.1061),
A.M. peak allocation = 0.5,

Annual cost = $400,000 × 1 × 0.1061 × 0.5
            = $21,220.

The total annual cost is thus $652,500.

4. FASTER TRAINS FOR BOTH STATIONS, NO CHANGE IN FREQUENCY

Equation (13.11) can be used to determine the number of new engines required:

Round-trip distance = 40 miles,
Frequency = 12,
Train speed = 55 mph,

$$T = \left\langle \frac{40.12}{2.55} \right\rangle = 5.$$

The annual cost is given by:

Cost per engine = $350,000,
Engines required = 5,
Engine life (CRF) = 30 years (0.1061),
Peak allocation = 0.5,
Annual cost = $92,840.

Again the existing passenger cars can be used.

5. FASTER TRAINS FOR THE PARK-AND-RIDE STATION, DOUBLED FREQUENCY

This project, implemented in conjunction with the last one, adds an additional 12 departures from the park-and-ride station, resulting in a total of 24 from that station and 12 from the suburban station. The number of engines required in addition to those determined previously is:

Round-trip distance = 34 miles,
Frequency = 12,
Train speed = 55 mph,

$$T = \left\langle \frac{34 \times 12}{2 \times 55} \right\rangle = 4.$$

The annual cost is given by:

Cost per engine = $300,000,
Engines required = 4,
Engine life (CRF) = 30 years (0.1061),

A.M. peak allocation = 0.5,
Annual cost = $63,660.

No new passenger cars are needed.

6. EXPANDED SUBURBAN PARKING STRUCTURE

The suburban parking structure can be expanded to 150 percent of its present capacity:

Cost per parking space = $4,520,
New spaces = 2,500,
Structure life (CRF) = 40 years (0.1023),
A.M. peak allocation = 0.5,
Annual cost = $578,000.

7. REVERSIBLE EXPRESS LANES

The existing expressway can be expanded by adding two reversible express lanes within the present right-of-way, and using the present structures:

Cost per lane-mile = $660,000,
Lanes = 2,
Distance = 15 miles,
Roadway life (CRF) = 30 years (0.1061),
A.M. peak allocation = 0.5,
Annual cost = $1,050,390.

8. EXPANDED CBD PARKING STRUCTURE

The CBD parking structure can be expanded to 150 percent of its present capacity:

Cost per parking space = $7,540,
New spaces = 2,500,
Structure life (CRF) = 40 years (0.1023),
A.M. peak allocation = 0.5,
Annual cost = $964,180.

9. INCREASING SUBURBAN STREET CAPACITY

The suburban street capacity can be increased 50 percent by widening existing arterials. The number of new lanes and lane-miles, by link, are shown in table 13.9. The annual cost is given by:

Cost per lane-mile = $470,000,

Table 13.9 Increase in suburban street capacity

Link	Number of new lanes	Distance (miles)	Lane-miles of expansion
111-113	2	2	4
113-114	1	3	3
113-115	1	1	1

Roadway life (CRF) = 30 years (0.1061),
A.M. peak allocation = 0.5,
Annual cost = $199,470.

10. INCREASING CBD STREET CAPACITY

The CBD street capacity can be increased 50 percent by widening the existing CBD arterial, the link from 215 to 213:

Cost per lane-mile = $750,000,
Number of lanes = 1,
Number of miles = 1,
Roadway life (CRF) = 30 years (0.1061),
A.M. peak allocation = 0.5,
Annual cost = $39,790.

13.9.3 Annual Costs of the Alternatives

The annual costs of the alternatives described in section 13.9.1 are shown below. In each case the costs are derived from those developed in section 13.9.2. The numbers of the projects are listed.

Alternative A (rail)

1	785,140
2	167,100
Total	$952,240

Since both the rail and park-and-ride operators benefit, the annual cost is charged half to each.

Alternatives B, B-1, B-2 (park-and-ride)

3	652,500
4	92,840
5	63,660
6	578,000
Total	$1,387,000

The rail operator shares in the benefits of this alternative. He is therefore charged $587,000. The park-and-ride operator is charged $800,000.

Alternative C (automobile)

7	1,050,390
8	964,180
9	199,470
10	39,790
Total	$2,254,000

The park-and-ride operator shares in the benefits of this alternative. He is therefore charged $1,250,000. The automobile operator is charged $2,054,000.

Alternative D (all modes)

1	785,140
2	167,100
6	578,000
7	1,050,390
8	964,180
9	199,470
10	39,790
Total	$3,784,000

The annual costs by mode are:

Rail	476,000
Park-and-ride	1,254,000
Automobile	2,054,000
Total	$3,784,000

13.10 PREDICTED IMPACTS

Selected operator and user impacts of the new set of alternatives are shown in tables 13.10 and 13.11. Figure 13.6 repeats the graph of figure 13.5 with the new alternatives added. The results of class runs can be added to figure 13.6 to compare their total net revenues and composite service levels with alternatives 1–5, A–D, B1, and B2.

■ *Question 13.6* Compare the impacts of the new actions. Which action is now to be preferred? Why?

■ *Question 13.7* Formulate a statement of goals for which you feel new alternatives should be designed. What new alternatives would

Table 13.10 Operator impacts

	Alt. A	Alt. B	Alt. C	Alt. D	Alt. B1	Alt. B2
Trips/Peak Period						
Rail	8,470	7,257	6,518	6,108	7,224	7,111
Park-and-Ride	7,100	8,501	6,497	7,723	8,670	8,509
Automobile	6,899	6,719	9,456	8,648	6,584	6,854
Total	22,469	22,477	22,471	22,479	22,478	22,474
Improvement Costs						
(10^6 \$/year)						
Rail	0.48	0.59	—	0.48	0.59	0.59
Park-and-Ride	0.48	0.80	0.20	1.25	0.80	0.80
Automobile	—	—	2.05	2.05	—	—
Total	0.95	1.39	2.25	3.78	1.39	1.39
Operator Net Revenue						
(10^6 \$/year)						
Rail	−0.45	−0.69	−0.18	−0.70	−1.27	+0.05
Park-and-Ride	−0.54	−0.65	−0.36	−1.22	−1.77	+0.03
Automobile	−0.03	−0.05	−1.74	−1.85	−0.07	−0.04
Total	−1.02	−1.39	−2.28	−3.77	−3.11	+0.04

Alt. A: Improve rail service. Alt. B: Improve park-and-ride service. Alt. C: Improve automobile service. Alt. D: Improve service for all modes. Alt. B1: Improve park-and-ride service and lower fares. Alt. B2: Improve park-and-ride service and raise fares.

you suggest be analyzed to further these goals? What impacts would you expect for your proposed alternatives? Why?

■ *Question 13.8* Do figures 13.5 and 13.6 provide a sufficient basis for making a decision?

■ *Question 13.9* Prepare an evaluation report (using the methodology of chapter 9), based on the data available in this case study.

■ *Question 13.10* Describe briefly what you consider to be the major limitations of this analysis of the Hometown–Loop City corridor. What changes in this analysis would you suggest? Why? (You may find it useful to choose two real communities with which you are familiar as a basis for answering this question.)

■ *Question 13.11* What assumptions does this analysis make about the effects of level of service on automobile ownership? On automobile occupancy (number of persons per car and degree of "sharing" of an automobile, as in carpooling)? What alternative assumptions might you consider, and how would you modify the analysis to reflect them?

Table 13.11 User impacts

	Alt. A	Alt. B	Alt. C	Alt. D	Alt. B1	Alt. B2
Rail						
Volume	8,470	7,257	6,518	6,108	7,224	7,111
IVTT (min)	23.6	23.7	40.8	23.4	23.8	23.7
OVTT (min)	31.3	33.9	32.5	30.4	33.9	33.8
OPTC ($)	0.60	0.60	0.60	0.60	0.30	1.00
CSL ($)	−1.16	−1.23	−1.37	−1.14	−1.16	−1.32
Park-and-Ride						
Volume	7,100	8,501	6,497	7,723	8,670	8,509
IVTT (min)	37.2	38.8	49.1	34.8	38.9	38.9
OVTT (min)	38.1	26.7	34.5	21.6	27.7	26.7
OPTC ($)	0.90	0.90	0.90	0.90	0.40	1.20
CSL ($)	−1.34	−1.07	−1.37	−0.90	−0.98	−1.14
Automobile						
Volume	6,899	6,719	9,456	8,648	6,584	6,854
IVTT (min)	80.5	78.0	54.9	45.5	75.4	80.8
OVTT (min)	25.5	24.1	20.9	16.5	23.0	25.2
OPTC ($)	1.55	1.55	1.55	1.55	1.55	1.55
CSL ($)	−1.37	−1.31	−0.99	−0.79	−1.25	−1.36
Total volume	22,469	22,477	22,471	22,479	22,478	22,474
Mode Shares						
Rail	0.38	0.32	0.29	0.27	0.32	0.32
Park-and-Ride	0.32	0.38	0.29	0.34	0.39	0.38
Automobile	0.31	0.30	0.42	0.38	0.29	0.30
Average Service Levels						
IVTT (min)	45.4	45.6	49.1	35.8	44.7	46.9
OVTT (min)	31.7	28.3	28.2	22.1	28.3	28.5
Time (min)	77.1	73.8	77.3	57.8	73.1	75.3
OPTC ($)	0.99	1.00	1.09	1.07	0.70	1.24
CSL ($)	−1.28	−1.19	−1.21	−0.92	−1.12	−1.26

Alt. A: Improve rail service. Alt. B: Improve park-and-ride service. Alt. C: Improve automobile service. Alt. D: Improve service for all modes. Alt. B1: Improve park-and-ride service and lower fares. Alt. B2: Improve park-and-ride service and raise fares.

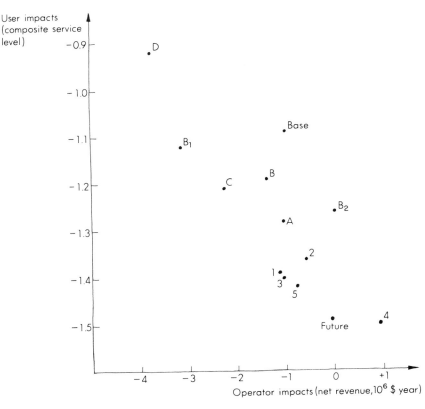

Figure 13.6 Trade-offs for eleven alternatives plus base and future cases.

■ *Question 13.12* The two goal variables used in this study are total operator net revenue, summed over all modes, and average composite service level, averaged over all groups of users (see sections 9.4, 9.5).

a. Critically appraise the use of these two goal variables. How relevant might they be in an actual corridor study? How would you alter them? What important issues might be overlooked if only these two goal variables were used?

b. Identify additional goal variables that you feel would be useful for this study. Discuss the various interests whose views would be important in such a study, and indicate which of your goal variables would reflect their views.

c. Define operationally the goal variables you have identified for which values can be determined with the data available and/or with reasonable additional assumptions (for example, air pollution emission rates).

d. Using these goal variables, develop the values for the alternatives studied; use impact tableaus, trade-off displays, and other forms of tables and graphs, where appropriate.

e. Prepare an evaluation report. Be sure to include recommendations for future work, including development of additional alternatives.

f. Compare the results with those of question 13.11. Did your views change? How? Why?

■ *Question 13.13* Develop one or more additional alternatives. State clearly the objectives you are trying to achieve with these alternatives. Predict their impacts. (Use TTP if available; if not, estimate impacts by interpolation and extrapolation of the preceding results, using the demand model and estimating an approximate equilibrium; describe the methods you use clearly.) Prepare an updated or interim evaluation report, giving the results of these new alternatives and referencing (or incorporating) your previous evaluation report.

TO READ FURTHER

Variations and extensions of this case study are given in the teacher's manual. Earlier versions of this case study used DODOTRANS, a subsystem of ICES. For a description of DODOTRANS see Manheim and Ruiter (1970). For a description of ICES see Roos (1966). Documentation of TTP is available from the author. See also Manheim and Ruiter (1973).

EXERCISES

13.1(P) Modifications that can be made to this case study include multiple user groups, multiple origins and destinations, and more exploration of operating and pricing options (as in chapter 5). Set up an expanded version of the case study and analyze appropriate options.

13.2(P) Set up a version of the case study for one of the following contexts:

a. An airport access problem in a city with two airports.

b. The planning of a new container port in a rapidly developing country.

14
Choice

14.1 THE CHALLENGE OF CHOICE

Until recently the dominant consideration in transportation decisions has usually been transport efficiency—how to get the greatest mobility for the lowest cost. Now, because of shifts in public values, many significant social, economic, and environmental factors must also be considered explicitly. People have become much more aware of the widespread effects of transportation system changes and of differences in opinion among various groups as to the ends that should be pursued; and a wider variety of interest groups than in the past have become effective at articulating their views in a politically effective manner.

Consider a plan to construct a major international airport in an economically depressed region. This project will provide significant direct benefits: more efficient movement of people and goods and increased mobility and access. These benefits to air travelers and shippers can be quite substantial. There will also be indirect positive effects, such as new employment opportunities in both construction and operation of the airport, an increase in the region's trade and industry, and other general multiplier effects due to the direct benefits accruing to users and to those involved in construction of the facility.

In the past these positive effects would have been balanced strictly against the monetary cost of the project in deciding on its desirability. Now, however, we realize that the "costs" of the project must include adverse effects on nearby individuals and communities, both quantitative and qualitative: increased noise levels in areas near the airport; takings of land, whether residential, commercial, industrial, agricultural, or undeveloped; increased traffic on local roads; and increased demands on local public facilities such as water, electricity, and sewage disposal. The project may also require destruction of resources of historical, cultural, or environmental significance, including farmland, wildlife refuges, or open spaces.

Moreover, the incidence of these effects on groups and interests will most likely be quite uneven: some will benefit greatly, others only slightly, and yet others will be adversely affected to a greater or lesser extent. In this example it is likely that the majority of the benefits will accrue to the business community and other high-income travelers, whereas most of the disbenefits will be experienced by residents of communities near the airport, few of whom will in general be either air travelers or employees of airport-related businesses.

Whenever such a differential incidence of effects occurs, there is a potential for political conflict. In recent years this potential has become realized in many transportation planning situations as more and more interest groups have come to recognize these effects and initiated political action to defend what they perceive as their interests. For example, in 1970 in Boston, Massachusetts, public pressure caused the governor of the state to call a moratorium on highway construction, to undertake a major restudy of metropolitan-area transportation priorities, and ultimately to redirect transport investment priorities from highways to transit (Gakenheimer 1976; see also *National Observer* 1969, Geiser 1970, Colcord 1970, 1971, Mauch 1973).

One result of this increased political activity has been, in many countries, the passage of new laws or promulgation of new regulations that significantly affect the transportation planning and decision-making processes. These laws and regulations address such issues as public involvement, coordinated comprehensive planning, special treatment of sensitive lands, and detailed documentation of the probable effects of proposed actions. For example, in the United Kingdom the Noise and Property Value Compensation Act of 1973 orders increased compensation for people suffering adverse social or economic effects from public works programs; the objective is to achieve a more equitable distribution of gains and losses by compensation of adverse effects (Brown and Deakin 1974).

In the United States emphasis has been placed on requiring a documented, open, participatory planning process and establishing specific performance standards for some impacts. Examples include the National Environmental Policy Act of 1969, which established the requirement for environmental impact statements; Section 4(f) of the Department of Transportation Act of 1966, which specified that certain publicly owned land cannot be used for highways unless there are no "feasible and prudent alternatives"; the Federal-Aid Highway Act of 1962, which established 3-C ("continuing, comprehensive, and cooperative") urban-area transportation planning; and the Clean Air Act of 1970 and its amendments, which established national ambient air quality standards and resulted in development of transportation control plans for various air quality control regions. Similar laws are in effect or under consideration in other nations.

How should transportation systems analysts respond to these issues? We must start with a recognition of the basic fact that transportation systems analysis is not and cannot be an apolitical process. Any major change in a region's transportation network will affect so many different people, as individuals and as groups, that a balancing of interests and a consideration of the distribution of benefits and disbenefits becomes an inevitable part of the decision process. When this balancing is done implicitly or in secret by analysts who view themselves merely as technicians, it is almost inevitable that the results will be socially inequitable, and it is likely that the choices they lead to will not be implementable because of political opposition. The consequence is widespread distrust of planners and analysts and of the decision makers who employ them.

If, however, the balancing is done in an open and explicit manner, with the views of all affected individuals and groups taken carefully into account and with their representatives kept informed and consulted at appropriate stages, the choices that are finally made can have a wide base of political support and therefore be implementable.

The role of the analyst is therefore of paramount importance in the process of choice, even though the decisions will generally be made not by the analyst but by those who employ him. This is the theme that we shall pursue in this chapter. We shall present a set of principles and guidelines for constituting the process of analysis in a politically conscious, open, and socially equitable manner. We shall adopt the perspective of a public-sector transportation planning agency, but our results will be applicable to operators and in many respects to private-sector agencies as well (see section 15.5). We start, however, with a look backward, at a "classical" model of transportation planning.

14.2 A CLASSICAL MODEL

It is useful to examine briefly a traditional view of the role of the analyst in the transportation planning and design process. The following description will be, to some extent, a caricature in that not all of the elements have been present in every past transportation study; unfortunately there have been all too many studies in which all of these elements *have* been present.

14.2.1 Impacts Considered

Until the late 1960s the primary impacts explicitly considered in the vast majority of transportation studies were those impacts on users and on operators that could be described in quantitative terms and given monetary values: for users, changes in travel times, out-of-pocket costs, vehicle wear-and-tear, and accidents; and for operators, the costs of construction and operation of a proposed project.

14.2.2 Evaluation Methods

The traditional evaluation methods were either pure judgment or, more recently, economic evaluation methods such as benefit/cost analysis. (The limitations of these methods are discussed in section 9.3.2.)

14.2.3 Participants in the Process

Almost always, the transportation analyst was hired and directed in a tightly structured way. The client was a single agency or individual, and the analyst had little or no interaction with other agencies or individuals (except to obtain technical data) during the process of analysis. Usually the first significant indication most interests had that there was a study under way (other than, perhaps, a press release) was when the legally required public hearing was held at the end of the study. (In many situations and regions even public hearings were not required!) At this point the alternatives had long since been defined, and the analyst's recommendation to the client organization was already firmly developed and usually the subject of the hearing. At such a point in the process issues raised by people who had not previously participated in the process would be met by defensive reactions on the part of the client agency or the analysts: "It's too late to consider that issue. The study is over and there isn't any time or money left," or "How can you question our analysis? We are trained professionals and have applied all our talents to the job," or "That's a good point, and it would have been useful to study it, but too much time has already been spent on analyses; it's time to make a decision because additional delays will cost X million dollars a day because of inflation, interest costs, etc." In other words, the process was a closed one, in which participation was limited, and if outsiders were allowed to insert their views at all, it was only at the end of the process when changes could not be accommodated without major disruptions.

14.2.4 Role of the Analyst

In this classical process the role of the professional was perceived to be that of an objective technocrat, free of value biases or "politics." The analyst was given the study task, went away and did his analyses, came back to the client, presented his results and his recommendations, and expected them to be accepted as a rational, objective, "professional" determination of the "best" course of action.

14.2.5 Critique

This classical model does not work anymore in most transportation analysis contexts, public or private. As we have already noted, a much broader set of impacts must now be considered, and the incidence on different interests of adverse and beneficial effects must be considered explicitly. Further, many people today do not accept the values and goals of transportation agencies, or of professional analysts, as their goals. Different groups have different goals; since there is no agreement on the objectives to be achieved, the analyst is often seen by some groups as reflecting the values of other, opposing groups, not as an objective participant in the process. Interests may feel that a study has been misdefined in the first place: for example, the right alternatives were never studied, or not enough attention was given to certain impacts (as when an urban study considers alternative expressway locations in a corridor but never considers transit improvements or arterial street improvements or measures to reduce the demand for travel by automobile, and fails to consider the effects of land takings or air-quality degradation). Today people want an open process in which they are involved from the beginning, so that they can influence all the elements of the study and thereby ensure that it addresses the issues they think are important.

Many transportation agencies have recognized the need for increased consideration of social, economic, and environmental factors and are improving their procedures for the identification and measurement of such potential impacts. However, the problem goes much deeper than simply a need for improved methods of technical analysis.

Today in many countries there is a crisis of confidence, in some cases in governments and other formal institutions, and in others in the role of technical professionals, the so-called technocracy, and especially engineers and planners. This crisis of confidence has many roots, some unique to a given country or region, others more general, such as the increased concern for environmental quality, a growing public mistrust of science and concern with the misuse of technology, and a general concern that more opportunities be opened up for private citizens to influence the governmental decisions that shape their worlds and life-styles. As a result many sectors of the public tend to reject the judgments of the technical professionals responsible for planning such major public facilities as highways, airports, and other transportation projects. Many citizens feel that transportation professionals and their organizations are out of step with the rest of society in that their proposals do not reflect the values and objectives those citizens hold and feel should influence transportation decisions.

For all these reasons the classical model is inappropriate in many situations today. It does not work, in short, because the politics of transportation have changed. It is also undesirable on grounds of professional ethics: the analyst must and should conduct his professional activities in a manner consistent with the spirit of the times.

14.3 OPENING UP THE PROCESS

We have seen that the classical model is no longer acceptable in many countries and many situations. In this section we suggest a set of six principles on which a more appropriate process should be based. Along with the statement of each principle we elaborate a set of guidelines for its application to the process of analysis.

14.3.1 Principle I: The Range of Alternatives

The range of alternatives to be analyzed should be sufficiently broad as to represent real choices and should always include the null option.

A wide range of both long- and short-term courses of action are available in every situation. In addition to direct transportation-system options, there are a variety of options for the activity system, including land-use controls and staggered work hours. Transportation options should be considered only as one part of a more comprehensive course of action and should be effectively coordinated with such nontransportation components as economic-development policies, social policies, and urban-design policies.

The null alternative is very important. Data on the effects of making no change in the existing transportation system should be developed to a level of detail consistent with that of other alternatives, to serve as a reference point for identifying, on a comparative basis, the adverse and beneficial effects of any other alternative.

Sufficient alternatives should be developed to demonstrate the key trade-offs that are potentially achievable among different combinations of positive and negative impacts. It is important that variations on alternatives, or basically new alternatives if necessary, be developed to minimize or avoid adverse social, economic, environmental, or urbanization impacts. Monetary compensation is one useful means of achieving equity, but there are others.

Suggestions from other agencies and from the public of alternatives to be studied should be as carefully considered as are the alternatives developed by the professional staff. Affected interests generally have a unique and valid understanding of their problems and of potential solutions and should be encouraged to develop their own proposals.

A wide range of alternatives should be developed and presented to all potentially affected interests throughout the course of the technical studies. The presentation of alternatives should serve as a catalyst to meaningful and constructive debate in the community of affected interests, to assist in bringing out issues and in clarifying community objectives. The presentation of initial alternatives should begin early enough in the process so that this debate can influence the development and refinement of additional alternatives.

14.3.2 Principle II: The Identification of Effects

All beneficial and adverse effects of each alternative, whether suggested by past experience, by judgment, by analysis, or by an affected interest, should be fully explored, and the information uncovered should be widely distributed.

The information developed for each alternative must include identification of the incidence of effects, that is, the specific groups and interests that are beneficially or adversely affected. It is essential that the differential effects of impacts be determined early so that effective programs to mitigate adverse effects can be developed.

This means that much greater attention must be given to effects that are qualitative and uncertain, such as social, aesthetic, long-term land-use, and environmental effects. The process of identifying, analyzing, and evaluating such effects must be designed to incorporate qualitative information and to deal with uncertainty.

Timely identification of impacts is essential in the planning process. Likely significant impacts should be identified sufficiently early in the technical studies that alternatives can be modified to take advantage of beneficial opportunities and to avoid or reduce potential adverse consequences.

Impact prediction should be carried out in association with public involvement activities because many impacts can be identified most readily through interaction with the affected community and because the significance of many impacts is dependent on personal values and priorities. Particular effort should be devoted to impacts that are perceived by particular sectors of the public as important to them. Other agencies can contribute much useful information and may be able to provide technical assistance and resources.

The level of effort to be devoted to identification of impacts, and the degree of detail for particular alternatives, should be that appropriate for each stage of the planning process. It is better, however, to err on the side of too much effort devoted to identification of impacts, rather than too little. Numerous procedures to predict various types of impacts are available, ranging from quick approximation methods to precise measurement tools. The prediction methodology chosen should be a function of the needs of the study and should be modified as needed during the study.

14.3.3 Principle III: Involving the Public

Each affected interest, individual or group, must be given ample opportunity to express its views in a timely and constructive manner and thus to influence the course of studies as well as the final actions taken.

Information about the existence, status, and results (interim and final) of studies should be made available to other agencies and to the public throughout the course of studies. Such information should be clear and comprehensible and should include the alternatives being considered, all the effects of the alternatives and their incidence, and the time schedule of major points in the process that are of public interest.

A program of public involvement should be developed to provide the opportunity for an open and constructive exchange of views between affected interests and the transportation agency throughout the process. There should also be appropriate institutional arrangements (formal or informal) to encourage effective participation throughout the process by other governmental agencies, such as environmental or housing agencies and local governments.

Conducting an effective program of public involvement requires special training for staff and, in some instances, the addition of new kinds of staff with skills not usually available in engineering and planning agencies.

Public involvement is an essential element in defining the goals to be achieved by transportation in a particular study and in developing information on values to be used in reaching a decision on a course of action to implement:

There is no single set of values underlying any community. Different groups of people can be expected to have different interests and different priorities, and the importance people attach to a particular factor depends on the context. For example, one group might generally prefer the development of recreation facilities to the preservation of wilderness areas; another group might generally prefer just the opposite. But in a specific instance, people who are usually supporters of wilderness preservation might prefer building a park.

While there may be consensus objectives, these are generally at such an abstract level as to be nonoperational from the point of view of the need for distinguishing among alternative actions. At the operational level, it can safely be assumed that different interests will have different priorities. Further, these interest groups have only a partial understanding of their objectives, and their priorities with respect to these objectives are dynamic, changing over time. As individuals are confronted with new issues or new opportunities to make choices, they clarify their understanding of their preferences, and perhaps change them, through the process of making choices.

Most people have difficulty in formulating meaningful, consistent statements of objectives. In fact, most people probably have preferences that are inconsistent, until that point where by having to make a choice they must impose a certain partial consistency on their preferences. In particular, if asked to express their preferences in the abstract in terms of the relative weights to be given to different attributes of highway projects—for example, construction cost versus safety versus parkland takings versus social disruption—most people will have difficulty formulating a complete, exhaustive, consistent set of weights.

When confronted, however, with a small number of explicit alternative actions or projects and also with statements of their likely impacts, most people can with some introspection reach a conclusion about their preferences for the several alternatives. This requires far less information about their underlying, partially known values; they need only express preferences about a small number of differences, not about all possible combinations. Thus, by examining and weighing the differences between alternatives, information about preferences and community values is gradually clarified.

It is clear, then, that trying to determine "community objectives" in the abstract (by certain kinds of opinion polls, for instance) is a futile exercise. Similarly, techniques such as linear scoring functions and cost/benefit analysis which assign different weights (that is, importance) to factors cannot be assumed to represent "public preferences." Not only do different people have different preferences, but any one person's preferences depend on the choices available and the specific effects of those choices. (Manheim et al. 1975b)

In short, the best way to find out about people's transportation preferences is to ask them how they feel about specific alternatives and why they feel that way.

Effective, informed participation of the community—federal, state, and local agencies, officials, interest groups, and individual citizens—is necessary in all phases of transportation planning, starting during the stage of initial system planning and continuing through location and design studies of particular projects and even into the stage of construction or other implementation activities. Such interaction helps the transportation agency to identify and predict both the incidence and the magnitude of social and environmental impacts and to learn what issues people consider important. Also, community groups can serve as a useful source of suggestions for solutions to transportation and related community problems.

Different levels of participation should be provided, depending on interest. Participation may range from general awareness to periodic attendance to intensive involvement.

A community interaction program normally will utilize several techniques simultaneously. Emphasis should be placed on face-to-face interaction with small groups and on the use of existing institutions and channels of communication. Agency staff must be trained to have an attitude of openness and responsiveness and be willing to listen to and learn from community inputs.

14.3.4 Principle IV: Equity

When adverse impacts result for some interests in order that benefits can be provided for others, those adversely impacted should be adequately compensated. Further, the benefits should be distributed broadly.

There are a wide variety of ways in which, in principle at least, adverse effects can be compensated, if not alleviated entirely, and benefits distributed more broadly. Consider the following hypothetical examples:

1. Expanding an airport extends the zone of aircraft noise to intrude on a previously quiet residential area, thus imposing an adverse impact on residences in order to benefit air travelers. Affected residents can be compensated by financial means—payments for adequate sound-proofing, payments in compensation for health effects, and payments to enable relocation to another neighborhood.
2. Building a new highway or transit line in an urban corridor requires substantial land taking and displacement of families and jobs. To help displaced families stay in the neighborhood, new housing and new industrial facilities with attractive rentals can be developed in the neighborhood by a community nonprofit organization with financial support from the transportation agency. Combined with appropriate training programs, such an activity can provide new employment opportunities for some local residents in construction and other areas.
3. Introducing a major technological innovation such as containeriza-

tion of marine freight transport will cause significant loss of longshoring jobs. Part of the increased profits from lower labor costs and greater revenues can be used to finance earlier retirements for a part of the labor force, more substantial pensions, aid in relocating or seeking other jobs, and, as a last resort, guaranteed job security for all presently employed labor.

4. A metropolitan area desires to undertake construction of a rail transit system in one corridor. To finance the system a tax is proposed (an areawide sales tax, an increment on the property tax, and/or an employer-payroll tax). All residents in the area will pay the tax, but only travelers in the transit corridor will benefit from the improved service. To provide a more equitable distribution of benefits, part of the tax receipts could be devoted to improving transit service in other corridors.

The key barriers to achieving more equitable distribution of impacts, once the issue is recognized, are institutional: lack of legal or administrative authority, explicit legal barriers, or administrative reluctance to innovate. All of these barriers can be overcome; recent legislative history has shown this conclusively (Bridwell 1969, S. L. Hill 1969, DEVELOPMENT AND COMPENSATION 1972, Brown and Deakin 1974).

The intellectual foundations of this principle are both theoretical and political. From a political perspective, in today's transportation world significant changes can rarely be implemented if they are inequitable, because of the significantly broadened distribution of political power and the increased openness of the decision-making process. From a theoretical perspective, this principle of equity is rooted in the Pareto criterion of welfare economics: "Any change which harms no one and which makes some people better off (in their own estimation) must be considered to be an improvement" (Baumol 1965, p. 376). Most action alternatives as initially formulated will not meet this criterion, but it is almost always possible to modify actions to make them substantially more equitable. Consider action E which gives benefits to interest X but causes adverse effects on interest Y. The principle of equity requires that some of the benefits to X be used to compensate Y, resulting in the modified action E'. This is the compensation principle (Baumol 1965, p. 376, Winch 1973, p. 143ff.) but carried out, not just "in principle" (see also Henderson and Quandt 1958, p. 219, Mishan 1970, Nwaneri 1970, Passonneau 1972).

Equity often costs more, but part of these costs can usually be covered by capturing some of the benefits to those interests most positively affected. Equity is a moral imperative, and in transportation it is often a political imperative as well.

14.3.5 Principle V: Dealing with Uncertainty
Uncertainties that may exist should be explicitly recognized.

In predicting impacts, it is essential that uncertainties be explicitly considered. For significant impacts, likely ranges of uncertainty should be indicated. This often means that extensive sensitivity studies must be done to determine the effect on predicted impacts of model parameters, model structure and logic, and assumptions about exogenous events.

Considerations of uncertainty should also influence the development of alternatives. Where uncertainties are likely to be significant, some alternatives should be designed to allow for maximum flexibility in implementation.

System plans refer to all of the facility, operating, and policy changes proposed over time for the transportation system of a particular geographic region or a particular operator. Changes in demand, in technology, and in values—both public and private—should be anticipated, and system planning should explicitly take into account the uncertainties inherent in long-range forecasts. To do this system plans should be defined as multiyear program plans (see chapter 1); implementation decisions should be made in stages over a period of time, thus enabling system-level options to be kept open longer (Manheim 1969, 1977a, Neumann and Pecknold 1973, Reno, Schneideman, and Manheim 1973, Neumann et al. 1974, Neumann 1976).

As portions of the system plan are implemented and as new or revised data become available, the implementation and decision-making schedule may be revised. Plans formulated in this way can more readily respond to changes in conditions and to new information than can target-year master plans based on highly uncertain estimates. Although a master plan for some future year has certain advantages in that it is tangible and easy to visualize, it tends to limit one's maneuvering room since it cannot be easily modified to respond to new information, revised impact estimates, or changes in such contextual elements as economic, demographic, sociological, and political events.

In evaluating alternatives, explicit attention should be given to identifying, for each, the options that are left open for possible future implementation and those that are foreclosed. Careful attention should be given to the relative advantages and disadvantages of strategies that preserve flexibility relative to other strategies (UMTA 1976a).

Periodic review and reassessment of transportation decisions should be built into all stages of system and project studies to provide a mechanism of accounting for new information and changes in previous assumptions or estimates. The structure of the decision process and the relationships among institutions should be specifically designed to stimulate this review and reassessment.

Programming is the process in which specific decisions are made about the initiation of implementation of system changes. The programming activity represents a key forum for reconsideration of system plans in light of ongoing project studies and also for reconsideration of current project studies in light of recent system planning (Manheim 1977a). Programming thus represents the most effective means of integrating system and project studies. The programming process should produce annually a single program document—the multiyear program plan introduced in chapter 1—as the central focus of periodic review and reassessment of transportation decisions.

14.3.6 Principle VI: The Decision Process

The process of reaching a decision should be open, participatory, and decisive, resulting in decisions that are implementable and implemented.

There are four important facets to this principle: organizational structure, the role of evaluation, management requirements, and the necessity of an interdisciplinary approach.

The organizational structures and interrelations of political and technical institutions influence the extent to which social, economic, and environmental effects are given serious consideration in transportation planning and decision making. Responsibilities for conducting studies, providing data, preparing reports, and making decisions should be allocated in such a way so as to maximize efficiency and effectiveness, to promote coordination, to encourage public input, to provide equal access to decision makers and the decision-making process, to clarify decision-making authority, and to permit an orderly process of appeal of transportation decisions.

Conflict is inevitable among interests and institutions, and the structure of the planning and decision process should make it possible for such conflicts to be resolved constructively.

In most cases many individuals and organizations have some role in the process of reaching a decision on implementing a change to the transportation system. Often the extent of involvement and interrelationships of these actors is unclear and confusing to the public, and sometimes even to some of the major participants in the decision process.

The structure of the decision-making process should be clearly defined. The public should know who has responsibility for the final decision and what role each of the major participants is to play. Moreover, they should understand the sequence of actions through which various participating organizations and individuals will be involved in the process of reaching a decision.

For the public to have confidence in the decision-making process, the public must be able to understand it. The structure of the process should be simplified as much as possible. This structure should be communicated to the public, so that citizens can understand what opportunities they have for presenting their views and otherwise affecting the process of reaching a decision.

More than anything else, the decision-making process must be such as to merit the public's confidence that the issues they consider important have been considered fully with all other relevant issues.

Central governments can often provide important incentives to other institutions—for example, at the regional and subregional levels—to participate more effectively in the decision-making process and to assume increased responsibility for transportation planning and implementation. A desirable pattern of institutional involvement is not something that can be determined in the abstract, however; it must be tailored to each specific national and local situation.

As discussed in chapter 9, evaluation is the activity of examining the available alternative actions in light of the possible goals, assessing the relative desirability of each action, and summarizing the key issues to be considered by interested parties in reaching a decision. An evaluation report should be prepared periodically throughout an analysis as a way of documenting the work performed and insights gained at key points and especially as a basis for informing decision makers of the key issues prior to their reaching a decision. A systematic evaluation process can be an important management tool in determining matters requiring further study, in controlling the quality of work performed, in setting priorities for subsequent activities, and in checking that all affected interests have had an opportunity to express their views.

In the approach described in chapter 9, evaluation involves the comparison of alternatives and the analysis of impact data, with account taken of the incidence of all significant impacts and the different viewpoints held by various organizations, officials, and concerned groups and individuals. This type of evaluation should assist in structuring the learning experiences of all the participants in the transportation planning process through identification of significant trade-offs, clarification of issues of choice, and indication of major areas of uncertainty.

Documentation of work performed and decisions made is crucial to an effective planning and decision processs. When such information is recorded in the form of evaluation reports, other required reports such as the environmental impact statements or the Analysis of Alternatives Reports of the U.S. Urban Mass Transit Administration (UMTA 1976a) become natural products of evaluation.

This principle also has important implications for the management of the process of analysis. Such a process should be decisive yet managed in a style that will enable it to be dynamic, flexible, creative, and responsive to changing conditions and to the needs of the community.

Personnel, fiscal, and time resources should be allocated periodically, based on an explicit choice of objectives and determination of needs. A major responsibility of process management is the development, and revision as necessary, of a process strategy and associated work program. The periodic preparation of an evaluation report is a useful aid in this activity.

In view of the wide variety of activities it must perform, it is clear that the planning team or organization must be staffed with individuals possessing a variety of professional skills. The staff may be from one organization or comprised of professionals on loan from several organizations. Regardless, it is essential that practical management procedures be utilized to ensure that the total planning process is conducted in a fully integrated, systematic, interdisciplinary manner with all relevant professional specialties influencing the course of studies and the final products. (In the United States the National Environmental Policy Act of 1969 requires the use of a systematic interdisciplinary approach. See also Devine 1971, Rogers 1968, TEAM CONCEPTS FOR URBAN HIGHWAYS AND URBAN DESIGN 1968, Parker and Panther 1974.)

Important qualifications for a project or study manager are the ability to manage an interdisciplinary group, to understand at least in a general sense the language and techniques of each discipline, and to work effectively and constructively with community groups.

Historically many transportation organizations, especially public agencies, have been dominated by engineers. The qualifications for project manager and for management at other levels within a transportation organization are much broader than simply a transportation engineering background. There is no reason why, because of their educational background, engineers are inherently more competent to deal with transportation problems than are many other kinds of professionals. Therefore these positions should be open to professionals other than engineers. This is not to say that engineers should be excluded from these positions; rather, no specific advantage or requirement should be given to people with engineering background as opposed to people with other kinds of relevant professional backgrounds.

14.4 IMPLEMENTATION

Full implementation of these principles and guidelines would require significant changes in most transportation organizations. Determining what change should occur is easier than determining how to bring about that change. Implementation of major changes of the nature described requires a carefully coordinated and sequenced set of changes in training, policy, personnel, and day-by-day practices, executed over a period of time.

The process of implementing changes is as important as the changes themselves (Schein 1969, Giel 1972, Bennis et al. 1976). A number of organizational barriers work against change in general and especially against the introduction of increased sensitivity to these issues within transportation agencies. Any such organization is a complex system, and a social system tends to react to suggested changes in ways that preserve old policies and practices. Major changes such as those implied by the foregoing guidelines tend to provoke complex and compensating reactions that may have the effect of subverting the changes. A coherent diagnosis of the organization can help those who initiate change to anticipate these reactions and to plan for them.

In spite of these difficulties (discussed further in section 15.6), these principles and guidelines have already been partially implemented in the United States. In the field of highway planning the Federal Highway Administration of the U.S. Department of Transportation has issued regulations to the state highway departments which reflect these guidelines (FHWA 1973a; see also Manheim, Suhrbier, and Bennett 1972, Report to Congress. . . 1972). In response, each of the 50 state transportation or highway departments has prepared a plan for improving its organization and procedures, and numerous changes and innovations have been implemented (California Department of Transportation 1973, Pennsylvania Department of Transportation 1973).

Under the sponsorship of the American Association of State Highway Officials, a manual has been developed which describes a number of specific techniques transportation agencies can use in implementing these principles and guidelines (Manheim et al. 1975b).

In the field of urban transportation several recent federal regulations also reflect these principles. The Urban Mass Transportation Administration of the U.S. Department of Transportation has promulgated a policy for major urban mass transportation investments (UMTA 1976a) which explicitly requires that transit systems be planned (1) for implementation in stages with periodic revision of long-range plans to respond to changing conditions (principle V), (2) with full opportunity for timely public involvement in the planning process (principle III), (3) with consideration of a wide range of alternatives, including improved management of existing transportation systems and measures to reduce the use of automobiles in congested areas (principle I), (4) with equitable distribution of transit service improvements throughout the metropolitan area (principle IV), and (5) with identification and evaluation of all significant impacts (principle II). In addition, UMTA and the Federal Highway Administration have jointly issued regulations on the urban transportation planning process which explicitly reinforce the emphasis on programming (principle V) (FHWA and UMTA 1975a; see also Reno, Schneideman, and Manheim 1973, Manheim 1977a).

In the field of airport planning the philosophy reflected here has been incorporated in an airport planning manual issued by the U.S. Department of Transportation (CLM Systems, Inc., 1972).

These principles and guidelines have also provided the basis for a major in-depth analysis of the organization and procedures of a major state highway department and have resulted in a number of specific recommendations (Manheim et al. 1972; Manheim and Suhrbier 1973).

14.5 SUMMARY

The changed context of transportation decisions calls for increased consideration of social, economic, and environmental issues and especially of the differential incidence of adverse and beneficial effects. If he is to be effective in bringing about change, the transportation systems analyst must recognize the depth of this change and its profound implications for everything he does. The decision process must be structured in such a way that the decisions reached are technically sound; decision makers, the public, and other interested parties have full confidence in the planning and decision-making process; and therefore the decisions taken are implementable, both technically and politically. This view requires significant changes from the classical role of the analyst in the planning and design process described in section 14.2.

A set of principles to guide the development of a process with the above features has been proposed. They are based on four premises:

1. The overall process through which social, economic, and environmental considerations are brought into transportation planning and decision making is as important as the particular techniques used for predicting impacts.

2. Issues of social equity must be explicitly recognized and taken into account.

3. Different groups of people can be expected to have different interests and differential priorities.

4. The role of the professional—the transportation systems analyst— is a key issue in designing a process.

These basic principles deal with the range of alternatives, the identification of effects, public involvement, equity, uncertainty, and the decision process. A number of specific guidelines based on these broad principles have been suggested.

Although full implementation of these principles and guidelines would require significant changes in many organizations, progress has already been made in implementing them in some contexts.

TO READ FURTHER
The theory behind the principles outlined in this chapter is described in more detail in Manheim (1973a,c), FHWA (1973a), and the other references in section 14.4.

On the diversity of effects to be considered see Sheehy (1974), Perfalter and Allen (1976), and Hyman and Manley (1977). On the changed context of urban transportation decisions see *National Observer* (1969), Organization for Economic Cooperation and Development (1969), Webber and Angel (1969), Colcord (1970, 1972), Demaree (1970), Geiser (1970), Mauch (1973), Brown and Deakin (1974), and Gakenheimer (1978). On public involvement see chapter 15.

Early work on uncertainty emphasized applications of decision theory; see Manheim (1966a, 1970d), Manheim, Bhatt, and Ruiter (1968), the paper by Wilson et al. in Organization for Economic Cooperation and Development (1969), Pecknold (1970), Khan (1971), Neumann and Pecknold (1973), and Knudsen (1977).

For the practical ramifications of the emphasis on programming see Reno, Schneideman, and Manheim (1973), Suhrbier and Bennett (1973b), Neumann et al. (1974), FHWA and UMTA (1975a), the report TRANSPORTATION PROGRAMMING PROCESS (1975), Forbes and Womack (1976), and Neumann (1976).

EXERCISES

14.1(C) Review PPM 90-4 (FHWA 1973a).
a. Compare with the guidelines suggested in this chapter. Discuss.
b. Suggest alternative approaches that might have been taken to implement the philosophy expressed in this chapter. Discuss advantages and disadvantages.

14.2(P) Obtain the action plan for a state highway or transportation agency. Evaluate it critically with reference to this chapter and to PPM 90-4.

14.3(P) Using the guidelines presented in this chapter, do a critical appraisal of an actual transportation analysis, either a study presently under way or a recently completed project for which documentation is available. (*Examples:* an airport planning study; a transit plan; or a proposal for changes in marine port prices, operations, or physical facilities.)

15
The Role of the Professional

15.1 INTRODUCTION

Our central theme in chapter 14 was that transportation decisions are essentially political. To choose a particular action entails choosing a distribution of beneficial and adverse effects. Because there is no rational or objective means of balancing benefits to one group against losses to another, this will involve a subjective judgment.

In most situations the responsibility for making a final decision will not lie completely in the hands of a single individual. Even in cases where the ultimate authority and responsibility does nominally reside in a single individual—the president of a private firm or public-sector enterprise, a minister or secretary of transportation, or a president, mayor, or governor—there will almost always be a number of other individuals and interest groups who have some influence over the decision.

The transportation analyst must see his role as being both technical and political. The *technical* role of the analyst is do an analysis that is valid, practical, relevant, and constructive in clarifying the issues that should be considered by all parties who will have some influence over the decision. The *political* role of the analyst is to serve as a constructive "catalyst" to the political processes in which individuals from many organizations interact in reaching a decision.

In this chapter we shall outline a basic model for the role of the transportation systems analyst in the political process. This model will be normative, that is, it will prescribe the structure and style of activities to be undertaken by the analyst and the technical team of which he is a member. As such, it reflects subjective judgments. While these judgments are based on the principles and guidelines of chapter 14, they are nevertheless subjective, and the reader should consider the model as a basis for thought and discussion and should examine it critically.

Our description of the model will be built from three major elements:

1. the objectives of the process of analysis;
2. a strategy for striving for these process objectives; and

3. the implications of this strategy for the role of the analyst.

The basic model will be outlined first in the context of public-sector transportation decisions, that is, situations in which the transportation analyst is working, directly or indirectly, for a public agency, such as a highway department, an airport or seaport authority, or a public transit operator. The applicability of the model to private-sector transport decisions will be discussed in section 15.5.

In this chapter we shall use the term "planning and design process" interchangeably with "process of analysis" as a general label for all of the activities in which the analyst and the technical team are engaged.

15.2 PROCESS OBJECTIVES

Based on the discussion in chapter 14 we now propose the following expanded version of the statement of objectives offered in section 9.1: *The objectives of analysis are to clarify issues of choice; to supply full and accurate information to the people charged with making decisions; to achieve substantial, effective community agreement on major elements of the planning and design process; and to achieve substantial, effective community agreement on a course of action that is feasible, equitable, and desirable.*

15.2.1 Clarifying Issues of Choice

The transportation analyst should work to clarify all issues in any way related to the given transportation study that involve choices among alternatives or the balancing of interests. He should explore these issues from many points of view in order to make explicit possible trade-offs among alternatives. This seemingly purely technical process will be effective only if it incorporates the following elements:

1. All interested parties should have an opportunity to get involved in the planning and decision-making process.
2. Alternative actions sufficiently different as to represent real choices should be investigated with the public.
3. Analysts, decision makers, and citizens should understand both the effects of each alternative and the distribution of those effects.
4. Opportunity for meaningful negotiation on what comprises an equitable distribution of gains and losses should be provided.

15.2.2 Supplying Full and Accurate Information

The analyst's sense of what information is essential for those who must make the final transportation decisions should be governed by an understanding of the issues involved in those decisions. Moreover, the analyst must always be aware of nontransportation ramifications of transportation decisions and should therefore supply input to decision makers with responsibilities in areas such as economic development, land-use planning, housing, and public utilities. The transportation analyst has a responsibility to make sure that *all* decision makers have sufficient up-to-date, accurate information on transportation proposals.

15.2.3 Achieving Substantial, Effective Community Agreement on Major Elements of the Planning and Design Process

Ultimately agreement is desired on a course of action to be implemented, that being the main objective of a transportation study. There are, however, other points in the process of analysis at which achieving agreement among the involved parties is important and may be helpful in reaching a final consensus. For example, agreement should be sought on the following items:

1. general aspects of the process, including the scope and timing of studies and the roles and responsibilities of various organizations, officials, and interest groups;

2. the community interaction program, including who should participate, the means for direct participation, the timing and format of major public events, and the availability of data and draft reports; and

3. interim decisions during the course of analysis, including what alternatives deserve further study, and whether new alternatives are needed; what impacts should be given highest priority for study and most importance in decison making; and whether the scope of studies or the schedule for decisions should be modified.

Agreement on these interim choices does not guarantee agreement on a final course of action. Full consensus may well be unattainable at any stage when the potential gains and losses involved are significant. But by striving for substantial agreement, the transportation agency is likely to unearth the major issues of choice and thus become better equipped to develop equitable solutions and pertinent information. Moreover, unless there is general agreement that the study process itself has been equitable, it will be much more difficult to achieve agreement on the final decision.

15.2.4 Achieving Substantial, Effective Community Agreement on a Course of Action That Is Feasible, Equitable, and Desirable

To clarify this goal we need to define its terms. Here the *technical team* is the organization of professionals that has responsibility for doing studies of alternative actions. This team might have as few as one or two professionals or as many as a hundred; it might be part of a national, state, or local agency, a metropolitan planning council, a consulting firm, or a private firm such as an airline or shipping company.

"COURSE OF ACTION"

The course of action that the analyst develops should be comprehensive. It should include both options directly affecting transportation and other actions that might usefully be coordinated with transportation-system changes to enhance the area under study. For example, a highway plan might be coordinated with plans for construction of replacement housing, air-rights construction, multiple uses of rights-of-way, new community facilities, urban redevelopment and other community action programs, job training, wildlife refuge development and other conservation measures, or rehabilitation of historical sites. This overall course of action will require coordination of many decision makers, both public and private.

"FEASIBLE"

The course of action must be feasible technically, financially, and legally. In some circumstances this may require actions by the technical team to stimulate changes in law or administrative interpretation.

"EQUITABLE"

To be equitable the course of action must adequately compensate people who receive undue negative impacts. For example, the traditional practice of compensating homeowners displaced by highway construction with "fair market value" is not equitable if equivalent replacement housing cannot be obtained on the open market at that price. Conditions such as limited housing supply or high interest rates or de facto segregation necessitate additional steps such as financial compensation over and above fair market value or even construction of replacement housing prior to highway construction (S. L. Hill 1969). Similarly construction of a new airport or shipping facility in a coastal zone may cause destruction of a nesting area used by waterfowl of an endangered species; an equitable plan would provide an alternative nesting area.

Equity considerations demand a structuring of the process of analysis in such a way that negative impacts are minimized. Compensation mechanisms will be necessary, but they should be employed only when it has been found impossible to identify other means of balancing negative impacts by positive benefits resulting from the course of action.

"DESIRABLE"

After the course of action has been so developed and tailored as to be feasible and equitable, the benefits should still be sufficiently great and broadly enough distributed to justify the costs that will be incurred if the action is implemented.

"COMMUNITY"

In our context the community consists of all those interests— individuals and groups—who will potentially be affected, positively or negatively, by any of the courses of action being considered. The community so defined is composed of diverse groups with very different values. For this reason it may not be feasible to get agreement on a statement of values, though it may well be possible to get agreement on a course of action.

"SUBSTANTIAL AGREEMENT"

It will never be possible to get total agreement from all of the interests affected. The technical team should nevertheless strive for this as an objective. The existence of a sizable group opposed to the course of action should be seen as an indication that a legitimate interest has not yet been adequately addressed. Major effort should be devoted to identifying and understanding this interest and developing a new component, or modification, of the course of action, or a new action, that is responsive to its concerns.

Under some circumstances the objective of seeking substantial agreement may be a conservative constraint. For example, it may happen that a particular strategy has unique and highly desirable effects even though it is opposed (or is likely to be opposed) by certain interests. In such situations the technical team has two responsibilities: to lay out the issues clearly for the responsible decision makers and to include in their presentation a careful assessment of both the advantages of the innovative strategy and also the disadvantages, especially the probability of failing to achieve implementation of the strategy and the consequences of that failure.

"EFFECTIVE AGREEMENT"

A course of action will be effective only if the whole community of interests is involved in the process of reaching agreement. Each group must be confident that its views, needs, and suggestions have been fully considered and taken into account; that the technical team is credible, open, and professionally knowledgeable; that there are no surprises or hidden arrangements; and that the agreed-upon course of action is indeed equitable and desirable from the points of view of the diverse elements of the community.

Another way of expressing the intent of "substantial, effective community agreement" is "sufficient acceptance of the action, by most interested parties, such that responsible decision makers are willing to take a decision and implement it."

15.3 A STRATEGY FOR ACHIEVING PROCESS OBJECTIVES

To achieve the process objectives the technical team must engage in extensive community interaction as well as technical analysis.

Technical analysis includes the collection and analysis of data, the development of alternative actions, the prediction of the impacts of each alternative on all the affected interests, and the analysis of these impacts.

Community interaction involves the manifold ways in which the technical team learns about the community in all its diversity, and particularly about the needs and values of its various segments; the community learns about the technical team and about the alternative courses of action and their consequences; and the community and technical team work together to achieve the objective of substantial, effective aggreement.

An effective community interaction program requires not only direct interaction but also information gathering and information dissemination. Some available techniques for each of these three basic activities are identified in table 15.1. The community interaction program should employ several techniques from each of the three basic areas (see Yukubousky 1974, Manheim et al. 1975b, Jordan et al. 1976).

Achievement of the process objectives involves careful coordination of technical analysis and community interaction. To indicate the kind of interplay that is required, a basic strategy has been formulated. This *process strategy* is a broad outline within which the

Table 15.1 A catalog of community interaction techniques

Information Gathering	Information Dissemination	Direct Interaction	Special-Purpose Techniques
Exploring existing sources	Posters, billboards, and signs	Small group meetings	Referenda
Working with local officials	Mail notices, brochures, newsletters, fliers	Working meetings	Technical assistance
Monitoring new developments	Newspapers (legal notices, advertisements, news articles, feature columns and articles, news releases, letters to the editor)	Workshops	Mediation and arbitration
Analyzing plans, programs, and reports		Hearings and other large public meetings	Ombudsman
Monitoring mass media		Field offices	Charrette
Fieldwork		Public information centers	
Surveys		Advisory committees, steering committees, other groups	
	Radio and television (announcements, news coverage, talk shows and community-oriented programs, documentaries)		
	Community organizations		
	Displays, models, maps		

Source: Adapted from Manheim et al. (1975b).

specific details will vary from situation to situation.

The basic strategy consists of four phases:

I. study design
II. exploration of issues
III. detailed analysis
IV. choice.

These phases are designed to promote a dynamic process in which knowledge and values change over time. Initially the technical team has relatively little conception of the issues and of the alternative actions open to it. As it works with the technical problem in interaction with various affected interests, the issues become clearer. As a range of meaningful alternatives is developed, negotiation of an equitable compromise can begin. In this negotiation process the team acts more or less as a catalyst, as local conditions warrant, while retaining that basic authority over technical issues which is its legal responsibility. Finally, either the objective of substantial, effective agreement is reached or, resources having been expended, the options are passed on to the relevant decision makers for their choice.

Within each phase of the process strategy, the resources of the technical team are assigned to the several ongoing activities according to the urgency of the activity and the particular talents and specialties of the team. The specific allocation of team resources will depend on the current issues at each point in the process, as well as on the scale of the project and the resources available. The organization and staffing of the process should be sufficiently flexible as to allow ready modification of priorities as new knowledge is developed.

15.3.1 Phase I: Study Design

The objectives of the study design phase are to propose initial definitions of the transportation problems to be addressed; to establish an initial data base; to acquire a basic understanding of the needs, plans, and objectives of potentially affected interests; and to develop a work program for the remaining phases.

The technical team will have some conception of the transportation problems of the area under study at the outset, especially since some perception of a "problem" will usually have led to the team's establishment. However, interested parties may have different views of their transportation needs and may be able to point out issues of which the team was not previously aware. It is necessary, then, to have public input in defining the transportation needs and desires that should be addressed in the study. To do this effectively the agency should publicize the initiation of the studies, make available the data that led to the studies, inform the public about prior transportation decisions and agency responsibilities, and establish mechanisms for public input.

The study design phase is the appropriate time to assemble basic data on social, environmental, and economic characteristics of the study area, as well as transportation and other technical data. Coordination with other agencies is vital; they will be a valuable source of data and will also provide input on their plans and objectives. Community interaction activities are an additional source of data and provide an initial sense of what the significant issues are likely to be.

The results of the study design phase are an initial definition of the scope of studies, including the types of alternatives to be considered, the roles and responsibilities of all participants in the process, and the shape of the community interaction program; and an initial work program, including identification of data needs, scheduling of technical studies—including model development, search, and prediction activities—and detailed design and timing of community interaction activities.

15.3.2 Phase II: Exploration of Issues

The objective of this phase is to develop an understanding of the major issues by discussing with affected interests a variety of alternative courses of action, each of which reflects different objectives. The intent is not to develop a final solution, but to bring out the issues involved in the particular study and to help all concerned to improve their understanding of the advantages and disadvantages of various alternatives. Because a wide range of possible alternatives is to be explored, "sketch planning" and approximate impact prediction techniques are often appropriate.

Extensive interaction with the public occurs during this phase, with special emphasis on bringing into the process all those who may be affected by or interested in the planning process. Information on alternatives and their impacts is presented, and the public's reactions and suggestions for modifications or for additional alternatives are gathered and fed back to the technical activities, leading to development of additional alternatives. Also, the transportation planning activities are coordinated with other community and regional plans.

Data collection continues throughout this phase. It is important to document the alternatives considered, their impacts, and the responses of groups and individuals. It may be useful to prepare interim evaluation reports summarizing results of the studies as they progress, for review by interested parties.

The exploration of issues requires intense interaction between technical analysis and community interaction activities. The results of analysis—the alternatives developed and their predicted impacts— are used in community interaction. The information gained from these interactions helps the team to better understand the various interest groups and their views and feeds back to the analysis activities, stimulating the search for further alternatives. By presenting the information about alternatives and their impacts to various groups, the team helps them to learn about the issues and demonstrates possible trade-offs.

Because the alternatives are relatively realistic, although preliminary, people can perceive the impacts on them and become motivated to involve themselves in the process.

During this phase the team and the interests involved in the process will develop a sense of what alternatives are deserving of further study, what issues must be addressed, and what additional data are needed. By the end of phase II the technical team should have achieved a heightened understanding of the issues in the community without the groups affected having made commitments to hardened positions. This understanding of both technical issues (the alternatives available and their impacts) and value issues (the incidence of impacts on different groups and the views of those interests) is particularly important to the team. The team's strategy for phase III should be based on its understanding of these issues. Modifications should be made as necessary to the scope of studies, the work schedule, and the community interaction program. The result of phase II is a clarification of the issues of choice, with a preliminary identification of a few alternatives that seem to have the greatest potential for acceptability.

15.3.3 Phase III: Detailed Analysis

The objective of phase III is to produce substantial agreement on a course of action. This will require a multifaceted program of action, including detailed development of actions explored in phase II and prediction of their impacts in order to develop feasible, equitable, and desirable courses of action.

In the technical analyses of this phase, many additional alternative actions are developed and their impacts predicted. However, whereas in phase II the emphasis was on a wide range of basically different alternatives, now there is a focus on variations of several basic alternatives in order to develop potential compromise solutions. For example, application of the criterion of equity will stimulate a search for means of modifying actions to reduce or eliminate inequities—through redesign, development of associated nonphysical program elements, or direct compensation.

In-depth prediction of the potential impacts of the alternatives under study is performed. By examining the incidence and magnitude of these impacts with the public, the team develops ways of modifying alternatives to alleviate negative impacts and to obtain additional beneficial impacts. Associated programs such as land-use control plans and relocation assistance are also developed in detail, and the funding

mechanisms for both transportation and related programs are determined.

In the community interaction activities the emphasis also shifts
from the clarification of objectives and the collection of information to
the start of constructive negotiations among conflicting interests.
Community interaction focuses on determining the acceptability of the
alternatives and associated programs and may suggest additional
impacts to be addressed and new alternatives or modifications to
alternatives to be considered. The agency works with the community
to find feasible compromises that will lead to more equitable and
desirable plans. Detailed evaluation reports are prepared periodically.

The results of this phase are one or perhaps a few detailed courses
of action—transportation proposals plus associated development,
coordination, and impact alleviation programs—that represent the
team's best efforts and that best reflect community preferences.

15.3.4 Phase IV: Choice

The objective of phase IV is to reach a decision on a particular course
of action. In this phase the team prepares a final summary evaluation
report, presenting the major alternative courses of action, discussing
for each alternative its advantages and disadvantages and the views
expressed by various groups and individuals, and pointing out the
main trade-offs among alternatives. Public participation in this phase
is useful for checking that the report is accurate and for obtaining
further input. (Very often the circulation of the summary evaluation
report in draft form for comment will meet important legal requirements; for example, in the United States it can serve as the environmental impact statement, as discussed in chapter 9.) A major element
of the community interaction program in this phase is often the legally
required public hearing, which provides an important opportunity for
interested parties to place their views on the record formally.

Finally, the responsible authority reaches a decision. Important
inputs to this decision will be the summary of the results of technical
analyses and community interaction presented in the evaluation
report and the views of interested parties recorded at the public hearing and in formal written comments on the evaluation report. Of
course, in almost all cases the individuals with formal decision-making
authority will have had prior knowledge of the process, since they will
usually have interacted with the technical team and with various
affected interests from time to time throughout the process.

If substantial community agreement has been reached on a particular course of action, the activities of phase IV provide an opportunity for documentation of that fact, through comments on the evaluation report and at the public hearing. The decision-making authority can then take the formal decisions that will initiate implementation of the selected course of action.

If, on the other hand, no clearly preferred course of action has been developed, the activities of phase IV bring the issues into focus. With the results of the process documented in the evaluation report and with clear expressions of the views of different interests, those with decision-making authority have the information necessary to reach a judgmental (political) decision.

15.3.5 Interrelation of the Four Phases

Although there is a general progression of the planning process from one phase to the next, there are a number of activities that are conducted throughout the process at various levels of detail. For example, impact prediction and community interaction would normally occur in each of the four phases. As new information becomes available, it may be necessary to cycle back to an earlier phase or level of planning and make revisions. Thus, although the intent of the study design phase is to gather basic data and determine the general scope of studies, much information will be obtained only in the later phases, and this information may require modification of the scope of studies. Similarly information on alternatives developed during the detailed analysis phase, or new alternatives suggested then, may necessitate a return to phase II. The point is that the dividing lines between phases should not be rigid; flexibility must be retained to allow work activities to be adjusted as new information becomes available. (This strategy is based on a particular set of hypotheses about the interaction of technical analysis with the political process; see Manheim 1973c.)

15.4 DUTIES OF THE ANALYST

The proposed process implies challenging duties for transportation systems analysts. In addition to their traditional responsibility for developing alternative transportation strategies and predicting impacts, transportation professionals also assume the following roles in this model:

1. *Community advisors:* Transportation professionals work with interest groups to develop alternatives that reflect their needs and

desires. They also help people clarify their objectives and broaden their perceptions of the impacts of alternatives on themselves and others.

2. *Ombudsmen and spokesmen:* Transportation professionals have an obligation to identify and voice interests that are not otherwise represented in the planning process. This will often mean speaking for national, statewide, or regional interests; for low-income communities who may not have the resources to participate effectively; for minorities, the elderly, and the disabled; and for those considerations (historic, aesthetic, or ecological, perhaps) for which no spokesmen have come forth. Professional responsibility includes the provision of technical assistance to interest groups and may extend to the development of alternatives responsive to their particular needs and interests.

3. *Impartial negotiators:* Transportation professionals must identify trade-offs and search for equitable compromises in situations of conflict. Their duties include promoting understanding of the positions, needs, and preferences of the various interests, stimulating negotiations among groups who are in conflict, and developing alternative packages through which compensation might be provided either in kind or as a quid pro quo to those who would be adversely affected by a particular proposal (for example, in the case of urban highways this might involve the development of industry along the highway right-of-way to provide new jobs in the community).

4. *Agents of, and advisors to, the decision-making authority:* Transportation professionals are responsible for fully informing decision makers on the alternatives, the impacts and their distribution, the reactions of different interests and segments of the public, and the issues being negotiated. They may also act as representatives of the decision-making authority during the course of studies.

15.5 APPLICABILITY OF THE MODEL TO PRIVATE-SECTOR DECISIONS

Our discussion of the model has so far adopted the perspective of public-sector transportation decisions. We shall now examine its applicability to private-sector decisions. Such situations would include privately owned transportation operations, such as an airline, railroad, shipping company, or automobile parking facility or transportation terminal, production facilities for transportation equipment and materials (including fuel), and organizations providing interface services between transportation operators and users, such as freight forwarders or travel agents.

The key characteristic of these situations is that the primary responsibility of the people to whom the transportation analyst reports is to a set of private individuals—the owners of the firm. The dominant concern of these individuals is usually profit—the return received by them on the capital they have invested in the enterprise.

Of course, the categories listed above need not be part of the private sector. An airline or railway may be an enterprise of a national government (as in fact most international airlines outside the United States are); a parking lot operator may be a municipal authority; and so forth.

Some situations may have elements of both public and private sectors. For example, transportation carriers that are government enterprises are often required to operate with a profit-maximization objective, at least to the extent that their net revenues should be sufficient to cover operating expenses. One major criticism of some U.S. public authorities is that while nominally public, they in fact behave like private firms. Many of these authorities obtain their financing through bonds that are backed by revenues from user fees (for example, the major revenues of an airport authority will typically come from fees charged to airlines for use of the airport, from rentals for space in the air terminal, and from automobile parking fees). Because of this financing mechanism such authorities tend to see their primary and dominant objective as maximization of their net revenues in order to keep their bonds attractive as investment opportunities for private capital.

The major premise on which the decision making of the private firm is based is that the sole objective is to maximize profit. (This may be measured in any of several ways; see the discussion of economic goal variables for operators in chapter 9.) From this premise it is then argued that the use of some such economic criterion of profit maximization is the *only* required—and appropriate—basis for evaluation of alternative transportation decisions.

This is rarely true in transportation. To put the problem in proper perspective the transportation analyst in a private firm should ask himself these questions:

1. Are there impacts that must be considered in the decision process in addition to those reflected in "profit"?
2. Are there affected interests outside of the organization that will receive some impacts as a result of the decision reached?
3. Are there affected interests outside of the organization that may be

able to influence the decision reached?

4. Is there more than one element within the organization that will participate in the process of reaching a decision?

If the answer to any of these questions is yes, then the use of profit maximization as the sole criterion for evaluation of alternative transportation decisions is inappropriate. To show this we shall discuss each of the questions in detail.

15.5.1 Impacts Not Reflected in Profit

Every transportation decision has a variety of impacts. Many of these can be translated into economic costs and revenues, and then their contribution to the net profit of the firm can be reflected appropriately in economic calculations. However, there are usually some impacts that, because they are significant even from the self-interest viewpoint of the private firm, will enter into the decision process even though they cannot be wholly reflected in a net-profit measure. Consider the case of a private shipping company, air carrier, or railroad pondering the introduction of a new type of vehicle that will allow changes in routes and services offered. Among the many impacts to be weighed in the decision process, in addition to those reflected in contributions to revenues, costs, and thus net profit, are these:

1. financial viability of the project in terms of its attractiveness to moneylenders (for example, the financing of vehicles is made easier by the fact that the source of money knows it can always obtain part of its funds back by repossessing and reselling the vehicles; investment in fixed facilities may not have the same convertibility);

2. effect on competitors in the same mode and in other modes and their likely responses;

3. possible difficulties in the transition to a new service pattern, especially with personnel; and

4. uncertainty of the predicted impact or the net profit and the degree of risk in the proposed action.

15.5.2 Range of Affected Interests

Many of the impacts of a decision will extend beyond the organization itself. Continuing the above list of impacts that may not be directly reflected in profit, we have:

5. effects on labor use (number of workers, job skills required, opportunities for advancement);

6. effects on users such as reducing the availability of service to

some users or providing especially favorable service (or rates) to certain groups of users; and

7. environmental and social effects such as increased noise, air pollution, or water pollution, changes in the community arising from the construction of new facilities, changes in service patterns, or changes in the viability of industries due to changes in the services provided.

15.5.3 Interests That Can Influence the Decision

If there are interests outside the organization that are affected by the decision, then from an ethical point of view one would argue that these interests should be consulted in evaluations of the alternative actions. Unfortunately the transportation analyst is not always free to adopt the procedures called for by his professional and personal ethics. Occasionally the management of a private firm will consider profit to the firm to be the only relevant criterion. In such a situation the analyst should ask the practical "political" question, Can any of the affected interests cause difficulty to, or even block, implementation of any of the proposed courses of action? If there is a possibility of this, then, as a practical matter, the impacts on these interests must be considered, even if the ethical argument for considering these impacts would be rejected by management.

Given the great public concern that has been manifested with regard to the social and environmental effects of transportation system changes, even wholly private enterprises must carefully consider any such potential effects of their actions. For example, a firm planning to introduce a new vertical or short takeoff and landing aircraft will quickly discover that such aircraft cannot be introduced into major metropolitan areas unless the noise effects are acceptable to communities near the proposed terminals. And development of new port facilities, even if wholly private, will still be subjected to careful appraisal on environmental grounds: a tract of coastal marshland that appears to be attractive for development because of its low purchase cost may be very expensive politically because it contains a unique ecological environment or plays a critical role in the region's groundwater cycle. Many other examples could be given.

15.5.4 Intraorganizational Elements Participating in the Decision Process

In almost every situation, even if the final decision is made solely by the chief executive of an organization, several other participants in the process within the organization will influence how the decision maker views the issues and reaches his decision. The exact balance of roles will depend greatly on personalities, organizational politics, the nature of the particular alternatives being considered, and a variety of external and internal pressures.

For example, the final decision about introduction of a new vehicle technology may well be made by a firm's president. But the vice-presidents for operations, for marketing, for finance, and for public relations will each have a different viewpoint on the decision, and they will influence the president's views in various ways, that being their role and responsibility. The president may also obtain views from several members of the board of directors and perhaps from other sources outside the organization, such as the institutions from which financing is sought.

Thus even when the impacts of a potential decision fall wholly within the firm and are seemingly all reflected sufficiently in terms of their consequences for net profit, the analyst must still consider the existence of several affected interests. It will rarely be possible to get agreement on values among these intraorganizational interests; because they have different roles, responsibilities, and personalities, they will have different values. It will therefore be important to work toward agreement on a course of action rather than on values; and the role of the analyst must be, as in the context of public-sector decisions, to bring out the issues of choice to assist the community of affected interests in reaching a decision.

15.5.5 Caveat and Conclusions

There should be one caveat to the above discussion. Obviously no organization—private or public—can function if *all* decisions, no matter how minor, must involve wide-ranging discussion and debate among a number of affected interests. There will, as a practical matter, be numerous "small" decisions that are wholly within the domain of a single decision maker at some level of management within the organization. These decisions can and should be made expeditiously; that is what delegation of authority and responsibility is all about.

The question of whether a decision is or is not "small" or "tactical" can be answered operationally by asking the questions we have just considered. Essentially, if the impacts of the actions to be implemented are wholly within the domain of authority and responsibility of the decision maker, *and* there are no significant impacts on any other affected interest (inside or outside the firm), *and* the existing policies and procedures and the past history of decisions have clearly established the relative values to be placed on the various impacts (that is, in the past there has been substantial agreement among the affected interests on the values to be applied in assessing alternative actions), *then* the decision maker should act on the basis of a technical analysis reflecting the net-profit criterion or its proxy at the particular organizational level of the decision maker.

For example, a railroad yardmaster can and should make train makeup and dispatching decisions on his own authority, using appropriate operational criteria, on a routine basis. Under some circumstances, however, those decisions can have significant impact on the level of service as perceived by users. Consider a situation where changes in the usage of different tracks in the yard are to be made in order to improve service for freight cars moving from origin region A through the yard to destination region B. These changes will also result in increases in average delays in the yard and therefore in a deterioration in service for freight cars moving from origin region C to destination region D. The consequences of this change in service for movement from C to D may be sufficiently great that only people from the marketing side of the firm can adequately assess the impacts in terms of their consequences for revenue.

Thus in the private firm the analyst must often take substantially the same approach to evaluation of alternative actions as an analyst in the public sector:

1. Many impacts must be considered, including some that are difficult to measure quantitatively.
2. The incidence of these impacts on the various affected interests must be considered.
3. The analyst must strive for agreement among the interests on a course of action.
4. The alternative actions must be viewed from the perspectives of each of the affected interests.
5. The analyst must work to clarify the issues, to assist the community of interests in reaching a decision, within the particular structure of the organization.

15.6 THE IMPLEMENTATION OF CHANGE

Full implementation of the principles and procedures described in this and the preceding chapter would require significant changes in most transportation organizations. Such organizations are often large, complex, and highly structured bureaucracies (whether in the private or the public sector), and each is unique in its history, its economics, its personalities, and its social and political environment. Change in such organizations is inherently complex, since attitudes and internal constraints will tend to inhibit innovation and experimentation and to encourage patterns that have worked well in the past, even in the face of signs that those patterns are not working well in the present.

Moreover, the changes required are complex, in that many elements of professional practice are involved. Indeed our definition of the role of the transportation professional requires a substantial shift in the professional's view of his own personal and professional objectives and of his organization's objectives.

Implementation of new approaches therefore takes time, measured in years rather than in days or weeks.

If it is to achieve its intended effect, the process of change must involve the individuals being asked to change. People in organizations cannot be forced to do things in which they do not believe. Changes, and particularly changes in attitude, will take place only if people can be convinced that change is necessary and that the proposed direction of change is useful and productive (Giel 1972, Bennis et al. 1976).

A university research team has examined in depth a large state transportation agency, which employed 17,000 people at the time (see S. L. Hill 1969, Legarra and Lammers 1969). This agency had already made a commitment, at the level of top management, to the principles and processes described in this chapter; this was no longer an issue. The key issue rapidly became the implementation of this view throughout the agency.

A number of barriers to change were identified by the research team, and specific steps were proposed to overcome each of these barriers (see Manheim et al. 1972, Manheim and Suhrbier 1973, Manheim et al. 1975b, p. 106ff.; see also CALIFORNIA REPORTS 1972, Colcord 1972, Giel 1972, Pecknold et al. 1972, Reno and Richardson 1972):

1. *Definition of mission:* Many transportation organizations were founded to perform a well-defined transportation function—for example, to build highways, airports, or transit facilities, or to operate a particular network of air, rail, or transit services. Further, growth and expansion are often accepted goals. The notions that a particular facility should not be built, that a system should be cut back rather

than expanded, or that improvements to existing services are preferable to major construction programs for new facilities, are all difficult for many transportation organizations to accept.

Often it will be necessary to reexamine the mission of the transportation organization, both explicitly stated and implicit in the way it actually operates, and perhaps to redefine that mission. For example, in the 1970s many state highway departments in the United States have had to shift away from a mission of building major interurban highways to a new mission of providing a variety of operational improvements to existing highways and to interurban and intraurban mass transportation services (see FHWA and UMTA 1975b).

2. *The reward structure:* The reward structure perceived by the professional staff is critically related to the success of planning procedures and is often related to the agency's definition of its mission (but sometimes may be counter to it!). For example, in agencies with a mission to build facilities, the planners or managers of a particular study will usually feel that their promotion and advancement opportunities within the agency are directly related to their success in getting a project built. Yet a major feature of the approach described here is that the decision *not* to build a project—selection of the null alternative—may in fact be the best decision, provided the community has reached that decision with full information about the alternatives and their consequences. Thus the perceived reward structure can be an effective barrier to change.

3. *Disciplines and status hierarchy:* Most transportation organizations employ professionals with specialized training in a variety of disciplines. Different status levels are often associated with different disciplines within the organization. For example, in this particular state highway department the status order ran as follows: At the low end, rights-of-way (that is, the acquisition of land for new facilities), followed by the environment (air quality, ecology, and other specialties), system planning (work on regional and statewide long-range plans), and route location (preliminary planning and location of a facility within a corridor). Design (the detailed engineering design of the facility) had the highest status (people spoke in awe of an engineer who had designed a multilevel, all-directional freeway interchange that was graceful and elegant as well as structurally sound). As a consequence, environmental and planning activities had several strikes against them at the outset.

4. *Personal style:* The process we have advocated requires certain attributes in the personnel of the technical team: openness,

willingness to accept criticism (sometimes unfounded, often emotional) from laymen, flexibility with regard to changes in ideas, procedures, and timetables. There is a great deal of ego involvement in any plan or design, and most professionals gain satisfaction from the amount of their work that is adopted or put into effect. In a process where a variety of alternatives must be considered, and many viewpoints are expressed, there is a danger that an analyst will view suggestions from others as attacks on his competence. Team members must be capable of viewing suggestions, requests for further work, and even reconsiderations of earlier decisions as stimuli to improvements of their technical work rather than as criticisms of their abilities or professional judgments. Team members must also work against the development of adversary roles vis-à-vis interests outside the team. If personnel feel threatened or under attack, they may develop elaborate defense mechanisms such as disregarding outsiders' comments, denigrating their "opposition," or avoiding community interaction altogether. Adversary roles may also develop among professional specialties within an agency when they are forced to work together closely in the more dynamic, more unstructured situations that this process often requires.

5. *Sequential production process:* An agency's procedures are often based on a concept of linear progression from "system" or "planning" studies to "design" to "implementation," thus establishing an inflexible process in which previous decisions and established timetables are assumed fixed almost regardless of information developed in later stages.

6. *Locus of decision authority:* Even when there is a clear assignment of *legal* responsibility for decisions to a particular individual or group, there may be so many organizations and/or individuals involved in the decision process in major ways that the locus of real decision authority is not at all clear. In such a situation many interest groups may seriously question whether their participation in the process will influence the decision in any way (Jones 1974, Davis 1975).

This brief overview of some of the barriers to change should suggest to the reader some of the complexity of the problem. This should not discourage the analyst, however. *Bringing about change in organizations is feasible.* Indeed substantial changes have already occurred in many transportation organizations.

The analyst needs to recognize the importance of organizational change. This is in fact one of the most exciting aspects of this profession: that within the broad domain of transportation systems analysis one can develop specializations ranging from technical methods for demand forecasting to bringing about change in large, complex organizations.

15.7 SUMMARY

Building on the principles and guidelines discussed in chapter 14, this chapter has explored the role of the professional in the process of analysis.

The transportation analyst must see his role as both technical and political. A model has been presented for how the technical and political elements should interact. This model is normative, prescribing the structure and style of activities to be undertaken by the analyst and the technical team to which he belongs. The major elements of this model are a set of objectives for the process of analysis, a strategy for striving for these process objectives, and an analysis of the implications of this strategy for the role of the analyst.

The objectives of the analysis process should be to clarify issues of choice, to supply full and accurate information to decision makers, and to achieve substantial, effective community agreement on major elements of the planning and design process and on a final course of action that is feasible, equitable, and desirable.

To achieve these objectives the technical team must engage in extensive community interaction as well as technical analyses. An effective community interaction program requires direct interaction, information gathering, and information dissemination and thus the use of several interaction techniques. The technical analyses and community interaction must be carefully coordinated.

The strategy described to illustrate these interactions has four phases: study design, exploration of issues, detailed analysis, and choice. This process strategy implies that, in addition to traditional tasks such as developing alternative transportation strategies and predicting their impacts, transportation professionals also assume the roles of community advisor, ombudsman and spokesman, impartial negotiator, and agent of and advisor to the decision-making authority.

Although the model was described from the perspective of public-sector transportation decisions, it is also applicable to private-sector decisions when many impacts on a number of different interests must be considered, when some of these affected interests are outside

the organization and have the capability to influence the decision, or
when more than one element within the organization participates in
the process of reaching a decision.

TO READ FURTHER

For a more detailed exposition see Manheim (1973c), from which
this chapter was adapted, and Manheim et al. (1975b).

On community interaction see Arnstein (1969), S. L. Hill (1969),
Legarra and Lammers (1969), TRANSPORTATION AND COMMUNITY
VALUES (1969), Wachs (1970), Bleiker, Suhrbier, and Manheim
(1971), Webber (1971), CITIZEN PARTICIPATION AND COMMUN-
ITY VALUES (1972), Park (1972), CITIZEN PARTICIPATION IN
TRANSPORTATION PLANNING (1973), Suhrbier and Bennett (1973a),
Lockwood (1974), Yukubousky (1974), CITIZEN'S ROLE IN TRANS-
PORTATION PLANNING (1975), Castle (1976), Jordan et al. (1976),
Symposium on public participation in resource decision-making
(1976), and Wellman (1977).

Particularly important case studies are provided by the Boston and
Toronto experiences (on Boston see Commonwealth of Massachusetts
1970, Gakenheimer 1976, Hansen and Lockwood 1976; on Toronto
see Soberman 1976, Steinkrauss 1976). For some of the problems
introduced by the changing environment of urban development
policy see Altshuler and Currie (1975).

On organizational change see Schein (1969), Giel (1972), and
Bennis et al. (1976).

EXERCISES

15.1(C) The following statement was made at a conference on
transportation education (Webber 1974, p. 50):
i. "Those of us who were trained in the natural sciences and in
engineering, and many of us who were trained in positivist social
science too, were trained to believe that there are correct answers
to problems. The frequency of the phrases 'problem solving' and
'optimization techniques' and the facility with which some can
speak of 'solving the urban problem' are dead giveways. We truly
believe that there are right answers to be found, that there are optimum
solutions to be discovered or invented."
ii. "I shall wish to argue that there can be no such answers or
solutions to societal problems or to societal systems, including such
societal systems as transportation and communication ones. The
only tenable answers to questions are those that come out of the

other end of the political processes. Especially where the outcomes are of the zero-sum sort, such that somebody loses because someone else wins, there is no way of knowing what is right. Indeed, there is no right. There are only political bargaining and the outcomes of those open political processes."

iii. "That may be the hardest lesson for scientists and engineers to learn. Contemporary and future transportation policy will specifically surround just these kinds of equity issues for which answers can never be found."

a. Discuss the three parts of this statement and the applicability of each to transportation systems analysis.

b. What do you believe?

15.2(P) Select a transportation organization or study for which you can obtain adequate source material, preferably by interviewing people inside and outside the agency and examining primary documents describing procedures and products of the organization or study. On the basis of your interviews and study of documents, describe the process and procedures being used and critically compare them with those described in this chapter and in the references. You may find it useful to use the guidelines as a checklist and to consult the U.S. Federal Highway Administration's "Action Plan" guidelines (FHWA 1973a).

16
Designing an Analysis: An Introduction

16.1 INTRODUCTION

In this volume we have explored the challenge of transportation
systems analysis in several directions. We have discussed the
theory and methods underlying the prediction of impacts, principally
the representation of transportation systems through performance
functions and the prediction of consumer response to the services
offered through demand functions. We have also discussed such
value issues as the methods used for evaluation, the principles and
procedures for structuring the process of choice, and the role of the
analyst in the process of analysis. These two themes come together
in the design of a transportation analysis to meet specific requirements.
The design of an analysis involves technical judgments, management
judgments, and, especially important, value judgments.

The *technical judgments* involve such decisions as what existing
data to utilize, what new data to collect, what types of models to
develop and how to coordinate the various kinds of technical analyses
to be done. The *management judgments* involve the overall
strategy of the study, including the allocation of resources (money,
skilled personnel, calendar time) and also the critical issue of how to
manage the study as it evolves.

The *value judgments* in designing a study involve such issues as
what is to be studied, who should participate in the study, what
role should technical analysis play, what role should judgment and
value decisions play, and what is the proper role of the technical team
in the process of analysis.

The value issues pervade all elements of transportation systems
analysis; even issues that at first appear to be largely technical or
managerial often contain significant value implications—even such
decisions as what models to develop and what data to utilize.

16.2 TECHNICAL JUDGMENTS

The technical elements in designing an analysis concern primarily
the different approaches to technical analysis that might be taken,

especially the alternative modeling approaches. We have placed particular stress in the foregoing chapters on the basic theory of transportation systems analysis. Building on this theory, we have also demonstrated a variety of ways in which transportation analyses can be done.

There is a misconception in the profession today that the practice of transportation systems analysis necessarily involves the use of large, complex models, substantial amounts of data, and elaborate computer software. This belief arose in part because in early years of the field this was in fact the basic style of analysis for urban transportation studies (as represented by the Urban Transportation Model System described in chapter 11), as well as for many other kinds of analyses and planning activities. By placing particular stress in this volume on demonstrating the diversity of styles in which the fundamental theory can be applied, we have specifically endeavored to demonstrate that the contrary is true.

Currently applicable styles include, of course, large-scale computer models, but also simple pencil-and-paper analyses, using elasticities or other incremental-analysis methods, pocket-calculator methods, and other relatively simple models and approaches. This diversity of styles means that it is possible to design an analysis appropriate to the issues to be clarified in a particular analysis situation. Simple methods can be used in some situations, more elaborate methods in others. In order to design any analysis, however, it is necessary to understand not only the basic theory but also the advantages and disadvantages of different ways in which that theory can be applied in practice.

We shall not discuss in this volume such important topics as procedures for developing models, for search, or for designing a technical analysis. Here we can only offer a few brief points:

1. Developing models involves more than just statistics. The choice of one from among several alternative modeling approaches, and of specific parameter values for the chosen models, involves a balancing of a number of criteria: relevance to the problem (in terms of ability to address the options, impacts, and causal relations that various interests may consider important); consistency with prior theory and empirical evidence; testability against data in the specific situation (that is, the model should be estimable); compatibility with other elements of prediction models; and feasibility within the resources available for development and use in analysis.

2. Models must be designed to be *used* in a systematic analysis; prediction is only one part of a technical analysis. Search procedures and other elements must also be designed.

3. It may often be desirable to have several sets of models: one for detailed analysis of a relatively small number of alternatives, and one (or more) for quick approximate analysis of a wide range of alternative actions ("sketch planning"). Different types of sketch-planning models may be useful for different types of actions (Manheim 1966a, 1969, Chan 1976, Kocur, Rushfeldt, and Millican 1977, Kocur et al. 1977, Martland, Assarabowski, and McCarren 1977).

4. A wide variety of search procedures are possible. Optimization models such as linear or dynamic programming are quite common in the technical literature, but many other types of search methods may be more useful in particular situations (Alexander and Manheim 1962, 1965, Moore 1970, J. C. Jones 1970, Alexander et al. 1975, Rapp et al. 1976).

16.3 MANAGEMENT JUDGMENTS

In addition to an understanding of the technical issues, one must also have a sense of strategy. By "strategy" we mean the interplay of the technical analysis with the community-involvement process. It is through this interplay that the technical team and the affected interests (including the decision makers) create a mutual learning experience, as described in chapters 14 and 15. To design a study with a sense of strategy requires understanding of the diversity of political and institutional issues that establish the context in which an analysis is taking place, as well as the issues underlying the technical judgments described in section 16.2. Among the issues to be considered are the following:

1. How much effort should be devoted to technical analysis and how much to community involvement?

2. How is the team's effort to be allocated among the major phases of an analysis (such as the four phases—study design, exploration of issues, detailed analysis, and choice—described in chapter 15)? What is to be the schedule of these phases?

3. Within technical analysis, how much effort should be devoted to the setup versus the analysis phase, that is, what is to be the split between getting set to do analysis and actually doing it?

4. Also within the technical analysis: How many cycles of search-prediction-evaluation-choice will be necessary to do a systematic

analysis of a range of alternatives? (See chapter 10.) Will the same prediction and search procedures be used in each cycle, or will there be several "levels" of analysis, utilizing both sketch planning and detailed procedures? (See Manheim 1966a, Kocur et al. 1977.)

5. What degree of flexibility should be built into the study design to allow major revisions if and when new issues surface that were not initially considered?

6. How is the analysis to be organized and staffed to achieve an effective multidisciplinary approach?

7. How is the process of analysis related to the ongoing processes of planning and implementation? Is this a one-time study designed to produce answers to a single set of questions, or is the study part of a continuing process?

8. How is the process of analysis related to the broader objectives of change in society? Is the product of the analysis strictly "technical," or is the analysis part of an overall strategy to bring about change?

16.4 VALUE JUDGMENTS

The importance of value judgments in the design of an analysis cannot be overemphasized. Value judgments permeate every element of a technical analysis. They begin with the overall conception of the study in terms of the sense of strategy just described and reach even into the question of the technical details of modeling approaches and assumptions. The design of elements of prediction that seem technical in fact reflect important value judgments: which options and impacts to model, which to leave out; whether to emphasize flow or nonflow impacts; whether to emphasize demand and activity shifts or system performance; whether to focus on the long term or the short term; what to aggregate and what to disaggregate. (This is why we emphasized, in our discussion of model development, the importance of criteria of "relevance" and of "prior theory." For further discussion see volume 2.)

There is no rational, objective way of deciding what is the best model for a particular application. The choice of a model involves significant value judgments in terms of what is included and what is excluded, in terms of the causal theories used to establish the functional specification of the model, in terms of the technical procedures used for data collection and for parameter estimation, and in terms of judging the relative acceptability of different models. While statistics and statistical methods can and should play an important role in assisting the analyst in making judgments, almost all of the judgments that go into designing a specific set of models are fundamentally value judgments. Technical expertise is a necessary precondition to making these judgments, but it is not sufficient. Technical expertise must be complemented by a thoughtful, perceptive appraisal of differences in perspectives among the interests who will be concerned with the product of the study, directly or indirectly, and of the various modeling approaches that can be used to take account of the value perspectives of those interests.

If prediction involves numerous value judgments, then other elements of the process must clearly involve even more. The design of search procedures requires numerous simplifying assumptions, each of which imposes potentially serious limitations on what alternatives will be examined and what will not be. Evaluation, goal formulation and revision, and choice involve value judgments heavily. *Analysis is not value-free; it is value-laden.*

16.5 SUMMARY

In the prologue we described the challenges of transportation systems analysis as follows: The *substantive* challenge is to intervene, delicately and deliberately, in the complex fabric of a society to use transport effectively, in coordination with other public and private actions, to achieve the goals of that society. The *methodological* challenge is to conduct a systematic analysis in a particular situation which is valid, practical, and relevant, and which assists in clarifying the issues to be debated. It is in the design of an actual analysis that these challenges must be effectively met through the interplay of technical, managerial, and value judgments.

TO READ FURTHER

The ideas of this chapter are developed in more detail in volume 2. There we lay out a heuristic strategy by which analysts can think through the issues involved in designing a transportation systems study. An early version of this strategy appears in Cambridge Systematics (1974, ch. 10). For an application to rail systems analysis see Martland and Terziev (1976).

EXERCISES

16.1(P) It is instructive to examine several transportation studies and to assess critically the advantages and disadvantages of the modeling and technical analysis approaches utilized. Choose several of the following examples:

a. Intercity passenger studies: the Northeast Corridor Project (NORTH-EAST CORRIDOR TRANSPORTATION PROJECT REPORT 1970, Miller et al. 1971, Wheeler 1978); Project 33 in Europe (Grévsmahl 1977).

b. National transportation studies in a developing country: the Harvard-Brookings Model System (Kresge and Roberts 1971, Schuster 1974); the FLOPATS approach (Mowll and Chiang 1973).

c. Urban transportation studies: the FEA sketch-planning manual (Cambridge Systematics 1976c); areawide network modeling (UMTA 1976b); other simplified methods (Toder 1976, Manheim, Furth, and Salomon 1977).

16.2(C) Consider the following statement: "The way to make policy models more useful in policy is through greater understanding and generally improved communication between policy modelers and policy makers.... The most successful modeling projects are ones in which the relationship between the policy staff and modelers is marked by trust, mutual respect, reasonableness, frank communication, and common purpose. The disappointments are marked by rivalry, contempt, unreality, lack of understanding, and confused or hidden motives" (Greenberger, Crenson, and Crissey 1976, p. 340).

a. Discuss the implications of this statement for transportation systems analysis.

b. Considering the ideas presented in chapters 15 and 16, what features would you build into the work program of a study in response to this statement?

Epilogue
The Ethics of Analysis

The transport sector is a major component of most national and regional economies. Transportation provides many jobs, is very visible in its impacts, and involves large budgets. As a consequence, public transportation agencies and private transportation firms are often very powerful, politically and economically.

As professionals working with or for transportation agencies or firms, analysts can have substantial impact and power. In addition to the leverage of the organizations themselves, there is the power of analysis. The techniques of transportation systems analysis, while far from ideal, are often more soundly developed than those of other sectors, and the large models and computerized, quantitative analyses employed sometimes convey an aura of technical sophistication that can overwhelm other perspectives.

Because of this impact, the perspective an analyst has on his objectives and role can have significant influence.

Everything a transportation analyst does has ethical implications. Even in the development of prediction models, subjective judgments play a far more central role than the most powerful statistical techniques and tests. In other elements of analysis, such as search, evaluation, or choice, the value judgments are even more significant. Even the appearance of objectivity and value neutrality in the use of economic evaluation methods or optimization methods turns out to be illusory. In short, objectivity is an ideal, never attained, in transportation systems analysis. Value judgments pervade all elements of an analysis.

The failure to achieve objectivity does not, however, argue for using analysis as a political instrument. Rather, it argues for a constant alertness and deep understanding, so that the analyst can strive for neutrality in an arena of conflicting values and perspectives. The best strategy is one of continual questioning, always seeking to uncover one's own biases, to expose "hidden assumptions," and to understand the perspectives of those with different values. The analyst should search aggressively for as neutral and as objective an analysis as can be achieved, recognizing that this will always be an unattainable goal.

To guide this search the analyst must have a professional ethic, by which we mean a set of values that will guide his professional behavior. In trying to formulate a personal value position, the analyst should consider questions such as these:

● What goals would I like to help society achieve?

● What does this mean for what I want to try to achieve in terms of changes in transportation?

● What do I think are the important interests whose needs, goals, and objectives should be given most consideration in reaching transportation decisions?

● What do I see as the role of analysis? With what professional role would I be most comfortable?

● Am I prepared to recognize limits to my technical expertise?

● Am I prepared to grow and change professionally as I encounter new professional opportunities and challenges?

Clearly these are value-laden questions to which each of us will have a unique set of answers. Yet it is important for each analyst to consider issues such as these in striving to clarify his own professional ethic.

In chapter 1 we emphasized the dynamic changes likely in a professional career in transportation. If we are always open to new ideas and new viewpoints, our views on these ethical questions will evolve as we grow and change over the trajectories of our professional careers. This evolution is natural; we should welcome it and indeed even seek out opportunities to be exposed to new value perspectives in transportation.

The most important element of the ethic of a transportation systems analyst is a sense of perspective: a perspective on the role of transport in society; a perspective on the role of technical analysis and on the role of the professional analyst; and a perspective on our own skills and values, which allows us to retain a sense of personal humility and flexibility as we seek to utilize the powerful levers of transportation to bring about change in society.

TO READ FURTHER

For the role an individual can (or once could) play see Caro (1974). On ethics in the sense used here see American Institute of Planners (1975), Marcuse (1976, 1978), Burco (1978), Manheim (1978b). On the relevance of analysis see Binder (1973), Bouchard (1973), Gakenheimer (1976), Ridley (1976), Wheeler (1978).

For critiques of systems analysis see especially Greenberger, Crenson, and Crissey (1976); also Goodman (1971), Benveniste (1972), Hoos (1972), Thoenig (1973), Cole et al. (1974), and Natural Resources Defense Council (1977). For the broader context see the debate on technology and technologists in the readings collected in Bereano (1976) and Teich (1977); see also the references in chapters 9 and 14–16.

For an example of the implications of alternative conceptual frameworks see Allison (1971).

EXERCISES

E.1(P) Numerous authors have raised issues about the relative usefulness of models (and modelers!) in light of the great uncertainties that sometimes exist about various key elements of the future (see, for example, Manheim 1970b, Mills 1971 [p. 133ff.], de Neufville 1976, Luchtenberg 1976). Select a particular situation—such as the study cited by Mills or another actual planning or policy study—and critically appraise the possible alternative roles of models and analysis. You may wish to consider these issues: the relative roles of scenarios and models; sensitivity analyses; simple versus detailed models; the distinction drawn in this text between systematic analysis and the use of formal models.

E.2(C) You are the project manager for an intercity passenger transportation study. You have played a major role throughout the project, working closely with the various specialists on your staff, which includes some very good and experienced people. The data collection and model development efforts went about as well as could be expected; the demand models that were calibrated seemed pretty good— the functional forms developed were consistent with theory and prior empirical knowledge, the coefficients of the estimated models were statistically significant and reasonable in magnitudes and signs, and so forth.

You are now on schedule, but your deadlines are very tight; you must make a presentation to the policy committee supervising your project in ten days, discussing the prediction of flows and other impacts for the first six or seven alternative transportation systems.

You have just received computer output with the predicted flows for three alternative future systems, and you have a problem. The travel volumes originating at three cities (out of twenty) seem much too high—double or triple the magnitudes you think "likely" for these systems and these cities. Your staff has already checked out the coding

of the networks and other aspects of the transportation plan specifications and the socioeconomic data for all the cities; no errors have been
found. Rough "hand" calculations indicate that the predicted magnitudes are not inconsistent with the calibrated demand models—but,
don't forget, the total prediction takes into account the competition
among multiple origins and destinations and the influence of network
topology and of congestion effects, all through the complex logic of
your battery of computerized prediction models.

You have the following options; each has its advocates on the staff
(there is no possibility of going back to respecify and reestimate the
demand models):

1. Continue using the models as now calibrated: The problem with
this is that the magnitudes of the flows originating at the three cities
will be noticed by the policy committee members. At the least this will
cause some embarrassment; in the worst case several committee members may question the validity of the whole effort, based on lack of
confidence in the predictive models.

2. Adjust the model outputs by hand: Simply take the tables of computer output and change some of the numbers before typing up the
material for presentation to the committee.

3. Modify the models: Introduce into the demand model an additional
coefficient that takes values specific to each city. For those cities in
which the flows seem valid, this coefficient would be set to a value
(such as 0 or 1) that leaves the volume predicted for the city as it is.
For the three cities that seem out of line, the values of the coefficients
would be set so as to scale down the magnitudes of the predicted
volumes.

What would you do? Why? Discuss the ethical issues as you see
them.

E.3(C) An internationally prominent transportation systems analyst,
Dr. X, is often called upon to describe a major transportation systems
modeling effort in which he was involved several years ago. This effort
involved the development of a large-scale transportation systems model
and the use of this model to analyze a number of alternative transport
investment programs. After this quite illuminating and entertaining
lecture the question is usually asked: "Were the results of this elaborate
modeling and analysis effort used?"

His answer goes like this: "During the development of the model
and the analysis of the transport alternatives, we met quite frequently
with the minister of transport for whom we were doing this study. The

minister was professionally trained and asked many pointed, intelligent, and constructive questions throughout this process. At the end of the project we summarized the models, the analysis, and the recommendations in our final report to the minister."

He continues: "The minister keeps this report in his desk. When a transport project is proposed which he supports and which was supported by our analysis, he pulls out our report, waves it in the air, and says that Dr. X and his team recommended it. When a project is proposed which he opposes but which we supported (or which he supports but our analysis opposed), he leaves the report in his desk and doesn't say anything about the study."

Discuss the ethical implications of this situation.

E.4(P) Select a transportation study reported in the literature (or presently under way in your region) such as an urban or regional transportation study or a regulatory proceeding on truck, rail, or air rate or route changes. Identify the ethical issues in the study. Which issues were recognized by some or all participants? Which were not recognized? How might recognition of these issues have changed the nature of the analyses and the results?

E.5(C) It has been suggested that there should be a code of ethics for systems analysts.
a. Review the codes of some of the engineering or other professional societies. Do they address issues you consider important for your profession? What is lacking?
b. Describe the features you would include in a code of ethics for transportation systems analysts. Try drafting a full code. (See the references listed at the end of the chapter for ideas.)

E.6(C) Discuss the following statements from Greenberger, Crenson, and Crissey (1976) in the context of transportation systems analysis:
a. "Models are to be used but not believed" (p. 18).
b. "The political setting in which a model is presented may be decisive in how the model is received by policy makers" (p. 20).
c. "Researchers [that is, analysts] and policy makers are usually representatives of different subcultures and sometimes contradictory interests" (p. 39).
d. "Professional standards for model building are nonexistent. . . . Modelers mostly build and run their own models: that is where the credits lie. Very few modelers run and analyze the other fellow's models in any systematic way. . . . [We propose] the development of a new breed of researcher/pragmatist—the model analyzer—a highly skilled

professional and astute practitioner of the art and science of third-party model analysis. Such analysis would be directed toward making sensitivity studies, identifying critical points, probing questionable assumptions, tracing policy conclusions, comprehending the effects of simulated policy changes, and simplifying complex models without distorting their key behavioral characteristics" (p. 339).

Appendix A
Values of Exponentials and Reciprocals

x	$\dfrac{1}{1+x}$	$\dfrac{1}{1+e^x}$	$\dfrac{1}{1+e^{-x}}$
0	1	0.500	0.500
0.05	0.952	0.488	0.512
0.10	0.909	0.475	0.525
0.15	0.870	0.463	0.537
0.20	0.833	0.450	0.550
0.25	0.800	0.438	0.562
0.30	0.769	0.426	0.574
0.35	0.741	0.413	0.587
0.40	0.714	0.401	0.599
0.45	0.690	0.389	0.611
0.50	0.667	0.378	0.622
0.55	0.645	0.366	0.634
0.60	0.625	0.354	0.646
0.65	0.606	0.343	0.657
0.70	0.588	0.332	0.668
0.75	0.571	0.321	0.679
0.80	0.556	0.310	0.690
0.85	0.541	0.299	0.701
0.90	0.526	0.289	0.711
0.95	0.513	0.279	0.721
1.00	0.500	0.269	0.731
1.05	0.488	0.259	0.741
1.10	0.476	0.250	0.750
1.15	0.465	0.240	0.760
1.20	0.455	0.231	0.769
1.25	0.444	0.223	0.777
1.30	0.435	0.214	0.786
1.35	0.426	0.206	0.794
1.40	0.417	0.198	0.802
1.45	0.408	0.190	0.810
1.50	0.400	0.182	0.818
1.55	0.392	0.175	0.825
1.60	0.385	0.168	0.832
1.65	0.377	0.161	0.839
1.70	0.370	0.154	0.846
1.75	0.364	0.148	0.852
1.80	0.357	0.142	0.858

x	$\dfrac{1}{1+x}$	$\dfrac{1}{1+e^x}$	$\dfrac{1}{1+e^{-x}}$
1.85	0.357	0.136	0.864
1.90	0.345	0.130	0.870
1.95	0.339	0.125	0.875
2.00	0.333	0.119	0.881
2.05	0.328	0.114	0.884
2.10	0.323	0.109	0.891
2.15	0.317	0.104	0.896
2.20	0.313	0.100	0.900
2.25	0.308	0.095	0.905
2.30	0.303	0.091	0.909
2.35	0.299	0.087	0.913
2.40	0.294	0.083	0.917
2.45	0.290	0.079	0.921
2.50	0.286	0.076	0.924
2.55	0.282	0.072	0.928
2.60	0.278	0.069	0.931
2.65	0.274	0.066	0.934
2.70	0.270	0.063	0.937
2.75	0.267	0.060	0.940
2.80	0.263	0.057	0.943
2.85	0.260	0.055	0.945
2.90	0.256	0.052	0.948
2.95	0.253	0.050	0.950
3.00	0.250	0.047	0.953
3.10	0.244	0.043	0.957
3.20	0.238	0.039	0.961
3.30	0.233	0.036	0.964
3.40	0.227	0.032	0.968
3.50	0.222	0.029	0.971
3.60	0.217	0.027	0.973
3.70	0.213	0.024	0.976
3.80	0.208	0.022	0.978
3.90	0.204	0.020	0.980
4.00	0.200	0.018	0.982
4.20	0.1923	0.0148	0.9852
4.40	0.1852	0.0121	0.9879
4.60	0.1786	0.0100	0.9900
4.80	0.1724	0.0082	0.9918
5.00	0.1667	0.0067	0.9933
5.20	0.1613	0.0055	0.9945
5.40	0.1563	0.0045	0.9955
5.60	0.1515	0.0037	0.9963
5.80	0.1471	0.0030	0.9970
6.00	0.1429	0.0025	0.9975

Appendix B
Basic Probability Formulas

DEFINITIONS

i, j: elements.

I: set of elements i.

J: set of elements j.

$p(i : I)$: probability of picking element i out of set I.

$p(i : I, j : J)$ or $p(i, j : IJ)$: joint probability of i and j (probability of picking both element i out of set I and element j out of set J).

$p(i : I | j : J)$: conditional probability of i (probability of picking element i out of set I given that j has been picked out of set J).

PROPERTIES

$$0 \leq p(i : I) \leq 1, \qquad 0 \leq p(j : J) \leq 1.$$

$$\sum_{i' \in I} p(i' : I) = 1, \qquad \sum_{j' \in J} p(j' : J) = 1.$$

RELATIONSHIPS

$$p(i : I) = \sum_{j' \in J} p(i, j' : IJ).$$

$$p(j : J) = \sum_{i' \in I} p(i', j : IJ).$$

$$p(i : I | j : J) = \frac{p(i, j : IJ)}{p(j : J)}.$$

Standard Abbreviations and Sources

The following abbreviations are used in the bibliography and text. For convenience in ordering publications, the detailed addresses are given.

CTS/MIT
Center for Transportation Studies
Massachusetts Institute of Technology
Cambridge, MA 02139

DOT
Department of Transportation
400 Seventh Street, Southwest
Washington, D.C. 20590

ECMT
European Conference of Ministers of Transport
33 Rue de Franqueville
75775 Paris, France

FAA
Federal Aviation Administration
U.S. Department of Transportation
400 Seventh Street, Southwest
Washington, D.C. 20590

FHWA
Federal Highway Administration
U.S. Department of Transportation
400 Seventh Street, Southwest
Washington, D.C. 20590

FRA
Federal Railroad Administration
U.S. Department of Transportation
400 Seventh Street, Southwest
Washington, D.C. 20590

GPO
Government Printing Office
Washington, D.C. 20402

HMSO
Her Majesty's Stationery Office
P.O. Box 569
London SEI, England

HRB
Highway Research Board (see TRB)

HRR
Highway Research Record (see TRR)

IBRD
International Bank for Reconstruction and Development
1818 H Street, Northwest
Washington, D.C. 20433

ICTR
PROCEEDINGS OF THE FIRST INTERNATIONAL CONFERENCE
ON TRANSPORTATION RESEARCH, Bruges, Belgium, June 1973
(Chicago: Transportation Research Forum, 1974).

IRT
Institut de Recherche des Transports
Ministries of Equipment and of Transport
2 Avenue du General Malleret-Joinville
B.P. 28, (94) Arcueil, France

ITS
Institute of Transportation Studies
University of California, Berkeley
Berkeley, CA 94701

ITTE
Institute of Transportation and Traffic Engineering (see ITS)

JTEP
Journal of Transport Economics and Policy
London School of Economics
Houghton Street, Aldwych
London WC2A 2AE, England

NCHRP
National Cooperative Highway Research Program
2101 Constitution Avenue
Washington, D.C. 20418

NUTC
Transportation Center
Northwestern University
Evanston, IL 60201

OECD
Organization for Economic Cooperation and Development
2 Rue Andre-Pascal
75775 Paris Cedex 16, France

PTRC
Planning and Transport Research and Computation Ltd.
109 Bedford Chambers
King Street
London WC 2, England

Transportation (journal)
Elsevier Scientific Publishing Company
P.O. Box 211
Amsterdam, The Netherlands

Transportation Research (journal)
Pergamon Press Ltd.
Headington Hill Hall
Oxford OX3 OBW, England

Transportation Science (journal)
Operations Research Society
428 East Preston Street
Baltimore, MD 21202

TRB
Transportation Research Board
(formerly Highway Research Board)
2101 Constitution Avenue
Washington, D.C. 20418

TRF
Transportation Research Forum
Box 330
Ocean City, NJ 08826

TRR
Transportation Research Record (papers series; formerly Highway
Research Record), published by TRB.

UMTA
Urban Mass Transportation Administration
U.S. Department of Transportation
400 Seventh Street, Southwest
Washington, D.C. 20590

USL/MIT
Urban Systems Laboratory
Massachusetts Institute of Technology
(reports available through CTS/MIT)

TRRL
Transportation and Road Research Laboratory
U.K. Department of Transportation
Crowthorne, England

WCTR
TRANSPORT DECISIONS IN AN AGE OF UNCERTAINTY: PRO-
CEEDINGS OF THE THIRD WORLD CONFERENCE ON TRANSPOR-
TATION RESEARCH, Rotterdam, The Netherlands, April 1977,
Evert J. Visser, ed. (The Hague: Martinus Nijhoff; available through
Kluwer Boston, Hingham, MA)

Bibliography

Adler, Thomas J., 1976. Modelling non-work travel patterns. Ph.D. dissertation, Department of Civil Engineering, MIT.

Adler, Thomas J., and Moshe Ben-Akiva, 1975. A joint frequency, destination and mode model for shopping trips. TRR 569 (TRB).

Aldana, Eduardo, Richard de Neufville, and Joseph H. Stafford, 1974. Micro-analysis of urban transportation demand. HRR 446 (HRB).

Alexander, Christopher W. J., 1966. NOTES ON THE SYNTHESIS OF FORM. Cambridge, MA: Harvard University Press.

Alexander, Christopher W. J., and Marvin L. Manheim, 1962. THE USE OF DIAGRAMS IN HIGHWAY ROUTE LOCATION: AN EXPERIMENT. Research report R62-3, Civil Engineering Systems Laboratory, MIT.

Alexander, Christopher W. J., and Marvin L. Manheim, 1965. The design of highway interchanges: An example of a general method for analysing engineering design problems. HRR 83 (HRB).

Alexander, Christopher W. J., Murray Silverstein, Shlomo Angel, Sara Ishikawa, and Denny Abrams, 1975. THE OREGON EXPERIMENT. New York: Oxford University Press. See also the other books in this series: THE TIMELESS WAY OF BUILDING and A PATTERN LANGUAGE.

Algers, S., S. Hansen, and G. Tegner, 1974. On the evaluation of comfort and convenience in urban transportation—A choice analytic approach. TRF Proceedings XV:1, pp. 470–481.

Allison, Graham T., 1971. ESSENCE OF DECISION: EXPLAINING THE CUBAN MISSILE CRISIS. Boston: Little, Brown.

Alonso, William, 1965. LOCATION AND LAND USE. Cambridge, MA: Harvard University Press.

Altshuler, Alan A., and Robert Currie, 1975. The changing environment of urban development policy. *Urban Law Annual* 10, pp. 3–42.

American Association of State Highway Officials, 1960. ROAD USER BENEFIT ANALYSIS FOR HIGHWAY IMPROVEMENTS. Washington, D.C.: AASHO.

American Institute of Planners, 1975. THE SOCIAL RESPONSIBILITY OF THE PLANNER. Washington, D.C.: AIP.

Anderson, J. Edward, 1977. TRANSIT SYSTEMS THEORY. Lexington, MA: D. C. Heath.

Arnstein, Sherry R., 1969. A ladder of citizen participation. *Journal of the American Institute of Planners* 35:4.

Arrillaga, Bert. 1978. Urban Mass Transportation Administration's experience with pricing to control traffic. Paper presented to TRB (January).

Atherton, Terry J., 1975. Approaches for transferring disaggregate demand models. M.S. thesis, Department of Civil Engineering, MIT.

Atherton, Terry J., and Moshe Ben-Akiva, 1976. Transferability and updating of disaggregate demand models. TRR 610 (TRB).

Atherton, Terry J., John H. Suhrbier, and William A. Jessiman, 1976. The use of disaggregate travel demand models to analyze carpooling incentives. TRR 599 (TRB).

Averous, Christian, Philippe Bovy, Jean-Raymond Fradin, and Marvin L. Manheim, 1977. LES TRANSPORTS A PARIS ET EN REGION ILE DE FRANCE. Case study for the Group of Experts on Traffic Policies for the Improvement of the Urban Environment. OECD Report ENV/UT/77.4.

Baerwald, John E., ed., 1976. TRANSPORTATION AND TRAFFIC ENGINEERING HANDBOOK. Englewood Cliffs, NJ: Prentice-Hall.

Bain, Joseph H., 1976. Activity choice analysis, time allocation and disaggregate travel demand modelling. M.S. thesis, Department of Civil Engineering, MIT.

Barton-Aschman Associates and Cambridge Systematics, Inc., 1976. LOS ANGELES CENTRAL BUSINESS DISTRICT: INTERNAL TRAVEL DEMAND MODELLING. Report prepared for the Community Redevelopment Agency, Los Angeles, CA.

Baumol, William J., 1965. ECONOMIC THEORY AND OPERATIONS ANALYSIS. Englewood Cliffs, NJ: Prentice-Hall.

Beasley, Michael E., 1973. URBAN TRANSPORT: STUDIES IN ECONOMIC POLICY. London: Butterworth's.

Beck, M., n.d. PREPARATION D'UN PROGRAMME DE SIMULATION D'UN AXE LOURD AMENAGE DANS UNE DIRECTION (SALAD). IRT.

Beckmann, Martin J., 1967. On the theory of traffic flow in networks. *Traffic Quarterly*.

Beckmann, Martin J., 1976. Equilibrium versus optimum in public transportation systems. In Florian (1976).

Beckmann, Martin J., C. B. McGuire, and C. B. Winston, 1956. STUDIES IN THE ECONOMICS OF TRANSPORTATION. New Haven, CT: Yale University Press.

Beimborn, Edward A., 1976. Structured approach to the evaluation and comparison of alternative transportation plans. TRR 619 (TRB).

Ben-Akiva, Moshe E., 1971. Public and private transportation in an urban corridor —The Southeast Corridor of Boston. M.S. thesis, Department of Civil Engineering, MIT.

Ben-Akiva, Moshe E., 1973. Structure of passenger travel demand models. Ph.D. dissertation, Department of Civil Engineering, MIT.

Ben-Akiva, Moshe E., 1974. Structure of passenger travel demand models. TRR 526 (TRB).

Ben-Akiva, Moshe E., 1977. Passenger travel demand forecasting: Applications of disaggregate models and directions for research. WCTR.

Ben-Akiva, Moshe E., and Thomas J. Adler, 1975. Social-recreation joint choice model. Working paper no. 8, CTS/MIT.

Ben-Akiva, Moshe E., Thomas J. Adler, Jesse Jacobson, and Marvin L. Manheim, 1977. Experiments to clarify priorities in urban travel forecasting research and development. Working paper, CTS/MIT.

Ben-Akiva, Moshe E., and Terry J. Atherton, 1977. Methodology for short-range travel demand prediction: Analysis of carpooling incentives. JTEP 11:3, pp. 224–261.

Ben-Akiva, Moshe E., and Frank S. Koppelman, 1976. AGGREGATE FORECASTING WITH DISAGGREGATE TRAVEL DEMAND MODELS USING NORMALLY AVAILABLE DATA. Report for Projectbureau Integosh Verkees en Verkoerstudies, The Netherlands. Cambridge, MA: Cambridge Systematics, Inc.

Ben-Akiva, Moshe E., Frank S. Koppelman, and Thawat Watanatada, 1976. DEVELOPMENT OF AN AGGREGATE MODEL OF URBANIZED AREA TRAVEL BEHAVIOR. Phase I report prepared for the Office of the Secretary, DOT. CTS/MIT.

Ben-Akiva, Moshe E., and Steven R. Lerman, 1978. Disaggregate travel and mobility choice models and measures of accessibility. In Hensher and Stopher (1978).

Ben-Akiva, Moshe E., Steven R. Lerman, and Marvin L. Manheim, 1976. Disaggregate models: An overview of some recent research results and practical applications. In PROCEEDINGS OF THE PTRC SUMMER MEETING (London: PTRC).

Ben-Akiva, Moshe E., and Martin Richards, 1975. Disaggregate multimodal model for work trips in The Netherlands. TRR 569 (TRB).

Bennis, Warren G., Kenneth D. Benne, Robert Chin, and Kenneth E. Corey, 1976. THE PLANNING OF CHANGE. New York: Holt, Rinehart and Winston.

Benveniste, Guy, 1972. THE POLITICS OF EXPERTISE. Berkeley, CA: The Glendessary Press.

Bereano, Philip L., ed., 1976. TECHNOLOGY AS A SOCIAL AND POLITICAL PHENOMENON. New York: John Wiley.

Bhandari, Anil, and Frederic Berger, 1975. THE HIGHWAY COST MODEL: APPLICATION TO THE DAR ES SALAAM-MOROGORO SECTION OF THE TANZANIA-ZAMBIA HIGHWAY. Draft report, Department of Civil Engineering, MIT (June).

Bhatt, Kiran U., 1971. Fundamental explorations in the comparative analysis of transportation technology. Ph.D. dissertation, Department of Civil Engineering, MIT.

Bhatt, Kiran U., 1976. Comparative analysis of urban transportation costs. TRR 559 (TRB).

Bien, Gerard, with Alain Bieber, Christian Bourgin, and Marvin L. Manheim, 1977. DOSSIER DE LIGNES D'AUTOBUS ET ETUDES DE RESTRUCTURATIONS LOCALES. I: PROPOSITION D'UN CADRE METHODOLOGIQUE GENERAL. IRT.

Bien, Gerard, Christian Bourgin, and Marvin L. Manheim, 1976. DOSSIER DE LIGNES D'AUTOBUS—NOTE METHODOLOGIQUE NO. 2. IRT (April).

Binder, Robert H., 1973. Major issues in travel demand forecasting. In Brand and Manheim (1973).

Bishop, Bruce A., et al., 1969. Socio-economic and community factors. In PLAN-NING URBAN FREEWAYS (report prepared at Stanford University).

Blackburn, Anthony J., 1970. A non-linear model of the demand for travel. In Quandt (1970a).

Bleiker, Hans, John H. Suhrbier, and Marvin L. Manheim, 1971. Community inter-action as an integral part of the highway decision-making process. HRR 356 (HRB).

Borman, Frank, 1977. Testimony before the Subcommittee on Aviation, Committee on Commerce, Science, and Transport, U.S. Senate, March 29, 1977. Miami, FL: Eastern Airlines.

Bouchard, Richard J., 1973. Relevance of planning techniques to decision-making. In Brand and Manheim (1973).

Boyce, David, N.D. Day, and C. McDonald, 1970. METROPOLITAN PLAN MAK-ING METHODOLOGY. Philadelphia: Regional Science Research Institute.

Boyd, J. Hayden, Norman J. Asher, and Elliot S. Wetzler, 1976, Evaluation of rail rapid transit and express bus service in the urban commuter market (abridgement). TRR 559 (TRB).

Brand, Daniel, 1973a. Travel demand forecasting: Some foundations and a review. In Brand and Manheim (1973).

Brand, Daniel, 1973b. Theory and method in land use and travel forecasting. HRR 422 (HRB).

Brand, Daniel, 1976. Approaches to travel behavior research. TRR 569 (TRB).

Brand, Daniel, and Marvin L. Manheim, eds., 1973. URBAN TRAVEL DEMAND FORECASTING. Special report 143, HRB.

Branston, David, 1973. Link capacity functions: A review. *Transportation Research* 10:4, pp. 223–236.

Braybrooke, David, and Charles E. Lindblom, 1963. A STRATEGY OF DECISION. New York: The Free Press.

Bridwell, Lowell K., 1969. Freeways in the urban environment. In JOINT DEVEL-OPMENT AND MULTIPLE USE OF TRANSPORTATION RIGHTS-OF-WAY, spe-cial report 104, HRB.

Brog, Werner, Dirk Heuwinkel, and Karl-Heinz Neumann, 1977. PSYCHOLOGICAL DETERMINANTS OF USER BEHAVIOR. Round Table 34, ECMT.

Brog, Werner, and Wilfried Schwerdtfeger, 1977. Considerations on the design of behavioural oriented models from the point of view of empirical social research. WCTR.

Brown, Richard A., and William Deakin, 1974. Development, people and compen-sation. ICTR.

Bruck, H. W., Marvin L. Manheim, and Paul W. Shuldiner, 1967. Transportation systems planning as a process. In PAPERS FROM THE EIGHTH ANNUAL MEET-ING, TRF.

Burco, Robert A., 1978. Some ethical problems in transportation agencies. Paper presented to TRB (January).

Burns, Lawrence D., Thomas F. Golob, and Gregory C. Nicolaidis, 1976. Theory of urban-household automobile-ownership decisions. TRR 569 (TRB).

Burrell, J. E., 1968. Multiple route assignment and its applicaton to capacity restraint. In W. Leutzbach and P. Barrow, eds., PROCEEDINGS, FOURTH INTERNATIONAL SYMPOSIUM ON THE THEORY OF TRAFFIC FLOW, Karlsruhe, Germany. Also in STRASSENBAU UND STRASSENVERKEHRSTECHNIK, Heft 86.

Burrell, J. E., 1976. Multi-path route assignment: A comparison of two models. In Florian (1976).

Burress, Michael J., 1975. Statement before the Interstate Commerce Commission. ICC Docket 35527.

California Department of Transportation, 1973. ACTION PLAN FOR TRANSPORTATION PLANNING AND DEVELOPMENT (June).

California Division of Highways, 1972. Transportation corridor/route location study procedures. Circular letter 72-10.

CALIFORNIA REPORTS, 1972. Series of eight volumes (reports numbered 72-2 through 72-9) prepared for the California Department of Transportation, TCV Project. USL/MIT. See also Colcord (1972), Giel (1972), Manheim et al. (1972), Pecknold et al. (1972), and Reno and Richardson (1972).

California State Transportation Board, 1973. Regional transportation plans: Guidelines, in response to State Assembly Bill 69 approving the creation of a department of transportation (April).

Cambridge Systematics, Inc., 1974. INTRODUCTION TO URBAN TRAVEL DEMAND FORECASTING. Four volumes: SUMMARY; DEMAND MODELLING; EVALUATION; DEMAND MODEL SELECTION MANUAL. Office of Research and Development, UMTA.

Cambridge Systematics, Inc., 1975a. THE DEVELOPMENT OF A DISAGGREGATE BEHAVIORAL WORK MODE CHOICE MODEL FOR THE LOS ANGELES METROPOLITAN AREA. Report prepared for the Los Angeles Regional Transportation Study and the Southern California Association of Governments.

Cambridge Systematics, Inc., 1975b. TRAVEL MODEL DEVELOPMENT PROJECT. Phase I final report prepared for the Metropolitan Transportation Commission, Berkeley, CA.

Cambridge Systematics, Inc., 1976a. A BEHAVIORAL ANALYSIS OF AUTOMOBILE OWNERSHIP AND MODES OF TRAVEL. Volumes 2–4. Prepared for the DOT.

Cambridge Systematics, Inc., 1976b. CARPOOLING INCENTIVES: ANALYSIS OF TRANSPORTATION AND ENERGY IMPACTS. Report prepared for the Federal Energy Administration.

Cambridge Systematics, Inc., 1976c. GUIDELINES FOR TRAVEL DEMAND ANALYSES OF PROGRAM MEASURES TO PROMOTE CARPOOLS, VANPOOLS AND PUBLIC TRANSPORTATION—STATE ENERGY CONSERVATION PLANS. Report prepared for the Federal Energy Administration.

Cambridge Systematics, Inc., 1976d. THE USE OF DISAGGREGATE TRAVEL DEMAND MODELS TO ANALYZE THE ENERGY CONSERVATION POTENTIAL

OF PARKING RESTRICTIONS WITHIN THE METROPOLITAN AREA. Report prepared for the Federal Energy Administration, Office of Contingency Planning.

Cambridge Systematics, Inc., 1977. MTC TRAVEL MODEL DEVELOPMENT PROJECT: FINAL REPORT. Three volumes. Prepared for the Metropolitan Transportation Commission, Berkeley, CA.

Cambridge Systematics, Inc., 1978. DOWNTOWN PEOPLEMOVER PLANNING MANUAL. Report for the DOT in process.

Campbell, G. C., 1977. An exercise in the management of traffic peaks. TRF Proceedings XVIII:1.

Canadian Transport Commission, 1970. INTERCITY PASSENGER TRANSPORT STUDY. Ottawa: Information Canada.

Caro, Robert A., 1974. THE POWER BROKER. New York: Knopf.

Castle, L. Lewis, 1976. Citizen participation in rapid transit planning. TRR 618 (TRB).

Chan, Yupo, 1976. A method to simplify network representation in transportation planning. *Transportation Research* 10:3.

Chan, Yupo, Kenneth G. Follansbee, Marvin L. Manheim, and John R. Mumford, 1968. AGGREGATION IN TRANSPORT NETWORKS: AN APPLICATION OF HIERARCHICAL STRUCTURE. Research report R69-39, Department of Civil Engineering, MIT.

Charles River Associates, Inc., 1967. A MODEL OF URBAN PASSENGER TRAVEL DEMAND IN THE SAN FRANCISCO METROPOLITAN AREA. Cambridge, MA: CRA.

Charles River Associates, Inc., 1968. AN EVALUATION OF FREE TRANSIT SERVICE. Report prepared for the DOT (NTIS PB 179 845).

Charles River Associates, Inc., 1972. A DISAGGREGATED BEHAVIORAL MODEL OF URBAN TRAVEL DEMAND. Report prepared for FHWA.

Charles River Associates, Inc., 1976. ESTIMATING THE EFFECTS OF URBAN TRAVEL POLICIES. Report prepared for the Office of the Secretary, DOT.

Chiang, Yu-sheng, and Paul O. Roberts, 1978. An empirically-determined level of service supply model of transit time and reliability for regular-route LTL trucking. In Florian (1978).

Chu, C., 1971. A review of the development and theoretical concepts of traffic assignment techniques and their practical applications to an urban road network. *Traffic Engineering and Control* (August).

Chudleigh, Peter, 1975. Economic potential of specialized wool shipping services. JTEP 9:3.

CITIZEN PARTICIPATION AND COMMUNITY VALUES, 1972. HRR 380 (HRB).

CITIZEN PARTICIPATION IN TRANSPORTATION PLANNING, 1973. Special report 142, HRB.

CITIZEN'S ROLE IN TRANSPORTATION PLANNING, 1975. TRR 555 (TRB).

Civil Aeronautics Board, 1975. AIRCRAFT OPERATING COST AND PERFORMANCE REPORT. Washington, D.C.: CAB (July).

CLM Systems, Inc., 1972. AIRPORTS AND THEIR ENVIRONMENTS: A GUIDE TO ENVIRONMENTAL PLANNING. Report prepared for the Office of the Assistant Secretary for Environment and Urban Systems, DOT (DOT P 5600.1).

Cohen, Harry Stuart, 1975. Evaluation of project-level transportation alternatives. Ph.D. dissertation, Department of Civil Engineering, MIT.

Cohon, Jared L., and David H. Marks, 1974. Multiobjective analysis in water resource planning. In de Neufville and Marks (1974).

Colcord, Frank C., Jr., 1970. URBAN TRANSPORTATION DECISION MAKING. PART 2. HOUSTON, A CASE STUDY. USL/MIT.

Colcord, Frank L., Jr., 1971. URBAN TRANSPORTATION DECISION MAKING. PART 3. SAN FRANCISCO, A CASE STUDY. USL/MIT.

Colcord, Frank L., Jr., 1972. TRANSPORTATION SYSTEMS PLANNING IN CALIFORNIA: INSTITUTIONAL ARRANGEMENTS OF STATE AND LOCAL GOVERNMENTS. Report 72-7, TCV Project, USL/MIT.

Cole, H. S. D., Christopher Freeman, Marie Jahoda, and K. L. R. Pavitt, eds., 1974. THINKING ABOUT THE FUTURE: A CRITIQUE OF "THE LIMITS TO GROWTH." London: Chatto & Windus/Sussex University Press.

Colony, D. C., 1974. Shifting the emphasis in engineering education. In MULTI-DISCIPLINARY EDUCATION IN TRANSPORTATION, special report 150, TRB.

Committee on Evaluation of Urban Transportation Alternatives, 1977. URBAN TRANSPORTATION ALTERNATIVES: EVOLUTION OF FEDERAL POLICY. Special report 177, TRB.

Committee on Principles of Decision-Making for Regulating Chemicals in the Environment, 1975. DECISION-MAKING FOR REGULATING CHEMICALS IN THE ENVIRONMENT. Washington, D.C.: National Academy of Sciences.

Commonwealth of Massachusetts, Steering Group, Boston Transportation Planning Review, 1970. STUDY DESIGN FOR A BALANCED TRANSPORTATION DEVELOPMENT PROGRAM. Washington, D.C.: System Design Concepts (November).

Cookenboo, Leslie, Jr., 1953. Economies of scale in the operation of crude oil pipelines. Ph.D. dissertation, Department of Economics and Social Science, MIT.

Cookenboo, Leslie, Jr., 1955. CRUDE OIL PIPELINES AND COMPETITION IN THE OIL INDUSTRY. Cambridge, MA: Harvard University Press, p. 26. See also Leslie Cookenboo, Jr., COSTS OF OPERATING CRUDE OIL PIPELINES (Houston: Rice Institute Pamphlet, 1954).

Copas, Thomas L., and Herbert A. Pennock, 1977. STAFFING AND MANAGEMENT FOR SOCIAL, ECONOMIC AND ENVIRONMENTAL IMPACT ASSESSMENTS: NCHRP Synthesis of Highway Practice 40. Washington, D.C.: NCHRP.

Council on Environmental Quality, 1973. GUIDELINES FOR FEDERAL AGENCIES UNDER THE NATIONAL ENVIRONMENTAL POLICY ACT. Washington, D.C.: CEQ.

Crow, Robert T., Kan Hua Young, and Thomas Cooley, 1973. Alternative demand functions for "abstract" transportation modes. *Transportation Research* 7:4.

Dafermos, Stella C., 1971. An extended traffic assignment model with applications to two-way traffic. *Transportation Science* 5, pp. 336–389.

Dafermos, Stella C., 1976. Integrated equilibrium flow models for transportation planning. In Florian (1976).

Daganzo, Carlos F., 1977a. Some remarks on traffic assignment methodology selection. Working paper 7703, Stochastic Traffic Assignment Project, ITS (May).

Daganzo, Carlos F., 1977b. On achieving stochastic user equilibrium on a transportation network. Working paper 7704, Stochastic Traffic Assignment Project, ITS (June).

Daganzo, Carlos F., 1978a. On the traffic assignment problem with flow dependent costs. *Transportation Research* (in press).

Daganzo, Carlos F., 1978b. Textbook in process.

Daganzo, Carlos F., Fernando Bouthelier, and Yosef Sheffi, 1977. Multinomial probit and qualitative choice: A computationally efficient algorithm. *Transportation Science* 11:4.

Daganzo, Carlos F., and Yosef Sheffi, 1977. On stochastic models of traffic assignment. *Transportation Science* 11:3.

Damay, Gerard, and Niels de Terra, 1974. Modelling non-business air travel demand in the north-south market. ICTR.

Dasgupta, Partha, Amartya Sen, and Stephen Marglin, 1972. GUIDELINES FOR PROJECT EVALUATION. United Nations Industrial Development Organization, Project Formulation and Evaluation Series, No. 2. New York: UN.

Davis, Sid, 1975. Public participation in transportation planning: An experiment in process change. In CITIZEN'S ROLE IN TRANSPORTATION PLANNING (1975).

Dawson, R. F. F., 1968. THE ECONOMIC ASSESSMENT OF ROAD IMPROVE-MENT SCHEMES. Road Research Technical Paper No. 75. HMSO.

Deen, Thomas B., Walter M. Kulash, and Stephen E. Baker, 1976. Critical decisions in the rapid transit planning process. TRR 559 (TRB).

Demaree, Alan T., 1970. Cars and cities on a collision course. *Fortune*, p. 124ff.

de Neufville, Richard L., 1976. AIRPORT SYSTEMS PLANNING. London: Macmillan, and Cambridge, MA: MIT Press.

de Neufville, Richard L., and Ralph Keeney, 1974. Use of decision analysis in airport development for Mexico City. In de Neufville and Marks (1974).

de Neufville, Richard L., and David H. Marks, eds., 1974. SYSTEM PLANNING AND DESIGN: CASE STUDIES IN MODELLING, OPTIMIZATION AND EVAL-UATION. Englewood Cliffs, NJ: Prentice-Hall.

de Neufville, Richard L., and Joseph H. Stafford, 1971. SYSTEMS ANALYSIS FOR ENGINEERS AND MANAGERS. New York: McGraw-Hill.

Department of the Environment, 1972. GETTING THE BEST ROADS FOR OUR MONEY: THE COBA METHOD OF APPRAISAL. HMSO.

DeSalvo, Joseph S., 1969. A process function for rail linehaul operations. JTEP 3:1.

DeSalvo, Joseph S., and Lester B. Lave, 1968. An analysis of towboat delays. JTEP 2:2, pp. 232–241.

DEVELOPMENT AND COMPENSATION—PUTTING PEOPLE FIRST, 1972.
HMSO.

Devine, E., Jr., 1971. MULTI-DISCIPLINE DESIGN TEAMS FOR TRANSPORTA-
TION FACILITIES. DOT report no. DOT-OS-00060.

De Weille, Jan, 1966. Quantification of road user savings. World Bank Occasional
Papers No. 2, IBRD.

De Weille, Jan, and Anandarup Ray, 1974. The optimum port capacity. JTEP
8:3.

Dial, Robert B., 1971. A probabilistic multi-path traffic assignment model which
obviates the need for path enumeration. *Transportation Research* 5:2.

Dial, Robert B., 1976. Urban transportation planning system: Philosophy and
function. TRR 569 (TRB).

Dickey, John W., et al., 1975. METROPOLITAN TRANSPORTATION PLANNING.
New York: McGraw-Hill.

Dix, M. C., 1977. Report on investigations of household travel decision making
behaviour. WCTR.

Domencich, Thomas A., Gerald Kraft, and Jean-Paul Vallette, 1968. Estimation of
urban passenger travel behavior: An economic demand model. HRR 238 (HRB).

Domencich, Thomas A., and Daniel McFadden, 1975. URBAN TRAVEL DEMAND:
A BEHAVIORAL APPROACH. Amsterdam: North-Holland/Elsevier.

Drew, Donald R., 1968. TRAFFIC FLOW THEORY AND CONTROL. New York:
McGraw-Hill.

Dreyfus, S. E., 1969. An appraisal of some shortest-path algorithms. *Operations
Research* 17, pp. 395–412.

Duguay, G., W. S. Jung, and D. McFadden, 1976. SYNSAM: A methodology for
synthesizing household transportation survey data. Working paper 7618, Urban
Travel Demand Forecasting Project, ITS.

Dunbar, Frederick C., 1976. Quick policy evaluation with behavioral demand
models. TRR 610 (TRB).

Echenique, M., A. Feo, R. Herrera, and J. Riquezes, 1974. A disaggregated model
of urban spatial structure: Theoretical framework. *Environment and Planning* 6,
pp. 33–63.

Edel, Matthew, and Jerome Rothenburg, eds., 1972. READINGS IN URBAN
ECONOMICS. New York: Macmillan.

Ehrlich, Morton, 1977. An airline management information system. WCTR.

Ellis, Raymond, and Alistair Sherrett, 1976. TRANSPORTATION SERVICE AND
TRAVEL BEHAVIOR IMPACTS OF BART: INTERIM FINDINGS. Berkeley, CA:
Metropolitan Transportation Commission.

Ellison, A. P., and E. M. Stafford, 1974. THE DYNAMICS OF THE CIVIL AVIATION
INDUSTRY. Franborough, U.K.: Saxon House, and Lexington, MA: Lexington
Books.

Faludi, Andreas, ed., 1973. A READER IN PLANNING THEORY. London: Pergamon
Press.

Farris, Martin T., and Forrest E. Harding, 1976. PASSENGER TRANSPORTATION. Englewood Cliffs, NJ: Prentice-Hall.

Ferland, J., Michael Florian, and C. Achion, 1975. On incremental methods of traffic assignment. *Transportation Research* 9, pp. 237–239.

FHWA, 1970. URBAN TRANSPORTATION PLANNING: GENERAL INFORMATION AND INTRODUCTION TO SYSTEM 360.

FHWA, 1971. Policy and Procedure Memorandum 90–1 (24 August; revised 7 September 1972).

FHWA, 1972. URBAN TRANSPORTATION PLANNING: GENERAL INFORMA-TION.

FHWA, 1973a. PROCESS GUIDELINES (SOCIAL, ECONOMIC, AND ENVIRON-MENTAL EFFECTS OF HIGHWAY PROJECTS). Policy and Procedure Memo-randum 90-4 (codified in FEDERAL-AID HIGHWAY PROGRAM MANUAL as Volume 7, Chapter 7, Section 1).

FHWA, 1973b. TRAFFIC ASSIGNMENT.

FHWA and UMTA, 1975a. Transportation improvement program: 23 CFR Chapter I, Part 450, Subpart A. In *Federal Register* 40:181 (17 September 1975, Part II).

FHWA and UMTA, 1975b. Supplementary guidelines on development of trans-portation system management plans under UMTA and FHWA joint regulations: 23 CFR Chapter I, Part 450, Subpart A, Appendix. In *Federal Register* 40:181 (17 September 1975, Part II).

Fleet, C. R., and S. R. Robertson, 1968. Trip generation in the transportation planning process. HRR 240 (HRB).

Florian, Michael, 1974. On modelling congestion in Dial's probabilistic assignment model. *Transportation Research* 8:1 pp. 85–86.

Florian, Michael, 1975. A TRAFFIC EQUILIBRIUM MODEL OF TRAVEL BY CAR AND PUBLIC TRANSIT MODES. Publication no. 32, Centre de recherche sur les transports, Université de Montreal.

Florian, Michael, ed., 1976a. PROCEEDINGS OF THE INTERNATIONAL SYMPO-SIUM ON TRAFFIC EQUILIBRIUM METHODS. New York: Springer-Verlag.

Florian, Michael, 1976b. Urban travel demand models and multi-modal traffic equilibrium. TRF Proceedings XVII:1.

Florian, Michael, ed., 1978. PROCEEDINGS OF THE INTERNATIONAL SYM-POSIUM ON TRAVEL SUPPLY MODELS. In press as a special issue of *Trans-portation Research*.

Florian, Michael, R. Chapleau, S. Nguyen, C. Achim, L. James, and J. Lefebvre, 1977. EMME: A planning method for multi-modal urban transportation systems. WCTR.

Florian, Michael, and B. Fox, 1976. On the probabilistic origin of Dial's multi-path traffic assignment model. *Transportation Research* 10, pp. 339–341.

Flusberg, Martin, and Nigel H. M. Wilson, 1976. A descriptive supply model for demand-responsive transportation planning. TRF Proceedings XVII:1.

Forbes, C. E., and Robert R. Womack, 1976. A new direction for the highway program, TRR 585 (TRB).

Foster, Christopher D., 1975. THE TRANSPORT PROBLEM. London: Croom Helm, second revised edition.

Frankel, Ernst G., 1977. PORT PLANNING AND DEVELOPMENT. Course notes (offset), CTS/MIT.

Frankel, Ernst G., and Henry S. Marcus, 1973. OCEAN TRANSPORTATION. Cambridge, MA: MIT Press.

Frankel, Ernst G., and Chang Bin Tang, 1977. Port capacity measures and port effectiveness modelling. In Frankel (1977).

Freeman, Fox, Wilbur Smith and Associates, 1971. CHOICE OF ROUTE BY CAR DRIVER Report prepared for the Mathematical Advisory Unit, U.K. Department of the Environment. London: Freeman, Fox, Wilbur Smith and Associates.

Fried, M., J. Havens, and M. Thall, 1977. TRAVEL BEHAVIOR: A SYNTHESIZED THEORY. Phase I final report for NCHRP Project 8-14. Washington, D.C.: NCHRP.

Fromm, Gary, ed., 1965. TRANSPORT INVESTMENT AND ECONOMIC DEVELOP-MENT. Washington, D.C.: The Brookings Institution.

Gakenheimer, Ralph, 1976. TRANSPORTATION PLANNING AS RESPONSE TO CONTROVERSY: THE BOSTON CASE. Cambridge, MA: MIT Press.

Gakenheimer, Ralph, ed., 1978. THE AUTOMOBILE AND THE ENVIRONMENT: AN INTERNATIONAL PERSPECTIVE. Cambridge, MA: MIT Press.

Gaudry, Marc, 1975. An aggregate time-series analysis of urban transit demand: The Montreal case. *Transportation Research* 9.

Gaudry, Marc, 1977. Notions of equilibrium and their implications for travel model-ling. Working paper no. 51, Centre de recherche sur les transports, Université de Montreal.

Gazis, Denos C., ed., 1974. TRAFFIC SCIENCE. New York: John Wiley.

Geiser, Kenneth, 1970. URBAN TRANSPORTATION DECISION MAKING. 1. POLITICAL PROCESS OF URBAN FREEWAY CONTROVERSIES. USL/MIT.

Gerlough, Daniel L., and Matthew J. Huber, 1975. TRAFFIC FLOW THEORY. Special report 165, TRB.

Giel, Robert L., 1972. TRANSPORTATION DECISION-MAKING AND ORGANIZA-TIONAL STRUCTURE. Report 72-9, TCV Project, USL/MIT.

Gilman, S., 1977. Optimal shipping technologies for routes to developing coun-tries. JTEP 11:1.

Golob, T. F., and Martin J. Beckmann, 1971. A utility model for travel forecast-ing. *Transportation Science* 5, pp. 79–90.

Goodman, Robert, 1971. AFTER THE PLANNERS. New York: Simon and Schuster.

Goodwin, P. B., 1976. Human effort and the value of travel time. JTEP 10:1.

Greenberger, Martin, Matthew A. Crenson, and Brian L. Crissey, 1976. MODELS IN THE POLICY PROCESS. New York: Basic Books.

Grëvsmahl, J., 1977. Conclusions from Action 33. WCTR.

Guenther, Karl, 1968. Transportation production process: An example. Discussion paper T-33, Department of Civil Engineering, MIT.

Haase, R. H., and W. H. T. Holden, 1964. PERFORMANCE OF LAND TRANSPORTATION VEHICLES. Report RM-3966-RC, The Rand Corporation, Santa Monica, CA.

Haight, Frank A., 1963. MATHEMATICAL THEORIES OF TRAFFIC FLOW. New York: Academic Press.

Hall, Frederick, and Marvin L. Manheim, 1967. Abstract representation of goals. In John De S. Coutinho, ed., TRANSPORTATION: A SERVICE (New York, NY: New York Academy of Sciences).

Hansen, Walter G., and Stephen C. Lockwood, 1976. Metropolitan transportation planning: Process reform, TRR 582 (TRB).

Harris, A. J., and J. C. Tanner, 1974. TRANSPORT DEMAND MODELS BASED ON PERSONAL CHARACTERISTICS. TRRL Supplementary report 65 UC.

Harrison, A. J., 1974. THE ECONOMICS OF TRANSPORT APPRAISAL. London: Croom Helm.

Hartwig, J., and L. Linton, 1974. Disaggregate mode choice models of intercity freight movement. S.M. thesis, NUTC.

Harvey, Thomas N., 1972. Estimation of user benefits for urban transportation systems. Ph.D. dissertation, Department of Civil Engineering, MIT.

Hauser, John R., and Frank S. Koppelman, 1976. Effective marketing research: An empirical comparison of techniques to model consumers' perceptions and preferences. Working paper, NUTC.

Hauser, John R., and Frank S. Koppelman, 1977. Designing transportation services: A marketing approach. TRF Proceedings XVIII:1.

Hausman, Jerry A., and David A. Wise, 1976. A conditional probit model for qualitative choice: Discrete decisions recognizing interdependence and heterogeneous preferences. Working paper no. 173, Department of Economics, MIT.

Hautzinger, Heinz, and P. Kessel, 1977. The state of mobility research. WCTR.

Hay, William W., 1961. AN INTRODUCTION TO TRANSPORTATION ENGINEERING. New York: John Wiley.

Heflebower, Richard B., 1965. Characteristics of transport modes. In Fromm (1965).

Heggie, Ian G., 1972. TRANSPORT ENGINEERING ECONOMICS. London: McGraw-Hill.

Heggie, Ian G., 1977. Putting behavior into behavioral models of travel choice. Working paper no. 22, Transport Studies Unit, University of Oxford.

Henderson, James M., and Richard E. Quandt, 1958. MICROECONOMIC THEORY: A MATHEMATICAL APPROACH. New York: McGraw-Hill.

Hengsbach, Gerd, and Amadeo R. Odoni, 1975. TIME-DEPENDENT ESTIMATES OF DELAYS AND DELAY COSTS AT MAJOR AIRPORTS. Report R75-4, Flight Transportation Laboratory, MIT.

Hensher, David A., ed., 1977, URBAN TRANSPORT ECONOMICS. Cambridge, U.K.: Cambridge University Press.

Hensher, David A., and Peter R. Stopher, eds., 1978. PROCEEDINGS OF THE THIRD INTERNATIONAL CONFERENCE ON TRAVEL DEMAND MODELLING. Oxford: Pergamon Press.

Hershdorfer, Alan M., 1966. Predicting the equilibrium of supply and demand: Location theory and transportation flow models. In PAPERS FROM THE SEVENTH ANNUAL MEETING, TRF.

Heymann, Hans, Jr., 1965. The objectives of transportation. In Fromm (1965).

Hide, H., et al. 1975. THE KENYA ROAD TRANSPORT COST MODEL: RESEARCH ON VEHICLE OPERATING COSTS. TRRL report LR 672.

HIGHWAY CAPACITY MANUAL, 1965. Special report 87, HRB.

Hill, D. M., and N. Dodd, 1962. Travel mode split in assignment programs. HRB Bulletin 347.

Hill, Donald M., Larry Tittemore, and David Gendell, 1973. Analysis of urban area travel by time of day. TRR 472 (TRB).

Hill, Morris D., 1967. A method for the evaluation of transportation plans. HRR 180 (HRB).

Hill, Stuart L., 1969. Century freeway (Watts). In JOINT DEVELOPMENT AND MULTIPLE USE OF TRANSPORTATION RIGHTS-OF-WAY, special report 104, HRB, pp. 68–74.

Hitch, Charles J., and Roland N. McKean, 1965. THE ECONOMICS OF DEFENSE IN THE NUCLEAR AGE. New York: Atheneum.

Hoos, Ida R., 1972. SYSTEMS ANALYSIS IN PUBLIC POLICY: A CRITIQUE. Berkeley, CA: University of California Press.

Huber, M., W. Buntwell, and D. Witherford, 1968. COMPARATIVE ANALYSIS OF TRAFFIC ASSIGNMENT TECHNIQUES WITH ACTUAL HIGHWAY USE. NCHRP Report 58, HRB.

Huddleston, John, and C. Michael Walton, 1976. Interurban transportation policy and the rural community. TRR 617 (TRB).

Humphrey, T. F., 1967. A report on the accuracy of traffic assignment when using capacity restraint. HRR 191 (HRB).

Hutchinson, B. G., 1974. PRINCIPLES OF URBAN TRANSPORT SYSTEMS PLANNING. New York: McGraw-Hill.

Hyman, William, and Steve Manley, 1977. Vegetation and wildlife impacts of railroad branch line abandonment. TRF Proceedings XVIII:1.

Industry Task Force on Reliability Studies and the Center for Transportation Studies, 1975. RAILROAD RELIABILITY AND FREIGHT CAR UTILIZATION: AN INTRODUCTION. Report CTS 75-8, CTS/MIT.

Isard, Walter, 1960. METHODS OF REGIONAL ANALYSIS. Cambridge, MA: MIT Press, chapter II (gravity, potential and spatial interaction models).

Isard, Walter, 1975. INTRODUCTION TO REGIONAL SCIENCE. Englewood Cliffs, NJ: Prentice-Hall.

James, F. J., ed., 1974. MODELS OF EMPLOYMENT AND RESIDENCE LOCA-TION. New Brunswick, NJ: Center for Urban Policy Research.

Jessiman, William A., and George A. Kocur, 1975. Attracting light rail transit ridership. In LIGHT RAIL TRANSIT, special report 161, TRB.

Jewell, W. S., 1967. Models for traffic assignment. *Transportation Research* 1:1.

Johnson, Michael A., 1976. A comparison of several methods of calculating travel time data for analysis of urban travel demand. TRF Proceedings XVII:1.

Jones, J. Christopher, 1970. DESIGN METHOD. New York: Wiley-Interscience.

Jones, Lyn, 1972. DEEP-SEA CONTAINER PORTS—SYSTEMS APPRAISAL AND SIMULATION MODELLING. Systems Behavior Course Module 1. Bletchle, Buckinghamshire, U.K.: The Open University.

Jones, Peter M., 1978. New approaches to understanding travel behavior: The human activity approach. In Hensher and Stopher (1978).

Jones, P. S., 1974. Citizen participation in Westside transportation planning. TRR 528 (TRB).

Jordan, D., S. Arnstein, J. Gray, E. Metcalf, W. Torrey, and F. Mills, 1976. EF-FECTIVE CITIZEN PARTICIPATION IN TRANSPORTATION PLANNING. Two volumes. FHWA.

Judge, E. J., 1974. Tests of assignment accuracy: An interurban case study. *Transportation* 3, pp. 25–44.

Kanafani, Adib, and Elisabeth Sadoulet, 1977. The partitioning of long-haul air traffic: A study in multinomial choice. *Transportation Research* 11:1, pp. 1–8.

Kanafani, Adib, Elisabeth Sadoulet, and Edward C. Sullivan, 1974. DEMAND ANALYSIS FOR NORTH ATLANTIC AIR TRAVEL. ITTE.

Keeney, Ralph L., 1972. Utility function for multi-attributed consequences. *Management Science* 18:5, pp. 276–287.

Kemp, Michael A., 1973. Some evidence of transit demand elasticities. *Transportation* 2.

Kemp, Michael A., 1975. Policies to increase transit ridership: A review of experience and research. Working paper 5032-1-3, The Urban Institute, Washington, D.C.

Kemp, Michael A., and Rebecca L. Rea, 1976. THE CONSEQUENCES OF TRANSIT FARE AND SERVICE POLICIES: A CLASSIFIED BIBLIOGRAPHY. Exchange Bibliography No. 1096, Monticello, IL: Council of Planning Librarians. Also available as working paper 5050-1-2, The Urban Institute, Washington, D.C.

Khan, Ata M., 1971. Transport policy decision analysis: A decision-theoretic framework. *Socio-Economic Planning Sciences* 5:2.

Kinstlinger, Jack, 1972. Relationships of areawide, subarea, and project planning in the urban transportation planning process. Paper presented to the Meeting of the AASHO Subcommittee on Urban Affairs and Socio-Economic Factors, Phoenix, Arizona.

Kneafsey, James T., 1974. THE ECONOMICS OF THE TRANSPORTATION FIRM. Lexington, MA: Lexington Books/D. C. Heath.

Knight, F. H., 1924. Some fallacies in the interpretation of social costs. *Quarterly Journal of Economics* 38, pp. 582–606.

Knudsen, Tore, 1977. Uncertainties in airport cost analysis. WCTR.

Kocur, George A., et al., 1977. DUAL MODE TRANSIT PLANNING CASE STUDY. Volume 1: PLANNING ANALYSES. Volume 2: TECHNICAL APPENDICES. Volume 3: TRANSIT SKETCH PLANNING MANUAL. UMTA.

Kocur, George A., Thomas Rushfeldt, and Rich Millican, 1977. A sketch planning model for transit system analysis and design. Paper presented to TRB.

Koppelman, Frank S., 1975. Travel prediction with disaggregate choice models. Ph.D. dissertation, Department of Civil Engineering, MIT.

Koppelman, Frank S., 1976a. Methodology for analysing errors in prediction with disaggregate choice models. TRR 592 (TRB).

Koppelman, Frank S., 1976b. Guidelines for aggregate travel prediction using disaggregate choice models. TRR 610 (TRB).

Koppelman, Frank S., and Moshe E. Ben-Akiva, 1977. Aggregate forecasting with disaggregate travel demand models using normally available data. WCTR.

Kraft, Gerald, 1963. DEMAND FOR INTERCITY PASSENGER TRAVEL IN THE WASHINGTON-BOSTON CORRIDOR. Washington, D.C.: U.S. Department of Commerce.

Kraft, Gerald, and Martin Wohl, 1967. New directions for passenger demand analysis and forecasting. *Transportation Research* 1:3.

Kresge, David T., and Paul O. Roberts, 1971. TECHNIQUES OF TRANSPORT PLANNING. Volume II: SYSTEMS ANALYSIS AND SIMULATION MODELS. Washington, D.C.: The Brookings Institution.

Kutter, Eckhard, 1973. A model for individual travel behavior. *Urban Studies* 10, pp. 235–258.

Lago, Armando M., 1968. Cost functions and optimum technology for intercity highway transportation systems in developing countries. *Traffic Quarterly* (October), pp. 521–553.

Lamm, Lester, 1972. An appraisal of urban transportation planning. Paper presented to AASHO.

Lancaster, Kevin J., 1966. A new approach to consumer theory. *Journal of Political Economy* 74, pp. 132–157. Reprinted in Quandt (1970a).

Landau, Uzi, 1976. Sketch planning models in transportation systems. Ph.D. dissertation, Department of Civil Engineering, MIT.

Lane, Robert, Timothy J. Powell, and Paul Prestwood Smith, 1971. ANALYTICAL TRANSPORT PLANNING. London: Duckworth.

Lang, A. Scheffer, 1977. Decision issues and research priorities in intercity freight transportation: A U.S. perspective. WCTR.

Lang, A. Scheffer, and Richard M. Soberman, 1964. URBAN RAIL TRANSIT: ITS ECONOMICS AND TECHNOLOGY. Cambridge, MA: MIT Press.

Larwin, Thomas F., and Darwin G. Stuart, 1976. Issue-oriented approach to environmental impact analysis. TRR 583 (TRB), pp. 1–14.

Lave, C. A., 1969. A behavioral approach to modal split forecasting. *Transportation Research* 3:4.

Lave, C. A., J. Mehring, and R. Kuzmyak, 1977. Price elasticities of intercity passenger travel. TRF Proceedings XVIII:1.

Lawson, John R., Marvin L. Manheim, and Darwin G. Stuart, 1976. Guideway transit for Southern California: A policy analysis. Minneapolis: Audio-Visual Library Services, University of Minnesota.

LeBlanc, L. J., 1976. The use of large-scale mathematical programming models in transportation systems. *Transportation Research* 10:6.

LeBlanc, L. J., E. Morlok, and W. Pierskalla, 1975. An efficient approach to solving the road network equilibrium traffic assignment problem. *Transportation Research* 9:5, pp. 309–318.

Lee, Douglas B., Jr., 1976. Cost-oriented methodology for short-range transportation planning. TRR 589 (TRB).

Lee, J. W., D. O. Covault, and G. E. Willeke, 1972. Framework for using social indicators to monitor, evaluate and improve a public transportation system. HRR 410 (HRB).

Legarra, John A., and Thomas R. Lammers, 1969. The highway administrator looks at values. In TRANSPORTATION AND COMMUNITY VALUES, special report 105, HRB, pp. 109–116.

Lerman, Steven R., 1975. A disaggregate behavioral model of urban mobility decisions. Ph.D. dissertation, Department of Civil Engineering, MIT.

Lerman, Steven R., 1976. Location, housing, auto ownership and mode to work: A joint choice model. TRR 610 (TRB).

Lerman, Steven R., and Moshe E. Ben-Akiva, 1975. A disaggregate behavioral model of auto ownership. TRR 569 (TRB).

Lerman, Steven R., Martin Flusberg, Wayne M. Pecknold, Richard Nestle, and Nigel H. M. Wilson, 1977. METHOD FOR ESTIMATING PATRONAGE OF DEMAND-RESPONSIVE TRANSPORTATION SYSTEMS. Report prepared by Cambridge Systematics, Inc., for the DOT.

Lerman, Steven R., and C. Manski, 1976. Alternative sampling procedures for disaggregate choice model estimation. Paper presented to TRB.

Lerman, Steven R., and C. Manski, 1977. An estimator for the generalized multinomial probit choice model. Paper presented to TRB.

Lerman, Steven R., and Nigel H. M. Wilson, 1974. Analytic equilibrium model for Dial-a-ride design. TRR 522 (TRB).

Lion, Paul Michel, and Richard M. Opperman, 1977. Operating tradeoffs in transit systems. Unpublished working paper, Department of Civil Engineering, Princeton University.

Liou, P. S., G. S. Cohen, and D. T. Hartgen, 1975. An application of disaggregate mode choice models to travel demand forecasting for urban transit systems. TRR 534 (TRB).

Litchfield, Nathaniel, 1966. Cost-benefit analysis in urban redevelopment: A case study—Swanley. *Regional Science Association Papers* 16.

Little, I. M. D., and J. A. Mirrlees, 1974. PROJECT APPRAISAL AND PLANNING FOR DEVELOPING COUNTRIES. New York: Basic Books.

Lockwood, Steven C., 1974. Transportation planning in a changing environment. *Traffic Quarterly* 28:4.

Lovelock, C. H., 1975. A market segmentation approach to transit planning, modelling and management. TRF Proceedings XVI.

LOW VOLUME ROADS, 1975. Special report 160, TRB.

Luce, R. D., and P. Suppes, 1965. Preference, utility and subjective probability. In R. D. Luce, R. R. Bush, and E. Galanter, eds., HANDBOOK OF MATHEMATICAL PSYCHOLOGY (New York: John Wiley), volume 3.

Luchtenberg, G., 1976. TRANSPORT PLANNING IN CONGESTED AREAS AND THE ROLE OF QUANTITATIVE MODELS. Report of the ECMT regional roundtable on transport economics. The Hague: Projectbureau Integosh Verkees en Verkoerstudies, Ministerie van Verkeer en Waterstaat (February).

McFadden, Daniel, 1974a. Conditional logit analysis of qualitative choice behavior. In Paul Zarembka, ed., FRONTIERS IN ECONOMETRICS (New York: Academic Press).

McFadden, Daniel, 1974b. Quantal choice analysis: Survey. Draft paper presented at the NSF-NBER Conference on Decision Rules and Uncertainty.

McFadden, Daniel, 1974c. The measurement of urban travel demand. *Journal of Public Economics* no. 3.

McFadden, Daniel, 1975. The revealed preferences of a government bureaucracy: Theory. *The Bell Journal of Economics* 6:2, pp. 401–416.

McFadden, Daniel, 1976. THE THEORY AND PRACTICE OF DISAGGREGATE DEMAND FORECASTING FOR VARIOUS MODES OF URBAN TRANSPORTATION. Report prepared for a seminar on emerging transportation planning methods, Daytona Beach, FL, December 1976. Office of the Secretary, DOT.

McFadden, Daniel, 1978. Quantitative methods for analysing travel behavior of individuals: Some recent developments. In Hensher and Stopher (1978).

McFadden, Daniel, and Fred Reid, 1975. Aggregate travel demand forecasting from disaggregate models. TRR 534 (TRB).

McGean, Thomas, 1976. URBAN TRANSPORTATION TECHNOLOGY. Lexington, MA: Lexington Books/D. C. Heath.

McGillivray, Robert G., Kevin Neels, and Michael E. Beesley, 1978. Toward rational road user changes. Paper presented to TRB.

McIntosh, Peter T., and David A. Quarmby, 1972. Generalized costs and the estimation of movement costs and benefits in transport planning. HRR 383 (HRB).

McKean, Roland N., 1968. EFFICIENCY IN GOVERNMENT THROUGH SYSTEMS ANALYSIS. New York: John Wiley.

McLynn, J. M., and T. Woronka, 1969. Passenger demand and modal split models. Report 230, Northeast Corridor Transportation Project, DOT.

Maine Department of Transportation, 1972. U.S. ROUTE 1A, HARRINGTON,

MAINE, FINAL ENVIRONMENTAL IMPACT STATEMENT. Report prepared by Edwards and Kelsey.

Major, David C., 1974. Multi-objective redesign of the Big Walnut project. In de Neufville and Marks (1974).

Major, David C., 1977. MULTI-OBJECTIVE WATER RESOURCE PLANNING. Washington, D.C.: American Geophysical Union.

Manheim, Marvin L., 1961. Data accuracy in route location. *Traffic Quarterly* 15:1.

Manheim, Marvin L., 1966a. HIERARCHICAL STRUCTURE: A MODEL OF PLAN-NING AND DESIGN PROCESSES. Cambridge, MA: MIT Press.

Manheim, Marvin L., 1966b. Principles of transportation systems analysis. HRR 180 (HRB).

Manheim, Marvin L., 1969. Search and choice in transport systems planning. HRR 293 (HRB).

Manheim, Marvin L., 1970a. A design process model: Theory and applications to transportation planning. In Moore (1970).

Manheim, Marvin L., ed., 1970b. TRANSPORTATION ANALYSIS, PAST AND PROSPECTS. HRR 309 (HRB).

Manheim, Marvin L., 1970c. Fundamental properties of systems of travel demand models. Working paper, Department of Civil Engineering, MIT.

Manheim, Marvin L., 1970d. DECISION THEORIES IN TRANSPORTATION PLAN-NING. Special report 108, HRB.

Manheim, Marvin L., 1973a. How should we respond to environmental issues in transportation? ICTR.

Manheim, Marvin L., 1973b. Practical implications of some fundamental properties of travel demand models. HRR 422 (HRB).

Manheim, Marvin L., 1973c. Reaching decisions about technological projects with social consequences: A normative model. *Transportation* 2, pp. 1–24. Reprinted in de Neufville and Marks (1974) and in the *Journal of Applied Systems Analysis* 5:1(1976).

Manheim, Marvin L., 1973d. Memorandum to Robert Dial: Proposed direct equi-librium approach using exponential functions (24 September).

Manheim, Marvin L., 1974. Societal issues and transportation education. In MULTI-DISCIPLINARY EDUCATION IN TRANSPORTATION (1974).

Manheim, Marvin L., 1976a. An overview of some current travel demand research. In Matzner and Ruesch (1976).

Manheim, Marvin L., 1976b. Transportation systems analysis: A personal view. *Transportation* 10:6, pp. 371–375.

Manheim, Marvin L., 1977a. The emerging planning process, neither long-range nor short-range, but adaptive and (hopefully) decisive. Paper presented to TRB.

Manheim, Marvin L., 1977b. How should transit options be analysed? Paper presented to the January 1976 meeting of the TRB (available from CTS/MIT).

Manheim, Marvin L., 1978a. Understanding supply in transportation systems. In Florian (1978).

Manheim, Marvin L., 1978b. Ethical issues in transportation analysis. Paper presented to TRB (available from CTS/MIT).

Manheim, Marvin L., John P. Attanucci, José Portuondo-Diaz, and Richard Shepherd, 1975a. RESEARCH PAPERS: GUIDELINES FOR FEDERAL POLICY ON ASSISTANCE FOR MAJOR MASS TRANSPORTATION INVESTMENTS. Prepared for the Office of Systems Research and Analysis, DOT, and the Office of Policy and Program Development, UMTA.

Manheim, Marvin L., K. U. Bhatt, and E. R. Ruiter, 1968. SEARCH AND CHOICE IN TRANSPORT SYSTEMS PLANNING: SUMMARY REPORT. Research report R68-40, Department of Civil Engineering, MIT.

Manheim, Marvin L., Peter Furth, and Ilan Salomon, 1977. Responsive analysis methods: Transportation analysis using pocket calculators. Working paper CTS-RAMP-77-1, MIT. Also in TRR (in press). [See also other reports in the RAMP series.]

Manheim, Marvin L., and Gary Hawthorne, 1974. GUIDELINES FOR PLANNING, IMPLEMENTING AND FINANCING A COMPREHENSIVE POLICY OF VEHICLE RESTRAINTS. Report prepared for OECD.

Manheim, Marvin L., and Earl R. Ruiter, 1970. DODOTRANS I: A decision-oriented computer language for analysis of multi-mode transportation systems. HRR 314 (HRB).

Manheim, Marvin L., and Earl R. Ruiter, 1971. Systematically analyzing transportation alternatives. In Daniel Brand, ed., URBAN TRANSPORTATION INNOVATION (New York: American Society of Civil Engineers).

Manheim, Marvin L., and Earl R. Ruiter, 1973. The transportation laboratory: Teaching fundamental concepts of transportation systems analysis. HRR 462 (HRB).

Manheim, Marvin L., and John H. Suhrbier, 1971. Community values in transport project planning. TRF Proceedings XII.

Manheim, Marvin L., and John H. Suhrbier, 1972. Community values: A strategy for project planning. In CITIZEN PARTICIPATION AND COMMUNITY VALUES (1972).

Manheim, Marvin L., and John H. Suhrbier, 1973. Incorporating social and environmental factors in highway planning and construction. In ENVIRONMENTAL CONSIDERATIONS IN PLANNING, DESIGN AND CONSTRUCTION, special report 138, HRB, pp. 9–22.

Manheim, Marvin L., John H. Suhrbier, and Elizabeth D. Bennett, 1972. PROCESS GUIDELINES FOR CONSIDERATION OF ENVIRONMENTAL EFFECTS. Report 72–11 prepared for FHWA by USL/MIT (June).

Manheim, Marvin L., John H. Suhrbier, Elizabeth D. Bennett, Lance A. Neumann, Frank C. Colcord, Jr., and Arlee T. Reno, Jr., 1975b. TRANSPORTATION DECISION-MAKING: A GUIDE TO SOCIAL AND ENVIRONMENTAL CONSIDERATIONS. NCHRP Report No. 156, TRB.

Manheim, Marvin L., et al. 1972. COMMUNITY AND ENVIRONMENTAL VALUES IN TRANSPORTATION PLANNING: SUMMARY OF FINDINGS AND RECOMMENDATIONS TO THE STATE OF CALIFORNIA. Research report 72-2, TCV Project, USL/MIT.

Manski, Charles F., 1973. The analysis of qualitative choice. Ph.D. dissertation, Department of Economics, MIT.

Manski, Charles F., and J. David Wright, 1976. Nature of equilibrium in the market for taxi services. TRR 619 (TRB).

Marcuse, Peter, 1976. Professional ethics and beyond. *Journal of the American Institute of Planners* (July).

Marcuse, Peter, 1978. Ethics and the "public interest" in transportation. Paper presented to TRB (January).

Martin, Brian V., and Marvin L. Manheim, 1965. A research program for comparison of traffic assignment techniques. HRR 88 (HRB).

Martin, Brian V., Frederick W. Memmott III, and Alexander J. Bone, 1961. PRINCIPLES AND TECHNIQUES OF PREDICTING FUTURE DEMAND FOR URBAN AREA TRANSPORTATION. Cambridge, MA: MIT Press.

Martland, Carl D., 1977. Smaller train crews: Better performance, not lower crew costs. TRF Proceedings XVIII:1.

Martland, Carl D., Richard Assarabowski, and J. Reilly McCarren, 1977. THE ROLE OF SCREENING MODELS IN EVALUATING RAILROAD RATIONALIZATION PROPOSALS. Studies in Railroad Operations and Economics 21, Transportation Systems Division, Department of Civil Engineering, MIT.

Martland, Carl D., Joseph M. Sussman, and Craig E. Philip, 1977. Improving railroad reliability and freight car utilization. TRF Proceedings XVIII:1.

Martland, Carl D., and Marc N. Terziev, 1976. RAILROAD RATIONALIZATION METHODOLOGY. Studies in Railroad Operations and Economics 18, Transportation Systems Division, Department of Civil Engineering, MIT.

Matzner, Egon, and Gerhard Ruesch, eds., 1976. TRANSPORT AS AN INSTRUMENT FOR ALLOCATING SPACE AND TIME—A SOCIAL SCIENCE APPROACH. Report no. 11, Institute of Public Finance, Technical University in Vienna.

Mauch, Sam. 1973. Origins and consequences of the overemphasis on hardware in transportation planning. ICTR.

May, Adolph D., Jr., and Hartmut E. M. Keller, 1967. Non-integer car-following models. HRR 199 (HRB), pp. 19–32.

May, Adolph D., Jr., and Maxence Orthlieb, 1976. Urban freeway corridor control model (abridgement). TRR 601 (TRB).

Mead, Kirtland C., 1973a. Resource allocation and the system planning process. HRR 467 (HRB).

Mead, Kirtland C., 1973b. Design of a statewide transportation planning process: An application to California. Ph.D. dissertation, Department of Civil Engineering, MIT.

Mead, Kirtland C., Marvin L. Manheim, and Arlee T. Reno, Jr., 1971. Basic issues in incorporating community and environmental factors in the transport system planning process. TRF Proceedings XII:1.

Meyer, John R., John Kain, and Martin Wohl, 1965. THE URBAN TRANSPORTATION PROBLEM. Cambridge, MA: Harvard University Press.

Meyer, John R., Martin J. Peck, John Stenason, and Charles Zwick, 1960. THE ECONOMICS OF COMPETITION IN THE TRANSPORTATION INDUSTRIES. Cambridge, MA: Harvard University Press.

Meyer, John R., and Mahlon R. Straszheim, 1971. TECHNIQUES OF TRANSPORT PLANNING: PRICING AND PROJECT EVALUATION, volume I. Washington, D.C.: The Brookings Institute.

Meyerson, Martin, 1956. Building the middle range bridge for comprehensive planning. *Journal of the American Institute of Planners* 22:2. Reprinted in Faludi (1973).

Miller, Fred, 1975. Sensitivity analysis of rate of return. TRR 550 (TRB).

Miller, Myron T., et al., 1971. RECOMMENDATIONS FOR NORTHEAST CORRIDOR TRANSPORTATION. Three volumes, DOT.

Mills, G., 1971. Investment planning for British ports. JTEP 5:2.

Mishan, E. J., 1970. What is wrong with Roskill? JTEP 4:3.

Mishan, E. J., 1971. COST-BENEFIT ANALYSIS—AN INTRODUCTION. New York: Praeger.

Moavenzadeh, Fred, Fredric Berger, Brian Brademeyer, and Robert Wyatt, 1975. THE HIGHWAY COST MODEL: GENERAL FRAMEWORK. Draft report, MIT.

Moore, Gary T., ed., 1970. EMERGING METHODS OF ENVIRONMENTAL DESIGN. Cambridge, MA: MIT Press.

Moore, Will T., Frederic J. Ridel, and Carlos G. Rodriguez, 1975. AN INTRODUCTION TO URBAN DEVELOPMENT MODELS AND GUIDELINES FOR THEIR USE IN URBAN TRANSPORTATION PLANNING. FHWA.

Morlok, Edward K., 1968. The comparison of transport technologies. HRR 238 (HRB).

Morlok, Edward K., 1969. AN ANALYSIS OF TRANSPORT TECHNOLOGY AND NETWORK STRUCTURE. Evanston, IL: Northwestern University Press.

Morlok, Edward K., 1976. Supply functions for public transport: Initial concepts and models. In Florian (1976).

Morlok, Edward K., 1978. INTRODUCTION TO TRANSPORTATION ENGINEERING AND PLANNING. New York: McGraw-Hill.

Mowll, Jack, and Yu-sheng Chiang, 1973. The FLOPATS concept. ICTR.

MULTIDISCIPLINARY EDUCATION IN TRANSPORTATION, 1974. Special report 150, TRB.

Mumford, John R., 1969. COMPUTER-AIDED EVALUATION OF TRANSPORT SYSTEMS. Research report R69-41, Department of Civil Engineering, MIT.

Munby, D., ed., 1968. TRANSPORT. Hammondsworth, Middlesex, U.K.: Penguin Books.

Murchland, John D., 1969. Road network traffic distribution in equilibrium. Paper presented at the Conference on Mathematical Methods in the Economic Sciences, Mathematisches Forschungsinstitut, Oberwolfach.

Nahmias, Jacques A., 1972. Airport: The design of a role-playing game in transportation. M.S. thesis, Department of Civil Engineering, MIT.

National Observer, 1969. Now the real fight begins (April 14).

Natural Resources Defense Council, Inc., 1977. The fundamental problem: An inversion of values. *NRDC Newlsetter* 6:2–3 (April).

Neuburger, Henry, 1971. User benefit in the evaluation of transport and land use plans. JTEP 5:1.

Neumann, Lance A., 1972. Time-staged strategy approach to transportation systems planning. M.S. thesis, Department of Civil Engineering, MIT.

Neumann, Lance A., 1976. Integrating transportation system planning and programming: An implementation strategy approach. Ph.D. dissertation, Department of Civil Engineering, MIT.

Neumann, Lance A., Marvin L. Manheim, Wayne M. Pecknold, and Arlee Reno, Jr., 1974. Integrating system and project planning for effective statewide programming of investments. TRR 499 (TRB).

Neumann, Lance A., and Wayne M. Pecknold, 1973. Application of the time-staged strategic approach to system planning. HRR 435 (HRB).

Nguyen, S., 1974. An algorithm for the traffic assignment problem. *Transportation Science* 8, pp. 203–216.

Nicolaidis, Gregory C., 1975. Quantification of the comfort variable. *Transportation Research* 9:1.

Nicolaidis, Gregory C., and Ricardo Dobson, 1975. Disaggregated perceptions and preferences in transportation planning. *Transportation Research* 9:5.

Niebur, Howard Duke, 1975. Minuteman access roads. In LOW-VOLUME ROADS (1975).

NORTHEAST CORRIDOR TRANSPORTATION PROJECT REPORT, 1970. Report NECTP-209, Office of High Speed Ground Transportation, DOT (April), NTIS number PB 190 929. See also the other volumes in this series: PB 190 930 through 190 945.

Nwaneri, V. C., 1970. Equity in cost-benefit analysis—Third London airport. JTEP 4:3.

Odoni, Amadeo R., and Peter Kivestu, 1976. A HANDBOOK FOR THE ESTIMATION OF AIRSIDE DELAYS AT MAJOR AIRPORTS (QUICK APPROXIMATION METHOD). Washington, D.C.: National Aeronautics and Space Administration.

Oglesby, C. H., B. Bishop, G. E. Willeke, and H. Henderson, 1970. A method for decisions among freeway location alternatives based on user and community consequences. HRR 305 (HRB).

Okita, S., 1972. Economic growth and environmental problems. In AREA DEVELOPMENT IN JAPAN, no. 5 (Tokyo: Japanese Center for Area Development Research).

Oliver, A. M., 1972. MODELLING A BUS ROUTE AND MEASURING REGULAR-ITY. Operational Research Report R188, London Transport (July).

Organization for Economic Cooperation and Development, 1969. THE URBAN TRANSPORTATION PLANNING PROCESS: IN SEARCH OF IMPROVED STRATEGY. Report of a Panel of Experts, OECD.

Organization for Economic Cooperation and Development, 1974. URBAN TRAFFIC MODELS: POSSIBILITIES FOR SIMPLIFICATION. OECD.

Overgaard, K. Rask, n.d. Traffic estimation in urban transportation planning. *Acta polytechnica scandinavica* (UDC 656, 021.2), p. 131.

Paquette, Radnor J., Norman Ashford, and Paul H. Wright, 1972. TRANSPORTA-TION ENGINEERING. New York: Ronald Press.

Park, Ki Suh, 1972. Achieving positive community participation in the freeway planning process. In CITIZEN PARTICIPATION AND COMMUNITY VALUES (1972).

Parker, John, and Warren Panther, 1974. Traffic and environment: The multi-disciplinary team and its working methods. ICTR.

Passonneau, Joseph, 1972. Full compensation in urban roadway construction: A necessary and practical objective. TRR 399 (TRB).

Pearce, D. W., 1971. COST-BENEFIT ANALYSIS. London: Macmillan.

Peat, Marwick, Mitchell and Co., 1973. TRANSPORTATION SYSTEM EVALUA-TION INDICATORS. Report prepared for UMTA.

Peat, Marwick, Mitchell and Co. and Market Facts, Inc., 1976. A MARKETING APPROACH TO CARPOOL DEMAND ANALYSIS. Report prepared for the Federal Energy Administration.

Pecknold, Wayne M., 1970. Evolution of transport systems: An analysis of time-staged investment strategies under uncertainty. Ph.D. dissertation, Department of Civil Engineering, MIT.

Pecknold, Wayne M., Kirtland C. Mead, Lance A. Neumann, Arlee T. Reno, Jr., James T. Kneafsey, Frank Koppelman, Albert J. Mailman, Cathy A. Buckley, and Marvin L. Manheim, 1972. TRANSPORTATION SYSTEM PLANNING AND COM-MUNITY AND ENVIRONMENTAL VALUES. Report 72-3, TCV Project, USL/MIT.

Pecknold, Wayne M., Nigel H. M. Wilson, and Brian Kullman, 1972. AN EMPIRI-CAL DEMAND MODEL FOR EVALUATING LOCAL BUS SERVICE MODIFICA-TIONS. Department of Civil Engineering, MIT.

Pennsylvania Department of Transportation, 1973. ACTION PLAN (September).

Perfalter, Michael, and Gary R. Allen, 1976. Diachronic analysis of social and eco-nomic effects of relocation due to highways. TRR 617 (TRB).

Philip, Craig E., 1978. FREIGHT CAR UTILIZATION AND RAILROAD RELIABIL-ITY: THE APPLICATION OF AN INVENTORY MODEL TO THE RAILROAD EMPTY CAR DISTRIBUTION PROCESS. Report CTS 78–2, CTS/MIT.

Pignataro, Louis J., 1973. TRAFFIC ENGINEERING: THEORY AND PRACTICE. Englewood Cliffs, NJ: Prentice-Hall.

Pollack, Maurice, 1974. Some aspects of the aircraft scheduling problem. *Transportation Research* 8:3, pp. 233–242.

Potts, Renfrey B., and Robert M. Oliver, 1972. FLOWS IN TRANSPORTATION NETWORKS. New York: Academic Press.

Pouliquen, L. Y., 1970. RISK ANALYSIS IN PROJECT APPRAISAL. Baltimore: Johns Hopkins Press.

Prokopy, John C., and Richard B. Rubin, 1975. PARAMETRIC ANALYSIS OF RAILWAY LINE CAPACITY. FRA.

Quandt, Richard E., ed., 1970a. THE DEMAND FOR TRAVEL: THEORY AND MEASUREMENT. Lexington, MA: D. C. Heath.

Quandt, Richard E., 1970b. Introduction to the analysis of travel demand. In Quandt (1970a).

Quandt, Richard E., 1976. The theory of travel demand. *Transportation Research* 10:6, pp. 411–414.

Quandt, Richard E., and William J. Baumol, 1966. The demand for abstract transport modes: Theory and measurement. *Journal of Regional Science* 6:2, pp. 13–26. Reprinted in Quandt (1970a).

Quarmby, David A., 1967. Choice of travel mode for the journey to work: Some findings. JTEP 1:3. Reprinted in Quandt (1970a).

Quinby, Henry D., 1976. Mass transportation characteristics. In Baerwald (1976).

Raiffa, Howard, 1968. PREFERENCES FOR MULTI-ATTRIBUTED ALTERNATIVES. Memorandum RM-5869-DOT, The RAND Corporation, Santa Monica, CA.

RAILROAD RESEARCH STUDY BACKGROUND PAPERS, 1975. Oxford, IN: Richard B. Cross Co.

Rallis, Tom, 1967. CAPACITY OF TRANSPORT CENTERS: PORTS, RAILWAY STATIONS, ROAD HAULAGE CENTERS AND AIRPORTS. Report 35, Department for Road Construction, Transportation Engineering, and Town Planning, Technical University of Denmark, Copenhagen.

Rapp, Matthias H., Philippe Mattenberger, Serge Piguet, and Andre Robert-Grandpierre, 1976. Interactive graphics system for transit route optimization. TRR 559 (TRB).

Rassam, Paul R., Ray Ellis, and J. C. Bennett, 1971. The n-dimensional logit model: Development and application. HRR 369 (HRB).

Ratcliffe, E. P., 1972. A comparison of drivers' route choice criteria and those used in current assignment processes. *Traffic Engineering and Control* (March/April).

Rea, John C., and James H. Miller, 1973. Comparative analysis of urban transit modes using service specification envelopes. Paper presented to HRB (January).

Reebie Associates, 1972. TOWARD AN EFFECTIVE DEMURRAGE SYSTEM. Report FRA-OE-73-1, FRA (PB 212 069).

Reichman, Shalom, and Peter S. Stopher, 1973. Disaggregate stochastic models of travel mode choice. HRR 369 (HRB).

Reno, Arlee T., Jr., 1972. Interaction procedures in the transportation systems planning process. HRR 394 (HRB).

Reno, Arlee T., Jr., and Barbara Richardson, 1972. INTEGRATION OF SYSTEM AND PROJECT PLANNING: THE ROLE OF TRANSPORTATION CORRIDOR STUDIES. Report 72-4, TCV project, USL/MIT.

Reno, Arlee T., Jr., Ben Schneideman, and Marvin L. Manheim, 1973. OPPORTUNITIES TO IMPROVE THE INTERRELATIONSHIP OF URBAN SYSTEM AND PROJECT PLANNING. Report 73-1, USL/MIT, prepared for FHWA.

REPORT TO CONGRESS ON SECTION 109(h), TITLE 23, UNITED STATES CODE—GUIDELINES RELATING TO THE ECONOMIC, SOCIAL AND ENVIRONMENTAL EFFECTS OF HIGHWAY PROJECTS, 1972. Committee on Public Works Print 92-45. GPO (August).

Richards, Martin G., and Moshe E. Ben-Akiva, 1975. A DISAGGREGATE TRAVEL DEMAND MODEL. Lexington, MA: Lexington Books.

Ridley, T. M., 1976. Research and decision-making, *Transportation Research* 10:6, p. 387.

Riedesel, G. A., and J. C. Cook, 1970. Desirability rating and route selection. HRR 305 (HRB).

Road Research Laboratory, 1965. RESEARCH ON ROAD TRAFFIC. HMSO.

Roberts, Paul O., 1970. Model systems for urban transportation planning: Where do we go from here? HRR 309 (HRB).

Roberts, Paul O., 1977. Forecasting freight demand. WCTR.

Roberts, Paul O., and Donald N. Deweese, 1971. ECONOMIC ANALYSIS FOR TRANSPORT CHOICE. Lexington, MA: D. C. Heath.

Roberts, Paul O., Donald S. Shoup, and J. Royce Ginn, 1971. The inter-modal transfer model. In Kresge and Roberts (1971), Appendix C.

Roberts, Paul O., and Richard M. Soberman, 1971. The highway cost-performance model. In Kresge and Roberts (1971), Appendix A.

Roberts, Paul O., Marc N. Terziev, James T. Kneafsey, Lawrence B. Wilson, Ralph D. Samuelson, Yu-sheng Chiang, and Christopher V. Deephouse, 1976. ANALYSIS OF THE INCREMENTAL COST AND TRADEOFFS BETWEEN ENERGY EFFICIENCY AND PHYSICAL DISTRIBUTION EFFECTIVENESS IN INTERCITY FREIGHT MARKETS. Report 76-14, CTS/MIT.

Robillard, P., 1974. Multipath assignment with dynamic input flows. *Transportation Research* 8:6, pp. 568–574.

Robinson, Ira M., 1965. Beyond the middle-range planning bridge. *Journal of the American Institute of Planners* 31. Reprinted in Faludi (1973).

Robinson, Richard, 1975. The Kenya road transport model. In LOW-VOLUME ROADS (1975).

Robinson, Ross, and Keith P. Tognetti, 1974. Modelling and port policy decisions: The interface of simulation and practice. ICTR.

Rogers, A. C., 1968. The urban freeway: An experiment in team design and decision-making. HRR 220 (HRB).

Romoff, Harvey M., 1977. Relationship of research to decision-making in intercontinental transport. WCTR.

Roos, Daniel, 1966. ICES SYSTEM DESIGN. Cambridge, MA: MIT Press.

Rothenberg, Jerome, 1961. THE MEASUREMENT OF SOCIAL WELFARE. Engle-wood Cliffs, NJ: Prentice-Hall.

Ruiter, Earl R., 1973a. Analytical structures. In Brand and Manheim (1973).

Ruiter, Earl R., 1973b. The prediction of network equilibrium: The state of the art. ICTR.

Ruiter, Earl R., 1976a. Network equilibrium capabilities for the UMTA transporta-tion planning system. In Florian (1976).

Ruiter, Earl R., 1976b. UMTA FUNCTIONAL AND DETAILED SPECIFICATIONS FOR A HIGHWAY NETWORK EQUILIBRIUM PROGRAM. Cambridge, MA: Cambridge Systematics, Inc.

Ruiter, Earl R., and Moshe E. Ben-Akiva, 1977. A system of disaggregate travel demand models: Structure, component models and application procedures. Paper presented to TRB (January).

Ruiter, Earl R., and George A. Kocur, 1976. Interfacing travel-supply models and equilibrium procedures with travel-demand models. In Stopher and Meyburg (1976).

Samuelson, Ralph D., and Steven R. Lerman, 1977. Modelling the freight rate structure. TRF Proceedings XVIII:1.

Sanders, D. B., T. A. Reynen, and Kiran U. Bhatt, 1974. CHARACTERISTICS OF URBAN TRANSPORTATION SYSTEMS—A HANDBOOK FOR TRANSPORTA-TION PLANNERS. DOT.

Schein, Edgar H., 1969. PROCESS CONSULTATION. Reading, MA: Addison-Wesley.

Schein, Edgar H., 1972. PROFESSIONAL EDUCATION. New York: McGraw-Hill.

Schneider, Lewis M., George P. Baker, and Robert B. Waldner, 1977. A pragmatic approach to railroad traffic forecasting. TRF Proceedings XVIII:1.

Schneider, Morton, 1973. Probability maximization in networks. ICTR.

Schuster, Helmut, 1974. Transportation planning techniques: Problems and pros-pects. *Kyklos* 27:3, pp. 583–600.

Sen, Ashish, and Chris Johnson, 1977. On the form of a bus service frequency supply function. *Transportation Research* 11:1, pp. 63–65.

Senior, Martin L., 1974. Approaches to residential location modelling 2: Urban eco-nomic models and some recent developments (a review). *Environment and Plan-ning* 6, pp. 369–409.

Sheehy, J. E., 1974. Highway displacement relocation experience in Massa-chusetts. *Traffic Quarterly* 28:2, pp. 209–226.

Sheffi, Yosef, and Carlos F. Daganzo, 1978. A unified approach to transportation forecasting: Hypernetworks and supply-demand equilibrium with disaggregate demand models. Paper presented to TRB (January).

Shephard, Lynn, 1968. The freeway revolt. A series of ten articles. *The Christian Science Monitor*.

Sherman, Len, Terry J. Atherton, and Wayne M. Pecknold, 1976. A preliminary assessment of the transportation impacts of auto restricted zones in U.S. cities. TRF Proceedings XVII:1.

Shortreed, John H., 1976. Transit and pricing policies. In URBAN TRANSPORTATION PRICING ALTERNATIVES (1976).

Simcock, B. L., 1972. Environmental pollution and citizens' movements: The social sources and significance of anti-pollution protest in Japan. In AREA DEVELOPMENT IN JAPAN, no. 5 (Tokyo: Japanese Center for Area Development Research).

Simon, Herbert A., 1960. ADMINISTRATIVE BEHAVIOR. New York: Macmillan, second edition.

Simpson, Robert W., 1969. SCHEDULING AND ROUTING MODELS FOR AIRLINE SYSTEMS. Report FTL-R68-3, CTS/MIT.

Simpson, Robert W., 1974. A theory for domestic airline economics. TRF Proceedings XIV:1.

Simpson, Robert W., 1977. Advanced airline planning models as a tool for developing regulatory policy. WCTR.

Simpson, Robert W., 1978. Modelling the supply function for public transportation. In Florian (1978).

Small, Kenneth A., 1977. Priority lanes on urban radial freeways: An economic simulation. Paper presented to TRB.

Smith, David G., Daniel P. Maxfield, and Stan Fromovitz, 1977. The inseparability of operational control, policy analysis and strategic planning in transportation: An experience with U.S. airports. WCTR.

Smith, Peter S., 1974. AIR FREIGHT: OPERATIONS, MARKETING AND ECONOMICS. London: Faber and Faber.

Soberman, Richard M., 1966a. Economic analysis of highway design in developing countries. HRR 115 (HRB).

Soberman, Richard M., 1966b. TRANSPORTATION TECHNOLOGY FOR DEVELOPING REGIONS. Cambridge, MA: MIT Press.

Soberman, Richard M., 1966c. Predicting supply functions for transportation. TRF Proceedings VII.

Soberman, Richard M., 1971. The railway cost-performance model. In Kresge and Roberts (1971), Appendix B.

Soberman, Richard M., 1976. Developing transportation and land use alternatives in Toronto. In TRANSPORTATION AND LAND USE PLANNING ABROAD, special report 168, TRB.

Spear, Bruce D., 1977. APPLICATIONS OF NEW TRAVEL DEMAND FORECASTING TECHNIQUES TO TRANSPORTATION PLANNING: A STUDY OF INDIVIDUAL CHOICE MODELS. FHWA.

Steenbrink, Peter A., 1974. Transport network optimization in the Dutch Integral Transportation Study. *Transportation Research* 8:1, pp. 11–27.

Steilberg, Chresten, 1973. The development and application of demand functions for intercity travel by railroad and bus in The Netherlands. WCTR.

Steinkrauss, W., 1976. Public participation in the metropolitan Toronto transportation plan review. In TRANSPORTATION AND LAND USE PLANNING ABROAD, special report 168, TRB.

Stopher, Peter, 1969. A probability model of travel mode choice for the work journey. HRR 283 (HRB).

Stopher, Peter R., and Arnim H. Meyburg, 1975. URBAN TRANSPORTATION MODELLING AND PLANNING. Lexington, MA: Lexington Books/D. C. Heath.

Stopher, Peter, and Arnim Meyburg, eds., 1976. BEHAVIORAL TRAVEL-DEMAND MODELS. Lexington, MA: D. C. Heath.

Stratford, Alan H., 1967. AIR TRANSPORT ECONOMICS IN THE SUPERSONIC ERA. London: Macmillan, and New York: St. Martin's Press.

Suhrbier, John H., and Elizabeth D. Bennett, eds., 1973a. PROCEEDINGS OF A PANEL DISCUSSION ON COMMUNITY INVOLVEMENT IN HIGHWAY PLANNING AND DESIGN. Office of Environmental Policy, FHWA.

Suhrbier, John H., and Elizabeth D. Bennett, eds., 1973b. PROCEEDINGS OF A PANEL DISCUSSION ON THE INTERRELATIONSHIP OF TRANSPORTATION SYSTEM AND PROJECT DECISIONS. Office of Environmental Policy, FHWA.

Sussman, Joseph M., 1975. Research needs and priorities in rail service reliability. In RAILROAD RESEARCH STUDY BACKGROUND PAPERS (Oxford, IN: Richard B. Cross).

Symposium on public participation in resource decision-making, 1976. *Natural Resources Journal* 16:1, pp. 1–236.

Syrnick, Joseph R., and Thomas N. Harvey, 1977. Assessing the distribution of user benefits from proposed transportation investments. *Transportation Engineering* 47:7 (July).

System Design Concepts, Inc., 1972. WEST SIDE HIGHWAY PROJECT: PRELIMINARY ANALYSIS OF ALTERNATIVE PROGRAM PACKAGES. Washington, D.C.: SDC (October).

System Design Concepts, Inc., 1974. WEST SIDE HIGHWAY PROJECT: ENVIRONMENTAL IMPACT STATEMENT. Washington, D.C.: SDC (April).

Systems Analysis and Research Corporation, 1963. DEMAND FOR INTERCITY PASSENGER TRAVEL IN THE WASHINGTON-BOSTON CORRIDOR. Boston: SARC.

Tagliacozzo, F., and F. Pirzio, 1973. Assignment models and urban path selection criteria: Results of a survey of behaviour of road users. *Transportation Research* 7:3, pp. 313–330.

Talvitie, Antti, and Ibrahim Hasan, 1978. An equilibrium model system for transportation corridors and its application. In Florian (1978).

Taylor, Charles E., 1977. Research issues in rail transport operations. WCTR.

Taylor, James, 1977. Load factor patterns, coach and economy class service: Domestic operations of the trunk airlines, 12 months ending June 30, 1976. TRF Proceedings XVIII:1.

TEAM CONCEPTS FOR URBAN HIGHWAYS AND URBAN DESIGN, 1968. HRR 220 (HRB)

Teich, Albert H., ed., 1977. TECHNOLOGY AND MAN'S FUTURE. New York: St. Martin's Press.

Terziev, Marc N., 1976. Modelling the demand for freight transportation. M.S. Thesis, Department of Civil Engineering, MIT.

Terziev, Marc N., and Paul O. Roberts, 1976. MODELS OF TRAVEL TIME AND RELIABILITY FOR FREIGHT TRANSPORT. Report 76-16, CTS/MIT.

Thoenig, Jean-Claude, 1973. L'ERE DES TECHNOCRATES—LE CAS DES PONTS ET CHAUSSEES [The era of technocrats]. Paris: Les Editions D'Organization.

Thomas, Edward H., and Joseph H. Schofer, 1970. STRATEGIES FOR THE EVALUATION OF ALTERNATIVE TRANSPORTATION PLANS. NCHRP Report 96.

Thomson, J. Michael, 1974. MODERN TRANSPORT ECONOMICS. Hammondsworth, Middlesex, U.K.: Penguin Books.

Tober, Ronald J., 1977. Improving service quality and efficiency through the use of service standards. In TRANSPORTATION SYSTEM MANAGEMENT, special report 172, TRB.

Toder, Eric, 1976. Highway capacity reduction and fuel consumption. TRF Proceedings XVII:1.

Train, K., 1977. A summary of the results of a validation test of disaggregate travel demand models. TRF Proceedings XVIII:1.

TRANSPORTATION AND COMMUNITY VALUES, 1969. Special report 105, HRB.

TRANSPORTATION PROGRAMMING PROCESS, 1975. Special report 157, TRB.

TRANSPORTATION SYSTEM MANAGEMENT, 1977. Special report 172, TRB.

Turvey, Ralph, and Herbert Mohring, 1975. Optimal bus fares. JTEP 9:3, pp. 280–286.

UMTA, 1975. INNOVATION IN PUBLIC TRANSPORT.

UMTA, 1976a. Major urban mass transportation investments. *Federal Register* 41:185, Part II (22 September 1976).

UMTA, 1976b. URBAN TRANSPORTATION PLANNING SYSTEM—REFERENCE MANUAL.

United Nations, 1958. MANUAL ON ECONOMIC DEVELOPMENT PROJECTS. New York: U.N.

URBAN TRANSPORTATION PRICING ALTERNATIVES, 1976. Papers presented at a conference held in May 1976. TRB (review draft).

U.S. Department of Housing and Urban Development, 1968. TOMORROW'S TRANSPORTATION. GPO.

Van Vliet, Dirck, 1976. Road assignment. *Transportation Research* 10:3, pp. 137–158.

Vickrey, William, 1967. Optimization of traffic and facilities. JTEP 1:2, pp. 213–236.

Voorhees, Alan M., and Associates, Inc., Cambridge Systematics, Inc., and Moore-Heder Associates, 1977. AUTO RESTRICTED ZONES. Final report, UMTA.

Vuchic, Vukan, 1976. Comparative analysis and selection of transit modes. TRR 559 (TRB).

Wachs, Martin, 1967. Relationships between drivers' attitudes toward alternate routes and driver and route characteristics. HRR 197 (HRB).

Wachs, Martin, 1970. Basic approaches to the measurement of community values. University of Illinois Center for Urban Studies Paper No. 8 (January).

Wachs, Martin, and Robert D. Blanchard, 1976. Life-styles and transportation needs of the elderly in the future. TRR 618 (TRB).

Wachs, Martin, B. M. Hudson, and Joseph L. Schofer, 1974. Integrating localized and systemwide objectives in transportation planning. *Traffic Quarterly* 28:2, pp. 159–184.

Wagner, Harvey M., 1969. PRINCIPLES OF OPERATIONS RESEARCH. Englewood Cliffs, NJ: Prentice-Hall.

Walsh, H. G., and A. Williams, 1969. CURRENT ISSUES IN COST-BENEFIT ANALYSIS. HMSO.

Walters, Alan A., 1961. The theory and measurement of private and social cost of highway congestion. *Econometrica* 29, pp. 676–699. Reprinted in Munby (1968).

Walters, Alan A., 1968. THE ECONOMICS OF ROAD USER CHARGES. Baltimore: Johns Hopkins Press.

Wardrop, J. G., 1952. Some theoretical aspects of road traffic research. In PROC. INSTITUTION OF CIVIL ENGINEERS, Part II, 1, pp. 325–378.

Warner, Sam B., Jr., 1962. STREETCAR SUBURBS. Cambridge, MA: Harvard University Press and MIT Press.

Warner, Stanley L., 1962. STOCHASTIC CHOICE OF MODE IN URBAN TRAVEL: A STUDY IN BINARY CHOICE. Evanston, IL: Northwestern University Press.

Washington, D.C., Council of Governments, 1974. ANALYSIS OF ZONAL LEVEL TRIP GENERATION RELATIONSHIPS. Technical report no. 10.

Watanatada, Thawat, 1977. Application of disaggregate choice models to urban transportation sketch planning. Ph.D. dissertation, Department of Civil Engineering, MIT.

Watanatada, Thawat, and Moshe E. Ben-Akiva, 1978. Spatial aggregation of disaggregate choice models: An areawide urban travel demand sketch planning model. Paper presented to TRB (January).

Waters, W. G., II, 1976. Statistical costing in transportation. *Transportation Journal* 15:3, pp. 49–62.

Watson, Peter, and Richard B. Westin, 1975. Transferability of disaggregate mode choice models. *Regional Science and Urban Economics* 5.

Wattleworth, J. A., 1976. Traffic flow theory. In Baerwald (1976).

Webber, Melvin H., 1971. ALTERNATIVE STYLES FOR CITIZEN PARTICIPATION IN TRANSPORT PLANNING. National Research Council, HRB.

Webber, Melvin H., 1974. Societal contexts of transportation and communications. In MULTIDISCIPLINARY EDUCATION IN TRANSPORTATION (1974).

Webber, Melvin H., and Shlomo Angel, 1969. The social context for transport policy. In SCIENCE AND TECHNOLOGY AND THE CITIES, Committee on Science and Astronautics, U.S. House of Representatives. GPO.

Wellington, A. M., 1891. ECONOMIC THEORY OF RAILWAY LOCATION. New York: John Wiley.

Wellman, Barry, 1977. Public participation in transportation planning. *Traffic Quarterly* 31:4, pp. 639–656.

Wheeler, Porter K., 1978. The Northeast Corridor: Has research influenced policy? WCTR.

Wigan, Mark R., 1976. Equilibrium models in use: Practical problems and pro- posals for transport planning. In Florian (1976).

Wilken, Dieter, 1978. European passenger travel demand analysis and strategy- responsive forecast. WCTR.

Williams, H. C. W. L., 1977. On the formation of travel demand models and economic evaluation measures of user benefit. *Environment and Planning A* 9, pp. 285–344.

Williamson, W. V., 1977. Freight car utilization: A look at some basic constraints and possible solutions. TRF Proceedings XVIII:1.

Wilmes, P., and E. Frankel, 1974. Port analysis and planning. ICTR.

Wilson, Alan G., 1967. A statistical theory of spatial distribution models. *Trans- portation Research* 1. Reprinted in Quandt (1970).

Wilson, Alan G., 1973. Travel demand forecasting: Achievements and problems. In Brand and Manheim (1973).

Wilson, Alan G., 1974. URBAN AND REGIONAL MODELS IN GEOGRAPHY AND PLANNING. New York: John Wiley.

Wilson, George, 1959. The output unit in transportation. *Land Economics* (August).

Wilson, Lawrence B., Paul O. Roberts, and James T. Kneafsey, 1977. Models of freight loss and damage. TRF Proceedings XVIII:1.

Wilson, Nigel H. M., 1978. Short-range transit planning: A new approach. Working paper, CTS/MIT.

Wilson, Nigel H. M., and Chris Hendrickson, 1978. In Florian (1978).

Wilson, Nigel, Wayne Pecknold, and Brian Kullman, 1972. SERVICE MODIFICA- TION PROCEDURES FOR MBTA LOCAL BUS OPERATIONS. Urban Observatory, Boston College.

Winch, D. M., 1973. ANALYTICAL WELFARE ECONOMICS. Hammondsworth, Middlesex, U.K.: Penguin Books.

Wohl, Martin, 1974. TRANSPORTATION INVESTMENT PLANNING. Lexington, MA: Lexington Books.

Wohl, Martin, and Brian V. Martin, 1967. TRAFFIC SYSTEMS ANALYSIS FOR ENGINEERS AND PLANNERS. New York: McGraw-Hill.

World Bank, 1972. TRANSPORTATION: SECTOR WORKING PAPER. IBRD.

World Bank, 1975. URBAN TRANSPORT: SECTOR POLICY PAPER. IBRD.

Worms, Vincent R., 1976. The implementation of a joint disaggregate demand model in an urban simulation. M.S. thesis, Department of Civil Engineering, MIT.

Wright, C. C., 1972. Some properties of the fundamental relations of traffic flow. In Gordon F. Newell, ed., TRAFFIC FLOW AND TRANSPORTATION (New York: American Elsevier).

Wyckoff, D. Daryl, and David H. Maister, 1975. THE OWNER-OPERATOR: INDEPENDENT TRUCKER. Lexington, MA: D. C. Heath.

Yagar, Sam, 1971. Dynamic traffic assignments by individual path minimization and queuing. *Transportation Research* 5, pp. 179–196.

Yagar, Sam, 1977. Minimizing delays for transient demands with application to signallized road junctions. *Transportation Research* 11:1, pp. 53–62.

Young, Steven C. K., 1976. The application of disaggregate demand models in urban travel forecasting. M.S. thesis, Department of Civil Engineering, MIT.

Yukubousky, Richard, 1973. CITIZEN PARTICIPATION IN TRANSPORTATION PLANNING—A SELECTED BIBLIOGRAPHY. Planning Division, New York State Department of Transportation (February).

Yukubousky, Richard, 1974. Community interaction techniques in continuing transportation systems planning: A framework for application. TRR 481 (TRB).

Index

(References to figures and tables appear in italics.)

Aggregation (continued)
See also Aggregate behavior;
   Aggregate demand functions
Agreement on actions, as process
   objective, 561–564
Airborne revenue hours, 252
Aircraft routing over a network,
   170, *170. See also* Operating
   plan; Vehicle trajectories
Aircraft utilization, effect on
   relative costs, 252–254, *253*
Airfreight, example of an
   operating plan, 305–308, *306*
Airline network, 302
Air pollution, 11, 19, 171, *172*, 542
Airport, link representation of, 167
Airport access
   and congestion, 501
   as example of market
      segmentation, 115
Airport planning
   choice issues in, 540
   and equity issues, 549
   evaluation issues in, 333–334
Air quality standards, 542
Air-rights construction, 562
Air transportation, example of
   analysis, 183–198
Allocation of costs, in network
   case study, 529–534
All-or-nothing assignment, 495–
   498, 502
Alternative actions, need for, 545–
   546
Alternative models, importance of,
   585
Alternative technologies, for a
   penetration road, 237–241
Analysis
   as a continuing activity, 40–45
   and implementation, 40–47,
      586
   cycles of, 38, 394
      in network case study, 522–529,
         535–539
      in operations planning case
         study, 407–414
   and study design, 585–586
   ethics of, 589–594
   iterative nature of, 38–40
   levels of, 586
   objectives of, 330, 560–564
   and the political process, 47, 589

(*See also* Choice; Role of the
   professional)
power of, 589
product of, 41–47 (*See also*
   Choice; Evaluation report)
value judgments in, 586–587
Analysis of Alternatives Report,
   554
Analysis summary form, 394, *395.
   See also* Evaluation report
Analyst, judgments of
   about applications of theory, 34
   about choice dimensions in
      demand models, 415
   in constructing economic goal
      variables, 371–372
   about demand functions, 121
   in demand-model calibration,
      406–408
   in demand-model development
      for carrier operations planning,
      405–407, 408–409
   about demand variation over
      time, 321, *403*
   in evaluation, 355
   about magnitudes of changes, 34
   about management issues, 583,
      585–586
   in model development, 586–587
   about operator equilibration, 326
   about performance functions,
      198–203
   as prediction procedures, 350
   about scenarios and models,
      325–326
   about the scope of analysis, 12
   and simple demand prediction
      methods, 142–147
   about technical issues, 583–585
   about travel-market equilibration,
      316–319, 465–466, 501
   values and, 583, 586–587
   and worksheet design, *398,* 399
Annual cycle, 221, *222,* 224–225,
   305
Annual net operating revenue, 371
Annual net revenue, 371
Approximate impact prediction, in
   process strategy, 350, 567
Approximation methods, 34. *See
   also* Incremental analysis;
   Simplified prediction methods
Arc elasticity, 127

Community (continued)
organizations, 565
role of analyst as advisor to, 570-571
values (*See* Societal values)
Community interaction, 546-549, 564-570
catalog of techniques, *565*
Compensation
for adverse effects, 546, 549-551, 568
in evaluation method, 352-355
for residential displacements, 562-563
in United Kingdom, 541
Compensation principle, and Pareto criterion, 550
Competition for services, in a network, 466
Components, of transportation systems, 164-166, *164*
Composite activity variables, 136-138, 418
Composite service level, 134-136, 418
as measure of user impact, in network case study, 516, 525
for path, 486, 487
See also Generalized cost; User impacts
Composite variables
and the consistency of sequential forms, 418, 423-424, 441, 457
in demand functions, 134-138
Computer models, 584. *See also specific names*
Confidence of the public
in the decision process, 553
in transportation professionals, 358-359, 542, 544-545
Conflicting values, 589
Conflict resolution, 565-566, 571
Conflicts
in evaluation, 353-355
among interests, 552
between users and operators, 178, *178*
See also Trade-offs
Congestion, 268-281, 295-300
and diminishing marginal productivity, 241
effects of, 218-220, 272-273, *272,*

278-281, *279, 281,* 297-300, *299,* 314-316, *315*
load-dependent, 277-281
load-independent, 276-281, 295-300
load-schedule, 277
load-vehicle, 277-281
models of, 273-276, 278-281, 295-300
transient conditions, 273
and vehicle cycle, 218-222, *222*
vehicle-facility, *169,* 276, 286-287, 295-300
vehicle-schedule, 276-278, 286-287, 305-307
Congestion toll, 273
Connecting services, 303
Consensus. *See* Agreement on actions
Consistency
of block-conditional model systems, 442-443
of demand functions, 421-425
internal, 425
of UTMS-1, 436-437
See also Choice dimensions
Constant-volume assumption, in equilibration, 23
Constraints on frequency, effects of, 290-292, *290*
Consumer, definition, 64
Consumer behavior
classical theory, 86-87
in MTC model system, 457
in path choice, 466-470
Consumer behavior model I, 64-82, 120
appraisal, 82-83
and path choice, 491
Consumer behavior model II, 82-86, 120. *See also* Disaggregate demand models
Consumer choices, represented as demand functions, 73-74, 79-81
Consumer decision process, 70-71
Consumer surplus, in evaluation, 376, *377*
Containerization, 10
and equity issues, 549-550
Continuing analysis process, 38-48, *40, 42. See also* Operations

Duties of the analyst, 570–571. *See also* Role of the professional

Ecological impacts, 11
  as resources consumed, 172, *172*
Economic analysis in evaluation, 360–361, 365–384, 589
  limitations of, 360–365
Economic capacity, 271
Economic concepts as goal variables, 366–384
  in network case study, 516
  in operations planning case study, 408
  role in evaluation, 383–384
Economic development, role of transport in, 14, 58–60. *See also* Activity system; Penetration road
Economic interests, perspective of, 172
Economies of scale, 236
Effective agreement, 564
Effects of transportation, on social and economic activity, 58–60. *See also* Impacts
Elastic behavior, 126
Elasticities, 125–133
  and composite variables, 137
  and prediction, 129–133, 142–147
  of prices, effect on revenues of, 194–195
  properties of, 128–129, *129*
  in transit analysis, 399
  types of, 127–128
  for urban passenger demand functions, 131, *131*
  See also Demand functions
Empty backhaul, 244
Energy, as resource consumed, 172, *172*
Energy conservation measures, 454, 458
Engineers, role in transportation organizations, 554
Entropy models, 120n
Environmental effects of transportation, 11
  as resources consumed, 172, *172*
  See also Impacts
Environmental impact statements, 541, 554, 569
  and evaluation, 355–356

Environmental interests, perspective of, 172
Environment of a system, in performance functions, 174, 176
Equilibration, 28–30, 312–327. *See also* Activity-system equilibration; Operator equilibration; Travel-market equilibration
Equilibrium analysis, 176–177
Equilibrium conditions, 314
Equilibrium flow pattern. *See* Travel-market equilibration
Equilibrium models
  in network case study, 515
  simplified, 327
  in travel-market equilibration, 30–31
Equilibrium volume, 21, 176
  and capacity, differences between, 177
  estimation using load factor, 199
  as measure of user impact, 182
Equity, 541, 542, 549–551
  barriers to, 550
  considerations in developing alternatives, 545–546
  of a course of action, 562–563
  in evaluation method, 353–354
Equivalent annual cost, 368, 371
Equivalent-day volume factor, 403
Equivalent-hour volume factor, 403
Equivalent-service approach, 248
Estimation of model parameters. *See* Model development
Ethics of analysis, 574, 589–590
Evaluation, 39, 330–387
  aggregation versus disaggregation, 381
  basic method of, 335–336, 348–356, *348*
  and choice, 331
  classical approaches, 360–365
  and decision process, 553
  definition, 331
  economic analysis in, 360–384
  and environmental impact statements, 355–356
  extension of basic method to large-scale problems, 366–385
  and goal formulation, 331
  government viewpoints, 381–383

Path
 of a user, 303, 464
 of a vehicle, 170, *170*, 220, *220*,
  303, 464
Path choice, 491
Path level of service, 473–474, 478,
 493
Paths, in network case study, 513
Path volumes, 493
Pattern of flows. *See* Flow
 patterns
Peak and off-peak services, 407
Peaking factors, 403, 404
Peaking problem, 320–322, *403*,
 404
Peak period, in network case
 study, 510
Peak-period demand, 404
Peak-period demand functions,
 410
Pencil-and-paper methods. *See*
 Manual methods; Simplified
 prediction methods
Penetration road, 237–241
People-mover systems. *See*
 Automated-guideway transit
Performance of a transportation
 system, 163–309
Performance functions
 definition, 174
 highway, 296
 and supply function, 200–203
 surface, 175, *175*
 use in analysis, 176–178
Performance model I, 178–182,
 182, 281
 and more detailed analyses, 205–
  206
Performance model II, 278–281,
 280
Performance model III, 286–291,
 289
 implications of, 291–300
Performance prediction, in
 operations planning case
 study, 412
Periodic review and reassessment,
 of transportation decisions,
 43–45, 551–552, 579. *See also*
 Multiyear program plan
Personal flexibility, need for, 9
Personal values, 590
Perspectives of various interests,

as complement to technical
 expertise, 587. *See also*
 Community interaction
Physical capacity, 271
Physical impacts, 18
Pipelines, cost functions for, 241,
 242
Pivot-point methods, for
 incremental prediction, 132,
 142–146
 with an assumed model
  structure, 144–146, *146*
 with elasticities, 142–144
 in operations planning case
  study, 399
Plan, 322. *See also* Long-range
 plan; Multiyear program plan;
 Options
PLUM, 455
Pocket calculator. *See* Calculators
Point elasticity, 127
Policy, 322
Political nature of transportation
 decisions, 47–48, 559
 balancing of interests, 19, 542
 conflicts among interests, 552
Political role of analyst. *See* Role
 of the professional
Pollution, 11
 as resource consumed, *172*
Port, link representation of, 167–
 169, *168*
Positioning, 243
 time, 221, *222*, 224
Posters, as community-interaction
 technique, 565
Potential, in demand models, 117–
 118, 420. *See also* Composite
 variables
Power of analysis, 589
Practical capacity, 271
Prediction, 38, 330
 of aggregate behavior, 121 (*See
  also* Aggregation)
 context of, 38–49, *39*
 with demand elasticities, 129–
  133, 142–147
 with disaggregate demand
  functions, 147–155
 of effects, 546–547
 in network case study, 513–515
 of operator response (*See*
  Operators)

Urban Transportation Model
System (UTMS-1), 119–120,
156, 426–437, 494, 584
appraisal, 433–437
conceptual structure, 426–429,
435–437
dimensions of choice, 426–427,
435–437
directions for improvement, 437–
438, 454–458
inconsistencies in, 32, 433–437
limitations of, 433–437
market segments in, 428
and network equilibrium, 494
sequential structure, 427–428
submodels, 32, 427–431
travel-market equilibration in,
419, 430–433
Urban transportation planning, 3,
32
Urban Transportation Planning
System (UTPS), 455
Urban travel models, new
directions, 443–458
User benefit/cost analysis, 361,
382–383, 548
User cost, 66
in evaluation, 376, *377*
trapezoidal approximation, 376–
377, *377*
See also Composite service level
User impacts, 18
differential incidence, 378–379,
380
economic goal variables and,
372–381, *373, 374, 375, 377*
expressed by service level and
equilibrium volume, 182
in network case study, 516, 525,
527, 528, 535, *537,* 538, *538*
options available, 14–15, 17
User-operator total cost, in
evaluation, 382
User-operator trade-offs. *See*
Trade-offs
User-optimizing flow distribution
rules, 490, 499
User perspectives
on alternative paths, 303–304
economic goal variables and,
372–381
on path choice, 473–474
on a transportation system, 171

See also Service variables; Trip
profiles
Utiles, 69
Utility, 69
choice-independent, 139
Utilization, 251, 262
effect on costs, 251–254
of a fleet of vehicles, 306–307,
307
and operating plan, 306–307
of railcars, 261–265
of vehicles, as a policy issue, 262
(*See also* Vehicle cycles)
UTMS. *See* Urban Transportation
Model System
UTPS. *See* Urban Transportation
Planning System

Value information file, 346, 350
Value judgments, in analysis, 583,
586–587. *See also* Analyst,
judgments of
Values, changes in, 10
Van pools, 10
Variable cost, 236
Vehicle acquisition cost, 295
Vehicle assignment to routes,
304–305
Vehicle availability, relation to
congestion, 277n
Vehicle cost, effect of utilization
on, 251–254
Vehicle cycles, 218–230, 250–265,
305–307
changes in, and effect on costs,
219–220
components of, 220–225
economics of, 250–265, *257*
in network context, *302,* 305
opportunities to affect, 229–230
Vehicle-facility congestion, *169,*
276, 286–287, 295–300
Vehicle-facility interactions, *169,*
286–287
Vehicle fleet
economics of, 254–255
management of, effect on vehicle
cycle, 229
Vehicle investments, 287
Vehicle links, 167
Vehicle operating-cycle time, *222,*
224
Vehicle options, 16, 186–191, *190*